The Life of

WILL
IAM

THIS ALARMING PARADOX, 1935–1962

FAUL
KNER

VOLUME 2

CARL ROLLYSON

UNIVERSITY OF VIRGINIA PRESS
Charlottesville and London

University of Virginia Press
© 2020 by Carl Rollyson
All rights reserved
Printed in the United States of America on acid-free paper

First published 2020

1 3 5 7 9 8 6 4 2

Library of Congress Cataloging-in-Publication Data

Names: Rollyson, Carl E. (Carl Edmund), author.
Title: The life of William Faulkner / Carl Rollyson.
Description: Charlottesville : University of Virginia Press, 2020. | Includes
bibliographical references and index. | Contents: Volume 1. The past is
never dead, 1897–1934. | Volume 2. This alarming paradox, 1935–1962.
Identifiers: LCCN 2019032254 (print) | LCCN 2019032255 (ebook) |
ISBN 9780813943824 (hardback ; volume 1) | ISBN 9780813943831
(epub ; volume 1) | ISBN 9780813944401 (hardback ; volume 2) |
ISBN 9780813944418 (epub ; volume 2)
Subjects: LCSH: Faulkner, William, 1897–1962. | Authors, American—
20th century—Biography. | Novelists, American—20th century—Biography.
Classification: LCC PS3511.A86 Z9619 2020 (print) | LCC PS3511.A86 (ebook) |
DDC 813/.52 [B]—dc23
LC record available at https://lccn.loc.gov/2019032254
LC ebook record available at https://lccn.loc.gov/2019032255

Cover art: Faulkner in 1943, on the terrace of his office on the Warner lot
in Hollywood, working on the screenplay for *To Have and Have Not,*
released in 1945. (Pictorial Press Ltd/Alamy Stock Photo)

Every so often, in spite of judgment and all else, I take these fits of sort of raging and impotent exasperation at this really quite alarming paradox which my life reveals: Beginning at the age of thirty I, an artist, a sincere one and of the first class, who should be free even of his own economic responsibilities and with no moral conscience at all, began to become the sole, principal and partial support—food, shelter, heat, clothes, medicine, kotex, school fees, toilet paper and picture shows—of my mother, . . . [a] brother's widow and child, a wife of my own and two step children, my own child; I inherited my father's debts and his dependents, white and black without inheriting yet from anyone one inch of land or one stick of furniture or one cent of money. . . . I bought without help from anyone the house I live in and all the furniture; I bought my farm the same way. I am 42 years old and I have already paid for four funerals and will certainly pay for one more and in all likelihood two more beside that, provided none of the people in mine or my wife's family my superior in age outlive me, before I ever come to my own.
—William Faulkner to Robert Haas, May 3, 1940

Contents

Gallery follows page 340.

Preface

After the publication of *Light in August* in 1932, race and history were no longer a given, a prologue to William Faulkner's life and work, but instead became a problematic part of his inheritance as a southerner and as a writer with a claim on the world's attention. He had to write a new kind of history in which history itself is the intense focus of his attention, as in *Absalom, Absalom!*, *Go Down, Moses,* and *Requiem for a Nun,* or a community's past had to be retold and reshaped and debated, as in the Snopes trilogy. *A Fable* and *The Reivers* may seem to stand aside from this historiographical dynamic, but *A Fable* applies the Yoknapatawpha novels' approach to historical understanding to a world-changing event, the First World War, which motivated Faulkner in the 1920s to see his native region in terms of global events, and *The Reivers* not only recapitulates much of Yoknapatawpha history, as do *Collected Stories, The Town,* and *The Mansion,* but Faulkner's last novel also returns to the motive force of *The Unvanquished* and *Intruder in the Dust* as part of his recalibration of history and its impact on several generations that are embodied in *The Reivers'* first words: "Grandfather said." *Intruder in the Dust,* the novel and the film, brought new audiences to William Faulkner.

Hollywood had a significant impact on the trajectory of Faulkner's fiction after 1932. Novelists of his generation often worried that Hollywood would change them for the worse, that they would be forced to produce made-to-order scripts for an industry that viewed writers as disposable, interchangeable, and at the command of producers and studio heads. Hollywood was never home, where the writer went when he was through with the picture business, or it was through with him. Although Faulkner might mount a seemingly invincible facade, Hollywood got to him, forcing him to improvise and sometimes to take his screenwriting back to Oxford, but it also provided the impetus for novels like *Pylon* and *The Wild Palms* that took the measure of Hollywood, creating a new kind of history that arose out of his collaborations with other writers. They do not appear by name in the novels, except for Sergei Eisenstein, but those writers' room meetings about story values, dialogue, and characterization had their impact on the scenarios that characters like V. K. Ratliff, Gavin Stevens, and Chick Mallison concoct. Faulkner did not publicly concede to Hollywood any of his fictional territory, but Yoknapatawpha characters and settings appear in his screenplays "War Birds," "Revolt in the Earth," and "Country Lawyer," and *A Fable* grew out of his Hollywood work and talks with a Hollywood director and producer. Faulkner described screenwriting as an interruption of his novelist's mission. But in truth that mission gradually changed the more time he spent in Hollywood, so that when he went out into the world again he produced a different sort of fiction. This is the story of how those changes got made and how the man and the artist emerged recognizably as the figure he had always been and yet a transformed writer all the same.

I began my work on Faulkner as an undergraduate, inspired by M. Thomas Inge at Michigan State University, and then continued on with Michael Millgate at the University of Toronto, producing a dissertation and my first book, *Uses of the Past in the Novels of William Faulkner.* The debt owed to these fine scholars is immeasurable. I owe many other debts to Faulkner critics, which I have acknowledged in my narrative and notes.

Right from the beginning, when I had only a book proposal and a sample chapter to show, I had the invaluable support of Linda Wagner-Martin, who wrote in support of my work and has been a continuing inspiration. In the summer of 2014, during a stay in Oxford, I had the pleasure of lunching with Jay Watson, the Howry Professor of Faulkner Studies at the University of Mississippi, who patiently listened to my plans for a new Faulkner biography and provided much-needed encouragement and the invitation to give a keynote talk at the summer 2015 Faulkner and Yoknapatawpha Conference. On that same trip, I met and interviewed Larry Wells, the husband of Dean Faulkner Wells, and a fount of information and contacts that I sorely needed. Larry generously put me in touch with William Lewis Jr., the current owner of Neilson's Department Store, where Faulkner was a customer. Mr. Lewis knew Faulkner and was most welcoming and informative during our interview. Just as important was Tommy Freeland, another Larry Wells contact and the son of Phil Stone's law partner. Mr. Freeland gave me a tour of the Stone law office and told me a good deal about his father's dealings with William Faulkner. Through Larry I was also able to contact Sandra Baker Moore for her memories of the Faulkners and of what it was like for her to live next door to Rowan Oak in the 1940s, when her mother, Kate Baker, owned a dress shop in Oxford. I have been extremely fortunate to find those still living with memories of Faulkner, including Salley Knight, whose recollection of Faulkner in Virginia came to me via my contact with Scott Beauchamp.

Thanks to Jay Watson's invitation to Gloria Burgess, who spoke at the 2016 Faulkner and Yoknapatawpha Conference, I was able to interview her and continue a correspondence that has yielded a significant insight into Faulkner's efforts to help people of color.

Steve Railton, who has done so much to further Faulkner studies with Digital Yoknapatawpha, helped me out at a crucial moment when a website went down and has been a strong supporter of my biography. I relied on the estimable Molly Schwartzberg, Curator of the Albert and Shirley Small Special Collections at the University of Virginia, not only for much help with the vast Faulkner archive but also with connecting me to members of the university and Charlottesville community who had memories of William Faulkner. Ellie Sohm shared with me her University of Virginia undergraduate paper about Faulkner's relationship with his daughter Jill at a crucial time in the development of my biography. Sara Barnes was a wonderful tour guide and all-around facilitator during my visit to the university to deliver the first William and Rosemary MacIlwaine Lecture in American Literature. That lecture, I'm happy to say, prompted an email to Richard Garcia from Donald Nuechterlein about his experience with William Faulkner in Iceland that was forwarded to me. After my lecture, "Faulkner's Virginia Persona," I had the pleasure of speaking with George Thomas about those Faulkner days on the University of Virginia grounds. Others in the audience for my lecture came forward with their own William Faulkner stories. I am grateful to all of them.

Robert Hamblin, former Director of the Center for Faulkner Studies at Southeast Missouri State University, has been an invaluable source of information as he guided me through their indispensable Faulkner collection. Christopher Rieger, the current Director, has been equally helpful and generous. He made available to me a grant that allowed extended stays at the Center for Faulkner Studies so that I could complete my research in a timely fashion. On the premises, I had the excellent help of Roxanne Dunne, and of the indispensable Tyson Koenig, who sorted out many of the photographs reproduced in this biography.

Archivist Rick Watson, the son of eminent Faulkner scholar James G. Watson, helped me navigate my way through the Carvel Collins Papers at the Harry Ransom Humanities Research Center, University of Texas at Austin. Rick saved me a lot of time by expediting my access to the papers. I owe thanks as well to Ned Comstock at the Cinematic Arts Library, University of Southern California. I have known Ned since the mid-1980s, and he has remained an important source of archival material for many of my biographies. He has sent me copies of vital items that I did not know existed. Jenny Romero and the rest of the staff at the Academy of Motion Picture Arts and

Sciences have always proven a boon to my research, and that was true in this case as well, pointing me to a script not mentioned in previous accounts of Faulkner's career. Todd Goddard at Utah Valley University hosted my talk on "Faulkner as Screenwriter" and secured funding for a trip to Salt Lake City so that I could examine the Faulkner-authored scripts in the Howard Hawks Collection at Brigham Young University.

Similarly, through a generous invitation from Faulkner scholar Stephen Hahn at William Patterson University, I was able to examine the important work Donald Philip Duclos did on William C. Falkner, the old Colonel.

Jennifer Ford, Jessica Leming, and Lauren Rogers, in Special Collections at the University of Mississippi Library, facilitated my work in its Meta Carpenter Wilde Collection and other choice items such as Faulkner's handwritten script "Wooden Crosses," a first-draft screenplay that became *The Road to Glory*. And thanks to Gerald Walton for helping me out on my interests in the Ole Miss golf course that Faulkner played on. I'm grateful to William D. Griffith for a splendid tour of Rowan Oak and for answers to my questions.

Elizabeth Sudduth, Director of the Irvin Department of Rare Books and Special Collections, University of South Carolina Libraries, made my visit to consult the Frederick R. Karl Archive and Malcolm Argyle Franklin Collection efficient and profitable.

Matthew Turi, Manuscripts Research and Instruction Librarian, Research and Instructional Services Department, Louis Round Wilson Special Collections Library at the University of North Carolina, helped to facilitate my work in the Robert H. Moore Papers.

Meredith Mann in the Brooke Russell Astor Reading Room for Rare Books and Manuscripts at the New York Public Library helped me navigate through the Joel Sayre Papers, as did Mary Catherine Kinniburgh in the Berg Collection for various Faulkner items.

David Harper and Jessica Stock made my visit to the M. Thomas Inge Faulkner Collection at West Point a delight and an edification. I was able to follow Faulkner's walking route to his talk.

Penny White, reference librarian, and the Digital Production Group at the University of Virginia Library aided in acquiring the volume 1 cover image and several of the images in the galleries.

Edward Perry and Marcus Gray, two Faulkner scholars, have stuck with me over several years, making important suggestions about items essential to this biography. I thank Patrik Andersson for answering my query about the correspondence between Faulkner and Else Jonsson, and John Waters for answering my questions about Jean Stein.

Other Faulkner scholars, including Ted Atkinson, Sarah Gleeson-White, Arthur Kinney, Claude Pruitt, D. Matthew Ramsay, Timothy Ryan, Stefan Solomon, and Sally Wolff-King have responded to my queries and have contributed to the completion of my biography. I'm grateful to Jack Elliott for sending me an advance copy of his valuable work on Faulkner's last days, and for his last-minute corrections of material relating to Faulkner's ancestry and his early years. I should have consulted Jack sooner.

For sound advice about matters related to Faulkner and publishing, I'm grateful to Craig Gill, the Director of the University Press of Mississippi.

My fellow biographers Jonathan Alter, James Atlas, Kate Buford, Betty Caroli, Mary Dearborn, Gayle Feldman, Anne Heller, Justin Martin, Marion Meade, Sydney Stern, Will Swift, and Amanda Vail have given me much good advice, encouragement, and items to mull over for this biography.

Thank you, Barbara Barnett, for helping me with my rudimentary French and figuring out a Faulkner caption, and William Crawley for speaking with me about Faulkner's visit to Mary Washington University. And to Rosemary Clark, for untold great finds and research assistance, I am immeasurably indebted.

Several research award grants from Baruch College and the PSC-CUNY Research Fund made it possible to travel to archives and to conduct interviews for this book. Biography is an expensive endeavor, and without such help I don't see how I could have taken on so many research projects.

I'm very pleased that my shrewd agent, Colleen Mohyde, and my astute editor, Eric Brandt, combined to make this a better book. To Susan Murray, my magnificent copyeditor, and to the vigilant Morgan Myers, my heartfelt thanks for making this book, line by line, and chapter by chapter, better than I could make it myself. And it is gratifying to say here how much I valued the support of the late Mark Saunders as Director of the University of Virginia Press.

Lisa Paddock, my wife and a wonderful Faulkner scholar, patiently listened to my plans for the biography and made many excellent suggestions. I'm sure it was a trial, at times, to put up with my obsession, but she has borne it pretty well.

The Life of William Faulkner

1

Faulkner's Shadow

Pylon, 1935

I have a title for it which I like, by the way: ABSALOM, ABSALOM; the
story is of a man who wanted a son through pride, and got too many of
them and they destroyed him.
　　　　　　　　—William Faulkner to Hal Smith, August 1934

If *Absalom* proves to be about the sins of the father, lines of descent, a
society's decline, and the burden of the Southern past, *Pylon* takes up
the irrelevance of sin (not to mention fathers), lines of ascent, a society's
transformation, and a weightless future.
　　　　　　　　—John T. Matthews, *William Faulkner: Seeing through the South*

A Hanger-on with High Flyers

By 1935, in several short stories, film scripts, and novels, Faulkner had already
connected the world of Yoknapatawpha to the high flyers of World War I
and the barnstormers of the postwar period in the figure of young Bayard
Sartoris, bereft of his place in traditional southern culture and willing to risk
all in the test-piloting that results in his death. Young Bayard and his twin,
John, belong to that reckless crew of aviators in "Death Drag," "Honor," and
other short stories. They live in the moment, unsure of the future, even as
they continue to engage in "mock heroic" actions.[1] On what terms, if any, can
the world of the gentlemanly ideal, still in the sway of the Falkner family and
their community, prevail in the modern world of airports and air circuses?
It is a question posed by Faulkner's own actions. In New Orleans, in 1925, he

accompanied Hamilton Basso, who was writing a feature story about "The Gates Flying Circus." Basso recalled that Faulkner seemed to relish the frightening flights in a rickety Wright Whirlwind two-seater: "Nobody *else* in our crowd had gone looping-the-loop in a bucket seat and open cockpit over the Mississippi River."[2]

In mid-February 1934, William Faulkner attended an air show at the newly dedicated Shushan Airport in New Orleans, named after Colonel A. L. Shushan, president of the Levee Board. Faulkner had flown there with his flight instructor, Vernon Omlie, and both received the royal treatment, including a big black Cadillac with a driver at their disposal. Later, when Faulkner showed Omlie the novel that resulted from their trip, the aghast flyer said: "But you are calling these people unpleasant, and you are attacking the people who set up the airport, the levee board and the rest, and they were so nice to us, putting the car at our disposal. Do you still want to do that?" Faulkner said, "Certainly." Omlie's wife later claimed that Faulkner saw *Pylon* as another potboiler like *Sanctuary,* "somewhat pornographic" and designed to make money.[3] Like the flyers he wrote about with such great fascination, he did what he loved to do in a world that put a price on everything, and in which he had to figure out the price he could exact for his work. That did not mean, as he told the Omlies, that he would not try to suit himself as well.

Faulkner keenly understood that like the flyers financed by Shushan and other businessmen, he was implicated in the commerce of book publishing and film production. In subtle ways, the novelist fashioned an objective correlative for his own ambition and how he compromised it in his depiction of the airport and its creator. Colonel H. I. Feinman, a "fine man," touts his project in terms reminiscent of the novelist's aspirations. The airport is the expression of an "Undeviating Vision and Unflagging Effort," an achievement "Raised Up and Created Out of the Waste Land at the Bottom of Lake Rambaud." It is not too much to read an allusion to T. S. Eliot's poem *The Waste Land* in this corporate announcement, or even to detect ironic echoes in the site of the lake-bottom airport of the name of that visionary poet Arthur Rimbaud, who regarded himself as a seer, who cultivated his own soul and reached for the unknown—to quote one of his famous letters. Like Feinman, Faulkner wrested his work out of the "limbo of imagination"—as would Thomas Sutpen in *Absalom, Absalom!,* establishing his kingdom, Sutpen's Hundred, just as Faulkner would create his Yoknapatawpha and deem himself its sole owner and proprietor on the map inserted into the novel. Like Feinman, Faulkner believed in the originality of his vision and remained steadfast in the great effort required to write great fiction. But all his effort had to be disseminated in a marketplace that touted, as in Feinman's case, the

"Cost of a Million Dollars." This novel may well be the "most devastatingly self-critical of Faulkner's whole career."[4]

This was the era of Governor Huey Long, whose administration promoted the construction of high-visibility projects that enhanced the profile of Louisiana and his own reputation as a politician who put people to work during the Depression while contributing to the progress that made modern life comfortable. Faulkner had little interest in Long. The governor's life could not be the basis of a great novel.[5] But the consequences of a regime that conjoined commerce and politics and cut corrupt deals, afterward staging celebrations purported to be for the public good, agitated an author who had become part of a Hollywood no less self-promoting and venal than Long's Louisiana.

The Shushan layout may have reminded Faulkner of a movie set. The airport had two large hangars not so different from sound stages, and a tower with murals commemorating the history of flight in high-relief depictions of airplanes and their daring pilots. And like a Hollywood studio emblazoning its logo, the airport had Shushan's name or his initials inserted in every available spot. In short, if you wanted to see the show, you had to put up with the advertising. And Faulkner was there for the show, indulging his keen interest in barnstorming pilots. He had organized his own local air shows, and flying was a Faulkner business, taken up by his brothers Murry, John, and Dean. The very idea of flight had captivated all of them since that day Faulkner had convinced them they could make their own air machine. That their dreams had crashed into a ditch did not dissuade the boys from pursuing the lift that flying always offered. And crashing, after all, was part of the excitement.

The Shushan show did not disappoint. Milo Burcham defied the rainy weather and demonstrated why he was the world champion at upside-down flying. The famous Michel Détroyat, on a calmer day, performed his air acrobatics, as did Clem Sohn, jumping from ten thousand feet with a flour sack he emptied to mark his descent. After some near-collisions and a forced landing, a pilot and parachute jumper plunged to their deaths in Lake Ponchartrain. In one case, the body could not be found; in another, no relatives could be located for the nomadic airman.[6]

Perhaps the anonymity of these deaths disturbed Faulkner and led to his writing *Pylon*. His own explanation is that *Absalom, Absalom!* had stalled, and he needed the relief that writing a different kind of novel provided.[7] But it "seems significant that the novel Faulkner wrote 'to get away from' the high modernist *Absalom, Absalom!* is a book patterned to a degree after Hollywood criteria."[8] In fact, in July 1934, Howard Hawks suggested to the stalled novelist that he should write about flyers, and Faulkner told him about "This

Kind of Courage," the story that evidently presaged *Pylon*. Hawks said, "That sounds good,"[9] and that seems to have been good enough for Faulkner. *Pylon* and *Absalom, Absalom!* are both about deracination and displacement. Like Thomas Sutpen, *Pylon*'s rootless flyers swoop down on land that has been converted into property, into the possession of one man, the not so fine Colonel Feinman.

With *Pylon,* Faulkner could dispense with *Absalom, Absalom!*'s genealogy of characters fraught with the intricacies of a narrative overwhelmed by the eruption of the past in the present. Faulkner's flyers—Roger, Laverne, and Jack—have, for most of the novel, no past. Their lives seem the work of happenstance. Their mechanic, Jiggs, is an unreliable alcoholic who is nevertheless devoted to them, which is all they seem to require. The novel's center of consciousness—always referred to as "the reporter"—is not even given a name. He is drawn to the aviators because they are so alive in the air. On the ground, their lives seem rootless and sordid. Roger and Jack share Laverne, who is married to Roger because he won the roll of the dice with Jack. Laverne is like the tough-talking women—Hildy Johnson in *His Girl Friday* and "Feathers" in *Rio Bravo*—who populate Howard Hawks's later films. She is also like Joan Crawford's character Ann in *Today We Live,* the female fulcrum of male triangles in the terse tension of war and romance.

Laverne Shumann is not the nymph pursued in Faulkner's early poetry. She is full-bodied—part of a life intensely lived, which means risking death, precisely what Dr. Martino urged upon Louise. Laverne is a woman possessed, the cynosure of male society, but also her own woman, dogged by a reporter who is a descendent of Keats's frail knight, "alone and palely loitering"—in effect, a knight manqué.[10] The war is mentioned only once in *Pylon,* when Jiggs buys "one of the pulp magazines of war stories in the air," which will give Laverne and her male companions "something to do on the train" that takes them to the air shows in which they will duel in the air with their competitors. If this is not the world of gentleman flyers, it remains, nevertheless, a kind of chivalric endeavor involving sacrifice and heroes, however corrupted for popular entertainment and profit.

Faulkner's treatment of the reedy reporter is original and yet probably based on Hermann Deutsch, a thin, tall journalist with a shambling gait whom Faulkner transformed into his shambolic, skeletal character. The two men first met in 1925 in New Orleans and were impressed with one another. Deutsch remembered Faulkner saying to him, "If somebody in the Yale Bowl was going to be shot, you'd be standing next to him."[11] It was a line Faulkner would elaborate on in *Pylon,* when the editor says as much to the reporter.

At the air show, the novelist spent a good deal of time in Deutsch's company, watching the journalist carry around on his shoulders a little boy who belonged to one of the aviators. Out of this meager material, Faulkner conceived of the reporter who becomes increasingly involved in the lives of the flyers he comes almost to worship because they seem solely intent on their air missions. They are "hooked on speed."[12] They are adventurers and likened to "immigrants walking down the steerage gangplank of a ship." They are refugees hazarding a trip into what was still then the new world of flight. They no longer have a secure place, a home to which they could return "even if it's just only to hate the damn place good and comfortable for a day or two."

It looks as though Faulkner patterned the besotted, drunken reporter on himself. Faulkner could become voluble when it came to talking about flying.[13] When he turned up in New Orleans after the air show, he looked as if he had slept in the gutter. "Yes, ma'am, I have," he assured writer Roark Bradford's wife. Faulkner claimed to have become involved with the flyers, sleeping and fighting. It was a "disjointed, confused, nightmarish tale of having been offered a ride by a man and woman riding a motorcycle, or perhaps riding two motorcycles, with stops to visit bootleggers," said Roark Bradford's son, who also remembered that Faulkner never forsook his "elaborately polite and chivalrous" manners: "He was the only person over the age of twenty-one who was allowed to call my mother 'ma'am.'"[14] Faulkner had not eaten for several days. He certainly acted like the starved reporter when he devoured three eggs and bacon she made for him. He talked about two women and three men living together indiscriminately,[15] which he compacted into the one woman and two flyers who become the reporter's obsession. This was Faulkner as hanger-on in this world of high flyers. To Vernon Omlie's wife, Phoebe, Faulkner was very much like the reticent reporter who goes along for the ride and puts himself at the service of the flyers. She said Faulkner had "no real desire . . . to be a precision flyer" or make flying a business. It became, instead, "a mental and emotional release"—as it does for the reporter who liberates himself from the grimy and gloomy environs of the newspaper office. Phoebe observed a "rather shy man who wanted to be left alone." In a "pair of old coveralls" he would lose himself in a "group of mechanics, and help out by washing parts or doing what he would around the general aircraft operation rather than be out where people could see him and lionize him."[16] In short, Faulkner craved the anonymity he confers on his reporter.

The reporter appears like an allegorical figure, almost like a ghost in a medieval mystery play. In the popular imagination, especially as it was fed by movies like *I Cover the Waterfront* (1931), the journalist is usually self-sufficient and cynical, manipulating the woman he loves and willing to do whatever it takes to get the story, which often involves corruption and solving a crime or a criminal conspiracy. The journalist is like H. Joseph Miller (Ben Lyon) in *I Cover the Waterfront* or Hildy Johnson (Pat O'Brien) in *The Front Page*. Both journalists are humanized and redeemed by beautiful women, who bring out the reporters' qualms about newspaper work. In fact, in Miller's case, he is a budding novelist—a sure sign that morally he is better than most crass reporters.

Faulkner forgoes the Hollywood sin-and-redemption scenario with characters who never do follow a conventional moral compass and are not bound by any community's standards of propriety. This air crew belongs nowhere and everywhere. It does not matter where they go so long as they can perform their show. By one definition, these are free spirits, not bound by any rules except those of the air races funded by capitalists like Colonel H. I. Feinman, Faulkner's version of Colonel A. L. Shushan. To emphasize the impurity of Feinman's power, he is identified as chairman of the Sewage Board. He is, in effect, the lord of a landfill, since the airport rests on reclaimed lake bottom. Ironically, the press treat Roger, Laverne, and Jack with fascination and scorn while spending not a moment inquiring into how the airport got built or what purpose the air race show fulfills in Feinman's master plan that includes stamping the letter *F* all over his property.

Only the reporter believes the story is the air crew themselves, not just their antics in the air. He is fascinated with how they live apart from the society they entertain. They seem to find it enough to be with one another. They work together as one unit, although Jack has a temper he expresses by kicking Jiggs, and Roger—even more than the others—lives to fly. Even as he expects to survive, he never discounts the danger. The reporter alone sees these characters as admirable—in part because he is a Prufrock, afraid to bring the moment to its crisis, to confess his love for Laverne and for what the flyers represent to him. As the reporter, he is a passive observer. He is repeatedly described as a scarecrow and a cadaver, one of the walking dead in T. S. Eliot's unreal wasteland city, one of the poet's impotent hollow men.

Faulkner is careful to provide almost no details about the reporter's life save for the mention of a thrice-married mother who does not care for her son. He is, in short, as deracinated as the flyers. But lurid newspaper ink circumscribes his world: "In the driver's seat there lay folded a paper: one of the colored ones, the pink or the green editions of the diurnal dogwatches, with a thick heavy typesplattered front page filled with ejaculations and pictures." This is the mediated prurient world of print culture, one that Faulkner had absorbed while hanging around newspaper offices in New Orleans writing his sketches of the city,[17] transmogrified in the novel into New Valois, the name of a French royal line, and a fitting irony for the tawdry city's aggrandizement of itself. Using journalistic jargon like "dogwatches" evokes the environs of journalism, but the novelist's compounded neologisms like "typesplattered" create a vocabulary that vitiates the reporter's profession. The stories journalists tell are a sensationalistic mess.

The factitious Feinman Airport opening is presided over by a disembodied amplified voice, "apocryphal, sourceless, inhuman." The newspaper office is similarly disquieting, a room right out of a film noir, with "down funneled light" from the editor's desk lamp. Journalism would not be depicted in such dim surroundings until the release of *Citizen Kane* (1941). In the hermetic "dusty gloom," the editor expresses a frustration with the reporter that many readers of the novel have also experienced:

> You have an instinct for events. . . . If you were turned into a room with a hundred people you never saw before and two of them were destined to enact a homicide, you would go straight to them as crow to carrion; you would be there from the very first: you would be the one to run out and borrow a pistol from the nearest policeman for them to use. Yet you never seem to bring back anything but information. Oh you have that, all right, because we seem to get everything that the other papers do and we haven't been sued yet and so doubtless it's all that anyone should expect for five cents and doubtless more than they deserve. But it's not the living breath of news. It's just information. It's dead before you even get back here with it.

Like the new journalists Tom Wolfe first touted in the 1960s, the reporter becomes part of the events and people he covers, latching on to just those characters who appeal to newspaper readers. But then he is unable to go beyond recording what they say to him. He cannot, in other words, turn his reports into stories, the "living breath of the news." But what the reporter wants to do cannot be contained within a newspaper article, any more than Faulkner felt his talent could be fully articulated in movie scripts or stories for popular magazines. Faulkner's "anxieties about his place in the world—as an artist and reporter on life, as a man subjected to the wiles of larger economic forces, as a frustrated novelist unable to focus entirely on his major vision— seem reflected in the figure of the reporter, who tellingly has no name. He is, in a sense, Faulkner's shadow," emanating from a "fantasy world Faulkner had created about himself."[18]

Faulkner's anomie in Hollywood is akin to the flyers who are confined to stunts and have neither the equipment nor the venue to show just how good they are. Journalism is a dead end for the reporter, and the editor explains, "patiently, almost kindly," why: "The people who own this paper or who direct its policies or anyway who pay the salaries, fortunately or unfortunately I shant attempt to say, have no Lewises or Hemingways or even Tchekovs on the staff: one very good reason doubtless being that they do not want them, since what they want is not fiction, not even Nobel Prize fiction, but news." Just substitute the "people who own this paper" for Howard Hawks talking about the "people who own this studio." The reporter, like the screenwriter, can never own his story, make it his sole property, or root himself in his own work. The flyers seek fulfillment only in flight, just as Faulkner sought fulfillment only in fiction, but both are bound, nevertheless, to paymasters who determine when they can fly and what he would write.

In the popular imagination, as depicted in *The Front Page* and *I Cover the Waterfront*, the conflict is between the wayward reporter and his disciplinarian editor. Seldom, until *Meet John Doe* (1941), did Hollywood take on newspaper owners. But in *Pylon,* the editor could just as well be a Hollywood producer advising Faulkner to stay within the conventional boundaries of a script. And the reporter's reaction, like Faulkner's, is to drink and subside into silence rather than engage any more deeply in the corporate culture that enmeshes him. The editor in *Pylon* is like Monroe Stahr in *The Last Tycoon* lecturing the recalcitrant writer about how to make movies. News, the editor implies, is not a narrative of lives and events per se but an account of a certain set of circumstances: "What I am paying you to bring back here is not what you think about somebody out there nor what you heard about somebody out there nor even what you saw: I expect you to come in here tomorrow night with an accurate account of everything that occurs out there tomorrow that creates any reaction excitement or irritation on any human retina; if you have to be twins or triplets or even a regiment to do this, be so." The newspaper reader has to get it all in one gulp, one documented day, in a you-are-there drama or movie. No flashbacks, Howard Hawks would say.

Of course, the repressed reporter romanticizes the flyers, who fascinate him because of their uninhibited sex lives, which the reporter as voyeur watches— but not with the journalist's practiced passivity. He yearns to be one of them, just as Faulkner coveted the role of war pilot, which his Hollywood buddy Laurence Stallings accorded him in a review of *Pylon*.[19] The reporter, escaping that dim newspaper office and the grind of a reporter's routines, gravitates to the open spaces that the deracinated Roger, Laverne, and Jack navigate with aplomb. The air is their world elsewhere come to grief on the wasted ground of New Valois.

The flyers forsake bourgeois values and live for their own sakes. They are willing to risk everything to pursue a society of their own. Such an uncompromising sense of self results in tragedy because of their human fallibility, which is caught up in modern mechanisms over which they cannot exert complete control. Even in the air this liberated trio is fixated on those pylons that enforce the boundaries of the racers' route. Roger, flying first an inferior plane, bests his competitors but crashes because the drunken Jiggs has not performed all of the necessary maintenance. Then, in a dangerously experimental plane, Roger plunges to his death. This flawed teamwork contributes to the flyers' fate as much as do Feinman's machinations. *Pylon* is not a parable of economic determinism. Faulkner's characters are too implicated in their own destiny to attribute their actions to forces outside themselves. Faulkner might rail against Hollywood, but he never forgot he chose to be there to pick up the check.

In the novel's closing chapters, the journalists cluster together to chew over the crash story, just like they do in countless newspaper movies—most memorably in *Citizen Kane,* a film *Pylon* anticipates by layering together reporters, editors, and their corporate masters. Unlike the star reporters in Hollywood dramas, Faulkner's reporter is hardly a hero. What he discovers makes him ill. "I could vomit too," one of the journalists says to the reporter. "But what the hell? He aint our brother." The irony, of course, is that the reporter wants to write about his fraternal feeling for Roger. When the reporter says, "you dont understand," he might as well quote Prufrock's lament that it is impossible to say just what he means.

The reporter's final effort to tell the story ends up in fragments the copyboy picks out of a wastebasket. Like an embryonic editor or budding scholar experiencing his first joy in deciphering an unpublished manuscript, the copyboy—bright, ambitious, and with a literary sensibility—pastes together the fragments, which "he believed to be not only news but the beginning of literature." After a bald summary of Roger's crash, the reporter observes that the pilot's "competitor was Death." Acknowledging Roger's honorable end—he deliberately steered his plummeting plane away from the people below—his two rivals circle the spot where he disappeared: "Two friends, yet two competitors too, whom he had met in fair contest and conquered in the lonely sky from which he fell, dropping a simple wreath to mark his Last Pylon." Less florid than the narrator of *Flags in the Dust,* the reporter nevertheless ennobles the aviators as knights of the air in a scene reminiscent of the romantic salute to war pilots in *Wings* (1927)—and also in the florid prose of Hermann Deutsch, who wrote about the dead aviator as "a gay cavalier of the skies" whose ashes are scattered from "scudding clouds," the remains of a man with "pulsing tissues" that had "once formed a living part" that had "clouded in the fine tingle of zestful living."[20] It is not hard to imagine Faulkner's scorn and yet affection for such romantic literary effects.

Reporters in Hollywood films—like H. Joseph Miller in *I Cover the Waterfront*—are often aspiring novelists chafing at the constraints of journalism, or playwrights like Stu Smith in *Platinum Blonde* (1931) seeking to evade the daily grind of the news. That they overcome the limitations of the trade and also, of course, win their ladyloves is precisely what Faulkner's novel contradicts as it shows how deeply mired the unrequited reporter is in events that he cannot surmount through literature. Thus the copyboy spots another draft on the editor's desk, a draft that is factual, detailed, specifying time, place, and outcome, but not the reporter's personal response: "At midnight last night the search for the body of Roger Shumann, racing pilot who plunged into the lake Saturday p.m. was finally abandoned by a threepiece biplane of about eighty horsepower which managed to fly out over the water and return without falling to pieces and dropping a wreath of flowers into the water approximately three quarters of a mile away from where Shumann's body is generally supposed to be since they were precision pilots and so did not miss the entire lake." Of this version, the reporter comments in a penciled note to the editor: "I guess this is what you want you bastard." The reporter's last words are directions to where he will be getting drunk, and where the editor can come with cash to pay for the drinks. This disgust with the higher-ups is typical of movie journalists, who delight in charging whatever they can to their bosses, and it is also, of course, the reporter's declaration of independence. His behavior is not so different from Faulkner's conflicted relationship with Hollywood producers, or with the aftermath of working on a story. In fact, after completing *Pylon,* Faulkner went off on one of his alcoholic binges. His mother called Dean: "William is drinking. He needs you." Dean came to Rowan Oak while his wife, Louise, remained with Maud.[21] The usual routine involved staying in Bill's Rowan Oak bedroom. Sometimes Dean took him for long country drives. Sometimes Dean did not know what else to do except drink with his brother until the bout subsided.

No one else intervened; no one else talked about such episodes. Remarkably few people, even family members, ever saw him intoxicated. His niece Dean Faulkner Wells wrote, "I never saw William Faulkner drunk." Her mother told her about the time in the Waco when after twenty minutes the liquored-up Bill gave up trying to land the plane and at Dean's request turned over the controls: "It was typical of the understanding between the brothers that William did not resent Dean's taking over. Nor did Dean judge his brother for losing his nerve."[22]

It is not surprising that Faulkner wanted to sell the novel to Howard Hawks. It contains crucial elements of their earlier collaborations: a love triangle in the fraught world of flyers. Tom Dardis goes so far as to argue that *Pylon* is an homage to Hawks.[23] It is an action story resembling the director's *Ceiling Zero* and *Only Angels Have Wings*. Faulkner's characters exhibit "all of the typical Hawksian virtues of professional competence before danger, combined with stoical endurance, qualities equally esteemed by Faulkner." That the reporter can only observe these taciturn figures from the outside is of course consonant with what the camera can capture. The reporter is, so to speak, the camera eye.

Why Hawks did not buy Faulkner's novel is not clear, but as producer Darryl Zanuck used to say, a movie had to develop a rooting interest for the hero, and neither the reporter nor Roger Shumann invites that kind of empathy or exudes the kind of charm that would make them, or characters based on them, attractive. Of course, Hawks could have had the novel rewritten, but under the new Production Code that was coming into full force in 1935, the sexual innuendo in *The Front Page* (1931) was impermissible. By having Roger and Laverne copulate in midair Faulkner goes well beyond anything the masterful Hawks could confect by way of bypassing the Breen office, enforcer of the Production Code. In fact, just then Hawks was going through elaborate rewrites on *Barbary Coast* because the film linked prostitution and gambling. So the scene in *Pylon* after Roger Shumann's death could not be filmed without radical revision, which would also have needed the backing of an independent studio boss like Sam Goldwyn,[24] willing to resist the kind of sanitization Breen demanded. *Pylon* features the kind of joking about sex and marriage prevalent in pre-Code films:

> "While you are supposing," the fourth [reporter] said, "what do you suppose his [Roger Shumann's] wife was thinking about?" "That's easy," the first said. "She was thinking, 'Thank God I carry a spare.'" They did not laugh; the reporter heard no sound of laughter, sitting quiet and immobile on his beer-case while the cigarette smoke lifted in the unwinded stale air and broke about his face, streaming on, and the voices spoke back and forth with a sort of brisk dead slap-slap-slap like that of the cards. "Do you suppose it's a fact that they were both laying her?" the third said. "That's not news," the first said. "But how about the fact that Shumann knew it too? Some of these mechanics that have known them for some time say they dont even know who the kid belongs to."

The Production Code forbid this portrayal of cynical and salacious journalists—even with the chastising comment that followed: "'You bastards,' the second [reporter] said. 'You dirtymouthed bastards. Why dont you let the guy rest? Let them all rest. They were trying to do what they had to do, with what they had to do it with, the same as all of us only maybe a little better than us. At least without squealing and bellyaching.'" The word "bastard" would never have made it to the screen.

Malcolm Cowley thought *Pylon* was constructed like a play: "The characters are easy to recognize: every time they walk on the stage, the author identifies them by phrases that have the same function as the catch lines or gestures of actors doing character bits. Thus, the reporter is known by his flapping coat, Jiggs the mechanic by his bouncing walk, and Laverne by her 'savage mealcolored hair.'" But Cowley's description, including his mention of the "quick, sharp, condensed" action,[25] is as applicable to a shooting script. Critics have complained about the lack of character development in the novel, but that is to measure *Pylon* by standards Faulkner is not observing in a work that does not probe motivation. In the hands of deft actors bringing to life the faces, gestures, and movements of his characters, *Pylon* might well succeed better on the screen than on the page. Douglas Sirk showed as much in his adaptation of the film, *Tarnished Angels,* which Faulkner liked.[26]

Peter Lurie calls the novel's basic elements—"the courageous pilots, the love triangle, and the boldface 'headlines'" used in Faulkner's own screenplays—"Hollywood fodder."[27] The absence of other salable features, however, argues for a more ambitious novel-cum-film. "*Pylon* evokes Weine's classic German Expressionist film *The Cabinet of Dr. Caligari,*" Susie Paul Johnson observes: "As the reporter appears for the first time, the narrator describes the way the other characters 'were now looking at something which had apparently crept from a doctor's cupboard and, in the snatched garments of an etherized patient in a charity ward, escaped into the living world.'"[28] Faulkner's antirealism in such passages countermands the journalistic imperative to record and document. So often in *Pylon* journalists resort to their lurid imaginations, which are stymied by what they cannot see when Roger, Laverne, and Jack are off-screen, so to speak. The novel is "a story trying to tell a story,"[29] and such films are rare in Hollywood and evoke the kind of hostile reactions Orson Welles had to confront after the release of *Citizen Kane.* The reporter himself pivots between elite and popular culture. He is the "sensitive go-between . . . alternately the tough, alert reporter of the American newspaper tradition or his more detached, urbane, Eliotic contemporary."[30] That kind of oscillation has perplexed certain readers of a novel Hollywood would have been hard put to homogenize. Without a clear denouement, separating fact from fantasy, the novel-cum-film founders. Even the ambiguous *Citizen Kane* required an RKO resolution, a Rosebud.

BACK TO BAILEY'S WOODS

Even though Hollywood did not purchase *Pylon,* Faulkner felt a little better about his circumstances, reimbursing the Bryants for taxes they had paid on his property. *Harper's* had published a short story, "Lion," in December, bringing in a little cash, and he expected a two-thousand-dollar advance from Smith and Haas (it arrived on February 5) for *Absalom, Absalom!* "We have spring to look forward to now; I think that the smell of plowed earth and the sight of greening willow buds and the sound of birds is always the best tonic which a man can have," he wrote to Will Bryant.[31] Faulkner still had his eye on Bailey's Woods, property adjacent to Rowan Oak where he had played as a child and that would serve as barrier to anyone encroaching on his domain from the side of his property close to the Ole Miss campus. He was as tenacious about property as Sutter or Sutpen, although he could not yet afford Bryant's purchase price. Faulkner's tone in his letters to Bryant is remarkable—so different from his letters to publishers and agents like Hal Smith, Morton Goldman, Ben Wasson, and Bennett Cerf. Faulkner may well have been mollifying Bryant until Faulkner could secure all the property he desired. But Bryant showed none of the skepticism or contempt that Faulkner's own family had often shown for his efforts. As property owner and literary man, Faulkner seemed to have Bryant's respect and even affection. And Faulkner wanted to please and impress him: "I have a great deal of respect for credit; if it had not been for that institution, I should not have now the home which I want. But I have too much respect for my credit now and in the future to abuse it. And to me, the taking on of this third obligation [securing more land without a down payment] with the first two (or neither of the first two) still undischarged, would be just that." *Pylon* would be out in a month, he told Bryant. "I have you on my list." The patient, encouraging Bryant replied: "I am watching your literary growth. Hope you see with me as to the Bailey Woods."[32]

Faulkner spent these first months of 1935 buggering up stories, to use his expression, and refusing to do a nonfiction book about Mississippi while assessing the state of his career, telling his agent, Morton Goldman: "I cannot and will not go on like this. I believe I have got enough fair literature in me yet to deserve reasonable freedom from bourgeoise material petty impediments and compulsion, without having to quit writing and go to the moving pictures every two years. The trouble about the movies is not so much the time I waste there but the time it takes me to recover and settle down again; I am 37 now and of course not as supple and impervious as I once was."[33]

Faulkner remained on cordial terms with Hal Smith, who visited Rowan Oak early in the year. The two men went hunting with shotguns and dogs in snow and mud, getting nothing but wet feet. Then Faulkner took Smith flying.[34] "All the ladies express bright pleasure and appreciation of the suave metropolitan breath which you brought to our snowbound and bucolic midst," Faulkner wrote Smith.[35] But another publisher, Faulkner hoped, might provide a better offer. Immersed in writing stories and still struggling with *Absalom, Absalom!*, he seems not to have paid any attention to reviews of *Pylon,* although they have their place in gauging his controversial reputation, especially since reviewers seemed bent on predicting Faulkner's extinction as a noteworthy writer.

Something Is Going to Bust

Smith and Haas published *Pylon* on March 25, 1935, just four months after Faulkner finished his typescript. The novel excited a small core of reviewers and disappointed many others. A "breathless adventure in reading," A. B. Bernd concluded in the *Macon Telegraph* (March 23, 1935). Ted Robinson in the *Cleveland Plain Dealer* (March 24), who had followed Faulkner's career with admiration, captured the novel's complex temper: "He adds the power of loving the people whom he scorns and of sparing us no brutality or vulgarity concerning the people whom he loves." Harold Strauss (*New York Times Book Review,* March 24) seemed prophetic, assessing *Pylon* as "an experimental book that contains a strong promise of leading to another major work." Faulkner had proven himself capable of turning to "any scene of human activity where there is tension and a wealth of nervous motion and treat[ing] it with persuasiveness, power, and imagination." Mark Van Doren (*New York Herald Tribune,* March 24) concurred: "Mr. Faulkner has never written a better story than this, or a more painful one." George Currie in the *Brooklyn Daily Eagle* (March 25) could not have known that he was trespassing on Faulkner's own experience when he described the novel as "reeking with the hot smell of engine oil" and with "alcoholic nausea." Faulkner had arrived in New Orleans after the air meet well-oiled, his exhaustion transmitted into the traumatic prose Currie quotes: "the garblement which was the city," featuring Laverne and "her strange little court of the knights of monkey-wrench and cotter-pins" in an "age in which a machine is more important than the hand which directs it."

In the *Nashville Banner* (March 24), the poet John Crowe Ransom, another frequent Faulkner reviewer, concluded it was a "bad book" that "seems to mark the end of William Faulkner." The reviewer deplored Faulkner's effort to make the flyers a mystery as a "hard lot but fearless." The novelist was one of those boys in the poolroom who admire "strong, silent, and vicious" types. Then Ransom resorted to the lowest form of criticism, biography: "Faulkner has never quite outgrown being one of those boys, but he likes to be a good deal more at the same time." The characters had no "depth or human dignity." They were just dirt, and not even country dirt—the kind that the Southern Agrarian Ransom preferred. The uncomprehending Ransom found the reporter "so limited" that "Faulkner is not in him either." This last phrase is striking because it is so proprietorial, so certain in its assertion of what is proper Faulkner. Similar sentiments came from a former admirer, William Soskin in the *New York American* (March 25), who spoke of his negative reaction to the novel as the "repudiation of an old friendship or a creed of thought or belief." *Pylon* invited epithets such as "disgusting, nauseating." Faulkner was now "passing out of the picture," declared Sterling North in the *Chicago Daily News* (March 27), a "genius astray," announced John T. Orr in the *Miami News* (May 26). John Bassett counted at least twenty similarly negative reviews.[36]

Several reviewers suggested Faulkner's prose was actually poetry, but only Malcolm Cowley showed how the sentences could be broken down into "separate lines as places where the voice instinctively breaks":

Above the shuffle and murmur
        of feet in the lobby
And above the clash and clatter
        of crockery in the restaurant
        the amplified voice still spoke,
        profound and effortless.

Cowley likened the "steady pulse-beat" of the poetic lines to the offstage tom-toms of *The Emperor Jones,* a play Faulkner admired—perhaps most of all for its atavism, its evocation of ancient and elemental forces that modern life cannot quite override with its amplified, technological voices. The new airport, described further on in the passage Cowley arranged as poetry, is a "steel-and-chromium mausoleum" juxtaposed against the "puny crawling painwebbed globe" emerging out of the "blind iron batcave of the earth's prime foundation." The airport, in other words, may seem to represent progress, an emergence from the cave, but it is a deathtrap, a cynosure of modernity that dooms the flyers. If Roger Shumann is "nearer to being a hero than any other character in Faulkner's eight novels," as Cowley claims, his fate chillingly reflects Faulkner's prophetic sense of how personal this novel had become, with its fatal denouement on November 10, 1935, when Dean's plane crashed. The reporter, a stand-in for the novelist, is instrumental in securing for Shumann the plane that will crash and end his life, just as Faulkner did for his beloved brother Dean, the only brother the novelist truly favored. And Dean reciprocated, worshipping William, telling his wife, Louise, that his brother and their mother came first. Dean's life had been disordered, and flying seemed to give him a mission. Faulkner, never really very adept at flying planes, conceded that lead role to Dean, a better pilot who, it was thought, could go into business for himself, avoiding the very corporate hegemony that Faulkner's novel deplores. Shumann, in Cowley's words, "preserves his integrity in the midst of disorder; he is capable, strong, devoted, ready to sacrifice himself and to protect others even when his plane is crashing [he steers away from the grandstand]. He is also the technician, the type of modern demigod. And he is killed partly by the business men who control the Airport Commission and partly by the interference of a literary weakling [the reporter]."

The drinking and flying in the novel and the drinking and flying among the Faulkners appeared obliquely in Lewis Garnett's review of *Pylon*: "Faulkner himself, I hear, is flying from airport to airport in the South with a sort of air circus; it may well be that he finds this rootless life lived on the rim of death far more to his taste than the fear-haunted clinging to mere life of the little towns whence these planes take off. For to Faulkner this life had always been a dreadful thing, and there is a certain glory in the mere act of escaping from it into the mists of alcohol." Glory, as in heroic drinking, and "mists," as in a world of imagination, and the novel as a kind of spell cast on the reader, an intoxicant, align Faulkner and the reporter. Garnett quotes the reporter "shrieking his I-am-I into the desert of chance and disaster." He is Prufrocked, asking, "Do I dare disturb the universe?" Or the speaker in Faulkner's favorite Crane poem, who announces, "Sir, I exist!" To which the universe replies, "The fact has not created in me / A sense of obligation."

Garnett captured the experience of reading the novel better than any other reviewer: "'Pylon' snatches you away from the daily world; and when you emerge at the end of the book, you are likely to feel with the reporter that 'Something is going to happen to me. I have got myself stretched too far and too thin and something is going to bust.' Maybe in his oblique way Faulkner is saying that his reporter is the world."[37] It may be that *Pylon*, more than any other novel Faulkner ever wrote, immerses you in what it was like for him to discover and track a story. Like the reporter, he was fond of saying his characters found him, and he had only to follow their lead.

A month after the publication of *Pylon,* on April 27 and 28, William and Dean Faulkner and Vernon Omlie held an air circus in Oxford. Five planes in the show featured wing walking and parachute jumping by the only black performer in the world, the *Jackson (MS) Clarion-Ledger* reported: "An added attraction will be given by Mr. Faulkner when he releases from the plane a copy of his latest book 'Pylon' attached to a miniature parachute. Mr. Faulkner is going to autograph this copy for the lucky person who receives it."[38]

Bill doted on Dean, as did their mother, especially after Murry Falkner's death. Bill worried that Maud would smother Dean, who was doing no more than pumping gas. Bill wanted his younger brother to have something of his own, which is why he had set Dean up with the Waco. Soon the brothers were taking long trips in the plane—as far as New York and Washington, D.C., luxuriating in the leather seats, each with its own ashtray. Dean turned out to be a pilot's pilot, earning Vernon Omlie's respect. Dean had the perfect timing of a superb athlete and often said he would rather fly than eat. On more than one occasion, when an engine failed in midair, he was able to safely guide the plane to the ground.

Although Estelle spoke of Dean's wild streak, others viewed him as far more open and compassionate than his brothers and without their brooding sense of family heritage. Certainly his outgoing nature appealed to his brother Bill, who teamed Dean up with Vernon Omlie in the brotherhood of the air and a thriving business: flying lessons, charter flights, aerial photography, sightseeing, and barnstorming.[39] In the summer of 1934, in Memphis, where Dean stayed while working with Omlie, he met Louise Meadow, easygoing and stylish, introduced to him by his cousin Sue Price. Soon Dean and Louise were joined by Bill and Estelle for get-togethers at the airport. On September 29, 1934, Dean and Louise married without telling anyone, apparently wanting no interference, especially from Maud, who had not taken to her sons' wives. A letter from Dean's aunt tacitly acknowledges as much: "Be a good sport and write to your little mother sometimes and just know that I'm always for you." In fact, Maud seemed to take the marriage well after Dean and Louise paid her a visit. "Thank goodness," Maud said, "I thought you'd never marry." Bill and Estelle were the next to know and the following week hosted a party for the newlyweds. "To the best wife of the best flier I have ever known," William Faulkner toasted. He would often appear in Memphis unannounced, Louise recalled, and if he did not show up, then Dean made his way to Oxford.[40] Sometimes the call was urgent: Bill had been drinking again, and Dean had to be there to watch over his brother, saying virtually nothing about it to anyone, not even his wife. Louise realized this Faulkner part of her husband's life simply did not admit anyone else. As Dean's daughter wrote, "My relatives were private people, building walls not only to shield themselves from outsiders but from one another."[41] The independent Louise seemed to have no problem coping with taciturnity and apparently kept her own counsel. Many years later she said Maud Falkner was an "extraordinarily self-centered, selfish, and demanding woman."[42]

The Faulkner who drank was the same man who wrote sober letters in the hot weather of July to Will Bryant: "It is with both pleasure and satisfaction that I send you the enclosed [another house payment] and so reply to your request of last month, if not to the full amount, at least sooner than I believed at the time I would be able." He was sorry to hear that both "Mr. Will," as he always addressed Bryant, and his wife, Miss Sallie, were not well. He mentioned "working steadily on a new novel [*Absalom, Absalom!*] which I hope and believe that you will like better than some, many, of the others."[43]

The day-to-day responsibilities that Faulkner took on with such grace also seemed to undo him, and drinking relieved the pressure until he reached a point when the drinking itself was his undoing. His recoveries were remarkable. Whatever Bill and Dean said and did during these debilitating bouts they kept to themselves. The point was to get on with it. During three weeks spent in New York in late September and early October 1935, Faulkner tried to raise money by selling manuscripts of *The Sound and the Fury, As I Lay Dying, Sanctuary, Light in August,* and *Pylon.* He did not want to part with this work, but he feared losing his home and land, as Sutter had done. With no takers, he hit up Hal Smith for a loan to be repaid by another stint in Hollywood. He had borrowed just enough to cover rent, taxes, insurance, and clothes for Estelle and the children. If Smith had not come through, Faulkner had been prepared to approach Harold Guinzberg at Viking Press. "I feel good and ready and 'hard-boiled' now, enough to cope with Shylock himself," Faulkner wrote Estelle. She was to be careful, paying cash for everything.[44]

He had some time to socialize, reporting to Estelle about seeing S. J. Perelman, one of his few Algonquin Round Table friends who was not in Hollywood working. He also maintained contacts with Smith's rival publishers Harold Guinzberg and his wife, Alice, Bennett Cerf, and Donald Klopfer— perhaps dangling in front of them the first four chapters of his novel. He also had time to see two Broadway plays, although he did not say which ones. He continued to work on short stories, gauging the market by meeting with a *Saturday Evening Post* editor.[45] By October 15, back in Oxford, he had started chapter 5, the halfway point of *Absalom, Absalom!*

Overhead on Friday, November 9, Dean Faulkner in the fire-engine-red, four-seater Waco biplane that his brother Bill had flown with Hal Smith aboard now made several low passes, leafleting Oxford to the delight of clapping children and excited adults, all set to watch, as Dean put it in his own words:

MAMMOTH ARMISTICE DAY AIR PAGEANT

Two days—Nov. 10–11, Two O'Clock.
Featuring Dean Faulkner and Navy Sowell.
THRILLING EXHIBITION OF STUNT FLYING
AND AERIAL ACROBATICS.
Death-defying parachute jumps by Navy Sowell.
See Pontotoc from the air.
Long rides, one dollar.
Landing field west of Pontotoc.
In case of inclement weather show will be held
the following week.

On Sunday, November 10, Dean took three farmers, Lamon Graham, Henry Graham, and Bud Warren, for a long ride. All three wanted an aerial view of their farms and talked about taking flying lessons. All had been drinking. They were a "rough type," Dean told his wife, but he needed the money.[46] Nearly an hour later, the plane had not returned. Louise, Navy Sowell, and two others drove along the plane's route and discovered the Waco crashed into a pasture. One of Dean's fellow pilots called William Faulkner, who turned to Estelle with the news and then called his brothers, asking them to meet at their mother's house. By the time they arrived, another pilot had already called her, and she simply gripped Bill's hand and said nothing next to her silent son. A little later, she said, "Did I ever do anything to make him unhappy?"

The crash had destroyed most of the plane. Interviewed by a local newspaper, Faulkner said Lamon Graham, who had some flying experience, was found with the wheel in his lap. Perhaps Graham had frozen at the controls.[47] The engine had been driven into the cockpit and into Dean. "Hell, Dean, is that you?," Faulkner was overheard to say. What was left of Dean? Faulkner claimed to have worked all night on his brother's face to make him presentable to his mother. But the casket, on a bier in Maud's front parlor, remained closed, and he told her, "I want you to remember him the way he was." Cho-Cho watched her grandmother Maud try to throw herself into the grave and be held back as the grave filled with earth.[48]

Exactly what happened has never been determined. E. O. Champion, an aviation mechanic, well disposed to Dean, who always "had a word for everyone," said Dean was "a fine flyer, but had been at it long enough to have grown careless in addition to the drinking at the time."[49] Decades later, Dean's daughter concluded, "Finding fault for the crash is beyond mortal consideration." But William Faulkner blamed himself—for all of it, getting Dean into the flying business and even supplying him with a plane. From now on Dean's widow and baby would be William Faulkner's responsibility. After the funeral on November 11, Armistice Day, Faulkner moved in with his distraught mother on 510 South Lamar, the home he had visited so often, and where Louise now recuperated. He drew a bath for her at night and brought her warm milk and a sleeping pill before bed. When she said at breakfast, "I can't eat. I dreamed the whole accident last night," he replied: "I dream it every night."

It was a bad time to be away from Rowan Oak, where Estelle was drinking heavily, Louise remembered. No one mentions what Estelle was going through at this time, or how isolated she may have felt as her husband withdrew into his own sorrow, focusing on his mother and Louise, especially when he moved into the house with his mother and brother's widow.[50] He slept on a cot and used the dining room table to work on *Absalom, Absalom!* Louise heard him at the typewriter steadily working every night. He began drinking three weeks after Dean's death. On the sofa, reminiscing with Louise, he began to cry and said, "I have ruined your life." She was only eighteen and five months pregnant. Maud appeared and said to the sobbing Louise: "You understand, Louise, he cannot help it. He could not stand it anymore. He had to have some relief." On Dean's gravestone, Faulkner saluted his brother with the same inscription he had given to John Sartoris in *Flags in the Dust:* "I bare him on eagles' wings and brought him unto me." This making of literature out of a life troubled Maud, who regarded the inscription as a monument to William Faulkner's grief. Dean had the Butler body. Only a few inches taller than Bill, he had grown a mustache like his older brother, written stories, and added a *u* to his name. Dean, the pilot's pilot, Vernon Omlie's star, had been a projection of William Faulkner's own dreams, and now Dean, "not yet thirty, had died in his stead."[51]

Dean's death occurred at the very time barnstorming was coming to an end, a relic, really, of the 1920s. Flying was a more orderly business now. Dean represented in his high spirits and daring what Faulkner had written about in his stories and also in "Flying the Mail," in which the pilot is regarded with "awed respect," a cavalier of the air.[52] Later Maud told her granddaughter, named Dean after her father, that the "merry wild spirit" attributed to John Sartoris emanated from the "warm and ready and generous" brother, who stood apart from Jack, John, and William, who had more of young Bayard's aloof and tormented character. William Faulkner rarely spoke of his youngest brother to Dean, born four months after her father died, although she remembered his telling her on one occasion, "Your father was a rainbow."[53] Fraternal feelings, so much a part of *Absalom, Absalom!*—figured into the way Henry Sutpen worships Charles Bon, the more worldly, accomplished brother—became the increasing focus of Faulkner's work in the last two chapters of his novel. So, too, did the focus on their sister, Judith, so self-contained like Louise and at the same time the object of their intense affections.

Faulkner's stepdaughter, Cho-Cho, said he had fallen in love with Louise, and Louise admitted to Cho-Cho that she was "very much drawn to him," but they did not become lovers.[54] Did his drinking in the wake of Dean's death relate to an ardor he could not express, or was it, as Louise supposed, because he now worried about leaving home for another Hollywood assignment, which also meant interrupting work on his novel? On December 4, he wrote to Morton Goldman that *Absalom, Absalom!* "is pretty good and I think another month will see it done." But he needed to get a movie contract: "I dont care how . . . just so I do." He did not "particularly want to go," but he had to repay Hal Smith.[55]

On December 10, Faulkner flew to California to work on a film adaptation of *Wooden Crosses,* a French novel about World War I. There he would meet a young woman whom he could love, far from home, who reminded him of home.

2

Transcendental Homelessness

Absalom, Absalom!,
December 1935–October 1936

Despite the deep connection to the history and tragedy of the American South that permeates all of his novels, William Faulkner remains, to borrow a phrase from Lukács, one of the most eloquent novelists of "transcendental homelessness."

> —Sean Latham, "Jim Bond's America: Denaturalizing the Logic of Slavery in *Absalom, Absalom!*"

Romance during a Mad Yankee Operation

The Twentieth Century-Fox lot, the largest in Hollywood, went on for acres—truly a world unto itself, with city streets, neighborhoods, fields, forests, a swamp, and huge sound stages, each enclosing a world of make-believe. It has often been said that Faulkner hated the artificial atmosphere of Hollywood; indeed, he said so himself. But it is unwise to think his word—or that of others—is the last to be uttered on the subject. In truth, even a great novelist, as F. Scott Fitzgerald would tell you, could be seduced by the romance of movie making. After all, a man from Mississippi had magnolia in his blood and was susceptible to the fragrant, blooming atmosphere of this wonderland in which he could create a new, idealized version of himself. But until December 1935, Faulkner, by then thirty-eight, had not found the woman willing to enter into courtship on the terms he had worked out in his imagination.

No wonder, then, that when he entered the outer office at Fox studios, he was startled at what he saw. He had arrived exhibiting his usual stony manner—honed during three previous Hollywood enlistments—like a soldier reporting for duty. At least that's how he appeared to twenty-eight-year-old Meta Carpenter, who thought she was not what he had been expecting. Apparently flustered, his usual aloof—some would call it disdainful—demeanor dropped from view as he just about managed to say he was William Faulkner and that Mr. Hawks was "kind of expecting me."

The Meta Carpenter he met for the first time had come a long way—in fact, just as far as he had. She had grown up on the Ussery plantation in Tunica County, Mississippi. She did not remember having running water until she was eight or nine. Until then she washed in a zinc tub in the kitchen. The family never did have electricity, just gas lights. She remembered cleaning coal oil lamps and chimneys and sleeping on feather mattresses. No central heat. Just big fireplaces. Turner, a black servant, would light the fire and bring in water for washing. A big bell would be rung as a signal for the black people to start their work in the fields and in the house. Mammy Adeline took care of Meta's mother and later Meta. Adeline had the right to switch Meta with a wet dishrag around the legs. This part of her upbringing especially intrigued Faulkner, who would tell Meta about his Mammy Callie.[1] Meta had liked jumping on the sideboard of wagons, playing with black children, and sinking into fluffy cotton, like sinking into down pillows, after it had been ginned and the seeds removed. She relished the hayrides, buggy rides, and horseback riding, waiting for the afternoon train from Memphis bringing the mail. All in all, it was a countrified version of William Faulkner's own upbringing that he and Meta liked to remember.[2]

A made-over Mississippian, but a Mississippian nevertheless, Meta blurted out, "*The* William Faulkner." She had seen him once before, on April 7, 1922, at the Ole Miss Cotillion Club's Easter Ball, featuring the music of the Magic City Syncopators. Fifteen-year-old Meta wore high heels for the first time, the first of many firsts, including her participation in a grand march and wearing a corsage. "That's Bill," someone said, pointing at a young man across the room. Who was Bill?, she wanted to know. "Bill Faulkner," she was told.[3]

This lowly script girl, as she called herself, understood the value of staying professionally cool when dealing with stars like Spencer Tracy, Loretta Young, and Will Rogers. But she had visited Oxford in her teens and had heard stories about the raffish writer who hung out with riffraff—and even with "darkies"—to the disgust of his fellow townsmen. This larger-than-life figure turned out to be small and poorly dressed in an ill-fitting tweed suit. But he overcame his disarray with the intensity of his brown eyes, which never left her face. Meta had already been caught up in his imagination, triggered by the South he heard in her voice. "Mr. Faulkner," she told him, "I'm not only from the South, I grew up in Mississippi"—to which he replied with the only appropriate southernism at hand, "I declare." She elaborated: "Tunica, Mississippi. In the Delta. Though I was born in Memphis." With hand politely extended, like one of his Sartorises, Faulkner pressed hers, saying what had to be said: "Well, I never." He took it as an "augury of something good that on my first day of reporting to a Hollywood studio, I meet a fellow Southerner." This flourish accomplished, he walked into Howard Hawks's office just like the southern gentlemen of her childhood, "the lower torso thrust forward, the upper part of him leaning backward, so that he was slanted in motion, almost tilted."

Meta Carpenter's "*The* William Faulkner" was a southern gentleman and also the author of *Absalom, Absalom!*, a work that not only reaches back toward the past but also, in its conclusion, projects into the future. This was the novel he had been working on and had hoped to finish before this third Hollywood trip. *Absalom, Absalom!* is about displacement and displaced persons: Thomas Sutpen removes himself from his West Virginia home to Haiti, and then to Mississippi in order to establish Sutpen's Hundred, a spectacular plantation he will design as if he and his creation are sui generis; Quentin Compson, far from his native southern ground in his cold Harvard dormitory room, ruminates over his ambivalent southern identity and about the meaning of Sutpen's story as told to him by Rosa Coldfield, who denounces the demonic Sutpen, and by Quentin's father, who seeks a rational explanation of Sutpen's rise and fall; Shreve, a Canadian warming to the Southern Gothic mystery he has to wrench out of his roommate, Quentin. And the history that Quentin and Shreve piece together has as its focal character the illusory Charles Bon of New Orleans and Haiti, who rides from Louisiana in the company of his best friend, Thomas Sutpen's son Henry, bound for Mississippi. In *The Cunning of History*, Richard L. Rubenstein suggests that the twentieth century consists of the history of displaced peoples. And the displaced author of *Absalom, Absalom!*, lately of Oxford, Mississippi, but by way of Toronto and New Orleans—not to mention stays on the campuses of Yale University and Ole Miss, and a European trip like the one his great-grandfather, also a novelist, had taken—embodies that history. Faulkner did not have to read the papers to learn that Hollywood was becoming home to refugees from Hitler's Germany and Stalin's Russia. At a Hollywood party, for example, he met Shura Cherkassky, "an enormously gifted pianist who had come from the stifling political climate of Europe to the United States and was all but starving."[4] Faulkner only had to look around—and he was famous for never forgetting what he saw.

Hollywood lots full of ostentatious facades that pretended to magnificence were not that different from the decaying house Faulkner had renamed

Rowan Oak. But of course Hollywood was not of his making, even though it had a bawdy pretentiousness not unlike what Sutpen wanted from his French architect, who tried to run away and was hunted down like a dog even while refusing, no matter what, to sacrifice his humanity to Sutpen's grandiose design. An infuriated Faulkner had done the bidding of Hollywood moguls, who employed writers the same way Sutpen did his French architect. Both the writer and the architect were high-priced talent treated like indentured servants under contract and susceptible to the whims of overlords who could arbitrarily terminate a career—or, in Sutpen's case, a life.

And now there was Meta, erupting in the story like a Faulkner character, carrying with her in this foreign clime a temperament formed elsewhere. Faulkner, until now, had been a sort of Coriolanus—abrupt, rude, and scornful of the writers, executives, and producers who lorded it over him, even though they were beneath him. Why should he make the gesture of obeisance the Hollywood scenario called for? Why should he parade his writer's wounds in the Hollywood square for all to see? No, like Coriolanus, Faulkner preferred his sulks and silences, as he went on in his irate and independent fashion. Where on a studio lot could he have found anyone who would appreciate his soft-spoken manner, when what Hollywood valued was the noise of fame, the music of celebrity, the dance of scandal? Hollywood was the cynosure of evanescent success. A career could flicker and flame out as quickly as a piece of celluloid.

Still drowning anxieties and anger in drink, he said, "Mornin', Miss Carpenter." Two days later he barely managed to say that much as he made his way carefully into the office, maintaining his dipsomaniacal gravity, remarking on the beautiful weather as he nearly tipped over into her lap. A glazed-over Faulkner, full of liquor fumes, invited her to dinner. Still very much the southern lady, Meta retreated to Howard Hawks's office and begged the director to tell Faulkner, whom she knew to be married, that she could not go out with him. "I'm not used to men who drink to excess," she added. Hawks took care of it—until the next day, when a sober Faulkner turned up to continue his conversation about the weather. She had not wanted to hurt his feelings, and apparently she had not done so. Or had he forgotten what had happened the day before? She couldn't tell. After conferring with Hawks, Faulkner announced, "I'd be very honored, Miss Meta, if you'd have dinner with me tonight." He took her refusal calmly, since from the moment he stood in the door looking at her, he told himself, "There she is!" It was a decision worthy of Thomas Sutpen, who paid no nevermind to rejection and went after what he wanted.

Meta seemed firm about her own decision not to go out with Faulkner. Then she received a letter from a Mississippi relative telling her all about

Faulkner's troubled marriage, the death of his first child, Alabama, and the birth of his daughter Jill, to whom he was devoted. So when Faulkner asked Meta out again, she rebuffed him even more strongly. But he responded with a nearly expressionless look and a steady gaze that reflected his unalterable design. As he later told her, he would have known she was "the one" for him no matter where or when they met. As in his fiction, place and time were but extensions of his own imagination. And like a fascinated Faulkner reader, she found the grandeur of his vision irresistible.

Estelle, of course, had once been the one. What Faulkner made of Meta, a southern woman on her own in Hollywood of all places, with a figure he liked to draw and with the manners of a proper lady in the service of an industry where no ladies need apply, he never said. At the same time, Meta, more pliable than Estelle and in terms of employment, subservient, no matter how well he treated her, paradoxically asserted her independence insofar as he had to court her, a challenge he welcomed, a prize he cherished.

Hawks gave Meta the first handwritten pages of Faulkner's screenplay "Wooden Crosses," later titled *The Road to Glory,* based on an award-winning French novel about trench warfare, and on a French film adaptation with spectacular battle footage that would be incorporated into the Fox film. Hawks scrapped the novel's ensemble cast of characters who one by one lose their lives, except for a few survivors, one of whom narrates their fate. Hawks favored instead a Shakespearean approach, with the two officers, La Roche and Denet, as comrades in arms and rivals in love, complemented by a group of soldiers as groundlings commenting on the action. But the director retained and embellished several of the novel's riveting scenes: the remnant of a regiment dreading their fate as they hear the Germans digging a tunnel and placing mines to blow them up; that same regiment's entrance into a cemetery, an "orchard of wooden crosses"; the anguished cries of a soldier in no-man's-land out of reach of his rescuers exposed to merciless machine-gun fire. This unflinching account, written by an infantry veteran, was hardly Hollywood's usual fare, yet Hawks drew Faulkner to this holocaust, counting on him to invent a story not only appealing to moviegoers but also acceptable to the censors. "We would also like to recommend that care be taken not to make any of the battle scenes, etc., unduly gruesome," cautioned Production Code czar Joseph Breen.[5]

Faulkner had been assigned by associate producer Nunnally Johnson to work on the script with Joel Sayre, whose initial treatment did not satisfy Johnson. Sayre was charmed by Faulkner and his work. "One of the pleasantest men to spend time with that he ever knew," Sayre told Carvel Collins. "Faulkner's voice was a wonderful relief in Hollywood, where so many people were speaking with such strident, overwhelming voices." A year earlier Sayre had been worrying that Hollywood would lower his status as a writer. In a diary dialogue with himself, he asked: "Ain't you afraid Hwd will get you? . . . You don't see no Dreisers, Lewises, Cabells, Anderson, O'Neills . . . out there, do you?" Even a journalist like Ben Hecht did not stick around but took the Hollywood money and departed, Sayre told himself. He had grown up dazzled by airplanes and enlisted in the Canadian army in World War I, but like Faulkner he had not seen action, although he had been assigned to the American expeditionary forces in Siberia. In short, the two men had plenty of experiences to share. Through a friend, Sayre had come out to do work on *Barbary Coast,* a Hawks picture, joking that he was one of eighty writers who had tried to write a script for it. Meta Carpenter remembered that Sayre and Faulkner treated one another with "mutual respect and admiration."[6] They also liked to drink together. Sayre's exuberance, the sheer thrill of working and playing with Faulkner, comes through in his oral history:

> He was so swell in so many ways. He drank, of course, but he was the best guy to drink with that I ever saw. The more he drank, the more good natured he got. By the time the bottle was empty, he would just be beaming like. Nobody would ever pick a fight with Faulkner. You couldn't think of any reason. He'd loosen up. He's quite reserved at the start, but gee, once he started talking about something he was interested in he was simply marvelous. . . . Hawks used to give him a job every now and then. He regarded this as a kind of mad Yankee operation that he couldn't explain. . . . He had a fantastic wife named Stell. She'd been a missionary's wife, I think, in China. I think she smoked the opium or something. She was quite nuts.[7]

Sayre makes Faulkner behave like the happily drunken Robert Young in *Today We Live.* Sayre could not have seen that much of Estelle, and like Meta, it is likely that Sayre viewed Faulkner's wife as the character Faulkner made her out to be. Perhaps, for the fun of it, Faulkner actually did say that Estelle was a missionary's wife. Faulkner regaled Sayre with Snopes stories. He impressed Sayre with his productivity, writing forty pages in one night, an unheard-of feat for a screenwriter. But the film "took a long time because Faulkner went to the hospital at least twice if not more times to get dried out."[8] Sayre revered this soft-spoken man's dedication and dreaded his frequent depressions. Dorothy Parker remembered how Sayre tried to protect his writing partner. Faulkner, so open, so vulnerable, needed professional help, Sayre concluded, suggesting an appointment with a psychiatrist. Sayre had a car ready to take Faulkner for treatment. "Will he give me a drink?," Faulkner asked, deciding not to go.[9]

Sayre remembered taking Faulkner to see Charlie Butterworth's comedy routine, which Faulkner enjoyed, practically falling in the aisle in his "almost silent suppressed laughter." Sayre introduced Faulkner to Butterworth, who lamented that his material was getting stale. Couldn't these writers come up with something? A week later Faulkner handed Sayre a "fistful of material," routines that involved Hitler and Mussolini, and even Stalin "got into the act somehow." Sayre doubted Butterworth could deliver the lines. They seemed "unactable," but Sayre was surprised that Faulkner would take the time to write for the comedian.[10]

Sayre was also surprised to learn that Dashiell Hammett and Faulkner were such good friends, especially since Hammett had done what Sayre supposed was impossible: pick a fight with Faulkner at a party. Hammett said Faulkner had been "a failure because he had refused to sign any liberal petitions or communist petitions or take any active interest of a political sort in the reform movements with which Dashiell Hammett was himself associated." Apparently, Faulkner did not mind the diatribe.[11]

David Hempstead, an assistant to Nunnally Johnson, a producer on *The Road to Glory,* noted that Faulkner was "incredibly naive. This was another reason why you loved him. You felt, 'Somebody will do this guy in if I don't personally watch out for him.' He was not cynical in his melancholy, viewing the spectacle with dispassionate humor—removed, looking at something taking place offstage."[12] Faulkner talked to Hempstead about his novels and never about his motion picture scripts. It was as though he had just left his characters in the "next room or he was about to rejoin them." Waitresses loved him. He was the very model of what a "gentleman was supposed to be. His courtesy was unprecedented. His manners impeccable. His consideration in tiny things that most of us do not bother about or just are not sensitive enough to bother about were deeply appreciated by people who were not accustomed to seeing him."[13]

Nunnally Johnson, a writer and fellow southerner, liked to tell the story of his first meeting with Faulkner in the grandest and most imposing office on the Fox lot, situated on three floors and approached by ascending two marble staircases and walking across a long-napped green carpet. Faulkner made this journey "like a man with a heap of walking to do and was in no particular hurry to get it done," eventually arriving at the producer's desk, hat in hand, to ask:

"Are you Mr. Johnson."
"I am."
"Are you Mr. Faulkner."
"I am."

After an awkward silence, Faulkner produced a new pint of whisky but had trouble opening it. Dropping his hat on the floor he used both hands to rip off the heavy tin foil, gashing a finger that dripped blood into his hat. Apparently unperturbed, he drank half of the open bottle and offered the rest to Johnson:

> "Have a drink of whisky?"
> "I don't mind if I do."

Johnson finished off the pint. This began the start of a three-week drunk that landed the producer and writer in an Okie camp, from which they were extricated by studio detectives.

The Faulkner–Nunnally Johnson escapade scene is worthy of a pre-Code film where so much drinking and so little dialogue would not be a problem, and where the visual impact of studio grandiosity in a what-price-Hollywood movie would be established. Roark Bradford, a Faulkner friend, relished the Okie camp denouement, adding, "I, for one, have made no effort to verify this story; I am not a man to spoil a good tale with statistics." The sober version is that writer and producer got along well.[14] They were born in the same year—Johnson in Columbus, Georgia, a town not that much bigger than Oxford, Mississippi. Faulkner told Johnson about his grief over Dean's death, elaborating a story about a nightlong struggle to reconstruct Dean's face that also seems pure Hollywood. The two shared a sensibility that Johnson's biographer sums up in a sentence about his subject: "Through his life, there was a tension in Johnson between the desire for the order and stability represented by the idea of home and the excitement and adventure represented by the idea of escape."[15]

Faulkner liked to make light of his Hollywood work. Dashiell Hammett told Lillian Hellman about Faulkner's claim that he was trying to sell to Darryl Zanuck an original script about a man raping a woman on the edge of a cliff—"just as he succeeds they fall off locked together. The movie was to be just about his struggle to get on top of her for the landing."[16] In fact, during those supposedly lost three weeks with Nunnally Johnson, Faulkner and Sayre not only cowrote a full screenplay but responded to numerous requests from Darryl Zanuck, head of Fox production, to make changes, some of which were done overnight to satisfy the studio schedule. Faulkner did not saunter to work, and he did not miss deadlines.[17] And as George Garrett observes, Faulkner thrived in an atmosphere of huge egos and talents—Hawks, Johnson, and Zanuck—"powerful and often contradictory presences." Faulkner is said to have later remarked to a fellow writer assigned to a film: "Don't take the work too seriously. But you take these people very, very seriously." "Too seriously" is the operative phrase. Unlike some writers who rankle when asked to collaborate or to change their work, Faulkner complied with studio dictates. That meant honoring demands with "complete, unstinting integrity . . . in every exercise of his craft." To do less than one's best is to demean the profession and the writer's own sense of self. That Faulkner would sometimes suggest otherwise—that he was writing tripe—might humor those who had "no right to understand the artist's choices." At all times, he had to maintain a distance from his Hollywood work. To take it too seriously would have harmed his devotion to *Absalom, Absalom!,* a work that grew apace in the early California mornings before he had to report for duty at the studio, where he worked with men as obsessed and passionate as himself.[18] Sometimes he worked at Ben Wasson's house, throwing pages on the floor as he worked while Ben's butler picked them up.[19] Complain about his Hollywood work? Certainly. But as Meta Carpenter said: "Bill was far too honest with himself, and far too wise to permit hate to becloud his genius. He reserved his anger for injustice and oppression."[20]

Faulkner's handwritten script, full of technical terms, reveals how he had learned to write in terms of a visual medium:

Full shot; Medium close shot; Medium shot: Medium long shot; Camera pans; Group shot: Camera trucks up; Two shot; Quick dissolve to; Medium close truck shot; Three shot; WIDEN ANGLE; Camera holds on; Reverse angle; Cut to; The camera moves back; Hand comes into camera; Aerial shot; Reverse shot; Camera trucks across courtyard; Double exposure begins to fade as camera comes back through gate; The camera picks up the group; The camera passes from face to face; The camera swings back up faster now; The camera swings back; the camera swings around; The camera picks up the group; Camera trucks and pans with her; The camera pulls back.[21]

His earlier screenplay treatments, following Hawks's advice, made minimal references to the camera, but now he seemed eager to write for the screen, constantly moving along the action and seeing it from different angles and points of view.

As in *Today We Live, The Road to Glory* obligated Faulkner to reckon with a romantic triangle not in the original material but put there by Joel Sayre at Hawks's direction. Like Ann in *Today We Live,* Monique is an army nurse loved by two men. Monique is devoted to Captain Paul La Roche, but then she falls in love with La Roche's second-in-command, Lieutenant Michel Denet.[22] La Roche is worn out by war. He is shown constantly swallowing aspirin and drinking cognac, barely managing to overcome his exhaustion.

But he is also a highly disciplined soldier who has hardened himself to death, unlike the softer Michel—a courageous soldier but also an artist, who woos Monique by playing the piano. He is witty; La Roche is earnest and unbends only in Monique's presence. She feels obligated to La Roche, who is taking care of her family, but she loves Michel. Monique resists Michel's advances. But slowly he breaks down her resistance—in part by paying deference to her resistance, her insistence on the integrity of her own person. Something like this scenario was playing itself out as Faulkner stood over Meta helping her to decipher his virtually microscopic text.

A war in which men must show their solidarity and even their love for one another, performing their duty, not indulging in their personal desires, has its parallel in the romantic triangle, as Denet vows to defer to La Roche after discovering that the woman he desires is his commanding officer's beloved. Denet strives to control his compulsions—to resist courting Monique, to resist his men's panic over the mine that might blow up their line. Denet executes La Roche's order that they stay in place until replacements arrive. Thus Denet subordinates his individual will to collective action. La Roche and Denet form a partnership, a collaboration like the Hawks-Faulkner brotherhood.

La Roche, like Claude in *Today We Live,* is blinded and no longer regards himself as Denet's romantic rival. Like Claude, La Roche forgives his beloved and declares, "I understand everything," a sentiment that is implied but not actually expressed in the released film. Subsequently, La Roche is blown up in a barrage he directs (with his father's help) on his own position, which is the only way to destroy the German assault. His father, a veteran of the Battle of Sedan in the Franco-Prussian War (September 1–2, 1870), sounded the last charge with his bugle. He deplores the lack of cavalry and bugle-blown attacks in modern warfare and might as well be one of those Civil War veterans who populated Faulkner's childhood. In fact, Sedan was a lost cause, marking a humiliating French defeat with the capture of Napoleon III. When La Roche's father sounds his horn just before he is blown up, he is evoking the "wild bugles and the clashing sabres and the dying thunder of hooves" that so permeated Gail Hightower's existence.

Many Hawks scholars comment on the cyclical nature of his work—not only his repetition of the same story lines, as in *Today We Live* and *The Road to Glory,* but also in his awareness that one man carries on another's work,[23] as Denet takes over from La Roche at the end of the film. Faulkner fulfilled a typical Hawks plot. But Hawks channeled Faulkner all the same, since the repetition of characters and wars is a feature of *Flags in the Dust* and *The Unvanquished,* and the solemn La Roche and the gay Denet bear some resemblance to the brothers Sartoris, young Bayard and John. As is often the case in film productions, it is difficult to ascertain exactly who wrote what—especially since Faulkner, Sayre, associate producer Nunnally Johnson, and Hawks himself all worked on the film's dialogue. But however you look at the film, Faulkner is fused to this collective authorship.

Meta struggled to read Faulkner's cursive strokes, "at once private and cryptic, now graspable, now unyielding." Like a literary scholar or biographer, she wondered, "Where had he learned to write like that?" Working on a Faulkner manuscript is frustrating and exhilarating by turns because it is almost like breaking a cypher, a decrypted code that in Meta's case opened the way to an intimacy. She called him at his hotel for help, and soon they were on a first-name basis, Bill and Meta. He was at her side in the Hawks office, looking over her shoulder as she typed out his words but also turning away, Denet-like, when she did not need his assistance, "a small, well-considered act of courtesy," she noted, from a man who faulted himself for her struggles with his handwriting.

As Meta quickly realized, Faulkner was seducing her with southernisms and with little confidences when their hands touched while handling his script. The scene resembles those moments in *The Road to Glory* when Michel is seducing Monique next to him on the piano stool as he plays Chopin while the bombs fall. Although Faulkner said he had no feeling for music, he was quite aware of how much classical music meant to the classically trained Meta Carpenter, who would later marry a classical pianist. They began stealing glances at one another, Carpenter remembered—she admiring not only those alert brown eyes but also his high cheekbones and thrusting chin, carefully matched with a moustache that hid his "small sensitive mouth," and he admiring her lithe ninety-two-pound figure, exactly the kind of trim woman he had often apostrophized in his poetry and prose. She could have been one of his creations, and, in a sense, she became one as the screenplay began to take shape.

Carpenter's comments on Faulkner's screenwriting are a revelation of the man and his work. She thought highly of his visual sense and his story lines, but his dialogue was a challenge to the medium of film because its length exceeded the norm. In Meta's experience, he took his job seriously, no matter how much he might decry Hollywood. She admired his uncompromising refusal to "write down to the medium."

Faulkner now remained sober in her company and seems to have hidden his depression from her. Or perhaps, in her presence, he experienced a recovery, a kind of therapy. No other woman in his experience had come so close to him in the very act of writing. She had been assigned to him because she was adept at working on the continuity that movie scripts required. In short, she did more than just take dictation.[24] He had offered handmade books to Estelle and other women as tributes, but none of them had been his amanuensis. Now, Meta wanted to know what every word meant, even as she still said no to his invitations—but with a quiet humor that became part of a game between them.

Then Meta's daily dose of Faulkner was withdrawn when Hawks decided she had mastered the screenwriter's illusory writing. Having cracked his code, she missed the man. The import of his work, and the man, overcame her, and the glamour of the stars entering the Fox office actually seemed to contaminate the atmosphere now that he was absent. The younger men in her company seemed like so many indistinguishable extras. She wearied of a world where she was just a girl, someone to say "hi" to without giving her a thought—or to be sent off on an errand by Howard Hawks to make purchases for a mistress.[25]

Faulkner had always dreamed of a woman he could woo with words. That was, he confessed, his reason for writing poetry. His aesthetic could be summed up in Poe's "To Helen." He appeared in the guise of Poe's poet: the "weary, way-worn wanderer" bearing the visions of his beloved to "his own native shore." Hadn't he told her, nearly every day, that she reminded him of home? And wasn't she now wishing for the man who mattered, and who mattered to her? She had begun to think so, detecting a note of boastfulness in her replies at the Studio Club, a sort of sorority for young women working in Hollywood, a "relatively inexpensive and clean and attractive" place.[26] She had a room there. Her friends teased her about working with this notorious author. She also noticed that when she typed his work, she made very few errors, as if this Hollywood scenario was a sacred book, a Talmud teaching her to say yes to him the next time he entered the office. In short, Meta had become as overwrought as a Faulkner sentence, and, wound up in his company, she said yes to yet another invitation to go out with him. She took the writer by surprise, because so far he had been feeding her a line the way an actor runs his sides with whomever happens to be available. He stammered for a moment, taken aback and looking like the awkward boy who had just had his invitation to the prom accepted, Meta remembered. And then the man came into his own—or as Meta put it, he became "a newly handsome William Faulkner."

Meta referred to her volte-face as "female perversity." How like her to use a phrase that could have been penned by Faulkner, the novelist who created Temple Drake, the arbitrary female par excellence, capable of forsaking her southern gentleman, Gowan Stevens, and bedding down with a gangster. Indeed, Temple epitomized the very character Meta's girlfriends had in mind when they gossiped about her doings with the outré author of *Sanctuary*. Had they read *Sanctuary* or at least the February 16, 1931, *Time* account of the "nightmare novel," or seen *The Story of Temple Drake*? "The odor of sleaze hung over the project from the start," writes film historian Thomas Doherty, who calls it the "most notorious vice film of 1933," which contributed to harsher enforcement of the Production Code.[27] In promotional material for the film, Faulkner's name appeared along with that of Miriam Hopkins, touting his "Flaming story," "daring" and "sensational" novel. On June 3, 1933, the *Los Angeles Times* reported on the huge crowd that had shown up in a theater "more than packed" to see Faulkner's "sensationally sordid 'Sanctuary.'" Even though it had been "kicked around censorially," the filmmakers had kept much of the original—"Which much is, bye the bye, quite sufficient." Meta made it worse for herself by auditioning, so to speak, for one of the "bad girl" roles that Miriam Hopkins often played and cultivated in off-screen stories about her divorces and feuds as an undomesticated virago.[28]

The demure Meta salved her conscience by telling herself Faulkner was not a disreputable sort at all but rather a southern gentleman and that her evening with him would be one that she could relate without compunction to his wife. Meta saw Faulkner as the antithesis of those Hollywood lechers who preyed upon young women. In the company of her courtier, she rose above the Studio Club gossip. He had rescued her.

He took her to one of his favorites: Musso & Frank's Grill on Hollywood Boulevard, within a short walking distance of Grauman's Egyptian and Chinese theaters. The restaurant remains today an intimate place to dine, where you can sink deeply into a red upholstered booth and concentrate on your beloved. Later, they always returned to the middle booth along the left wall, where no one entering the restaurant would see them. An Italian small-town southern waitress with "crimped hair and an over powdered skin" took their order as these two great-grandchildren of slave owners, steeped in the sayings of Robert E. Lee and Stonewall Jackson, reminisced about their "own South." Taking in her family's claim to descent from an Irish king, he said, "Your ancestors were a lot more aristocratic than mine." Like Estelle, Meta played the piano and had taken ballet lessons. She climbed trees like Caddy Compson. But it was not all nostalgia. When Meta mentioned the plantation commissary, where the black sharecroppers obtained percale, muslin, potatoes, corn, and molasses, he murmured, "Course they got royally overcharged and cheated." He did not argue the point when she objected.[29] Many years later, reading *Go Down, Moses* and about the estrangement between Roth Edmonds and his black childhood friend, she wondered if Faulkner had drawn on her account of a similar breach of white/black boyhood on the

Ussery plantation. She wondered if Faulkner's own sense of "misplacement" beckoned him to her. He wanted to know all about the Ussery and her family, the Dohertys, and how they lived during Reconstruction, a period he had continued to explore in *Saturday Evening Post* stories.[30]

Faulkner ordered a good white wine. He knew his vintages. And then he seemed to withdraw into a gloom she would often see overcome him in Hollywood. Only a month earlier, he later told her, his youngest brother, Dean, had died in an air crash in the Waco plane Faulkner had given him. It was so like Faulkner, his heart's desire before him, to feel the counterpull of melancholy—in this case the burden of supporting Dean's wife and infant daughter. In front of Meta, he had suddenly switched from acting the courtly and gallant suitor to playing the diffident male, reversible roles that expressed the alternating currents of his personality.

That first evening Meta smiled at him and just waited, realizing that to ply him with questions would do no good, would not penetrate that deep reserve that in years to come would disconcert so many people trying to engage Faulkner in conversation. She noticed his hands, "small and strong and with a kind of grace, the way he handled his pipe, the way he handled the flatware at the table and would pick up a glass."[31] She studied the menu and asked for his recommendation. This question seemed to lift his gloom. "I set great store by their Cassoulet Toulousin," he said, smiling. Faulkner did not smile easily. One of Meta's most treasured pictures showed him smiling, sealed in a moment of rare, pure happiness. This classic French dish, made with various cuts of pork, white beans, carrots, celery, and tomatoes, simmered in duck fat and served as a stew with a hardy crust, was a full-bodied meal that Meta had never tried. She instantly ordered. Faulkner's silence had unnerved her. Relieved to follow his cue, she abided by the terms that would govern their affair. He would never tell her anything simply because she asked him. She would learn about him as she talked about herself and how she arrived in Hollywood.

Meta had come to Howard Hawks's attention because of her crisp efficiency and willingness to follow him from Universal Studios to the Goldwyn lot to Twentieth Century-Fox, typing scripts and also organizing his offices, all the while keeping intact her charming "magnolia-voiced" competence. She filed and she babysat for the director. Faulkner listened to her with his full attention as Meta drew herself into his world. He wanted to know if she liked working in Hollywood and why she did not devote herself to music, her first love. When she admitted she was not good enough to be a concert pianist, he expressed the hope that she would find some other way to work in the music business. You had to be, in one way or another, near your heart's desire.

After dinner, the couple walked along Hollywood Boulevard. "We felt like exiles in Hollywood, and we would talk about home," Meta recalled.[32] They watched moviegoers file out of the Chinese and Egyptian Theaters and pass the lit-up Hollywood and Roosevelt Hotels. Those glory days are gone from the Boulevard, but the theaters remain, and actually what Meta observed then, "an overgrown small-town thoroughfare, tacky, dinky, funky, bland," has become only more so in the decades since. With the lights turned off, this strip of Hollywood seemed then, as now, commonplace, a figment of the imagination dispelled in daylight. Faulkner told her as much when he said at dinner she would not see him on the set of *The Road to Glory*. "Lord, no, hon, I'll be long gone from Hollywood by then, I'll be back in Oxford." No one saw Hollywood as more illusory than did William Faulkner. However much he would be there for her, he could never be *there,* not really.

Faulkner took Meta into the Stanley Rose Bookshop and purchased a copy of *A Green Bough* for her as he grinned, noting that critics thought poorly of his poetry.[33] As he said good-night to her in front of the Studio Club, she accepted his invitation to go out with him again the next night. This was a couple already in heat, as she admitted in her memoir when she described the electricity of his touch. He had romanced her with stories of his World War I flying escapades. Not until after his death did she learn they were not true. After their first date, she fell asleep dreaming of him in an "airman's helmet flying low in a warplane over a foreign land." The image is quintessential Faulkner—not merely the lure of danger and derring-do, but the depiction of an ace alone in the firmament, unable to settle in one place but managing nevertheless to seem all hers, as she fantasized taking possession of him with her own hands, her own art, her fingers "moving thunderously over a piano keyboard."

This passage suggests an aspect of the relationship that Meta downplays in her memoir—that, in some respects, she was as much in control of Faulkner as he was of her. When she showed several portraits of herself to her coauthor, Orin Borsten, he asked her which one Faulkner wanted: "The one I wanted him to have," she replied. "I was sometimes rather high handed with Bill." She laughed, amused at herself, perhaps, or slightly embarrassed by her boldness, or both. She had a charming forthright quality I felt when I met her, a woman in command of herself.[34]

William Faulkner had met his match in this woman, whose imagination he could trigger in the same way he had once ignited Estelle, another artist who felt she was not quite good enough and who burned her first novel, resolving to become, instead, Mrs. William Faulkner. And he played the first evening with Meta just right. He did not try to paw her, let alone bed her, as so many

Hollywood men were in the habit of doing. He did not even kiss her. This man who scorned Hollywood had nevertheless acted like a proper leading man. She could imagine him trying to take advantage of her, but she also supposed "one look of reproof" would turn him apologetic with embarrassment. She did not realize that in certain respects he was Hollywood all over, with his bunkum about wartime flying that, for her, put him in the company of the stunt flyers she had met on the job for Hawks. Meta had met Amelia Earhart and thought William Faulkner was of the same ilk. To make the irony even stronger, Meta had actually flown a World War I Jenny in Memphis, which is more than Bill could truthfully claim he had done. What is more, she had done some barnstorming, like his characters in *Pylon* and his short stories. She was also better at the wheel than Faulkner, whom she considered a poor driver. On weekends together she preferred to drive her little green Chevrolet to Santa Monica for hotel stays with him.[35] "She drives a car with the style of someone well-acquainted with machines and knows physically where she is at the moment in relation to the rest of the universe," an impressed Carvel Collins wrote.[36] She had also ridden horses bareback, an impressive feat that William Faulkner, saddled up on his childhood pony, could not match.[37] Perhaps that is why Faulkner had to assert his own bogus prowess. After describing combat missions during the war, he told Meta, "When I crashed, I thought I'd never fly again." When his words elicited her tender touch on his sleeve, he grinned, tapped his head, and told her: "There's a silver plate in my skull. The sterling in my head is worth more than I am down at the Oxford bank." Even after Meta knew the stories to be false, she had trouble relinquishing her romantic vision of Faulkner falling to earth, the incorruptible man in a corruptible world.

On their second date, Bill brought Paris and New Orleans and New York to the table, as he examined the wine list like a display of names of old friends. He ordered a Pontet Canet, then an expensive eight dollars (one that would set you back more than a hundred now), a red wine described as having a "stunning richness" and a "60 second finish."[38] He thumped the table twice with an open palm, signaling, in Meta's words, a "boyish pleasure." She knew he couldn't help himself, even though he was trying to save his hard-earned Hollywood money and would normally have kept to his hotel room to work on *Absalom, Absalom!* It is revealing that she thought of his work on the novel as coming out of a "great furnace," because *Absalom, Absalom!* is his most superheated book. It did not seem to trouble her that he was giving a performance, relating his Mississippi stories with, as she said, "the skill of an actor." But this display was not all just for Meta's benefit. As his daughter Jill later said, she could never be sure when her father was not acting.

This William Faulkner production was staged at La Rue's on Sunset Strip, one of the playgrounds of the stars and not the usual haunt of writers. But he had picked this pretentious place, with its obsequious waiters, as though he needed it as an encore to their first night out. Meta called La Rue's an "unlikely setting—the shining silver, the china, the gleaming linen, the expensive clothes of its patrons—for tales about dirt farmers, Memphis whores, termagants, bootleggers and ruffians." But wasn't that always the way with Faulkner, combining the refinement of his prose with the rawness of his characters and settings?

Bill and Meta were now seeing each other three times a week, although Faulkner wanted her every night—a demand, she later admitted, that frightened her. Sometimes in the early morning he would walk a distance of about two miles from his Knickerbocker Hotel to the Studio Club, arriving at six or six thirty, and then sit on the curb waiting, while the women watched him from their front windows and told Meta he had arrived. They would go to breakfast together and then to work.[39] He drew pictures of their outings, one with them enjoying a big pile of pancakes, another of them playing ping pong, which they often did at the Studio Club and other places. A proficient player, he nevertheless drew a scene of himself lying on the floor, perhaps unconscious, with a victorious Meta bending over him.[40] He would tell her: "You save my damned life out here, Meta. I swear you do. You keep me alive and sane." It sounded like the flattery it was, but she could not resist him, even when he finally began to talk about Estelle and that as a married man he could not give Meta anything. But she needed him as much as he needed her.

They took long drives, during which Faulkner recited Housman and Swinburne. At other times his silence seemed just as eloquent, although she wondered if he might be thinking of Estelle and Jill. He only had to touch her now for her to feel a surge of love. As she put it, "he took full possession of my thoughts." For the first time, she felt secure in her relationship with a man who treated her as something more than "fair game" or the "unreal union" that had been her first marriage. Part of what made her pairing with Faulkner work is that he was so much like Howard Hawks, with a British reserve and correctness of manner so at odds with the factitious gregariousness of the Hollywood lot. The two men would huddle together in quiet, conferring on scripts.

Meta knew well enough not to press her lover for details. She would have to make her discoveries about him almost in the same way as a reader absorbs Faulkner: through fragments, glimpses, and inferences that gradually coalesced into a narrative that proceeded by intuition and surmise. In retrospect, she thought that Faulkner had divined how she would react to his manner. She did not know what gave her away. "My voice, my head, my back straight in the lady posture I had been taught"—were these the attributes that told him she would not pry or try to manipulate him into more of an affair than he desired? "It was Bill who had come slamming into my life, not I into his," she says in an evocative passage of *A Loving Gentleman*. Faulkner's forcefulness calls to mind that of Thomas Sutpen, who would overwhelm even the maidenly Miss Rosa Coldfield in a novel about a man who wanted the world only on his terms. Rosa Coldfield felt the power of his attraction but could not abide such a man; Meta Carpenter gave herself to such a man, accepting what she herself called his "terms of limitation."

Bill called Jill precious, his heart's darling, whom he wanted to see grow into "a fine young woman and a happy one," he told Meta. He worried that a drunken Estelle, given to binges, would bring the house down with a carelessly discarded cigarette or match. He had been writing about the smoking ruins of Sutpen's Hundred, and now he was reeling that drama back into his own life. Estelle was never really alone. She had not only Mammy but also a household staff and her two children by Cornell Franklin. The fire was in Faulkner's mind, the story told for his new confidant, Meta.

But talk of Jill was just a prelude to telling Meta how special she was. He had stopped talking when she had left it to him to tell her as much as he liked. He paused, and with his bright, level gaze he told her that he no longer slept with Estelle. They had not had sex since Jill was born. Meta had not expected such a confession. All she could do was nod when he asked if she understood him. She wanted to hold him after he let out a deep sigh. "It's God's truth I've told you," he said. Was it? Meta apparently never inquired about Faulkner's sex life, and Faulkner was not forthcoming. Was he implying that Estelle had withheld sex from her husband, or that he had simply ceased to find her attractive? All of Estelle's pregnancies had been difficult, and childbirth hazardous. It took her a long time to recover after Alabama's death. She had "reason to avoid pregnancy" and perhaps sex as well.[41]

Meta, past wanting to doubt Faulkner, had not pressed him about his marriage or expected revelations from a man who doled out the details of his life in tiny increments. She could not sleep, thinking about what her lover had told her: "A door had opened on the dark, airless, hidden part of William Faulkner's life, and while I had wanted it to be ajar, I was not prepared for the nature of his revelation or for the wrenching cost of it to him." She imagined that, like her, he could not sleep after making his uncharacteristic confession. It would have been more like him, she thought, to simply say, without further ado, that he and Estelle were an estranged couple no longer in love. But as Meta herself realized, his disclosure had drawn her even deeper into his life. In his telling, "It was Estelle who was the drinker, not

Bill." Surely an alcoholic would not call his own wife a drunk, she reasoned, as she rid her memory of seeing him staggering that one time, dismissing it as "clearly unimportant." Was Faulkner truly suffering over his marriage and in love with Meta?[42] His revelations to her had a calculated effect: "The knowledge that Bill was without physical love, that he had been without normal sexual outlet for some time, pervaded my sensibilities," Meta wrote. She now watched his movements in a "wholly new way." As she realized, "in one stroke he had removed the wife as a love rival." In this cunning foreplay he did not press her for sex, but only held her hand at parting, letting her feel the strain of his attraction to "a desirable young female," as she put it.

Many dinner dates followed at different restaurants, but Faulkner favored Musso & Frank's because of its decent prices and what Meta called its "honest ambience" and "friendly, unaffected waiters, most of them foreign-born." To be served by the displaced, so to speak, appealed to his own foreign sensibility. That he had a special affinity for immigrants is apparent to anyone who has read the Quentin section of *The Sound and the Fury*, in which he holds the hand of a little Italian girl who is as lost as he is. And yet Musso & Frank's was also Old Hollywood—old for Hollywood anyway—established in 1919 and frequented by other writers, including Nathanael West, Dashiell Hammett, and Lillian Hellman. The restaurant had a back bar where writers gathered on Saturday afternoons. Although Faulkner did not mingle or talk that much, he seemed happy among his fellow writers, Meta noticed, while he drank and smoked his pipe: a writer among writers but also apart, an alien among aliens.

As they walked out of their favorite restaurant, he pressed her hand firmly, and she felt a pressure of her own. She did not resist when he steered her toward his hotel room and locked the door. To her, he seemed a man overtaken by the pleasure of a passionate encounter, which he had not experienced for a "long, long time." Although he was only five and a half feet tall, he was powerfully built, she observed, with a massive chest, strongly muscled arms, and a thick waist. "His feet were very beautiful," she remembered. "They looked as if he had never worn any shoes, no blemish, no distortion of any kind. . . . He had a kind of boyish pride in them,"[43] which is perhaps why there are so many stories about him going barefooted. He told her again that she had saved him.

While Meta admitted to feeling some guilt over her coupling with a married man, his gratitude and her pride in saying to herself that William Faulkner was her lover overrode all else. He wanted her all to himself. Whenever they did stray into other territory—an art gallery, for example—she realized that he found it almost unendurable to meet people, even her friends who asked him to name the titles of his books and tried to make small talk. He would just turn his back on them, much to Meta's chagrin.

An especially painful episode occurred at a liquored-up Hollywood party omitted from *A Loving Gentleman.* Hayden Rorke, later a featured player in film and television, and Jud Addis, a voice coach, decided they should play "Pin the Tail on the Donkey." Faulkner, who had not wanted to attend the party, stood out, a sober figure among the "loose and buoyant" crowd. He drew the short straw. They blindfolded him and shoved him forward with a paper donkey tail in his hand:

> Hayden gleefully held a large jar of cleansing cream inches away from him. As Bill plunged the donkey tail into it, raucous laughter broke over the room. Blindfold off, Bill looked blankly at the convulsed thigh-slapping actors and their friends, wiped his greasy fingers on his sleeve handkerchiefs, and thanked our hosts for an enjoyable evening.
>
> Later, on our way home, I said, "I'm sorry, honey—it was just a gag."
> Bill nodded.
> "Everybody was high."
> "No harm done, dear love."
> "You don't like practical jokes, do you?"
> Bill slouched in the passenger seat of my car. "I don't mind it when the joke's on me. But I resent being gunned, as we say back in Miss'ippi. There's a difference."
>
> He hated being played for a fool. His fellow writers were the worst offenders. To defend himself, he would pretend not to understand that he was being ragged. Feigning solemnity and humorlessness, Faulkner could dampen any high jinks directed at him by refusing to get the point of it.[44]

How many times, in other circumstances, did Faulkner disguise his real feelings?

The reserved, aloof Faulkner never showed up in Meta's bed. The rapture of lovemaking made him talk bawdily and adopt the language of *Lady Chatterley's Lover,* his gift to her. He would pun about their sexual parts like a screenwriter trying to evade the censors who enforced Hollywood's Production Code. This was also the man who made erotic drawings of their lovemaking.[45] They enjoyed oral sex, including soixante-neuf, "not so common as it apparently is today," Meta said.[46] She never saw the slightest sense of guilt on his part: "After sex, we talked animatedly, found much to be amused at in the Hollywood of that day, went out for a night snack, and all this time Faulkner's face was the face of a fulfilled, happy man."[47] And at these happy moments he would quote his own poetry, especially the lines from poem XXIV in *A Green Bough:*

Then flowed
Beneath my hand thy body's curve, and turned
To me within the famished lonely dark
Thy sleeping kiss.[48]

Meta desired a more open, public life. She even dreamed of being Faulkner's consort, cheered by crowds as they stepped off trains—which were never traveling south in the direction of his home. But she never pressed him about marriage and vehemently rejected one biographer's claim that she was a model for Charlotte Rittenmeyer. Meta did not see herself as the "aggressive, insistent and fearless" woman depicted in *The Wild Palms*. She dreaded what a marriage to Faulkner would mean for her if she returned with him to Oxford.[49] Although she had been married very young, she considered herself still sexually inexperienced when she met Faulkner, who brought out the mature woman in her. She resented one biographer's speculation on the ribbon Faulkner bought for her hair. "I regularly wore such ribbons then to avoid the expense of hairdressers," she told Carvel Collins. They cost her fifteen cents.[50] "Faulkner, who was broke most of the time, gave me the ribbon as an inexpensive loving joke. He did not seem in any way to be trying to transform me by the gift into Alice in Wonderland or Shirley Temple." And she scorned the notion that she "was for Faulkner an amalgam of the 'daughter of his mind, the sister of his imagination, perhaps even his dark mother,'" saying that were that true she "seriously doubt[ed] that he could have achieved an erection." She might seem biddable, but she would have refused an invitation to move in with him. As she put it: "I needed to believe in myself, needed the Mississippi sense of being half-virtuous at least."[51] She also supposed that any proposal on her part to move in would have been met with, "My dear, you are a lady."[52] At a later time, when she casually mentioned the idea of their returning together to Mississippi to tour the land they loved, she could tell by his "tensed face" that she had "said the wrong thing."[53]

Meta exposed another side of the man she loved when she introduced him to John Crown and Sally Richards. It had taken all her coaxing to get this "old mud turtle," as he called himself, to meet her friends. He did not see why they had to "accommodate to others." But in the company of these musicians, both pianists, Faulkner relaxed, enjoying the outgoing John and the unassuming Sally, a fellow southerner who had known Meta while growing up in Memphis. Faulkner liked conversation with an artist as passionately devoted to his music as Faulkner was to writing.[54] They talked about the "meaning of life and the importance of leaving something behind."[55] Crown remembered a gracious man who made time for one of Crown's students. Faulkner impressed the composer with an extensive knowledge of wine and food. Faulkner, who had often praised Thomas Wolfe's work, admitted to Crown that he had never been able to get all the way through any of Wolfe's books. Crown listened. He did not pry or probe. Faulkner worried that academic life would ruin Crown's gift for music as it did professors who wanted to write. "John Crown says," Collins wrote in a note to himself, "Faulkner would sing pleasantly as they traveled in the car" and would "join them all when the four of them acted," as Crown said, just like a "bunch of kids."

Meta could see that her lover admired a man gifted at his own form of storytelling. John and Sally took Bill on his own terms and did not ask about his writing or his personal life. He had been accepted as Meta's friend, not as William Faulkner the writer, and now he was their friend, "part of them, as I was," Meta said. Faulkner, like Hollywood stars, constantly met people who responded to "William Faulkner," not really to him. He hated the idea of performing as The Writer, merely an object of fascination, because it made him nothing, really, as a person. Howard Hawks loved to tell about the time he took Faulkner and Clark Gable hunting. At one point Gable asked Faulkner about which writers the star should read. Faulkner mentioned several writers and then added himself to the list. A surprised Gable said he did not know Faulkner wrote. To which Faulkner replied, "And what do you do, Mr. Gable?" Faulkner and Gable hunted together and saw one another over the next decade, and in all likelihood both men enjoyed not having to act like William Faulkner and Clark Gable.

Bill inscribed *A Green Bough* with a line unlike any other in the book: to "Meta who soft keeps for him his love's long girl's body sweet to fuck." He called her "my heart, my jasmine garden, my April and May cunt; my white one, my blonde morning, winged, my sweetly dividing, my honey-cloyed, my sweet-assed gal." He quoted Joyce's love poetry to her and wrote a version of "Ode on a Grecian Urn" that included her name. In effect, he enveloped her in his own emotional and literary universe in ways she did not then understand. It puzzled her, for example, that he tended to make more of their ten-year age difference than she did. To him, she seemed to grow younger the more he desired her, as if he could reverse time the way he had done in his novels. Although nearing twenty-nine, she could pass for nineteen as an image of the idealized lover on the Grecian Urn, the image of the white woman he had created in his earliest poetry and stories. "I never protested," she admitted, "and my acceptance of his vision of me as a maiden nourished his fantasy."

During the beach weekends with John and Sally, it seemed to Meta that she and Bill now were a married couple, sharing a hotel room together and cavorting in the Pacific. He covered her bed with gardenia and jasmine petals in a romantic scene that would have made Howard Hawks "groan," Meta confessed. When William Faulkner wanted to, he could out-Hollywood Hollywood. She became, in her own words, a "pedestaled" woman. They had their arguments, to be sure, Meta reported. But always courteous, he would dissent: "But no, Ma'am," or "But no, honey." He played the courtly lover, the suffering artist, the knight who would ride in and out of Hollywood, and in and out of her life, like the characters in *Absalom, Absalom!* who disappear and reappear in different guises and from different camera angles.

Absalom, Absalom! is a restless novel written by a restless man, one who paced Howard Hawks's office going over the lines in his screenplay as Meta typed, sometimes asking him to repeat himself because he was so soft-spoken. No one else ever got so close to Faulkner the writer, who would lean over Meta's shoulder, brush her hair with his lips, and contemplate what she had typed and what he should say next. When she asked him about something he said in the script, he would reply: "I didn't say it. The character said it." Even with the movie work he said he despised, he regarded his scripts as having an integrity of their own, and he granted his characters a sacrosanct independence. This was his high-modernist credo, in which the god of art stood apart from his creations. But it was also the expression of a man who did not want to be made vulnerable by those who claimed he had a responsibility to explain his characters. Faulkner wanted to own his work, but he did not want that work to own him.

During this final phase of his work on *The Road to Glory* and nearing the conclusion of their first thrilling month together, Meta sensed he was pulling away, thinking of going home for Christmas. She blurted out, "You can't help yourself?" He said, "no." When he had given her an inscribed copy of *A Green Bough,* he had his epitaph: "Though I be dead / This earth that holds me fast will find me breath." Meta had been with him every day and still did not know what plans he intended. Would he leave his wife? Marry Meta? After searching a face as "locked" as Sutpen's impassive countenance, she dared not ask.

They made love on their last night together. She presented him with a photograph of herself. He gave her a double-breasted, full-length brocade evening coat, an extravagance she treasured, although she knew he was saving his salary for obligations back home. When she finally broke down and asked, "What about us?" he turned away, said nothing, then put one finger to her lips as if to silence her protests with the seigneurial gesture of a

Sartoris or of a silent Sutpen. When Meta began to cry, her startled lover abruptly wheeled around, walking away with head bent "as if braced against a whipping cold wind."

When they parted at the train station the next day, he asked her to write him care of Phil Stone, and he promised to write in return. The rest was silence as he boarded his Pullman car. She sent a wire, "I will wait for you forever. Love, Meta," to be delivered at one of his train stops. Although she spent hours wondering what she meant to him, in the end she believed in the certainty of his love, even though he had made no promises to return. She thought of him giving up everything—like Robert Taylor did for Joan Crawford, playing the innkeeper's daughter in *The Gorgeous Hussy* (1936)—and knew it for a fantasy.[56]

Aboard the Golden State Limited, he had wired his "dear, dear love," confessing, "I had to be cold and still when we said goodbye; if I had let myself go and held you, I would not have let you go and boarded the train." Letters followed, assuring her that they had just begun to love. She saw him as the "stable force" in the shifting, gossipy atmosphere of Hollywood. She lived in expectation of his return—with Chloe, the puppy he had insisted on purchasing for her. As Meta wrote, "There was a counterpull to me in Hollywood." He wrote her he was unhappy and hoped for their reunion. She wrote to him about the production of *The Road to Glory* and about Chloe, as though his departure had been only a temporary interruption in their life together. She read his books inscribed to her. She read the contemporaries he recommended—notably Thomas Wolfe, whose hero experienced the conflicting passions now part of Faulkner's bifurcated life.

Unhappy at Home

William Faulkner came home to an unhappy wife. He was always saying how much he loved home, so why was he always leaving it? When at home, he wanted no interruption, no radio, no phonograph, and he would not answer the telephone. Estelle remembered lines from Sir Walter Scott's *The Lay of the Last Minstrel:*

Breathes there the man, with soul so dead,
Who never to himself hath said,
This is my own, my native land!
Whose heart hath ne'er within him burn'd,
As home his footsteps he hath turn'd
From wandering on a foreign strand!

Estelle sent her own mocking version to her sister Dorothy:

> While he in dignity sits alone,
> Aghast at the sound of e'en a trombone.
> And whiles his joyless hours away
> Reading a book—or maybe a play
> That very few people save he—understand—
> This breathing soul is my own husband!

Estelle played the piano, studied French, made scenes that did not impress her undemonstrative husband. He could be engaging, of course, and dinner could be a lively affair. But while working, he passed some dinners in silence, as if he were not there.

In early January 1936, Faulkner completed a draft of *Absalom, Absalom!* that he now began meticulously to revise and retype. This arduous process meant that he would have little time to confect stories for popular magazines, like the *Saturday Evening Post,* on which he depended for a steady income. Returning to Hollywood as soon as work on the novel ended seemed inevitable—not only because Meta awaited him but because, much as he claimed to despise studio employment, Hollywood piecework suited him. He wrote quickly and to order, helping Howard Hawks with revisions, suggesting solutions to problem. His rewrites of scripts by others often improved them, even when his contributions did not result in filmable product.

Faulkner's letters to Meta emphasized his unhappiness with Estelle, but he did not tell Meta about his drinking, or why he did it. After completing his work on *Absalom, Absalom!* on the last day of January, his dipsomania followed the usual pattern. Intense absorption in a novel had left him depleted and depressed. He visited his mother every day, but he did not find enough relief in her company. His brother Dean's wife, due to deliver her baby in two months' time, remained part of his torment over his youngest brother's death.

A trip to the hunting lodge owned by Helen Baird and her husband did nothing to alleviate the strain. He had written her a curious, suggestive letter addressed to "Dear Skipper," recalling a spill she had taken out of a sailboat, after which she berated him for not jumping in after her but instead staying aboard to right the ship and then pick her up. He treated the incident as a turning point: "I should have gone overside . . . and you would have saved me and so ever after you would have had to keep me in parched corn and tobacco and I would not have had to go to Hollywood as I am about to do in a week or so." Helen remained his unrequited love, the elusively beautiful lover like those depicted in Keats's "Ode on a Grecian Urn," a poem never far from Faulkner's consciousness and quoted at length to Helen, Meta, and Estelle.

After a week of binge drinking, nursed along by his stepson Malcolm, Faulkner righted himself and walked over to Phil Stone's law office, just off the courthouse square. He read to Stone and his wife, Emily, parts of *Absalom, Absalom!*

HOLLYWOOD ON THE MISSISSIPPI

In late February, little more than six weeks after leaving Meta, Faulkner returned to Twentieth Century-Fox to work on *Banjo on My Knee*. "Great first treatment," hard-to-please Darryl Zanuck wrote.[57] The studio head expected, and Faulkner delivered, a template for the film. Meta Carpenter said that even when the studio did not use his dialogue, the underlying structure of a Faulkner composition remained. In this case, he broke down the treatment into six sequences, with minimal dialogue and camera directions. At a glance, in other words, Zanuck could see the whole picture. The released film would include virtually all of Faulkner's characters intact and most of his plot points as well. He evidently produced a script as well. David Hempstead claimed that Faulkner wrote "magnificent . . . practically blank verse," two or three pages at a clip that Nunnally Johnson did not like and that he rewrote. The setting on a Mississippi River shanty boat just above Memphis fitted Faulkner perfectly, as did the scenes in the New Orleans Creole Cafe. Walter Brennan (Newt Holley), who specialized in crotchety yet charming old men, plays his one-man-band contraption at the shanty boat wedding of his son Ernie (Joel McCrea) and Pearl (Barbara Stanwyck). The rest of the film is the story of how this quarreling couple split up, reunite, and split up again, frustrating Newt's hopes for a new generation. In the end, the couple reconcile, realizing they cannot live without each other, and without the river. The story, and especially the patriarch's place in it, appealed to Faulkner's "concern with genealogical transmission, with the preservations of memories and values from one generation to the next."[58] As Newt avers, both his father and grandfather have drowned in the Mississippi, and he expects no less for himself. He says so as a point of pride, regarding such deaths as natural.

Faulkner's script has not survived, but the spirit of the released film suits his own sense of the interplay between his white and black characters. At a pivotal moment on a New Orleans wharf, a black chorus and lead singer perform the "St. Louis Blues" in an escalating melancholy, a sense of unbearable loss: "I hate to see that evening sun go down / Because my baby he done left this town." The black ensemble makes Pearl's feelings about leaving home, abandoning her husband, and wanting to return all that more poignant, especially since Newt has played the "St. Louis Blues" at her wedding, as Faulkner specified in his treatment, calling W. C. Handy's composition the film's "theme song."[59] The black stevedores sing as they load a ship with huge sacks on their shoulders, burdens they carry in a solemn manner onto the ship that, Pearl later learns, would have taken Ernie away yet again. The black people are a sideshow, local color, and yet they are central to Pearl's misery at that moment. They express her plight. They know suffering, and, as in Faulkner's fiction, they are, for all their separateness, integral to the action. Then Pearl's spirits rise when she hears nearby Newt banging his way through an exhilarating medley of Stephen Foster tunes and "Dixie," capping off his contagious performance by donning a Confederate cap, the emblem of pride and loss, that Faulkner put at the heart of his treatment. This vignette is set in a city that invites all kinds of entertainment and mixing of styles, just as it welcomed Faulkner, and as it welcomes a river man who has never been in a restaurant let alone performed in front of an audience other than his family and friends. All these elements of the film seem to be Faulkner's even if he did not write them.

While Meta celebrated a reunion with Faulkner, he wrote to Estelle on March 2 that his work was going well. On March 9, he sent another letter proposing a two-week vacation in New Orleans after he completed his Hollywood tour of duty, a rendezvous that would be a kind of reconciliation—like the one between fractious Ernie and Pearl: "Hurrah for the letter yesterday. When things are going all right with you, I know that Little Missy is well and happy."[60] The next day Faulkner turned in a revised treatment. On the set every day, he told Estelle, he wanted to be home "still in the kitchen with my family around me and my hand full of Old Maid cards. . . . In haste, but with much love." The longing for home and family is palpable in Faulkner's *Banjo on My Knee* treatment because that is where people, whatever their ignorance and shortcomings, have a "certain integrity. . . . Leaving the river, to them, is almost the same as plunging into a life of shame."[61]

He did not sound like a man on the verge of divorce, as Meta believed him to be. But for William Faulkner, it mattered deeply that Meta believed in his unhappiness, because her belief made that unhappiness more real, more dramatic, and palpable not only to himself but to others. Years later, Meta realized a mutual friend had been watching them and learning from their story. In the 1970s, in the heyday of the auteur theory, whereby the director is deemed the author of his films, Meta began reading about the "archetypal Hawks heroine—Jean Arthur in all her variations, incapable of guile or artifice where her man was concerned, straight-shooting, accommodating, undemanding, sweetheart and pal all in one. Clearly, Howard Hawks knew more about his blonde secretary and her relationship with William Faulkner than I had deduced from his uninquisitive manner and masklike face." Hawks did not want to get mixed up in the Meta-Faulkner romance, he told Carvel Collins. "I only knew that she was a bright, sensitive girl and the kind that would appeal to him and they got along very very well."[62]

Six weeks, from late February to early April, resolved nothing for Meta or for Faulkner. Removed from *Banjo on My Knee,* he spent a little more than a dispiriting month at RKO, where writers were practically chained to their desks in an atmosphere far different from that of Howard Hawks's benign dictatorship. But Faulkner collected a thousand dollars per week and found time to do some hunting on Catalina Island with Nathanael West, who relaxed Faulkner with talk about guns.

"Getting along. All right and working hard. Have got my weight down to 140 and feel (and I hope, look) much better," Faulkner wrote to Estelle on April 26, asking for news about home and "my dear gal baby."[63] On May 16 to "Dear Pappy's own," he announced: "I think I will be coming home about June 1, am about done with R.K.O. Picture, and have agreed to write short synopsis for Gloria Swanson. Will see her Monday and find out about that. Love to you and my chillen. I ought to see you pretty soon now. Damn this being an orphan."[64] Nothing seemed to have come of the Swanson assignment.

Faulkner socialized with Hollywood friends before returning to Oxford in time for Jill's birthday in June. He visited Ben Wasson, working then as an agent. To his old friend, Faulkner declared that he loved Meta and wanted to marry her. Then he departed from Hollywood with a six-month contract, starting August 1. She would wait for him, even though she had met another artist, Wolfgang Rebner, "as sure of his talent as Faulkner was of his." She could share her passion for music with Rebner as she could not with Faulkner, who claimed not to have much feeling for it. Meta and Rebner did not become lovers. John Crown, their mutual friend, said to Meta that nearly all of Rebner's life had been "spent at the piano—practicing, rehearsing, playing, composing. Dalliance requires time. And time away from the piano is a commodity that he has never had."

Rebner, a Jewish exile from Hitler's Germany, a displaced person like William Faulkner—and like Meta Carpenter—pointedly asked her how she felt about Jews and if she had Jewish friends. She did and was used to working with Jewish directors and actors. She was acutely conscious of an impending disaster every time she walked onto a movie set and witnessed the "narrowness and bigotry of the typical Hollywood union crew—Jew-haters, Roosevelt-cursers, Communist-fearers, denigrators of Catholics and black people and Mexicans, espousers of the Silver Shirts." This organization claimed to have fifteen thousand members, with headquarters at the Murphy Ranch in the Los Angeles hills. They awaited the fascist takeover of the world, sharing a mentality that Faulkner had portrayed in Percy Grimm and that he would explore in later screenplays. He had yet to meet Wolfgang Rebner, but the pianist was the kind of man, the displaced dedicated artist, that the novelist would immediately take to.

COUNTERPULL

The period between December 1935 and August 1936 was especially unsettling for Faulkner as he shuttled between Oxford and Hollywood, wondering what would become of his art, but daring to imagine what life would be like beyond the boundaries of his marriage to Estelle. As he drew the map of Yoknapatawpha that would be inserted into *Absalom, Absalom!,* he continued to work on restoring Rowan Oak and wrote to Will Bryant, thanking him for some material Bryant had sent about Mississippi Indians, which "recalled the pleasant summer afternoons we spent while I heard you tell this word-of-mouth, which does lend the breath of life even to the dead men and the dead times in which they lived." The words could have almost been copied from *Absalom, Absalom!,* with Faulkner and Bryant talking out their stories like the characters in Faulkner's fiction. He was broke at present, he told Bryant, but an agent had five stories to sell and checks in the mail that would yield several hundred dollars that would satisfy the thousand dollars owed to Mr. Will.[65]

At the same time, Faulkner kept up his clandestine correspondence with Meta, who continued to send her letters to Faulkner in care of Phil Stone. Estelle was entering her forties, and drinking had taken its toll on her countenance, which began to show the strain that resulted from marriage to an alcoholic husband who always seemed at least halfway to somewhere else. The prospect of a fresh start with Meta beguiled Faulkner, then writing about Thomas Sutpen, who had uprooted himself twice while pursuing what he called his design. The very first copy of *Absalom, Absalom!,* only a few months away from publication, would be inscribed to Meta even as Faulkner observed the seventh anniversary of his marriage to Estelle on June 20. Two days later, in the *Memphis Commercial Appeal,* he ran an ad: "I will not be responsible for any debt incurred or bills made, or notes or checks signed by Mrs. William Faulkner or Mrs. Estelle Oldham Faulkner."

This public humiliation not only of his wife but of her family, which had fallen on hard times and was dependent on Faulkner's help, exposed much more than Estelle's extravagant spending and desire for the luxurious style of life to which she had been accustomed not only in her previous marriage to Cornell Franklin but during her upbringing as a southern belle. The ad was not the act of a gentleman but of an angry man who had not only forsaken the proprieties but also seemed determined to commit some kind of outrage that would drive wife and family away. The decision to join Meta could, in effect, be made for him. He acted like a man with a Hollywood contract held in escrow, so to speak, for a quick getaway. Not only did the ad declare his independence, it also made him an apostate. His mother's father, Charlie Butler, had abruptly left Oxford never to be heard from again after he had become involved, it was rumored, with an octaroon. What Faulkner knew about this family secret—the kind of secret a whole southern town would be aware of but never openly discuss—has never been established. But cases of men just picking up and disappearing were known to happen. What Maud, Faulkner's mother, thought of his ad has not been recorded. But her son knew that she disliked Estelle and the entire Oldham clan, a group of Republicans who looked down upon the Falkners (yellow-dog Democrats) and had, until recently, prospered, while her husband, Murry Falkner, never seemed to regain the power and prestige his father and grandfather had maintained.

Estelle, divorced once already, understood the damage that Faulkner's departure would exact, and she refused to fight with him. She nursed her hurt with alcohol and, in effect, played the victim, making it virtually impossible for her husband to leave. For Faulkner to abandon Estelle now would have been deemed not only unchivalrous but downright despicable in his own estimation—let alone in the community where his family had to keep up appearances. Instead of asserting her independence, Estelle made her husband feel more guilty and troubled about his family responsibilities. In the time of Faulkner's great-grandfather, such a public act of repudiation could easily have led to violence, a duel to defend the Oldham family honor. Instead, Estelle's father, Lem, rebuked his "lowdown" son-in-law. The silent Faulkner simply walked away from Oldham's diatribe.

Two days later, on June 24, Faulkner helped Estelle celebrate Jill's third birthday. He could play the doting father, drawing pictures for Jill and reveling in outdoor activities with her. This may also have been when he took a series of photographs—a sequence of five resembling film stills—starring Jill that powerfully evoke not only his attachment to her but also the cinematic nature of his imagination. Her first appearance is arranged like a high-angle crane shot, as she enters a sylvan scene, striding confidently, her arm swinging out, looking down at the ground so that we can't make out her features. She is at the apex of the picture, with ten-year-old Malcolm shown in three-quarter profile. He is positioned diagonally below her looking at the center of her body, the cynosure of the picture. In the second photograph, a medium close-up, a smiling Malcolm turns toward the camera while

Jill is seen only from the back in what Judith Sensibar felicitously calls her "sunsuit." Malcolm is the admiring audience, a stand-in for us but also, of course, for Faulkner. Like all good filmmakers, Faulkner understood the importance of the reaction shot. The third photograph, a low-angle medium close-up, shows Jill standing tall, her arms at her side, gazing down at the pooling water. Malcolm is there by synecdoche, with only his right arm bent at the elbow intruding into the shot. The fourth photograph, a reverse-angle medium close-up, again catches Jill moving, her back to the camera, both arms and legs in motion, fully animated, with Malcolm on all fours watching her approach him. In the fifth photograph, she bends over, looking into the water, her bottom more prominent, with Malcolm, just barely visible in front of her. She is in command of this world, utterly at home. On her first visit to California, just ahead of her, she played in the surf, and when she was hit by a strong wave, Meta heard her say, "Pappy, I like the creek at home better."[66]

In *Faulkner in Love,* Judith Sensibar treats the photographic sequence in terms of Caddy and her muddy drawers—an inevitable comparison, especially since Jill is never shown frontally or in full close-up, so that she is just as elusive as Caddy herself. In this Eden—probably Bailey's Woods, which Faulkner would purchase shortly—Jill is not only herself but, as Sensibar supposes, a "wood nymph," and a figure like those appearing in Faulkner's early poetry. But it is Hollywood that showed him how to catch the natural light that plays on her hair and on the water, Hollywood that taught him how to position bodies in space on the diagonal for the most dynamic sense of life, of motion—a term that Faulkner would prize in his later interviews. The very word "camera," so ubiquitous in his treatments and screenplays, and the word "photograph," as employed by Mr. Compson to describe Charles Bon's palpable and yet evanescent appearance, suggest how fused Faulkner became to his literary and filmic work.[67] Later one of his screenwriter friends recalled Faulkner's fascination with the "creative possibilities in films . . . that he would like somehow to have just a camera and himself and they would go out and sort of write the thing, the work of art, directly on the film by the camera and he liked this idea very much."[68]

Can too much be made of what may be the accidental art of family photographs? Perhaps, although Sensibar calls attention to a letter Faulkner wrote to Estelle on July 21, 1934: "I'm hoping to wangle via the studio, the camera I have wanted, the little one with the German lens that takes pictures indoors and out both. The good ones cost $200, but I hope to be able to get one for about $75. If I can do so, I may buy it. Then we can keep a regular diary of the children and Rowanoak [*sic*]." This writer, so conscious of posing for the camera in the Odiorne Paris sequence, chose this camera, or one very like it, to make the symbolic sequence composed or discovered in the course of his location work far, but not too far, from Hollywood.

Although the day after Jill's birthday the *Oxford Eagle* printed Faulkner's incendiary ad, he signaled his defeat when he canceled scheduled reprintings. When *Time* told the country on July 6 about the ad, Faulkner blandly said he worried about incurring more debt. In a funk about having to write "trash," sometime in June he told his agent, Morton Goldman, that he was thinking of taking a popular magazine story, changing the names and locale, and publishing that—although doing so took "hard work too and requires skill, but I seem to be so out of touch with the Kotex Age here that I can't seem to think of anything myself."[69]

Less than a month later, on July 15, Faulkner left for Hollywood, taking Estelle, Jill, two black servants, and a cook with him. He had apparently overcome certain qualms, since he had told Dean's widow that because Jill was "a pigtailed little girl of great beauty and charm at that point looking like Cinderella," he was "afraid she might be picked up as a child star and might get caught up in the Hollywood thing which he did not want her to have anything to do with."[70]

They traveled in a new Ford phaeton, a sporty convertible sedan with a powerful V8 engine that vaulted Ford ahead of Chevrolet in sales for 1936. This was a striking purchase for a man who complained that his wife and her retinue were bankrupting him. How could he do this, accommodating his wife in the style she expected, but that he had supposedly rejected? Well, husband and wife liked the finer things in life. Jill's friends could never remember a meal that was not served on polished silverware and good china. Although Faulkner could certainly dress down, even appearing in shabby clothing, he also had his gentleman's well-tailored wardrobe.

Faulkner's own explanation for taking Estelle along for the ride—the one he would give to Meta—was that he could not reject Estelle without also losing Jill. Estelle would never permit him to take their daughter away, and though Faulkner did not say so, he had to know the law would surely side with his wife. He did not want to leave his daughter after such a short and disruptive stay in Oxford. Even so, taking Estelle and Jill with him to Hollywood? In spite of all, was he trying to save his marriage? Was he atoning for his cruel ad?

Faulkner rented a house in Santa Monica, which suited Estelle well enough, she wrote to her children Malcolm and Victoria, although she missed the family silver. Her reaction to Southern California was remarkably like her husband's: "You have to ask a policeman where all these suburbs start and stop—Hollywood, Beverly Hills, Glendale and Santa Monica all look alike to me, except that *our* village is practically on the beach." From upstairs she could see mountains and the sea. The beautiful sameness of her surroundings seemed only to increase her yearning for home.[71] Say what he would about Estelle, Faulkner shared a sensibility with her, no matter how many times he pretended they no longer had anything in common.

Faulkner now began an exhausting triangulated life, split between working on uninspiring studio projects, trysts with Meta, and trials of strength with Estelle, who, Faulkner claimed, would get so worked up she would scratch his face or have a go at him with a croquet mallet. He did not tell Meta that this combat occurred during his drinking bouts with Estelle.[72] Then Faulkner upped the ante by taking Jill to spend afternoons with Meta while Estelle was drinking. To Meta, it seemed Faulkner depended on her for a lifeline. "As you see, I am in California again up to my neck in moving pictures," he wrote Morton Goldman on September 4.[73] Faulkner read the galleys of *Absalom, Absalom!,* but he had no other novel to work on. He confronted the bleak prospect of spending an entire year on Hollywood piecework.

Estelle could not compete with a woman in her twenties. She had spent her own twenties (1918–28) with Cornell Franklin. Then Estelle had been, and in a sense remained, the missing woman in her husband's life, and now she embodied the decaying image of his lost youth. Estelle, the social butter-fly, had become a wraith-like presence. Faulkner sometimes portrayed her as a kind of specter haunting his hours with Meta. When Meta met Estelle, in an encounter Faulkner engineered by having Ben Wasson bring Meta to his rented Santa Monica home as Ben's date, Meta saw "a pale, sad, wasted crea-ture." Photographs of Estelle's hollow-eyed and skeletal face and body certainly enforce that impression. Actually, Meta's unpublished reaction was harsher: a "spastic, blubbering, helpless wreck."[74] Estelle seemed to know instantly that Meta was Faulkner's lover, not Wasson's. Estelle may have known Wasson was gay, even though in Hollywood he dated Miriam Hopkins.

The story told in *A Loving Gentleman* is not quite right. At one point in her sessions with Orin Borsten, Meta lowered her voice and said, "How do you think we can deal with the evening that I went to the house for dinner?" Then she spoke up and added: "With everything I've said up to this point it seems so out of character for me to have done that, you know. He asked me to do it."

Orin: We can leave it out.

Meta: The fact that he was willing for me to go into his house as a guest at his table. Doesn't that seem strange?

Orin: It does. It also seems strange that you invited Bill and Estelle to the reception.

Meta: The reception of my brother's wedding at the Studio Club and they came.

Before the encounter between Estelle and Meta, Bill had invited Meta to a party at Marc Connelly's house. Borsten suggested that afterward it got around that Bill and Meta were a couple.

Orin: You think it got back to Estelle.

Meta: I know it got back to Estelle.

Orin: Let's try to do it without the other two instances [the two times Meta met Estelle] because if you don't do the thing about the Studio Club and your brother, who's going to say anything?

Meta: It did appear as a social item in the *Citizen News,* but who is going to look that up?

Orin: It's a better structure, looking at it as a screenplay, just the one meeting between you and Estelle is plenty.[75]

Orin speculated that Estelle had seen the notice in the paper: "And then she went back and saw the picture, she would have known who the hell you were."

To Meta, as to Ben Wasson, Faulkner's reasons for wanting his wife and mistress to meet were mysterious. Meta could only speculate: He wanted to punish his wife; he was comparing the two women; he was experiencing a "sexual thrill playing a dangerous game." She said she never blamed him for the awkward and painful evening with Estelle, and he never brought it up.[76] Ben concluded that the incident signaled Faulkner's intention to divorce Estelle and marry Meta. Meta certainly hoped so. Yet Faulkner held back. Certain unresolved elements in his attitude toward women projected Meta and Estelle as opposing archetypes in the allegory of his love life. Setting up their encounter in his Hollywood residence virtually assured a conflict he could not resolve.

In *Count No 'Count: Flashbacks to Faulkner* (1983), Wasson observes that during their college days together, his friend "liked to stage a scene." Faulkner had to be in charge and set the conditions in which he could be observed. In this scene with Ben, Meta, and Estelle, he was giving full play to the counter-pull of his character, bringing together his childhood sweetheart and wife, his Hollywood mistress, and his college confidant, who also served as his New York agent and Hollywood buddy. Finally, there was Jill, the daughter as offstage presence, who had been to the beach with Meta. In one setting he had managed to gather together the significant elements of his life—just like a tableau in one of his novels. In such circumstances Faulkner could expect Estelle to play the protective wife. Did he want protection from Meta? She wanted to marry him, and he seems to have employed Estelle as a buffer between himself and his lover.

The dialogue Wasson gives Meta and Estelle during a "half-hearted toast" vividly enacts the division in Faulkner's character:

> "To Hollywood," Estelle said. She was twitching nervously.
> "No, to Mississippi," Meta said.

Each woman is portrayed as making a gesture toward the other, with Estelle perhaps weakening but then recovering her position by addressing Ben: "I hope you take this pretty child out a lot." To Estelle, Meta may have appeared to be a neophyte in this battle for her husband's affection.

Estelle, no matter how enfeebled or neurasthenic she might look, worked diligently to get the better of Meta. Meta held her own. Faulkner remained impassive throughout this rencontre, observing this drama of his own contriving. His stance may be interpreted as a "rather strong distrust of women," as his step-granddaughter, Victoria Fielden Black, observed.[77] Having the women compete in front of him deflected pressure from himself. He had once mentioned to Wasson his belief that relationships between women were like a contest, and Wasson remembered Faulkner's remark when his friend's wife and mistress met: "[Estelle] and Meta, when I introduced them, gave one another the femininely characteristic once-over, and I was reminded of Bill's comment so many years before that even small girls, when they meet for the first time, looked one another over, and knew everything about each other." If Estelle did not lose Faulkner, it was partly because she refused to give him up. She is supposed to have told him, "You can keep your Miss Carpenter, but I shall keep your name."[78] Did he take a perverse pride in his name and his wife's attachment to it? She was gallantly combative, and it seems likely that Faulkner, who wrote with admiration about similar characters in his fiction, welcomed the battle she gave him.

The Estelle-Meta bout had a sort of coda on October 11, 1936, during a party at 2217 Canyon Drive, the home of John Crown's parents. In front of everyone, including Meta, Estelle startled them into "an enormous embarrassed silence" by abrupt announcing, "Billy is going to teach me how to write."[79] Perhaps this outburst brought on the next stage, two weeks later, of the marital discord.

FAULKNER V. FAULKNER

On October 23, 1936, Estelle's attorney, Joseph L. Gainer, sent a letter to Hubert Starr: "In accordance with our telephone conversation this morning I am herewith enclosing a copy of summons and complaint in the above entitled action. I understand that you are accepting the service of these papers for your client, William Faulkner." Gainer had filed in the Superior Court of the State of California in and for the County of Los Angeles, an affidavit for "Order to Show Cause in re Attorney's Fees, court Costs, Alimony Pendente Lite [temporary support during divorce proceedings], Allowance for Support and/or Custody of Children, and Restraining Order." Estelle had, her attorney noted, "good and sufficient cause of action against her husband for divorce."[80]

She listed her husband's income as $6,000 per month and her necessary monthly expenses as $1,750 per month. She declared she had no income of her own and did not know what her husband needed to live on each month. She claimed his net income as approximately $78,000 from all sources in the past year. She had no employment and with a baby to care for did not expect to work. She lived in a seven-room house with her husband, baby, and two servants, rented for $175 a month. She wanted custody of her child since she would be at home to take care of Jill while her husband was at work. She did not want to entrust the child to strangers. She requested $1,125 for her own support. As assets she listed Rowan Oak, which she valued at $20,000, but she had no idea what other money or assets her husband might have.

Her husband countersued, citing a "good and sufficient cause of action against his wife for separation; as will appear more fully from his answers & cross complaint." He cited the $300 per month "alimony from at least one prior husband." His "temporary" weekly income was $671.46. He valued Rowan Oak at $10,000 and his equity as $4,000 and cash as $3,000. To the question, "Has your wife any organic disease or major physical defect?" he answered with one word: "dipsomania." As to himself, he admitted to no organic disease or defect. As for his wife's "necessary monthly expense," he listed $100 for "baby & servants" and $20 for her clothes and cleaning. He paid the rent, the utilities, and the help. His necessary annual expenses were $1,948.15, and $155 for the baby, $200 for "living & auto upkeep," house rent $175 monthly, the servants $70, "phones & utilities" $25. He declared Estelle had received $3,600 in alimony for the past year. He listed his net income for the past year as $6,273.76. As to whether his wife could support herself, he answered: "She doesn't know how to do anything; has never done anything; the colored servants do all the work; her present mental and physical condition is that of incompetence." He wanted custody of Jill, noting his "colored servant" cared for the child, "my wife never had done anything." Given Estelle's incompetence, it was best for Jill to stay with him, especially since Estelle had two children by a previous marriage to care for. He would allow Estelle visitation rights. Crossed out was his statement, "she never cared for the child." He would pay $150 for her attorney's fees and $15 for court costs, $100 a month alimony, and $75 for child support.

Faulkner did not sign his affidavit, a document that reflected the couple's wildly different perceptions and expectations and his deep anger, which he decided not to indulge anymore in legal papers. Along with his affidavit is this undated note to his attorney:

Herb

Do not send that paper to Gainer until you hear from me. Will explain tomorrow. Can you stop at hotel tomorrow a.m. or call me early as possible. Will wait for you. Do not send that paper. Something else has come up. Take no step at all until I see you. I am at home, maybe there until 8. Try me on phone, then at hotel. Must see you tonight if possible.

5:30 p.m.

On October 26, Starr wrote to Estelle's attorney that his client wanted to modify "certain statements which he thinks might be construed by some busybody as uncomplimentary to Mrs. Faulkner." Here the divorce trail ends. Nothing else in Starr's papers points to any subsequent action.

Meta evidently never knew that Faulkner had come this close to a legal separation, if not a divorce from Estelle. Meta also would have been surprised to learn that Estelle, not Faulkner, had initiated the divorce action and that it was Faulkner who apparently had second thoughts. Estelle seems to have called his bluff. Much later, Faulkner would comment that Hemingway's mistake was to think he had to marry the women who became his lovers. Perhaps he wanted "both Rowan Oak and Hollywood, a respectable family in Oxford *and* a young, beautiful mistress with whom to spend his weekends on the beaches of California."[81]

INTO THE DARK HOUSE OF HISTORY AND RACE

The confrontation between Estelle and Meta, followed by the aborted divorce action, occurred even as *Absalom, Absalom!* went into production for publication on October 26, 1936. The first pages of the novel are as challenging as anything Faulkner had written since the opening section of *The Sound and the Fury,* in which the "hitting" the idiot Benjy describes is only later understood as golfers attacking their balls. Faulkner forces the reader to make a story out of his character's perceptions. Similarly, in *Absalom, Absalom!,* Quentin Compson is trying to make sense of Rosa Coldfield's garbled story of a planter, Thomas Sutpen, and the domain he establishes in Jefferson, Mississippi. Sutpen erupts in her narrative with the force of creation itself: "The *Be Sutpen's Hundred* like the olden time *Be Light.*" Quentin is about to leave for his first year at Harvard, but Miss Rosa believes it is essential to his education that he learn about Sutpen because, to her, Quentin is not just a young man; he is a repository of the past who will carry with him what becomes, by the end of the novel, the burden of southern history itself. Or, as the narrator puts it, there are two separate Quentins, a man "still too young to be a ghost but nevertheless having to be one for all that."

The inescapability of the past is, of course, the essential theme of Faulkner's work, but this novel, more than any other, exemplifies his own plight as a modern man and as a vestige of an earlier epoch. He seemed old school in his manners but also contemporary, wooing Meta Carpenter with wines of recent vintage, writing about a horse-and-buggy age while buying a Ford phaeton. Even as a boy William Faulkner acted older than his age, yet he was also unwilling to grow up—at least in the usual sense—and become a conventional member of his community. He was, in short, like Thomas Sutpen, an outsider establishing his own Sutpen's Hundred in Rowan Oak, itself a relic of a bygone age Faulkner insisted on re-creating, even as he installed electric lighting and indoor plumbing.

As crucial as the story of Thomas Sutpen is to *Absalom, Absalom!,* another character, Charles Bon, is, for biographical purposes, even closer to his creator and, in the twenty-first century, even more relevant to understanding William Faulkner and the key position he occupies in a world that remains racialized. Charles Bon of New Orleans, studying at the University of Mississippi, is an outsider, like Sutpen. Sutpen grows up in West Virginia, then departs for the West Indies when he is told by a slave that he is white trash and must go to the plantation owner's back door. He then descends on Jefferson, Mississippi, because, somehow, his dynastic plans have gone awry elsewhere and he has to begin again. Quentin and his Canadian roommate, Shreve, advance and complicate the Sutpen story by concentrating on Charles Bon and his devoted friend, Sutpen's son Henry, who eventually kills Bon. As Shreve badgers Quentin about the details of Bon's biography, the Canadian simultaneously hectors Quentin about the quaintness of the South, its outlandish romanticism, which seems, in the cold, sober New England dark of their dormitory room, fantastic and unreal—as unreal as the South had to seem to Faulkner in Toronto in 1918, a thousand miles from Oxford, Mississippi, or nearly twice as far in Hollywood, where neither the climate nor the architecture gave Faulkner a sense of the season or of the place where he was writing *Absalom, Absalom!*

In a novel about a series of displacements in time, in place, and in sensibilities, with the point of view of each narrator very much tied to his or her place in a culture and generation, Faulkner explored his own sense of deracination and identity. There was the Faulkner who had been happy away from home with Meta Carpenter, who reminded him—sometimes unhappily—of home. There was the Faulkner unhappy in Hollywood in a home with his wife and child who was happily seeing Meta on the side and yet could not think to do anything better than invite his lover to meet his wife. This was conflicted behavior worthy of Charles Bon, who courts his half sister, not only defying his father, Thomas Sutpen, but outraging his devoted half brother, Henry—so Quentin and Shreve conclude, although the nature of Bon's identity, they eventually speculate, goes beyond the question of family and into the fraught ideology of race. What is finally at stake is Bon's color, which, in a sense, is no color at all, since when looking at him there is no reason to suppose he is black. Yet to be identified as black in Faulkner's white world is to be unacknowledged, marginal, and without home or family—an ostracism that William Faulkner himself found he could not accept as his own fate. Charles Bon, in short, strains the concepts of family, brotherhood, and race, to the breaking point—like the crisis Faulkner himself approached when Meta Carpenter walked into his Hollywood home and into the lives of his wife and child.

Charles Bon is, of course, a projection of each narrator, in the same way that William Faulkner was a projection of the perceptions of others. We get to know Bon as he enters the stories of other characters' lives, and as we factor in the biases and insights of different narrators, much as Faulkner was aware that the observations and interpretations of others informed his own character. As a conscious role-player, he encouraged these varying perceptions of him much as Bon seems to do in his various guises as lover, husband, brother, and son. At each decisive point in the novel Bon emerges as a different character. And in his one extant letter, he reveals that he is a consummately self-conscious character, writing in a style close to Faulkner's own.

Quentin and Shreve begin to realize how crucial Bon is to understanding the Sutpen story when they connect Sutpen's sudden departure "on business" to Bon's return to New Orleans after spending "a week or so" at Sutpen's Hundred. Quentin's grandfather had learned from Sutpen himself about Sutpen's trip to New Orleans, necessitated because, in Sutpen's opaque language, something had occurred that endangered his design. Because Sutpen, the "biggest single landowner and cotton-planter in the county," confides in no one, his success is suspect. His fellow citizens believed "there was a nigger in the woodpile somewhere," some secret, which Quentin and Shreve will eventually identify as Charles Bon himself, the mixed-blood son come home to claim if not his birthright, then at least his father's acknowledgment. They surmise that Sutpen, who has set up Henry as his heir, cannot abide the appearance of an elder son born of a woman of black blood whom Sutpen has rejected. It takes, however, virtually the entire novel for Quentin and Shreve to work out this version of what happened to Sutpen's design.

Family secrets are at the core of *Absalom, Absalom!,* and perhaps of all dysfunctional families, secrets like the existence of black Falkners, fathered by Faulkner's great-grandfather, who were unacknowledged and whom Faulkner himself could not recognize because their existence had been, in every meaning of the word, unspeakable. In the black community, it was another story. When Anthony Walton decided to return from the North to visit his black relatives in New Albany, where his grandmother had been born, his mother, taking a night-school course, started asking him questions about William Faulkner, whom she wanted to read. "Why Faulkner?" he asked. "Why not Richard Wright, James Baldwin or Zora Neale Hurston?" His mother said, "We're kin to some Faulkners." Walton laughed and told her, "*this* Faulkner was white." She smiled and said, "So?"[82] Faulkner's novels perceive the world in terms of a color line, even in seemingly trivial moments, as when Quentin notices his father's hand "looking almost as dark as a negro's against his linen leg."

Quentin Compson cannot speak about what he knows. He has so much trouble simply saying what he thinks happened at Sutpen's Hundred that Shreve has to take over the narration at key points. Over and over again, Shreve fails to rouse Quentin, whose frequent silences and seeming imperviousness to Shreve's hectoring asides are reminiscent of Faulkner's own taciturnity, which put up an impenetrable barrier not even Meta Carpenter managed to break through. At such moments, Faulkner seemed lost to her, lost to the world. What was he holding back from her?

Faulkner in Hollywood was a man out of order, like Charles Bon, who is sophisticated, elegant, self-assured, handsome, and too old to be attending a "small new college in the Mississippi hinterland and even wilderness, three hundred miles from that worldly and even foreign city," New Orleans, where Faulkner himself had shed the last vestiges of his provinciality. He could affect the ease of manner that Mr. Compson, Quentin's father, attributes to Bon, who has a "swaggering gallant air in comparison with which Sutpen's pompous arrogance was clumsy bluff and Henry actually a hobble-de-hoy." In this backwater, Bon stands out as a nonpareil—just as Faulkner did, returning home with new airs that confounded the locals.

Absalom, Absalom! is saturated with the voice of a community trying to make sense of the Sutpens, just as Oxford gossiped about the Falkners and their notorious scion, who wrote novels that outraged their sense of how a gentleman should comport himself and the way the world should work. The story of Sutpen—who is no gentleman, but who nevertheless expects his son Henry to behave like one—disturbs Jefferson once again when it learns of the showdown between Sutpen and Henry that results in the latter's renouncing his birthright and riding away in the night with Charles Bon. This development, as Mr. Compson relates it, defies explanation. So certain is the town of its sense of reality that it supposes Henry's action was "just the fiery nature of youth, let alone a Sutpen, and that time would cure it." Otherwise, the world is out of order, and the understanding of how families behave becomes unhinged and frighteningly unfathomable—exactly the way many of Faulkner's fellow townspeople regarded his novels, which they found unresolvable and therefore disconcerting. As a man and writer, he seemed forever to be displacing the community's sense of itself, while creating for himself a double life, as Charles Bon does, when his betrothed, his half sister Judith, finds on his body a photograph of an octoroon woman and child. The photo reveals that Bon had been intending to become a bigamist, leaving behind a family just as Thomas Sutpen did when he cast aside his wife in the West Indies. Mr. Compson speculates that Judith discovers what Henry already knew from having talked to his father about what Sutpen learned about Bon in New Orleans. It is Mr. Compson's contention that Henry's break with Sutpen results from Henry's will to believe in Bon. Indeed, it is Sutpen's assault on Henry's devotion to Bon that causes Henry's displacement. Henry cannot repudiate Bon without also forsaking the world Henry has made of their bond, which he wants to share with Judith, who is more like a fellow cadet than a sister, as Mr. Compson suggests. The sense of all three of them belonging together has underpinned Henry's identity. He does not want to choose between them. Even though he has left Sutpen's Hundred for New Orleans with Bon, he is bound to return, making the kind of to-and-fro journeys that marked Faulkner's own cross-country existence. To forsake all by departing from Sutpen's Hundred, as Henry dreads doing, and to claim all, as Bon has done by arriving there, articulates the very dilemma that Faulkner himself faced most dramatically when he invited Meta into his Hollywood home. "But who knows why a man, though suffering, clings, above all the other well members, to the arm or leg which he knows must come off?," Mr. Compson asks when contemplating

Henry's predicament, sensing that what his father said is true but wanting to believe it is a lie. Bringing Estelle to Hollywood meant putting her in the arena with Meta, even if Meta never actually asked Faulkner to leave his wife. Even if Estelle expressed, as she later did, a willingness to let Faulkner go, he knew that was not the end of the story.

It takes Henry four years to make up his mind about what to do with Bon, and it would take Faulkner far longer than that to sort out his feelings for Meta. In both cases, the idealization depended on departing from home and led to terrifying depression and displacement. And in both cases, only a return home—however dreadful and at whatever cost—could result in some modicum of peace in a dysfunctional family and in a disordered community riven with strife over the color line. Faulkner himself, with two mothers, one black and one white, projected his own divided nature into characters like Joe Christmas and Charles Bon, and understood what it meant for a man to deny any part of his nature and rearing.

Faulkner could not forsake his family for Meta, which would have meant living in some world elsewhere—a New Orleans of the imagination, a place where Charles Bon was free to live with his octoroon woman and their child while also courting Judith Sutpen. Bon is a doomed man, not only because his father will not acknowledge him but also because his brother cannot permit a marriage to their sister. A union of black and white is inconceivable in their world, even though their world, like Faulkner's, was rapidly changing and could not sustain the racial divide. Bon himself notes, with heavy irony, that his letter to Judith is written on notepaper that bears "the best of French watermarks dated seventy years ago . . . and written upon in the best of stove polish manufactured not twelve months ago in a New England factory." The present is bound to write over the past, as Shreve tries to tell Quentin at the end of *Absalom, Absalom!:* "So in a few thousand years, I who regard you will also have sprung from the loins of African kings." The Faulkner who thought a truly integrated world was at least hundreds of years away, who conceived of a sophisticated, mixed-race, seemingly foreign and yet thoroughly American figure (let's call him Barack Obama) who could be other than the tragic mulatto (a "mongrel," as Obama once called himself), sees Bon's demand for change as more than Henry or his culture can bear. But as Bon writes to Judith, "We have waited long enough."

Faulkner created a fully realized mixed-race character who refuses to be bound by the biases of his age and so hazards his life on behaving, like Joe Christmas, as no man, black or white, was then expected to behave. Like Joe Christmas, Bon does not run away from his fate. He welcomes it and thereby mounts a challenge to his society and to the author of his fate, William

Faulkner, dismayed by the alarming paradox of his own life—which he could imagine surmounting only in his fiction.

THE POWER OF LOVE

Absalom, Absalom! had a long, troubled gestation period during which Faulkner was working on at least four movie scripts, beginning his romance with Meta Carpenter, grieving over his brother Dean's sudden death, and struggling with his marriage and other family responsibilities. Even as Faulkner disliked having to put in so much time as a Hollywood hack, he also could not abide the tensions at home. Although his conflicted state of mind and time-consuming troubles may have seemed to threaten his creativity and achievement, just the opposite may also have been true. His hostility to Hollywood, his erotic arousal, his guilt over Dean's crash in the plane Faulkner had given him, and his disregard of Estelle seemed to have suffused him with greater narrative powers, resulting in the "intricacy, force, and intensity" of *Absalom, Absalom!* The novel demonstrated to him that he had not been "shackled and defeated in his role as an artist."[83] He had a certain role to play, making a construct out of himself that could endure pain and triumph and overcome his doubts and miseries. But all this took time. As Faulkner wrote to one of his editors in August 1934, the book was "not quite ripe yet; . . . I have not gone my nine months, you might say."[84] It seems unlikely that the Faulkner of 1934 could have produced a work of genius that rivaled and perhaps surpassed *The Sound and the Fury.*

Hollywood work that resulted in frustration nevertheless meant more than remuneration and an interruption in Faulkner's work on *Absalom, Absalom!* On April 9, 1936, on loan out to RKO, Faulkner worked on narrative outlines and a treatment for *Gunga Din* (1939), although the film, directed by George Stevens and starring Cary Grant, Douglas Fairbanks Jr., and Victor McLaglen, showed no trace of Faulkner's work.[85] The film amalgamated Rudyard Kipling's poem "Gunga Din" and his short-story collection *Soldiers Three,* featuring an Irishman, a Scot, and a Cockney. Tragedy and comedy were blended together in a buddy picture suffused with nostalgia for the British Empire and fast-talking, battling characters set against panoramic landscapes of the Indian subcontinent.

Faulkner knew the Kipling poem quite well. Gunga Din is a bhisti, a water carrier for the troops, who dies in battle hoping he has slaked the thirst of his white superior. A heroic servant of nobility, Gunga Din is memorialized: "Of all them black-faced crew / The finest man I knew / Was our regimental bhisti, Gunga Din." The poem can be taken as the epitome of imperial condescension, but it is also a tribute to courage over color, and a sense of human solidarity that Faulkner felt applied to his own experience with black people, which transcended social status and racial consciousness. Gunga Din becomes, in the end, a minister to suffering humanity: "'E'll be squattin' on the coals / Givin' drink to pore damned souls, / An' I'll get a swig in Hell from Gunga Din!" He is clearly superior to the callous, racist white soldiers. The poem's final line has become a proverbial expression: "You're a better man than I am, Gunga Din!"

Faulkner once referred to his magazine adventure stories as "third-rate Kipling," but his treatment eschewed the picaresque portrayal that Hollywood ultimately favored. Instead he wrote up notes that reflected the solemn, tragic spirit if not the plot of Kipling's poem. Captain Holmes has a son, Das,[86] by an Indian woman Holmes abandons. Das, in turn, rejects his dying father, refusing to rescue him. Holmes's other white son serves alongside Das in World War I. Not only do they remain loyal to one another even after their kinship is revealed, but Das sacrifices himself for his British regiment. For Faulkner, it was not enough to make Gunga Din carry water for the British. As with *Absalom, Absalom!,* he transforms the story of war and fraught family relationships into a probing exploration of loyalty, courage, and honor—all of which are explored in Kipling's poem, but without the compelling consanguinity of Faulkner's treatment. You cannot set aside part of the human race, Faulkner implies, by simply ennobling the singular Gunga Din. But Hollywood did not want a multiracial Gunga Din story, preferring Sam Jaffe in a brown body aping British military drill and playing a comic figure throughout most of the film, a sidekick to the antic and avaricious Cary Grant, obsessed with the golden temple that Gunga Din discovers. Gunga Din does redeem himself near the movie's end. Almost dead from a battle in which he defends his British masters, he struggles upward on the temple's golden frieze, blowing the horn that alerts British troops and their Indian allies to the ambush that awaits, planned by the followers of Kali, the goddess of a sect set on conquering all of India and driving out the British. Of course, the British overcome their nefarious enemies, and at the end Kipling himself makes an appearance penning his famous poem, part of which is read out to commemorate Gunga Din's sacrifice. Faulkner did make futile efforts to conform to Hollywood expectations, but after a month, he was taken off the picture, supposedly for writing dialogue deemed turgid for the screen. Meta remembered driving to the RKO lot to pick up a scowling Faulkner, who told her, "The trouble with the script is that these damned fool people [he gestured toward the administration building] don't begin to realize that Gunga Din was a colored man." Isn't this what he could have said about the white response to Charles Bon?[87]

The abrupt starts and stops in Hollywood were of a piece with a career that sometimes seemed to have gone to pieces in short stories, several of them unpublished, that did not quite jell, or that hardly seemed to be driving toward the novel that became *Absalom, Absalom!* As Noel Polk observes, "Five of the novel's important structural components—Sutpen's background before coming to north Mississippi; his friendship and then fatal contretemps with Wash Jones; the stories of his children's lives; the narrators' various relations to each other and to the story they are collectively telling; and the Compson family—seem to have been invented more or less independently of one another."[88] How could such material, created at different times and circumstances, coalesce in one novel? It is not certain that before 1935 Faulkner had even contemplated a work that could do so.

It is traditional in Faulkner criticism to show how various stories and fragments of stories culminated in Faulkner's novel.[89] He began writing *Absalom, Absalom!* early in 1934, interrupted it to write *Pylon*, and then resumed work in March 1935, completing at the end of January 1936 what Michael Millgate calls Faulkner's "most carefully articulated novel."[90] *Pylon*, as Millgate shrewdly observes, was not so much an intermission in the writing of *Absalom, Absalom!* as it was a working out of what became Faulkner's principal concern in the post-*Pylon* period: the "instability and malleability of fact."[91] As he acknowledged at the University of Virginia, arriving at the right approach to his masterpiece was an arduous process. Like the narrators of his novel going over the Sutpen saga, he had to relive and retell the experiences of his characters over the course of more than two years, including an extensive rewriting of chapter 1 after it had been sent to his publishers.

In one two-page précis, Faulkner seems to have first conceived of the novel as a triangular drama set in 1858 on a plantation involving Colonel Sutpen and his two children, Henry and Judith. They appear in the first sentence of "Dark House," a handwritten fragment found several years after Faulkner's death in his home. Reading "Dark House," now deposited in Special Collections at the University of Virginia, is fascinating and intriguing and frustrating as one tries to figure out Faulkner's minute handwriting that holds the same kind of mystery and power as the novel he was just beginning to imagine.

At college Henry meets Charles Bon, a charming and cosmopolitan man sent to the University of Mississippi by his guardian. Bon is aloof and yet "does like Henry as much as Bon is capable." Already, Faulkner has conceived of an enigmatic character who never quite reveals himself to Henry or to anyone else for that matter. Henry invites Bon home, where the sophisticate courts Judith just to "pass the time," and Colonel Sutpen seems impressed with Bon because he is such a gentleman. After Henry and Bon return to college, Bon receives letters from Judith in a "light and casual way." After a two-month stay with the Sutpens, Bon is accepted as Sutpen's prospective son-in-law, and much to Bon's surprise he realizes he has fallen in love with Judith. Then Henry accompanies Bon to New Orleans and discovers that Bon has a wife and child and that the wife has black blood. Henry returns home a "changed" man, convinced that Judith must "break with Bon." But Henry will not say why, and Judith, who "has spirit," defies her brother. Henry says he will kill Bon if Judith sees him again, and Colonel Sutpen tells Henry he cannot stay at home if he will not give a reason for his opposition to the marriage. And yet after he returns to college, Henry finds it impossible to repudiate Bon. As the two men ride once again to Henry's home, Bon taunts him, challenging Henry to ride ahead and presumably tell the Sutpens about Bon's other life. Henry and Bon draw lots, which results in Henry coming home first to see Judith waiting for Bon, who then arrives and takes her in his arms. Henry is ashamed of his behavior, but he fails to act, and Bon weds Judith—or so Faulkner wrote before crossing out the line that had them marry, and breaking off his work.

In another handwritten version, Faulkner reveals more about the Henry-Charles friendship. Bon discloses that his guardian has sent him to "rusticate" in a country college and to keep him out of trouble. Henry is obviously attracted to this "man of the world." The draft also has the Sutpens assuming that Bon has become Judith's suitor, although Bon does not declare such an undertaking. This time Faulkner emphasizes Henry's shock when he learns that Bon is married to an octoroon and has a child. An unapologetic Bon explains to Henry that such behavior in New Orleans is not uncommon and suggests this should not alter his relationship with the Sutpens. This fragment breaks off when Henry returns home and declares his opposition to Bon but will not give a reason to Judith or his father, both of whom demand an explanation.

Sutpen's character, undeveloped in "Dark House," eventually assimilates elements of Dal Martin in "The Big Shot," an unpublished story from the late 1920s.[92] Martin is turned away from "the big house" by its owner, who tells him to "go around to the kitchen door and tell one of the niggers what you want." Martin does not deliver the message and begins his quest to become the "boss" who has humiliated him. Faulkner had not yet figured out that the insult Martin-cum-Sutpen suffers could be intensified by having a slave deliver the rebuke instead of the white master. Like Sutpen, Martin seeks to elevate his progeny—in his case a daughter—into a privileged society, but also like Sutpen's brood, Martin's daughter comes to grief when she is run over by the gangster in Martin's employ.[93] The ambition to dominate the society that has denied him his dignity has resulted in the disintegration of his dynastic design.

But neither the notes for "Dark House" nor the quick irony of "The Big Shot" had the epic power Faulkner ultimately achieved in *Absalom, Absalom!* In "Evangeline" (ca. 1931), an unpublished story, Faulkner attempted to reorder, once more, and still at a much lower level of intensity than the novel, the key elements of the Sutpen tragedy. The story's dialogue between a character named Don and his unnamed journalist friend sounds a good bit like the exchanges between Quentin and Shreve:

> "It seems that this bird—his name was Sutpen—" "—Colonel Sutpen," I said. "That's not fair," Don said. "I know it," I said. "Pray continue." "—seems that he found the land or swapped the Indians a stereopticon for it or won it at blackjack or something. Anyway—this must have been about '40 or '50—he imported him a foreign architect and built him a house and laid out a park and gardens (you can still see the old paths and beds, bordered with brick) which would be a fitten setting for his lone jewel."[94]

The effort to find the right words, the interruptions, the bluff speculation, and the isolation of the grandiose main character, about whom so little of what is palpable is also provable, are akin to the portrayal of Sutpen in *Absalom, Absalom!* But this passage, so near the beginning of the story, lacks the demonic version of Sutpen that a bemused Quentin is trying to absorb during Miss Rosa's furious indictment in chapter 1 of the novel. In "Evangeline," Sutpen appears as an exotic, a curiosity, but without the historical heft he acquires through the generations of narrators who confect his story in *Absalom, Absalom!* In "Evangeline," Sutpen does not yet have a Gothic girth but instead seems almost comic: "a florid, portly man, a little swaggering."

Even so, a mystery pervades the Sutpens of "Evangeline," who are involved in a secret that no outsider has been able to reveal. Judith's brother Henry objects to her marriage to Charles Bon, but, according to Judith, Henry and Charles, the closest of friends who bonded at the University of Mississippi, come to some sort of accommodation after she marries Bon. "They have got over that now," Judith says without spelling out what "that" is. The journalist wants to sentimentalize the story with details like the rose in Judith's blonde hair, although the rose has no basis in fact. The story, like the novel that would come of it, is burlesquing the romances of the Old South that were still popular when Stark Young published *So Red the Rose* in 1934, which Hollywood released as a movie at the end of 1935. Young's novel also has two young southerners who meet at school and develop an intense friendship.

Like his characters in "Evangeline" and *Absalom, Absalom!,* Faulkner had to work through the conventions of popular film and fiction, steadily rejecting them to recover a more real, if still elusive, past. He wanted to "keep the hoop skirts and plug hats out," he confided to his editor.[95]

As in *So Red the Rose,* the male couple in "Evangeline" congregates around the desirable female: "Here are Henry and Charles, close as a married couple almost, rooming together at the university, spending their holidays and vacations under Henry's roof, where Charles was treated like a son by the old folks, and was the acknowledged railhorse of Judith's swains." The incestuous nature of these liaisons is part of Faulkner's demolition of the moonlight-and-magnolia school of southern literature. Presumably the reference to Bon as a railhorse means he has the inside track on Judith's affections.

But if Judith married Bon, and then Henry returned from the war with Bon's dead body, who is the ghost the journalist has come to find at the derelict Sutpen plantation home? The journalist had been expecting Judith to pine away for a lost love. Much of the suspense is dispelled when the journalist discovers the skeletal figure of Henry, a living relic of the past. The journalist has been led to this denouement by Raby, a Negro Sutpen who is transformed into the enigmatic Clytie in *Absalom, Absalom!* The journalist learns that Charles already had a wife in New Orleans while he was courting Judith. And yet that does not solve the mystery: "It seemed that there was something about the New Orleans business that, to Henry anyway, was more disgraceful than the question of divorce could have been." As in *Absalom, Absalom!,* the story's plot has to be reconceived moment by moment because it disrupts the predictable story line that readers crave. If the story is still not all that gripping, it is because the narrator/journalist and Don have very little invested in the story; they are not, as are Quentin and Shreve, implicated in how the story is resolved.

When Judith invites Bon's first wife and child to the Sutpen plantation, all is revealed to Judith as soon as Raby and Judith see the boy, although Raby refuses to spell out the revelation to the narrator. But then Raby's daughter shows the narrator the picture that Charles Bon carried with him during the war. That picture is of Bon's octoroon, "the mouth rich, full, a little loose, the hot, slumbrous, secretive eyes, the inklike hair with its faint but unmistakable wiriness—all the ineradicable and tragic stamp of negro blood." The color line has tragically divided Henry and Charles, resulting also in separating Charles from Judith.[96]

To have the story resolve itself as a matter of no more than a journalist's persistence is for the reader of *Absalom, Absalom!* a letdown but also a link to that obsessed reporter in *Pylon.* In "Evangeline," the journalist's discovery is not an act of the moral or historical imagination, or even the work of literature that the reporter in *Pylon* desperately desires to create. The story in "Evangeline" does not reverberate; it is only a mystery that has been solved. In *Absalom, Absalom!* what truth there is resides in the ambiguities. The novel, in other words, is not only about the process of interpreting and fashioning a narrative of the past; the novel also conducts an investigation into itself, so to speak: "What we seem to be listening for, and what we are moved by, are those ways in which Faulkner's text talks to itself: how it whispers its own divisibility."[97]

The point can be extended to considering the way that *Absalom, Absalom!* and *The Sound and the Fury* talk to each other. Quentin's effort in *The Sound and the Fury* to preserve his sister's Caddy's purity, even as he desires to violate it, is paralleled in his imaginative reconstruction of Henry and Judith Sutpen's eroticized relationship that has its foundation in the biblical story of Absalom, who kills his brother Amnon for raping their sister Tamar. And these repetitions, which provide so much mythic breadth to the novel, are amplified still more by Faulkner's exploration of race and history, for the Quentin in *The Sound and the Fury* who is identified in Cambridge as speaking like a colored man is also the Quentin in *Absalom, Absalom!* who portrays Charles Bon as tainted by the black blood that repels Henry. The struggle of father and son, Sutpen and Bon, and brother and brother, Henry and Charles, "merges with the Civil War," and the "struggle between David and Absalom turns into a civil war that divides the kingdom."[98]

But to get to this powerful story of incest, miscegenation, and a divided family and nation, Faulkner had more work to do on Thomas Sutpen. Connecting Sutpen's story to Faulkner's concern with caste and hierarchy did not occur until the fall of 1933, when he wrote "Wash," parts of which were incorporated in *Absalom, Absalom!* In this story Sutpen emerges as the "fine figure of man," with an epic grandeur absent from his earlier avatars. In both novel and story, Wash is the white trash refused entrance to the Sutpen house, and as such he is a parody of the young Sutpen turned away from the planter's front door. But he is also another example of how those oppressed by the plantation economy identify with their exploiters and attach themselves to what they believe is the sovereign seat of power. Like the narrators of *Absalom, Absalom!,* the Wash of Faulkner's story aggrandizes Sutpen:

He is bigger than all them Yankees that kilt his son and his wife and taken his niggers and ruined his land, bigger than this hyer durn country that he fit for and that has denied him into keeping a little country store; bigger than the denial which hit helt to his lips like the bitter cup in the Book. And how could I have lived this nigh to him for twenty years without being teched and changed by him? Maybe I ain't as big as him and maybe I ain't done none of the galloping. But at least I done been drug along. Me and him kin do hit, if so be he will show me what he aims for me to do.

Only when Wash realizes that Sutpen does not acknowledge Wash's place, however humble, in the economy of Sutpen's design—when Wash hears Sutpen reject Wash's granddaughter, who has borne a daughter and not the son Sutpen sought—does Wash cut down Sutpen with a scythe, finally taking down this "demon" who has tried to defy time itself in his attempt to restore the Sutpen line. In "Wash," the murder is one of a deeply disappointed and outraged lover: "'*I'm going to tech you, Kernel,*' Wash said in that flat, quiet, almost soft voice, advancing." In the novel, Faulkner downplays the story's intimate, almost erotic, death scene that segues into another horrible yet tender moment, when Wash slits his granddaughter's throat, so that our attention shifts away from Wash's tragedy to the sound of Sutpen's whip, which does not stop Wash, followed by the soundless scythe: "no whistling air, no blow, nothing since always that which merely consummates punishment evokes a cry while that which evokes the last silence occurs in silence." In *Absalom, Absalom!* Sutpen's death is shockingly sudden, evoking not simply his demise but "the last silence in silence." He has not just come to his end; he has been voided. In both novel and story, however, Sutpen has so profoundly "teched" (commanded) the characters that they seek to get in touch with him and his story.

Now with all the elements of the novel in place, Faulkner still had to create a narrative that bound them together. In the end, he would fashion a novel that never does tie up all the loose ends, a novel that in fact is as fragmentary and elusive as the past itself, a past that can be only partially reconstructed and then made whole only by the imagination, which defies—or should I say supplements? transcends?—reason. So why not have the novel itself rewrite the story, again and again, just as Faulkner himself reworked his drafts? The novel would become, in some ways, like those story meetings in Hollywood, where a group of writers would argue and collaborate over a story, except, of course, that in this case Faulkner would assert an authority and control that Hollywood denied writers, turning them into a species of house slave—well-paid but beholden to the studio hierarchy. At RKO, screenwriter Corey Ford, a Faulkner friend, only half-joked: "RKO gave us considerable freedom. We were allowed to speak to each other as we passed in the corridor, take our daily exercise in the yard without supervision by guards, and eat at noon in the same commissary with the producers and directors and actors, although at an isolated table in the rear."[99] It is too much to say that Hollywood's own caste system inspired *Absalom, Absalom!,* but all the same during his sojourn there Faulkner was writing against the regime that exploited his genius. During his "envy, fascination, frustration, contempt" for Hollywood, Faulkner produced a novel that often seems to be projected, as on a screen, rather than written on a page.[100] Remember Shreve's enjoyment of the Sutpen scenario: "It's better than Ben Hur, isn't it. No wonder you have to come away now and then, isn't it." Ben-Hur, a Jewish prince and slave in the thrilling silent movie, has been bested in multiple roles by mixed-race Charles Bon. Shreve's commentary also connects to Faulkner and his brothers, excited by silent film, and to the Faulkner who had to "come away now and then" from Oxford, from the South, to Hollywood not only to make money but, at times, for a release from the burden of history and family that Quentin Compson cannot endure.[101]

Why Faulkner could not let go of the Sutpen story and kept adding so many disparate elements to it is one of the biographer's obsessions. What concatenation of events and circumstances eventuated in the writer's decision to embark on an epistemological novel, an inquiry into the nature of narrative itself, which he had to realize would baffle many readers? He knew that he had created a work of genius: "I think it's the best novel yet written by an American," he told David Hempstead. That Faulkner would say this to a fellow screenwriter is also suggestive, since Quentin Compson sees Sutpen emerge out of a "quiet thunderclap," or very much like his entrance in a silent film. Quentin is like a screenwriter given a story idea to develop, a treatment that has many holes to be plugged, many scenes yet to elaborate:

> *It seems that this demon—his name was Sutpen—(Colonel Sutpen) Colonel Sutpen. Who came out of nowhere and without warning upon the land with a band of strange niggers and built a plantation—(Tore violently a plantation, Miss Rosa Coldfield says)—tore violently. And married her sister Ellen and begot a son and a daughter which—(Without gentleness begot, Miss Rosa Coldfield says)—without gentleness. Which should have been the jewels of his pride and the shield and comfort of his old age, only—(Only they destroyed him or something or he destroyed them or something. And died)—and died.*[102]

Hollywood reified Faulkner's tendency both to romanticize and ridicule the South of fiction and film. What was he playing at when he met Meta Carpenter? She presents him as the Southern Gentleman Extraordinaire, even resorting to some of the clichés anyone watching a movie about the South could mouth, resulting in something like "an innocent teenage romance." And yet she also conveys an exalted portrayal of their "doomed relationship with heartbreaking dignity and sadness." Part of this bifurcated response has to do with her sincere desire to be faithful to her experience even as she was working with an old Hollywood hand, a coauthor seeking to shape her story into the popular convention of a memoir, complete with heightened dialogue. Matthews is right to think that Faulkner is no mere projection of her imagination: "Meta was Faulkner's Hollywood—young, seductive, modern, emancipated, and even Southern. He loved her, but he couldn't bring himself to give up his past love (or love of the past?) for her."[103]

If there are two separate Quentins in *Absalom, Absalom!* in that famous passage so often quoted from the novel, there were at least two Faulkners, also positioned in more than one world at a time. Faulkner in Hollywood might even have said of his novel, as Quentin in his Harvard dormitory says of the Sutpen saga, "If I had been there I could not have seen it this plain." *Absalom, Absalom!* is a narrative that "incorporates the conflict between being too close and too far at the same time."[104]

Like Charles Bon, Faulkner was a sincere man practiced in deceit. And he had an anthropologist's sensibility—using all of his experience in Oxford, New Orleans, the North, Canada, Italy, and France to create the characters of his greatest novel. What did love, as he expressed it to Meta Carpenter, mean to William Faulkner? Love, as much as race, is a construct in *Absalom, Absalom!,* issuing from the imagination of a man who would be conflicted about love and race his entire life. And in Charles Bon, love object and "nigger," Faulkner created a character cognizant of his own doom and at the same time unwilling to relinquish his desire to live and to love.

In Hollywood, Faulkner was the "other"—as Charles Bon was in Jefferson, Mississippi. Faulkner had Hollywood friends, to be sure, but which of them could claim to know the retiring and reserved William Faulkner? He arrived and departed in mystery, leaving behind, as did Bon, traces of himself—more letters than Bon did but not enough evidence to be dispositive. To be himself, Faulkner had to hold back something. To be William Faulkner was a matter of intrigue; to be Charles Bon meant much the same thing. "Bon is the most extravagantly reinvented character in the novel" and its "erotic center."[105] Bon is an exotic, as out of place in Mississippi as Faulkner was in Hollywood, and yet, like Faulkner, somehow functioning in an alien world. Like Bon, Faulkner's manners, his demeanor, the way he walked, how he was observed—were all a matter of considerable, if thwarted, fascination. What director, other than Howard Hawks, could claim to have hunted with Faulkner and talked at length with him? And it can hardly be said that Faulkner unburdened himself to Hawks, given the colorful but limited nature of Hawks's anecdotes about Faulkner. Faulkner seems to have disclosed less to Howard Hawks than Thomas Sutpen did to General Compson. Even with Meta, Faulkner was circumspect in certain matters and downright duplicitous about others. She waited for him to open up, and he never quite did, even though she waited for him longer than Judith Sutpen waited for Charles Bon.

Bon is, in a sense, the character all the narrators have been waiting for and projecting themselves into: "A white world is created in broad historical outline and sufficient psychological depth to subsume the myths of the Negro, but that world fails, and the vision creating it is reduced to an emotional paralysis. Henry . . . and Quentin . . . are both catatonic figures at the conclusion of the novel; their condition is one result of their joint creation of Charles Bon as 'nigger.'"[106] Bon, you might say, is a necessary creation, one that rectifies the limitations of the white world, especially its conception of the "nigger." More than that, Bon speaks to the yearning that all of the characters—even the bigoted Miss Rosa—express in their conflicting versions of the Sutpen story and in their own conflicted natures. Bon is the something more, a heart in the darkness, the adumbrations of a more human, more complex figure than the psychological and ideological makeup of these various character-narrators can quite encompass. Even Shreve's *Gone with the Wind* notions of the South dissipate when he bears down on who Bon is and what he represents. In the end Bon, if he remains in some unreconstructed sense a "nigger," is also the "nigger" brother and son, husband and father, functioning in all these roles as a familial cynosure and the crux of what tears not only the Sutpen family but a civilization apart. But he is also what unites the family and the narrators in a common history.[107]

The tensions Faulkner himself felt as brother, son, father, and husband are an indelible part of his fiction, and of Charles Bon, especially, since Bon shares with his creator a wry humor, a melancholy sophistication and sense of tragedy that no other character quite matches. Bon functions as Henry's mentor just as Faulkner functioned for his younger brother Dean, and this bond between brothers was strengthened in the last three chapters of *Absalom, Absalom!,* written after Dean's fatal plane crash.[108]

Bon enters the story via New Orleans, an octoroon mistress, and son. Faulkner joked in New Orleans that he had fathered children on the side, so to speak, that he stood apart from traditional and bourgeois customs, but his fabulation has its fruition in Charles Bon's fatalistic acceptance of his multicultural, multiracial role. He is the alien who elects to join a society that at once rejects him and yet cannot relinquish the idea of him. Bon fights for a South that has no place for him, and yet a place must be found for Bon in the narrative precisely because he will not be denied a place.

Bon is the dark part of the story, the elusive mystery that has to be elucidated because his reality has been obscured by his blackness, by the mythology and abstractions about the "Negro" that Faulkner grew up with in his own home and community. After Dean's death, Faulkner sat at his mother's dinner table, working on those last chapters of his novel. And like Bon, who finds it so difficult to reveal himself, what could Faulkner have said to his own family about his deepest feelings, knowing that his own mother would reject them? Dean's daughter, whose memoir did not appear until 2010, reveals how profoundly racist Faulkner's mother, Maud, was. When Dean, named after her father, recited the Declaration of Independence, Maud pointed out that the "all men are created equal" phrase did not apply to "Negroes." Maud broke her Nat King Cole records when she learned he was black.[109] And yet this was the mother Faulkner shared a meal with at least once a week—and sometimes every day—while in Oxford.

When I interviewed Larry Wells about his wife's memoir, I asked why it had taken her so long to publish. I first met her in Oxford in 1975, and though she was willing to share memories about her family, what she has to say in her book reveals many more of the darker aspects of the family's history. "She was waiting on Jill," Larry explained. It was Jill's turn to tell the story and not Dean's place to precede her. The Faulkner family was hierarchical, Larry noted. When Jill died, Dean at last felt released, like the last Sutpen, to tell what she knew.

The back-and-forth of narration and counternarration, adopting and discarding interpretations, assessing the narrators and evidence at the same time, dismantles Sutpen's hierarchical worldview that begins with Miss Rosa in the first chapter,[110] even though she never quite made it into the Sutpen family. She suggests to Quentin that he is auditioning for the role of writer, since she proposes that one day he may want to write up what she has to tell him for the money he may need to support his family. Even the reclusive Miss Rosa knows that the South has become a "property"—in Hollywood parlance. Does she know the hard-up Compsons have sold a piece of land to send Quentin to Harvard? The question might occur to readers of *The Sound and the Fury* and the "Compson Appendix."[111] At any rate, she knows that tales of the South—such as those Faulkner published in the *Saturday Evening Post*— could provide a living.

Quentin's father doubts Miss Rosa's stated reasons for contacting Quentin. In the first of many instances when the motivations for telling a story are questioned, Mr. Compson speculates that Miss Rosa feels Quentin is implicated in the Sutpen story since his grandfather, General Compson, was as close to a confidant as Sutpen ever had. In short, perhaps Miss Rosa thinks she will learn something from Quentin that will make Sutpen's mystifying and troubling behavior understandable. Like all such explanations,

Mr. Compson's is open to challenge.[112] He seems so much calmer than her and with a sense of perspective she lacks. But he is also condescending and even a bit of a bore, going on about the "closed masonry of females." Perhaps some readers now lose patience with him after so much has been written about his patriarchal attitudes. "He thus controls the excessive and powerful Rosa with the myth of the 'Southern lady,'" one critic concludes. Miss Rosa, remember, is the proactive one, not the effete Mr. Compson. She wants Quentin to accompany her out to Sutpen's Hundred—to encounter what, she does not say. But in her very desire to confront what is in the Sutpen house she blunts Mr. Compson's thesis that she cannot cope with reality. She seems to want to own the story and the house and take her place in the Sutpen hierarchy.[113]

Even though Quentin does not put pen to paper, he confronts Faulkner's dilemma: how to comprehend and articulate the past that implicates him. Like the characters Faulkner said appeared to him with a life of their own, Miss Rosa commands Quentin's attention—even when he prefers it were otherwise. She is, however fitfully, finally making the effort to deal with a shuttered history through the filtered light of memory, behind those drawn blinds in her house that stripe her narrative and make a latticework of her house's exterior walls—like a chiaroscuro scene in a film noir. History is occluded in the blinkered consciousness of an old woman shut up in a dark house. Time has stopped in her "schoolprize water color" version of the sulphur-reeking Sutpen with his "band of wild niggers" and his manacled French architect. Miss Rosa reflects the "tendencies of the individual to place the past and the future on a mythic, indeterminate scale in an attempt to stand outside history."[114] Sutpen, as far as she is concerned, has defiled her family and community. She is working out for Quentin her provincial outrage, the "barbarism of the American dream" that insists on "the need for cultural purification from influences considered 'outside.'" Miss Rosa's house, like Sutpen's, harbors "dark and deeply ingrained familial and cultural structures that contain the seeds of the novels' major crises."[115]

If a good deal of Miss Rosa's narrative is suspect, she nevertheless adumbrates a structure and language for the Sutpen story that is sustained through the succeeding narratives, no matter how often her point of view is challenged and modified.[116] Her centrality only becomes more important upon rereadings of the novel, so that she becomes part of what might be called a family of narrators, providing clues that Faulkner deeply embeds in her narrative, such as her reference to Henry as "murderer and almost a fratricide."[117] What Miss Rosa "knows" is questionable, but not her profound impression that Henry and Bon were as close as brothers. She writes the text, so to speak, which subsequent interpreters absorb through annotation and correction.[118] Could they be wrong? Faulkner does not exactly endorse the Quentin/Shreve interpretation, but he did say at the University of Virginia that they come closer to the truth than anyone else, and the novel, in my view, does not allow us to overturn their interpretation, whatever gaps and dubious speculation remain in their account. Race and family and love are part of the unresolved tensions of *Absalom, Absalom!* just as they were in Faulkner's own life.[119]

Mr. Compson explores that nature of family strains in chapter 2, after his son's encounter with Miss Rosa. Mr. Compson's commentary suggests that if we cannot know exactly what happened in the past, we can certainly enlarge our frame of reference, opening up and layering the story that Miss Rosa flattens out. Unlike Miss Rosa's spectacle-and-tableau approach that pinions Sutpen to the ground of her imagination, Mr. Compson liberates Sutpen, allowing him to emerge, almost moment by moment, in the company of General Compson, the Coldfields, the townspeople, and even outsiders who disrupt Sutpen's wedding to Ellen Coldfield. History as process is initiated in sentences such as, "Now there began a period, a phase, during which the town and the county watched him with more puzzlement yet." This phase entails finding a wife after he has built the shell of Sutpen's Hundred. Miss Rosa's demon is no more, but Sutpen's inscrutability—a major aspect of her story— remains intact. And her outrage is ratified, so to speak, in Mr. Compson's evocation of "public opinion in an acute state of indigestion." The conventions Miss Rosa favors are, after all, those of her neighbors who are aghast at the rapidity of Sutpen's rise to wealth and power. No one—not even General Compson at this stage (1833–38)—is taken into Sutpen's confidence.[120]

He disrupts the community's sense of its own identity. He has displaced the story of manifest destiny with his brand of imperialism, bilking the Indians out of their land and settling it with African slaves. In effect, "Sutpen and his Haitian slaves expose a history that the South has repressed, though not erased." Slavery is not a peculiar American institution but the manifestation of "a larger Euro-American history of imperialism and subjugation."[121] If Sutpen seems like a primordial force in Rosa's depiction of his eruptive entrance into Jefferson, it is because he is reenacting the rapacity of the land's first white settlers. Sutpen's own displacement, we later learn in his talk with General Compson, has simply made him want to displace the native population as part of his design. What planter needs to wrestle with his slaves? Only one who acts as though he is creating slavery de novo. The planters liked to think that white supremacy had been long established, although, in fact, Sutpen arrives in Jefferson less than two years after Nat Turner's bloody slave revolt in August 1831.

Sutpen is a throwback in time, his wrestling with his wild "Negroes" a recapitulation of the rebellion he suppressed in Haiti, an anachronistic element in the novel since slavery had been abolished in 1804, twenty years or so before Sutpen arrived. This misdating seems deliberate, since it allows Faulkner to telescope history, linking the imperialistic origins of slavery with Sutpen's arrival in Jefferson.[122] Sutpen's first imperialistic design disintegrates for reasons he does not specify, although to General Compson he concedes that, in Mr. Compson's telling, Sutpen made a "mistake which if he had acquiesced to it, would not even have been an error and which, since he refused to accept it or be stopped by it, became his doom." This reference to what Quentin and Shreve later develop as their main contribution to the Sutpen story—that he set aside his wife because he discovered she had black blood—is so oblique that only an especially attentive reader or a repeat reader is likely to register what Mr. Compson is relating to his son.

It would seem that as long as Quentin has only his father and Miss Rosa to draw on he cannot get beyond a certain impasse in the story, although it remains vivid for him since he can hear and sense the same scenes that Sutpen experienced. Quentin has "grown up in a world not much changed from that in which Sutpen lived."[123] But Mr. Compson has a tendency to romanticize, to put back in the hoop skirts that Faulkner said he was removing from his novel. Hoop skirts, in fact, came into fashion some twenty years after 1833, but Mr. Compson cannot resist putting in the picture of Jefferson women floating down the street—their ankles and feet covered by anachronistic hoop skirts—any more than Hollywood, or the courtly Faulkner himself, could resist putting on a performance of the Old South, or the idea of the Old South, for Meta's entertainment and his own. History and myth and the popular versions of the South coagulate with Mr. Compson's classicism as he compares Sutpen's comings and goings, and the community's speculation about him, as the strophe and antistrophe of a Greek choral drama, with Sutpen's name invoked over and over again as the cynosure of Jefferson's anxieties.

Some of Mr. Compson's classical allusions make of Sutpen an almost supernatural creature, a mystery akin to Miss Rosa's. Sutpen's seed, Mr. Compson opines, is like dragon's teeth, an herb that is incredibly fertile and, in the myth of Jason and the Argonauts, produces seeds that germinate into fully armed warriors. The potent Sutpen's progeny include not only Clytie and Henry and Judith but also "the one before" this brood. Who is that? And how does Mr. Compson know?[124] We are only in chapter 3 of the novel, and yet, like Miss Rosa's allusion to fratricide, another element of the narrative appears out of nowhere, like Sutpen himself. We might as well be dealing with a torn fragment of papyrus, given the jagged and truncated accounts of the novel's first two narrators. What aren't we being told? Parts of the narrative seem to have been luxated. "Let's start again" might well be the cry of readers still in their novitiate. We are all postulants when it comes to the order—or orders—of the Sutpen story. Such moments endow *Absalom, Absalom!* with a unique authority as a work of fiction, as though it really draws on a history outside of itself, and we become the historians piecing together narratives. When Faulkner discussed the novel at the University of Virginia, he also acted as though he was responding to a history that even he could not entirely account for. Similarly, the unnamed narrator also treats the characters and the past they probe as autonomous. Neither the narrator nor Faulkner himself ever claims a privileged authority.[125] Consequently, the very idea of the author-narrator who can exercise absolute control over the fiction is subverted in *Absalom, Absalom!* Part of the reason for the massive commentary on this novel— whole books, not to mention thousands of articles, have been devoted to its elucidation—is surely a talmudic effort to supplement or supplant previous interpretations, just as the character-narrators in the novel absorb and supersede previous narratives.

Mr. Compson leads the way in this hermeneutical process, reporting on the interpretations he has heard. For example, he refers in chapter 3 to the community's suspicion that Sutpen's success as the largest landowner and cotton planter in the county is due to some nefarious maneuver to "juggle the cotton market" or to some kind of supernatural power associated with his "wild niggers" who can "conjure more cotton per acre from the soil than any tame ones had ever done." Mr. Compson acknowledges a more rational reason—Sutpen's "singleminded unflagging effort"—and yet he also reports the community's suspicion that "there was a nigger in the woodpile somewhere."[126] We are well on our way to linking the "nigger" with the sudden appearance of Charles Bon, who is somehow going to spike Sutpen's design.

Bon first appears as an elegant figure who puts in high relief the crudity of Sutpen's grandiosity:

Charles Bon of New Orleans, Henry's friend who was not only some few years older than Henry but actually a little old to be still in college and certainly a little out of place in that one where he was—a small new college in the Mississippi hinterland and even wilderness, three hundred miles from that worldly and even foreign city which was his home—a young man of a worldly elegance and assurance beyond his years, handsome, apparently wealthy and with for background the shadowy figure of a legal guardian rather than any parents—a personage who in the remote Mississippi of that time must have appeared almost phoenix-like, fullsprung from no childhood, born of no woman and impervious to time and, vanished, leaving no bones nor dust anywhere—a man with an ease of manner and a swaggering gallant air in comparison with which Sutpen's pompous arrogance was clumsy bluff and Henry actually a hobble-de-hoy.

For all their differences, of course, Sutpen and Bon are flamboyant outsiders with shadowy backgrounds of an almost supernatural import. Both men displace any conventional rendering of their biographies. But the dislocated Bon has more style and more mystery and is thus a refinement of Sutpen as anomaly.

What we know about this stage comes from Sutpen's wife, Ellen, who for six months bruits about the engagement of her daughter Judith and Bon until Henry abruptly vanishes, Mr. Compson reports: "And then something happened. Nobody knew what: whether something between Henry and Bon on one hand and Judith on the other, or between the three young people on one hand and the parents on the other." Then, according to Mr. Compson, the Sutpen slaves let it be known that Henry renounced his birthright after a showdown with his father and rode off with Bon. Mr. Compson pictures a prostrate Ellen unable to cope with "reality." But what is the reality of this contretemps? And what did Judith know? Miss Rosa, Mr. Compson says, can't help because she was not told anything. What Mr. Compson does know is that Judith and Henry, like Henry and Bon, were very close, and the intensity of their bond, as Mr. Compson describes it, has a powerful impact on Quentin and Shreve, who later elaborate a very complicated incest story involving Henry, Judith, and Bon. But what does all of this have to do with Wash Jones, who shows up at the end of chapter 3 to ask, "Air you Rosie Coldfield?" At so many turns in the novel, a new development or piece of evidence emerges but is not, as in the traditional detective story, immediately factored into the narrative.

Mr. Compson's arguments can be dismissed as misogyny and grandiose speculation, but far more important is his tenacity and desire to understand, to drive the narrative forward. Without his effort at turning inference into narrative, Quentin and Shreve cannot proceed. The narrator notices Mr. Compson's "hand looking almost as dark as a negro's against his linen leg," as if to signal the black shadow that will eventually dominate the story of what happened to Sutpen and his brood, which is also the story of what happened to the South, although Mr. Compson's words have more implications than he realizes. Part of what seems like *only* Mr. Compson's speculation in chapter 4 is given confirmation later when he produces Bon's letter—and later when Bon's wife and child show up at Sutpen's Hundred. So we have to work back from later phases of the narrative to fully grasp passages like this one in chapter 4: "Because Henry loved Bon. He repudiated blood birthright and material security for his sake, for the sake of this man who was at least an intending bigamist even if not an out and out blackguard, and on whose dead body four years later Judith was to find the photograph of the other woman and the child." Phrases like "the iron dark of that Christmas morning" when Henry repudiates his birthright are echoed in the iron dark of Quentin and Shreve's Harvard dormitory room. In other words, the narrative, for all its detours in conjecture, builds a momentum toward what is not a resolution in the conventional sense of certainty as to what happened but rather toward a preponderance of the evidence that leads to persuasive, if not absolute, conclusions. To say the novel does less than that is to say history is just another fiction—an argument that can be made of course, but not one that this novel sustains. What is at stake, ultimately, is Faulkner's seriousness and sincerity. If he had no faith in facts per se, he did believe in truth—no matter how tentative and subject to revision.

Mr. Compson supplies wording and feelings that are certainly his own creation and yet speak to Henry's existential dilemma: *"I will believe; I will. I will. Even if it is so, even if what my father told me is true and which, in spite of myself, I cannot keep from knowing is true, I will still believe."* Henry's vehemence, rendered in italics, is an invention, to be sure, representing Mr. Compson's working back to the scene in which Henry repudiates his father's claim that Bon is already married. Mr. Compson's passionate reconstruction here—quite different from his customary studied commentary—stimulates Quentin and Shreve's search for better explanations of what happened at Sutpen's Hundred, and to put that story, ultimately, in its largest frame.

When Mr. Compson describes, in chapter 4, the scene between Henry and his father and ponders what Judith knew, if anything, about her brother's renunciation of his inheritance, Mr. Compson uses the word "armistice" twice to characterize the four-year suspension of the conflict over Bon's wish to marry Judith. The irony of employing such a word is apparent: these two young men face a common enemy and fight to preserve the very system—call it a color line that exists, slavery or no, a division within families—that is sundering a nation.

Mr. Compson portrays Judith as an independent woman, willing to abide by Henry's objections only so long as she deems fit:

Judith acquiescing up to that point, who would have refused as quickly to obey any injunction of her father as Henry had been to defy him yet who did obey Henry in this matter—not the male relative, the brother, but because of that relationship between them—that single personality with two bodies both of which had been seduced almost simultaneously by a man whom at the time Judith had never even seen—she and Henry both knowing that she would observe the probation, give him (Henry) the benefit of that interval, only up to that mutually recognised though unstated and undefined point and both doubtless aware that when that point was reached she would, and with the same calm, the same refusal to accept or give because of any traditional weakness of sex, recall the armistice and face him as a foe, not requiring or even wishing that Bon be present to support her.

That this is not Mr. Compson's fanciful conception is established when we finally get to read Bon's letter to Judith, a piece of evidence that clearly shows the confidence he has in her own judgment. Mr. Compson's Judith is also the same child who does not shrink from her father's wrestling with slaves as Henry does.

Mr. Compson delays actually showing the Bon letter to Quentin because, like all the narrators, he wants to exert his command over the story and put whatever he knows into his own interpretation—or design, as Sutpen himself does. Mr. Compson's sensitive reading of family relationships revealed in his passage about Judith is reminiscent of Faulkner's assertion of his own authority even as he bowed, at strategic points, to Estelle's will and the demands of maintaining a family. The dynamics of what it means to be yourself and at the same time preserve a family suffuse both his novel and his life.

Bon's status in the Sutpen family eludes Mr. Compson. He speculates that Bon seduced Henry and Judith and simply awaited Sutpen's revelation to his children of Bon's New Orleans wife (mistress?) and child. Bon also waited for Henry and Judith to make up their own minds. That Bon might have had an even closer connection to brother and sister does not figure in Mr. Compson's surmises. At an impasse, Mr. Compson contents himself with evoking Bon's "fatalistic and impenetrable imperturbability," although he also magnifies Bon's charisma, reporting that he mesmerizes several other undergraduates like a "hero out of some adolescent Arabian Nights."

Mr. Compson's suggestive narrative opens up gaps to be filled—when he notes, for example, that Bon paid Judith the "dubious compliment" of not ruining her (taking her virginity) even though he was known for his "prowess" with women. Why he holds back will become, in Quentin and Shreve's retelling, a key factor. Unable to advance his interpretation any further, Mr. Compson delivers his famous lament on the unknowability of the past: "It's just incredible. It just does not explain. Or perhaps that's it: they dont explain and we are not supposed to know. We have a few old mouth-to-mouth tales; we exhume from old trunks and boxes and drawers letters without salutation or signature, in which men and women who once lived and breathed are now merely initials or nicknames out of some now incomprehensible affection which sound to us like Sanskrit or Choctaw." These doubts are hardly a reason for Quentin and Shreve to give up their own reconstruction of the past. Mr. Compson's skepticism, while warranted, is also inadequate, since the point of *Absalom, Absalom!* is that the truth is not singular but is rather the product of the cumulative and incremental efforts of the character-narrator historians over several generations. However readers react to Quentin and Shreve's story, Mr. Compson's conclusions about that past—"their acts of simple passion and simple violence, impervious to time and inexplicable—Yes"—cannot stand.

As soon as Mr. Compson produces Bon's letter in chapter 4, Bon's own voice countermands Mr. Compson, which is perhaps one reason why Mr. Compson delays so long in allowing Quentin to see it. "We have waited long enough," Bon announces to Judith. His declaration is made either in the full certainty that she will agree or in his own decision to take control of their fate—or both. At any rate, he is hardly the passive creature Mr. Compson depicts, although he is as sophisticated and even world-weary as Mr. Compson supposes. The Bon in this letter is compelling. He has no illusions about the outcome of the war or about the fragility of human life and the onset of change. It is easy to see how he exerts such a hold on Henry and Judith, and why Sutpen rightly reacts to Bon as a threat to his design.

Bon has the sensitivity of an artist, writing to Judith with an extraordinary immediacy on "a sheet of notepaper with, as you can see, the best of French watermarks dated seventy years ago, salvaged (stolen if you will) from the gutted mansion of a ruined aristocrat; and written upon in the best of stove polish manufactured not twelve months ago in a New England factory."[127] He understands how the world has changed and sends her no uplifting note but instead a declaration of love and purpose that simply exists beside his sense of defeat and what he knows to be her own love: "I do not insult you by saying that only I have waited, I do not add, expect me. Because I cannot say when to expect me. Because what WAS is one thing, and now it is not because it is dead, it died in 1861." He believes they are "doomed to live," but in their very survival resides their tragedy.

Bon's decision sets up the ultimate confrontation with Henry, one that Mr. Compson attempts to re-create and that Quentin and Shreve will fully realize: "the defiance and the ultimatum delivered beside a bivouac fire, the ultimatum discharged before the gate to which the two of them must have ridden side by side almost: the one [Bon] calm and undeviating, perhaps unresisting even, the fatalist to the last; the other [Henry] remorseless with implacable and unalterable grief and despair." Mr. Compson even supplies some of the words Quentin and Shreve will build on: *"Dont you pass the shadow of this post, this branch, Charles;* and *I am going to pass it, Henry."*[128] This drawing of the line will be echoed later in Clytie's barring the way to Miss Rosa mounting the steps of Sutpen's Hundred to discover who has been hidden there, Miss Rosa claims, for four years.

Mr. Compson's dominant narrative voice throughout chapters 2–4 is challenged in chapter 5 by a return to Miss Rosa's powerful monologue. Or is she, in fact, speaking? Generations of readers have puzzled over her italicized words that make up most of the chapter. Her vocabulary is extraordinary, as if she had been reading a Faulkner novel. Some commentators describe this chapter as Quentin's own distillation of what she tells him. Still others suggest the italics are meant to render the import of what she says—not her literal wording.[129] What matters, however, is that we become displaced, since the words in chapter 5 are not given a location. We are in some never clearly defined mental territory. Why? It would seem that the words in this chapter are meant to be taken as a set-aside—that is, a realm unto itself, emerging from Miss Rosa's consciousness but not pinioned by her own voice. This "narcotic" and "surreal" prose resists "objective representation." It is the language itself that dominates and not the experience to which it refers.[130]

Why dislocate a novel this way? Faulkner took a tremendous risk, but one he felt compelled to pursue because Sutpen's story is a boundary breaker that a conventional narrative—Mr. Compson's mode of rational inquiry—cannot comprehend. He, too, has been straining to get more out of the Sutpen story, but not until chapter 5 do we get a narrative that is now confounded with an almost phantasmagoric fable, beginning with Miss Rosa's railing against *"the brute,"* Wash Jones, who announced Charles Bon's death. Jones is the unworthy messenger, a degraded Sutpen, in fact, who *"until Ellen died was not even permitted to approach the house from the front."* Miss Rosa is, of course, not aware of the story we have yet to hear of Sutpen's own turnaway from a planter's front door. And the novel's first readers can't yet know that Miss Rosa is sore because Sutpen turned from her to Jones's granddaughter Milly, on whom Sutpen expected to sire a male heir. In a further irony that Miss Rosa cannot appreciate, she is outraged at Clytie *"barring the stairs"* that Miss Rosa wants to climb to see what is hidden at Sutpen's Hundred. Sutpen's own experience continues to be repeated even before we know the experience is his—when, that is, he vouchsafes his opaque autobiography to General Compson in chapter 6. Time may be linear, in one sense, but in another its ramifications extend to all periods at once. We perpetuate what we do not know has already happened to others.

Clytie begins to hover over Miss Rosa's narrative in this chapter as an exemplar of a *"brooding awareness and acceptance of the inexplicable unseen inherited from an older and a purer race than mine"*—an astounding comment coming from Miss Rosa, who as a child could not bear to touch Clytie's toys. Like Sutpen's "wild niggers," Clytie is aboriginal, a reminder to Miss Rosa that she is secondhand and outranked even though society treats Clytie as an inferior. Like Lucas Beauchamp in *Go Down, Moses,* Clytie is never less than her own person regardless of the servile circumstances that confine her. Clytie owns a part of the Sutpen story that Miss Rosa cannot possess. What is worse, Clytie remains, in Miss Rosa's own words, Sutpen's black replica—immune to insult and *"decreed to preside upon his absence."* Clytie is as unyielding as her white father, which results in a displacement of Miss Rosa's own authority as a white woman over this *"inscrutable coffee-colored face."* That Miss Rosa cannot read one who is supposed to be her inferior is phenomenally frustrating. When Clytie says, *"Dont you go up there, Rosa,"* addressing Miss Rosa as an equal, she is also echoing what her white half brother Henry says to Bon: Miss Rosa can invoke her authority by saying to Clytie, *"Take your hand off me, nigger,"* but she already knows Clytie's touch has shattered the *"eggshell shibboleth of caste and color."*

Miss Rosa knows, as chapter 5 reveals, that the past cannot sustain her. More than one of her Charles Bon–like sentences begins, *"Once there was."* Her presumed stable world vanished in the Civil War, and all that remains, she asserts, is faith and love—surely the same sentiment Bon conveyed in his letter to Judith. In the new dispensation, Miss Rosa briefly experiences a kind of union forbidden in her antebellum upbringing: *"It was as though we were one being, interchangeable and indiscriminate, which kept that garden growing, spun thread and wove the cloth we wore, hunted and found and rendered the meagre ditch-side herbs to protect and guarantee what spartan compromise we dared or had the time to make with illness, harried and nagged that Jones into working the corn and cutting the wood which was to be our winter's warmth and sustenance;—the three of us, three women."* Sutpen's return and his offer to marry Miss Rosa disrupts this momentary colligation. He offers neither faith nor love when he returns home, and yet he still represents the desire to create the world anew. In that sense, he is all that Clytie and Judith and Miss Rosa have. Why Miss Rosa agrees but then spurns Sutpen's proposal she does not exactly say, although his recourse to Milly Jones suggests, as Shreve will later speculate, that a marriage to Miss Rosa was predicated on coupling with her first to produce a son.

At the end of chapter 5, Quentin is aroused from his reverie by Miss Rosa's declaration that there is *"something hidden in that house."* For Quentin, the Sutpen saga stalls while he contemplates the confrontation between Bon and Henry, who bars the way to Judith and Sutpen's Hundred. Quentin cannot proceed without the displacement that his removal to Harvard enforces, or without Shreve, his "insurgent narrator."[131] In chapter 6, Shreve suddenly expands the saga's narrative, taking it to Hollywood in his references to "it's better than Ben Hur," to the silent films that promulgated the myths of the Old South. The querulous Shreve commands: "Tell about the South. What's it like there. What do they do there. Why do they live there. Why do they live at all."

Shreve is reminiscent of bumptious Morris Ankrum, a fine character actor who pestered a reluctant Meta to introduce him to Faulkner. Promising to be on his good behavior, Ankrum could not help himself and tried to question Faulkner about his work, to engage with a dour, retiring writer not so different in such circumstances from the reticent Quentin Compson. However uncomfortable Faulkner felt in Hollywood, however much he longed for home, that home and its history could not be brought into proper perspective without his departures and returns, and the rude questions about his native land. *Absalom, Absalom!*, beginning in chapter 6, is a series of departures and returns—to the past, to the South, to Harvard, and, ultimately, to a vision of history and of the future.

The Canadian Shreve who puts his abrupt questions to Quentin in a Harvard dormitory room expands the transcontinental trajectory of Sutpen's biography and its consequences, preparing us for Shreve's concluding prediction about race and history at the end of the novel. Both of these undergraduates are displaced persons attracted to a story about deracination, with characters who have to cope with situations unprecedented in their cultures. Henry contends with the cosmopolitan Bon, and Judith struggles with trying to bring up Bon's son as . . . what? White or black? Clytie waits on Bon's octoroon mistress—or she may be his wife—even though her role is to serve white people, even though she sleeps next to Judith as an equal. None of the characters act in terms of their society's conventions. Sutpen is hardly a typical slave owner in his dealings with his human property and with Wash Jones, who becomes a kind of court fool to Sutpen's throne.

From Harvard, Quentin and Shreve are thrown back into the past. To a biographer, Faulkner's choice of Harvard is also curious. Why not Yale? Faulkner knew it well from his stays with Phil Stone. Both Yale and Harvard began as educational institutions for Congregationalist ministers. But Harvard is older—indeed the oldest institution of higher education in the United States—and just that much closer than Yale to the Boston elites and New England Puritanism. Quentin's quasi-Puritan sensibility, like Henry Sutpen's, is challenged by outsiders like Bon and Shreve, who come from times and places that permit them a freedom to which neither Quentin nor Henry can adjust. Quentin is stuck at that moment when Henry confronts Bon, which is also Quentin's moment when he must go through that door at Sutpen's Hundred, where, Miss Rosa insists, something is hidden. Shreve tries to shame Quentin into action: "Good Lord yes, let's dont find him or it, try to find him or it, risk disturbing him or it." Although Shreve differs from Mr. Compson in so many respects, he is nevertheless like Quentin's father—"just like father" Quentin thinks—because Shreve will not let the story alone and is determined to fill in its blanks. Shreve recapitulates much of what Mr. Compson told Quentin while also extending the saga to include Bon's confused angry son, whom Judith and Clytie bring up, and who refuses to pass as white but who cannot settle into any community, picking fights with black and white alike. Bon's grandson, who becomes known as Jim Bond, is mentally incapable of understanding his fraught heritage. The anomaly that Sutpen represents is magnified in Bon's son and grandson, who become the reductio ad absurdum of the South's caste, class, and race system. Their anomie is the Sutpen agony, the plight of having no certain identity. Quentin remembers that as a young boy approaching Sutpen's Hundred, he witnessed the consequences of displacement before he understood what he was seeing: "you didn't see the old woman [Clytie] at all at first because you were watching the boy, the Jim Bond, the hulking slack-mouthed saddle-colored boy a few years older and bigger than you were, in patched and faded yet quite clean shirt and overalls too small for him, working in the garden patch beside the cabin." What Quentin now understands is not yet vouchsafed to Shreve. In fact, Shreve tells him to "wait," since Shreve wishes to work out for himself what has been repressed in Quentin's consciousness, and what lies behind that door Quentin finally opened at Sutpen's Hundred. Shreve is, in effect, helping Quentin throw open the door of the unconscious mind, the dark house that haunted so much of William Faulkner's imagination.[132]

As an outsider who knows little about the South, Shreve is, in a way, prepared to identify with Sutpen's own "innocence," as it is called when he begins to tell his own story to General Compson. And so Shreve's recapitulation of the West Virginia Sutpen's early days—of his first awareness of class and caste and race—is especially appealing to this Canadian who sees something other than Miss Rosa's devil: "So he didn't even know there was a country all divided and fixed and neat with a people living on it all divided and fixed and neat because of what color their skins happened to be and what they happened to own." This is Sutpen emerging out of a state of nature into society, a Sutter-Rousseau, about to fall into the world of good and evil. Sutter, the disciple of Rousseau in Faulkner's screenplay, becomes like the corrupt society that Rousseau deplored. Similarly, Sutpen's awareness of class and social structure deprives him of his natural egalitarianism when he learns he is white trash turned away from the planter's front door and told to go around to the back by a liveried slave, who by virtue of his dress and position can tell a white man what to do. Sutpen never delivers his father's message because Sutpen has been given another message in terms of his rejection: "He had learned the difference not only between white men and black ones, but he was learning that there was a difference between white men and white men," Quentin reports, explaining what Sutpen told Quentin's grandfather. Sutpen, unschooled in the ways of this world, at the mercy of his father's perpetual displacement of the family in treks across country, confesses to General Compson, "he knew neither where he had come from nor where he was nor why."

What Sutpen does know is that he wishes to be in a position to be his own man, which to him means he can act with the same arbitrary power that has been used against him. As Quentin tells Shreve, Sutpen "just told Grandfather how he had put his first wife aside like eleventh and twelfth century kings did: 'I found that she was not and could never be, through no fault of her own, adjunctive or incremental to the design which I had in mind, so I provided for her and put her aside.'" No justification is needed for Sutpen's action; this is how the world works, as far as he is concerned. History is not something that happens to him: "it was to him—a spectacle, something to be watched," Quentin reports.

As we learn about the French architect who flees from Sutpen's megalomania and wonder, as do the character-narrators, why he would ever consent to do Sutpen's bidding in the first place, the architect's capture reveals the escapee's affinity for Sutpen's design: "then [he] flung the hand up in a gesture that Grandfather said you simply could not describe, that seemed to gather all misfortune and defeat that the human race ever suffered into a little pinch in his fingers like dust and fling it backward over his head." The architect cannot escape his fate any more than Sutpen can avoid his, but both men act as though history cannot deter them. In defeat, they proclaim their victory—as Sutpen will do again when he returns from war and monomaniacally begins to restore his Hundred.

Quentin and Shreve reassemble the Sutpen saga in their "snug monastic coign," joined by their "geologic umbilical," the Mississippi River that traverses a continent from the Deep South to Alberta, Canada. Through narrative they seek to reintegrate the displaced elements of the Sutpens— all the conflicting characters who have to be subsumed in a story that also reflects Quentin and Shreve's own "transubstantiation"—to use Faulkner's word for the way the two of them become one with a religious intensity. Like monastics they suffer through the cold and sleepless night not in prayer exactly but certainly in devotion to their story. Shreve's deep breathing in the cold with his shirt off and the window open suggests a kind of ritual- istic self-mortification that Quentin evinces in his sullen, close to catatonic moments when he often repeats the same words like a mantra: *"Maybe we are both father."* Nothing ever just happens once, Quentin muses, in his famous metaphor of the "umbilical water-cord" that connects all of the characters and narrators, no matter how their temperatures, molecularity, and rhythms differ. The metaphor is in itself an effort to overcome displacement. When Quentin says that maybe it took all of the characters in the story to make Sut- pen, or that Sutpen made all of them, he is not only repeating this umbilical water-cord metaphor but also expressing the unity in difference that is the ultimate meaning and art of *Absalom, Absalom!*

Sutpen cannot see the unity in difference and so sets aside his first wife and child, but that is a conclusion about his motivations that can be made only after reading chapter 8. In chapter 7, he tells General Compson repeat- edly that a certain "fact" was withheld from him, a fact he discovered after his child was born. Quentin will later admit that he somehow discovered Sutpen's reason for rejecting his firstborn, and Shreve, for all his skepticism and ridicule, never challenges Quentin's laconic acknowledgment of what he learned in Miss Rosa's company at Sutpen's Hundred. We are moving toward a story with a closure dependent on the joining together of Quentin and Shreve in their narrative umbilical. But they are not simply tied together in their story; they are feeding off one another, sharing a story that Sutpen par- tially withholds from General Compson, and in the withholding expresses the very nature of his inability to attain a full humanity and demonstrates why his displacement makes of him the demon Miss Rosa calls out.

Shreve is now so immersed in the Sutpen saga that he says quite emphat- ically: "So that Christmas Henry brought him [Bon] home, into the house, and the demon looked up and saw the face he believed he had paid off and discharged twenty-eight years ago. Go on." The operative words "into the house" powerfully express Sutpen's vulnerability to what he thought he had cast aside, displaced. Bon is the return of the repressed. Sutpen thinks only that he has made a mistake and that General Compson's legal mind will help to locate the error. But Sutpen's "mistake" is his denial of part of himself. He displaces part of his own identity. Sutpen is self-defeated. He vanquishes the outsider, the displaced person, who is a product of Sutpen's own flesh, the homeless human being looking to create a home. And Sutpen turns into his opposite, into the figure he most wanted to jettison, for in turning away his own son he becomes like the slave who turned him away from the plantation front door. He has "become black,"[133] and part of a black diaspora, a dispersal of himself that he is incapable of recognizing.

In using the words "fact" and "factor" Sutpen withholds the mention of race: "The omission that interrupts Sutpen's narrative, then, the effacement of race, allows the narrative to continue."[134] The repressed black double "returns to soil and spoils the point of view of white autonomy and dominance." And this is what bothers Sutpen: he loses control of the story, the design, the dynasty he wants to fashion in his own Sutpen way. The Freudian paradox is that the more he seeks to repress the black spot on his immaculate design, the darker that blemish becomes—at least in his imagination. This is the colossal irony that Toni Morrison points out: "Faulkner in *Absalom, Absalom!* spends the entire book tracing race, and you can't find it. No one can see it, even the character who *is* black can't see it. As a reader you have been forced to hunt for a drop of black blood that means everything and nothing. The insanity of racism."[135]

The ideology of racism becomes Sutpen's psychology when he confesses to General Compson that the design can be completed, but "in such fashion as to be a mockery and a betrayal of that little boy who approached that door fifty years ago and was turned away, for whose vindication the whole plan was conceived." That boy, in Sutpen's mind, is a victim, and he feels victimized by the way his design will be completed. Sutpen will say no more, however, and instead speaks to Henry, precipitating the final confrontation between Charles and Henry that Quentin and Shreve re-create in chapter 8. They have to excavate what Sutpen has tried to bury. But even without their discoveries, Faulkner has already revealed why Sutpen is a failure: "His own total commitment to the design's implementation is thus a perversely 'moral' commitment to an ideology and it may be Faulkner's veiled commentary on the major contending ideologies of the 1930s—Capitalism, Fascism, and, especially, Communism; indeed, it is not difficult to imagine Sutpen, as he is depicted by Rosa especially, as a ruthless dictator."[136] A ruthless fascist dictator, since he cannot rule without his sense of racial superiority intact. But the obsession with Sutpen's ruthlessness obscures the one element lacking in Miss Rosa's and Mr. Compson's accounts. In chapter 8, Shreve goes beyond assimilating what he has heard and radically reorients the story: "'And now,' Shreve said, 'we're going to talk about love.'" Out of the intense bond formed with Quentin during their exploration of the Sutpen saga, Shreve creates a Bon who recognized his own features in Henry's face and sought in Sutpen some sign of recognition that they were family. Shreve has turned the saga into a romance.

In Shreve's narrative, Bon, to his own surprise, exclaims, "apparently I am a good deal younger than I thought." When he sees no recognition in his father's face, Bon is devastated. It is as if his existence has no consequence and his desires cannot evoke even the slightest emotion. This nullification of Bon's humanity is what Bon cannot abide. His only recourse, in Shreve's telling, is to go through the gates of Sutpen's Hundred. He does not turn away from the big house, as Sutpen did, in order to create some kind of alternative world for himself. Bon alone forces the issue, making Henry react, as Shreve compels Quentin to pursue the Sutpen story to its end. The love Shreve speaks of, the narrator suggests, has emanated from the union of these roommates and their "happy marriage of speaking and hearing wherein each before the demand, the requirement, forgave condoned and forgot the faulting of the other—faultings both in the creating of this shade whom they discussed (rather, existed in) and in the hearing and sifting and discarding the false and conserving what seemed true, or fit the preconceived—in order to overpass to love, where there might be paradox and inconsistency but nothing fault nor false." Without this love, this fusion of Henry and Charles and Quentin and Shreve into one couple, there can be no comprehensible outcome of the Sutpen saga. The factor that Sutpen never names is, ultimately, not Bon's black blood but love, which has no place in his design or his vocabulary.

Finally, it is the nature of love that transfixes not only Shreve and Bon but also William Faulkner, writing on the foreign soil of Hollywood and thinking of his fleeting moments with Meta Carpenter, and then writing in the voice of another foreigner, Shreve, imagining the passion of another foreigner, Bon, spending his first spring in northern Mississippi, "a little harder country than Louisiana," and musing on the "vain evanescence of the fleshly encounter; who has not had to realise that when the brief all is done you must retreat from both love and pleasure, gather up your rubbish and refuse—the hats and pants and shoes which you drag through the world—and retreat since the gods condone and practise these and the dreamy immeasurable coupling which floats oblivious above the trammelling and harried instant." The hats and pants and shoes are not only the clothing discarded and then put on again in lovemaking but also the accoutrements of Bon's other life, in New Orleans, and of Faulkner's in Mississippi.

All Bon wants to do in those deeply imagined italicized scenes that Shreve and Quentin create is to *touch flesh* with Sutpen, and Sutpen never reciprocates any more than Miss Rosa does when Clytie touches her on Miss Rosa's way up to Henry's room at Sutpen's Hundred. When Wash Jones finally touches Sutpen, it is, of course, too late for that touch to be anything other than murderous, since Sutpen cannot imagine a world in which he can be touched. The thwarted pattern of love, so reminiscent of Amy Lowell's "Patterns," becomes inescapable in the penultimate chapter of the novel, with those references to Judith and Bon strolling in the garden in *"that slow rhythm where the heart matches the footsteps and the eyes need only look at one another."*

Bon is no longer the passive cosmopolite Mr. Compson depicted. Only love, Shreve insists as he overcomes Quentin's skepticism, can account for Bon's refusal to forsake Judith, a love that yearns for some kind of acknowledgment from Sutpen himself, even if, as Shreve imagines, the acknowledgment will result in Bon's agreement to depart and never return to Sutpen's Hundred. In the climactic scene that Quentin and Shreve create, they interpret the confrontation between Charles and Henry as Bon's final bid for recognition not only as Henry's brother and Sutpen's son but also as "the nigger" who is going to marry Judith. When Henry Sutpen kills Charles Bon rather than permitting him to marry Judith, Bon's belief that the color line cannot be crossed is confirmed. So is Henry's doom since he has, in Quentin's and Shreve's account, acted against his love for both Judith and Charles even as Henry acts in accordance with the dictates of white supremacy.

Trying to understand Quentin's connection to these events, Shreve, for once, drops his bluff pose and exclaims in chapter 9: "Listen. I'm not trying to be funny, smart. I just want to understand it if I can and I dont know how to say it better." Quentin tells Shreve, "you can't understand it. You have to be born there." But in all honesty Quentin has to admit almost immediately that he does not understand it himself, which is to say that Quentin cannot understand himself.

Hovering over *Absalom, Absalom!*, as any reader of *The Sound and the Fury* knows, is Quentin's unspoken death. Shaken by the Sutpen saga, Quentin withdraws into himself, overcome by a hysteria and depression that will culminate in his suicide. When Quentin hears Henry announce his imminent death in the scene between them near the end of the novel, Henry is addressing his "future self. . . . Henry's words put an end to Quentin's future as surely as Henry's shot ended Charles Bon's life and his own future in the South."[137] To intensify the approach of Quentin's own death, Faulkner places the scene with Henry within the "tomblike room in Massachusetts." Faulkner's first impulse had been to begin *Absalom, Absalom!* with Quentin's fate in mind: "This was the summer when Quentin died," as several early fragmentary drafts of the novel reveal.[138] Ultimately, the novelist decided it was more powerful to withhold that vital event just as he delayed revealing so many of the crucial events in the narrative—not only to intensify suspense but to displace our conventional expectations of how a story develops. "This is damned confusing," Hal Smith, Faulkner's editor, wrote on one of the drafts of chapter 1. Faulkner only went partway to clarifying the confusion, adding some punctuation and clarifying pronouns,[139] because he wanted his readers to experience, as Shreve does, the turmoil of Quentin's dislocation, which was also the South's inability to get past its past, which "my people haven't got," Shreve says: "Or if we have got it, it all happened long ago across the water and so now there aint anything to look at every day to remind us of it."

In the unsettled debate about Quentin's discovery of the ghostlike Henry whom Clytie secludes at Sutpen's Hundred, some readers argue that Quentin learns more than is represented on the page, and others contend, as I do, that Quentin is incapable of saying anything more to the wasted man except to confirm his name and his impending death.[140] Henry seems to have exhausted his identity, his reason for being, by killing his brother: "Sutpen and Bon nominated Henry to the task of destroying the taint [of Negro blood], and none of the three could rationalize any other solution to the tragic situation."[141] It is difficult to imagine Henry answering more than the questions Quentin puts to him. The shaking but immobile Quentin tells Shreve he is "fine," but he seems nearly as debilitated as Henry. Quentin is finally aroused by Shreve's prediction that in time the differences between white and black will bleach out and disappear. Isn't this why Shreve asks that final, abrupt, and shocking question, "Why do you hate the South."[142] Isn't Shreve implying that the southern code of race relations will one day seem nugatory and that the notion of white superiority will no longer pertain—even though the Jim Bonds of the world, with the slightest amount of black ancestry—will continue to bedevil white people for whom race matters?[143] The irony is palpable since Jim Bond knows nothing of his ancestry even as he is defined by it. He is the "nigger left standing," because he cannot be shaped by white people as white or black but can only be himself.[144] *Absalom, Absalom!* is right at the summit of Faulkner's achievement as man and artist: "that a white Mississippian raised during the apogee of segregation would see fit in 1936 to substitute Jim Bond (the very name effuses integration) for Jim Crow might stand as an act of Faulknerian heroism dwarfing all the others."[145]

Jim Bond's presence thwarts any resolution of the Sutpen saga that is acceptable to Quentin, who is, in fact, a prisoner of Reconstruction in "a novel of southern masculine defeat and renewal in the three decades immediately following Reconstruction, a period typically referred to as the nadir of black experience."[146] As postwar segregation is codified in medieval-like laws, white and especially male supremacy is instituted. The novel begins with that oft-quoted passage on Quentin as the barracks of back-looking ghosts, his body an "empty hall echoing with defeated names." He is one of T. S. Eliot's hollow men whose freedom is "that of impotence," the novel's narrator asserts. As a "commonwealth," Quentin bears a huge symbolic burden, which he detests, as Shreve divines, but which Quentin cannot even bring himself to admit.

Suddenly, the depleted Quentin at the end of the novel recasts the significance of those early scenes in which Henry shrinks from his father's fighting with slaves and behaves with a defeated squeamishness reminiscent of Quentin's failure to preserve his sister Caddy's honor and to uphold the code of the Old South. He is like Scott's Quentin Durward, born too late to fulfill the medieval idea of knighthood.[147] Shreve tries to shake the shaking Quentin out of his anachronistic posture: "Quentin's failure to embody the hope of national redemption (despite leaving the South) or to produce a vision of sustainable collective futurity is caused by his inability to imagine an interracial national polis in which black men and women are regarded as equals in sociopolitical, juridical, economic, and humanistic terms."[148] Quentin's failure, in other words, is another version of Sutpen's failure. Quentin's humorless rigidity is the opposite of Charles Bon, who writes that letter to Judith using stove polish on stationery liberated from the ruins of a plantation house. Bon adjusts to the "flux of existence . . . relishing whatever small degree of mastery can be attained in the face of daunting odds."[149]

Unlike Quentin in *The Sound and the Fury,* Henry is able to defend his sister's honor. But Judith cares no more for honor or the chivalric code than Caddy does. Judith does not mind her father's grappling in the dirt with his slaves. At the same time, she falls for Bon, the very ideal of the aristocratic gentleman and every inch a man who has no need to exert the rugged energy of the southern masculine code.[150] In effect, Bon refuses a duel with Henry, refuses to kill his brother in arms, while Henry asserts his culture's demand that he act like a man and like his sister's brother. Quentin is paralyzed by Henry's plight as a murderer who has become his own victim, and a victim (Bon) who has become a victor, for Bon asserts a humanity and regard for human feeling that Quentin can imagine but cannot sustain or fulfill.

At the end, Shreve seems to be implying that the South is not really Quentin's problem, and Quentin, in his vehement response that he does not hate the South, affirms as much—or does he?—since he protests too much and cannot, in the end, remove himself from Mississippi mores, no matter how coldly Shreve tries, in the end, to put the Sutpen saga in the perspective of world history.

With *Absalom, Absalom!*, Faulkner was putting himself on a global stage, inviting the kind of international attention that would attend his winning of the Nobel Prize thirteen years later. As much as Faulkner disliked the role of public figure, this novel, more than any other, shows the making of the author as envoy, engaging the world outside of Yoknapatawpha even as he probed more deeply into his native land's races and history.[151]

3

The Dividing Line

October 1936–February 1938

FLANNEL UNMENTIONABLES

"Breathless," "chaotic," "abnormal" are the adjectives applied to *Absalom, Absalom!* by A. B. Bernd, a follower of Faulkner's work, in the *Macon (GA) Telegraph* (October 25), reflecting the tone of reviewers overwhelmed by the novelist's "imagination and power." Words catapulted at the reader with a "driving," "tremendous" force: "You will find yourself absorbed, aroused, profoundly stirred, completely removed from your familiar world into the semi-lunatic asylum which is Mr. Faulkner's Mississippi." It took the reviewer six paragraphs to get to a plot synopsis, concluding: "Essentially this is the familiar tale of the rise and fall of a Southern planter," told, however, with "freshness and new beauty."

Bernd recognized but did not elaborate on the novel's achievement: "Racial and sexual relations dominate the world of his brain; and he penetrates them and exposes them as no other American writer does." What Faulkner exposed seemed beyond the remit or perhaps the ken of contemporary reviewers, many of whom could detect no clear motivation in the novel's characters. A fed up Bernard De Voto (*Saturday Review of Literature,* October 31) dismissed the "familiar hypochondria of Mr. Faulkner's prose. . . . In book after book now he has dropped tears like the famed Arabian tree, in a rapture of sensibility amounting to continuous orgasm." Sentences that went on for more than a page and studded with parentheses marked a "style in process of disintegration." Cameron Shipp in the *Charlotte (NC) News* (November 1) confessed he was "lost and terrified in the shadows and thunders" of Faulkner's "involved prose" and yet called the novel his "master work."

Outrage over a "disgusting" novel erupted in the *Fort Wayne (IN) News* (November 7)—also called "morbid" (*San Diego Union*, November 15), "macabre and sadistic" (*American Spectator*, February–March 1937), a "wearying welter of degeneracy and extravagant sordidness" (*Hartford Courant*, November 15), and full of "gratuitous horror" and "race fears" (*Pseudopodia*, Winter 1937). The *El Paso Herald-Post* (October 30) announced: "he has done his worst." Under the headline "Dusk in White Faces," C. L. Sonnichsen summed up: "The negro is the center of the problem. On the final page of the novel there is a prophecy that 'in a few thousand years' there will no longer be any pure white blood in the Western Hemisphere." Hermann B. Deutsch, the journalist who served as a model for the reporter in *Pylon*, wrote in the *New Orleans Item* (January 24, 1937) that such reactions amounted to "a sort of Faulkner-phobia." These reviewers, Deutsch suggested, were like those who could not bear to refer to long underwear other than as "flannel unmentionables."

No reviewer seems to have considered that *Absalom, Absalom!*, given its title alone, is not simply a "violent tale of the South," as Winfield Townley Scott put it in the *Providence Sunday Journal* (November 22). That the novel had national, let alone international and universal implications never occurred to reviewers, although Deutsch noted: "Absalom, it will be recalled, murdered his brother for the rape of their sister, Tamar, and lost his life in revolt against his father. Just why the one tale should be morbid and the other not, is unclear to this reviewer." Wallace Stegner, born in 1909, a year before Quentin's suicide, and about to publish his first novel in 1937, caught on to Faulkner's epistemological purpose, noting in the *Salt Lake City Tribune* (November 29) that "we arrive at our knowledge—or rather, our surmises—of other people through these approximations, these driblets of information, from six or 600 sources, each driblet colored by the prejudices and emotions of the observer." Readers craved certainty: "Accustomed to having our fictional characters complete, fully rounded, we feel cheated if an author rejects the omniscient lie at the basis of most fiction." As such the novel represented, notwithstanding its faults, "a significant contribution to the theory and art of fiction"—"more searching, more profound and (in the progressive spell of inescapable doom which it lays upon the reader no less surely than upon the hapless characters that people its pages) more dramatic than anything Faulkner had hitherto given us."

Malcolm Cowley (*New Republic*, November 4) helpfully placed *Absalom, Absalom!* in the tradition of the Romantic novel, singling out Sutpen as a

Byronic hero, although at the same time the critic succumbed to a saga-of-the-South line that occluded Faulkner's larger purposes. Perhaps the map Faulkner included, as well as the chronology and genealogy, abetted this idea that he had written a provincial work. Peter Monro Jack in the *New York Sun* (October 30) noted the Yoknapatawpha statistics on the map: "Area, 2400 square miles; population, whites, 6,298; Negroes, 9,313." That Faulkner named himself the "sole owner and proprietor" provoked Jack to comment: "A queer sort of county" that apparently deformed its owner's sensibility, making him think he could make it a "symbol of the world."

It is remarkable that reviewers paid scant attention to Shreve, to his Canadian background, and to the significance of the Harvard dormitory-room setting. Paul Anderson, an exception in the *San Mateo Times and Daily News Leader* (December 5), regretted the "verbose collegian['s]" prediction that "in time the southern negro will have become part of all the races of the Western Hemisphere. Unfortunately the author has chosen an idiot halfbreed to symbolize his meaning. The inference is as irresponsible as it is unavoidable."

That *Absalom, Absalom!* had a continental thrust and, ultimately, a world-historical vision escaped contemporary notice. With so much of literature and film treating the South as a peculiar anomaly in the national experience, Faulkner's aims were almost entirely misconceived. William Troy in the *Nation* (October 31) did, however, point toward the future reception of the novel: "History and geography affect the *form* of the Sutpen saga, but its meaning will be found in a much deeper and broader interpretation of life as a whole. According to this interpretation, everything that has happened could have happened anywhere else in the world. The little drop of Negro blood that runs through Sutpen's destiny becomes no more than the symbolical materialization of that irrational element which exists to thwart the most carefully planned designs of the human will." Troy concluded that the book seemed "not only the best he has yet given us but one of the most formidable of our generation." Other brief flashes of insight appeared in Lewis Gannett's review (*New York Herald Tribune,* October 31): "I suspect that Mr. Faulkner is not really talking about the South at all but about a region of his own and kindred minds; and that if any war oppresses and burdens his imagination it is not the Civil War but the World War." On December 28, Faulkner wrote to Bennett Cerf, thanking him for sending Basil Henry Liddell Hart's *The War in Outline, 1914–1918.*[1]

Several generations of Faulkner scholarship have remedied the tunnel vision of the reviews. One scholar notes that Sutpen's one hundred square miles created out of swampy bottomland measure up precisely to the dimensions of Washington, D.C., also designed by a French architect, with white houses built by slaves that are burned down. Sutpen's failed design, it has been argued, is America's fatal flaw. The Hundred's architecture is never specified, never made southern, which allows for an ironic reading of Faulkner's intention—showing how the South is integral to an understanding of what America has become, not the backwater many of Faulkner's northern contemporaries disparaged in their reviews of his work. Washington, D.C., in its earliest years resembled the mudbound and ramshackle first years of Sutpen's foray into the wilderness. Sutpen's Hundred models Washington's own crude yet arrogant aspirations to greatness. The very name of the nation's capital identifies it with the father of the country, its progenitor, who did, in a manner of speaking, create a dynasty, with several Virginia presidents and the southern domination of government that ultimately came to grief in the Civil War. And so Sutpen's Hundred, in telescoped form, mimics and mocks the nation's destiny, a future that Quentin cannot contemplate because he is so fixated on the southernness of his experience. The South, set aside in Quentin's mind from the rest of the country, is, in fact, inside as well as outside American history, distinctive and yet of a piece with the entire country. Sutpen is a Virginian, after all—*the* Virginian in a horrid way that revolts Miss Rosa, educated, as Faulkner was, in the sacred memory of Robert E. Lee. Coming from what became West Virginia, the part that went to the North, Sutpen is an outsider who becomes an insider, even if he is never quite accepted by his neighbors. His status, though, is in no doubt because of his association with General Compson, who acknowledges in Sutpen an equal. As General Compson's confederate, Sutpen has to uphold what even today is the white pure-blooded notion of what the White House stands for. Yet no reviewer even thought to raise miscegenation and Sutpen's downfall as an *American* phenomenon directly applicable *then*. Instead, Faulkner's novel, begun during the U.S. occupation of Haiti (1915–34), was admired or deplored as a species of Southern Gothic, with virtually no understanding that Sutpen's triumph and his tragedy result from the recognition of one race and the repudiation of another in the service of imperial nation building on land originally occupied by other nations.[2]

SLAVERY AND WAR THE HOLLYWOOD WAY

Negative reviews did nothing to damage Faulkner's reputation, especially since influential reviewers considered *Absalom, Absalom!* Faulkner's greatest work so far. And he was already considering a new book, *The Unvanquished*, a collection of six stories about "a white boy and a negro boy during the civil war,"[3] he told his new publisher, Bennett Cerf, who had bought out Hal

Smith and Robert Haas and had been delighted to publish *Absalom, Absalom!* Faulkner did not use the customary phrase, "the war between the states." Did it matter that he was writing to a northern publisher? At any rate, he would revise the adventure stories, his "third-rate Kipling," written for the *Saturday Evening Post* and *Scribner's*.

Work on *The Unvanquished* straddled the fall of 1936 and the first part of 1937, when his Fox contract raised his salary from $750 to $1,000 per week. Faulkner finished "An Odor of Verbena," in the last chapter of which Colonel John Sartoris comes to terms with his violent, dictatorial nature, telling his son he will go unarmed to confront his adversary. Sartoris refuses to kill again and is determined to do a little "moral housecleaning." At nearly the same time,[4] Faulkner dealt directly, for the first time, with the slave trade in *The Last Slaver,* a novel adapted for the screen and released as *Slave Ship* in June 1937. Captain Lovett, played by Warner Baxter in much the same mood as his Captain La Roche in *The Road to Glory,* is seemingly inured to evil and yet capable of recovering his humanity for the love of a young woman who cares for him. For his beloved Nancy (Elizabeth Allan), Lovett renounces slave trading, confessing: "I went into it when I was a boy. All it meant to me then was excitement. Boys have no sense. Then it was just my life—life farming in somebody else's life. I never thought any more of it than that—and then I was older, before I knew it, and I met you. That told me what I—what I was, and what I was doing." Lovett could almost be recounting the youthful experiences of Bayard Sartoris in *The Unvanquished,* reflecting on his own part in the iniquity of the war and resolving, like John Sartoris, to renounce what has been, in Lovett's words, "dirty" and "filthy."[5]

The released film does not include Lovett's speech, unfortunately, and it transforms the moral complexity of Faulkner's script in a more anodyne drama. Whereas in Faulkner's version Lovett goes down with his burning, sinking ship in a conflagration reminiscent of Sutpen's burning mansion, in the film Lovett successfully quells the mutiny of his slave-running crew, frees the slaves from the hold of his ship, and lives happily ever after with his Nancy on a Jamaica plantation. No Hollywood hero could be as complicit in evil as Colonel Sartoris or Sutpen and yet remain a figure to admire. In *The Unvanquished,* Faulkner works against the very Hollywood myths he had been hired to perpetuate. Just who is working that Jamaican land is a question the film never asks or answers.[6] Even so, some of Faulkner's work remained, including his description of the slave hold: "dark, cramped, lighted by torches" with slaves "packed like spoons in tiers."[7]

Another script, "Splinter Fleet," worked on in collaboration with a Fox screenwriter, Kathryn Scola, eventually made it to the screen as *Submarine*

Patrol (1938), stripping out precisely those aspects of Faulkner's work that would have made it a much more formidable film. Scola worked on the story line and Faulkner on the dialogue.[8] The title referred to the World War I submarine chasers, made out of wood, assigned the nearly impossible task of sinking U-boats. The film's hero is a Harvard-educated playboy, Perry Townsend III, whom no one takes seriously but who shows his mettle as an engineer, running the ship's engines while under attack and helping to sink a U-boat. Faulkner maximizes the tensions between Perry and the working-class crew and complicates the story with a rivalry and a fight between Perry and Fender, whose girl, Susan, falls in love with Perry when he accidentally encounters her before reporting for duty. Perry rejects the offer of a safe desk job in the military, declaring: "This war is the biggest thing that will happen in our lifetime. If I dodged it, I'd never forget it. . . . Not what people would say about me after it was over and you and I had settled down—but what I would think about *myself*—the excuses I'd have to give myself that I couldn't believe." The words come right out of William Faulkner's own biography, his characterization of Julian Lowe in *Soldiers' Pay*, and what Faulkner would say to his nephew Jimmy about doing his part in World War II. The speech is also the most effective way to demonstrate why it is imperative for Perry to show the sub-chaser crew that he is one of them, notwithstanding his wealth and privilege.

Faulkner's script presaged a series of films he would write in the 1940s—all aimed to unite the American people in a war meant to overcome class and racial differences. Class is a constant feature of conflict in the script, and it is exactly what Darryl Zanuck ordered five writers to root out. Instead, Perry is transformed into a bland if well-meaning hero whose main worry is not German and Austrian U-boats but overcoming the opposition of Susan's father, captain of a merchant ship. Captain Leeds rejects Perry because he represents the crass materialism of the upper class that uses up women like his daughter for their sybaritic pleasures. All that stands in Perry's way is this father—not the crew who soon take to him and treat him, unrealistically, as just one of them. Absent from the film is Faulkner's Perry, who looks at the crew "staring at him with hostile eyes—conscious that he is not one of them."[9] Faulkner shows him uneasy in a bar, "his obvious air of breeding, a little incongruous in this lusty atmosphere."[10] Susan, at first reluctant to accept Perry's attentions, refers to his Park Avenue upbringing and says, "I belong to the—common people." References to finger bowls and having tea add to the jibes at Perry's genteel heritage. Especially revealing is Fender's jibe that Perry is a Park Avenue "gentleman." Such comments reflect Faulkner's increasing understanding that modern warfare had no place for aristocrats and the gentleman's code.

In effect, Perry proves himself by becoming a grease monkey, making sure the engines of the ship run. He becomes Faulkner's version of the upper-class man as Eugene O'Neill's hairy ape, on whose power a whole ship moves. Perry, in Faulkner's script, proves himself by getting his hands dirty, as Faulkner did working with mechanics at the airport and in his brief stint on a locomotive. Such gritty details are entirely absent from *Submarine Patrol,* as is a scene with a prostitute that the Production Code would have prohibited and that could have been taken from one of O'Neill's nautical dramas.

BREAKUP

Faulkner continued to live in Hollywood with Estelle, accustoming himself to Meta's realization that he would not marry her. In a canceled passage from *A Loving Gentleman,* Meta reflects with some bitterness on Estelle, "scarred by the realization that she was one of those dowries whom successful men marry in their youth, long before they have any real intimation of the renown into which they will come . . . attempting to pull herself upward to his level."[11] In the published book Meta explains that she turned to Wolfgang Rebner, who spoke to her love of great music in a way that Faulkner could not, and accepted Rebner's marriage proposal in September 1936. Faulkner seemed resigned to losing her, but not without one last effort to dissuade her:

> "I should have known it was coming," he said after a stunned moment, "but I just wouldn't let myself admit that it could happen."
> "Wish me happiness."
> "I do. I want you to always be happy. You know that."
> "No question."
> "You don't feel that you can wait it out with me?" His eyes seemed to slowly darken, the whites shading into a sick gray.
> "Before I know it, I'll be thirty."
> "Give us a little more time, dear love."
> "For what?"
> "I don't know. The great unforseeable. A lightnin' bolt out of the sky."
> "You don't really believe that, Faulkner."
> "No, ma'am. I can't say as I do in our case."

The spare dialogue would work well in a movie, with just enough physical business for the actors to elaborate: "He looked down at my fingers cross-hatched on his own, limp and unmoving." What saves the scene from just being a scene is her full acknowledgment of all the complicating factors: Faulkner's concession to and then his rebuttal of Meta's feelings. "You can't live in Hollywood," she told him. "No more than I can live in Oxford." He agreed but persisted, saying it was not enough that Wolfgang, then a thousand miles away on an American tour, was a "fine person" who wrote passionate letters. She did not know him well enough. She brought up Jill, but he put his hand on her mouth to silence her. Then he relented, only to call her later proposing a meeting at her place. She said no: "I am not going to sleep with you anymore." She had to endure his beseeching look and his plea for "one last time," saying her attachment to Rebner reflected the "flush of pure romantic fantasy." She was, after all her lapses, still a properly brought-up southern woman, the product of a "long matriarchal chain." He seemed to accept her decision, but after a week he exploded, declaring he was not a monk.

Meta admitted it had been tempting to forsake her principles, which is why she called on her Aunt Ione to stay with her until she married Rebner. Sitting down to dinner with Meta and her duenna, Faulkner finally accepted his defeat in a scene he could well have written, with Aunt Jenny instead of Aunt Ione. Two days before her wedding, however, he showed up at midnight, bloody-faced, outside her apartment. "Estelle's signature," Meta said. He only shrugged, asked for a drink, but then said his wife had attacked him while they were driving, because he said Meta's wedding made no difference. He still wanted her. He had lost his temper when Estelle had thrown a twenty-five-dollar compact out of the window. "I think she wanted to kill me, if not herself," he concluded.

Meta married Wolfgang Rebner on April 5, 1937, and they departed for Europe. A letter to Meta from Henriette Martin, a friend of hers and Faulkner's, reported he had gone on a "nonstop drinking binge," resulting in an emergency visit to a Los Angeles hospital and a six-week convalescence. In May, Estelle and Jill departed for Mississippi. Cho-Cho had just married and had become pregnant, and Estelle wanted to be near her daughter. Estelle left behind a wasted-looking Faulkner, who remained in the rented Santa Monica house, attended by Narcissus McEwen, Jill's nurse, who also cooked for him. At the end of June, he wrote to Estelle: "I've had such nice letters from Rowanoak that I have stopped worrying and now I can concentrate on just missing everybody. I am still in the house. Thought I might just as well stay . . . Have given two dinners . . . one last week for Coindreau . . . I want to hear about birthday party. Much love."[12]

He worked on the script for *Drums along the Mohawk*, and on *The Unvanquished*.[13] To an agreeable Will Bryant, he wrote to say he was now prepared to buy the rest of the property (four lots) surrounding Rowan Oak.[14] When he thought of home, he thought of "Negroes" and became "animated and euphoric," telling Henriette Martin about the ones at Rowan Oak and saying they had "courtesy of the heart."[15]

A Voodoo Version of *Absalom, Absalom!*

It seems that sometime in the summer of 1937, William Faulkner met Dudley Murphy, then part of an independent production company, Associated Artists, organized as a profit-sharing scheme that provided an alternative to the hegemony of the studio system. The project never succeeded, but it lasted long enough for Faulkner to become involved, producing "Revolt in the Earth," an adaptation of *Absalom, Absalom!*

Murphy's approach to film, making the artist into a central figure, is beautifully realized in his haunting silent *Soul of the Cypress* (1921), set on the California coast on a cypress-covered cliff. A beautiful dryad is held captive, the title card explains, in the "gnarled and twisted branches of the oldest tree." A musician is shown in silhouette piping his composition, like one of those faun-like figures in an early Faulkner drawing. His music is so enchanting that it melts the heart of the tree, liberating the dryad, who looks like the epicene dancing figures that Faulkner liked to depict. Drawn nearer to the music, she dances, swirling in ecstasy in her diaphanous dress and cape as if she might take flight. As she approaches the musician, seated high atop a boulder, the title card announces: "Unfortunate is he, the legend tells, who falls in love with a Dryad—and more unfortunate he who tries to capture her." As he pursues her, she dances away, as Estelle danced away from Faulkner, as the figures on Keats's Grecian urn pursue but never possess one another. The spirit the artist has summoned eludes him, a figure of the imagination he cannot catch. She longs to feel a human touch but also dreads what she has never experienced. She escapes into the ancient cypress, telling the musician he can be with her forever, an immortal, if he throws himself in the sea. The artist is torn between his overpowering love for the dryad and his "desire for life." In despair he climbs to the cliff top and sways over it and plunges into the sea, his spirit becoming the song of the sea and uniting with the Soul of the Cypress.[16]

How Faulkner met Murphy and what Faulkner knew about Murphy's work not even his biographer seems to know.[17] Was Faulkner familiar with *Soul of the Cypress,* a nine-minute parable of the power of art and its demands on the artist? The film expresses a sensibility keenly attuned to Faulkner's own aesthetic, and one that Faulkner had seen reflected in *He Who Gets Slapped.* Perhaps because of the abortive work on *Slave Ship* and the lack of studio interest in *Absalom, Absalom!,* Faulkner turned to a collaboration with

Murphy, who had worked with European modernists like Ezra Pound and Fernand Léger. Murphy had also collaborated with Paul Robeson on the film *The Emperor Jones* (1933), a work Faulkner greatly admired and emulated. Who looked at "Revolt in the Earth," other than producer Robert Buckner at Warner Brothers in 1943, is not known. Buckner thought very little of the work and even wrote to Faulkner, "I hope you had nothing to do with it." Buckner advised against sending it around.[18]

The film opens on a marble statue of Sutpen striking a grandiloquent pose not so different from the old Colonel's in the Ripley cemetery. Clytie, aged twelve, is shown gazing raptly at the statue, calling to mind, at least in a biographer's mind, those black Falkners in the graveyard the white family did not acknowledge. The film periodically returns to her at the statue as the cynosure of the story. The sound of galloping horses dissolves into a shot of a black family's cabin. It is the scene of Clytie's birth, where a swaggering Sutpen scoffs at the "nigger voodoo" of an old black woman who calls the child a devil's spawn, presaging a "revolt in the earth till Sutpen land has swallowed Sutpen's birth." The prophecy of Bon's death and Henry's disappearance—"one will die and one will ride away"—is only understandable, at this point, to readers of *Absalom, Absalom!* Nowhere is it explicitly said that Clytie is Sutpen's child, or that Bon is Sutpen's son and Henry's brother. Faulkner had to know that in all likelihood the Production Code would not have permitted a film about miscegenation, and yet the script shows white people drawn to black people and to their doom, signified in the voodoo rites that subvert Sutpen's supremacy. Both Henry's and Judith's treatment of Clytie implies kinship, as does her attendance at Sutpen's statue long after he is dead and slavery has ended so that she owes no fealty to her master. Clytie and other black women are given a voice that is absent from the novel.[19]

Sutpen's racism is blatant. He says a newborn calf is "worth a dozen of you niggers." Another set of scenes show Sutpen rejecting his white daughter as well, born from his mating with Wash's granddaughter, but Wash only threatens Sutpen, who walks away in disgust. He is now shown in conference with Henry as they watch Charles Bon in the garden courting Judith—without permission, Sutpen notes. Henry assures his father that Bon is a gentleman and will do the right thing, but Sutpen counters, "How well do you know him?" Sutpen tells his son he has been duped into admiring those urbane qualities in Bon that Henry lacks. Judith is called and told that Bon is a blackguard. She is defiant and seems to know more than either Sutpen or Henry do about Bon's intentions.

In the background during these early scenes the sound of "nigger laughter" is heard, and then, as Bon enters Sutpen's library, the sound of tom-toms erupts, as in *The Emperor Jones,* along with an ambient laughter and drumming that grows ominously louder. But Sutpen is apparently satisfied with Bon's representations, and Henry and Charles depart for New Orleans aboard a steamboat to the accompaniment of more sensuous "negroid" music. A dissolve returns the scene to Clytie beside Judith as the half sisters watch preparations for Judith's trousseau. The black women laugh and make snide references to the old black woman's prediction about the devil's spawn. In New Orleans Henry and Charles attend a quadroon ball that is also engulfed in "negroid" music while women parade in masks that make it impossible to know if they are black or white. Henry is shocked at Bon's duel with the man who has escorted the beautiful octoroon Bon unmasks at the ball. She is Bon's wife, and her escort is shot dead. When Henry is made to understand what has happened, the sound of the tom-toms recommences. An outraged Henry is introduced to Bon's son by the octoroon as the background laughter rises and Henry rushes home to prevent Judith's marriage to Bon, although he refuses to give his reasons but instead looks directly at Clytie. Sutpen declares the marriage will go on, and Henry departs to murder Bon, returning to announce that now Judith cannot marry him. On Bon's body Judith finds the locket that she presumes holds her daguerreotype but that contains, in fact, one of Toinette, the octoroon wife.

Sutpen has banished Henry, but the two meet again as Henry is dying on a Civil War battlefield with shells sounding like the savage beat of tom-toms as the film segues to a voodoo ceremony in a jungle on the periphery of the Sutpen house, where the black women talk about how the prophecy has come true as Judith paces in the house to the beat of the drums and then is shown after a dissolve on a battlefield with her dead father. She is taken away by a northern soldier and in a subsequent scene is shown in a delivery room in a northern hospital, where she has given birth even as her head turns from side to side to the beat of drums only she can hear. Clytie, too, has survived the war, found a mate, and produced a child.

What takes a whole novel to relate becomes the first act of the movie, which now flashes forward to a seventy-year-old Clytie staring at the statue, which is overwhelmed by jungle growth. The film cuts to a bayou where Charles and Henry had once traveled on a houseboat, which is now a wreck that Wash's son, also named Wash, occupies. In the next scene, set in 1910, the Sutpen house is now a ruin inhabited by Clytie, who gazes at a photograph of Judith and a baby, her granddaughter, Miriam. This memento, inscribed to Clytie, comes from another world, where Judith inhabits an English garden like a "grand lady" and is present at the wedding of Miriam to an English clergyman, Eric. Judith is grateful that she has escaped the Sutpen curse, which her progeny will never know, although a dissolve to Clytie activates the drums as the telegram from Judith announcing Miriam's marriage is read to her black aunt as yet another dissolve segues to black people singing spirituals at Miriam's wedding. The music excites Miriam as Judith assumes the same pose as Clytie hearing about Miriam's marriage. So disturbed is Judith that she grabs Miriam and takes her home.

At the wedding Eric has heard about a white voodoo doctor in a New Orleans bayou, who is seen in a cut to be a Kurtz-like figure who has gone native in a jungle drum scene, which, in turn, cuts back to a theater box where Eric and Miriam are entranced by a play about "a white man making himself a black king in a white country." A fascinated Eric proposes they visit Judith's ancestral home, exactly what Judith has feared. Miriam exclaims: "No, no! It would kill Grandmama for me to go back. She won't even let me talk to her about it." Yet Miriam sways and pants in a movement that is "completely negroid." She is taken by the art on the stage exactly as Murphy's dryad was driven to the music by the sea. An aghast Eric is embarrassed as Miriam's "face is animal." As she writhes against him and the tom-toms beat, he capitulates to her plea that they go to the bayou. "Now! Tonight!"

The second act reveals a white witch doctor (Wash's grandson) in a voodoo ceremony wearing cow horns and a Prince Albert coat. He cuts a woman's throat, and several scenes follow of Judith aboard ship evidently in pursuit of Miriam as she rides through a swampland frightened by snakes but urged on by Eric, who does not seem to hear the tom-toms. Then Clytie and Miriam finally meet at the Sutpen house, recognizing one another instantly. Now everyone hears the drums from the voodoo ceremony. Miriam listens and is "restive." Eric spots the voodoo witch doctor, now in overalls, as Miriam grows frightened and demands that they leave. But Eric is thrilled to see and hear the real thing, so much better than the stage show at the Albert Hall. The besotted Eric is willing to pay for a voodoo service just as Wash shows up and Miriam, nearly hysterical, wants to leave. Clytie, refusing to indulge Eric's desire for a voodoo service, tells him, "You go home." But Eric persists as Miriam shuts herself in the house. The second act ends as he plans his excursion, even though Miriam pleads with him not to leave her.

The third act opens with Eric, now a "tropic-exploring Briton" aboard a boat on the way to witness a baptism. Miriam tries to follow in the jungle and almost falls into quicksand, saved from death by Wash, who nonetheless frightens her because of his sinister "faun-like" expression. "You belong to this land," he tells her. Miriam runs back to the Sutpen house but in a frenzy dashes into the garden where an "inhuman" Wash lurks. Cut to Miriam in Wash's cabin, a prisoner saying to herself she must be "mad." And then she enjoins Wash: "I must go back. Let me out!" But to the increasing sound of the drums she sways next to Wash, who dances with abandon.

Clytie has sent a message to Eric requesting his return to the Sutpen house. She tells a baffled Eric he must take Miriam away with him. Against a chorus of rising and falling laughter, an outraged Eric declares he will discover what Clytie is hiding. Like Judith, Miriam is now tormented by the drums Eric cannot hear. She begs him to take her away before nightfall. He won't leave because he is determined to write a book about what he has seen. Out in the jungle, awaiting the start of another ceremony, Eric is accosted by Clytie, who tells him he must take Miriam away by daybreak: "Ain't you know dis place done run her whole family out?" Miriam, evidently released from Wash's cabin and unable to sleep, is shown again at the Sutpen house, calling for Eric, who is out in the jungle, crop in hand like a European explorer surrounded by Africans he is "trying to intimidate by his sheer lack of skin pigment." He rushes at them, but they simply vanish into the jungle. Clytie confronts Wash in the garden, raising a rib from a pig she has slaughtered, which terrifies him, and he strikes her down. As Miriam paces madly in her room, Eric is lost in the jungle. Cut to Wash picking up Clytie's rib and plunging into the jungle, followed by Miriam, whose voice Eric hears crying out to him as she sinks into quicksand. Dissolve to Wash beside the houseboat wreck wearing the white witch doctor's headdress as the scene dissolves into daylight with Clytie once again brooding before Sutpen's statue. The laughing, chanting blacks are heard repeating the Sutpen curse. To them it sounds like a joke. "It do sound funny," one of them says. "Whut you reckon it mean?" Another says: "I don't know dat. I do well to 'member how to say it." Amid laughter one says, "Ain't dat a fack." Then a snake "writhes down from the statue and away into the jungle."

This horror-movie version might well disappoint readers of the novel,[20] and anger some with all the references to "nigger laughter," but not so for Faulkner, who saw adaptations of his fiction as entirely autonomous work in which he and others could change the nature of his characters and rewrite plots and themes, as he did with the Sartoris twins in "War Birds." Clytie, who seems to have a knowledge never revealed in *Absalom, Absalom!*, remains in "Revolt in the Earth" an enigmatic, inscrutable figure, the unknowable Sutpen, the survivor, the Clytemnestra whose role in the murder of Agamemnon (Sutpen) is occluded, as it is in different versions of her actions in Greek mythology and drama. She stands in "Revolt in the Earth" as a kind of medium, attuned to the forces that undo the white people, who are surrounded by black people they do not comprehend, notwithstanding white claims to superiority. The relentless laughter and drumming serve as an abiding mockery of white mastery. And though the script does little to develop the white witch doctor, it is apparent that Wash, who refers to himself as a poor white, has more in common with the blacks—or fears he has more in common with them—than he allows himself to admit except when he dons the witch doctor mask. For all its melodramatics, "Revolt in the Earth" powerfully presents the black rebuke to white power in a work that is akin to Sherwood Anderson's *Dark Laughter,* also set in New Orleans. Black sensuality, as depicted in that novel, and in Faulkner's script, may seem offensive—equating black people with animality—but African Americans also represent a life force, a closeness to nature from which Sutpen is separated and which he tries to defy by treating both his slaves and Wash's granddaughter (he calls her a heifer) as merely animals. Their animality is human, and white people are in the sway of it as much as black people, but the white people seek to deny that truth by mastering black people. Even Judith, who tries to escape the family's fate, cannot resist writing to Clytie and sending photographs of Miriam, acknowledging their bond even as she tries to attenuate it by staying away.

The juxtaposition of jungle and garden scenes, the cultivated and the elemental aspects of existence, overcome some of the limitations of the horror-movie format, as do the scenes in England, on the stage, and other scenes in New Orleans at the octoroon ball, where Henry cannot function in a civilization built on the masking that the old Colonel exploited in *The White Rose of Memphis.* In "Revolt in the Earth," Charles Bon dies not because of his black blood—at least not so as the censors would notice—but because of his easy commerce with color that so offends Henry's notion of a gentleman. Bon's unmasking of himself—showing to Henry that the courtesies and manners and ceremonies (including marriage) are so many masks that are the accoutrements of a gentleman—leads to his murder. And Miriam, never told about her family history, is bound to sink in the quicksand of its dodgy identity. In short, the Sutpen saga is a voodoo horror show, a curse of the Sutpen arrogance and inhumanity. Sutpen's statue is not crumbling like Shelley's Ozymandias, but the jungle (nature) reclaims it. The earth has revolted against those who have sought to dominate it.[21] In the voices and laughter of the black people chanting about the earth swallowing up the Sutpens, the history of their white rule "remains only in the talkings of the black descendants."[22]

That Hollywood in the late 1930s and early 1940s would film anything resembling "Revolt in the Earth" seems inconceivable. How it seemed to Faulkner is impossible to say. Even so, that he went ahead anyway and produced, along with Dudley Murphy, a Eugene O'Neill–inspired script, is testimony to his desire to do more than just pick up his check.[23]

In Mississippi in the fall of 1937, Faulkner believed he was done with Hollywood. "I don't like scenario writing," he told an interviewer: "I don't know enough about it. I feel as though I can't do myself justice in that type of work, and I don't contemplate any more of it in the near future."[24] He had made $21,650 for the year. During the winter of 1937–38, he purchased Bailey's Woods, adjoining Rowan Oak, and a 320-acre farm seventeen miles away. "I am home again," Faulkner wrote to Will Bryant on September 2, "returning to my house and oaks and cedars with the same pleasure, the same lift of the heart which, God willing, the sight of it will always give me and which I shall very likely take into the earth with me when my time comes."[25] And yet he kept finding reasons to leave home.

In September, he had begun to work on a new partitioned novel, *The Wild Palms,* and by the middle of the month he was in New York, where he met Meta's new husband and inscribed for her copy number 1 of *Absalom, Absalom!* A month later, he met his new sympathetic editor, Saxe Commins, who took care of him in New York City as he suffered through one of his worst alcoholic bouts, passing out and burning himself badly on a radiator in his hotel room. Meta's husband, Wolfgang Rebner, remembered seeing Faulkner in his hotel room still drinking and repeating, "It was ludicrous."[26]

Yet Faulkner's writing went well, but a little more slowly, he said, for a forty-year-old.[27] By November, back home, he wrote Robert Haas at Random House that he had "got myself mentally together."[28] He spoke as a man and novelist who had tried to be in several places at once and found it torturing, as his painful back kept reminding him. He would need to have some skin grafting done, he told Eric Devine, his old New York friend.

Faulkner never seems to have regretted the dire consequences of his drinking—in company, at least, treating it lightly. After one of his benders he would say to Donald Klopfer, Bennett Cerf's business partner, "Well, Donald, I've been a bad boy."[29] Phyllis Cerf told the story of meeting Faulkner at a party and pointing out his dirty trench coat and a hole in his socks. "I know," was all he said. He charmed everyone, including Mrs. Vincent Astor, Mrs. William Paley, and journalist Quentin Reynolds and his wife, Virginia. Enchanted with the company, he had a wonderful time. Writer Robert Sherwood's wife, Madeleine, admired Faulkner's perfectly shaped head, and he offered to give it to her when he died. She said she did not believe it. So he wrote it out, "I, William Faulkner, hereby bequeath my head when I am dead to Madeleine Sherwood." Bill always giggled about it, Cerf recalled. Then he got drunk and did not show up the next day. Bennett said: "Bill it's so horrible. You've had ten days in New York and you've spent the entire time, because of getting drunk, in a hospital"—to which, Faulkner rejoined: "Bennett, it was mah vacation and I can spend it anyway I want to and I had a good time." He said good-bye to the Cerfs and went home.[30]

Revising *The Unvanquished* in Hollywood, Oxford, and New York placed Faulkner right on the dividing line of his commercial and literary careers, which were constantly crossing over one another, as he made entertaining *Saturday Evening Post* short stories into serious fiction.[31] The first sentence of "Ambuscade" (summer 1862), the first chapter of *The Unvanquished,* introduces a vivid, immediate retrospective: "Behind the smokehouse that summer, Ringo and I had a living map." The narrator is Bayard Sartoris, the old Bayard of *Flags in the Dust,* reminiscing about his youth, when along with his black companion he fashions a ground map of the Vicksburg siege. Compared to *Absalom, Absalom!, The Unvanquished* may seem a minor work, an adventure story along the lines of a Hollywood product—like *Slave Ship*—with a very selective treatment of the peculiar institution and characters you can root for and others you can despise. But like *Absalom, Absalom!, The Unvanquished* explores a broken-up past that is fitfully recalled. Its chapters are episodic, historic moments rather than a continuous, integral narrative of a historical period as in traditional historical novels such as *The History of Henry Esmond* or in films like *Slave Ship* and *Drums along the Mohawk.* Unlike Thackeray, Faulkner does not attempt the portrait of an age. Historical figures rarely make an appearance in his fiction, as Generals Marlborough and Webb do in *Esmond.* And Faulkner makes no sustained effort to disguise his narrative as a memoir or to employ archaisms—a favorite ploy of Scott, Thackeray, and many other historical novelists. As in *Absalom, Absalom!,* Faulkner essays an approach to the past knowing full well that the whole of it cannot be recaptured.

Whereas the boys assiduously water their evaporating miniature trench to mimic the terrain of battle, the older Bayard as narrator muses on the tyranny of time that the boys and all mankind battle. The earth will absorb life faster than the boys can live it. Loosh, Ringo's uncle, sweeps away the chips the boys have employed like toy soldiers and announces: "There's your Vicksburg." He "kind of surged up out of the darkness right beside us," Bayard recalls in a phrase that suggests Loosh is the black reality, the slave owners' defeat, which is about to change their lives. Loosh is drunk and perhaps celebrating the Union victory, presaging freedom for Loosh and his fellow slaves, although Bayard does not say as much or acknowledge that he is exploding the fanciful myth of loyal darkies, the staple of post–Civil War sentimental fiction and movies. A character like Loosh is inconceivable in *Slave Ship,* where the slaves are simply shown as whipped victims of white slavers, or even in the nostalgic reminiscences of the war in *Flags in the Dust,* in which slavery is merely a backdrop to the main action of the white characters. *The Unvanquished,* hardly begun, is bowled over by a black man. The boys are baffled. How could a slave know more than Bayard's father, Colonel Sartoris? Loosh is presented with very little darkie dialect. He may be a slave, but he has articulated his independence and sense of equality even if he does still refer to "Marse John." If Bayard reaffirms his father's authority to Ringo, he nevertheless confides to himself: "niggers know, they know things." In *Absalom, Absalom!,* General Compson pieces together important parts of the Sutpen story by talking to his slaves. This novel matured in the mind of the young boy who listened to Callie Barr and other black people and understood they were intelligence agents, no matter how bound they were to white masters.

Bayard and Ringo are black and white brothers in all but blood and alternate at impersonating Union and Confederate generals in their war games. As children they can enjoy what Henry Sutpen and Charles Bon could not share as soon as an awareness of race separates them: "Ringo and I had been born in the same month and had both fed at the same breast and had slept together and eaten together for so long that Ringo called Granny 'Granny' just like I did, until maybe he wasn't a nigger anymore or maybe I wasn't a white boy anymore, the two of us neither, not even people any longer: the two supreme undefeated like two moths, two feathers riding above a hurricane."

When Colonel Sartoris, Bayard's father, returns home, his son announces that Loosh has news, a startling development to the father whose son regards him with awe. But the Yankees have the Colonel on the run, like the game little Confederate in Faulkner's schoolroom cartoon. *The Unvanquished* retains some of that youthful identification with the Lost Cause, but the Yankee officer who enters the Sartoris home after the boys shoot at one of his soldiers is a gentleman who treats Bayard's Granny with respect and chooses to ignore the boys, who hide under her skirts. A few years later, Dana Andrews would play just such a courtly Union soldier in *Belle Star* (1941), reflecting what Faulkner had already shown: a tremendous need for Americans to honor heroes on both sides of the war.

Colonel Sartoris realizes he is fighting a lost cause and that his slaves will soon be released from their fealty to him: "Father said that Louvinia would have to watch him [Loosh] too, that even if he was her son, she would have to be white a little while longer. Because if we watched him, we could tell by what he did when it was getting ready to happen." Ringo wants to know what "it" is. He does not understand that Colonel Sartoris anticipates that Union troops are coming to occupy his land and that Loosh will know about their arrival sooner than anyone else. In Colonel Sartoris's absence, Loosh proclaims: "Ginral Sherman gonter sweep the earth and the Race gonter all be free!" Biographies of Sherman say as much: Slaves deserted masters and supplied Union troops with what they knew about the movements of Confederate troops.[32]

Colonel Sartoris is gallant, courageous, fatally flawed, doomed, and he knows it. He has to reckon with a world he has made and is now being unmade. Like Sutpen, Sartoris is not destined for a happy ending. He knows it better than Granny, who tries to preserve the world she has known by recovering property appropriated by Union soldiers while taking advantage of Union army incompetence. She forges documents that enable her to acquire more mules to sell back to criminal black marketeers who eventually murder her. The incorruptible Granny who washes the boys' mouths out with soap for various infractions is caught in the chicanery of war, having started out to do nothing more than to protect and preserve her family. She is aided by the family's slaves, especially Ringo, who completely identifies with the southern cause, thinking of Yankees only as invaders intent on destroying his homeland.

The first draft of "Retreat" (summer 1863), the second chapter of *The Unvanquished,* began in much simpler form, focused exclusively on action, on what could be shown on a movie screen:

> Joby set the lantern down and he and Loosh dug up the trunk where we buried it last summer. Granny carried the lantern and it took Ringo and me both to help carry the trunk back to the house but I dont believe it weighed a thousand pounds. Joby began to bear away toward the wagon.
> "Take it into the house," Granny said.[33]

This *Saturday Evening Post* version is replaced with the novel's evocation of a remembered scene, filtered more problematically through Bayard's consciousness, through the struggle to reclaim the past and to reflect how phantasmagorical the scene seemed to a boy trying to assimilate a conflicted family's effort to sustain itself in war:

> Then they stopped—Joby and Granny, and while Granny held the lantern at arm's length, Joby and Loosh dug the trunk up from where they had buried it that night last summer while Father was at home, while Louvinia stood in the door of the bedroom without even lighting the lamp while Ringo and I went to bed and later I either looked out or dreamed I looked out the window and saw (or dreamed I saw) the lantern. Then, with Granny in front and still carrying the lantern and with Ringo and me both helping to carry it, we returned toward the house.

Before we reached the house Joby began to bear away toward where the loaded wagon stood.

The "we" in the first passage becomes "they" in the second, for the story of *The Unvanquished* becomes Bayard's studied witness to a past he participated in but did not fully understand and that he will have to rectify in the novel's last chapter, "An Odor of Verbena."

With every previously published story that became a chapter, Faulkner added similar complexities, exploring Bayard's shock as his world disintegrates. The first draft, "And then Ringo and I looked at one another because we heard the key turn in Granny's lock."[34] becomes "Then Granny shut the door behind us and then Ringo and I stopped dead in the hall and looked at one another. Since I could remember, there had never been a key to any door, inside or outside, about the house. Yet we had heard a key turn in the lock." Bayard struggles with memory—"since I could remember"—and is as confused as his black companion. What kind of world of locks and keys does he now live in? The powerful disruptions of the war are rendered in the most homely details, not in dramatic battles, which play no part in the novel except as hearsay. That is why Loosh's knowing comments are so disturbing. How can a slave be in control of the information that Bayard and Ringo have to absorb? The two boys are constantly playing catch-up to discover what Loosh already knows. House slaves like the loyal Louvinia are there, just as they are in *Gone with the Wind*. She still wears the master's cast-off hat, but the life that Bayard and Ringo have counted on is in retreat. Loosh senses the momentous changes about to occur. When he declares his freedom and refusal to help safeguard the family silver, Granny tells him that it belongs to John Sartoris and asks, "Who are you to give it away?" Loosh replies: "You ax me that? Where John Sartoris? Whyn't he come and ax me that? Let God ax John Sartoris who the man name that give me to him. Let the man that buried me in the black dark ax that of the man what dug me free." The novel never mentions the slave trade, but the "black dark" is redolent of the dark, crammed human cargo holds of slave ships. In *Slave Ship,* the slaves have no voice; in *The Unvanquished* Loosh looses his.

Part of the authority that Colonel Sartoris and other slave masters exercise is a fiction, a system of tyranny that is a collaborative enterprise between white and black people, an improvisatory ruse that the war will bring to an end. The McCaslin twins, Buck and Buddy, focal characters in *Go Down, Moses,* appear in "Retreat" trying to retreat from slavery, living in a two-room log cabin and turning over their fine manor house to their slaves, driving them "into the house and lock[ing] the door with a key almost as big as a horse pistol; probably they would still be locking the front door long after the last nigger had escaped out the back." The McCaslin regime is comic but also calamitous. They are a joke but also a parable about the folly of supposing that, in the end, slavery can survive as a rational and logical system—even as a kind of socialist enterprise, share and share alike in a kind of parody of 1930s Communist politics. Before the war, the brothers were eccentrics, but now they are the remnants of what was always an absurd system they could not entirely do without any more than Faulkner could maintain his family without his black retainers. Colonel Sartoris says the McCaslins are "ahead of their time" because they believe they belong to the land, not that the land belongs to them, a theme Faulkner would develop in *Go Down, Moses,* even as he identified himself on the map of Yoknapatawpha as its sole owner and proprietor and steadily increased his Rowan Oak domain.

"Raid" depicts the disintegration of slavery and the plantation system. "'Raid' kept my thoughts on Robert Peel, Manager of Polk Plantation, whose farm hands in 1866 took up a march of religious fervor to cross the Jordan & go over into Canaan. They got as far as Yocona river & some crossed tho Peel retrieved most of them," Will Bryant wrote to Faulkner.[35] The chapter was written in the wake of the Great Migration of African Americans to northern cities that began with World War I and continued into the 1970s, bringing six million African Americans northward in a racial tide. Although Ringo regards himself as apart from what is happening to his people, Bayard, in retrospect, realizes the boys were caught up in a mass movement that overwhelmed their own efforts to keep the Sartoris domain intact:

> the motion, the impulse to move which had already seethed to a head among his [Ringo's] people, darker than themselves, reasonless, following and seeking a delusion, a dream, a bright shape which they could not know since there was nothing in their heritage, nothing in the memory even of the old men to tell the others, "This is what we will find"; he nor they could not have known what it was yet it was there—one of those impulses inexplicable yet invincible which appear among races of people at intervals and drive them to pick up and leave all security and familiarity of earth and home and start out, they dont know where, empty handed, blind to everything but a hope and a doom.

Bayard treats mass migration as problematic, but are these migrating black people "blind to everything" any more deluded than Bayard and Ringo, grounded in their own mythology? In retrospect, Bayard seems aware if not exactly attuned to the changes that are about the transform his native land.

Gradually, *The Unvanquished* becomes less about the war itself—the battles and the heroics—and more about the displacement of white and black people. Bayard, Ringo, and Granny are on the move, following the trail of the advancing Union army. They begin to "pass big fires, with niggers in wet clothes crouching around them and soldiers going among them passing out food," even as Granny and her gang rely on Yankee largesse. When a Union soldier looks at the commanding officer's order to supply Granny, he comments: "I guess the General will be glad to give them twice the silver and mules just for taking that many niggers." It is an accurate reflection of Sherman's own belief that the liberated slaves were an encumbrance.

"Riposte in Tertio" (October–December 1864), a fencing term for a counterthrust that comes after parrying an opponent's thrust, alludes to Granny's final deal with outlaws so that she can recoup enough money for John Sartoris to start again after the war. "Southern men would not harm a woman," she reckons wrongly. In "Vendée" (December 1864–February 1865), an allusion to the counterrevolutionary, royalist region of western France, Bayard and Ringo hunt down Grumby, the outlaw leader who has murdered Granny. They restore the family's honor, and Bayard is hailed as his father's worthy successor, scion of his noble line. But this revenge tragedy in "Skirmish at Sartoris" (spring 1865) seems, by the end of the novel, anachronistic, a holdover of old world values that no longer pertain now that the "men had given in and admitted that they belonged to the United States." Only the women, like Drusilla, the Colonel's consort, behave as though the war has not been lost, and that the ancien régime prevails.

Faulkner knew how much it had cost his family to pretend that the past was their future, perpetrated in titles like "Colonel" that the post–Civil War generation had not earned but simply assumed as they took power. How much had changed during Reconstruction is alluded to in John Sartoris's desperation: "We were promised Federal troops; Lincoln himself promised to send us," Bayard overhears his father say to Drusilla. "Then things will be all right."[36] Without those troops, from Sartoris's point of view, he is at the mercy of carpetbaggers and abolitionists, the same ones who appear in *Light in August*: "two Burdens from Missouri, with a patent from Washington to organise the niggers into Republicans." Bayard notes that "Father and the other men were trying to prevent it." Lincoln's death, a catastrophe for the South, meant that Reconstruction, from the southern point of view, would not be advanced as a unified Union project but rather as the opportunistic campaign of one political party. It is at this point that Sartoris murders the Burdens.

The cycle of violence finally ends twelve years later in "An Odor of Verbena" (October 1873). An unarmed Bayard, now twenty-four, studying law, confronts but refuses to shoot Redmond, his father's murderer, who flees the scene, confirming that a new era has come. The past that Colonel Sartoris, Drusilla, and Ringo justify and celebrate is dead; Bayard destroys the pattern of a "succinct and formal violence" by a succinct and formal act of his own. After a confused moment, even his father's lieutenant George Wyatt understands that "maybe you're right, maybe there has been enough killing in your family." In effect, Wyatt and later Drusilla, who leaves a sprig of verbena in tribute to Bayard's courage before she leaves the house, ratify his deed as worthy of a gentleman, of a Sartoris.

At the end of *The Unvanquished* it appears that the direct sources of the Colonel's peculiar power over the Sartorises are being revealed. The Colonel who sits before his "cold hearth" with a "dead cigar" is reminiscent of Bayard himself in *Flags in the Dust,* an old man who has not only inherited his father's title but has also come to resemble him, especially in the scene between Bayard and his grandson, where his cold cigar is symbolic of his exhaustion, worn out by time and approaching death. In this same scene the continuity between generations of Sartorises is also emphasized by the "hawk-like planes" of young Bayard's face, which resemble the Colonel's "hawklike face." In *The Unvanquished,* the Colonel's library includes a set of Dumas, who is Bayard's favorite reading in *Flags in the Dust.* Even the Colonel's habit of sitting with his muddy boots in the library is part of the aging Bayard's routine. The old Bayard of *Flags in the Dust* and the young Bayard of *The Unvanquished* are consanguineous: "Bayard has not changed the Old Order and its ways, Bayard is the Old Order bereft of firebrand violence."[37]

The gentlemanly code, the Sartoris/Faulkner noblesse oblige still obtained and would inform William Faulkner's life and work right to the end of his days. This heritage was hard to square with Hollywood, where no gentleman need apply, even though its films were full of gentleman heroes impersonated by the likes of Warner Baxter and Ronald Colman and more raffish versions perfected by Clark Gable, Faulkner's hunting companion. MGM bought the rights to *The Unvanquished* for twenty-five thousand dollars. Louella Parsons reported that screenwriter Frances Marion had been assigned to adapt the novel,[38] but the film never went into production, even though Faulkner's emphasis on individuals and skirmishes might have made for a good, low-budget B movie that would have stripped out Bayard's musings. In the *Nation* (February 19, 1938), Louis Kronenberger called the book "high-romantic stuff, cinema stuff, though where *Gone With the Wind* is purely Hollywood, *The Unvanquished* is coated with the expressionism of the foreign studio." Granville Hicks (*New Masses,* February 22) deplored an "enthusiasm for Confederate heroes almost as unadulterated as that of Margaret Mitchell or

Stark Young." To Clifton Fadiman (*New Yorker*, February 19), "these stories, despite their nervous brilliance or manner, are in a class with those hysterical and gushy lost-cause fictions that pudgy, middle-aged English ladies used to write about Bonnie Prince Charlie and the Jacobites." Such verdicts are overturned in a much later assessment of the novel's "mood of feral desperation, a kind of wild determination to survive no matter what, which just pulverizes any pretense to genteel mannerliness."[39]

Most reviewers liked *The Unvanquished* but did not take it too seriously: "This is not the hard-boiled Faulkner of old. This is a southerner and sentimentalist and, for all his pretense, he is a sentimentalist, writing sincerely and effectively about his home country," concluded Charles C. Clayton in the *St. Louis Globe-Democrat* (February 19). C. L. Sonnichsen (*El Paso Herald-Post*) hailed the novel as the first one that readers of Stark Young's "magnolias and moonlight" work might enjoy because it does not include the usual "dirt and denigration." Faulkner, after all, cherished a "deep feeling for a ruined country and defeated countrymen." "Toned-down and brushed up Faulkner," announced Ted Robinson in the *Cleveland Plain Dealer* (February 20). Only the killing of Grumby seemed "truly Faulknerian"—a comment that revealed a need to keep the novelist well within the boundaries of previous novels. In *Canadian Forum* (June), Earle Birney was almost alone in setting the mass exodus of the slaves against contemporary history, arguing that "Faulkner can see no real motive, no suffering negro race, behind the phenomenon. He looks at the black still through the dulled and provincial eyes of a slaveholder, ignorant of the humanity he surrounds himself with, ignorant of the essential anachronism of plantation feudalism, and ignorant of the real barbarousness of the equally outdated wage-slavery under which the contemporary black groans." That it is Bayard whose consciousness Faulkner is rendering seems not to have impressed Birney.

Read in the context of his previous fiction, Bayard emerges as a new kind of Faulkner hero: self-aware and self-critical and not so prone to the self-defeating thoughts and actions that doom Quentin Compson and Henry Sutpen.[40] Could it also be that Bayard's understanding of his father's plight became an easier subject for Faulkner to contemplate after his father's death? Murry Falkner, needless to say, was nothing like John Sartoris, and yet his death brought on Faulkner's own reckoning with his place as his family's patriarch. Murry, for all his complaints against his eldest son, had been an indulgent father and set an example that Faulkner followed as well in his attempts to care for all of his family, no matter what he thought of them individually.

And what to make of Ringo? Reviewers by and large ignored him, although he is Bayard's other self—the one that remains committed to the old Sartoris code, like a family retainer who does not follow Loosh into freedom. All around him, Faulkner had such characters, family servants with strong personalities who nevertheless subordinated themselves to their white-supremacist employers. Meta met one of them, Jack Oliver, in California on his first trip out of Mississippi, and she noted Faulkner's cautioning her that Oliver had to acclimate to this new world. On arrival in Los Angeles, Faulkner said to Oliver, "Why don't you park the car and walk around and see what you can see." Jack answered: "Mr. Bill, I've got the weak trembles. It's the first time I've ever set foot in a foreign country." Estelle remembered how "the weak trembles" delighted her husband. Amusing, yes, but also reminiscent of the master in Estelle's story "Dr. Wohlenski," who delights in his slave's sayings. As Oliver became more accustomed to his new surroundings, he became "uppity," provoking in Faulkner an irritation not so different from old Bayard's in *Flags in the Dust*. Estelle remembered Jack answering the phone, saying, "This is Mr. Oliver speaking," not, "This is the Faulkner residence." Faulkner shouted at Jack, who dropped the phone. Faulkner said that if Oliver answered a call that way, then he could find another employer.[41] Jack Oliver remained in California after Faulkner returned to Mississippi.

For every Ringo remaining in the past, a Loosh, a Jack Oliver looked to the future. Bayard "carries within him the hope of another, new South, more peaceful, more civilized, if not more fraternal."[42] In *The Unvanquished*, Colonel Sartoris treats Bayard and Ringo as equals, suggesting, even, that Ringo might be smarter than Bayard. Are the boys, in fact, brothers? So some readers have concluded, based not so much on one novel but on a close reading of *Flags in the Dust* and "There Was a Queen." Paradoxically, the abolition of slavery separates white and black brothers in spirit, and perhaps in blood.[43] Ringo and Bayard part company as Bayard initiates a new kind of history Faulkner was beginning to imagine for the second half of his career. What he ultimately thought of *The Unvanquished* is not clear. When asked at the University of Virginia, twenty years after the novel's publication, which of his books should be read first, he said, "maybe *The Unvanquished*" in a rising voice that sounds more like a question than an answer.

4

Grief

February 1938–January 1939

How shall we sing the Lord's song in a strange land?

—Psalm 137

I saw this screenplay of his for "Drums Along the Mohawk" . . . written in longhand in that little tiny funny handwriting of his and, because it was Faulkner, I sat down and I read it and it was good and you know he could write a screenplay. . . . He didn't sneer at it.

—Budd Schulberg

It is worth considering that his experimental fiction was a reaction to the discipline of his scriptwriting—that it was an acting out of an impulse of "manic defense."

—Paul Theroux, *Deep South*

FAMILY COMPLICATIONS

Even as William Faulkner had surveys done of his domain and extended his property, he wrote with a badly burned back that refused to heal. The skin grafts failed and became infected. He could not sleep, and he could not forget—not only Meta but also Helen Baird, whose physical appearance and bearing resemble Charlotte Rittenmeyer's in *The Wild Palms*. While in Hollywood in 1935 he had written to say he could not accept Helen's invitation to a literary conference in Louisiana because he was still scurrying about to "make money to boil the pot." His frustrated, lingering desire for her seemed to come out in his confession that "I do wish to hell I didn't have to wait 10 years between seeing you." In another letter, he seemed almost to panic: "What have you been in hospital for? You couldn't have been sick. . . . Sick to me anymore than you can get old. It must be something else. Is it another child?" His obsession climaxed in his closing address: "Helen Helen Helen Helen."[1] Charlotte Rittenmeyer's life would end in a botched abortion. Helen Baird did not die, but, now married with two children, she was lost to William Faulkner. "'Between grief and nothing I will take grief' . . . is the theme of the whole book," Faulkner told Robert Haas at Random House about *The Wild Palms*.[2]

When he was not writing, he was farming or hunting. Slowly his back healed. He did some flying mainly to look over his land. Faulkner did little of the manual labor on Greenfield Farm, putting his brother John in charge. The farm, adjacent to land owned by black families, put Faulkner in touch with a community of stalwart and independent African Americans, some of whom worked for him. They seemed to take him in stride as he seemed to take them. "It was cool" to have him around, said Trudy McJunkins, one of his African American neighbors.[3]

Keeping accounts as a farmer suited him:

> *July 9, 1938*
> *$10.00*
> *On or after Nov 15, 1938 I promise to pay to Falkner Bros the sum of ten dollars ($10.00) at 8% interest the above amount is secured by 1 hog which is owned sole by me.*[4]

Long periods went by—Malcolm called them the "silent days"—when Faulkner wrote and seemed to do nothing else, except to take long walks during which, Malcolm believed, certain plots and characters were worked out. Sometimes the noise of projects the neighborhood children created excited his attention, and he would pitch in.[5]

He also had to care for Malcolm's sister, Cho-Cho (Victoria), whose husband, Claude Selby, had deserted her just after she had given birth during the Christmas season of 1937–38. She had always regarded Faulkner as her "special friend." For her eighth birthday, he had given her *The Wishing Tree* with a hand-lettered label, calling her his "dear friend." He was "Billy" to her and only "Pappy" after Jill's birth. After Alabama's death, Cho-Cho began to feel neglected and jealous of anyone who drew Pappy's attention away from her, and that included her mother and her drinking. Cho-Cho's devotion to Faulkner had, perhaps, a sexual subtext. Friends of the Faulkners who visited Rowan Oak frequently said that "when William Faulkner had a little bit to drink Cho-Cho had to keep the door of her bedroom locked, and another rumor had it that she was his mistress."[6] Then Cho-Cho, sent away to boarding school in Holly Springs, watched Jill depart with her mother and Pappy for Hollywood. "Suddenly Mama had nothing where she [Estelle] had had it all," Cho-Cho's daughter, also named Victoria, said. "I know my mother felt abandoned and, most likely, somewhat betrayed."

She was not the only one. "I think Pappy felt he had been taken advantage of by my mother, by her elopement, and getting pregnant while Pappy was in California," Victoria said. Selby, at least temporarily, had made Cho-Cho feel desired.[7] Faulkner overcame his upset over Cho-Cho's behavior, realized she was heartbroken, and began reading Keats to her. Together they played games and worked on crossword puzzles. "He kept me alive," she later said. Neither one wanted a rift, and perhaps Faulkner understood that his stepdaughter "adored men; she didn't like women," Victoria said: "She did not like me, she didn't like her mother, and she did not like Jill." To Victoria, the situation was hardest on her grandmama Estelle, "a lovely human being, a lady who cared deeply about her children, her husband, and who was proud of the simplest pleasures in life." Cho-Cho destroyed two hundred of her mother's letters, trying to erase, Victoria claimed, a rounded sense of Estelle's positive role in the Faulkner family—in effect helping to perpetuate Faulkner's own nullification of his wife's importance.

According to Victoria, Faulkner traveled on a bus all the way to Michigan's Upper Peninsula, where Cho-Cho had gone to retrieve her wayward husband, who refused to return to Mississippi. Faulkner accompanied mother and daughter home and wrote to Cornell Franklin, suggesting a trip to see Franklin in Shanghai would do Cho-Cho some good. Franklin agreed, realizing perhaps how hard it was on all concerned. "Just read Pappy's 'A Rose for Emily' if you really want to know how the town reacted to anything and everything even slightly out of the ordinary," Victoria pointed out.[8]

On June 17, 1938, Faulkner wired Random House: "NOVEL FINISHED. SOME REWRITING DUE TO BACK COMPLICATIONS. SENDING IT ON IN A FEW DAYS." It had been a steady, slow haul, with frequent interruptions, almost like the structure of the book itself, which swerves not only between two stories but gets caught up in the Great Flood of 1927, with Faulkner holding on to his painfully wrought design as doggedly as his convict in "Old Man" who holds on to his boat in raging waters.

On July 8, the relieved author wrote to Robert Haas: "I was glad to read your letter. I have lived for the last six months in such a peculiar state of family complications and back complications that I still am not able to tell if the novel is all right or absolute drivel." It felt like he had been writing blindly and between two worlds—one he was living while he imagined another. It was rare for him to put into words what such bifurcation meant to him: "To me, it was written just as if I had sat on the one side of a wall and the paper was on the other and my hand with the pen thrust through the wall and writing not only on invisible paper but in pitch darkness too, so that I could not even know if the pen still wrote on paper or not." The elements of his conceit—the pen thrusting through a wall and writing on invisible paper in pitch darkness may have derived from his Hollywood work. Writers were, in a sense, walled off from what they created, which, in turn, was projected into darkness by invisible means with which they had no contact. Hollywood also manufactured plenty of love-story drivel, including coincidences, chance encounters, accidents, strokes of luck—all the stuff of popular fiction and film and of *The Wild Palms.*

The novel also seemed an expression of Faulkner's desire to incarcerate his love for Meta Carpenter. The counterpoint to the claustrophobic love story of Harry Wilbourne and Charlotte Rittenmeyer—the convict's fervent desire to avoid "family complications" that come flooding upon him—reflected an aspect of Faulkner's anomie. *The Wild Palms* expresses as much of Faulkner's emotional geography and different writing experiences as any novel he would write.[9] The tall convict, seemingly Faulkner's physical and mental opposite, has read too many robbery pulps and put himself in prison by presuming they are primers of success. Like his creator, "writing has been his prison house." Similarly, Charlotte tells Harry that she finds validation for their love from what she has read in books.[10]

Sometime during the final preparations for the novel, Faulkner uncharacteristically broached the idea of a memoir, a form of writing he would attempt only once, years later, in his essay-length semifictional reminiscence, "Mississippi," for *Holiday* magazine. An enthusiastic Bennett Cerf replied immediately: "Excited and extremely pleased at your idea of your book of memoirs. I agree with you that such a book should be illustrated both with photographs and your own sketches. You don't say anything about your war adventures. Wouldn't you include them at all, and would there be any chapters about New York and Hollywood?"[11] Perhaps the questions were enough to dissuade Faulkner, who would have to explain what he did during the war.

By the fall he was in New York. Some words in *The Wild Palms* had to be changed, Haas wrote. Faulkner proposed that "Women, shit," the last two words the convict speaks, could be changed to "Women, ...," a dot standing for each deleted letter. He spent part of September and October in New York, staying at the Algonquin Hotel, working on other details. On October 10, he wrote home revealing how much his family remained in his thoughts. He described an Army vs. Columbia football game at West Point, asking Estelle to relay to Malcolm the action and the statistics, including Columbia's "steady drive of 80 yards, 9 plays, 5 first downs on 4 20 yd. passes, wins." He expected to leave for home in a few more days after finishing the galley proofs.[12]

On December 3, Robert Cantwell arrived in Memphis to do a cover story for *Time* to mark the publication of *The Wild Palms*. Faulkner apologized for arriving late, saying his wife had received Cantwell's telegram on an especially busy day. Cantwell observed that a healthy-looking Faulkner carried himself like a military man, erect with his head thrown back. He looked at you intensely with dark-black eyes before he spoke softly and slowly in an unexcited voice. Cantwell blurted out: "The convict is wonderful. The best thing you've done." Faulkner smiled for the first time and said, "I kind of liked him myself." Cantwell followed up by dropping names—Lyle Saxon and Hal Smith: "No response." Cantwell's first impression: "A cold fish—extremely cold, perhaps cruel." He noted Faulkner's extremely thin lips. The hotel was crowded with noisy, drunken football fans who took their enthusiasm right into the elevator. "They must have rented the elevator space too," Faulkner remarked.

Outside they got into a Ford touring car with a soft front tire and one broken side curtain. In the back sat Malcolm and Faulkner's nephew Jimmy. Faulkner said staying at the hotel that night would be like sleeping in a fraternity house. He pointed out Beale Street, and Cantwell tried again: In one of his books Faulkner had said "four or five blocks of Beale Street made Harlem look like a movie set." Quoting Faulkner to Faulkner seemed to make Faulkner uncomfortable. While Malcolm and Johnny talked about Beale Street— unsafe for white people any time of day or night but with good bargains in pawn shops—Cantwell finally engaged his subject in talk about the Civil War, family history, plantations, and farming, as Faulkner carefully drove the swaying car, clenching and unclenching his gloved hands—nervous man, Cantwell suspected, keeping himself under rigid control, a carefully confected personality groomed as meticulously as his sloping mustache. Faulkner "never laughs," Cantwell noted, but he was amiable, if taciturn, answering yes or no to exploratory questions, often seeming to seek refuge in long silences, unwilling to open himself up to further inquiry, or perhaps proud, prone to see slights, unwilling to pass the time in the "small change" of conversation that might lead to more "fundamental matters." As they drove along Cantwell decided that "Faulkner must be the greatest listener in American literature."

On one subject, Faulkner became voluble: the old Colonel—perhaps because of the recent publication of *The Unvanquished*. He said his great-grandfather "had no humor and probably no sensibility," a surprising comment given some of the amusing scenes in *The White Rose of Memphis* and

Rapid Ramblings in Europe. Or did Faulkner mean only the man, not the author? In full flow, Faulkner spoke too quickly for Cantwell to record direct quotations: "There is a rare eloquent quality to his talk when he gets animated. The phrases are composed and telling, and although there is no change in his voice, in its tone, or in his manner, the words could go down on paper exactly as he utters them, and would fall into place as if they had been worked over and revised."

The car crested rolling hills and sometimes came upon black people walking along the road, which had few cars on it. In the distance Cantwell could see settlements with dimly lit, tumbledown cabins of black people and patches of cleared land looking desolate with washed-out gullies, eroded hills, and scrubby pines. Faulkner preferred talking about Ole Miss football with his stepson and nephew to answering questions about Hollywood. He wouldn't even mention the movies he had worked on, saying only that he was no good at screenwriting and that Joel Sayre liked to get drunk and pick a fight with the bartender.

After a short stop at a service station in Holly Springs, more talk about the war, and a drive through the Oxford square in the evening, they pulled into Rowan Oak's cedar-lined drive. As they approached the lighted front porch, Jill ran out to meet them, but then stopped, waiting for her father to approach her. Obviously happy to be home, he greeted her affectionately. She turned gravely to Cantwell, who was impressed with her self-possession and pale beauty. She had won a nickel on the football game and then announced she had learned to ride her bike and seemed grieved to learn that she was not unique—that Cantwell's daughter had done the same. He asked her when she would go to school. She said it was up to her mother and Pappy to settle it as she sprawled out, saying, "I certainly like to lie on the floor."

Then Cantwell turned to Estelle: "aging, dressy, hospitable, with a warm, engaging, careless manner, proud of her children and of Faulkner and—apparently—a little afraid of him." Estelle apologized for her inexperienced servants. She had lost Jill's nanny, Narcissus McEwen, and Jack Oliver, an old couple devoted to the Faulkners. In California they were called "Mr. and Mrs., and it went to their heads so they stayed there." Billy had paid four hundred dollars for Narcissus's operation, but when the hospital staff called her Mrs., "she never got over it." To Cantwell, Estelle remained a puzzle he worked on for some time:

She was cheerful and nice but continually disappeared, changed her dress, and returned abruptly from upstairs or the kitchen as if she had discovered you were there. She would say absent-mindedly, "I must show you the whole house." Or when I was outside looking over the grounds, she would lean from an upstairs window and say cheerfully, "I hope you slept well."—this being startling because you could not tell where the voice was coming from. So you would have a little conversation with a row of windows, standing out under the trees and looking up self-consciously while she seemed to talk and at the same time go about some household task.

Does this say as much about Cantwell as it does about Estelle? Why he thought she feared Faulkner is never explained, and why she might have felt uneasy about this prying reporter in the house never seems to have occurred to him. Until the *Time* cover story, the Faulkners had remained incognito so far as the national media were concerned, with no major interview with Faulkner conducted in Faulkner's home until now. What role was Estelle supposed to play? What limits had to be placed on southern hospitality? How was one supposed to treat this northern reporter with his transparent ploys at immediate familiarity? Just watching this stranger prowling the precincts of Rowan Oak tested her and Faulkner in a new way. Was she supposed to drop everything and just fawn over him? Was her talk about servants an indication of how unsettled this visit had made her? Her world was out of order, but wasn't she trying awfully hard to cope with this intruder? The Cantwell episode had begun with Faulkner apologizing for his tardiness but also saying he had been busy. Was it Faulkner's oblique way of saying, "We will try to fit you in"? Cantwell was a sharp observer of manners but a poor analyst of motives and behavior.

At dinner the Faulkners talked about fishing—about how Billy always threw the fish back, saying they were too small. Estelle did more fishing than Billy, prompting Malcolm to say to his mother: "You fish like a nigger. You keep everything no matter how little." After dinner, in the study, Faulkner seemed relaxed, assuring Cantwell that he really did read *Don Quixote* in the winter: "It's a winter book." On rainy nights, he'd get a drink, roll some cigarettes with home-cured Kentucky tobacco, and read nearly until midnight. Favorites? *Henry Esmond, Richard III, Henry IV,* and occasionally Henry James and the Bible. "I'd expect you to like *Lear*," Cantwell ventured. "I read to come to Falstaff and Doll Tearsheet [Falstaff's whore]," Faulkner returned. "I think Marlowe is better than people acknowledge, and I like Campion."

Gradually Cantwell drew out of Faulkner much of the family history and an account of his early career that would be potted for the *Time* feature, published on January 23, 1939. For public consumption, however, Cantwell concentrated on Faulkner as the cynosure of a southern literary renaissance: "For the last nine years he had been successful, regarded by critics as the most talented but least predictable Southern writer, by his fellow townsman as an enigma, by himself as a social historian, who hopes that by recording the minute changes in Oxford's life he can suggest the changes that are transforming the whole South."

THE BAD BOY OF AMERICAN FICTION

Reviews of the novel were decidedly mixed, but the widespread coverage, beginning with Cantwell's *Time* feature story, brought results. By early March, a fifth printing had been announced, with more than twenty-one thousand copies in print—an even higher sales figure than *Sanctuary*'s.[13] "In his latest book," Robert E. McClure announced in the *Santa Monica Evening Post* (January 20), Faulkner "no longer shocks for the sake of shocking, no longer reminds us of an over-imaginative youth too long exposed to the reptilian terrors and malarial fevers of a southern swamp, without benefit of sunshine and fresh air." To the tragic story of a passionate couple overcome by their physical attraction, he pitted the convict reluctantly helping a woman about to have a child. They are in same boat, capsized twice, in the "raging main stream of the Mississippi and the hillbilly is still in prison stripes," an inmate of Parchman prison sent there for trying to be another dime-novel Jesse James, and now assigned to rescue work. "That is what the movies call a 'story situation,'" McClure noted. "If you can improve on it for suspense you may go to Hollywood right now." The "emotional pitch and intensity" of Charlotte and Harry's romantic agony "swept [one] along to the final tragedy with a sensation of being hypnotized by a powerful drug." The very extravagance of Faulkner's prose reminded McClure of the Elizabethans, even if he did not know that Christopher Marlowe was one of the novelist's favorites. Similarly, Wallace Stegner in the *Virginia Quarterly Review* (summer 1939) observed that the "love story, full of stripped and quivering passion that never relaxes, is almost too harrowing to be read through consecutively. Mr. Faulkner's power of evocation is so great, his voltage so high, that the love story, in spite of its pitiful beauty, would exhaust a reader. The convict story, though intense itself, furnishes relief because the tensity in this second tale is pure muscularity, pure determination, without the emotional strain of the other."

Reviewers tended to see the love story as overdone or sordid, the flood tale as brilliantly picaresque or preposterous, with the convict as a "low-life Quixote" (Mary Carter Roberts, *Washington Sunday Star*, January 22). The mix of the two stories befuddled some, irritated others, and, in general, seemed forced. Others, like Malcolm Cowley (*New Republic*, January 25), steered readers away from the southern-specific, observing that Harry and

Charlotte "fall in love, instantly and fatally, like two characters in a late-Elizabethan tragedy, forsaking security for passion even as the convict forsakes passion for security." The liberated Harry and Charlotte invert the convict's desire to return to prison so that he does not have to make the decisions that freedom requires. Cowley noted that the tall convict is the "ideal soldier for a fascist army."

Even the negative reviews of the "bad boy of American fiction" (*Bakersfield Californian,* May 19) compared reading it to a "psychological spell" (S. W., *Philadelphia Inquirer,* February 11), a "powerful anesthetic" (Michael March, *Brooklyn Citizen,* January 27), "something overwhelming and terrible. . . . An evil spell so unutterably fascinating that one cannot escape its black magical power." In the *Huntington (WV) Advertiser* (February 5), Bruce Catton summed up: "Take it or leave it, it is unforgettable fiction." After calling the novel a "lexicon of obscenity" because it dealt with "childbirth, abortion, and other aspects of sex," and complaining about structure and sentence construction, "Diogenes" in the *Winnipeg Free Press* (February 4) said the "reader will be surprised how difficult it is to lay it down." Why, exactly, is never explained, although C. L. Sonnichsen in the *El Paso Herald-Post* (January 28) noted the novel's "keynote" succinctly: "the agonizing struggle of living organisms in the grip of mighty forces." The reviewer, like so many writing for the newspapers, neglected to specify those forces: sex and nature, although one referred to the two stories as examples of "sex attraction" and "sex repulsion" (*Minneapolis Star,* February 4).

Edwin Berry Burgum in the *New Masses* (February 7) saw the two stories as not merely opposites but integral parts of a single allegory ending "within the 'security' of prison walls." Neither the pursuit of freedom nor the pursuit of conventionality has proven satisfactory, he concluded. Faulkner was rarely viewed as a political novelist, but Burgum made his case: "The 'wretched of mankind' are in no mood to arise in Faulkner, but they have at all events escaped that pretense of freedom which our competitive world sets up as an ideal and translates, as these two stories hint, into the actuality of the undernourished body and the neurotic personality." Tortured in mind, tortured in body, the doctor and the proletarian, each seeks an escape from routinized society that, ironically, drives them both to prison.

The novel occasioned two reviews that have often been reprinted as early examples of the critical response to Faulkner's achievement that opened up new ways of looking at his work. Given the many reviews deploring Faulkner's sensationalism, the first sentence in George Marion O'Donnell's "Faulkner's Mythology" (*Kenyon Review,* summer 1939) is startling: "William Faulkner is really a traditional moralist, in the best sense." O'Donnell argued that the novels are "built around the conflict between traditionalism and the anti-traditional modern world in which it is immersed." Sartorises and Snopeses, the first proponents of an ethical code, however flawed, and the second, entrepreneurial in every sense of the word, which means jettisoning morality. O'Donnell saw the characters in terms of a mythology, or allegory, which set aside the complaints of those critics who regarded many of Faulkner's characters as improbable or extreme. Their objections, O'Donnell implied, were beside the point. The "Sartoris-Snopes conflict," he concluded, is "fundamentally a struggle between humanism and naturalism." So Harry and Charlotte were "natural, amoral . . . insisting upon the entirely physical nature of their love" and are "defeated by the very naturalism to which they have fled." The convict, rescuing the pregnant woman and then returning to prison, has "fulfilled his ethical obligation." Ingenious, perhaps, but Procrustean. O'Donnell's chief contribution was to take Faulkner out of the rut of reviews that failed to see any ethical element in his fiction.

Conrad Aiken, in "William Faulkner: The Novel as Form" (*Atlantic Monthly,* November 1939), offered one of the classic descriptions of Faulkner's style of *"deliberately withheld meaning,"* the almost perverse refusal to end a sentence because he wanted the "keep the form—and the idea—fluid and unfinished, still in motion as it were, and unknown, until the dropping into place of the very last syllable." Aiken's further elaboration is reminiscent of the flow of film: "What Mr. Faulkner is after, in a sense, is a *continuum.* He wanted a medium without stops or pauses, a medium which is always of the *moment,* and of which the passage from moment to moment is as fluid and undetectable as in the life itself which he is purporting to give." Those reviewers who wondered at the spell of his books did not have Aiken's perspective, which saw the fiction whole, in perpetuity, and not just as a book to shut and declare, "the end." *The Wild Palms* carried a "living *pulse.*" Fixated on subject matter, reviewers did not see the intricate form of the novels, and, in fact, lost in his sentences, they called them formless. Aiken understood the Faulkner who sat up until midnight reading Henry James, for like him, Faulkner implied that it is "practically impossible to make any real distinction between theme and form. . . . The novel as revelation, the novel as slice-of-life, the novel as mere story, do not interest him: these he would say, like James again, 'are the circumstance of the interest,' but not the interest itself." Southernness hardly interested Faulkner at all, Aiken contended, giving the boot to most reviewers and devotees of allegory like O'Donnell. Aiken's thinking applied to the "fugue-like" *Wild Palms:* one story's form was a comment on the other's; one chapter's form a response to the next one. Compare forms, in other words, as well as characters.

The staggered chapters, operating like an alternating current, put off certain reviewers because Faulkner upset the order of conventional storytelling, the very order that he had been called on to replicate in his work on *Drums along the Mohawk,* an adaptation of Walter D. Edmonds's best-selling novel, set on the frontier during the Revolutionary War. Faulkner turned in a twenty-six-page treatment to Twentieth Century-Fox on March 15, and then a much longer dialogued treatment on June 13, 1937, around two months before he began to write *The Wild Palms.* To read Faulkner's scripts and his novel in their sequence of composition is to realize how he sought to exploit and subvert Hollywood and mainstream fiction conventions.

In the film, released in November 1939 without a writing credit for Faulkner, two separate stories of love and war are jammed together in absurd and yet popularly acceptable ways. Gil Martin (Henry Fonda) takes his new wife, Lana Borst (Claudette Colbert), from her grand Albany home to settle their new homestead in territory contested by American rebels, Tories, and their Indian allies. Lana is shocked by the primitive conditions, by Blue Back, an Indian (even though he is friendly), and has to overcome hysterics, eventually holding her own, shooting an attacking Indian on the British side and becoming a full partner in Gil's ultimate triumph, as he bravely runs through a hostile Indian encampment and outpaces his murderous pursuers to summon the victorious American army.

But this is not what Faulkner wrote in two treatments. He liked the novel,[14] and followed Edmonds's lead, showing American settlers at odds with the nascent nation-state (akin to the big-government New Dealers Faulkner opposed). As his short stories written during the Second World War demonstrate, he believed in hardy individualism and distrusted any notion of a welfare state that would deprive people of the motivation to provide for themselves. The federal government had no business dictating what farmers could grow and market, and his opposition to a centralized bureaucracy is evident in his *Drums along the Mohawk* script.

The settlers simply want to farm their land, and they resent the intrusions of the Continental Congress, which pays their militia poorly, takes the settlers' grain, and delays sending armed forces to help protect the land from the depredations of the British and their Indian allies. "God save us from the Continental Congress," declares Bellinger, a militia leader. In effect, two colonial powers with different policies are in contention. Bellinger tells the colonel in the regular army: "You're going to lay waste to their [the Indians'] country, destroy their towns and drive them from the land—men women and children. Then I suppose you'll turn around and march back to Albany? What do you think the Indians will do then?" In a long and quite detailed screenplay, Faulkner stripped away much of the patriotic sentiment featured in the released film and the novel. When a militia man gets his first look at the nation's new flag, he remarks: "Thirteen stars. Thirteen. That's unlucky, ain't it?"[15]

The Faulkner of the Indian stories and also the critic of colonial settlement that will emerge in *Go Down, Moses* appears in the screenplay, in which Indians are viewed more as Native Americans, with Lana commenting on their family friend Blue Back:[16] "He has lost everything now. Even the land his ancestors lived on. While we have so much." The Indians are driven by other Indians and American militia and regulars toward Indian encampments on the Niagara frontier, a retreating force reminiscent of the South's retreating armies in the Civil War. "What would you do if you had been driven out of your country," Bellinger asks the regular army colonel, and "had looked back to see your house and fields burned, driven back on some folks that are the same color and speak the same language as the ones that drove you out? And you sitting there with nothing to do but feel your stomach getting more and more like a walnut, let alone having to look at the eyes of your women folks and the faces of your children every time you turned your head."[17] This is the kind of Faulknerian speech often deemed too long for the movies—at least for the major studios, although an independent producer like Walter Wanger might well have worked in this kind of speech, as he did in *Canyon Passage* (1946), an unorthodox western that includes a white man punished by his community for raping an Indian woman.

The tense Martin marriage in Edmonds's novel and in Faulkner's scenario is nothing like the final sentimentalized Hollywood version. In his first treatment Lana refuses sex after a miscarriage, and her husband loses patience and takes her by force, effectively raping her. Gil considers asserting his manhood by bedding the nubile Nancy, a servant girl, later excised from Faulkner's careful examination of colonial class structure. In true Hollywood fashion, Faulkner's Gil remains faithful to Lana, but he is taunted by Helmer, a strapping eligible single male who pretends to wipe mud off Gil after witnessing Lana rebuff her husband. "You lost your yoking match, too," Helmer tells Gil, adding, "I'm just wiping the mud off for you." That kind of sexual joke could not survive the Hollywood Production Code.

In a second, longer "dialogued treatment," Faulkner cuts the rape scene, but the sexual threat remains. Mrs. McKlennar, who employs Lana and Gil after Indians torch their home, advises Lana to submit to her husband, and when Lana refuses, Mrs. McKlennar grudgingly admits to admiring Lana's independence: "Still, I must say you did pretty well." In the released movie the love story capitulates to a rousing war epic, incorporating Lana as essentially a new recruit. In Faulkner's two treatments the love story heads one way and the war another, reflecting a polarity akin to *The Wild Palms* even if, in the end, Faulkner had to rein himself in to produce a happy ending. As a character in Faulkner's dialogued treatment declares, "To be young and to be in love—there is no wilderness then." In his first treatment he had written that the film's ending needed "whatever sappy stuff . . . about love conquers all things, etc."[18]

The Wild Palms rewrote *Drums along the Mohawk,* resulting in a far different wilderness/civilization diptych and a fraught reading of romance and love. "The Wild Palms" begins in a beach cottage, the place for a temporary stay by the sea that Faulkner knew well from his Pascagoula time with Helen Baird, his honeymoon with Estelle, and his weekend getaways with Meta on the Pacific coast. A middle-aged doctor who marries the wife his father picked out for him and lives in the house his father had built and smokes a pipe because his father said cigarettes were for dudes and women has rented his cottage to Charlotte and Harry. Charlotte stands out because she wears men's pants, tight in just the right places. She is alluring but also in command, and as such she fascinates the doctor and his real estate agent. Charlotte is a bolder Lana. Mrs. McKlennar, who employs Lana and her husband after Indians burn their home, says to Gil: "I'm interested in seeing just how much longer it will be before you decide just which one of you wears the pants in your family." The real estate agent is sure Charlotte and Harry are not married to each other, although he suspects (rightly) that Charlotte has a husband, and the doctor speculates (rightly) that she has children. Charlotte sits in a beach chair all day long "watching the palm fronds clashing with their wild dry bitter sound against the bright glitter of the water while the man carried driftwood into the kitchen." Calling Harry "the man" emphasizes his gender, which is second in importance to his subservient role. The "natural" order of things, as expressed in *Drums along the Mohawk,* has been reversed, or, rather, the subtext of Faulkner's screenplay, which emphasizes the paradox involved in the yoking of men, women, wilderness, and civilization, becomes paramount in "The Wild Palms." As Dr. Petrie observes in *Drums along the Mohawk:* "Women are strange creatures, Gil. The frontier is no place for them. Yet it can't exist without them. Else there would be no reason for us to make it livable."[19] Harry, the parody of a pioneer, walks barefoot on the beach, like Faulkner, a drifter. The minimalist cottage, devoid of much furniture and containing only the basics in mismatched utensils and cracked cups, suits a twosome stripped bare of accoutrements. Their settlement is no better equipped than the Gil Martin–Lana Borst household. Harry and Charlotte, living on the fly, are the very definition of what Rowan Oak was not but also the exemplum of the vagabondage Faulkner found appealing. Harry and Charlotte are a pioneering couple, with no Oxford that Bill and Meta had to worry about. Of course, Charlotte and Harry outrage the proper doctor's wife. They do not behave, however, like lovers but more like the Faulkners on their estranged honeymoon with something between them that intrigues onlookers.

Charlotte stares at the doctor with "blank feral eyes" as he does his Christian duty, delivering a bowl of gumbo to the uncivilized couple. He is like the placid frontier types who welcome Lana and Gil. Charlotte is, in fact, in a position similar to Lana's in *Drums along the Mohawk,* having forsaken, in Charlotte's case, not a comfortable Albany estate but the comforts and status of a married woman with children in Chicago. She has given up everything for love, and what has it brought her? She is in a wilderness of her own bitterness and isolation that cannot be perversely turned around in a Hollywood treatment. That was, in truth, Lana's plight, and her anger and depression are given full scope in Faulkner's scripts. But Claudette Colbert, playing Lana, could hardly hint at her anger and depression, since her marriage, like the war, had to be won on Hollywood's terms.

The doctor could well be a conventional Hollywood character suddenly confronted off-screen by a woman unwilling to behave according to the script men put women in: *"What is it that man as a race can have done to her that she would look upon such a manifestation of it as I, whom she has never seen before and would not look at twice if she had, with that same hatred through which he must walk each time he comes up from the beach with an armful of firewood to cook the very food which she eats."* The alienated Charlotte is on the frontier of the doctor's consciousness, of all that he must repress in order to please his father and his wife and remain respectable and a man. Charlotte is a revelation to him, a character that heretofore he could not imagine watching in the movie he has made of his life. In his encounter with Charlotte, the doctor detects a "sense of imminence, of being just beyond a veil from something, of groping just without the veil and even touching but not quite, almost seeing but not quite, the shape of truth." In her presence, he has begun to reflect on the grounds of his own existence as he struggles toward insight: *"Something which the entire race of men, males, has done to her or she believes has done to her."* Any moment now, he will realize that the issues joined are pregnancy, childbirth, and abortion.

The male prerogative that Gil Martin and his Hollywood begetters take for granted is at risk, and no reviewer seems to have considered the novel's reversal of gender roles. Harry has brought Charlotte to this figurative wilderness, the end of the line, but even more than Lana, Charlotte does not want to surrender. "The fool. To bring her here, of all places. To sealevel. To the Mississippi coast," remarks the doctor's censorious wife when informed that Harry has knocked on their door asking for medical assistance because Charlotte is bleeding. No female character in *Drums along the Mohawk* appears to tell Gil much the same—that he has no business bringing his wife to a warring frontier where she miscarries. The novel is about another kind of frontier conflict, the one within the human heart, the storm center the doctor has entered, objectified in the "unimpeded sea-wind which thrashed among the unseen palms." What would be a cliché in a motion picture—"the invisible wind blew strong and steady among the invisible palms, from the invisible sea"—becomes in Faulkner's prose human palms and a sea of emotions.

The doctor behaves like a character observing the limits of the Production Code. He only recognizes his "barricade of perennial innocence"—how much knowledge he has blocked out like a redacted film script when he picks up on Harry's hint that Charlotte's bleeding is where a woman bleeds, not from the lungs as the doctor first supposed. Now the doctor's veil is parting, an apt choice of words for a man—really a civilization—that blinds itself to a woman's suffering and also puts women in veils (ignorance) such as those that characters like Caddy and her mother wear.[20] But it is just as much the doctor who is the woman, the violated one, as it is Charlotte. And his wife might as well be Mrs. McKlennar implying that Gil is a fool for not disciplining his wife.

Before the doctor attends to Charlotte, the novel switches to the tall convict's story—another outraged innocent like the doctor. The inmate is convicted of an attempted train robbery after reading too much pulp fiction that he foolishly regarded as a foolproof guide to showing he was the "best at his chosen gambit." He shares a cell with a short, plump robber and murderer unfit for much of anything, so "in a long apron like a woman, he cooked and swept and dusted in the deputy wardens' barracks." In films of this period, the towering John Carradine, with his mournful good looks, could have played the tall convict, and Edward Arnold the short, plump one. This couple subsists in conditions even more elemental than Charlotte and Harry's. The convicts read about the approaching disaster: the Great Flood of 1927. They farm land that nature at any moment may reclaim, just as the settlers in *Drums along the Mohawk* worry that their burned-out homes and fields will return to wilderness. As the levee breaks, the prisoners are told to turn out. The chapter ends, like the first one, on the very cusp of a momentous event. Reviewers spoke of the novel's orchestration, perhaps sensing that the chapters were like movements in music. Did Faulkner, for all his telling Meta he cared nothing about music, actually absorb what he needed not only from her but from her composer friend John Crown?

The next chapter delays the denouement between the doctor and Charlotte again, flashing back to Harry's childhood and medical training, shadowed by his father's early death and Harry's scrabbling to fund his education, sacrificing any pleasure to be had outside of his studies. A twenty-seven-year-old intern in New Orleans, he is celibate and virginal, and now convinced that he will remain without passion, practically a solitary like the tall convict in his cell. A fellow intern invites Harry to an artist's party in the French Quarter, one of those casual drop-in affairs that Faulkner occasionally attended at about the same age. Harry resists getting involved: *"You have peace now; you want no more,"* he tells himself. Harry is in for trouble—you just know it—in the heavy, sultry city air that is part of the party spirit. Of course he meets Charlotte, who stares at him with "speculative sobriety like a man might." In this informal setting she looks at him and says it looks like he is slumming. Without a plan or pose, Harry just blurts out that he is twenty-seven, it is his birthday, and he is in borrowed formal clothes. She takes him in hand, "ruthless and firm." She is a sculptor, and her talk about displacing air and water with her work is reminiscent of those conversations about art in *Mosquitoes.* Faulkner's experience in New Orleans in 1925 left him with a yearning that fastened on Helen Baird. He spent his time writing obsessively the beginning of a poem he could not complete, with variations on two lines, one version of which began: "You and your verse! O man's vanity! / To think I gave my kiss for any line!"[21]

Charlotte wants to fill existence with her creations. Her romance with Harry, never spoken of, just begins when she asks, "What to do about it, Harry?" He doesn't know: "I never was in love before." When Harry confesses to his roommate, Flint, that he knows nothing about sex but now needs to know, Flint exclaims, "You have come out, haven't you?"—as if Harry is a debutante. Flint's refusal to counsel Harry is of a piece with the novel's view of males as the secondary sex: "There aint any advice that Don Juan or Solomon either could give the youngest fourteen-year-old gal ever foaled about this kind of phenagling." Flint does say, however: "She could turn up with a bag of her own and a coat and a veil and the stub of a Pullman ticket sticking out of her handbag and that wouldn't mean she had done this before. That's just women." When Charlotte does turn up to meet Harry, she is wearing a coat but no veil because, of course, her appeal to Harry is that she has always been open to him.

Charlotte is disturbed by their flight to a tawdry hotel: "Not like this, Harry. Not back alleys. I've always said that: that no matter what happened to me, whatever I did, anything anything but not back alleys." She is speaking of illicit romance, not abortion, but it comes to the same thing since she senses they are heading toward tragedy: "But Jesus, Harry, how I have bitched it for you." Unlike Faulkner, who could not forsake a wife and child for Meta, Charlotte is prepared to abandon her children and a Catholic husband (all of them described as ordinary) even without a divorce, which he won't give her. She has taken the initiative all along, turning Harry into the "other woman."

Harry thinks conventionally, supposing that Charlotte is worried about leaving her children. With no money, Harry can offer Charlotte no support. Then he finds nearly $1,300 inside a wallet in a trash bin. It is Saturday, so Harry can't mail the money back to the address he finds in the wallet. Back in his room he tries to read and thinks: *It's all exactly backward. It should be the books, the people in the books inventing and reading about us—the Does and Roes and Wilbournes and Smiths—males and females but without the pricks or cunts.* Harry reads like the helpless Faulkner, envisioning his characters even as his characters watched him, writing what Hollywood wanted while also writing for himself, putting in the pricks and cunts in his drawings of himself and Meta, worrying about money and writing letters that sometimes come close to Harry's sense that he utterly lacks the resources to act upon his desires and that it is all *"exactly backward."*

Faulkner's typescripts and manuscripts reveal he wrote the novel as it was published, with the chapter of one story breaking in upon another like a wave about to hit shore, or like the oscillation in Faulkner's own life between Hollywood and home, Meta and Estelle, with Faulkner in rented rooms feeling utterly bereft after hours on duty as a scenarist interned in a studio instead of in Harry's hospital, sending money home to Oxford just like Harry sends two dollars to his sister. If "every time we move [in *The Wild Palms*] from one story to another, we are required to renegotiate our relationship with the text,"[22] so it may have seemed to Faulkner, having to recalibrate his reactions to Hollywood and home. Life turns into a text, and the text turns into a life.

Harry's found money is enough for him to run away with Charlotte. When Harry meets Charlotte's grieving husband at the train station, he realizes that *"they both stood now, aligned, embattled and doomed and lost, before the entire female principle."* Neither man wants to live without her, and therefore they want to do the best for one another—as Faulkner seemed to do for Wolfgang Rebner. When Meta's husband mentioned his difficulties with English and how important it was to have his advertisement in a Los Angeles newspaper well worded, Faulkner took over, making sure Rebner's copy was correct.[23] When Carvel Collins mentioned to Meta that he thought Rebner and Faulkner were "pretty good friends," she smiled, "as if this were a rather special thing," Collins noted.[24]

The *"entire female principle,"* whatever else it might mean, is an abiding awareness that life is impossible, in principle, without women, which is exactly what troubles but also ennobles Gil Martin in *Drums along the Mohawk.* He cannot conceive of going on without Lana. That both Harry and Charlotte's husband should act nobly may be one reason why reviewers called the characters improbable, but they were not by the standards of the story Faulkner had to tell, which was not about just this threesome but about the male conception of women upon which all the men in the novel comment.[25]

When the story's events occur is also important, Faulkner emphasizes. Alone, in the drawing room of the train, Charlotte faces Harry in the "scant feminine underwear of 1937." She undresses first, unknots his tie, "pushing aside his own suddenly clumsy fingers." He is, again, the woman, the virgin, who has also fumbled with the lock on their door. The scene is like none that could be filmed in 1937 on screens that dared not expose the female principle. What goes on behind a locked door can be revealed only in the novel, although because it is 1937, no graphic sexual scene follows.

The flood arrives in the next chapter to envelop the convicts just as Charlotte has been thinking about how much she loves water and how death by water would "wash out of your brain and out of your eyes and out of your blood all you ever saw and thought and felt and wanted and denied." The flood the plump convict has been reading about is upon the convicts being ferried away from the prison ground in a truck. As the road disappears in the swelling water, a convict cries out against the death by water Charlotte welcomed. They make it through the water and perch on a railroad embankment watching civilization whirl away. The water rushes backward; the train they eventually board travels backward, receding against the "liquid plain" of the flood, and the tall convict is swept backward and underneath his boat and presumed drowned—everything moving away from, not toward, a destination, just as Charlotte and Henry's train ride is a retreat from the fixed world that holds no place for them. As integral to itself as "Old Man" is within the confines of the novel, "Old Man" seems propelled by "The Wild Palms" and the retrograde force of the first chapter.

The convicts are swept up in the moment, and Charlotte does not want to see beyond the moment. It has to be "all honeymoon," she tells Harry, in a life dedicated to love. Harry is not so sure. Like the tall convict, who is reported to have been drowned, Harry is out of his element: *"Maybe I'm not embracing her but clinging to her because there is something in me that wont admit it cant swim or cant believe it can."* In Chicago, Charlotte rents a studio and in collaboration with a friend, McCord, creates what is, in effect, a Faulkner portfolio: marionettes for McCord's photographic magazine layouts. McCord functions, as Howard Hawks did, as the artist's impresario and employer. Her Quixote puppet has "a gaunt mad dreamy uncoordinated face," her gross Falstaff has the "worn face of a syphilitic barber," and her Cyrano, with his flaring nostrils, looks like a low-comedy Jew in vaudeville. These figures—all Faulkner favorites—are created in a "sustained rush of furious industry—a space of time broken not into successive days and nights but a single interval interrupted only by eating and sleeping." Her industry is not so far removed from Faulkner's rapid writing of screenplays and handling of stereotypes—like his Indian in *Drums along the Mohawk* who actually says, "How." Charlotte's exploitation of stereotypes for commercial purposes even as she sets herself apart from society is a Faulknerian sensibility. She has an aloof self-containment that Faulkner tried to maintain for himself and that he admired in Helen Baird. Charlotte earns money to fund her life of love, and as soon as the fashion season changes, her "puppet business ended"—a market swing Faulkner experienced in writing for the slicks and Hollywood.

Charlotte's art, like Faulkner's prose, is part of a world she despises but also caters to in order to survive, to keep her head above water—the cliché is inescapable. Although biographers have treated Faulkner's Hollywood sojourns as a digression, they were all of a piece with the rest of his life, just like Charlotte's Chicago marionettes: "component parts like the parts of a tableau or a puzzle, none more important than another." As a life to be lived, all of Faulkner's work all the time was in a sort of fluid suspension, even if, in retrospect, he did, of course, favor or disparage some works than others. Like Charlotte, he staved off grief with his writing, but Harry has no such option, and after losing his job, with only a hundred or so dollars left, finds refuge in a lake cabin their photographer friend McCord provides, so that Harry and Charlotte can hold out until sometime in the fall, when, as Harry puts it, he awaits "the first cold, the first red and yellow leaves drifting down, the double leaves, the reflection rising to meet the falling one until they touch and rock a little, not quite closing." To this melancholy poeticism, McCord ripostes: "For sweet Jesus Schopenhauer. . . . What the bloody hell kind of ninth-rate Teasdale is this?" The reference to Sara Teasdale (1884–1933), who committed suicide, and Schopenhauer, who wrote about suicide, is McCord's way of mocking Harry's self-destructive streak, which is premature, McCord, says, since "You haven't near done your share of starving yet. You haven't near served your apprenticeship to destitution." McCord's earlier reference to a "sea of Hemingwaves," when he is drinking with Harry and Charlotte in a bar, alludes to another Harry in "The Snows of Kilimanjaro," kept by his wealthy wife. The Hemingway-Teasdale-Schopenhauer triptych converges on Harry Wilbourne's self-defeating sulk.[26] He is a man on the verge of despair but holding it back, as Faulkner so often did, by employing, paradoxically, the language of suffering. Something about McCord—maybe it is his bluff chafing of Harry—is reminiscent of Hal Smith's bolstering of William Faulkner.[27]

In effect, McCord warns Harry against a self-pity that will lead to inauthenticity, a series of actions unworthy of the couple's striking out on their own. Charlotte is acutely aware of what McCord means. She carries with her to the lake cottage the figure of the "imbecile clown," which she calls the "bad smell" and also the "old man," which is also a name for the Mississippi and the rising waters that will engulf the tall convict. Charlotte's art is a talisman that she keeps in a cigarette-carton coffin much as Faulkner put his misery between the covers of a book so that he would not be overwhelmed. Harry knows that it is nature, not civilization, that he should attend to when he hears the cry of a loon and thinks, "how man alone of all creatures deliberately atrophies his natural senses and that only at the expense of others; how the four-legged animal gains all its information through smelling and seeing and hearing and distrusts all else while the two-legged one believes only what it reads." The "old man" is nature that we ignore at our peril. When Charlotte gives her talisman away, it is to Bradley, the departing neighbor with a predatory look who spies the old man and seems to want it, as if Bradley is their bad smell. He has brought food, but his eye has been on Charlotte. Her offering of the figure to Bradley perhaps forestalls Harry's hostility to the intruder. Sending him off with the effigy clears the air, so to speak. She calls Harry Adam as if they have re-created a prelapsarian world, having just banished the devil.

Faulkner may as well be addressing his studio bosses when he has Harry watching Charlotte undress, noting the "grave simple body a little broader, a little solider than the Hollywood-magazine cod liver oil advertisements, the bare feet padding across the rough boards, toward the screen door." The boards, the screen, the theater and cinema of their romance is exactly what Faulkner could not work on in Hollywood but does so in a book that declares his freedom to write as he likes.

So now it is Harry's turn to write pulp fiction in "one sustained frenzied agonising rush," as they depart their lakeside idyll, after their money and food run out, and return to Chicago, where Charlotte once again puppets herself for department stores. What was to be all honeymoon has become a grind and Harry just another husband—actually a housewife, taking care of the apartment as Charlotte sets off for work. As Harry tells McCord, "She's a better man than I am."

So Harry takes Charlotte west, where he works as a medical attendant in a Utah mine—once again away from civilization. As he parts from McCord—both realizing they will not see one another again—he tells McCord that McCord and Charlotte have parented him. He does not explain, but it seems that Harry has felt both love and security in their company even as he believes that he and Charlotte are doomed—that the choices are to conform or die. What has McCord done for Harry? McCord has offered employment and sometimes a place to live, but more importantly an unfettered friendship. McCord is like the Hal Smith who looked out for Faulkner and his place in the world in ways no one else would ever again be able to do in quite the same way. Smith had traveled on trains with Faulkner. They walked down teeming city streets together. Smith sent Faulkner off to Florida to recuperate and brought him back again to start anew. Smith was always *there,* like a parent, for Faulkner's send-off.

Harry's plan is to go west, like Faulkner's father wished to do, to mine what is there while it is there, as Faulkner did in Hollywood, no matter how unsatisfactory it might seem. Harry rages against a splintered, fragmented world of newspapers and radio that deters people from love—from, in effect, concentrating on themselves. Modern life is a diversion that he desperately tries to defeat by remaining constantly on the move and thinking exclusively in terms of his devotion to Charlotte. Modern life is an interruption, an invasion of self and home that Faulkner himself tried to subvert by not answering the phone and forbidding radios and phonographs in Rowan Oak. So much of life, *The Wild Palms* suggests, is a pattern of thwarted desire.

The Utah mine is accessible only by the train that takes away the ore. The freedom of location that Harry seeks is a spatial liberation that overwhelms the convict in the flood. His world is turned upside down as his boat capsizes and nearly brains him. Darryl Zanuck had doubted Faulkner knew enough about nautical terms to write a script for *The Last Slaver/Slave Ship.*[28] Well, here is an example of what Faulkner *could* do: "he [the convict] grasped the stern, the drag of his body becoming a rudder to the skiff, the two of them, man and boat and with the paddle perpendicular above them like a jackstaff." The convict grabs at the gunwale of the boat as it spins away from him. Then floored to the bottom of the boat by another spin, the convict sees nothing, and then hears a voice, coming from a pregnant women up in a tree, telling him it was about time he has returned—a perplexing comment to a man who did not think of himself as going anywhere in particular. But she has been high enough to get a perspective on his struggle. She was the woman he was sent to save. At this late date in his life, the convict, an innocent without sexual experience is, like Harry, confounded by his predicament. But perhaps his reading of the "pulp-printed fables," like those penned by Harry ten years later, has prepared the convict: "who to say what Helen, what living Garbo, he had not dreamed of rescuing from what craggy pinnacle." Reality offers him yet another rebuke when he realizes she is pregnant: *"And this is what I get. This, out of all the female meat that walks, is what I have to be caught in a runaway boat with."* Relieved of his imprisonment, the convict nevertheless yearns to return to the world of "shotguns and shackles," since the very idea of accompanying this woman, close to giving birth, disgusts him.

The flooding river obliterates landmarks and geography itself as the skiff flows over everything—dead animals, houses, even bridges—and past the debris of civilization as the couple cling to life, to the elemental properties of existence that Harry and Charlotte would like to think of as sufficient for their love. By contrast, the convict longs to rid himself of the woman on a piece of level ground where she can give birth, so that he can return to the barracks, the fields he plows, the friends, the prison food in the one place he feels secure, the location to which he is fixed, the very point of existence that Harry and Charlotte try to desert. The last thing the convict wants, he declares, is to escape.

In the swelling water time seems anachronic as the convict is swept backward and forward in profound disorientation, suspended between possibilities limited only by his refusal to let go of the woman, his mission given to him by a prison authority, just as Harry won't let go of Charlotte, his self-authorized love. This part of the story is retold back in prison, making the convict's experience a fairy tale destined for, in his terms, a happy ending, even though in the telling his efforts to reach safe ground are repeatedly foiled—first by an outlaw couple who want nothing to do with a convict they would have to turn in to the police along with the pregnant woman, and then by men shooting at him as if he is an escapee. Like Harry, he feels himself doomed, a refugee. As the convict finally strikes firm ground and is catapulted onto shore, the woman gives birth, and time resumes its relentless course into the novel's next chapter.

At the mine, Harry and Charlotte meet the brash and voluble Billie, a part Faulkner could have written for Marie Dressler, Wallace Beery's better half, here outfitted with the name Buck. Billie is the perfect name for a whore, Charlotte chips in, sounding like a Hollywood pre-Code tough talker. Then they are escorted to their cabin by a giant Pole—a good role for Beery—friendly but without any English to help explain their setup. Soon they learn from Buck that they will be cold all the time, no matter what they do, just as the convict remains wet. That Faulkner had film in mind is apparent when Harry sees the mine for the first time, "something out of an Eisenstein Dante." Faulkner would have seen Eisenstein's drawings for *Sutter's Gold* accompanying the screen treatment. Harry sees the equivalent of a Hollywood soundstage: a "small amphitheatre, branching off in smaller galleries like the spread fingers from a palm, lighted by an incredible extravagance of electricity as though for a festival—an extravagance of dirty bulbs." Eisenstein had left Hollywood after a tryout with movie mogul William Fox, finding American cinema an uncongenial environment for the kind of vision Faulkner presents in this mine, abandoned by its Chinese and Italian workers, and now manned by Poles alone, who think they are working for overtime pay, even though no payroll has been issued for months, which is why the other workers left. The mines, the world of *Sutter's Gold,* and even the wording of Eisenstein's treatment—"the sounds of the picks" echo in Harry's imagining of the frenzied miners with their "picks and shovels."

Buck says the "chinks" and the "wops . . . smelled it"—that they were working for nothing. "Like niggers," Harry responds. All along, "niggers" have been used as a baseline. Harry and Charlotte sleep in a "bed in which his [the doctor's] wife said she would not ask a nigger servant to sleep." Charlotte does not want Harry to carry his own bag after their meeting in a hotel for that "nigger to snigger at." Harry imagines himself "draw[ing] the old routine up over my head and face like niggers do the quilt when they go to bed." One of the flood refugees complains: "I saw that launch and them boats come up and they never had no room for me. Full of bastard niggers and one of them setting there playing a guitar but there wasn't no room for me." The very definition of demeaning routine and the lowest position is "nigger," yet "niggers" have a cunning understanding of exploitation and diminished status. For Harry, as for Faulkner, the world was not comprehensible without the "nigger" category, a standard by which to measure one's place in the world, a place that for Harry is always precarious, which is why he has "niggers" on his mind. In prison, the inmates read of a kind of forced integration, obliterating the fixed social/political coordinates of their world: "conscripted levee gangs, mixed blacks and whites working in double shifts against the steadily rising water."

Harry is there, Buck tells him, mainly to satisfy mine inspectors who require that a doctor be available to workers. But why does Buck stay?, Harry wants to know. Billie is pregnant, and they can't afford a child, and Buck is hoping that for a hundred dollars Harry will perform an abortion, although the word is never used. Harry refuses, even when the fee is raised by another fifty dollars. Out of his element, like the tall convict, Harry wants no further entanglements. Harry tells Charlotte he refuses to do the operation not out of fear or offense at the money offered, but she does not press him for an explanation. So why does Harry hold back? It seems that an abortion is what he has been taught a doctor ought not to do. He thinks in terms of his training and not in the terms of this particular couple, just as the convict does not think of that particular pregnant woman but of the unarticulated principle that a life should be preserved, no matter the cost to him. The two couples, Buck and Billie, Harry and Charlotte, sleep in the same room, not fifteen feet apart, and then with mattresses together when it becomes even colder (41 degrees below zero). It is as if they are in the same boat surrounded by the drenching wet of "Old Man." Charlotte convinces Harry to perform the abortion for the departing couple, asking him to imagine themselves in the same predicament, implying that Harry would do it for love, even if, in this case, it is not for their love.

Now with only the food in the commissary to last them until spring, Harry becomes, in effect, the "white man": "another representative of that remote golden unchallengeable Power in which they [the Poles] held blind faith and trust." It is a curious place, this site of "frenzied and unabated work" Faulkner invents, the mine a production unit with a commissary in a nonunionized industry. Meta could never get him to talk about politics, and politics per se is not the issue here, and yet the consequences of working and living for yourself alone are devastating. Harry and Charlotte have one another, but their bodies never generate quite enough heat. Harry thinks the Poles are happy living on an illusion, but are they so different from Harry and Charlotte? She creates her own moving pictures with crayons on paper tacked to commissary shelves, explaining in several scenes what has happened to the now comprehending Poles, who take the rest of the supplies.

Then Charlotte becomes pregnant, having used no protection since her douche bag froze and burst. Harry reacts like the convict, disgusted that all of his life had led to this point: *"And this is the price of the twenty-six years, the two thousand dollars I stretched over four of them by not smoking, by keeping my virginity until it damn near spoiled on me."* To Charlotte, however, this abortion is a logical outcome of their passion, her unwavering allegiance to the love principle making her once again, in Harry's words, a *"better man and a better gentleman than I am, she is a better everything than I will ever be."*

Harry and Charlotte travel through the West from Utah, a year since their departure from New Orleans, heading south again displaced against a memory of the film world that Faulkner could not quite leave behind: "the lunch rooms with broad strong Western girls got up out of Hollywood magazines (Hollywood which is no longer in Hollywood but is stippled by a billion feet of burning colored gas across the face of the American earth) to resemble Joan Crawford, asleep or not he could not tell." How many stories, including

Drums along the Mohawk, ended with "love conquers all"—a foregone conclusion with stars such as Claudette Colbert, not to mention Joan Crawford? It has often been said that Faulkner wrote only one story about Hollywood, "Golden Land," but this is clearly not the case, since Hollywood was on the frontier, in Chicago, Utah, along the Mississippi—unavoidably everywhere.

The Production Code that forbid the treatment of abortion reflected a society that withheld certain kinds of knowledge even from medical professionals like Harry. His desperation is measured by his resort to a San Antonio brothel, where he hopes to obtain a pill that will end Charlotte's pregnancy since he does not want to do the procedure himself. The madam, who misunderstands Harry's mission, offers a Spanish girl: "It's the influence of the moving pictures, I always say," apparently alluding to the white appetite for the exotic and the off-color. But he is thrown out since his request has brought the brothel into disrepute! The five pills he purchases for five dollars in a pharmacy and a night of drinking and dancing fail to induce a miscarriage. The very thought of having or giving away Harry's child hurts too much, Charlotte tells him. At the start of her fourth month, to a trembling Harry, instrument in hand, she tries to soothe him: "What was it you told me nigger women say? Ride me down, Harry." Harry botches the abortion, and she weakens from loss of blood and infection, fearing the worst and yet refusing treatment, because she knows that Harry will go to prison, and she will lose him, although the understanding between them is never put into words. She says good-bye to her husband and children as Harry, sitting on a Jackson Park bench in New Orleans, imagines the scene of her fatal farewell, sealed off from her family as firmly as Harry parted from McCord.

The compounding irony of the novel is the convict's delivery of a child done in ignorant dedication at the woman's commands, gathering together the basic implements (a tin can he uses to cut the umbilical cord) and warm water. He watches the woman wash the baby in the water he has heated with matches. On the dreaded Mississippi he has reenacted his entrance into a world he cannot, even yet, locate: *"And this is all. This is what severed me violently from all I ever knew and did not wish to leave and cast me upon a medium I was born to fear, to fetch up at last in a place I never saw before and where I do not even know where I am."* Even so, he is reborn.

The woman and baby and profusely bleeding convict are picked up by a steamboat full of refugees, attended by a doctor who tells the convict he is a hemophiliac, which in the convict's prison tale strikes the plump convict as insulting, since he mixes up the word with hermaphroditic, a comic misunderstanding that emphasizes the convict's female midwife's role. The doctor has the convict inhale a phial with an ammoniac smell that stanches the blood. When Charlotte's hemorrhage stops in the previous chapter, she regards it as an ominous sign, while Harry decides to seek refuge on the same Mississippi coast where the convict debarks after he learns the boat is going to New Orleans, not anywhere near Parchman. On a land again that he does not recognize, he is taken in by a wiry old man, a Cajun, who gives the woman and baby refuge in his river shack and takes the convict along on alligator hunts, a thrashing wild-eyed sort of struggle that is nothing like the Al Jackson tall-tale spoofs confected so long ago in New Orleans. The rapport between the Cajun and the convict is described in words that also apply to the convict and woman he has rescued: "two people who could not even talk to one another made an agreement which both not only understood but which each knew the other would hold true and protect (perhaps for this reason) better than any written and witnessed contract." The convict hardly ever talks to the woman, and even less with the Cajun, whose language he does not understand, and yet they are all bound together more closely than Sherwood Anderson and William Faulkner ever were with all their talk about swamp creatures. The Cajun-convict pair bond and divide up their hunting, arranging it in bastard English and French, like "two members of a corporation facing each other across a mahogany board table," or like the division of labor at a writers' conference in Hollywood, lasting, in this case, ten days until the Cajun departs because, as the convict soon learns, when a launch picks up his party and his boat, a levee is about to be dynamited that will drown them all if they do not move out, which they do, setting the convict on dry land once again, where he delivers the woman he was charged with rescuing to a deputy.

A life saved and one taken: "You have murdered her," the outraged doctor tells Harry, who has dared to experience "this bright wild passion which had somehow passed him [the doctor] up when he had been young enough, worthy enough, and to whose loss he believed he had not only become reconciled but had been both fortunate and right in having been elected to lose." Harry waits for the ambulance and the police to arrive, thinking *"I have made a bust even of that part of my life which I threw away."* No last-minute Hollywood redemption is possible in those final ten minutes of a film when a reversal of fortune is required. Harry and Charlotte have run away from everything except the responsibility for what they have done to themselves.

A remarkable moment occurs when Faulkner tracks back all the way to his childhood as Harry tries to "remember something out of a book, years ago, of Owen Wister the whore in the pink ball dress who drank the laudanum and the cowboys taking turns walking her up and down the floor, keeping her on her feet, keeping her alive, remembering and forgetting it in the same instant since it would not help him." Why it doesn't help is not disclosed, but

in the Wister novel, *Lin McLean* (1897), the whore, a strong woman, succumbs, outside the boundaries of respectability but supported by the men she
has serviced. All the doctor's wife cares about is that Charlotte be removed,
walked out of her proper cottage by whatever means necessary.

Harry accompanies Charlotte to the hospital, expecting to be handcuffed
but instead is treated kindly and allowed to view her body after the unsuccessful operation. He has never intended to leave her, not even when her husband
arrives and posts bail. Like the convict he seeks incarceration, utterly incapable of pursuing a larger life without Charlotte. From his cell he looks at the
concrete hull of a 1918 emergency ship and thinks of the war and *"the waste.
Not of meat, there is always plenty of meat. They found that out twenty years ago
preserving nations and justifying mottoes—granted the nations the meat preserved are worth the preserving with the meat it took gone."* Mottoes? Saving the
world for democracy? It doesn't seem as if the world can be saved, so far as
Harry is concerned. And he does not want to save himself. After Charlotte's
husband makes a plea to the judge for mercy—all for Charlotte's sake—he
visits Harry's cell and offers him a cyanide pill. But Harry does not see how
his suicide will help. It is her memory that keeps him alive and that alone is
worth his living. He remembers her "body, the broad thighs and the hands
that liked bitching and making things," as Faulkner made things for Meta
in those drawings of their lovemaking. And he will remember right into old
age: "memory could live in the old wheezing entrails: and now it did stand to
his hand, incontrovertible and plain, serene, the palm clashing and murmuring dry and wild and faint"—words that echo their passion and stimulate his
erection as he remembers her.[29] *"So it is the old meat after all, no matter how
old,"* he realizes. But more than the physical sensation, the body that is no
longer, is the passion of memory. Or as he puts it in his last words, *"Between
grief and nothing I will take grief."*

The novel's final chapter is a coda, a tale of how the convict made his way
back to prison, forsaking various opportunities to remain free, thinking not
only of the woman in tow but also the sweetheart who had abandoned him
while in prison. Although his plump, voluble sidekick thinks it a terrible blow
to have ten years added to the tall convict's sentence (he has been declared an
escapee) just to satisfy authorities who would otherwise have to free him since
he had been pronounced dead, the tall convict accepts his sentence, clearly
relieved that he does not have to live in a world that includes females who
have given him so much grief. Or, as he puts it in his final words, "Women,
shit." He does not want to escape his fate any more than Harry does in his cell.
It may seem odd to say, but both the convict and Harry are gentlemen, accepting the consequences of their actions and taking their punishment without

whining or exculpation. They never think of themselves in chivalric terms, and yet they are far nobler, in Faulkner's world, than those Hollywood heroes he had to confect. Occasionally Harry and the convict give way to self-pity, as did their author, but in the main they shoulder an individual responsibility as tenacious and supple as Faulkner's own. They also join their author insofar as the convict's sentence terminates in 1937, the year Faulkner began writing the novel and Harry enters prison.

The symmetrical ironies of "The Wild Palms" and "Old Man" are tragicomic when they are not farcical. Life floods through this novel as it is never permitted to do in movies, as one story floods or spills over into another, and the novel replicates the Mississippi, "doubling back upon itself over and over as it moves south."[30] A flood almost wrecks the family home in *Banjo on My Knee,* but it is preserved by landing on a sandbar not long after Faulkner is taken off the picture. Neither Hollywood nor the rest of the world is built to comprehend stories such as Harry and Charlotte's, let alone the tall convict's. His fellow prisoners presume he would enjoy the company of women after having been deprived of them for so long. The doctor can only think of Harry as a murderer. No one, except perhaps Charlotte's husband, has any idea of the dimensions of the story. This is a novel that humbles the world it depicts, a world of limited imagination. This is the world as lockup, which is why Harry has no place to go, no other life to begin anew. Prison is exile for both Harry and the convict, the exile Faulkner alluded to in his original title, *If I Forget Thee, Jerusalem,* taken from the 137th Psalm. Harry will not forget, and the price of not forgetting is his exile. And in his own way, the convict comes to the same understanding: There is no way for him to just be—to live—outside of prison.

The Wild Palms is ultimately the work of a writer who felt similarly trapped by conventional plotlines and pieties, in Hollywood and Oxford, and overcame his incarceration by writing about it and also by drawing his way out of his separation from Meta in eight pages of erotic line drawings that testify to the consubstantiality of the flesh—at least in his art.[31] In pose after pose, in vertical, horizontal, and diagonal entanglements, the lines of their bodies flow together and converge, atop one another, side by side, elevated, and on their knees, his penis entering her vulva or her mouth always as an integral culmination of their movements together as he buries his head in her vulva, girdled between her legs. He takes her from behind; she grabs his penis; her legs encircle his midsection; he holds her up on his shaft. Some of the action is acrobatic, with Meta's legs lifted to his shoulders as her body descends on his member. Faulkner only outlined their faces. They kiss but do not talk. They perform. The drawings are about the dynamism of this inseparable duo. The epigraph to *A Loving Gentleman* are lines from *A Green Bough:* "A singing fire that spun / The gusty tree of his desire / till tree and gale were one." Meta reported that he said to her, "it's always this way with you—with you and no one else." Twenty-four different drawings are displayed, sometimes three to a page in frames or panels that make up a sequence that has an ending: Faulkner is prone, his hand between Meta's thighs as she sits on his chest, her back to him as she holds his flaccid penis with the caption: "THAT'S ALL."[32] The drawings, like film frames, are full of medium, long, and close-up shots, from low and high angles. On these pages, they could watch the story boards, the cinema of their love.

5

Up from Feudalism

The Hamlet, 1938–1940

EXILE AND EXHAUSTION

The haunting image of Harry in his cell also depicted the prison house of William Faulkner in exile. He did not want to forget Helen Baird or Meta Carpenter. While working on *The Wild Palms,* he vacationed with his family in Pascagoula. And he met with Meta Carpenter and her husband in New York. Rebner was no more jealous of Faulkner than Charlotte Rittenmeyer's husband had been of Harry. Faulkner and Rebner got along just fine in the company of the woman they both loved, apparently saying as little about their feelings as the characters do in "The Wild Palms." Meta watched Faulkner responding to Rebner's erudition, even conversing in French, yet she recalled his "great mournful gaze" and "eyes burning into mine." After this meeting he succumbed to the alcoholic binge that resulted in his passing out and burning himself so badly on a hotel radiator. Sometimes it was no better at home. During this period one of Faulkner's fraternity brothers and his wife visited Rowan Oak, and Jill greeted them at the door, saying that "if we could step over 'Papa' and come into the Parlour 'Mamma' was looking for us. Bill was asleep (drunk) in the main hall." Children of alcoholics grow up treating such episodes as a way of life, only later realizing the import of their upbringing.[1]

Faulkner and Meta would meet several times between 1938 and 1939 in New York City, sometimes alone and sometimes with her husband, who was attempting to establish himself as a concert pianist in the United States. As a Jew he could no longer perform safely in Germany or, soon, in Nazi-occupied Europe. Through Rebner and Meta, Faulkner met many exiles from fascist Europe. In May 1938, he joined more than four hundred other writers in reacting to the Spanish Civil War: "I most sincerely wish to go on record as being unalterably opposed to Franco and fascism, to all violations of the legal government and outrages against the people of Republican Spain."[2] The following October he wrote to journalist Vincent Sheean, offering the manuscript of *Absalom, Absalom!* as a contribution to the Spanish loyalist government. He would later create an antifascist character, the redoubtable Linda Snopes.

The Rebners struggled to support themselves, and Faulkner sent Meta money and introduced Rebner to influential friends such as Hal Smith and Bennett Cerf.[3] A downcast Meta, feeling her marriage under strain, remembered Faulkner admonishing her: "Buck up, Carpenter. I've never seen you like this." His rebuke hurt, she confessed, since unlike her own hypercritical husband, Faulkner had always been so supportive and curious about her inner life.

Faulkner's marriage to Estelle was no better, he confided to Meta. If he did not choose to run away from it, he did arrange a romantic rendezvous with Meta in New Orleans, where he wanted her to stay, where he pinned gardenias to her pillow and ministered to her feverish rundown condition. But she returned to Rebner, making the choice that Charlotte Rittenmeyer had resolutely rejected. Faulkner, too, returned home. Life was not, after all, a Faulkner novel.

Sometimes he made the best of it at Rowan Oak, enjoying special occasions and holidays and dressing up for parties. Random House was a second home, providing him with advances that were never enough, given his appetite for land and also his generous loans to Phil Stone, burdened by paying off his father's debts. Saxe Commins, now Faulkner's editor, revered him and catered to his needs, housing Faulkner during dipsomaniac periods and also indulging the author's idiosyncrasies. Asked by the president of Harvard what he did, Saxe said, "cleaning and repairing."[4] Sometimes Greenfield Farm settled him, although Bill did not get along that well with his brother John, who felt like a secondhand Faulkner, never receiving his elder brother's praise for the farmwork or encouragement with his writing.

THE RISE OF THE REDNECK

For the first time, Faulkner began to say he might be written out. When he said as much to Phil Stone, no longer as close to Faulkner or as sure of his genius, Stone advised returning to the long-delayed Snopes saga, which had first been conceived in the mid-1920s.[5] Perhaps finally getting down on paper all those Snopes stories he had been telling for years marked a return to first principles, a regrounding in the land displaced by the upheavals of Hollywood that had infiltrated the composition of *The Wild Palms.* Even so, Faulkner had taken his oral history of the Snopes saga to Hollywood, regaling fellow writers with the clan's exploits. Joel Sayre said Faulkner always had more stories to tell—more, even, than Sayre ever found in his friend's books.[6]

In a letter to Robert Haas, written in mid-December 1938, Faulkner outlined the Snopes trilogy, which would take him more than two decades to complete. He had a running start on the first part, to which he gave a Balzacian title, "The Peasants," with three short stories he had already published. Flem Snopes, first seen in *Father Abraham,* dominated the story, rising from the village Frenchman's Bend to a "foothold in Jefferson," forty miles from his origins. The second volume, "Rus in Urbe" (country in the city), traced Flem's trajectory from his rusticity to part ownership of a "back street restaurant" to a bank presidency. The third volume, "Ilium Falling," suggested the grand finale to this provincial epic: the Snopes invasion and conquering of Jefferson (Troy), displacing the aristocratic Sartorises and corrupting local government with "crooked politics" while subdividing the land.

This was *the* story, the "rise of the redneck," that Stone had been urging Faulkner to write all along. And while Faulkner never abandoned this saga of rapacity, it had taken him a good fifteen years to put even part of it down on the page, a time during which Stone wondered why the Snopeses remained on the margins of Faulkner's major work. So what had changed? Why was Faulkner now, suddenly, animated to project this tripartite tale, providing a detailed treatment for his editor, as he would for a Hollywood studio? Although, as always, he needed money—the farm was not really a paying proposition, and he had so many dependents—all he could think about was his novel. *The Wild Palms* had become Faulkner's best-selling novel, but it was hardly a bestseller, and he had turned away from Hollywood as a quick source of revenue.

On March 17, Haas received a letter from Faulkner admitting, "I tried last month to put the novel aside and hammer out a pot-boiler story to meet this [insurance] premium with, but I failed, either the novel is too hot in my mind or I failed to keep from stewing over having to make a home run in one lick, to cook up a yarn."[7] On March 22, Faulkner cashed in an insurance policy and asked for another advance from Haas so that he could relieve the pressure on Stone over a lawsuit demanding payment of a seven-thousand-dollar note. Stone's troubles, in other words, had become Faulkner's, just as the depredations of Snopesism had always been their joint enterprise. By March 29, Faulkner had three thousand dollars from Haas, telling him that the novel would be on the way soon to Random House and that he had "enough stories to make another volume. What do you think about it?" The urgency to produce the grand design of the trilogy (perhaps, in part, as a way of extracting a larger advance) and Stone's pressing need for money, coupled with Faulkner's renewed sense of the origins of his turn to prose and to his native soil, had converged. It was now or never to make good on the promise made to Phil Stone and to himself at the conception of the Yoknapatawpha chronicle.

To a reporter in April, Faulkner revealed yet another way of looking at the trilogy—as an implicit comment on modern America: "The South seems to be the only place in the country that is interested in art these days.... Maybe it's because the North is more industrialized than we are. Maybe in 80 years we'll be as highly industrialized and we'll quit turning out art." Oxford at the turn of the century was not Frenchman's Bend, but even so there might be something in the surmise that *The Hamlet* "mythologizes Faulkner's childhood in the self-contained South at the turn of the century."[8] The novel approaches the classic perspective of the pastoral poet, presenting a rural, even retrograde movement, a flowing back to natural sources like the convict swept back by the mighty Mississippi. If Faulkner felt impelled to continue the Snopes saga, perhaps it is because he found himself in another place, mentally and physically. In 1931, during that writers' conference in Virginia, he had said: "The South? Nothing of any real value is likely to come out of it in the next twenty-five years at least."[9] Now the velocity of change made it increasingly impossible to regard his heritage as stable or permanent.

Literary life was more likely to be rejuvenated by a "Keats coming out of the backwoods," declared the 1939 Faulkner. He scoffed at the writers in the French Quarter, declaring that the "fellows who are going places are too busy working to sit around and talk about it." The need to boil the pot had delayed the writing of the trilogy about "a poor white who comes to a little Southern town and teaches the populace corruption in government and..." Apparently he did not finish his sentence. Six months later, at the Plaza Hotel in New York City, he appeared to a *New York Post* reporter as a tweedy English country squire until he began to speak, drawling out his Snopes stories, including one that would not make it into print until *The Town* (1957). He described the family as creeping over Jefferson like "mold over cheese and destroying its tradition and whatever lav'liness there was in the place."

"The Peasants," retitled *The Hamlet,* published on April 1, 1940, neither advanced nor detracted from Faulkner's formidable reputation. Many reviewers had difficulty reconciling regionalist realism with a romanticism that went beyond the bounds of the decorum and structure expected in fiction, and that Faulkner had flouted—most recently in *The Wild Palms.* In general, they picked apart the novel, praising the rise of Flem Snopes as though Faulkner were writing *The Rise of Silas Lapham* (*Chicago Daily News*, April 3), and deplored the reverie of Ike Snopes, "a mindless imbecile" in love with a cow: "Why, but for the gratification of the author's perverted judgment, should any reader endeavor to interest himself for 60 pages in a minute description of a gruesome creature who grovels habitually in filth?" (*Cleveland Plain Dealer*, April 14). Eva Lou Walton in *New Masses* (April 16) found that same Ike Snopes interlude unforgettable: "sheer primitive myth—apocalyptic poetry, too." She also grasped the importance of the most outrageous episodes, like the spotted horses and their mad frenzied race through barns, bridges, and even houses. This exciting and symbolic episode counterpointed the lives of most men "caught in part by their own stupidity, in part by poverty." In the *Santa Barbara News-Press* (May 6) Maurice Swan acknowledged Faulkner's "sheer genius to ignite images that cut open new worlds upon our sensibilities." The reviewer understood the unities of the novel, the contrast between Flem and Ike, the former with the "bow-tie [that] gives the neck decorum, the neck through which the cells in the cortex shape schemes to tangle people into harness by the immutable civil laws of man," and the latter a "seminal stream" of "unbridled sex of the unconfirmed, untutored virgin." Eula, the voluptuous daughter of Will Varner, is sold to Flem "like a cow," Swan notes. She is the Venus of a myth brought to earth, "wrangled and mangled by money and sex."

That Faulkner operated within traditions of the tall tale and frontier humor seems to have escaped most reviewers, although George Marion O'Donnell applied a corrective in the *Nashville Banner* (August 21). He focused on Ratliff, a sewing machine salesman, as the principal narrator. Neither a Snopes nor a Sartoris, he stands between, the reviewer observed, in the middle and able to mediate between two extremes, a "village custodian."[10]

A dismissive reviewer in the *Times Literary Supplement* (September 24) referred to Flem as Faulkner's "lunatic marionette of a hero," unwittingly pointing to exactly what makes the character so powerful in his string-pulling monomania to make money and get ahead. "He moves them around like puppets," observed William J. Walters Jr. in the *Central New Jersey Home News* (April 7), admiring the novelist's energy and perhaps realizing how the characters' vitality depends on endowing them with only a narrow range of animating features. Flem is Ike's denatured opposite. As Robert Penn Warren explained in the *Kenyon Review* (Spring 1941), "The structure of the book depends on the intricate patterning of contrasts," a method carried over from *The Wild Palms*. But Warren remained in the minority. Most reviewers, like Desmond Hawkins in *John O'London's Weekly* (September 20), could find no "structural purpose" in the novel. *The Hamlet* utterly baffled George Orwell

(*Time and Tide,* November 9). "Disjointed" but "fantastic and compelling," Wallace Stegner concluded in the *Virginia Quarterly Review* (Summer 1940).

In *College English* (May 1941), Warren Beck rebuked the legion of reviewers who had deplored Faulkner as amoral, immoral, melodramatic, incoherent, and sensationalistic. "A virile critical approach will first recognize the coherent rationality and humanity of Faulkner's point of view." That so many did not suggests how unprepared for war they were, how blinded they chose to be when they gibbered about Faulkner's "nihilism," Beck concluded: "Such ostrich tactics become increasingly ridiculous in a world where a recrudescence of irrationality and brutal passions have pointed up for even the most impercipient those melancholy facts about human nature and progress which Faulkner has confronted all along and has unequivocally attacked." In short, Faulkner could see it coming, the fascism that would engulf the world, and that his own fiction, a new kind of history, had done so much to expose.

"Flem"

In book 1, "Flem," the first paragraph corresponds to the map of Faulkner's domain that had become fixed in the minds of his regular readers. No previous passage had been quite so close in spirit to Scott's Waverley novels that had done so much, Mark Twain contended, to shape the South's own sense of itself:

> Frenchman's Bend was a section of rich river-bottom country lying twenty miles southeast of Jefferson. Hill-cradled and remote, definite yet without boundaries, straddling into two counties and owning allegiance to neither, it had been the original grant and site of a tremendous pre-Civil War plantation, the ruins of which—the gutted shell of an enormous house with its fallen stables and slave quarters and overgrown gardens and brick terraces and promenades—were still known as the Old Frenchman place, although the original boundaries now existed only on old faded records in the Chancery Clerk's office in the county court house in Jefferson, and even some of the once-fertile fields had long since reverted to the cane-and-cypress jungle from which their first master had hewed them.

Like Scott, Faulkner situates his story in the recent past—in the late nineteenth/early twentieth century in a pocket of the past, and from a pastoral point of view among ruins that the Romantics found so evocative. Decaying plantation grandeur, the traces of something that had once been "tremendous," is now a relic with remains retrievable only in "old faded records," themselves a sign of a culture reverting to its primitive state. Civilization has come and gone in this Babylon, once the preserve of oppressors, leaving no trace of their power and oppression except for "fallen stables and slave quarters."

Into this indeterminate territory, lacking exact boundaries, a foreign Ozymandias built his establishment, and its decayed remnant is now ruled by Will Varner, who has bought up the land from Jefferson bankers and presides over the remnants—the "walnut newel posts and stair spindles, oak floors which fifty years later would have been almost priceless"—and the legend of a buried treasure. "Somebody is always digging for treasure since the Civil War," John Cullen told scholar Floyd Watkins.[11] In the novel, the past is prologue to a new rapacious generation—not yet announced in the narrative—and its leader, Flem Snopes. Varner is the landlord and the law of this land, a shopkeeper, mill owner, justice of the peace, and election commissioner. The ballots are stuffed his way. He lends money and tends to animals, a veterinarian as well. No one gins cotton or grinds meal outside of Varner's regime. He sits, apparently indolent, watching the Old Frenchman place, wondering why any man would need such a colossal residence just to sleep and eat in. It dismays Varner that the Old Frenchman place is the only property he has never been able to sell and that people have tired of dismantling.

Will Varner rules more like a feudal lord than a capitalist. While he drives a hard bargain and has the consolidating mentality of a capitalist, he also has a warmth and genuine interest in his fellows that is absent in the man who will become his business partner: Flem Snopes. Will is neighborly, humorous, insightful, and a student of human nature. He may exploit people, but he has some sense of community and obligation to others as well. He even inspires respect, or at least deference, among those beholden to him and to whom they must account.

Faulkner understood this sort of man very well because he had done business with him. Will Bryant had sold to William Faulkner a modest version of the Old Frenchman place. He had been patient in extending the terms of repayment and had taken an interest in Faulkner's writing. Faulkner, in turn, enjoyed not only talking with Will Bryant about Indians and the history of their region, he felt beholden and accountable to this landlord. In letter after letter addressed to "Mr Bryant" and later "Mr Will" and "Miss Sallie," Faulkner gave an accounting of himself to a couple who addressed him as "William" or "William Faulkner," never Bill. On September 2, 1939, for example, Faulkner explained that he was "short of cash" and could not pay the installment due that month because of an additional assessment of his 1937 taxes: "Is it convenient to allow me some more time on this next payment." He wanted an extension to January 1, 1940. The same letter includes two columns of eleven handwritten dates and amounts paid to the Bryants.[12] The meticulousness of these letters, their author's mixing of business and pleasure, and his unvarying deference to the Bryants were reciprocated in their tolerant and even generous responses to his pleas for more time to settle his debts. They represented, in short, the very world that Flem Snopes dismantles piece by piece.

The dreams of the past that the Old Frenchman place represents are dead. New wealth will be generated some other way—and not by Jody Varner, the ninth of Will's sixteen children, who oversees the family operation. He is the epitome of the "masculine Singular" gone to flab. His incompetence is "a nuisance in the operation of Varner's businesses but to the Varner legacy Jody is a threat."[13] Jody's malfeasance will provide an opportunity for Flem. Jody initiates his debacle by supposing he can shortchange Flem's father, Ab Snopes, holding Ab's reputation as barn burner over him, since Snopes has engaged to work Varner's farm so late in the season and will have nowhere else to go. But Ratliff, who has followed Snopes's history, explains how much trouble Snopes caused his previous landlord, Major de Spain, ruining an expensive rug by walking on it with manure-laden boots, then ruining it again by having it harshly cleaned, then suing De Spain and finally burning down his barn—although De Spain could not prove arson. In short, Ab Snopes thwarts the traditional sharecropping system that is supposed to keep men like him in thrall. This is the first sign that doing business as usual will no longer be possible now that Ab and his family have arrived. They are as unpredictable as the wild spotted horses Flem brings from Texas in what is the founding event of the Snopes trilogy established in *Father Abraham.* The unruly horses are an import upsetting the community's way of doing business and establishing an economy that no longer can be controlled by the old school Varners, a family that depended on the deference and cooperation of peasants (Faulkner's original title for the novel). Creating a market with those unbroken horses sets up a competitive, subversive dynamic that diminishes the very idea of privilege that the Varners have perpetuated.

Jody Varner, now scared of what Ab will do, rides out to the Snopes farm to assuage Ab: "just send me word and I'll ride right up here as quick as I can get here. You understand? Anything, just anything you dont like—." Ab declares his truculent independence: "I been getting along with fifteen or twenty different landlords since I started farming. When I cant get along with them, I leave. That all you wanted?" Ab is immovable, except when he wants to move. On his return home, Varner looks at the contract he had made with Snopes and thinks it "must have occurred in another time"—exactly so, since Snopes is the new dispensation.

Historical change, mainly the subject of fascinating asides in *Flags in the Dust,* flashbacks in *Light in August,* a murky subtext in *Absalom, Absalom!*

that suddenly emerges in Shreve's prediction of the future, now becomes the dominant narrative that will pick up apace in *Go Down, Moses, Intruder in the Dust,* and *Requiem for a Nun.* *The Hamlet* is at the forefront of this new kind of history, which is no longer the subtext as in *The Sound and the Fury,* where Jason fulminates about an unpredictable commodity market, and *Sanctuary,* where Popeye's predations occur on the grounds of a ruined plantation. Characters like Jody Varner and Ratliff see change coming and comment on it as the shaping force of their lives.

Ratliff, in particular, embodies the neoteric phase of Faulkner's fiction that continues all the way to *The Reivers.* Whatever Ratliff's limitations and misperceptions, his temptations and renunciations, he follows a moral compass, fitfully and imperfectly, but without the preconceptions of a Horace Benbow or Gavin Stevens, his competitors in working out an ethical approach to the developing history of Yoknapatawpha. Ratliff is tenacious, if not always successful, in his opposition to Flem Snopes, who represents a "devastating threat to principled existence that cannot go unchallenged by men committed to justice and equity in human affairs."[14]

Flem's first appearance in the novel signals how history is about to change. Jody Varner has only seen Flem through the window of Ab's house, and now meets him in a scene typical of Flem's ability to waylay his marks while apparently doing nothing: "One moment the road had been empty, the next moment the man stood there beside it, at the edge of a small copse—the same cloth cap, the same rhythmically chewing jaw materialised apparently out of nothing and almost abreast of the horse, with an air of the complete and purely accidental which Varner was to remember and speculate about only later." Even the shrewdest observers, like Ratliff, have to catch up with Flem, who appears and acts before they can spot or deter him. Flem has a broad flat face and eyes the "color of stagnant water." If he is not as menacing as Popeye, he is just as inhuman and mechanical—the marionette that one reviewer complained about. Flem gives nothing away: "His face was as blank as a pan of uncooked dough." Varner has to do all the talking, trying to smooth things over with the Snopeses. Like Ab, the monosyllabic Flem does not carry the conversation forward. To Varner's allusion to the family's moving around and its dissatisfactions, Flem remarks, "There's a right smart of country." That sounds innocuous, but it can be interpreted as a warning: Everything is available and all of it can be a Snopes business. Flem, in other words, cedes no ground and acknowledges no fiefdoms. Varner tries to buy Flem off with the offer of more farmland. But Flem finds "no benefit in farming. I figure on getting out of it as soon as I can." Flem then breaks through Varner's palaver with a question, "You own a store, don't you?" It doesn't take

Varner long to understand that Flem wants to be a store clerk, a job he has secured without having to ask for it. By the end of the first chapter, Flem's business plan and his way of doing business have been revealed without his saying more than sixty-eight words. At the same time, chapter 1 has covered fifty or so years of history from the Civil War to Reconstruction to the post-Reconstruction period that coincided with the rise of the redneck and the politics of populism that overcame the Faulkner way of doing business in the decades to come. The last thing Flem would think to do is restore the Old Frenchman place, a dilapidated relic grander than Rowan Oak, since he craves employment as store and bank clerk, the very occupations William Faulkner disdained.

"Evening, Uncle Will," Ratliff says at the beginning of chapter 2, "in his pleasant, courteous, even deferent voice." "Deferent" is the operative word, reflecting a code of courtesy and respect that Flem and his family do not honor, starting with the Civil War, when Ab Snopes in *The Unvanquished* gets the better of Rosa Millard in a mule trade and then leads her into the trap that results in her murder. "Ab had to withdraw his allegiance to the Sartorises, and I hear tell he skulked for a considerable back in the hills until Colonel Sartoris got busy enough building his railroad for it to be safe to come out," Ratliff reports. Flem's clerkship is actually a sinecure, a marvel to Frenchman's Bend since the store is a casual self-service enterprise needing no help. Ratliff grew up watching Ab curdle, bilked in a horse trade with the infamous Pat Stamper, and now mistrustful of humanity itself. Ab relies on his son Flem to take away Jody Varner's advantage, and now Ab has a team of mules he has not had to trade for, except insofar as Flem himself is the commodity traded, so to speak, for the mules. Flem is a comer acting, as Ratliff says, as if he was "raised store-keeping." Ratliff gets around in his sewing machine business, absorbing the lay of the land and its people's lore as he adds his own eyewitness to events, past and present. No other character in Faulkner's fiction has such reach, such disinterested curiosity in how events will turn out, and how the community will react to change. Snopesism is the catalyst, but it is just one driver of history, a fundamental point so many reviewers missed in their fixation on Faulkner as southern novelist.

In chapter 3, the sinecure becomes a cynosure for the community as members purchase items to get a good look at the new novelty clerk. When Will Varner arrives, he orders Flem to bring him some chewing tobacco. Flem stands there while Varner continues with a story but is disturbed by Flem at his elbow. "What?" Varner asks. "You aint paid for it," Flem responds. The transaction, not the person, is the principle Flem propounds. The ancien régime relinquishes its authority to Flem's strict accounting. Jody Varner made mistakes, usually in his favor, but had always been generous with customers, too. Now no leeway, no credit, is offered by Flem, whose arithmetic is meticulous. Jody begins to neglect the store. When Flem turns his attention to the cotton gin, suddenly it is Jody who must mind the store, while months later Ratliff figures out that Flem has "passed" Jody, becoming more indispensable to Will Varner than Varner's own son. When it is time to settle accounts with farmers, Will Varner, who has always done it alone, now has Flem at his side. They resemble a "white trader and his native parrot-taught headman in an African outpost." The colonial, imperialistic nature of the enterprise has been established on a new basis, with the headman "acquiring the virtues of civilization fast." Soon Flem is operating as essentially a payday lender, doling out anywhere between twenty-five cents and ten dollars "if the borrower agreed to pay enough for the accommodation." Then he begins importing family members to run other businesses, like the blacksmith shop. A hapless Jody Varner exclaims: "How many more is there? How much longer is this going on? Just what is it going to cost me to protect one goddamn barn full of hay?" Of course, Flem does not answer. His mind is on more than a protection racket.

Ratliff tries to beat the Snopeses at their own game but is swindled nevertheless, accepting from Mink Snopes, Flem's cousin, a promissory note that Ratliff cannot collect on because, Flem tells him, it has been signed by an idiot, Isaac (Ike) Snopes, a helpless victim Ratliff does not care to exploit. These transactions do not just reflect the rise of the redneck that obsessed Phil Stone. This is a change from feudalism to capitalism—from the liege lord Will Varner to the banker Flem Snopes—the complications of which took Faulkner more than a decade to work out as he meditated on the implications of the spotted-horses episode in *Father Abraham* and the changes in the national and local economy that occurred during the Depression. Ratliff's insistence that Ab Snopes "soured" after the Civil War marks the breakdown of deference and the destruction of the comity—no matter how fragile—that kept communities together. Ab's anomie becomes Flem's opportunity. He builds his business one client at a time, spreading his risk, never depending on specific properties or allegiances that make owners like Jody Varner vulnerable.

"Eula"

What is missing in book 1, "Flem," called the "female principle" in *The Wild Palms,* is supplied in abundance in book 2, "Eula." In chapter 1, Jody Varner, outraged that his sedentary and already well-endowed eight-year-old sister does nothing, drives her to school but is aghast at the spectacle she arouses, a scent she gives off if a man is within one hundred yards of her. His dilemma is macrocosmic: "He had a vision of himself transporting not only across the village's horizon but across the embracing proscenium of the entire inhabited world like the sun itself, a kaleidoscopic convolution of mammalian ellipses." Eula is an eruption, an affront to a dollars-and-cents economy, the careful calculation of profit and loss, and an interruption of business as usual. She can be factored into the monetary mind only as an acquisition. The trouble is she cannot be quantified like hard currency. Her appeal is incalculable.

In the Sleepy Hollow of Frenchman's Bend, Labove, the besotted school-teacher—as much of an anchorite as Harry Wilbourne before he encounters Charlotte Rittenmeyer—is undone by his infatuation with Eula. Labove's drive and intelligence has caught the interest of Will Varner, who is looking, it seems, for an heir to usurp Jody's place, now that no other male Varner is available.[15] The ambitious Labove is no Faulknerian poet, but until teaching Eula he has wanted to be "fiercely free," sharing Faulkner's "'sardonic not-quite belief' in the unreality of the university and its systems of values."[16] Labove also resembles Flem insofar as he, too, is the son of a dirt farmer determined to leave the farm behind. But unlike Flem, Labove is undone by the female principle that diverts his steady, determined pursuit of a college degree and a place in the law profession. Eula is impervious to his clumsy effort to seduce her. Pushing him aside, she sums up what she has learned at school, telling him to stop pawing her, "You old headless horseman Ichabod Crane." Eula conflates the two characters of Washington Irving's story—one looking for the head he lost in battle, and the other fleeing after his courtship of a wealthy farmer's daughter fails. Labove is both, since he has lost his head over his passion for Will Varner's daughter, and like Crane he disappears in defeat. Labove's frustration is akin to what Faulkner himself felt, it would seem, during those years when he inscribed his handmade books to the married Estelle. Labove comes to believe he is no more "a physical factor" in Eula's life "than the owner's name on the flyleaf of a book."[17]

Eula becomes Flem's prize as he consolidates his position and place, and an ornament of his power and prestige. She is as much the "centrice" in her world as Flem is the center of his, her child by another man no trouble to a Snopes who now possesses, thanks to a transaction with Will Varner, the seigneurial rights to the Old Frenchman place in this farce of a knight, the semblance of a frog prince, saving the damsel in distress. Eula, the community property of every male's sexual fantasy, becomes a Flem Snopes asset.

Flem's rescue of the Varner pride, if you want to call it that, provokes in Ratliff a fantasy of Flem as a Faustus with a used-up and much-reduced soul who bargains with the devil for hell itself, which the devil has no capacity to offer, but which Flem feels is the price of the note payable by the devil for Flem's work. Confronted by the unrelenting Flem, the Prince of Darkness screams, "*Take Paradise!*" In Ratliff's book, Flem outdevils the devil, arrogating to himself a sovereignty that none of the other males who salivate over Eula can imagine, let alone assert.

"The Long Summer"

Chapter 1 of book 3, "The Long Summer," cuts across the cash nexus of Flem's career with Ike Snopes's romance. This erotic attachment to a bovine beauty baffled most reviewers, many of whom deplored the sensationalism and perversity of an author they presumed only wanted to shock his readers. He did—but not in quite the way they supposed. He offended their sense of propriety, to be sure, but in the service of establishing the very ground of love lacking in the transactional world of Flem Snopes. The inarticulate Ike, who cannot even pronounce his last name, pursues the cow as the female principle, "speaking to her, trying to tell her how this violent violation of her maiden's delicacy is no shame, since such is the very iron imperishable warp of the fabric of love." Like Benjy, Ike is sensate and devoid of shame and purely loving without pretext, finding his equilibrium in the cow's company in a world he otherwise has trouble negotiating—like the steps he falls down at home. That domesticated world roars back at Ike when Houston catches him with the cow in the creek and slashes at the cow, calling it a whore, and strips Ike of his fouled clothing, which Houston throws into the water and scrubs with a stick on the grass, shouting at Ike to go home. But not even this terrifying rebuke and assertion of propriety deters Ike from resuming his courtship as he returns to the cow to milk her and feed her and eat along with her. The leaves and blossoms and petals Ike strews upon the ground forming an "abortive diadem" are reminiscent of Faulkner doing the same when he garlanded Meta's bed. What Faulkner felt in her caress is the same tenderness Ike feels for his beloved, wishing to crown the ground for her. Like Ike, Faulkner found his love in a transactional world that told him what to do even as he made his paradise of it as others like Flem made the same world a hell. In the bed of nature, Ike is sovereign. In the hour between sunset and dark Ike lies down with the cow at the very time that Houston, four years a widower, misses his wife the most. The private nature of Houston's grief retroactively suffuses the coupling of Ike and the cow, which, in turn, becomes a public spectacle to which Ratliff puts a stop. Ratliff, a fastidious bachelor, seem incapable of joining in with crude barnyard humor.[18] He appeals to I. O. and Eck Snopes, arguing they must buy the cow (another transactional solution) and dispose of it to preserve the family's honor, although no such honor exists but only Ratliff's shame that Ike's passion should be a matter of public entertainment. In place of his living love, Ike is given a toy cow. Like Eula Varner, the "object of love has been turned into an object."[19]

The shift in chapter 2 of "The Long Summer" is at first puzzling. How does Houston's story impinge on the Snopes saga? Love is part of the answer—not a love that conquers all but love that is simply indispensable, even though it plays no part in Flem's rise to wealth and power any more than love has a role in Sutpen's ascent. Houston grows up with Lucy Pate, the woman he marries, and when she dies six months after they wed, he is inconsolable and raging. She is nothing like Estelle Oldham; Houston is nothing like William Faulkner, but matrimony nevertheless binds both as chosen men: "It was as though she [Lucy] had merely elected him out of all the teeming earth, not as one competent to her requirements, but as one possessing the possibilities on which she would be content to establish the structure of her life." Estelle had done as much—even if she had chosen someone else first—and her election of Faulkner made it nigh on impossible for him to repudiate her, no matter how hard he tried. He was her destiny—just like Houston's wife, still waiting for him after he returned from thirteen years away from home. He is not an easy man to love—torn as he is between his desire to be let alone and to have her support: "It was a feud, a gage, wordless, uncapitulating, between that unflagging will not for love or passion but for the married state, and that furious and as unbending one for solitariness and freedom." Houston, a paradox like Faulkner, is pinned between these alternatives.

Then Mink Snopes shoots and kills Houston over a cattle dispute, with repercussions that continue right to the end of the trilogy in *The Mansion*. So much for the family honor—although Mink believes he has asserted his dignity and delivered a blow against that "conspiracy to frustrate and outrage his rights as a man and his feelings as a sentient creature." Mink has subsisted on the rented land and meager resources that Flem has repudiated in his rise. Mink is the sum of bitterness, with no plan or purpose, other than to survive—as he proves when his food runs out and he eats the shavings in a grain barrel. His vulnerable and impecunious condition is precisely what Flem has sought to surmount. Mink's sense of honor leads him to murder Houston not for money, and not even with the idea of escaping his punishment—as his wife urges him to do—but as an assertion (as paradoxical as it sounds) of his humanity. He does not consider what is to his own advantage, or to his family's well-being. He rejects Lump Snopes's offer of an alibi. It seems that anything that might compromise the principle of self-determination involved in Houston's murder must be rejected. Only pride of self matters to the uncompromising Mink, who refuses to accommodate himself even to the idea of self-preservation, except for his bungling attempts to hide Houston's body.

Just as uncompromising in his own way is Lump. He can think only of the fifty dollars he is sure that Mink forgot to retrieve from Houston's body. Lump cannot conceive of a crime that does not involve money, and he wants to split the proceeds with Mink, doggedly pursuing his cousin, playing checkers with him for six hours while trying to cajole him into going back for the Houston loot. Lump even lies to the sheriff about Mink's whereabouts, even after Mink knocks Lump down and ties him up. Even though Lump thinks Mink may assault him again, all he can think about is the money. Lump's pecuniary personality—the Snopes brand, you might say—drives him forward like an eighteenth-century humors character. Mink has more in common with the proud man he murders than with his covetous cousin.

Money was never far from William Faulkner's concerns, although not for its own sake. Even so, the scheming, playing games, ingratiation—none of which he was very good at or even wanted to perfect—were an inescapable part of his experience as family man and enterprising writer, even though his family (no Snopeses, to be sure) could not figure out the motivations of a man who was as silent about himself as Mink is with his wife, with Lump, and with everyone else he encounters. In fact, what it meant to be William Faulkner, and what it meant to be Mink Snopes, coincided in the most crucial way: Both depended on silence to remain themselves, to be at an essential remove from the commerce of the world. It is no wonder then that Mink engaged Faulkner as a character he would be compelled to return to in the most brilliant passages of *The Mansion*.

In jail, after the sheriff and deputy have caught up with Mink trying to dispose of Houston's body, Mink says to a group of incarcerated black men that he was all right "until it started coming to pieces," meaning the disintegrating body. The black men want nothing to do with this white man's confession. And Mink, entirely absorbed in the cultural determinants of what constitutes his rights, watches them rush the stairs toward the smell of food, and thinks: "Are they going to feed them niggers before they do a white man?"

Mink awaits trial in chapter 3, not bothering to defend himself or hire a lawyer. Everyone supposes he is waiting for Flem to somehow get him out of jail. But Flem remains in Texas on his honeymoon and does not return with Eula, leading Ratliff to suppose that Flem will wait until Mink's case is closed. Ratliff provides a home for Mink's wife and children even as the rest of his kin stay away from him as someone who has detracted from the family brand. Their absence, for all their clannishness, is telling. Mink is simply not worth anything to them. Only Mink, right to the last, believes that the traditional clan code will save him from the life sentence imposed during Flem's truancy.

"The Peasants"

In chapter 1 of book 4, "The Peasants," Faulkner finally circles back to the precipitating event of the Snopes saga, the sale of the spotted horses. He told an audience that he drew on a childhood experience. To hear him tell it is to realize how much he enjoyed the impracticality of buying such an animal: "That the man even in a society where there's a constant pressure to conform can still be taken off by the chance to buy a horse for three dollars. Which to me is a good sign, I think. I hope that man can always be [tolled] off that way, to—to buy a horse for three dollars."[20] So much commentary emphasizes how the men are gulled into buying the horses, but the spirit of those ponies appealed to Faulkner, who became unusually loquacious, almost a little boy, when he remembered his own experience in such a wholehearted way that his audience fell in love with him:

I bought one of these horses once. [*audience laughter*] They appeared in our country. Every summer somebody would come in with another batch of them. They were western range-bred ponies, pintos. Had never had a bridle on them. Had never seen shell corn before. And they'd brought—be brought into our town and auctioned off for prices from three or four dollars up to six or seven, and I bought this one for four dollars and seventy-five cents. I was—[*audience laughter*] oh, I reckon ten years old. My father at that time ran a livery stable, and there was a—a big man. He was six feet and a half tall. He weighed two hundred pounds, but mentally he was about ten years old, too. And I wanted one of those horses. My father said, "Well, if you and Buster can buy one for what money you've saved, you can have it." And so we went to the auction, and we bought one for four dollars and seventy-five cents. We got it home. We were going to gentle it. We had a two-wheel cart made out of the front axle of a buggy with shafts on it, and we fooled with that [creature]. It was—was a wild animal. It was a wild beast. [*audience laughter*] It wasn't a domestic animal at all, and finally Buster said that it was about ready, so we had the cart in a shed. Estelle probably remembers this. We put a croaker sack over the horse's head and backed it into the cart with two niggers to—to fasten it in, to buckle traces and toggles and things, and me and Buster got in the seat, and Buster said, "All right boys, let him go." [*audience laughter*] And they snatched the—the sack off the horse's head, and it went across the lot. There was a big gate. The lane had turned at a sharp angle. It hung the inside wheel on the gatepost as it turned. We were down on one hub then. Then about that time, Buster caught me by the back of the neck and threw me, just like that, and then he jumped off. [*audience laughter*] And the cart was scattered up that lane, and we found the horse a—a mile away run into a dead-end street. All he had left on him was just the hames, the harness was gone. [*audience laughter*] [But] that was a [pleasant] experience. But we kept that horse and gentled him to where I finally rode him. But I loved that horse because that was my own horse. I bought that with my own money. [*audience laughter*]

This is rare Faulkner, the Faulkner we can see growing up when it was all right to talk about "niggers" as he does without a second's reservation or embarrassment. To be a fool about a horse did not lower a man or boy in Faulkner's estimation. In fact, in *The Hamlet* he has a boy, Eck Snopes's son, who constantly gets too close to the bucking ponies so that Eck has to tell him to stay back. For Faulkner, those spotted horses evoke the wonders of his childhood, and a story his own father told too—without the addition of Flem Snopes.[21] The laughter, which can be heard on the website recording, is robust, and it helps to animate Faulkner. When he gets to the part about the cart, his voice picks up speed, and then by the time Buster catches him by the back of the neck, you can hear Faulkner's amusement and imagine his smile as the audience laughs along with him. In this reliving of his childhood, he re-creates a kind of community in this University of Virginia classroom that gives you some idea of the collective experience with horses Faulkner and his contemporaries shared and that is so much a part of *The Hamlet*. And how very rare of Faulkner to put Estelle in the story, if only as a bystander, as if to corroborate and make even more real his relish of the past for its own sake and for the sake of those like him who did not mind seeming impractical, as artists are always impractical. Estelle would not only remember, but he could be sure she would think, always, of that gallant, impractical boy she fell in love with the first time she saw him parading down a street on a horse. And don't forget Faulkner's tolerant father, so often shown as misunderstanding his son, but who allowed his eldest boy's fantasy to fructify in this livery stable period, providing for his son not only the pleasure of his own purchase but with a memory that turned into such literary profit. Faulkner's emphasis on "my own money" and "my own horse" and how much he paid for that horse link him to all the poor childlike men who will buy Flem's horses out of their meager savings, wanting to own some part of that wild spirit, much to their wives' consternation.[22]

The fun Faulkner had as a child would be put to a more serious purpose in *The Hamlet:* The spotted-horses auction marks a momentous change in the economy of Frenchman's Bend, disrupting traditional, normative practices and launching Flem's takeover not only of business but of the way to do business, commanding the greed and power dynamics incipient in a populace he knows how to exploit, creating a spectacle that diverts his audience even as they hand over their treasure to him, including Henry Armstid's last five dollars to take possession of a horse he cannot control but that has become the same as an assertion of his will. He puts his wife in danger and strikes her when she cannot head the horse in Henry's direction. The Texan auctioneer offers to return the five dollars to Armstid's wife, but Flem halts the offer, saying he wants to honor the sale—if such a word can be employed to describe Flem's cupidity. In effect, the auction has become a bet on horses as in a race where most of the betters are losers but cannot resist the idea of winning. The horses break loose when the owners come to collect them. All along Mrs. Littlejohn has been doing her chores, barely glancing at the auction, until one of the wild ponies scrambles onto the porch and she bashes it with a washboard. As an injured Henry Armstid is carried into her house, she declares, "You men." This practical-minded woman, as Faulkner explained, watched these men "committing puerile folly for some gewgaw." Her disgust is palpable at seeing the beaten man who has beaten his wife: "See if you cant find something else to play with that will kill some more of you." Her comment is apt coming after the antics of Eck Snopes and his boy besotted with catching the "free" horse the Texan bestowed on them at the auction. Several times the menagerie of wild horses has been called Flem Snopes's circus. He has put on a show appealing to these boy-men who also want to be animal tamers and exert their need to dominate. As Will Varner says, "You take a man that aint got no other relaxation all year long except dodging mule-dung up and down a field furrow. And a night like this one, when a man aint old enough yet to lay still and sleep, and yet he aint young enough anymore to be tomcatting in and out of other folks' back windows, something like this is good for him." The tall-tale tradition and the dime novel converge in Ratliff's comment when he refers to the Texas auctioneer as "Dead-eye Dick."

The episode ends on a sour note, with Flem pretending he does not have the five dollars Mrs. Armstid asks him for, claiming the Texan has taken all the sale money. Flem makes his meanness even plainer when he gifts a sack of five-cent candy to Mrs. Armstid for the children. Fed up with trying to ameliorate Flem's depredations, a revolted Ratliff refuses to do any more for the hapless Armstids, announcing: "I never made them Snopeses and I never made the folks that cant wait to bare their backsides to them. I could do more, but I wont. I wont, I tell you!" His vehemence suggests that he will nevertheless do something, just like Faulkner helped out his brother John, with a wife and two children, by giving him the farm to manage even as Faulkner complained about the added responsibility.

In the aftermath of the horse mayhem, causing Armstid's injuries and Tull's, whose wife brings a suit against Eck, whose gift horse caused the trouble, the judge cannot decide in favor of Mrs. Armstid since it cannot be proven that the horses are Flem's. Even worse, Lump Snopes swears Flem gave back Mrs. Armstid's five dollars to the Texan. And Mrs. Tull is outraged when the judge decides Eck never really owned the horse that upset her husband, since no deed of ownership was drawn up. The only recompense offered to Mrs. Tull is possession of the very horse that has brought her to sue Eck. Behind it all, Flem Snopes remains impervious and beyond the law, as chapter 1 concludes with Mink in the courtroom shouting out the absent Flem's name, the name of the one man he thought could save him from a life sentence.

Flem, now the obsession of just about everyone in Frenchman's Bend, is observed at night digging for the treasure supposedly buried by the original owner of the ruined property that Varner deeded to Flem when he married Eula. Varner has dangled the possibility of selling the Old Frenchman place before Ratliff, without actually putting up the property for bidding. It may well be that Varner and Flem, as business partners and family members, are colluding in an effort to bilk Ratliff: "Like characters in the novel, the reader will never have quite enough information to be certain that he knows what is going on. The narrative voice is shrewd, secret, and, if he seems to be entertaining, seems as well to hide as much as he reveals." In one of his most cunning novels, Faulkner implicates readers in these transactions. How good are you at figuring the deal that is about to go down? Caveat emptor. As Claude Pruitt observes, "This is a level of verisimilitude that transforms the novel into a horse trade and the reader (along with the folks of Frenchman's Bend) into unwary buyers likely to be 'skinned' in the deal."[23]

Ratliff arrives with Armstid and Bookright, who hear Flem's pickaxe, all certain that he would not waste his time if he had not come near to discovering a fortune. "Just look at what even the money a man aint got yet will do to him," Ratliff realizes even as he digs deeper, the men finding three bags of silver coins with the aid of Uncle Dick Bolivar and his silver-detecting equipment. Certain that they will have to return the next night for more digging, they pool their resources to buy the property from Flem, never questioning why he would want to sell. And so they dig—grave deep—their own doom, with only Ratliff suspecting but not yet admitting they have been had. Flem had even set up a relative, Eustace Grimm, as a decoy, letting the trio of treasure hunters suppose Flem had another prospective buyer. Only the maniacal Henry Armstid refuses to believe the truth: "Get out of my hole," he tells his partners, who know only too well what holes they have put themselves in.

Ratliff, one of the principal critics of Flem Snopes's rise, succumbs to Flem's monetary scheme of values, believing he can become rich with one quick strike. Ratliff did not arrive in time for the spotted-horses auction, and now he has another opportunity to participate in the "thrill of competitive acquisition."[24] All along, he has been twitted by the community about his know-it-all attitude, and now he has been brought low—into a ditch, in fact, soiled with Flem's money-grubbing chicanery.

Ratliff's greed is not so different from Faulkner's first reaction to Hollywood gold, when he wrote home to Estelle to say he could make several thousand dollars writing for Tallulah Bankhead. Although Faulkner quickly soured on Hollywood, the urge to make a quick buck in the Hollywood go-round never deserted him for long. Like Ratliff, he could come and go in the economy of his world, selling his wares, remaining somewhat aloof, and yet realizing how deeply implicated he was in everybody's business. The whole business, in fact, leads one reader of Faulkner's life to conjecture: "Madly digging for gold before an audience on the lawn of his antebellum mansion, Armstid is made in the image of his creator's sometimes outraged image of himself at work at Rowan Oak."[25]

Chapter 2 of "The Peasants" concludes with Flem's move to Jefferson. Eula appears in the "first tailored suit ever seen in Frenchman's Bend," as part of her husband's new profile as a townsman entering modern life with the vestiges of the village life he is leaving behind: "the weathered and creaking wagons, the plow-galled horses and mules, the men and women and children entering another world, traversing another land, moving in another time, another afternoon without time or name." This departure and new beginning, a part of historic changes taking place in Faulkner's land and across the South, will become an increasing part of this novelist's concern, the new kind of history he and his characters will make. The South of decaying plantations, the Civil War–haunted characters, will begin to recede from subsequent narratives, if not, certainly, expunged from the latter-day consciousness of old and young alike. The image of Henry Armstid still digging after two weeks, a holdover of the past searching for its treasures, closes out the story, if not the history of Frenchman's Bend. He makes a spectacle of himself—like Flem's spotted horses—drawing "the rapt interest of a crowd watching a magician at a fair." His faithful wife continues to bring him food in a pail, and the couple become a staple of community conversation while people also gather to watch Flem leave town, marking the end of an era.

But not the end of Ratliff, who is already climbing out of the hole, like Faulkner, daring failure to become a success. Faulkner's own comments about Snopesism show how closely he aligned his own efforts as an artist with Ratliff's opposition to Flem:

> When the battle comes, it always produces a Roland. It doesn't mean that they will get rid of Snopes or the impulse which produces Snopes, but always there's something in man that—that don't like Snopes and objects to Snopes and, if necessary, will step in to keep Snopes from doing some irreparable harm. There's whatever it is that—that keeps us still trying to paint the pictures, to make the music, to write the books. There's a great deal of pressure not to do that because certainly the artist has no place in—in nature, and almost no place at all in our American culture and economy, but yet people still try to write books, still try to paint pictures.[26]

Faulkner, acutely aware of his own marginality during most of his lifetime, with no more status, in some respects, than an itinerant sewing machine salesman, a hired hand in a Hollywood studio, on the sidelines of an economy that favored the bottom line, began to see with the advent of the Snopes trilogy that his writing, while not designed to uphold conventional morality, could nonetheless enact a moral purpose. The impulse to battle Snopesism became the same as creating his books.

6

Was

Go Down, Moses, 1940–1942

WAY DOWN IN EGYPT LAND

On January 21, 1940, as Faulkner perused the galleys of *The Hamlet,* Mammy Callie died. A paralytic stroke had felled her a few days earlier. Estelle and Caroline Barr's children, grandchildren, and great-grandchildren watched over her. She was near a hundred as far as anyone knew. She had ailed from time to time, and Faulkner had always soothed her suffering with ice cream, her favorite that he obtained on late-night trips to a juke joint. She had a small house behind Rowan Oak where a live-in couple tended to her, making sure she had enough "wood and such," and help if she took sick. She ate her meals at Rowan Oak and took care of seven-year-old Jill.[1]

Faulkner arranged the obsequy in the Rowan Oak parlor, delivering a three-hundred-word funeral address to her weeping family, calling her a "fount of authority" who had kept him secure with love and devotion. On February 3, the *Memphis Commercial Appeal* quoted him: "As oldest of my father's family, I might be called her master. That situation never existed between 'Mammy' and me."[2]

Faulkner wrote on February 5 to Robert Haas, sending back the galleys late, explaining: "I have had little of heart or time either for work." Until the stroke she could still "hear perfectly and thread needles and sew by lamplight, and would walk for several miles. . . . She couldn't have gone better, more happily." A few days later he sent Haas his eulogy, remarking, "it turned out to be pretty good prose."[3] He put a marker on her grave:

MAMMY
Her white children
bless her.

He dedicated *Go Down, Moses* to her:

TO MAMMY

CAROLINE BARR

Mississippi
[1840–1940]

Who was born in slavery and who
gave to my family a fidelity without
stint or calculation of recompense
and to my childhood an immeasurable devotion and love

What William Faulkner felt deeply he turned into literature—at some cost
to the life out of which his words arose. Barr's family were grateful that he
covered all their expenses, but another view prevailed among Barr's relatives:
"And then he had the funeral in the living room! In his living room! And I
think he had the Community Choir of Oxford. I think they call that choir
to come down and sing and then he let us brought her to the Baptist Church.
He come with it [the body]. Him and Miss Estelle had the funeral and carried
her on out there and buried her." They wondered why Faulkner had not given
his eulogy in their church or home—"even at the bitter end, he couldn't let
go of her, couldn't let her be with her family." In 1940, it would have been
difficult for Barr's family to speak up, but their resentment several decades
later remained palpable.[4] In 1940, perhaps it was inconceivable to Faulkner to
hold the service in Barr's home or church. Caroline Barr seemed "an emblem
of those traditional relationships unchanged by the Civil War,"[5] and in fact
still operative in Jill's upbringing.

To the Falkners, the head of the family had shown Caroline Barr deep
respect. Aunt Bama wrote to her nephew Vance Broach, enclosing a clip-
ping from the *Memphis Commercial Appeal* (February 5, 1940), "Rites Held
for Former Slave in Novelist Faulkner's Home." The headline alone, for
that time, was startling. Bama also enclosed a letter from Mary Bell, one of
Barr's relatives, thanking him for "giving Mammy such a fine funeral." Bama
wrote parenthetically to Broach, "Have you been away from Dixie too long
to appreciate that?" Faulkner had answered Bell's letter, Bama wanted her

nephew to know, adding: "For him to take the time to write to this lowly, obscure negro is an index to the real Faulkner & for that reason I wanted you to read it."[6] Bama's letter evokes the eighteenth-century world of deference, when the word "condescension" meant the nobleman's gracious acknowledgment of the lower orders.

Faulkner admired Caroline Barr's independence and realized she did not always coincide with the Falkner line. But he made no mention in his funeral oration of her several efforts to strike out on her own, which always ended in her return to the Falkners. They may even have admired what might be called her race pride. "And if Mammy [Callie Barr] could have seen that Decoration Day parade," Faulkner wrote to his mother on June 2, 1918: "The colored troops were there, veterans of the civil war, dolled up in blue suits and cigars and medals until they all looked like brigadiers."[7] The condescending ("dolled up"), nevertheless, is part of paying respect to these black men in blue. To Faulkner, perhaps, Caroline Barr's decision to remain in service to his family was more than they deserved but also a comfort in supposing her very presence redeemed their own complicity in slavery. Exactly what Faulkner shared with his mother at this moment is hard to get at and yet should not be overlooked.

Caroline Barr's death is a poignant and painful moment in Faulkner biography since, like *Go Down, Moses,* her death exposes what whites mistook about the black people who worked for and lived among them. Faulkner himself, for all his sensitivity, could fail as his characters failed to acknowledge the full humanity of more than half the population of Lafayette County cum Yoknapatawpha: 6,298 whites and 9,313 "Negroes," according to the map drawn for *Absalom, Absalom!*—another searing indictment of the white people who reject the invisibly black Charles Bon.

On May 3, 1940, in a letter to Robert Haas, Faulkner confessed that Barr's death set off a vehement train of reactions to the deaths of Murry, Alabama, and Dean: frustration, anger, dismay, and wonder at "this quite alarming paradox": He had shouldered responsibilities that interfered with his ambition and genius, developed as much away from home as within it, as a solitary man and a scion. He had carried it all—the Falkner and Oldham debts, the dependents—"white and black," without inheriting land or money, and with no expectation of recompense. The unreconstructed Falkner also made an appearance: "What I need is some East Indian process to attain to the nigger attitude about debt. One of them is discussing the five dollars he must pay before sunset to his creditor, canvasses all possibilities, completes the circle back to the point of departure, where there is simply no way under heaven for him to get five dollars, says at last, 'Well, anyway, he (the creditor) cant eat me.' 'How you know he cant?' the second says. 'Maybe he won't want to,' the first says."[8] "Pantaloon in Black," published in *Harper's* (October 1940), included in *Go Down, Moses,* portrays a tragic black man with a harrowing dignity. Writing as William Faulkner in a letter he seemed in a different realm, writing about a world in which he played a compromising part.

Unable to write what he called trashy short stories, he began to conceive of works that would eventually become *Intruder in the Dust* and *The Reivers,* although committing himself, even for six months, to a novel bothered him because he had so many pressing obligations. His letters to Robert Haas, full of dollar-sign amounts, signified his month-by-month calculations as to how he could manage his debts and continue to write.[9] He opted for a short-story collection comprising already published magazine fiction and new material giving that work a greater dimension and integrity, just as he had done for *The Unvanquished.*

It took more than a year to work out what to do with interrelated short stories. He fretted about "this business in Europe"—the war. "What a hell of a time we are facing," he wrote Haas. Faulkner could still fit into his World War I uniform: the "wings look as brave as they ever did. I swore then when I took it off in '19, that I would never wear another, nohow, nowhere, for no one. But now I don't know. Of course I could do no good, would last about two minutes in combat. But my feeling now is better so; that what will be left after this one will certainly not be worth living for. Maybe the watching of all this coming to a head for the last year is why I cant write, dont seem to want to write, that is. But I can write"—by which he meant he was not written out and still wanted to "scratch the face of the supreme Obliteration and leave a decipherable scar of some sort." The very technology that could destroy a thousand lives, he proposed, might also "preserve, even by blind mischance and a minute fault in gears or timing, some scrap here and there, provided it was ever worth preserving."[10] This Second World War heightened his historical sensibility just as the first one had, driving him to think more deeply about slavery, bondage, and all forms of oppression. Civilization was at stake. In the heart of *Go Down, Moses,* in the fourth section, "The Bear," Ike McCaslin and McCaslin Edmonds debate no less than the nature of their heritage and the values on which their patrimony was founded.

At the same time, the housebound writer had tried and failed to get a Hollywood assignment, reflecting his desperation as he stewed about his insupportable circumstances: income tax, insurance premiums, bank notes, his and his mother's household expenses, and his unprofitable farm. "I need $4,000.00 more by Jan 1," he wrote Haas on June 7, 1940, acknowledging the $3,000 advance for a novel not yet delivered. Then he resorted to his only remaining financial resource, saying he did not want to be a Random House burden, especially after "You and Don and Bennett have been my good friends for a long time." Rather than spoil it all, he had considered contacting a publisher (Harold Guinzberg of Viking Press) who had "intimated" years before Faulkner's connection with Random House, that "I could almost write my own ticket with him. This may not even hold now. But it is one thing more I can try before I decide to liquidate my property and savings."[11] Guinzberg did make an offer but also agreed that Faulkner should stay with Random House if the Viking Press offer could be matched. Bennett Cerf wrote Faulkner, explaining they had 2,500 copies of *The Hamlet* to sell and a tremendous stake in his career: "All of us are absolutely sick at heart at the thought of your leaving Random House."[12] After Guinzberg calculated the cost of buying Faulkner out of his Random House contract, he withdrew his offer.[13] Then Harold Ober sold some short stories and even held back his commission on one to help his client.

Farming, flying, and doing some work as an advisor with Ole Miss's flying school seemed to lift Faulkner's spirits, although he brooded on race in "this destruction-bent world. Saxon fighting Saxon, Latin against Latin, Mongol with a Slav ally fighting a Mongol who is the ally of a Saxon-Latin ally of the first Slav; nigger fighting nigger at the behest of white men; one democracy trying to blow the other democracy's fleet off the seas. Anyway, it will make nice watching when the axis people start gutting one another." This conflicted network of disrupted relations would figure into the genealogies of *Go Down, Moses* as Faulkner began to dilate on the nexus between North and South, white and black, and intrafamilial dramas that would engulf the McCaslin and Edmonds descendants.[14]

Mired in the here and now, he retreated to the woods: "off there hunting, I dont fret and stew so much about Europe." But the wilderness was no solution to his worries. He was the same man, sometimes separating from fellow hunters and drinking himself sick. On one trip he had to be evacuated from camp by motorboat. It had been a close call, his doctor told him. And yet, as usual, he recovered in short order. The world elsewhere, especially the war, could not be denied: "I'm only 43, I'm afraid I'm going to the damn thing yet."[15] The woods would form the backdrop of *Go Down, Moses,* the world Faulkner had grown up in but that was vanishing as dramatically as the war came upon him. But he had not yet worked out a sufficiently complex view of what historical change had wrought and what it portended. But it was all around him: the demolition of an Oxford church to make way for a supermarket, the tearing down of an old hotel that had been a part of the community for a hundred years, and the elimination of train service in and out of Oxford, where he had arrived and departed for forty years.

"The Tall Men," one of the *Saturday Evening Post* stories published during this period to pay off back taxes, reflected Faulkner's siege-like psychology and vision of a world coming after him, as it comes after the McCallum brothers, Anse and Lucius, who have not registered for the draft. This is the family in *Flags in the Dust* that takes in young Bayard Sartoris after he wrecks his car, in which old Bayard has his fatal heart attack. The pastoral setting is akin to the backwoods environs of *Sergeant York* (1941), featuring a war hero who begins as a draft resister, a film with sentiments similar to Faulkner's about the sturdiness of rural America and its core values. In "The Tall Men," the old deputy, Gombault, accompanying a government agent arresting two draft resisters, extols independent cotton farmers who brook no interference from government programs and the New Deal farm subsidy programs. The McCallums "still believed in the freedom and liberty to make or break according to a man's fitness and will to work," and not according to what the government paid them for planting or not planting crops. Anse and Lucius are patriotic but resist the draft so long as the country is not actually at war. Their attitudes jibe with Faulkner's own anti–New Deal opinions voiced by Gombault. Like Sergeant York, the McCallums do not want to shirk their duty. Ultimately they decide "it was time to go, because the Government had sent them word."[16]

In letters, and in the limited range of stories like "The Tall Men," Faulkner did not have the capacity to confront issues that could not be neatly divided up between antinomies like big government and individual liberty. On May 1, 1941, he finally announced his plan for *Go Down, Moses,* the "general theme being relationship between white and negro races here." But the stories still required an encompassing argument that would put them within the panorama of history. Not until November did Faulkner find the core story of the novel, "The Bear," a reworking of "Lion" (1935) that would unite all the chapters. The fourth section of "The Bear," taken out in the *Saturday Evening Post* version, created the dialectical argument that radiated throughout *Go Down, Moses,* a culmination of the short story–novel structures he had built up cumulatively in *The Unvanquished* and *The Hamlet. Go Down, Moses,* completed in December 1941, reflects a heroic effort to coalesce his conflicted life and work on several fronts—at home, in Hollywood, in mass-circulation magazines, bringing together every aspect of his biography, family, regional, national, and world history in a series of concatenating chapters that recover a past that suffuses the present, beginning with "Was."

Part 1 of "Was" introduces "Isaac McCaslin, 'Uncle Ike,' past seventy and nearer eighty than he ever corroborated any more, a widower now and uncle to half a county and father to no one." His cousin McCaslin Edmonds, from whom Ike derives the past events that are about to be narrated in part 2, is "descended by the distaff" but inherits the plantation, even though Ike belongs to the male line of McCaslins who originally held the title to the land granted from the Indian patent. Ike finishes his life, however, in a "cheap frame bungalow in Jefferson," the gift of his wife's father.

In part 2, Cass Edmonds tells the story of Ike's father, Uncle Buck, hunting for his part-white McCaslin slave, Tomey's Turl, even as Miss Sophonsiba Beauchamp hunts Buck for a husband. The fox horn blows, indicating that Buck and Cass are near the Beauchamp plantation, where they will "den" Tomey's Turl, and Miss Sophonsiba will "den" Uncle Buck. Caught in Sophonsiba's room, Buck must gamble for his freedom and for the "niggers," according to a wager by Miss Sophonsiba's brother, Hubert. Beauchamp would like to pursue a simple, rustic way of life, but he is forced to accommodate himself to his sister's claims of aristocratic descent and adherence to a chivalric code. The snares of family and heritage, so familiar to Faulkner as head of his clan, are played to comic effect, but in the novel's historical context, race, family, individuality, and property become inextricably mixed and inescapable, full of the paradoxes that Faulkner put so plaintively in his letters.

After having "won" Sophonsiba through losing the card game, Buck sends for his brother Buddy to help him escape the marriage. In the meantime Buck is reduced to acting like a "nigger," telling Cass that "if they pushed him too close . . . he would climb down the gutter too and hide in the woods until Uncle Buddy arrived." Although Buddy successfully extricates his brother from an entangling alliance, the ending of "Was" suggests that eventually Buck will be caught in Miss Sophonsiba's trap. For when they return home, the old dog "Old Moses" is found with the fox's crate around his neck—surely a symbolic forecast of foxy Miss Sophonsiba's yoking that other old dog, "old Buck," as Tomey's Turl calls him.

Ironic reversals of power dynamics, the woman commanding the man, the slave eluding the master, the white man acting as "nigger," and later more than one black man acting with the authority of a white man, turn both past and present, the antebellum and postbellum worlds, upside down as befits a Faulkner who revolted against his responsibilities even as he continued to uphold them. He keenly understood the ironies of his own life, many of them self-made, and others inherited, in a frustrating cycle that runs all the way through his letters to Random House, just as characters like Buck and Tomey's Turl remain on the run.

The next chapter, "The Fire and the Hearth," centers on a contemporary figure, Lucas Beauchamp, a proud black descendant of old Carothers McCaslin, nearly as old as Ike, and the oldest McCaslin Negro on the plantation. Lucas is planning to dispose of George Wilkins, his young competitor in the moonshine trade and his daughter Nat's fiancé, who is a "fool innocent of discretion." Lucas is worried that George will expose the illicit black business that the white people, Zack Edmonds and his son, Carothers (Roth), have forbidden. Near where Lucas has planned to bury his still, part of a plot against George Wilkins, Lucas discovers a gold coin in an Indian burial mound. As canny and pecuniary as Ratliff, Lucas succumbs to treasure-hunting fever.

But the search for buried treasure is interrupted twice by episodes from Lucas's past, providing insights into his present attitudes and the state of the McCaslin family and plantation. In the first episode, forty-three years earlier (1898), Lucas had risked his life to save the life of Roth Edmonds's mother, but she died, and Lucas's wife, Mollie, took her place in Zack Edmonds's household. Believing that Zack had taken Mollie as his mistress, Lucas demanded that the white man return her. Mollie had come back, but with Zack's child (Roth) as well as her own. Roth Edmonds only knows that Lucas achieved an unusual degree of independence stemming from a confrontation with his father about a woman, and Roth is frustrated by that awareness because it inhibits his own authority on the plantation, especially since his mother died in childbirth and Mollie is the only mother he has known. The separation from her as he becomes an adult is painful and confusing and provoking.

The second interruption of treasure-hunting deals with an even earlier time (1895), when Lucas, turned twenty-one, came to Ike to ask for the legacy left him by old Carothers. Although he should have been in the inferior position of a black man, his proud demand for the legacy transformed it into a debt owed to him and a responsibility Ike had shirked. Ike, living in a little bungalow in town, supported by fifty dollars per month from his cousin Cass, realizes that he is powerless to aid Lucas in any other way than by simply dispensing a legacy that had been in his trusteeship. Lucas's cold and distant response prompts Ike to think: *"Fifty dollars a month. He knows that's all. That I reneged, cried calf-rope, sold my birthright, betrayed my blood, for what he too calls not peace but obliteration, and a little food."*

As Lucas gives up the hunting days of his youth and young manhood, Ike dwells more and more on those very same experiences. Lucas accepts his McCaslin heritage, even though white people treat him as an inferior; Ike relinquishes a position of respect and authority in his family and community that is his by birth. Lucas matures into a position of self-importance, his age a considerable factor in his dealings with the much younger Roth, who is continually reminded of Lucas's claims as head of the family, but who is much more than that: *"I am not only looking at a face older than mine and which has seen and winnowed more, but at a man most of whose blood was pure ten thousand years when my own anonymous beginnings became mixed enough to produce me."*

Faulkner's own bifurcated biography, his identity as a solitary writer and his obligations as landowner and head of family, his unwillingness to permanently move away from Oxford or repudiate his heritage and his compulsion to claim his status within his family and community are writ deeply into *Go Down, Moses*—as is his understanding of bondage and deliverance and of the desire to be set free from the past. But renouncing ownership, as Ike does, results in powerlessness. It is, then, the vexed relationship between past and present that Faulkner kept trying to get right as he wrote his new kind of history.

"Pantaloon in Black" completes a trilogy of chapters seeking different ways of connecting past and present, and black people to white. It is, in some ways, the most remarkable chapter in the novel, since it closes in on a black consciousness in ways reminiscent of Richard Wright, Faulkner's African American and Mississippi-born contemporary.[17] Rider and his wife build a "fire on the hearth" on their wedding night "as the tale told how Uncle Lucas Beauchamp, Edmonds' oldest tenant, had done on his forty-five years ago and which had burned ever since." Lucas Beauchamp's heritage survives into the 1940s. Just as losing Mollie to Zack Edmonds provoked a crisis in the life of twenty-four-year-old Lucas, so now, forty-three years later, twenty-four-year-old Rider's loss of Mannie leaves him bereft of any reason to go on living and convinced that he is "bound to die." Rider, like Lucas and Ike, is set apart from both black and white people by the special integrity of his personality and his unusual bond with nature. All three are proud, solitary men, but Lucas and Rider curb the vanity of their own strength by cooperating with their wives in the union of marriage. "Pantaloon in Black," an ironic allusion to the buffoon of commedia dell'arte, repudiates the denigrating stereotype of the foolish black man that lingers in *Flags in the Dust* and in Faulkner's later letters. After Mannie dies, Rider no longer cares what happens to him. He no longer conforms to his subordination as a black man. He cuts the throat of a white man cheating black men at dice.

The grief of a solitary and proud man, so familiar to Faulkner, infuses Rider's despair. However straitened Faulkner's marriage to Estelle had become, the continuity he craved always brought him back from the temptations to leave her. He could not imagine life without the rituals and traditions of family life and home. Without them, in Hollywood, a despondent Faulkner dreamed about playing cards in the kitchen with his family. Rider's self-destructive inability to stop drinking, like Faulkner's binges, reflects a sensibility beyond the help of anyone's intervention.

In another of the novel's many ironies, a white deputy puzzles over Rider's suicidal behavior, which is as unaccountable as Nelse Patton's when he cut the throat of a white woman well known to him, and with whom he had done business before. The deputy, like the exhausted Rider on his last day, is "spent now from lack of sleep and hurried food at hurried and curious hours and, sitting in a chair beside the stove, a little hysterical too." The stove, the deputy's modern fire and hearth, reflects what should be the center of domestic harmony. Unfortunately he cannot imagine that Rider's acts were those of a man who had lost precisely what the deputy is looking for from his inattentive wife: some comforting response to allay the trauma of the last several hours. The deputy is caught in a system of prejudice he did not create, no matter how much his own actions may perpetuate it. The very force of his concern with Rider's story suggests that he is genuinely troubled by this black man's fate and is searching for some way to explain it to himself. Like Rider, the deputy cannot stop thinking, nor can he help looking for the meaning of what he has just witnessed. So he repeats Rider's last words and then addresses a question of his own to his wife, unconsciously echoing Rider's own puzzlement: "'Hit look lack Ah just cant quit thinking. Look lack Ah just cant quit.' And what do you think of that?" She does not think anything of it: "'I think if you eat any supper in this house you'll do it in the next five minutes,' his wife said from the dining room. 'I'm going to clear this table then and I'm going to the picture show.'" She wants to be diverted, entertained, as Faulkner well knew from all the picture shows he had written. By failing to understand her husband's desperate obsession with Rider's last desperate words, the white deputy's wife is as "lost" to her husband at this moment as Mannie was to Rider. These are characters and marriages for which the modern screen had no use, which is to say that in *Go Down, Moses* Faulkner relieved himself of his own bondage to unreal scripts and redeemed his vocation as a writer.

"The Old People" reverses the trajectory of the first three chapters by returning to the terrain of the Indian stories, establishing a genealogy and line of authority that is an alternative to the white Edmonds/McCaslin ascendancy. Faulkner had told Will Bryant he would write a novel about the Indians and now made them central to the historical vision of *Go Down, Moses*. Sam Fathers, the part-Negro descendant of an Indian chief, is Ike's spiritual guide. The chapter includes Ike's experiences from his eighth to his twelfth year that he will still remember at eighty, but the predominant time is 1879, when Sam marks Ike with the blood of the buck he has just slain, initiating the twelve-year-old boy into the order of nature, just as Cass Edmonds was initiated into the life of the plantation at the age of nine in "Was." Even though Sam Fathers has also initiated Cass in the woods, Cass had become an unwitting accomplice in Uncle Buck's hunting of Tomey's Turl. The circular pattern of "Was," in which Tomey's Turl eventually returns to Tennie's cabin and Uncle Buck returns to the Beauchamp plantation and Sophonsiba's bed chamber, conforms to Sam's reading of the buck's path in which "he will circle back in here about sundown to bed." But "Was" has no equivalent to Ike's awareness of "the buck moving in it [the wilderness] somewhere, not running yet since he had not been pursued, not frightened yet and never fearsome but just alert also as they were alert, perhaps already circling back, perhaps quite near, perhaps conscious also of the eye of the ancient immortal Umpire." The timeless quality of the woods fosters the identification of hunter and prey with one another that can never be acknowledged in the slave hunts, or in the distinctions of society and family that Faulkner forsook on his own in the wilderness.

In "The Bear," Ike first becomes aware of "Old Ben," not by sighting him or even hearing him but through participating in the sensation of the hounds: "a little different—an eagerness, passive; an abjectness, a sense of his own fragility and impotence against the timeless woods, yet without doubt or dread." Ike's primordial feelings occur in a wilderness that "looked exactly as it must have looked when the first ancestor of Sam Fathers' Chickasaw predecessors crept into it and looked about him, club or stone axe or bone arrow drawn and ready." Ike relinquishes his gun, compass, and watch in order to get his first look at the bear, and to experience "a condition in which not only the bear's heretofore inviolable anonymity but all the ancient rules and balances of hunter and hunted had been abrogated." But once he has done so, Ike is lost. To find his way back to where he has abandoned his watch and compass, he makes, as Sam has "coached and drilled him," a "cast to cross his backtrack." When he does not find the point at which he originally began, he makes the next circle in the opposite direction and much larger, so that the pattern of the two of them would bisect his track somewhere. He finds the watch and compass, and then he has his privileged vision of the "dimensionless" bear. Old Ben becomes for Ike all-encompassing. The watch and the compass are time- and space-bound, whereas the bear appears to move in neither time nor space. Where the watch and compass divide and separate time and space into units, the bear and the wilderness coalesce, soundless and solidified. Putting aside the instruments of civilization foreshadows Ike's renunciation of his white heritage. To him, his family line depends upon a very short chain of cause and effect, whereas the bear seems ancient and ubiquitous. For Ike, the bear does not vanish, is not lost; rather he simply recedes back into his element, always there, always present, in a changeless universe. Yet the first pages of "The Bear" announce that the wilderness is doomed.

In part 2, Ike is caught in the paradox of hunting Old Ben, symbol of the immortal wilderness. Ike's confusion is apparent in his failure to shoot the bear when the little fyce turns Old Ben toward Ike. Old Ben, the "epitome and apotheosis of the old wild life," is also just an aging bear. Ike senses the fatality the hunt enacts, but he passively accepts its consequences as though he were just an observer of historical processes that he is, in fact, helping to bring about as both the wilderness and Old Ben are inseparable from his initiation into the meaning of life.

Old Ben's death also marks a turning point in McCaslin history. Retrospection on the events related in "The Bear" has begun even before the events themselves can properly be said to have ended. Groups of men, very carefully chosen for the representativeness of their experiences in or beside the wilderness, gather around the old bear to remember the past, as though they instinctively understand that Old Ben's death is a historical event like the closing of the frontier, which can be preserved only through the imagination. Ike is sixteen. In two years he will set out on his attempt to locate the son of Tomey's Turl and Tennie Beauchamp, Tennie's Jim, who left home at twenty-one before collecting his thousand-dollar legacy. This is the same ubiquitous Tennie's Jim of "The Bear." Ike and Tennie's Jim run forward to witness the death scene, with their valiant dog Lion gutted by Old Ben. Although the main action concentrates on Boon Hogganbeck's care for the dying Lion and on Sam Fathers's sudden collapse, the repeated appearances of Tennie's Jim help to define the kind of world that dies along with the major figures in the story. No reason is ever given for the disappearance of Tennie's Jim two years after this scene, but the scene itself argues that the world, and the place Tennie's Jim occupied in it, has been destroyed. All along Faulkner has carefully associated the whole life of Tennie's Jim with these wilderness scenes, just as he grounded Lucas's life in his loyalty to the plantation.

Tennie's Jim is a part of many memorable scenes in "The Bear." He holds "the passive and still trembling bitch," who, in Sam's words, "would have to be brave once so she could keep on calling herself a dog." Tennie's Jim pours the whiskey, which is like a sacrament to the hunters. He holds the hounds on leash, saddles the mules, wakes Ike up on the morning when he and Boon go into town for whiskey. Tennie's Jim is the black man who pulls the towsack off of the horse that Boon and Ike purchased, and he is the one who is sent to the doctor for Boon, Lion, and Sam. He stays with Sam after the white men leave. Tennie's Jim's departure from the scene, from Ike's life, and from his native land suggest his quest for a new world in which to forge his identity while Ike remains fixed on the past.

Part 4 shows that Ike's vision of history is seriously damaged, if not wholly discredited, by his inability to accept the change that is dramatized in the first three parts of "The Bear." Instead of continuing the sixteen-year-old Ike's development from the killing of Old Ben to his last visit to Major de Spain's hunting camp when he is nearly eighteen (which is treated in part 5), part 4 begins with Ike's rejection of his patrimony on his twenty-first birthday, and it then ranges from his sensitive reading of the commissary books at sixteen, to his attempts to "free" Fonsiba (Tennie's daughter) when he is eighteen, to Lucas's acceptance of his legacy when Ike is twenty-eight, to Hubert Beauchamp's bequest to Ike, and finally to Ike's refusal to share his McCaslin legacy with his wife by rejecting her plea that he assume the ownership of the plantation. Ike is an isolated figure, retreating from family responsibilities and estranging himself from those like Cass and his wife who might have been his closest confidants.

Part 4 includes the powerful debate between Ike and Cass Edmonds. Ike presumptuously speaks of a divine purpose transcending a loyalty to family heritage, while Cass stubbornly interprets history from the point at which his family took possession of the land. Ike invokes higher laws operating in contravention of his cousin's obsession with regional history, while Cass chides Ike for relinquishing his responsibility as the sole heir to the McCaslin plantation in favor of a faith in God's purposes that does not seem warranted in light of the very history Ike invokes, and that he then puzzles out in Buck and Buddy's commissary books.

The twin brothers had originated the family debate by both accepting and then trying to modify the legacy left to them by their father, old Carothers. They move out of the big house, the conspicuous symbol of a slave economy, and move into the one-room log cabin, "refusing to allow any slave to touch any timber of it other than the actual raising into place the logs which two men alone could not handle." Even so, Buck and Buddy treat their slaves as animals, herding them "without question protest or recourse, into the tremendous abortive edifice scarcely yet out of embryo."

Because the commissary books are, in a sense, the past itself—"the yellowed pages and the brown thin ink in which was recorded the injustice and a little at least of its amelioration and restitution faded back forever into the anonymous communal original dust"—they give to Ike's investigation a sense of immediacy found nowhere else in Faulkner's fiction.[18] Buck and Buddy use their ledgers as business accounts, journals, diaries, and chronologies. In the process of accustoming himself to the varied uses of the ledgers, Ike is also accustoming himself to the thought patterns, the sense of history, and indeed the heritage he had debated with Cass. Ike's obsession with the ledgers, with an accounting of the past, also reflected Faulkner's own ledger-keeping at Greenfield Farm. Keeping accounts straight mattered deeply for financial and emotional reasons.

The ledgers reveal that Buck and Buddy do their best to put together a complete account of what they know about their family as it had been established by their father and grandfather. After their father's death, the twin McCaslins conscientiously attempt to free their family's slaves in the only way they know how—through business transactions recorded in the family ledgers. That the slaves are more than just property, more than just a part of plantation "business" to Buck and Buddy, is clear from the entries in which Buck notes that neither Fibby nor Roskus wants to leave the plantation and that Thucydus wants to earn his freedom.

Buck makes sure that the 27th and 28th of June 1837, the days on which "A.@ T. McCaslin" tried to free their slaves after their father's death, are fully and precisely recorded. Two entries in the ledger, one by Buck and one by Buddy, seem to have been Ike's first insight into why it was so important to free Thucydus on the very day after old Carothers died: *"Eunice Bought by Father in New Orleans 1807 $650. dolars. Marrid to Thucydus 1809 Drownd in Crick Christmas Day 1832."* Buddy's entry is easily the most dramatic in all of the ledgers, for it is made without preface or explanation and reaffirmed after Buck's skeptical reactions two days later:

> *June 21th 1833 Drownd herself*
>
> *23 Jun 1833 Who in hell ever heard of a niger drownding him self*
>
> *Aug 13th 1833 Drownd herself*

Buck brings out the truly shocking nature of Buddy's statement by expressing an assumption of his time, that a slave had no life of his own that he could think of ending. Buck is not reflecting on the particular circumstances of Eunice's death (note his change from "herself" to "him self") but is betraying his notions about black people in general.

Ike does not share his father's attitudes toward black people, and so the nature of his questions is different. It is not quite so surprising to him that Eunice should commit suicide, but he is perplexed by Uncle Buddy's insistence on the point. Additional entries record that Eunice died six months before her daughter Tomasina (Tomey) gave birth to a child (Turl). On June 21, 1833, perhaps after the birth of Tomey's Turl, Buddy realized she had committed suicide. On June 28, 1837, four years later, and a day after old Carothers died, Thucydus, Eunice's husband, was offered his freedom. Once Ike looks at his grandfather's will, he realizes that old Carothers "made no effort either to explain or obfuscate the thousand-dollar legacy to the son [Tomey's Turl] of an unmarried slave-girl." If never stated by old Carothers, it is nevertheless clear to Ike, as presumably to Buddy, that old Carothers would have left such a legacy only to his own son, and that he shifted the burden and the consequences of his sin to the next two generations of his family rather than directly acknowledge his responsibility to his black son.

But why would Eunice commit suicide? Ike reads in the ledgers that Eunice's daughter died in childbirth. Old Carothers, Ike conjectures, impregnated his own daughter, and that is another reason why he could not directly acknowledge his son. Ike strengthens his shocking inference by noting that his grandfather, who "never went anywhere more than his sons in their time ever did and who did not need another slave, had gone all the way to New Orleans and bought" Eunice. Ostensibly seeking a mate for Thucydus, old Carothers had evidently obtained a mistress for himself. Ike then shifts to the only other concrete evidence he has: remembering the light-skinned Tomey's Turl, his father Buck's unacknowledged half brother. Buddy's insistence on Eunice's suicide finally makes sense. Tomey's Turl received his white blood from Carothers's intercourse not only with Tomasina but also with her mother, Eunice. Faulkner himself had no doubt that Ike is right: "The ledger excerpts in Go Down, Moses were a little to set a tone and an atmosphere," he wrote to historian Bell Wiley, "but they also told a story of how the negros became McCaslins too. Old McCaslin bought a handsome octoroon and got a daughter on her and then got a son on that daughter; that son was his mother's child and her brother at the same time; he was both McCaslin's son and his grandson."[19]

Buddy's brief but insistent record of Eunice's suicide drives Ike to imagine Eunice's last moments: "He seemed to see her actually walking into the icy creek on that Christmas day six months before her daughter's and her lover's (Her first lover's he thought. Her first) child was born, solitary, inflexible, griefless, ceremonial, in formal and succinct repudiation of grief and despair who had already had to repudiate belief and hope." In an act of empathy, Ike creates a scene akin to Rider's despair after his wife's death. Ike invests Eunice with a dignity and integrity that are only hinted at in the historical record and that Buck and Buddy seem to have only partially recognized.[20]

The "rank dead icy air" in which Ike asks himself why Eunice drowned herself is reminiscent of Quentin in the cold, tomb-like room asking himself why Henry killed Bon. For both young men the past is of immense importance to their sense of identity; they cannot live in the present without reckoning with the past. Neither Quentin nor Ike proves capable of living a full life. Their plight, so familiar to what Faulkner confronted with his own family's occluded racial history, was his only way of acknowledging a deep affinity with black people like Eunice and Rider. *Go Down, Moses* implicitly recognizes the crucial importance of his black kin in his life and work.

In part 5 of "The Bear," Ike retreats from his heritage in the guise of repudiating change. He is disturbed at the new signs of progress represented by the planing mill that will tear down the wall of wilderness as part of the unceasing encroachment on nature and the mania of ownership that estranges Ike from the present. He seeks refuge in the unceasing round of nature, although an immersion in it is the antithesis of history.

In "Delta Autumn," which is very specifically set a year before America's entry into World War II (November 1940), Ike, now seventy-three, serenely rejects Roth's low opinion of mankind and his bitter tirade against the degeneration of the nation unfit to fight Hitler and too susceptible to homegrown fascism and superficial patriotism: "singing God bless America in bars at midnight and wearing dime-store flags in our lapels." Ike notes that the country has always had its defenders: "My pappy and some other better men than any of them you named [Roosevelt and Willkie] tried once to tear it in two with a war, and they failed." Although Ike believes that man always has the potential to be just a little better than his circumstances allow him to be, he acknowledges his disappointment in man's failure to take advantage of his God-given opportunities. But his own refusal to accept responsibility for the plantation makes him an ineffective counter to Roth's vision of tyranny, both in public and private life, and he is disturbed by his own responsibility to the "does," the women who, according to Ike, make fighting for one's country a meaningful act of self-defense. All along Legate, Roth's hunting buddy, has been referring to Roth's black lover as a "doe," and Roth is perhaps more irascible than usual, voicing a somewhat darker view of humanity than he expresses in "The Fire and the Hearth." In that chapter he shows his other side, his devotion to Mollie Beauchamp, inspired by Callie Barr, who taught Roth to be a gentleman.

Neither Ike nor Roth can quite fulfill their responsibilities. Ike acts as Roth's agent in paying off Roth's mistress, who had had a child by him. Ike assumes that her return to the hunting camp is motivated by feelings of revenge, but the woman's responses show how unfair Ike has been to the couple: "I would have made a man of him. He's not a man yet. You spoiled him. You, and Uncle Lucas and Aunt Mollie. But mostly you." Cutting himself off from the present has only meant that Ike repeats the past, failing to recognize his own kin, so the woman has to tell him she is a descendant of Tennie's Jim. Ike responds in "amazement, pity, and outrage," "You're a nigger!"

This is a powerful, paradoxical moment that tests Ike's capacity to empathize. He sounds surprised and also brutal, especially after his haunting re-creation of Eunice's suicide. And for Faulkner himself? What did this moment mean? He used the word "nigger" frequently, and "Negro" appears in the novel more than a hundred and "Negress" thirteen times, in both lowercase and uppercase, perhaps signaling "a moment of transition in the development of his political consciousness."[21]

To Ike, this "nigger" is as inconceivable a match for Roth as Charles Bon was for Judith: *"Maybe in a thousand or two thousand years in America, he* [Ike] *thought. But not now! Not now!"* And her response might as well be Bon's: "Old man, have you lived so long and forgotten so much that you dont remember anything you ever knew or felt or even heard about love?" He gives her cynical advice to go north and take revenge on "a black man" and surrenders to a bitter condemnation of the present, equating the loss of the wilderness and the degradation of humanity.

Like the ending of *Absalom, Absalom!,* which projects into the North, into the Western Hemisphere, and into the future, the novel's coda, "Go Down, Moses," shifts to a Chicago jail where Butch Beauchamp, a convicted murderer, awaits execution. Beauchamp, born a McCaslin black man, now in the numbers racket, answers the census taker's questions in a "voice which was anything under the sun but a southern voice or even a Negro voice." He is imprisoned in a "steel cubicle" and lives in a denatured atmosphere, the antithesis of Ike's wilderness experience, in which all of the color, other than that of the steel fixtures, comes from the overdressed prisoner himself: "He wore one of those sports costumes called ensembles in the men's shop advertisements, shirt and trousers matching and cut from the same fawn-colored flannel, and they had cost too much and were draped too much, with too many pleats."

The scene is a manifold contrast to the world presented in previous chapters—the integrity that Rider's black voice gives to his experience, the natural beauty of the wilderness, the economy and frugality of Ike and the other hunters. Against Butch's "sports costume" sit Lucas's fifty-year-old hat and Lucas's "small metal dispatch box which his white grandfather, Carothers McCaslin himself, had owned almost a hundred years ago," and in which Lucas kept the "knotted rag tight and solid with the coins, some of which dated back almost to Carothers McCaslin's time, which he had begun to save before he was ten years old." In the second part of "Go Down, Moses" there are references to Gavin Stevens's "rumpled linen suit" and the newspaper editor's "old fashioned boiled shirt." On the other hand, Butch's "steel cubicle" may stir memories of Ike's "rented cubicle" in "Delta Autumn." In part 1 of "Was," Ike sleeps on an "iron cot"; in part 1 of "Go Down, Moses," Butch lies on a "steel cot" in striking contrast to Rider, who tears his iron cot "clean out of the floor it was bolted to." Although on opposite ends of a moral and historical and racial scale, both men are McCaslins who have, each in his own way, repudiated a heritage and tried to seal off the agony of loss that impels Rider's violence. In a sense Butch has also taken Ike's advice to Roth's black lover and gone north.

In "Go Down, Moses," Gavin Stevens, another outsider, like the deputy in "Pantaloon in Black," is largely ignorant of the relationships between black people in his own community. Stevens is more sensitive and compassionate than the deputy, but his perceptions of black people are largely abstract and patronizing. He treats very lightly Mollie's accusation that Roth Edmonds sold her Benjamin into Egypt because he does not understand the significance of Roth's throwing Butch off the plantation for breaking into the commissary store. Butch offends against the laws of property and against the established order the commissary represents, but Roth is equally wrong in denying responsibility for Butch's fate, so that both violate the plantation tradition of interdependence and mutual obligation, which Faulkner carried on in his own extended family at Rowan Oak. Roth's sense of duty and his complaints about his patriarchal role are not that different from Faulkner's own tirades against his dependents.

Stevens attends Butch's funeral in the black community in a setting Faulkner obviated in his services for Caroline Barr. Like Stevens, Faulkner remained an observer, building out his story after watching a coffin come into town on a train.[22] Stevens cannot share the traditions embedded in the communal mourning of his black neighbors. He panics in a manner reminiscent of the white deputy's hysterical reaction to Rider and wants to resume the status quo. Stevens's parting words—"'Come on,' he said. 'Let's get back to town. I haven't seen my desk in two days'"—match Buck's last words to Uncle Buddy in "Was": "Go on and start breakfast. It seems to me I've been away from home a whole damn month." Stevens, like Buck, is a man of his time, but his attitudes are also continuous with Buck's.

Faulkner's concern with change is embodied in the artistic and technical aspects of his work in the sense that he links character development to the processes of time. Here the historical dimension of Faulkner's imagination is the same as in *Absalom, Absalom!,* in which what a character's actions come to signify depends on the time from which they are viewed. Lengthen, shorten, or abolish the historical perspective, and the meaning of human actions and human character changes. How we perceive a character, then, depends very much upon how we adapt to the novel—upon, that is, the imaginative level reached. In both novels there is always another level, more intricate than the previous one, so that character creation becomes a historical exploration of the interaction between our past and present perceptions of specific figures.

The progressive nature of Faulkner's exploration of the past is especially apparent toward the end of *Go Down, Moses,* as parts 4 and 5 of "The Bear" and "Delta Autumn" all read like possible conclusions to the book that are superseded, each in its turn, by another attempt at closure. The book's meaning expands through these conceivable conclusions, but it does not end in any finite sense. Still another conclusion, beyond "Go, Down, Moses," is possible, although Faulkner thought that with this ending he had achieved a structure for the work that would at the end be sufficiently apparent to return us to "Was" and to a sense of the past as still transforming and perfecting itself in our minds.

Stand apart from the seven individual chapters of *Go Down, Moses,* and from the ways they are connected to each other, and look at a larger structural dynamic: The first three chapters deal with plantation life in the South and with the history of race relations between the dominant white master class and their repressed black slaves. The wilderness out of which the white man carved this world is a minor theme. In the next three chapters, the major and minor themes are reversed, and the world of white civilization is seen through the perspective of the wilderness as an encroaching set of future conditions. The resolution of this dialectic of wilderness and civilization is accomplished in the last chapter, briefly set in Chicago and then in Jefferson. In the town and the city, however, the same problems of white-black relationships occur, the same consequent question of what constitutes a genuine human community is posed. The white man's invasions of (in turn) the wilderness, the plantation, the town, and the city are successively the focal turning points that define his increasing distance from his own sources. For Ike, man's evil increases with the distance in time from man's initial violation of the wilderness. But *Go Down, Moses* itself seems to argue that good and evil are the basic, unquantifiable antinomies of all stages of history. Butch Beauchamp, for instance, is not corrupted in the city. He goes to the city because he is already corrupt, and because he has as a result been expelled from his native land. The census taker who inquires after his real name and background is just as shocked as a member of Jefferson would be to hear that Butch does not care about his family and does not concern himself about the disposal of his body. Although the census taker is also in a "numbers racket," he does not treat Butch merely as a number but responds to Butch's own inhumanity as might any sensitive human being. Gavin Stevens, with his Heidelberg Ph.D., is not less humane than Ike, who has been schooled in the wilderness. A sense of humanity, in short, is not tied to a particular place, and Ike's assumption to the contrary (that the wilderness is the special preserve of universal moral values) renders him powerless in a changing world. As in *Absalom, Absalom!,* past and present are not joined by emphasizing the sameness of any two periods of time, but by dramatizing history as a human process that is going on at all times and all places.

"Our Most Distinguished Unread Talent"

So said the reviewer in the *Boston Globe* (May 6, 1942), seconded by the *Trenton Times* (May 9), which deemed *Go Down, Moses* Faulkner at his best. His difficult style and subject matter that put some people off also relegated him to a niche even among the literati who had yet to absorb the implications of his work. In short, unlike Hemingway, Faulkner was not a digestible appetizer for a literary party let alone for mass consumption. Even a distinguished critic like Lionel Trilling in the *Nation* (May 30) could not fathom the novel's purpose or structure, calling "Pantaloon in Black," for example, an inferior story unrelated to the rest of the volume. But one critic, Malcolm Cowley in the *New Republic* (June 29), began to come around, admitting that "there is no other American writer who has been consistently misrepresented by critics, including myself."

A few reviewers, like John Temple Graves in the *Saturday Review* (May 2), saw that the South per se is not really the point: "Reading the stories with Hitler's war going on tends to make you give certain names to certain of their motifs. You seem to recognize the stern and bloody surviving which the Nazis preach, the pure democracies Walt Whitman sang, and the fatal heredity and environment which made the late Clarence Darrow pity all men for their crimes." Graves understood that in order to triumph in the war, Americans had to understand their own criminality, what Americans had done to Americans of different races, which the pure democracy of the woods could not wipe out, as Ike's own reactionary politics demonstrate. "We who are now called on for our instincts of survival," Graves argued, "can feel the click of words like these": "It was of the men, not white nor black nor red but men, hunters, with the will and hardihood to endure and the humility and skill to survive, and the dogs and the bear and deer juxtaposed and reliefed against it, ordered and compelled by and within the wilderness in the ancient and unremitting contest according to the ancient and immitigable rules which voided all regrets and brooked no quarter;—the best game of all, the best of all breathing." Ed Werkman in the *Pittsburgh Press* (April 26) quoted, without comment, a passage from Ike's speech in "Delta Autumn" that revealed the novel's reach:

This Delta. This land which man has deswamped and denuded and derivered in two generations so that white men can own plantations and commute every night to Memphis and black men own plantations and ride in jim crow cars to Chicago to live in millionaires' mansions on Lake-shore Drive, where white men rent farms and live like niggers and niggers crop on shares and live like animals, where cotton is planted and grows man-tall in the very cracks of the sidewalks, and usury and mortgage and bankruptcy and measureless wealth, Chinese and African and Aryan and Jew, all breed and spawn together until no man has time to say which one is which nor cares.

Ike's own pride in his heritage, no matter how much he deplores it, is set against the chaotic, contradictory, and paradoxical nature of modern life. The "deswamped and denuded and derivered" land leads to the ecological disaster of *The Wild Palms,* and up North he sees an exploitive economy and interracial coupling that is mindless and rootless. Reviewers were not pre-pared to recognize, let alone deal with, Ike's diatribe. Most of them praised "The Bear" but failed to see how "Delta Autumn" severely compromised Ike's moral position, which itself grew out of the interaction of three races: red, white, and black. Ike's outrage is the voice of panic—almost a prediction of what was in store for the world after the Pearl Harbor attack, when America opposed Hitler's rendition of purity but remained racist. The global import of *Go Down, Moses,* published five months after America's entry into the war, went unheeded and unread.

7

War

July 1940–June 1942

VISITATIONS, CORRESPONDENCE, AND EXHIBITIONS

Historian Bell Irvin Wiley, teaching at Ole Miss, became a friend of the family and visited Rowan Oak frequently. He called his host a "very kind and gentle man" who was just wonderful with children. Faulkner only turned cold when asked about his books. Wiley never heard him swear and admired his impeccable tweeds that reminded him of a country squire. Wiley never saw him drunk, but he drank socially and liked to sing Negro spirituals. Wiley admired his voice, and Faulkner was often called on to sing his favorite, "Water Boy," first recorded by Fats Waller in 1922 and Earl Hines in 1941. The song that seems to have originated in Georgia is a call for water from a parched convict pounding rock, or in other versions a slave in the field, crying out, "Water boy / Where are you hiding?" No one pounds that rock like the voice that warns the elusive water boy: "I'm gonna whoop this rock, boy / From here to Macon / All the way to the jail." It is at once a mournful, boastful, and relentless song: "If you don't come right here / Gonna tell your pa on you."

The lives of black folk intrigued, troubled, and amused William Faulkner. Some of his behavior fell into the rhythmic, repetitive routines of folk songs. He liked to walk in to the Oxford square on Saturdays when country people in their wagons came to town. A black man called Obed would approach Faulkner and would invariably say that "Mr. Luke Pegees had said to Obed that William Faulkner was 'the prettiest little man in this whole town.' And then he would ask William Faulkner for the loan of twenty-five cents. And

William Faulkner would 'loan' Obed twenty-five cents."[1] Closer to home there was Uncle Ned. Faulkner had directed him to slaughter Black Buster, a stud bull that had proved disappointing. At the barbecue, Faulkner noticed that another bull, pedigreed and highly prized, was missing but that Black Buster was in the field, as Ned admitted when Faulkner asked him. Faulkner looked down at his plate and asked, "who's this? I thought I told you to kill Black Buster and I thought you told me you did." Ned, backing away swiftly, said, "Master, I calls them all Black Buster."

Wiley did not think Estelle got enough credit for being the "balance wheel," running the house superbly, cooking magnificent meals, taking care of her children with affection, and dressing her daughter in exquisite hand-made clothes. And yet it was Estelle's drinking, not her husband's, that Wiley observed. Estelle could be falling-down drunk two or three weeks at a time. To Wiley, Estelle was a wife so supportive of her husband that she broke down, unable to cope with a literary genius.[2]

July 19, 1940: An aspiring poet hitchhiked to Oxford, Mississippi. He asked a truck driver for directions to William Faulkner's home. The farmer?, the trucker asked. "No, he's a writer," Dan Brennan replied. "Don' know him." Brennan went to the local drugstore, not knowing about Mac Reed, and found the name in the phone book. A woman answered, soft-voiced and pleasant. "Does Mr. William Faulkner live there?" After a beat, she answered guardedly, "Who's calling please?" Brennan knew enough to keep it casual: "I'm just a college student from up north. I've always liked Mr. Faulkner's books, and I'd like to meet him. I'm passing through." Another beat. "Will you hold the line, please?" Brennan waited and then heard a man's voice, "slow and measured": "Yes?" Later Brennan pictured "those black, motionless eyes," holding back and then saying, "Why don't you come out in the morning? About nine."

Brennan remembered the sunlight coming through the cedar trees in "thick yellow shafts" along the driveway. As he approached this southern mansion that belonged in a book, not to mention an MGM movie, a "short, black-eyed, hawk-nosed" man approached leading a pony ridden by a child with hair that shone in the golden light of morning and with the kind of "pink and white face made for a cameo brooch." Faulkner appeared all in white—duck trousers, shirt, and tennis shoes. He had finely wrought hands and an aristo-cratic air. Change the nose, Brennan thought, and you had Ronald Colman, the model of the gentleman hero for actors like Dana Andrews and writers like Norman Mailer. In the enchanted world of Rowan Oak, Jill greeted the visitor with a "bell-like, light, airy, a fairy-tale voice." Yet just beyond the drive was a paved, modern street.

Brennan tried to make small talk and waited a good long minute before Faulkner answered his question about how long Jill had been riding horses. "Three years." As Faulkner gazed down the drive, he said, "You know, a woman should know only how to do three things." He paused, shifted his pipe in his mouth, musing: "tell the truth, ride a horse, and sign a check." Brennan played along and asked if Jill could sign a check. Faulkner did not change his quiet expression when he answered, "That's the last thing you want to teach a woman." Jill's second-grade report card (1940–41) extolled her independence, careful work turned in on time, her lively reading aloud, her courtesy, initiative, and growing vocabulary. She read more books than the average child.[3]

Faulkner let Brennan look around the house and stay while Faulkner continued to type two stories that day, allowing the literary pilgrim to salvage sheets of discarded drafts, chapters from Go Down, Moses. "Do you feel your work is getting better?," Brennan asked. "Ten years ago I was much better," Faulkner said, smiling. "Used to take more chances. Maybe I'm tired. I've had insomnia lately." He had his mind on Estelle's lunch: "peas, corn bread, fried chicken, and a green salad." Then Faulkner, along with Jill, took Brennan deep into the woods, where they fished in a pool, Faulkner threading worms onto the hook of Jill's cane pole. After a brief stop at Greenfield Farm, where Faulkner spoke with a black tenant farmer about a brood sow and said he wanted to buy more land, they went into town. As they drove past red-brick school buildings, Faulkner said: "The wounded were brought in here from a battle up at Holly Springs. You can see the shell marks in the wall in day time." "Come back again," Faulkner said as they ended their day, with the moon overhead and the frogs piping.[4]

The Faulkners, judging by Estelle's letter to Brennan, were charmed by the visit: It had been a "sincere pleasure to have you here." She had wanted to send him an Ole Miss yearbook, but "until *now* hadn't the remotest idea where to send it!?!? You see, my dear young man—*I am old enough to reprimand you*—But speaking of being old—don't you for a minute let your friends think that I look like that scandalous picture—Promise?"[5] This vintage Estelle, complete with underlinings and exclamation marks, captures her vivacious, flirting, actressy persona. She may have been joking, but her age and her appearance mattered to her a great deal. Visiting Rowan Oak a decade or so later, Dorothy Commins discovered that "Estelle had every known jar of cream in her bathroom that had ever been invented for your face to make you look younger and all."[6]

June 18, 1941: Nearly a year after Brennan's visit, Ben Wasson arrived at Rowan Oak with Shelby Foote, who had briefly met Faulkner in 1939. Then eighteen-year-old Foote showed up at Rowan Oak—much to the consternation of his traveling companion, Walker Percy—with a "cover story," asking how Foote could obtain a copy of *The Marble Faun*. Faulkner replied: "I don't know where you can get one. Maybe Leland Hayward [an agent Ben Wasson worked for] could find you one. I can give you his address." He asked Foote where he was from. When Foote answered Greenville, Faulkner invited him to take a walk, saying: "I just finished a book about your country over there. . . . It's called *If I Forget Thee, Jerusalem*."[7]

On his second visit, Foote found Faulkner to be even better company. Estelle greeted Wasson and Foote, the "ebullient and perfect hostess," who announced in the parlor: "Billy and Jill are puttering out there in the barn, whatever that means. Lord knows, they spend enough time out there." Ben noticed Maud's portrait of young Bill over the mantel, and Estelle's hangings and other items from China. Faulkner came in and exchanged a few words about Delta planters and their rich soil: "I just have a small dirt farm. Got to scratch for what I get out of it—beans, corn." On the side porch, overlooking the rose garden, where it was cooler, Bill said: "That's Estelle's doing. She's good with all kinds of flowers. Has a sho-nuff green thumb." He sat there thinking about how the land flowered for women while men "brought in the meat" as Estelle served the drinks. Not many visitors paid much attention to Estelle, but in Wasson's company she brightened up, talking about her old-fashioned roses: "I don't go in much for the newfangled varieties." She turned to Foote: "Shelby, I hope you have a girl." He did not have a "special one," he told her. "And you, Ben? Whatever became of your movie star romance? I read about it in the movie magazines, and Louella Parsons wrote about it, too, didn't she?" Estelle may have been referring to Wasson's dates with Miriam Hopkins. "Those days seem long ago, now," Wasson said. "Hollywood," Faulkner muttered. Estelle changed the subject: "I tried my hand at a novel a long time ago, but Ben and Billy both said it wasn't good enough, so I stopped trying." As Wasson recalled, her "mouth dropped petulantly." Wasson evidently did not have a word to say about this sore point.[8] As Foote and Wasson were departing in the late afternoon for the SAE fraternity house on the Ole Miss campus, Estelle urged Bill to tell the boys about what their cook had said about the yard man. Bill laughed and said, "He puts me in mind of a long dusty black snake, just run out from under a stump."

July 6, 1941: Faulkner wrote an unusual letter to critic Warren Beck, who had sent three articles, "Faulkner and the South," "Faulkner's Point of View," and "William Faulkner's Style," which had appeared in March, May, and the spring of 1941 in the *Antioch Review, College English,* and *American Prefaces.*

Beck, far better than any other contemporary, identified Faulkner's stance: "a Mississippian who has transcended provincialism without losing artistic devotion to a locale; he is a Southerner who had become disinterested without losing interest."⁹ He cherished with Swift "the idea of a man as a creature capable of rationality or he would not be so intolerably affronted by the evils he contemplates, nor would he be so diligent in searching out their historical and psychological roots, nor would he create protagonists like Benbow and Hightower." Quentin Compson, the reporter in *Pylon*, Bayard Sartoris in *The Unvanquished,* and Ratliff in *The Hamlet* all embodied their author's "systematic protest against those evils, as well as an expression of his personal disenchantment." Beck responded to those critics who believed Faulkner's faults had been excused by his idolaters, noting his awareness of Faulkner's mannerisms and repetitions, although the latter often worked well in describing the mania of characters like Miss Rosa, and even Faulkner's prolixity had a cumulative power: "He may be unfashionably rhapsodic, but he seldom falls into the preciosity that lingers over a passage for its own sweet sake."¹⁰ Florid passages are sustained by their brilliant imagery and "colloquial bits," speaking with the "tongues of themselves and of William Faulkner."¹¹ Beck quotes several passages from the novels to demonstrate Faulkner's mastery of diction and rhythm. The word for Faulkner that Beck repeats throughout the discussion of style is "fullness" in its effort to speculate and report and dramatize.

Faulkner responded directly: "Thank you for sending the articles. I agree with them. You found implications which I had missed. I wish that I had consciously intended them; I will certainly believe I did it subconsciously and not by accident." No critic could wish for a better vindication not only of his particular work but of criticism itself, and no biographer could be happier since Beck also suggested he was reading Faulkner's temperament, which he likened to a melancholy Hamlet. Faulkner then stated his credo, one that would be expressed again in the short stories he would write during the war: "I have been writing all the time about honor, truth, pity, consideration, the capacity to endure well grief and misfortune and injustice and then endure again, in terms of individuals who observed and adhered to them not for reward but for virtue's own sake, not even merely because they are admirable in themselves, but in order to live with oneself and die peacefully with oneself when the time comes."¹² To Beck's discussion of faults, Faulkner replied: "I have found no happy balance between method and material. I doubt that it exists for me." He speculated that perhaps formal schooling would have made a difference, but mostly he blamed his defects on writing "too fast, too much. I decided what seems to me now a long time ago that something worth saying knew better than I did how it needed to be said, and that it was better said poorly even than not said. And besides, there would always be a next time. . . . Excuse all the I's," Faulkner concluded. "I'm still having trouble reconciling method and material, you see."

July 1942: *New York Times* critic Brooks Atkinson visited Oxford. The mayor, Branham Hume, an old friend of Faulkner's, insisted they go out to Rowan Oak. Hume, the son of Ole Miss's chancellor, had been part of a Faulkner secret society, the M.O.A.K.S, the Mystical Order of—no one seemed to remember of what. They sported one-dollar canes on club occasions. At football games and other events they showed up with their canes and derbies. They golfed together. At musicales Hume played a ukulele.[13] Now Hume was about to take a leave of absence to serve in the navy.[14] Atkinson remembered their drive up to the house with barking dogs and children, black and white. Faulkner answered Hume's knock and extended a reserved greeting to Atkinson, perhaps concerned that he was to be interviewed. But they settled into unhurried talk about local affairs that reminded Atkinson of the torpid pace of Frenchman's Bend and Jefferson, with Faulkner sounding like Ratliff, "a reliable citizen of long standing." A charmed Atkinson wrote, twenty years later, "I have always been glad that he [Hume] insisted."[15]

Atkinson said nothing about the state of repair at Rowan Oak, but it seems that it required more attention than Faulkner could afford to give it. One visitor mentioned its dilapidated condition, typical of old southern homes at the time. "The porticoes seemed to be a little rotting and the wallpaper over the stairway and along the side of the stairway was hanging down in festoons."[16]

That summer of 1942, Robert Daniel at Yale University organized the first major exhibit of Faulkner's work and career. He wrote to Phil Stone about what might be available. Copies of *The Marble Faun* were hard to find. Stone reminisced about how hard it had been to unload copies of the book: "It is most amusing nowadays to see some of these same people trying to get autographs out of Faulkner, when they refused to pay $1.50 for their autograph presentation copy of 'The Marble Faun.'" He set Daniel straight about Faulkner's bogus war record and revealed their growing estrangement: "I am disappointed that he has not developed into a better writer and I am afraid he has already reached his peak."[17] A delighted Daniel received Faulkner manuscripts from Aunt Bama and told her: "These are just right; and the notes you made are most helpful. I was also very glad to get the poems: unpublished poems are always fascinating, especially 'juvenilia.'" The summer exhibition included five illuminated upright cases. Students were taken with the movie stills but seemed to look at everything, including a sixth flat case.[18]

In her memoir, Dean Faulkner Wells remembered she was six going on seven in 1942, when she attended the formal Faulkner dinners. Her uncle presided, as houseboys brought out Estelle's excellent curries and chutneys served on delicate china, along with silver bread-and-butter plates and silver goblets set down on hand-embroidered linen place mats. Adults had to choose between smoking and drinking wine. The smokers would have their glasses turned upside down. Smoking, Faulkner explained, dulled the palate. Everyone stood until Estelle sat down. No one ate until Estelle took the first bite, "just in case the food was poisoned," Faulkner said. No one left the table unless he granted permission to be excused.[19]

During the summer months, almost every night, Maud took Dean to the movies at the Lyric Theater in Oxford, and Faulkner often did the same with Jill, right at the time when his finances were again precarious. He was not selling enough stories. "I am broke," he wrote to Robert Haas.[20] "Sure enough, do you know of anyone who wants to send a missionary to California for a few weeks?," he asked Bennett Cerf.[21]

The radio brought the war into everyone's home. That's how in Frenchman's Bend the nine-year-old narrator of "Two Soldiers" learns about Pearl Harbor and the Japanese and runs away from home to join his brother, Pete Grier, who cannot bear to miss the action and has enlisted in the army in Memphis, which to the narrator seems "like about a dozen whole towns bigger than Jefferson . . . set up on one edge in a field, standing up into the air higher than ara hill in all Yoknapatawpha County." Here is the description of an elevator: "a little room without nothing in it but a nigger dressed up in a uniform a heap shinier than them soldiers had, and the nigger shut the door, and then I hollered, 'Look out!' and grabbed, but it was all right; that whole little room jest went right on up and stopped and the door opened and we was in another hall." Pete convinces his brother to return to Frenchman's Bend. A soldier drives the boy home in a fast car—so fast that the boy is disoriented, his sense of time and space collapsing—and as he reaches home, he exclaims, "it was like I hadn't never been to Memphis a-tall." The boy begins to cry—why he does not say, but it seems that the rapidity of changing places, of running past them so quickly in the car, has undone the security of home and his place in the world.

"Shall Not Perish," narrated by the same boy, now slightly older, is about Pete's death and the deaths of other Yoknapatawpha young men. Like "Two Soldiers," this story is as much about the advent of the modern world as it is about the war. Pete had sent home from San Francisco a satchel with gifts inside closed up with a zipper, a device the family has never seen before and that they slide up and down its clicking track—the miniature locomotive of change in their remote rural lives. This poor country family brings the satchel with the shoes they are going to wear to funeral rites in town, where the wealthy Major de Spain mourns his aviator son's death. "The war years, 1941–45, were great levelers," Dean Faulkner Wells notes.[22] De Spain is bitter about his son's death: "He had no country: this one I too repudiate. His country and mine both was ravaged and polluted and destroyed eighty years ago, before even I was born. His forefathers fought and died for it then, even though what they fought and lost for was a dream. He didn't even have a dream. He died for an illusion. In the interests of usury, by the folly and rapacity of politicians, for the glory and aggrandisement of organized labor!" Against this southern outcry the narrator remembers his grandfather, a Civil War veteran, who cries out during a western picture show that the cavalry are coming. The narrator, his father, and Pete are embarrassed, but Mrs. Grier upbraids them: "He wasn't running from anybody! He was running in front of them, hollering at all clods to look out because better men than they were coming, even seventy-five years afterwards, still powerful, still dangerous, still coming!" De Spain's diatribe is overwhelmed in the story's patriotic devotion to fighting for home:

> the places that men and women have lived in and loved whether they had anything to paint pictures of them with or not, all the little places quiet enough to be lived in and loved and the names of them before they were quiet enough, and the names of the deeds that made them quiet enough and the names of the men and the women who did the deeds, who lasted and endured and fought the battles and lost them and fought again because they didn't even know they had been whipped, and tamed the wilderness and overpassed the mountains and deserts and died and still went on as the shape of the United States grew and went on. I knew them too: the men and women still powerful seventy-five years and twice that and twice that again afterward, still powerful and still dangerous and still coming, North and South and East and West, until the name of what they did and what they died for became just one single word, louder than any thunder.

Two world wars had changed the nature of the Civil War for the Falkners, who now regarded it in terms of what "shall not perish." Dean called Maud "obsessively patriotic": "During WWI, she had placed two stars on a piece of red, white, and blue felt and hung it in her window to show that she had sons serving in the armed forces—one for Jack, a marine who fought in the Argonne Forest in France—and one for William."[23] All the Falkners went to the movies for the newsreels and war news. One night in the theater much later in the war, Maud watched a newsreel about the invasion of Sicily and jumped up and said to the projectionist, *"Bob, run it back!"* Dean saw Uncle Jack, "in army uniform, a .45 pistol in his hand, wading ashore with the invading troops. . . . By the third or fourth invasion the audience was on their feet clapping and cheering 'That's our Jackie!'" As they walked home, Dean "felt completely safe and secure. Jack had saved Sicily from the Nazis and Pappy would save us from the Japanese."[24] Her response, very much like the narrator's in "Shall Not Perish," suggests that Faulkner's war stories reflected the pride many families felt about their part in the war.

At 6:00 p.m. every day, Maud opened the double doors of the console in her parlor and switched on the CBS News with H. V. Kaltenborn. She read a daily newspaper and subscribed to *Time* and *Life*. Faulkner probably heard about the news from his mother on his regular visits. His nephew Jimmy (John's son) trained with the Marine Corps and became the fighter pilot Faulkner had pretended to be. At forty-four, Jack Falkner managed to get a military intelligence assignment, much to the chagrin of his brother Bill, who could not get a commission from the navy.

Faulkner somehow attained the title of head of Home Defense in Lafayette County, charged with informing the rural citizenry about preparations for war. "But I'm not a speaker," he said to Charles Nelson, a local history teacher. "Would you do some speaking for me?" Nelson agreed, so Faulkner drove Nelson and his son out to Tula, sixteen miles from Oxford. They arrived at a "rusty, tin-roofed store" in this hamlet, and Faulkner hunched over with the men, telling them a story about a whiskey still that made them laugh. "He could easily have been taken for one of them, for his clothes were quite similar," Charles Nelson Jr. recalled. After his father gave a forty-five-minute talk, men gathered to talk with Nelson and a transformed Faulkner, "amiable" and nothing like the "introverted" figure the son, with aspirations to write, had usually encountered: "I thought of Stevenson's Dr. Jekyll and Mr. Hyde."

On the way home there were more surprises. Although Faulkner was well known as an anti–New Dealer, he spoke enthusiastically about the Tennessee Valley Authority and rural electrification. Even more remarkable was Faulkner's talk about his father, the model of a gentleman, Faulkner said, and "extremely kindhearted. He seemed to have a reverence for his father as sort of Godlike." Perhaps this was the beginning of a softening attitude that would result in the gentle portrayal of Murry as Maury in *The Reivers*.

On a second outing, as they drove along the winding highway through hills, ravines, and woodlands, Faulkner described the landscape in words that were "beautiful." They arrived in Abbeville, eleven miles from Oxford, to an empty schoolhouse where Nelson was supposed to speak. The men were all huddled together at the local garage listening to a Joe Louis heavyweight championship fight, and even afterward the men seemed in a daze and could not be gathered for a talk about home defense.[25]

Faulkner also went on neighborhood patrols as an air raid warden, wearing an official armband. His niece Dean remembered that a "blackout was in effect. Any sliver of light could provide a beacon for German or Japanese bombers. The fear of invasion in 1942 and '43 was very real." Sometimes she accompanied her uncle on his rounds when they would visit a Rowan Oak neighbor, Kate Baker, once a week. Faulkner would spot a light, and Baker would dutifully draw down a shade at his instructions. Kate would wink at Dean and invite them in for cake and coffee. "'No, no,' Pappy replied," Dean recalled. "We had rounds to make. I shrugged, wishing I could have some cake, yet intensely pleased with myself for serving my country." Much later, Dean would wonder just what was going on between Kate and Bill. As Dean tells it in her memoir, the light seemed like a welcoming signal. Kate was Estelle's good friend, and to Kate's daughter, Sandra, the idea of an affair between her mother and Faulkner seemed unimaginable. Dean thought otherwise.[26] Kate Baker went to New York twice a year to stock her Oxford square shop with the latest fashions. She dined at the restaurants Faulkner favored. It just seemed to Dean that the stylish Kate Baker belonged with William Faulkner. Dean herself was Faulkner's delight, reminding him of his swashbuckling brother. "We would discuss her father as if he was in the room," said Larry Wells, Dean's husband.[27]

ESCAPE FROM DEBTOR'S PRISON

Although full of patriotic fervor, Faulkner had another reason for wanting to enlist. "I am stale. Even a military job will dig me up and out for a while," he confessed to his agent, Harold Ober: "I have been trying for about ten years to carry a load that no artist has any business attempting: oldest son to widowed mother and inept brothers and nephew and wives and other female connections and their children, most of whom I dont like and with none of whom I have anything in common, even to make conversation about. I am either not brave enough or not scoundrel enough to take my hat and walk out. I dont know which." Did it cross his mind that his mother's father, Charlie Butler, had been scoundrel enough to dash out with the whole caboodle— the town's tax money and an octoroon mistress to boot? Butler, a topic never broached, Dean Faulkner Wells noted in her memoir, seemed a fitting precedent. Faulkner confided to Ober: "I believe I have discovered the reason inherent in human nature why warfare will never be abolished: it's the only condition under which a man who is not a scoundrel can escape for a while from his female kin."[28]

The debts mounted: unpaid grocery and telephone bills, a huge back tax bill, and another large bill due at Neilson's Department Store. Faulkner enclosed a check for ten dollars and would send more on account when he could, as he explained in a January 31, 1941, letter that is now proudly framed and displayed in the store, where attendees to the annual Faulkner conference and other visitors can view it. The exasperated debtor truculently concluded: "If this don't suit you, the only alternative I can think of is, in the old Miltonic phrase, sue and be damned. If you decide on that step, be assured that I shall do my best to see that the people who have fed me and my family will be protected, and after Uncle Sam gets through his meat-cutting, J. E. Neilson can have what is left. You may even get an autographed book. That will be worth a damn sight more than my autograph on a check dated ten months from now."[29]

Faulkner even asked Ober to find a magazine assignment, preferably in California, while he awaited a studio offer.[30] In the meantime, Bennett Cerf came up with his own proposal:

> Full half a dozen people have asked us, in course of the past month, whether or not we couldn't persuade you to do a whole novel about the present war that would be in the manner of your great short story, TURN-ABOUT. I don't know how you feel about a suggestion of this sort, but I do think I ought to pass it on to you. I know that, if you wanted to, you could deliberately write a book intended for a big sale and, if you ever do it, I promise that we'll whoop it up for you to the very limit of our ability. I remember that, in your introduction to the Modern Library edition of SANCTUARY, you explained that you had written this book with the laudable idea of making some real money out of it. Maybe you would like to take another whack at the old jackpot!

Such a book, the publisher wrote at the end of June to his unresponsive author, would "simply leave the boys like Fadiman with their pants down." Sales of *Go Down, Moses* were respectable, Cerf reported, but hardly enough to relieve Faulkner's financial distress.[31]

Although he had made as much as a thousand dollars per week working for Universal and Fox, he did not think he had been "or ever will be worth that to movies. It just took them five years to find it out. I will take anything above $100.00. I must have something somewhere, quick. For a month now I have had no cash whatever. I have borrowed a few dollars each week from my mother to pay the cook and laundry with." He had cashed in his life insurance. "Once I get away from here where creditors cannot hound me all the time, I think I can write and sell again," he wrote to Ober at the end of June.[32]

Faulkner complicated Ober's efforts to find work in Hollywood for his client by having earlier acceded to William Herndon's offer to look for a movie assignment. Just when Ober began to make headway, Herndon, after a five-month silence, claimed the exclusive right to represent Faulkner in negotiations with Warner Brothers. Faulkner had assumed Herndon had been unsuccessful, and chagrined by Herndon's accusation that Faulkner had been underhanded, the novelist sought to negotiate some fair and equitable arrangement with both agents, because he had been remiss in not writing to Herndon and severing their business together. Ober generously declined his commission and advised Faulkner to deal directly with Warner Brothers.

On July 18, he wrote to James J. Geller, head of Warner's story department, mentioning a letter he had received from Robert Buckner about working on a screenplay about Charles de Gaulle. "It is a good idea," he told Geller, "and I will be proud to work with it and I hope and trust I can do it justice." On July 22, Faulkner wired James Geller at the studio: "ACCEPT DEAL MADE BY HERNDON. WILL ARRIVE MONDAY SUBJECT TO TRANSPORTATION DELAYS. WILLIAM FAULKNER."[33]

8

Soldiering On

July 1942–January 1943

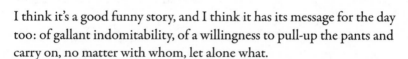

I think it's a good funny story, and I think it has its message for the day
too: of gallant indomitability, of a willingness to pull-up the pants and
carry on, no matter with whom, let alone what.
> —Faulkner to Harold Ober concerning "My Grandmother Millard
> and General Bedford Forrest and the Battle of Harrykin Creek"

"THE PRISON HOUSE OF WARNER BROTHERS"

Faulkner's Warner Brothers salary, three hundred dollars per week, shocked
his fellow writers. How could a writer so much their superior command so
little respect? The word passed down to Meta, now divorced from Wolfgang Rebner, was blackballed. Her friend Henriette Martin reported that
after Meta's marriage, a shattered Faulkner, surly, rude, and drunk, had been
deemed utterly unemployable. The studios might savage one another, but
they banded together to ban anyone labeled unreliable. "Poor Bill, he doesn't
know," Meta said, and following her friend's advice, she did not tell him.
Faulkner's extant letters do not reveal what he knew. His eagerness to settle
for so little may also have been a factor in determining his low salary, since
"you must never on any account show you want to go to Hollywood. If you
do, you will be simply devalued," wrote Ivor Montagu after his work as an
associate producer at Paramount. "If you are big enough, and it appears that
you do not want to go, or at least do not care whether you go or not, then
Hollywood will be after you with a cheque book."[1] Faulkner had finally been
hired by Jack Warner, who bragged about his big catch with small bait, saying

at parties that he had the best writer in America for three hundred dollars. At a Musso & Frank's reunion dinner, Faulkner explained to Meta, "I've been told that if I behave myself, stay sober, turn out the work, cause 'em not one scintilla of trouble, they'll tear up the contract and give me a new one."[2]

Before arriving he had sent Meta "unabashedly erotic" love letters that made it difficult for him to sleep: "I weigh 129 pounds and I want to put it all on you. . . . And as much in you as I can can can must must will will shall." He rejected her suggestion they live together to economize. He wanted to preserve "the mystery of each other," and his "Southern rectitude," which she found amusing in the author of *Sanctuary*. But she understood, remembering how he ran the water in the bathroom to "cover the evidence of his animality, bathing each time we made love." It was the southern gentleman's "need to pedestal the female, to spare her the indelicacies and harshnesses." She had no need of protection. "I would have loved him profane, but he didn't know it and it would have shocked him had he guessed."

But all was not as it had been. "What kind of love story did it become? Did you just fall right back into the pattern again?," asked Carpenter's collaborator, Orin Borsten. "Not exactly," Meta said. "Too many things had happened to me. There had been a maturing process. . . . An inner awareness was becoming part of my life's experience." Her second failed marriage had depressed her, and the six-day-a-week movie schedule, compounded by an allergy, exhausted her. The "early romantic feeling when it was all new and wonderfully exciting" had dissipated. Faulkner had expected as much, she surmised. "So I didn't think it was any great shock to him that I was a different kind of person."[3]

Talking about Jill was the only comfortable way this couple could deal with Faulkner's homesickness. It pleased Meta that Jill was taking piano lessons, but Faulkner seemed proudest of her horsemanship. He sent her a set of paints: "Granny will help you with them. If the 2 brushes dont paint like you need them to ask Granny to get you one that will." In late September he responded to her paintings: "Finest birthday I ever had." He thought he might "make a panel to hang on my office wall of my pictures one picture painted by Jill, one picture painted by Granny of Jill painting a picture . . . and a handkerchief embroidered by Mama with my natural signature on it." He sent his love home and told Jill: "I certainly am proud of your letters. Write to me and tell me about everything. I sure do miss home." And he tried to tell her at least a little about his doings: "The man I work with is named Mr. Buckner. He is from Virginia. He has a barbecue pit and a swimming pool. I go to his house and spend the night and we barbecue steak and swim. Wouldn't you like that?"[4]

He wanted his daughter to picture his life at the Highland Hotel. He had breakfast sent up to his room by an "oldish Negro waiter who likes me fine and brings me extra sugar." On a small terrace outside his room he ate his meal of orange juice, coffee, and toast with Estelle's homemade marmalade. This small establishment had a desk clerk, a bell boy, and one waiter who catered to old actresses whose talk made the meals noisy. He took a bus to the studio, although sometimes a fellow screenwriter picked him up in a car. He felt all right. He ate dinner in the cafe and wished "you and Mamma there too, so you and I could eat steak and roast beef and sometimes chicken and a lot of time fish together."[5]

He comforted Estelle: "You are doing all right. I am not worrying at all. Just spend it well, so we will have as much cash as we can save when I come home. I know things are high, and will be higher, I'm afraid. So don't worry. Hold down best you can, but don't worry about it."[6] He did not want to live without that jam: "would like some more preserves if you can spare it. I have a coffee pot in my office and will eat some preserves and bread too. Gave all other jam to Mrs. Buckner." Then he reminded her to get the furnace fixed.[7]

Faulkner joined Richard Aldington, Albert Maltz, Alvah Bessie, Jo Pagano, Al "Buzz" Bezzerides, John Collier, Stephen Longstreet, Steve Fisher, Tom Job, and other screenwriters in the "prison house of Warner Brothers," as Pagano put it. Pagano and Bezzerides probably saw more of Faulkner than the other writers. Meta observed that unlike the quiet and easygoing Pagano, Buzz was "big, outgoing, opinionated, his voice filled the room. He could overpower one in a conversation unless you were very direct. He would break into a conversation and you would just subside. He wasn't trying to be rude. He was so interested in the conversation that he was breaking in."[8] Faulkner admired Job's prodigious memory and ability to quote literary work at length, but Job thought Faulkner was easily his match. Meta remembered that Faulkner liked to be with Job and "liked to talk to him."[9] Faulkner listened to Fisher, a good-looking screenwriter in his mid-twenties pulling down an $1,800 weekly salary, describe his seduction of Hedy Lamarr, often called the most beautiful woman in Hollywood. Faulkner stood up and said, "I don't like it here," and left, never returning to that table, said screenwriter and novelist John Fante, who watched the walkout.

The well-read James J. Geller, head of the story department at Warner, admired Faulkner's fiction and invited him to parties. Sometimes Faulkner would show up and sit quietly while Geller did all the talking with guests such as Christopher Isherwood. These were good parties, according to Stephen Longstreet, who watched two black servants who would "do an Uncle Tom for William Faulkner."[10] Faulkner rarely seemed impressed with the company, although he made an exception for Mrs. Goldwyn. Clearly taken with her, he called her "quite pleasant."[11] Longstreet did not always know how to take Faulkner. What he said might be received as kidding or "truculent cruelty" and "sadistic humor." He seemed "a little sad, shabby, and I think he felt he had missed the boat. He had moments of silent lassitude."[12]

Jo Pagano, who had heard Jack Warner boasting about his bargain-basement acquisition of William Faulkner, remembered that at Warner Faulkner preferred to lunch with the grips, lighting men, and other film crew members. At their Toluca Lake home, Jo and Jean Pagano liked to entertain the courtly southerner, who sometimes brought Meta with him—a sure sign of how comfortable he felt in the Pagano home. "You know, Jo," Faulkner said to his soft-spoken friend, "in a lifetime of observing people, I've known few as nice as you are." He was always "Will" to them. After the Paganos hosted a dinner with Hedy Lamarr, Faulkner said, "I don't think she's so pretty, not as pretty as Miss Jean." She did his horoscope and detected a melancholy disposition. She told him he should write a book that would give people hope. He said, "I'll make a note of that, Miss Jean."[13] Pagano and Faulkner were a tweedy twosome, drinking quietly together in the aroma of tobacco.

Not all the drinking was quiet. Buzz claimed that he tried to keep Faulkner sober but also admitted to a spree with a sailor shipping out. This was probably the night that Faulkner treated them to an all-night-long rendition of a bawdy old Scots song:

There was fucking in the cowshed
And fucking in the cricks
You couldna hear the music
For the swishin of the pricks.

Bezzerides took Faulkner, recovering from a drinking binge, on an all-day car ride. At a light, two girls in a car looked at them, and Faulkner said, "You know, I could do with a strange woman." Stephen Longstreet said Bezzerides fawned on Faulkner, who hated Buzz but found him useful.[14] Meta said that Buzz and Bill had "rather severe disagreements," often over literary and personal matters, with Buzz then feeling Faulkner was "arrogant about his own status as a writer compared to Bezzerides."[15] Jo Pagano did not believe Faulkner had that much respect for Longstreet, who made too much of his own friendship with Faulkner.[16]

Longstreet said he first met Faulkner in New York in 1937, typing in a Random House office where Bennett Cerf had taken Longstreet. "This is Stephen Longstreet. He's going write a novel for us," Cerf told Faulkner, who did not even lift his head. Later, out on the street, Longstreet heard a voice, "Where can you get a drink?" It was Faulkner, "in that tweed jacket with the patches and everything." Longstreet mentioned an Irish bar on Third Avenue. There Faulkner drank a bourbon, holding up the glass "so the bartender would come over and fill it." Three hours later all that loopy Longstreet could remember was some talk about white lightning and coon hunting. There was "no literary conversation at all." On a later New York outing, Longstreet told Faulkner that Cerf still wanted Longstreet, a graphic artist, to write a novel. "Well," Faulkner said, "Bennett is a con man. He is the greatest salesman. I don't think he reads any of the manuscripts. But do it." Longstreet did not know how to write a novel, to which Faulkner replied: "Ten words make a sentence. Ten sentences make a paragraph. Three or four paragraphs make a page. Ten pages make a chapter. Twenty pages, twenty chapters, and you've got a book." Longstreet said, "That easy." Faulkner said, "That's that easy."[17] Too neat, perhaps, in the telling.

Of all the writers, Buzz Bezzerides put in a special claim on Faulkner. From his first frustrating reading of *As I Lay Dying* in 1931, when he could not put the book down, he continued to read Faulkner, "always with the same fury." Bezzerides described a writer but also a man who was holding out on him, leaving something vital unstated. Bezzerides had first seen the master in the Pig-'n-Whistle, still a going concern on Sunset Boulevard, and did what so many others could not help but do, approaching Faulkner's booth and saying: "Sir, you haven't the slightest idea who I am, but I know who you are; you're William Faulkner, and I have read everything you have written. I think you are a great writer." Faulkner stood up and said, "Thank you, sir." They shook hands, and an embarrassed Bezzerides returned to his booth. The setting could almost have been a movie, where the booths defined the different realms these two writers occupied. Bezzerides would never quite overcome this reputational dichotomy. It was something of a shock, then, for Bezzerides to encounter Faulkner for the first time in the Warner Brothers writers building, sporting a big knife, no less, that Faulkner said he was going to use on the agent who had obtained such a poor contract for him.[18]

Whatever the differences between these writers and their perceptions of Faulkner and of one another, they, along with Meta, formed a kind of cordon sanitaire around him, walking him off studio property when "he was in trouble with the bottle." He remained, even drunk, "impeccably courteous." She would take him to a steam bath on the corner of Yucca and Cahuenga Boulevard to get "boiled out." Even "dead drunk" he would turn to her as she left him, bow low from the waist, and kiss her hand. Then he would go inside for treatments, including a coffee enema, that might last two or three days.[19]

He could not have continued at Warner Brothers if those in charge like James Geller did not cover for him.

HOLLYWOOD GOES TO WAR

The drinking stories should not serve to minimize just how much work Faulkner turned in, without fuss, as his fellow writers observed when they car-pooled, with Bezzerides doing the driving. During one conversation about scripts and producers and the travails of writers, Faulkner said: "I don't understand why you fellows have these troubles. I just write."[20] Geller and producer Robert Buckner expected Faulkner to deliver for them on a special assignment from Jack Warner himself. President Roosevelt had told the studio head, "Jack, this picture *must* be made, and I am asking you to make it." Warner replied: "I'll do it. You have my word."[21] For the next five months, Faulkner would work on a story outline, a story treatment, a revised story treatment, and two complete screenplays, in an epic effort to tell the story of General Charles de Gaulle. During this period, Faulkner concentrated exclusively on screenwriting, with no novel in production or in the composition stage. For the first time in his career, he worked, in effect, on a government project, doing an assignment, in a sense, for the president of the United States, and having conferred on him a level of responsibility he had not experienced in Hollywood or anywhere else, for that matter.

This was not a property especially suitable to Faulkner's talents or to his aesthetic, even though it was a war movie with the kind of military subject matter appealing to him and set in France, like *The Road to Glory*. He had traveled in the country and admired its literature. But his work avoided the explicitly political, and historical figures rarely appeared in his work. He had never written a biopic. Usually writers already adept in the genre would be added to such a project. But Buckner, raised and educated at the University of Virginia, a playwright, short-story writer, and screenwriter as well as a producer, perhaps believed he could work it all out most efficiently with just Faulkner, who "had no meanness about him," Buckner recalled: "He was not petty. He took things at their face value. He was not superior about Hollywood.... He wasn't quite sure of the terminology. He would use dissolve for fade and cut for dissolve. He used these terms with more facility than accuracy, like a cook who felt that seasoning was needed."[22]

Faulkner liked Buckner. A prestige writer for a prestige project? Perhaps that consideration also entered into Jack Warner's approval of using the risky Faulkner. Geller and Buckner regarded Faulkner as their rehabilitation project and told him so.[23] Warner Brothers, more than any other studio, had produced anti-Nazi films, making Faulkner's work there welcome. Buckner understood, perhaps better than other producers, how William Faulkner's integrity would enhance their work. He would bring "verity to an important picture that was contaminated by false values and false relationships and make the whole picture better," Buzz Bezzerides said. "Sometimes a whole picture can be made in a few scenes. WF would have worked more in this town if this was understood."[24]

This probity is exactly what Faulkner brought to Howard Hawks's *Air Force* (1943), taking two days to rewrite a Dudley Nichols death scene that the director had not liked. In the original version, a dying bomber pilot had plaintively said to his crew: "Wait a minute ... don't go ... Don't go ... Wait for me, fellows." In Faulkner's version, the duty-driven dying man's last effort is a terse, monosyllabic, workmanlike inventory of their mission: "Everybody in, chief? ... Doors closed? ... Here we go. Lock 'em ... Wheels up ... They sound like they're gonna run all right, Robbie ... Monk. Monk, what's our course? ... That's right ... That's right, into the sunrise. Right into the ... the sunrise." The moving ending arises out of the matter-of-fact details of flying that Faulkner himself had mastered. If Buckner trusted Faulkner, it is because he recognized that this supposedly aloof writer had a "collaborative persona," one that is expressed in Hawks's own loving portrayal of their collaboration.[25] That Faulkner valued his contribution to *Air Force* is evident in his letter to Bill Fielden, recommending the film and pointing out the death scene and also "where the men in the aeroplace heard Roosevelt's speech after Pearl Harbor."[26] Dudley Nichols received an Academy Award nomination for best screenplay. Faulkner received no screen credit, although his scene helped to make the film a hit.

Buckner seems to have relied on Faulkner as much as Hawks did, and Faulkner reciprocated. In a story outline, he noted, "We can use the method Mr. Buckner suggested" to show how in May 1940 De Gaulle's agents helped to organize the Free French forces after the fall of France and the installation of a Nazi-controlled Vichy government. "I am now trying to follow a suggestion of Mr. Buckner's," Faulkner reiterated: "This was to paint a big canvas to show the growth and scope of the Free French moment and indicate that its limit is boundless, that one strip of film cannot possibly contain it, that it will run over the edge and will go on and on until its aim is accomplished."[27]

In a one-page abstract, Faulkner set the terms for "The De Gaulle Story" that recall *Absalom, Absalom!*'s "strophe and antistrophe," "brother against brother," and "blood against blood":

This is the story of Free France, told in the simple terms of a Breton village: the collapse of France and the hopes and struggle for rejuvenation as seen through the eyes of villagers, told by means of village characters who are themselves the common denominator of France. The village is the strophe with its passions and bafflement and divisions of brother against brother and blood against blood, that it may continue to exist as a symbol of home, security, happiness and peace which is man's heritage; France is the antistrophe, with its passions and bafflement and division of Frenchman against Frenchman in the national terms of a people struggling to survive and to keep alive their traditions and glory as a nation. It is a thesis that lust and greed and force can never conquer the human spirit.[28]

Faulkner decided against the format of the typical biopic. De Gaulle would be present at only strategic moments—beginning with a scene in his tank school that features De Gaulle's commitment to mobile warfare, overturning the obsolete World War I establishment of entrenched positions that led to the creation of the Maginot Line, which the French mistakenly believed would blunt a German offensive. In the story outline, revised on July 29, De Gaulle and Churchill are shown briefly on a plane staring ahead: "Each knows that the other has not given up." De Gaulle's aggressive influence is shown through one of his young recruits, Georges, "a replica of De Gaulle himself," fighting to protect his "little house and garden." Faulkner aimed to bring the war right down to the ground of everyday lives and a village community. Georges is a firebrand, enthralled with De Gaulle, and as such he has to be countered by a moderating figure—almost his opposite, as Faulkner realized when he turned his story outline into a treatment.

Faulkner expanded the familial context, pairing the bold, even reckless Georges with his cautious, reasonable brother, Jean, creating both a conflict and symbiosis similar to the dynamic tension between the Sartoris twins. The Mornet brothers are Bretons, a northwestern province of France famous for its Celtic independence. It is an enclave culture bearing some resemblance to Faulkner's South, which overcame its sectionalism in both world wars to join a national effort—as do the Bretons. Catherine, courted by both brothers, is one of several strong women's voices: "Bretons have suffered before this for Brittany. And if there are still Frenchman left who are willing to fight and die for France, at least we who can't fight can stay here and suffer too." Georges recognizes the women's courage: "Because of the land, their homes, the security of their homes and children." Madame Mornet, the stalwart mother, presides over a divided household—Jean becomes a collaborator, believing this is the only way to save France, while Georges remains a staunch Gaullist.

Catherine sides with Georges and characters like the priest who speaks of an "immortal spirit" the Nazis cannot conquer in tones that would ultimately be heard again in Faulkner's Nobel Prize address. "This man, this Hitler, is nothing: a little clod of rotten dirt before God," the priest declares. Ike McCaslin had said as much in *Go Down, Moses*—that his country "will cope with one Austrian paper-hanger, no matter what he will be calling himself."

De Gaulle is presented as Christ-like, insofar as he calls the "dead back to life," reviving the hopes of the defeated and summoning "battalions and regiments" that "live again." But not much is done to humanize this aloof figure, who is depicted as having one mission: to save and integrate France once again as one nation. In effect, De Gaulle's duty is to avoid a civil war. He is a Lincoln-like figure inasmuch as he wants to bind up the nation's wounds, like the presidential figure Faulkner first encountered as a boy in Oxford watching *Birth of a Nation*.

Jean, who had not wanted to risk his country's destruction, is won over to De Gaulle's side when he realizes the Nazis want only to rule, not govern, which means he can find no place within the Vichy regime that does not associate him with murder and plunder. De Gaulle welcomes Jean and "says nothing at all about Jean's past actions and convictions," citing the Bible: "More rejoicing in heaven over one sinner that repents than over a hundred who did not sin." On a first-name basis with his privates, De Gaulle is the antithesis of German "iron-bound rigidity." The collective forces of the Free French strike back as the picture ends, with villagers marking the fields for De Gaulle's bombers while Georges's resistance fighters set fires. A pilot exclaims, "All France is on fire, blazing—"

The revised story treatment preserves the first version but emphasizes the weak French government unable to match De Gaulle's spirit of resistance and succumbing to Nazi hegemony. Jean has turned collaborationist because he believes the French have been weak and put too much trust in their feckless leaders. The Nazis provide a strong counterweight to the defeatism that seems to overcome the French people. But for Georges, the spirit of freedom simply has to be awakened by De Gaulle, who gathers fresh forces even as the Nazis rule by terror. Resistance to occupation grows as the Vichy government weakens, unable to establish order. The terribly compromised Jean is nevertheless welcomed onto his brother's side.

For the first time in his career, William Faulkner was writing government propaganda. He had been a writer who avoided politics and political figures certainly not worth his time as a novelist. Now he was shaping a Gaullist agenda and taking on a responsibility of a different order from just collecting a Hollywood studio salary. He read the available biographies and historical works, putting himself at the service of a new kind of history, one that in all likelihood he never imagined writing—and certainly not for five months with De Gaulle and France as the only subject, with Faulkner alone, except for consultations with Buckner, having to create the history that had yet to be made—since the second front, the actual Allied invasion of Europe, had not yet begun. To say he was on the cutting edge of events hardly captures the momentous impact of this project and how it would shape William Faulkner's sense of himself as a world citizen with an attendant set of responsibilities that he could not shirk, no matter how much he might have wanted to return to his pre-Vichy, southern world. The French would have to reconstruct their nation and overcome the hard feelings between north and south that had marked William Faulkner's life. Whatever else his fiction did, it would have to speak to the rest of the country in a new mode, a form of direct address that would puzzle and disappoint certain readers who preferred the pre–World War II Faulkner.

"I feel pretty well, sober, am writing to the satisfaction of the studio," he wrote Cho-Cho on September 19. "The script I did now has the official O.K. of De Gaulle's agent and of the Dept. of State, so nothing to do now but write in the dialogue. This is confidential, please. Don't tell publicly what I am even writing."[29] It may have been sobering to submit to higher authority. Was Faulkner just asking his stepdaughter to be discreet, or was he, as well, proud of the part he had been called on to play in the war effort? His professional redemption in Hollywood had become, perhaps, a gratifying personal vindication and something of a secret mission—not to be discussed in Oxford— although how could anything his stepdaughter said to anyone really matter?

Faulkner's first complete screenplay resembles Lillian Hellman's script for *The North Star* (1943). It is possible he showed her or told her about his work during one of her frequent visits to the writers' bar at Musso & Frank's. Their Breton and Ukraine villages are alike in their proud independence epitomized by rugged, outspoken peasants, especially Coupe-tête (Chopine in Faulkner's story treatment) and Hellman's Karp—played by a sardonic Walter Brennan, who could have served just as well for Faulkner's wry character, who tells Jean, "Save your speeches for a softer ear than this (*he flips his hat brim beside his ear*)." Violation of home ground, as in the Civil War, pervades both scripts. Both writers focus on the plainspoken truths of peasants—the salt of the earth so much sounder than the wavering politicians unable to act upon De Gaulle's terse advocacy of a full frontal tank attack on the invaders. Later Jean observes the German advance from an airplane just as Kolya (Dana Andrews) does in *The North Star* in a scene that depicts the German superiority in the air but also the determination of the villagers to resist. Georges has become less obnoxious and more devil-may-care—more like, in other words, an insouciant Hollywood hero but also like the effervescent twin John Sartoris. Later Georges is forced to kill a German in his own backyard, bringing the war home as Hellman does when her antifascist hero, Kurt Muller, murders a Nazi sympathizer in his wife's Washington, D.C., house in *Watch on the Rhine* (play, 1941; film, 1943).

Faulkner dramatizes the clash between Pétain and De Gaulle, between capitulation and resistance, by having their voices broadcast in brief, interrupted radio addresses in a French cafe. How the two men identify themselves is telling:

> I recognize that the fate of the French people will be harsh and hard. But I, your leader, Pétain, Marshal of France—

> I, General De Gaulle, French soldier and chief, assume the right to call upon all of you. Soldiers of France, wherever you may be, arise.

Pétain's demoralizing rationalizations, it is implied, require more words that are cut off by the trenchant De Gaulle. Earlier Georges had said, "We have already crucified the man who tried to warn us." The resurrected De Gaulle also calls his nation, like Lazarus, to live again. Georges's "we" is crucial because De Gaulle accuses no one and accepts everyone enlisted in freeing France. Faulkner created this De Gaulle, speaking directly to the French people for the first time on a microphone in London, at the suggestion of Buckner, who remained deeply involved in the creation of the first complete screenplay.[30]

Even as De Gaulle in a BBC broadcasts says, "We didn't need you, Marshal, to obtain and accept conditions of slavery," the general tells a doubtful Lord Halifax in London that he accepts the Vichy agents of a government that has declared him a traitor because "those who accept Free France must do it of their own will and desires. . . . I want to be chief of all Frenchman who want to be free." De Gaulle is not so much fighting a war or a political battle as he is leading a liberation movement, so he treats his former enemies just as Lincoln did in his "malice toward none" speech and in his Reconstruction policy of reconciliation. The lessons Faulkner had learned—not in the classroom but in those Lincoln scenes in *Birth of a Nation*—are played again in his film.

Even as Jean is asked not only to collaborate but to inform on the underground, Georges is dispatched on a secret mission from England to France, announcing to his family that Roosevelt, "the friend to all of us in Europe who have suffered," has been elected to a third term: "Don't you see what that means? . . . It's like all America spoke to us when they elected Mr. Roosevelt and said to us, "We are with you. Go ahead—" Faulkner, notwithstanding his anti–New Deal politics, was now Roosevelt's man, on a mission, like Georges, and reconciled to the renewed nation state, like Jean, who refuses to betray his own brother at the behest of the Gestapo.

In a *Tale of Two Cities* ending, Jean arranges to have Georges freed from a Gestapo cell, dressing him up in Jean's clothes, while Jean, Sidney Carton–like, takes the place of Georges, who has been drugged so that he cannot interfere with Jean's scheme. In the last scene, Allied bombers appear as the Underground sets fires to welcome them.

In September 1942, Adrien Tixier, the Free French ambassador to the United States, provided a critique of the De Gaulle script, pointing out several errors that would not have troubled most Hollywood productions but that had to be addressed because they came from an important American ally. Tixier objected to making the ardently patriotic Bretons sound disaffected—of course not realizing that Faulkner was, in effect, making them southerners, creating a compelling scenario for Americans who had to overcome their own Civil War. De Gaulle's radio address, the fulcrum of the screenplay, occurred much later—but, of course, Faulkner focused on the dramatic arc of his story. It was "too early to speak of collaboration," or of an Underground, Tixier pointed out, concerned only with facts and not with the dramatization of issues that preoccupied Faulkner.

Buckner's report to Faulkner accepted many of Tixier's criticisms, acknowledging that most French people did not know about De Gaulle's book on tank warfare, which the French generals had ignored, or about the split between Pétain and De Gaulle over the armistice with Germany. Buckner believed that Tixier understood the dramatic value of Faulkner's script, but De Gaulle's representative still insisted that the slower development of events had to be respected, Buckner noted: "There are too many people who know the facts, and particularly in England we would be open to serious criticism of the picture."[31] A Faulkner checked by the facts is what he had always sought to avoid but could not do so when writing in the service of others.

A longer critique in November 1942 by Henri Diamant-Berger, another De Gaulle agent, repeated many of Tixier's criticisms but also rejected the story of the two brothers, noting, in particular, that it took Jean much too long to realize he could not collaborate with the Nazis. Like Tixier, Diamant-Berger wanted to see more of De Gaulle and pointed out many lapses in Faulkner's understanding of French manners. Such a response, of course, reflected no familiarity with the Hollywood that employed Faulkner. Hollywood specialized in making foreign settings familiar by Americanizing them. If Buckner had wanted an authentic, historically accurate script, he might well have employed a French émigré, or at least a European writer. Hollywood cared about facts only insofar as they accorded with its own conveniences.

Faulkner produced a revised screenplay on his own terms, although he did correct many misconceptions about France and the war that his French critics identified. His own thinking about how to treat the war was also evolving toward the position he would take in *A Fable*. Georges, for example, is far less militaristic: "it's men like me, young enough to have reason enough to hate war enough, who will finally put an end to war." The young have been betrayed by the "false reasoning of old men whose hearts are dead." The film is less parochial, less French, and addressed more directly to Americans. In church, a priest sermonizes: "We must endure. Rapacity cannot be bribed."

Faulkner heightens the conflict between Pétain and De Gaulle before the latter departs for England. At various points he adds notes to his French consultants, invoking "poetic license" and dramatic economies, but also sometimes asking for their advice on the authenticity of a scene, displaying the kind of diplomacy he would later exercise on his foreign travels for the State Department. The scope of the screenplay can be suggested by the deleted scenes set in a concentration camp in Syria and scenes with De Gaulle in Brazzaville, Africa. For all the changes made in the revised screenplay, however, the concept of the film, as Faulkner first announced it in his one-page abstract, remained intact.

Faulkner, a servant of two masters but now also fully invested in his screenplay, responded to Buckner on November 19: "Let's dispense with General De Gaulle as a living character in the story." Then they could be free to "make a picture which the American audience whose money will pay for it will understand and believe and not find dull." De Gaulle's representatives wanted a "document . . . not a story which will create in the hearts of the foreigners who will buy the admission tickets, a feeling of warmth and affection and pride toward people like themselves who suffered from the fall of France and have struggled and resisted and are rising from it." Following the French lead would mean sacrificing "dramatic values" and "poetic implications and overtones." He wanted to "choose among facts" and use them "in American terms" to "instruct, or perhaps uplift even by reaffirming in the value of human suffering and the belief in human hope." As to putting more of De Gaulle into the story, Faulkner objected, saying the historical hero "becomes colorful and of dramatic value only after he has been dead for years, because only then can a dramatist make him dramatic without challenge from the people who knew him in the flesh and who insist on fact." Even in Hollywood, Faulkner the artist stood firm, concluding, "It seems to me that any Free Frenchman would be glad to help us in this, not by obscure ukase and prohibition, but by grateful advice when requested of him."[32]

Faulkner's problems with his French consultants, with seeing the war their way, paralleled Roosevelt's and Churchill's disputes with De Gaulle, a troublesome ally at a time when attention had shifted to Russia and the making of another Buckner-produced film, the pro-Soviet *Mission to Moscow* (1943). Roosevelt and De Gaulle first met in Casablanca (January 1943) with "sparks flying," as one Roosevelt biographer puts it. "It's quite possible FDR was hostile to any movie hero-icizing of deG."[33]

Reading the script for the first time forty years later, Buzz Bezzerides commented on Faulkner's state of mind: "He actually enjoyed inventing the story lines, filling them in with dialogue. . . . Faulkner really thought he could write scripts, thought that he could do stories that were meaningful, and he landed on heavy subjects to do, but they never came off. He had to be bitterly disappointed."[34] "The De Gaulle Story," Bezzerides said, did not progress: "Things are discussed rather than made to happen."[35] The story could not be organic to Faulkner: "He was writing about things that he knew very little about. He knew little about the people. He knew little about De Gaulle, less about Churchill, so when he tried to write about them, they didn't ring true; they were two-dimensional." Bezzerides, in effect, said the script lacked authenticity: "How would Faulkner know what a village in France goes through when it's being occupied by the Nazis unless he were there?"[36] But this is to overstate the script's faults and Faulkner's lack of experience. In fact, he knew what it was like to live in an occupied land. And he never meant for De Gaulle or Churchill to be fully realized characters. The story, Faulkner's story, was about two brothers, which is why he said, in the end, the picture could do even without De Gaulle. As to lack of action, the psychological tensions within a family were Faulkner's focus. A director like Jean Renoir, with whom Faulkner would collaborate in a few years, would have understood. Films are not just about scripts but about the collaboration between writer, director, actors, and crew—as Howard Hawks had proven before and would again in *To Have and Have Not* and *The Big Sleep*. In short, Bezzerides expressed attachment to Hollywood conventions, especially the hero or star who carried the picture. Faulkner observed many of those conventions, but he also tried to circumvent them in his more ambitious scripts.

Where did this failure to go into production leave Faulkner at the end of November 1942, as he was preparing for his six-week furlough home? In a way he had come closer to the center of military power than ever before. Quiet, politely aloof, he never seems to have shared his feelings about the aborted project with anyone. Buzz Bezzerides said Faulkner never talked about his screenplays, so it came as a surprise to Buzz when he was told years later about "The De Gaulle Story."[37] Faulkner had written about tank battles, the political chicanery in France resulting in De Gaulle's exile, the Allied evacuation at Dunkirk, the establishment of the Vichy government, and a projected second-front invasion of Europe, while in Hollywood shortages of butter and meat prevailed, wardens patrolled the streets enforcing a blackout, and barrage balloons, searchlights, and hidden anti-aircraft batteries reflected fears of bombing. At the same time, the movie industry acted as though gas rationing did not exist and used their coupons as if fuel would not run out. He deplored the "parasites who exist only because of motion picture salaries, including the fake doctors and faith-healers, and swamis and blackmailing private detectives who live on the people who draw motion picture salaries." He did not realize, or perhaps did not care, that these phonies saw themselves as part of the war effort.[38] He was "afraid the same old stink is rising from this one as has risen from every war yet." He had in mind Churchill's determination to hold on to the British Empire. Yet he encouraged his stepson, Malcolm, to enlist in the "biggest thing that will happen in your lifetime. All your contemporaries will be in it before it is over, and if you are not one of them, you will always regret it." Faulkner still had the desire to join up (although all such efforts would prove fruitless). But he understood it would take young men to fight for liberty. Afterward, though, with the war won, he foresaw another role, one that he would seize in the "time of the old men . . . [t]he ones like me who are articulate in the national voice, who are too old to be soldiers, but are old enough to have been vocal long enough to be listened to, yet are not so old that we too have become another batch of decrepit old men looking stubbornly backward at a point 25 or 50 years in the past."[39] That Faulkner, forward-looking, owed much to his five-month mission to write the story of the Free French.

FURLOUGH

Christmas 1942 at Rowan Oak was an especially exciting and invigorating time for William Faulkner. Cho-Cho had remarried, and her husband, Bill Fielden, "a first-rate man,"[40] was a Faulkner favorite. The season began by gathering in the Rowan Oak library for the expedition to select and chop down a tree, chosen by Pappy. He picked one of the smaller cedars, leaving room for other trees to grow in Bailey's Woods. A family servant, Andrew, took an axe to the tree, and they placed it on a tarp, trimming branches near the base so that Pappy, Mama, Malcolm, and Bill Fielden could take turns dragging the heavy tree through the woods, with the tarp helping to protect its branches. Malcolm remembered returning to Rowan Oak in the late afternoon as a "cold sharp light" filtered through the living room windows. The ladies decorated the tree as menfolk made suggestions about where to place the ornaments. A fire, a bottle of bourbon on a silver tray, with cut-glass tumblers reflecting the fire. Later Christmas greens and mistletoe gathered near a Chickasaw boundary line completed the first phase of the Christmas ritual. Then Bill would drive Estelle to Oxford to do Christmas shopping.

For the Christmas Eve banquet, another servant, Norfleet, would appear, bowing to Faulkner as he set a water pitcher on a tray next to the bourbon. Friends would stop by bearing gifts, eating from the buffet, and drinking. Later, around eleven, Bill and Estelle went upstairs to stuff stockings as other family members went to a midnight service at St. Peter's.

On Christmas morning, Bill would appear in Estelle's bedroom, dressed in an "elegant and ornate Chinese robe," and start the stocking-opening ritual. Estelle took a light breakfast in bed while Bill had a full meal of eggs, bacon, grits in melted butter, and coffee. She would then appear downstairs in a "lovely Chinese wrapper in soft, muted pastel shades." Everyone gathered around the Christmas tree, including the black servants, and Pappy, still in his Chinese gown, "officiated," beginning with a prayer. Then began the distribution of packages. Christmas gifts often included a collection of multicolored pipe cleaners for Pappy—it's all he would accept, except for handkerchiefs from Mama. "Colored members of the family," as Malcolm put it, "went merrily off to the kitchen to open their gifts. There were pints of bourbon for our colored friends: Henry Jones, Wade Ward, and Wallace, who hunted with Faulkner, and of course Andrew."

Christmas Day featured punch, a William Faulkner creation (apples, bourbon, dry burgundy, and soda water on ice), in a glistening ruby-red bowl arranged with flowers. Malcolm remembered the punch cups on the "ornate lace table cover." In scenes not out of place in *Go Down, Moses,* black people came to call, shouting "Christmas Gif!," and were given drinks and rides home for those who "could no longer navigate." Dr. Culley, the very physician Faulkner had once said he had shot, came along with his surgical nurse, who had often attended Faulkner after drinking bouts. So did Colonel Baker and his "charming and vivacious" wife, Kate, whom Dean Faulkner Wells later supposed had been her uncle's lover. Maud never showed up. Family had to come to her. Faulkner would spend an hour on Christmas afternoon with her and then return home to dress in white tie and tails for dinner, preceded by drinks and toasts in the parlor. Then it was Estelle's turn to say, "Billy will you do the honors?"

Faulkner would stand at the head of a long table covered with an "elegant linen cloth," linen napkins, and lighted candelabra that "cast uneven shadows on the polished silver." Children were given their own two tables as chairs were held for the ladies and Faulkner graciously directed them to their seats. Then the white-coated, smiling Norfleet entered with a large platter of turkey and served the company. Faulkner would then taste the wine before walking around the table to fill glasses. Next came Boojack with a large bowl of rice, with Broadus just behind with a bowl of giblet gravy. For side dishes: broccoli with a cheese sauce, sliced buttered potatoes, and ham and broiled quail. Dessert began with Norfleet carrying ambrosia in a large cut-glass bowl and setting it before Mama. This would occasion Faulkner's story, as Malcolm recalled it, of a friend with a cook who was "asked if she would like to go to heaven when she died." Silent for a few minutes, she smiled and said, "No Sir, I don't believe I want to go to heaven, cause all I'd be doing up there every day for Eternity is grittin up coconut for the white folks' ambrosia." Fruitcake and after-dinner coffee, followed by cognac in "delicately patterned small brandy glasses," signaled the end of Christmas.

The period between Christmas and New Year's was less eventful, although Faulkner welcomed friends to Rowan Oak and went out quail hunting. Nearing midnight on New Year's Eve, Estelle would play the piano and her sister Dorothy would turn on the Christmas tree lights one more time. Estelle liked to play a W. C. Handy song, "Where the Southern Crosses the Yellow Dog"—actually about the crossing of two railway lines, the Southern and the Yazoo, the "dog" slang for a branch line. Like most blues songs, it conveyed yearning and comfort as in a 1927 recording by Sam Collins:

Be easy mama, don't you fade away,
Be easy mama, don't you fade away.
I'm goin' where that Southern cross the Yaller Dog.[41]

Malcolm agreed with Bell Wiley that Faulkner's performance of "Water Boy" was "outstanding." Then everyone accompanied Faulkner out the front door, some with champagne glasses in hand, for the fireworks, especially his favorite: Roman candles. Skyrockets and firecrackers and sparklers finished the show. New Year's Day, a much more casual affair than Christmas, featured a dinner of hog jowls, black-eyed peas, and cornbread. The company ended the day with a fishing expedition.[42]

Faulkner brought Hollywood home with him, working on a script, "The Life and Death of a Bomber," based on his visit to a San Diego aircraft factory—yet another assignment that took him beyond the boundaries of Yoknapatawpha and into the regularization of wartime industry at a time when he found himself also part of a Hollywood machine. His report on November 14, 1942, reflects his subaltern status: "Arrived San Diego Friday afternoon, the 13th, with Mr. Joe Berry of Location Dept. Received permission to enter plant at 10:00 a.m. . . . . All personal contacts with publicity department very pleasant. Four hour tour of plant with one hour break for lunch. I was permitted, courteously and without challenge, to examine as long as I liked any phase of the work I was shown."

Faulkner made detailed comments on every part of the plane. He watched women doing "all types of work" including spot welding, painting, and sewing linen. People seemed relaxed, calm, confident, "all seemed happy, perhaps proud of the ships they are making. Busy but not frenzied. Set up seems simplified, not complex, to a layman like me. Quite clean and pleasant working conditions and surroundings. People do not seem to be in one another's way, work busily but quietly . . . all seem to know what to do."

On January 21, 1943, a week after returning to Hollywood, Faulkner turned in a twenty-page screenplay outline. Smith, a trained engineer, falls in love with an employee married to the foreman, Halliday. Smith is on assignment to observe the production of a new aircraft that will save many American lives. Halliday's wife wants to preserve her husband's peace of mind as he works on his important job. Halliday discovers his wife's involvement with Smith, but neither he nor his wife wants to do anything rash. Halliday opposes Smith's idea of speeding up production, which a worker has suggested. The labor union wants the factory owners and stockholders to return their increased profits from speeding up production to the government. The owners refuse. Smith says to a worker, "While you people are squabbling about who gets the money, soldiers are dying." A workman says: "Some of them are our sons too. . . . But at least our sons die so that their kin and descendants will have a better world to work and earn their bread in: not just to increase and preserve the cash which their parents did not even work to earn." Smith turns against Halliday, telling his wife that her husband is hurting war production. She defends Halliday "doing right for the sake of labor, the men from whom he rose, etc. both of them are excited, worked up. So far she has held him off, until she can settle matters. The scene ends with them in their first embrace. At this moment Halliday enters. This is the blow-off." Halliday does not want to lose his wife but agrees to separate for the time being. Halliday speeds up production, even though a defect has been detected. On a test flight, Smith and Halliday remain with the plane as the crew parachutes before a crash landing. The two men survive the crash, but Halliday's hand is crushed. The plane is now behind schedule, "all because of the mistakes which the three of them brought about. They are all to blame." The wife returns to Halliday. A second act attributes to the repaired bomber a mind of its own, taking the controls over from the pilot and crashing on an enemy-held island. The crew manages to get the plane into the air again, but it has "now cost the lives of three men, as well as the foreman's hand." Act 3 opens with the bomber at the front, the only ship with the suicidal task of holding off an enemy in force. The bomber completes its bombing run before being shot to pieces. The bomber did its job. At the ceremony for the bomber and the dead crew, Halliday speaks about "the story of a bomber that arrived too late, because the people who made it let their private selfish motives intervene; they failed where the young men who died to fly the bomber had no opportunity or choice to let their private wishes intervene between them and the risk of death and the job to be done. This must never happen again." Faulkner closes with Halliday's words: "I'm not speaking to just us, here. I'm talking to all America, to all the men who are building the guns and planes and ships." The bombers take off. Halliday tells the shift to go back to work.[43]

As with the De Gaulle script, Faulkner, hired hand and now instrument of a private/public war effort, expressed considerable ambivalence and yet also commitment to a new role, becoming the national voice of a people committed to their mutual defense but also still driven apart by their personal passions. How to do both, be yourself and part of a greater cause, had become an especially acute dilemma. The conflicts on the factory floor, the desire to profit even at the cost of human lives, led Faulkner into the territory of Arthur Miller's *All My Sons,* the electrifying postwar play about a factory owner who turns out defective planes that crash, horrifying his son, who tells his father he has murdered all his sons.

Faulkner had always been a contract employee, but over the past decade he had come and gone on the basis of short-term employment agreements, operating like a freelancer. Now he was just like a stabled horse, part of what was called "the Ward" at Warner Brothers. On October 2, 1942, his option had been renewed at $300 per week, commencing October 26 for thirteen weeks with seven more options escalating from $350 to $1,250 if all options were renewed. On January 7, 1943, his option was picked up for another twenty-six weeks at $350.[44] This was not the new contract that Buckner and Geller had promised if Faulkner behaved himself. Perhaps this is one reason why he drank even as he produced one script after another on the studio assembly line. Saying he was on "furlough" perhaps made his Hollywood contract a little more palatable. Faulkner was soldiering on.

9

Yoknapatawpha Comes to Hollywood

January–August 1943

THE WAX WORKS

By mid-January, Faulkner had returned to Hollywood. "I had a pleasant time at home, hated like hell to come back," he wrote his agent Harold Ober.[1] He tried to avoid the writers' table at the Warner Studio restaurant, divided down the middle between left and right. He called the place "The Wax Works." On a visit there to pick up his lunch, Faulkner encountered Alvah Bessie, a Communist and veteran of the Spanish Civil War. Bessie spotted Faulkner's watch, saying the Russians would find it useful. "Yes, they would," Faulkner said and left without picking up his lunch.[2] John Crown remembered some political discussions but could not say much about Faulkner's views. It was "very difficult to know . . . what he thought and felt" because he "could not be snared easily into getting involved in such discussions." Crown called Meta a "bleeding heart . . . in the finest sense of the word" and thought Faulkner "might have hurt Meta a little by not being willing to get too involved with social matters which seemed to her to cry out for reform."[3] She represented to him not Hollywood but "a way of going home," Buzz Bezzerides said. "Bill was a very lonely man when he was here, very lonely."[4]

Faulkner sometimes attended the long writers' Saturday lunches at Musso & Frank's, even showing the bartender how to make a mint julep.[5] He was quiet, so quiet that waiters had to lean forward to take his order. With Meta he dined at the Knickerbocker Hotel, in the Spanish Colonial Revival style, on an open porch in days when traffic was not such a problem. A little later, at La Rue's on Sunset Boulevard, they had a favorite table—the one at the second window from the end that curved around toward the east and the north. At Imperial Gardens in West Hollywood on a high hill they liked to sit at a table in an open garden. They would watch Charlie Chaplin with a sizable entourage come into Henry's on Hollywood Boulevard, a restaurant the actor helped to finance. Faulkner liked to dine with William McKelvey Martin and his wife. Martin, who later became director of the Brooklyn Academy of Music, was "simple, direct, intelligent" and did not "bug" Faulkner about writing. The two pipe smokers talked about tobacconists and Faulkner's favorite in Hollywood—Richardson's—and about "when and how to light a pipe."[6] It is easy to see why the shop appealed to Faulkner, an establishment frequented by Clark Gable and other stars. Dudleigh Richardson, an English tobacconist, moved his business from London's Bond Street to Hollywood in the 1920s and carried the Dunhill line that Faulkner favored—stamping his pipes with the label: "P. Dudleigh Richardson/Hollywood–Beverly Hills."[7]

Faulkner took Meta on the rounds of bookstores—including the Satyr, where Stanley Rose got his start and also ran into trouble for peddling pornography. A shop clerk there remembered the couple happily going through the shelves and making purchases.[8] The Pickwick on Hollywood Boulevard was another favorite, and of course Stanley Rose's, next door to Musso & Frank's—perhaps the inspiration for the bookshop in *The Big Sleep*. Rose, a fabled raconteur, often showed up at the restaurant, establishing a creative synergy between the two establishments.[9]

On February 17, sounding almost jaunty, Faulkner wrote to Robert Haas, "I am well and quite busy, surrounded by snow, dogs, Indians, Red Coats, and Nazi spies."[10] He was referring to a Mountie movie, *Northern Pursuit,* starring Errol Flynn—"an avalanche of adventure," the trailer announces, "bigger than the Northwest."[11] Flynn, a Mountie of German descent, is charged with exposing Nazi infiltrators who have landed in Canada via a submarine that surfaces through the Hudson Bay ice. It is hard to tell what Faulkner contributed to the script. He seems to have been used in his screen doctor role. Credit ultimately went to Frank Gruber and Alvah Bessie, the latter getting his name on the picture with the help of fellow Communists—much to Faulkner's disgust.[12]

Deep Valley, which became a film starring Ida Lupino and Dane Clark, oscillated between a California farm and a convict camp somewhat in the mode of *The Wild Palms.* A convict petitions to be released so that he can join the convoys in the hazardous North Atlantic, confronting German submarines, ice fields, and mines, ferrying materiel to the Soviet Union and Britain. Although the film became a conventional love story that did not include Faulkner's work, *Deep Valley* addressed Faulkner's wish to volunteer:

"When I finish this job [on *Northern Pursuit*] I want to try for the Ferry Command," Faulkner wrote to Haas.[13] The RAF had established the Ferry Command in July 1941 to transport aircraft and pilots by ship at a time when transatlantic flights were problematic.[14] Work on *Northern Pursuit* and *Deep Valley* meant more than perhaps Faulkner could say. He wanted to put himself in harm's way, although all his efforts to do so floundered. He was too old and unqualified for active service. His aborted work on *Northern Pursuit* and *Deep Valley* parallels his thwarted efforts to charge into the thick of a military mission. But then two projects, "Country Lawyer" and "Battle Cry," provided the challenge and scope that only "The De Gaulle Story" had promised.

AT HOME AND WAR

In March, assigned to adapt Bellamy Partridge's best-selling *Country Lawyer,* a memoir about growing up in Phelps, New York, Faulkner transferred the story to Jefferson, Mississippi, beginning in 1890 and spanning both world wars. Lawyer Partridge (Faulkner soon changed the name to Sam Galloway) is an "outlander," a type that would later get Faulkner's full attention in *Requiem for a Nun.* The black people notice he is a "man without background of breeding, land, etc." He is determined to marry Edith Bellamy, the daughter of a prominent family, even though she is engaged to the scion of another prominent Jefferson family. With locals not willing to engage his services, he works in a livery stable. When a "middle-aged Negro, a local character" vaguely reminiscent of the unflappable Lucas Beauchamp, is accused of setting fire to the Hoyt family's stable, Galloway defends him, although the black man, who has "some of the snobbery of the white villagers," says he "had almost rather be sent to jail by what he calls 'folks' than to be cleared by 'trash.'" But Galloway wins the case and the respect of country people who "are of his own kind, who had quickly recognized his value to them, because of his honesty and the fact that he is not a blue-stocking aristocrat, and among Negroes to whom he has become a champion, seeing that they receive justice even when he will get no pay from them." They call him "Judge," a typical southern way of showing respect, although Galloway continues his solo practice. In short, he becomes a center of moral and legal authority that is otherwise absent in the community.

"Country Lawyer" reflects Faulkner's increasing awareness that the South had to change. So Edith (she might as well be called a Compson) is drawn to Sam Galloway: "Some female instinct might have seen in Sam's peasant blood that strength which was exhausted in her own blood." Sam Galloway anticipates the liberal southern lawyer who would later capture popular attention in the figure of Atticus Finch, although Faulkner does not make his hero southern by birth or saddle him with the bloviations of Gavin Stevens, who would figure so largely in *Intruder in the Dust, Knight's Gambit, Requiem for a Nun, The Town,* and *The Mansion.* Gregory Peck should have played Sam—not only because of his later celebrated performance in *To Kill a Mockingbird* but because of his key role in social-issue pictures like *Gentleman's Agreement* (1947), which "Country Lawyer" anticipates. As Faulkner says in his treatment: "We want to show a man who believes in the innate soundness of mankind, people, and in the simple verities of honor, dignity, justice, courage, etc." The "we" helps to explain what happened to Faulkner in Hollywood. He no longer spoke only for himself or for Hollywood but for the collective voice of humanity, a voice that would makes its way especially into the dialogue and narratives of *Requiem for a Nun* and *The Town.*

Edith breaks her engagement with the Hoyt scion and chooses Sam, but neither she nor Sam can win the approval of haughty Hoyt senior. Sam, the consummate gentleman, does not retaliate when Hoyt senior strikes him with a whip. Instead, Sam marries Edith and resumes his practice: "The Hoyts and the town cannot beat him." The Galloways' son, Samuel Bellamy Galloway, grows up playing with the son of a black family servant, named Sam Galloway Moxey, nicknamed "Spoot." Moxey's mother, Rachel, and another black family servant, Caroline, who "fed the white baby at her breast along with her own," roughly reflect the nurturing Faulkner received. The boys are treated equally—not at the insistence of Sam but of Rachel, who whips them both when they disobey and then feeds them cake afterward, wiping away their tears.

Sam junior follows the same trajectory as his father, falling in love with a Hoyt, but this time the enmity between Hoyt senior and Galloway senior is such that it breaks up this second-generation union of feuding families and results in Sam junior's estrangement from his father. Sam senior nevertheless remains the sympathetic patriarch, driving downtown to a drugstore to buy a quart of strawberry ice cream for the ailing Rachel just like Faulkner did for Caroline Barr.

Sam junior and Spoot enlist in the army in 1918, with the former put in charge of black troops because he is a southerner and presumably understands them. Sam junior says to his commanding officer that he "didn't know what there was he wanted understood about them; that maybe any human being was his own enigma which he would take with him to the grave, but I didn't know how the color of his skin was going to make that any clearer or more obscure." The color line in Faulkner's work is not erased in this treatment so much as it made to seem irrelevant—no more than a societal or institutional construct. When Sam junior and Spoot are reunited during the war, they become "once more the two boys who fed at the same breast, who hunted the bird nest, and stole the pig and were whipped for it, who slept in the same bed until after they were both so big they would have to sleep together by stealth to keep old Rachel from catching them, who hunted together and had never been separated until Sam went to Yale." Such scenes go beyond white boy–black boy scenes in *The Unvanquished* and *Go Down, Moses* and beyond anything Faulkner would attempt to imagine in *Intruder in the Dust*. Only the Hollywood Faulkner writes this plainly about "two men of different races" and "how little the difference in race means to them when they are alone." When Sam and Spoot come under German fire, Spoot "tries to cover Sam's body with his own as the machine gun bullets seek them out and kill them both." What would have happened, in terms of Hollywood and Yoknapatawpha history, if such a film had been released midwar? The coda to this death scene is the funeral for Rachel in Sam senior's parlor with a black choir and Sam senior delivering the oration. "Will use one I delivered in like circumstances over an old Negro servant of my family," Faulkner added parenthetically.

The film jumps from World War I to World War II. Sam senior is now seventy, and yet another Galloway is romantically involved with a Hoyt—"the old, old story of Montague and Capulet. But this time" the older generation will not have its way. Spoot junior is thinking of enlisting: "He says there is a squadron of Negroes being trained to fly at Tuskegee. That's what he would like to do, believes he can do." Lally, Edith's daughter, offers to help Spoot junior with his exams. She also tells Sam senior, still feuding with the Hoyts, "a few truths. He gets a new picture of young people of 1942, who have the courage of their mistakes and . . . an ability to face truth which old Sam begins to realize that perhaps he has not." She then delivers a speech similar to one given in Lillian Hellman's play *The Searching Wind* (1944; film, 1946)[15] that really leads to the suspicion that Hellman and Faulkner had some important discussions at Musso & Frank's bar. Lally tells Sam "calmly how it was the old people like him, with their greed and blundering and cowardice and folly, who brought on this war, brought about this situation in which Carter [Hoyt] and Spoot, Junior, will have to risk their lives and perhaps lose them, as her Uncle Sam and Spoot, Junior's, father did in the last war." Old Sam, for the first time in the film, is "speechless with amazement, is convinced by her very calmness and courage that perhaps young people do know what they are doing." Faulkner was well on the way to creating another outspoken younger person, Chick Mallison, and his black companion, Aleck Sander, important counterweights to Gavin Stevens, the retrograde progressive in *Intruder in the Dust.* This generational story forecasting what it would be like after the war anticipated films like *The Best Years of Our Lives,* in which the old ways of doing business would be severely challenged. As old Sam tells old Hoyt: "How can two outdated stupid old men like them save the good name of people who are already braver and stronger than they have ever been? What is there that such old men can do, that these young people can need?" Carter Hoyt and Lally Calloway marry, and the films ends, as it might in a Lillian Hellman play, with Caroline dismissing the two white patriarchs and telling Lally: "Come on, honey. Don't nobody care whether them two eats or not, but you got to eat. Come, on, now."

"I have come to like this picture, am trying to make a good job of it," Faulkner wrote to his mother.[16] But his script remained unproduced—nobody seems to know exactly why. Had it been otherwise, perhaps the "sympathetic, compassionate, and deferential respect of white toward black, black toward white, would have been sacrificed. In 1943, American audiences would have been disquieted, some outraged; all would have found the premise unrealistic, not 'true to life.'"[17] And yet it was what William Faulkner could imagine to be true, and what he would spend much of his remaining life insisting could be actually true.

Near the end of writing "Country Lawyer," Faulkner wrote an unusually long letter to his nephew Jimmy about war and their part in it, and about the next generation that had taken over in Faulkner's most recent screenplay. He wanted Jimmy, serving as a combat pilot, to have the lieutenant's pips from his RAF uniform as a "luck piece." Apparently still not able to get over missing the action, Faulkner perpetuated the myth about his own wartime derring-do "crack-up in '18": "I think the Gestapo has it [his dog tag]; I am very likely on their records right now as a dead British flying officer-spy." He could have put that story in an Errol Flynn Hollywood scenario. He warned Jimmy against "foolhardiness": "A lot of pilots dont get past that. Uncle Dean didn't." Foolhardiness was often a response to fear. "The brave man is not he who does not know fear; the brave man is he who says to himself, 'I am afraid. I will decide quickly what to do, and then I will do it.'" Jimmy just had to keep at it, with "trained reflexes" and "natural good sense." This was a preachifying letter, Faulkner admitted, but he gave advice based on his own meticulous studies: "Learn all you can about the aeroplane: how to check it over on the ground. Aeroplanes very seldom let you down; the trouble is inside cockpits."[18]

Cho-Cho's husband, Bill Fielden, wrote Faulkner about home. "Your letter moved me very much," Faulkner replied. "I too like my town, my land, my people, my life, am unhappy away from it even though I must quit it to earn money to keep it going to come back to." He admitted that "Big Miss" (Estelle) had "done fine" without him. He expected he would have to write another "good picture" before he would get home in July.

That "good picture," "Battle Cry," a Howard Hawks project, appeared in the spring of 1943. Meta remembered Faulkner "in a state of contained excitement": "His step was jaunty. He was not drinking to excess. Never one to talk shop . . . [h]e did tell me that his screen treatment, with pages and pages of dialogue, was coming along with only minor hitches." He even began speaking of actors who could play various roles. He wrote home to Jill about the "big picture" that would run three hours, cost between three and four million dollars, and feature several big stars. Unlike so many letters home, this one did not strike the mournful, yearning note of homesickness, although Faulkner did spend a paragraph mooning over Jill's hair that was about to be cut for the first time, apparently: "your hair can be cut like you want it, and it can still be like Pappy wants to think of it, at the same time. . . . I want you to enjoy it and write me about it." He wanted her to realize that she remained always in his thoughts even if he had to leave her: "Pappy knows and can remember and can see in his mind whenever he wants to every single day you ever lived, whether he was there to look at you or not, why any time he wants to he sees in his mind and in his sight too every single one of those days, and how you looked then." Then he told her more about what it was like in Hollywood, having to get his own breakfast now that the black man who served him had left for a better job in an aircraft factory. Faulkner took his breakfast at Musso & Frank's—orange juice, toast, marmalade, and sometimes "little fellows" (sausages)—and then waited on a corner for "Mr. Bezzerides and Mr. Job to come along in a car, and I go to the studio and walk into my office, and there on my desk is a letter from Mama and my Jill. That makes me feel just fine." Such letters gave a strong visual sense of his world and how much he wanted her to be part of it. He promised to write her more about the "big picture" later.[19]

This was a heady time for Faulkner and Hollywood, with Harry Warner, now a colonel, calling his studio a war industry: "Hollywood was alive with the pulsations of war, and something in him needed to be in the dead center of it." Everywhere he looked, men and women in uniform were all over Sunset Boulevard. He read the newspapers, visited an aircraft factory on assignment, and during pauses in writing the script listened to Edward R. Murrow and William L. Shirer on the radio reporting on their experiences in London and Berlin. Meta remembered that the "tensions and turbulence of wartime Los Angeles stretched Faulkner like a fine wire." Planes roared over Burbank. During blackouts huge blankets and tarpaulins covered sound stages.

Everyone was fingerprinted and issued ID cards. By 1943, Warner Brothers had lost something like a thousand employees, and anyone with a foreign accent excited suspicion: "There was talk of a fifth column." These were times of "tribal identification,"[20] but also of an expansive sense of the world struggling to be free that Faulkner labored to put into his panoramic screenplay.

He was not writing from scratch—instead adapting several published stories and a radio play and at strategic points introducing Earl Robinson's Lincoln cantata. Like Robinson, some of Faulkner's collaborators were Communists. Faulkner was perforce assembling and modifying the dialectic of public discourse about war coming at him from different angles and attitudes, deploying the drama of different peoples and cultures in strategically built-up scenes, with Robinson's choral commentary on the drive for liberty, beginning with the Civil War.

The work began on April 7, in consultations with Howard Hawks in June Lake, California. Faulkner reported home to "Big Miss and Little Miss" about this "dude resort," with "mountains all around with snow on them, and hot noons and nights like fall, so that we sleep under blankets." He worked in the mornings and fished for trout in lakes and creeks. He had taught Mrs. Hawks how to clean fish, which they cooked right beside a creek to eat—just as they did back home with Mamma and Missy and Buddy (Malcolm) hunting for rattlesnakes. Here, too, there were woods with deer and stripe-tailed chipmunks. The studio paid for this holiday for "only the price of turning out a few typewritten pages a day."[21]

Meta remembered that Faulkner had resisted departing from her for two weeks, but she said it would not be wise to disappoint Hawks, who had let go the other writers working on "Battle Cry" and had placed all his hopes in Faulkner. When he returned to her, he complained about "story parlays" that went on from morning to midnight. Back with Meta, he enjoyed sitting on his terrace, relaxed and self-absorbed and barely hearing what she had to say, as he returned to his fiction, she supposed, putting it all into place.

It took Faulkner only two weeks to produce a 143-page treatment, with an expanded treatment completed on June 2, and a revised screenplay on August 15, "new in form, cycloramic, with jumps in time and place, and with the camera utilized beyond any previous attempt."[22] This film would have been the most ambitious war picture Hollywood ever produced, an epic covering virtually every theater of war. Warner Brothers had produced the first anti-Nazi film set in the United States, *Confessions of a Nazi Spy* (1939). Fox released *Four Sons* (1940), about a Czech family split apart between fascist and antifascist brothers. In *The Mortal Storm* (1940) and *Escape* (1940), MGM exposed Hitler's concentration camps. Chaplin's *The Great*

Dictator (1940) confronted Hitler directly, as did Fritz Lang's *Man Hunt* (1941). Studios like Paramount geared up to report on the American preparation for war (*I Wanted Wings,* 1941), followed by action pictures such as *Dive Bomber* (1941), *A Yank in the RAF* (1941, dramatizing Dunkirk), *Wake Island* (1942), *Across the Pacific* (1942), and, of course, *Air Force* (1943). But none of these feature films—or those made during the rest of the war—had the scope or the comprehensive ideology that Faulkner incorporated into "Battle Cry."[23] Just as Faulkner had incorporated and modified the forms of popular fiction in *The Unvanquished,* he assimilated Hollywood tropes and conventions while creating aural and visual montages that went well beyond what Hollywood expected and beyond his own previous treatments and screenplays.

Faulkner's expanded story treatment began on a train platform in Springfield, Illinois, in early 1942. Soldiers are waiting for a train. A draftee, Fonda, has the "look of Lincoln as a young man."[24] Faulkner has in mind, of course, Henry Fonda, a war hero in *Drums along the Mohawk* and the star of *Young Mr. Lincoln* (1939). Fonda had also starred in *Blockade* (1938), about the Spanish Civil War, playing a pacifist farmer forced to defend his land. Naming Fonda is just the first instance of Faulkner's deliberate effort to draw on Hollywood history, choosing an actor who exemplified the common man as noble figure—Fonda, for example, as Tom Joad, a Depression-era hero in John Ford's adaptation of Steinbeck's *The Grapes of Wrath* (1940).[25] But like Gary Cooper's Alvin York in *Sergeant York* (1941), another Warner Brothers–Hawks production, Fonda is a reluctant warrior, telling his gung-ho grandfather, reminiscent of the grandfather in "Shall Not Perish": "I bet you wouldn't feel so chipper if it was you that had to go." But the old man announces the film's message: "You're going to fight for the folks that ain't free, that have been enslaved." He quotes Lincoln in a speech that also recalls the commissary books in *Go Down, Moses.* The old man invokes Lincoln's half slave/half free speech that he wrote "across the page of America, across the whole ledger of human bondage, in his own blood, so that no folks anywhere can ever forget it." Lincoln's words, like Faulkner's, are built to last. As writers, Lincoln and Faulkner coalesce, or dissolve into one another, in the montage of freedom.

Writing this film was William Faulkner's reckoning with the Civil War as he wrote a new kind of history—this boy who had grown up in a southern classroom drawing a picture of Lincoln as ogre, listening to the tales about the tyrant, as he was commonly described in southern poetry during the war. When Fonda objects to the Civil War talk, saying, "But that was 1865," he might as well be addressing audiences who went to see *Gone with the Wind,* who were able to set the Civil War aside as grim but also colorful and above all, *over!* Fonda says of that time: "The world was smaller, folks seemed to know then. At least, they never had to go to the end of the world to fight slavery." To which his grandfather responds, "That's jest where we want slavery: right at the ends of the earth!"

The Springfield scene segues to North Africa with Fonda (renamed Corporal Flynn) running with other soldiers in the desert in a shot that dissolves into the sound of tramping feet and the "sound of the Freedom Train," first mentioned by the old man describing Lincoln's cross-country funeral cortège. A voice announces the theme of Earl Robinson's Lincoln cantata: "They were the people. He was their man. Sometimes you couldn't even tell where the people left off and Abraham Lincoln began." Robinson's music suffuses the film, from beginning to end. He was a believer in the Popular Front that united all parties in the fight against fascism. For Faulkner, the war meant the restoration of brotherhood that had broken apart at the gates of Sutpen's Hundred. As Robinson's music dissolves into a banjo "playing a rollicking bay tune, American and Negroid," an American soldier, a white southerner, Akers, carries a wounded black soldier into a house to safety. Shot in the spine, the black man cannot move, and the "white boy" entertains them both on a dulcimer he has found in the house, "playing the rollicking merry tune." Faulkner uses natural sound, emanating from the scene itself, rather than a soundtrack, similar to the methods of World War II documentary filmmakers like Humphrey Jennings. The music keeps the men in two worlds—the one they come from and the "waste of the African desert" that the southerner watches through a window as he plays.

The southerner—in effect a nurse—makes a bed for the wounded, immobilized black man, whose name, he insists, is America, a name that could not have been used in Yoknapatawpha and would have made moviegoers think "black" whenever the country is named. Not only is North Africa where Americans were first battle tested, but it is also where black and white men fought the enemy to save one another, a solidarity contrasted to a captured German who sneers at an Italian captive: "Did you ever know a member of his race who didn't run from the sight of armed men?" Endemic racism still lingers in the southerner's speech, as it did in Faulkner's. Akers says, referring to the black man, "ain't going nowhere," and then adds, "Are you, nigger?" The question marks the very racial divide that the war is meant to overcome and that Akers himself is in the process of surmounting.

The North African scenes are counterpointed with the many voices of the Lincoln cantata telling the story of Lincoln's assassination and the people's fight to spread his legacy:

The slaves are free, the war is won
But the fight for freedom's just begun
. . . .
Freedom's a thing that has no ending
It needs to be cared for, it needs
defending.

This call includes all peoples and occupations: "A Kansas farmer, a Brooklyn sailor, / An Irish policeman, a Jewish tailor." "Battle Cry" anticipates Lewis Milestone's *A Walk in the Sun* (1945), a film that uses Robinson's choral commentary on battle scenes, with songs like "The House I Live In," famously sung by Frank Sinatra, extolling America's democratic ethos.

The action shifts to a Russian village in February 1942 in a section titled "Diary of a Red Army Woman," based on a radio script by Violet Akins and William Bacher. Tania becomes a pilot, like her beloved Semyon, who is engaged in trying to halt the German invasion on June 22, 1941. Her intrepid military career is followed in dissolves to other scenes of action in Moscow, Leningrad (August 1941), Sevastopol (December 1941 and February 12, 1942), Kuibyshev (June 1942), and Stalingrad (September 1942). Throughout it all, and even after Semyon's death, Tania, having given birth to a son, declares: "It is not only for Russia we women are fighting, my baby—Beyond Russia, beyond Stalingrad—there is a world of suffering people I must try to help." Her words meld into the cantata soundtrack, which itself serves as a transition to North Africa again. The sneering German might as well be Goering at Nuremberg, whose agile intellect troubled American prosecutor Robert Jackson (a Supreme Court justice). The German baffles the Americans, who conclude there is no way to answer the maniacal logic of fascists: "They are monsters. There is no hope for them, no place in the world for them and us too. We will have to destroy them to save ourselves." As the Americans bury one of their officers, the sound of their shovels mimics the beat of the Freedom Train that, in turn, dissolves into shovels digging a grave in China.

The next scenes, briefly described in the treatment, deal with Mama Mosquito, a shape-shifting figure who miraculously avoids the Japanese invaders. She is an old woman, like Granny Millard in *The Unvanquished,* working by stealth, disguise, and dissembling, organizing the labor of a people "moving by hand . . . [a]n entire munitions factory, piecemeal back into the hills where the Japs can't bomb it, on to where General Chiang decorates her." Mama Mosquito, a Harriet Tubman figure, is one of several women in Faulkner's script who become vital to the cause of freedom.

The interplay between the North Africa and China scenes is accomplished through musical montage, with the Italian prisoner of war learning to play an American tune and another soldier playing "When Johnny Comes Marching Home." Faulkner intended a "build-up to a definite lift: young men who may not even see tomorrow playing the old tune about when they will march triumphantly through the village streets of America." That very scene would appear at the end of *The Purple Heart* (1944), when American prisoners of war march in sync to the stirring music that expresses their defiance of Japanese torture and execution. At the same time Akers remembers a night "in the woods, an old church—niggers" singing about the Freedom Train.

> DISSOLVE begins.
> SHOT of moving 1865 train
> SHOT of small, shabby Negro church
> **1st SOLO**
> Just a pulpit and some wooden benches
> And Mr. Lincoln sitting in back,
> Listening to the sermon,
> Listening to the singing.

The next shot—the interior of the church—features a preacher and his congregation, as he cries out: "We got a new land! / Ain't no riding boss with a whip . . . No high sheriff to bring us back!" The black church settings in *Soldiers' Pay*, *The Sound and the Fury*, and *Go Down, Moses* that had often shown the chasm between black and white people serve here as a kind of Whitmanian catalogue of union, a heterogeneous group gathered at Lincoln's catafalque: "CLOSE SHOT of an old Negro woman decently dressed, but poor, in shawl and widow's bonnet, at the coffin. Behind her a cotton speculator, a gambler type, in frock coat, etc."

In Faulkner's double-column screenplay, song set to words is accompanied by the democratic exchanges of the dance:

Lincoln was down in Kansas town
Swinging his lady round and round!

A country barn dance, rustic, 1860–80, Two fiddlers, a triangle, a banjo; on crude platform, dressed in Sunday clothes, a caller. The dancers are farmers, young, middle-aged, the old people sitting in chairs, or on benches along the wall. Lincoln's figure is superposed, or he is one of the dancers maybe.

Lincoln in this sequence, Faulkner notes, is Fonda. The reluctant warrior has become the national hero who is also a "nigger" named America.

In scenes reminiscent of *Today We Live,* Faulkner has Fonda (the name Flynn has been dropped) walking through English streets in 1941, exciting the "astonishment and annoyance and a little contempt" from Englishmen who feel America has come to the war too late. Then the action shifts again to *The Hornet,* an aircraft carrier ferrying a load of Spitfires to Malta. Faulkner, the RAF trainee who worked on meticulous drawings of aircraft, focuses on the new planes, some of which have to make incredibly short landings on carriers, and others like the "long-range-Focke-Wulf with four engines and a big range from shore." Anyone can fly Hurricanes, says Ackroyd, who makes a miraculous Spitfire landing on a carrier, although he is told to jump and jettison the plane. Hurricanes were reliable, if less exciting than Spitfires. Such detail reveals the Faulkner who told his nephew Jimmy to learn about how his planes were put together. For Faulkner, this attention to mechanical detail, and to the ingenuity of pilots, was a crucial aspect of the fight for freedom. His suspenseful sequence in which a dinghy is rigged with explosives and has to be guided through a German minefield to blow up German warships anticipates the daring denouement of *Crash Dive* (1943), which concludes with an attack on a German submarine base.

In an alternative sequence, Fonda, stationed in England, visits a Sussex village, as Faulkner did in the fall of 1925. Fonda observes the women of all ages who have organized a factory. He also joins "one of the oldest hunts in England," now run by women: "He realizes that this, this preservation of a sporting club, is a part of the 'England' which these people are fighting and suffering privation for, and that maybe this is one of the symptoms of what has made them tough, made them able, out of all Western Europe, to resist the Germans." Did Faulkner remember such scenes when he went fox hunting in Virginia more than a decade later? Was the war, the idea of tradition itself, what kept him saddling up? He was quite aware, as is Fonda, of the differences between classes and hunts: "In Fonda's country, when anybody went fox or coon hunting, anyone who wanted to or heard the dogs and horses went along." The Willingham Hunt, on the other hand, is invitation only, although that too, he is told, will change. Fonda remains Fonda, incorrigibly American, sitting in "country fashion" on his horse, "slack-rumpled, his legs dangling practically, holding the reins in one hand as if he were holding a fishing pole." Faulkner compares the performance here to Gary Cooper's folksy Alvin York while working in yet another Hollywood staple, a cocksure American war correspondent—"John Garfield type"—in Malta wooing a British woman working in an air raid shelter and canteen.

Fonda, who has been to North Africa, to England, and back to North Africa, quotes heavyweight champion Joe Louis, "a man of America's people"—a phrase referring to both the wounded black soldier, America, and the country: "There's a heap wrong with this world, but Hitler can't fix it."[26] Louis's words provoke the Italian prisoner of war to tell the story of mountain villagers in Nazi-occupied Serbia hiding their ancient bell so that it will not be melted down for war materiel. Their refusal to collaborate results in their murder and the decimation of their town, which dissolves into a scene with the "cold contemptuous German officer" listening to the Italian prisoner of war, who has lived in America and seen "America's people" herded into "tenements in Harlem and Chicago and Detroit," refugees from the Jim Crow South in a country that has failed to live up to its Emancipation Proclamation. Americans have to "clean their own house a little," he admits, although, as Faulkner well knew, "it is not that simple, not that easy to turn your back on the land, the earth where you were born and where the only work you know is and where your mother and father and sisters and brothers and children, too, are buried—even if it is only a tenement in Harlem or Chicago or Detroit or a farm in Jim Crow land."

The forces of freedom and resistance are reasserted in a brief scene in Stevenson, an American village that adopts, in a town hall meeting, the name of an obliterated Serbian village, Cincovci, mispronounced as Sinkovski—perhaps Faulkner's wry comment on how so much of world history is actually a part of the American experience, no matter how mangled that history becomes in American parlance. The soldiers who have heard the Italian's Serbian village story vote against retreat as the Germans are closing in. This democratic solidarity is similar to that expressed in the scene in *The Purple Heart* (1944) when the American crew votes to continue its resistance to Japanese torture. Did Darryl Zanuck, who wrote the screenplay for *The Purple Heart*, and to whom the makers of "Battle Cry" reported, borrow from Faulkner's work?

Several morally compromised characters, some of whom would not have passed Breen office censorship, become part of the Freedom Train music played on Ayer's dulcimer, which dissolves in a street scene in Paris in 1938. Clemente, forced into prostitution to support herself and looking like a femme fatale to Albert Loughton, the Englishman who has befriended Fonda, ultimately becomes Loughton's beloved, whom he has to leave during the evacuation at Dunkirk, shown in a quick montage that includes the arrival of De Gaulle in London "with nothing but a clean shirt and razor." Just as Loughton supposes he has lost Clemente forever, a fade-out segues to a long sequence labeled "Mama Mosquito." She helps direct the flow of Chinese refugees fleeing the Japanese invasion, pictured as a "swollen flood of people flowing toward the west" with the "whole screen . . . filled with people carrying bedding, bits of machinery, looms, spindles, household furniture." This is a civilization on the move, broken up and yet surmounting the destruction of their ruined villages, led by this old woman "grim and implacable." Her marching scenes evoke the spirit of the Freedom Train as she outwits and deflects the depredations of the Japanese. In her person she is like Granny Millard: "so little and frail looking" and yet "strong and capable and calm."

While Mama Mosquito has become the symbol of Chinese fortitude and resistance, Clemente in occupied Paris and then Holland is like the Caddy that Faulkner will write about in the "Compson Appendix," who has become a German officer's woman. Clemente is "now a symbol of France itself: conquered, debased, prone and dazed and for a time apathetic beneath the conqueror's heel." Yet she recovers her dignity even as an apolitical Dutch boatman becomes a saboteur—both, "in an original idea of mine," Faulkner writes, will become effective enemies of fascism even as a fade-in returns to North Africa showing Akers tenderly moving the wounded America to a safer place. As the German tanks approach, the choruses of the Lincoln cantata merge into the firing, commemorating Lincoln's death but also his voice saying, "How to make the war and the Word agree." At this point Faulkner seemed to balk, perhaps concerned that "Battle Cry" had become unduly sentimental and pious and more propagandistic than he could tolerate. After Earl Robinson's Lincoln says, "I think God must have loved the common people; He made so many of them," Faulkner inserts a parenthesis: "If I remember correctly, Lincoln said, intent humorous, 'God surely must love the poor people: He made so many of them.' Am a little inclined to think the author stopped being a musician at this point in order to insert a little foreign matter." The foreign matter, it seems, was Robinson's collectivism, which annoyed the conservative and highly individualistic Faulkner. An aggrieved Robinson rejected Faulkner's "insinuations," saying Lincoln's statements, as Robinson reported them, could be documented.[27]

In spite of this small kerfuffle, Robinson thought Faulkner was well on the way to an "honest-to-God great picture," with "scenes that will really be new and startling but at the same time simple and true and embodying real people and believable characters and situations." One of the producers, William Bacher, said of Faulkner's work: "I think he's a swell craftsman. Mr. Hawks and he'll come through with a great job on it."[28] Nevertheless parts of the expanded story treatment were "spotty and confusing," Robinson noted.

Whatever quarrels Faulkner had with Robinson seem minor compared to their agreement. To his stepson, Malcolm, in a letter postmarked July 4, Faulkner wrote about the Tuskegee airmen:

> They are in Africa now, under their own negro . . . on the same day a mob of white men and white policemen killed 20 negroes in Detroit. Suppose you and me and a few others of us lived in the Congo, freed seventy-seven years ago by ukase; of course we can't live in the same apartment hut with the black folks, nor always ride in the same car nor eat in the same restaurant, but we are free because the Great Black Father says so. Then the Congo is engaged in War with the Cameroon. At last we persuade the Great Black Father to let us fight too. You and Jim say are flyers. You have just spent the day trying to live long enough to learn how to do your part in saving the Congo. Then you come back and are told that 20 of your people have just been killed by a mixed mob of civilians and cops at Little Poo Poo. What would you think?
>
> A change will come out of this war. If it doesn't, if the politicians and the people who run this country are not forced to make good the shibboleth they glibly talk about freedom, liberty, human rights, then you young men who live through it will have wasted your precious time, and those who dont live through it will have died in vain.

Faulkner suffered thinking of the male members of his own family in peril. Robert Haas at Random House had just had a son killed in the war, and Faulkner told Malcolm about it and about Haas's daughter flying planes in the Women's Ferry Squadron: "All Jews. I just hope I dont run into some hundred percent American Legionnaire until I feel better."[29]

In a second temporary screenplay, completed on July 5, Faulkner built up the role of the German prisoner of war and through him voiced a critique of a capitalist and consumer-oriented society, but also the doom of the Nazi Social Darwinist credo:

> Timber! Mines! Electric power! Bank accounts! Radios, cars, ice cream and picture shows! Pay. Let me tell you what I see. Power: the sinew of strength, the reins to control the force which only the strong dare handle—not for the moiling worthless mass of mankind, but for the power and glory of that race which has the strength to declare its own godhead, and so becomes godhead. America. An empty continent waiting for its master as a woman waits for hers. No wonder your hold on it is so tenuous that you have had to come to this African desert to defend it. The wonder is that she suffered you at all.

At this point, an outraged American soldier is prevented by his fellow officers from shooting the German in a scene that reflects precisely the humanity the "Japs and Germans" have tried to extinguish. But that struggle for freedom and democracy is precarious. A quarrel breaks out between Fonda and Akers about the Civil War. When Akers is told to "forget it," he responds: "Yeah. If I was a Yankee, I'd want to forget it, too." Fonda stares at Akers and says: "We can afford to forget it. We won." It takes another American officer, Corporal Battson, an orphan who does not see himself as either northerner or southerner, to say a new nation was born not in 1776 but in 1861–65, out of Lincoln's own words: "the suffering, the agony, the blood and grief and travails out of which rose a nation which can become in reality the shape of man's eternal hope and which, for that reason, must not and shall not perish from the earth."

Faulkner saw the war as a way of bridging the North/South divide, as he revealed in a letter to Robert Haas about the loss of his son, a carrier-based bomber pilot like Ackroyd. To the New York–born and Yale-educated Haas, Faulkner mentioned that his nephew Jimmy, an eighteen-year-old pilot, had just been posted to carrier training. Jimmy had captured his uncle's attention the same way, say, Ronald Reagan as the second lead in a war movie might.[30] Jimmy had the dash that brought Faulkner back to his dreams of glory, as he consoled Haas: "Then who knows? the blood of your fathers and the blood of mine side by side at the same long table in Valhalla, talking of glory and heroes, draining the cup and banging the empty pewter on the long board to fill again, holding two places for us maybe, not because we were heroes or not heroes, but because we loved them."[31]

Faulkner simplified his expanded story treatment and began the film much more simply and swiftly with a shot of a troop train, smoking and steaming ahead, accompanied by music from the Lincoln cantata and a voice-over: "Battle cry is that which rises out of man's spirit when those things are treated which he has lived by and held above price and which have made his life worth the having and the holding: the integrity of his land, the dignity of his home, the honor of his women and the happiness of his children:—that he and they be not cast into slavery which to a man who has once known freedom is worse than death." Instead of a chorus, the figure of Paul Robeson dominates the screen, using his bass baritone to shout the word "freedom," and then, in a close-up, he sings:

A lonesome train on a lonesome track,
Seven coaches painted black;
Carrying Mr. Lincoln home again,
—Only Mr. Lincoln wasn't on that train.

He is wherever the story of freedom needs defending, a "great long job" for which there is no ending.

The compacted story treatment was in part in response to the studio estimate, delivered at the end of July, that the film would cost over $4 million. *Sergeant York* had cost $1.4 million and had come in over budget, with delays attributed to Hawks. On August 1, Faulkner moved into Hawks's plush house on the studio lot so that they could work undisturbed, readying the film for shooting on September 15. They had big plans for afterward: to create an independent production unit, selling their product to the highest bidder. "I am to be his writer," Faulkner announced to "Big Miss" (Estelle). "He says he and I together as a team will always be worth two million dollars at least." Faulkner told her he would not come home until Hawks was "completely satisfied with his job. . . . This is my chance." Faulkner had not been so excited about his prospects since he had first been asked to write a treatment for Tallulah Bankhead. Although Bacher had a hand in the new opening of "Battle Cry," and another writer contributed a new section set in England, everything else remained Faulkner's adaptation, his masterwork for the screen.

Even so, he told Estelle: "I'm so impatient to get home, I am about to bust. Thank the Lord, I have work to do, something I believe in."[32] Estelle replied on August 4:

> Your letter sounded so cheerful that it made us all feel good. I've a notion that Mr. Hawks must have his old secretary back and that once again you're finding California worthwhile—Don't misunderstand this, and write back that I begrudge you pleasure—I truly I do not.
>
> Suppose I've lived so long now with the knowledge that it has become a familiar and doesn't frighten me as it did.
>
> With lots of love
> Big and Little Miss

This was not the wife who had gone at him with a croquet mallet, and what Faulkner made of such a letter, it is impossible to say.[33] Was it enough for her to attend to Rowan Oak and her family, certain that her husband would return?

Estelle's letter seems of a piece with her chatty and warm letters to her son, Malcolm, away from home on military service. She told him about enjoying *Dixie* with Bing Crosby, who played the author of the famous southern anthem, and about Jill's doings—making sure all the dogs had collars when she heard of a campaign to pick up stray pets. "My letter seems to be made up of exclamations, which Billy thinks a serious fault, but I do love to emphasise," Estelle wrote on August 12.[34] Like so many women during the war, Estelle did everything she could make the men in her life happy. Faulkner, in his better moods, appreciated it, and Malcolm adored her for it: "Mamma, your letters & faith in me during the last three months made all of my training seem easy for I love you so very much."[35]

On August 13, shortly after Faulkner moved into Hawks's studio lot house, Warner canceled "Battle Cry," and according to Faulkner's contract, he was "suspended for approximately 4 months."[36] If it was devastating to see so much work abruptly dismissed, it was wonderful to go home—although not before one more project suddenly materialized. William Bacher, no longer involved with "Battle Cry," pitched to Faulkner a story idea that been talked about in Hollywood since the early 1930s: What if the unknown soldier was Christ on his second coming? Had Faulkner mentioned to Bacher that he had been to the Pantheon and visited the unknown soldier?

Bacher "fired up" director Henry Hathaway, saying Faulkner was "the only man to write it."[37] Hathaway remembered that Bacher had talked for two or three hours to Faulkner. "I'd love to do it. I think that's a great idea," Hathaway remembers Faulkner saying. "But I don't really write screenplays." Hathaway said: "Well, don't write a script. Just write a treatment. 90 to 120 pages of something and just block it out for us and scripting is the easiest part of it if you've got the meat." Faulkner said, "Fine." He would go home and do it.[38] Bacher advanced him a thousand dollars, proposing they work on the picture "independently, and own it between us, share and share alike." Faulkner decided the story could be both a film and a novel. Elements of the Christ story appear, of course, in Faulkner's earlier fiction and screenplays, but why, exactly, a Hollywood pitchman and a director other than Hawks would have such an impact on a writer who would eventually, after a decade, produce the project as *A Fable* requires some explanation. According to Stephen Longstreet, Bacher, with his "wild, piercing eyes and wild red hair," was "a combination of General Patton and Harpo Marx." "Short, continually pulling up his pants," he never stopped talking. "He was a remarkable salesman, the world's greatest salesman. . . . Bacher had probably convinced WF that this was the greatest story since the gospels. . . . Bacher made the thing jell in WF's mind."[39] Maybe, although Hathaway, a veteran director, probably had as much influence as Bacher.

Even so, it seems improbable that a writer like Faulkner could be sold by force of personality or even the promise of profit on a shopworn subject. Perhaps in his work on "Battle Cry," which pictured the war effort in universalist terms not connected to a specific locality and reflected on freedom, which had no geographical limitation, he believed he had found a way to portray a new kind of history of a world he had not mapped before.

10

Fables of Fascism

To Have and Have Not,
August 1943–May 1944

REIGNING AT ROWAN OAK

"I called Nannie [Maud Falkner] tonite and she told me Pappy arrived today. I know how happy the house is now," Malcolm Franklin wrote to his mother, Estelle, on August 22. Malcolm, training in Oklahoma, missed the dove hunting with Pappy and told his mother: "I can hardly wait to hear about Pappy killing the deer. Write me all about it & ask him to."[1] As Malcolm's later diaries reveal, his visits to Rowan Oak were not perfunctory. They were occasions to be noted and celebrated. "What I would have given to have been at Jilly's Halloween party," Malcolm wrote to his mother:

> I know that an excellent time was had by all, as with all of our parties of
> the past—how I remember them. Granddaddy [Lem Oldham] wrote me
> a letter telling about the party: "Jill had her Halloween Party Sat. nite.
> Her costume was a beautiful one in spite of the fact that she played a
> 'witch.' Imagine a girl with her lovely face and girlish figure a 'witch.'"[2]

Missing Christmas at Rowan Oak was worst of all, although Malcolm comforted himself on a trip to New York City by hearing "A negro basso-baritone who was very good and sang some of Pappy's favorites—Water Boy—among them."[3]

William Faulkner as patriarch still rankled the Oldhams, especially the status-conscious Lem—resentful that he now had to rely on the largesse of the son-in-law he had not wanted his daughter to marry. On his stationery, Lem continued to glory in better days, still designating himself in October

1943: "United States Attorney, Northern District of Mississippi, 1921–1925." To Malcolm's sister, Cho-Cho, Oldham wrote: "I am anxious that Cornell will view Malcolm through our spectacles with the result of seeing his first son developed into a refined, cultured gentleman, a reflection of his ancestors, and I might add to a marked degree, the Franklin side." Cornell Franklin was still Lem Oldham's ideal.[4]

"He made our childhood," Vicki (Cho-Cho's daughter) and Faulkner's niece Dean said about life at Rowan Oak. Outdoors and on moonlight rides he predicted, "This is gonna be a good night for shooting stars." They would stay up late, and he would spot the stars for them. He would turn to Estelle and say, "The fish are biting today Stelle, want to go & catch fish?" Just walking down the Old Taylor Road with him was fun. Nothing escaped his notice: "That shack has a new water faucet. See it?" By ten or eleven, you were expected to "know things, to know about a man if they brought him up in conversation." Games included reciting the names of the twelve Caesars, the vice presidents, the Kentucky Derby winners, the six wives of Henry VIII. They became privy to confidential information: Anne Boleyn had a deformed finger and had sleeves especially designed to conceal it. They had a favorite parlor game, Twenty Questions, popularized in a 1940s radio program. How exactly they played it is not clear, but it usually involved an "answerer" who picked an object that the questioners had to guess—for example, "Is it bigger than a breadbox?" The successful questioner then became the answerer. The point was for the answerer to stump the questioners, winning if twenty questions did not yield the correct answer.

When Vicki showed her first short story to Faulkner, he asked, "Why did the young man do that?" Vicki didn't know. You have to know why, he told her. Then they worked on improving the story. He could be brutal, tearing up a story and making her rewrite it. They sometimes resented his discipline, but he was always there for their "emotional upheavals." They learned how to comport themselves in an adult world. At Thanksgiving the children, served first, drank watered wine at their own card table. Pappy would come to them and show them how to toast. Then Norfleet would enter, humming to himself, holding a platter. When Broadus replaced Norfleet, he was permitted to wear his white jacket only if he had served well the night before. They all had to be "on their mettle" if Aunt Bama visited.[5]

For much of this period Faulkner continued to work on "a fable, an indictment of war perhaps, and for that reason may not be acceptable now," he told Harold Ober. After all his schemes to get into military service, his account of a pacifist hero might seem odd, but this correspondence and certain stories revealed his anger over the desire to go to war, even when he joined in. By the end of October he had projected a ten- to fifteen-thousand-word "synopsis" he would send to Ober—adding, "if anyone wants it, I'll rewrite and clean it up." Three weeks later he had fifty-one pages for Ober, stipulating that screen rights were not for sale and that he was willing to rewrite the story as a play or "novelette-fable, either or both of which, under my leave of absence from Warner which reserved me the right to write anything but moving pictures while off salary." He even proposed converting the synopsis into a magazine story.[6]

Faulkner's letter to Robert Haas on January 15, 1944, contained a further elaboration of the fable:

> in the middle of the war, Christ (some movement in mankind which wished to stop war forever) reappeared and was crucified again. We are repeating, we are in the midst of war again. Suppose Christ gives us one more chance, will we crucify him again, perhaps for the last time.
>
> That's crudely put; I am not trying to preach at all. But that is the argument: We did this in 1918; in 1944 it not only MUST NOT happen again, it SHALL NOT HAPPEN again. i.e. ARE WE GOING TO LET IT HAPPEN AGAIN? now that we are in another war, where the third and final chance might be offered us to save him.

No reply from Haas is extant, and a month later work on the fable ceased as Faulkner returned to Hollywood and Hawks.

What Price Hollywood?

"Yes, I'm back again," Faulkner wrote to Harold Ober. "I have done nothing with the story [*A Fable*]." Work on *To Have and Have Not* would continue until the middle of May. "I dont know when I shall get at it, maybe then," Faulkner told his agent. "War is bad for writing." War had "dragged back into daylight" all the "cave instincts." Faulkner confessed he was still young enough to be attracted to the fanfare of war, and yet he was too old to do the fighting. He still believed in his "considerable talent, perhaps as good as any coeval." But he was forty-six, so "what I will mean soon by 'have' is 'had.'"[7] The words echo the title of the film he was working on, featuring a hero, Harry Morgan, played by Humphrey Bogart, who was only a few years younger than Faulkner and would see action and get the girl—just the kind of Hollywood denouement that Faulkner despised and yet that he wished for himself.

A few weeks after beginning work on *To Have and Have Not*, Faulkner wrote Estelle an extraordinary letter describing an experience that never happened to him but that he wanted her to believe was true. As he had with his nephew Jimmy, Faulkner continued to act as though he had seen action in World War I:

A curious thing happened to me yesterday. When the aeroplane crashed in 1918, I didn't feel anything. I just saw the ground getting closer, and then I woke up inside a house with a fearful headache. When I tried to stand up, my right leg just folded up but it never did hurt much. All of a sudden yesterday afternoon, with no warning, I felt all that I didn't feel while it was happening. But the curious thing is, it's my back and my left leg. I try to take a step, it feels all right, then too late I find that the leg is not going to hold me up and I have to grab something. So I bought myself a stick, a piece of malacca, a good piece. I dont have to limp on it, I just carry it handy to catch myself on. I just walk a little stiff, enough for people to ask me if rheumatism and old age have got me at last, to which I agree. I hope it will pass away soon. I imagine it will. It doesn't bother me much, only now and then. The strange thing is, finding again 25 years later the moment that I thought I had lost out of my conscious life.

This complete fantasy, after so much work on war pictures, apparently remained necessary in order to project a complete image of himself as the wounded warrior, the veteran that Cadet Lowe in *Soldiers' Pay* wanted to claim as his own experience even if it meant blindness and death.

Faulkner was living with Buzz Bezzerides, who had offered Faulkner a place to stay rent-free, although the subject of payment never came up. Faulkner would stay nearly six months. Bezzerides would sometimes hear the typewriter at three in the morning, working on his "new fable," he said. Buzz, used to watching his friend's slow-paced, erect, almost tilted backward walk, was startled by "an explosion of movement" as Faulkner darted across the room and grabbed the toppling high chair that baby Peter had pushed back from the table. "This man was so intense behind that seemingly quiet surface, almost seething," Bezzerides said. Bill was friendly to the family, and yet was never quite *there*, even though he often ate dinner with them.[8]

Meta had been assigned as script girl (that was the term then) on *To Have and Have Not*. She wondered how much Hawks knew about her and Bill. "Hello Howard," she said, "as breezy as the archetypal Hawks girl." He had not changed: "The princely reserve was the same as Faulkner, as much a part of him as his erect carriage and clipped speech." Hawks later said he had no intention of intruding on his friends' affairs.

Hawks had Jules Furthman's script for *To Have and Have Not* but "threw it away and asked for me," Faulkner told Ober. Faulkner exaggerated. Furthman's script served as a template that Faulkner took apart and reassembled in a more efficient piece of construction, limiting the action of the story to three intense days and simplifying locations—putting Harry and his love interest, Marie, in the same hotel, making her entrances and exits all the more enticing and intimate. "Rested, clear-eyed Bill knew what to do straight off," Meta remembered. Hawks-to-Faulkner-to-Carpenter—it was a sort of reunion, although with a difference: word got around about Faulkner's powerful performance, even though he worked for a pittance, compared to Furthman's $2,500 weekly salary. Faulkner alternately enjoyed and deplored the newfound respect. He told her: "All this head bowing and foot scraping. . . . Nobody looked at me before this, and if it's a flop, none of them will look my way again." He understood the precarious studio regime, as he wrote home to Estelle: "Warner seems to be in some state of almost female vapors. He fired his main producer, Mr. Wallis, and all Wallis' writers. Two other producers are about to quit. I think Warner has forgotten me. But someday he will look out his window and happen to see me pass, so I may be fired too. None of us know what's going to happen. Half the writers are gone now, and the whole shebang might blow up at anytime."[9]

Hawks had been in a jam because of U.S. government concerns about the film's location, Cuba, and the possibility of embarrassing the Batista regime and thwarting President Roosevelt's "Good Neighbor" policy. When Hawks told Faulkner the setting would be changed to Martinique, Faulkner suggested the "political interest would be the conflict between the Free French and the Vichy government."[10] Here, then, was yet another opportunity to get into production the antifascist critique that had been stymied in "The De Gaulle Story" and "Battle Cry."

A rewrite had to be produced by February 22, and the director started shooting March 1, with Faulkner on the set doing more rewrites and working with the actors. It was an amicable set. Faulkner enjoyed watching Bogart and Bacall fall in love and developed a scene that Hawks had trouble staging. In her screen test, Bacall had delivered her famous line to Bogart: "You don't have to do anything. Not a thing . . . Oh, maybe just whistle . . . You do know how to whistle, Steve. You just put your lips together and blow." Hawks remembered they had an "awful time" finding the right moment and setting. Faulkner said, "If we put those people in a hotel corridor where nobody else is around, then I think we can make that scene work." In fact, Bacall delivers the lines as she heads toward the door of Harry's room. She turns back as the door opens to the corridor and then launches the lines at the sitting Bogart, whose whistle just after she leaves shows how powerfully she has struck him. It is likely that the actors and Hawks worked up the business of the scene, but Faulkner provided the impetus. "I wrote the line," Hawks said, "but he [Faulkner] wrote the stuff that led up to it."[11]

Bogart's no-nonsense manner appealed to Faulkner. Hoagy Carmichael's earthy talk and piano playing were also entertaining. Carmichael often played character parts that made his music one of the romantic links between the male and female star. This time, his celebrated "Hong Kong Blues," romantic and plaintive, spoke to the plight of displaced characters:

> It's the story of a very unfortunate colored man
> Who got arrested down in old Hong Kong
> He got twenty years privilege taken away from him
> When he kicked old Buddha's gong.
> . . . .
> I need someone to love me.
> I need somebody to carry me home.

Faulkner always seemed to be on set when Carmichael performed.[12] Stephen Longstreet tried to get Carmichael to talk about his interactions with Faulkner, but Hoagy was as reserved about Bill as Bill was about himself. By design or by virtue of their very natures, both men created a mystique about their appearances in Hollywood, standing apart, and like Bogart, liking it that way.

Hawks, known for asking actors to suit dialogue to their way of speaking, also subordinated Faulkner to the same methods. When Bogart read over Faulkner's dialogue, the actor asked, "I'm supposed to say all that?" Hawks intervened and cut down the scene, consulting with his star. Faulkner had to "keep ahead" of Hawks "with a day's script." In this respect, he had Meta's invaluable help, since she had a meticulous sense of continuity that kept the director and writer straight on the changes made nearly every day. Furthman looked over Faulkner's work, but the two writers did not collaborate as such.[13]

Bogart's Harry is a supreme individualist as filtered through Hemingway to Faulkner. Harry is cold, says Helene de Bursac, the American wife of the Gaullist freedom fighter Harry is hired to rescue with his fishing boat. She even calls him unfeeling. Harry just wants to run his fishing boat for hire and rejects political engagements. He wants to be let alone. But he also wants to be free. To that extent he tells the saloon owner, Frenchy, that he is on Frenchy's anti-Vichy side. But it is the money, Harry claims, that motivates the rescue mission.

Harry is wary of women, "dames," who are a drag and get in the way, although Hawks toned down the misogyny in Faulkner's script. Harry calls Marie, the pickpocketing femme fatale who pursues him, "Slim," the nickname of Hawks's wife, who had recommended Bacall for the role. Bacall is alluring and yet almost masculine in her descent into the lower registers of her voice, making her a perfect match for the skittish hero. Harry's studied understatement hides (doesn't it?) a certain suspicion, if not dread, of what women might do. After all, he is clearly attracted to Marie and yet buys her a plane ticket so he no longer has to deal with her, which is why, as she says, she decides to stay and even put herself in danger in a vicious Vichy stronghold. How could the romance between the older Harry (Bogart) and the younger Marie (Bacall) not make for an enticing project for the Meta-besotted Faulkner? During the making of the film, hard-drinking Bogart had to fend off his alcoholic wife's physical attacks (she had also tried to commit suicide) as it became apparent that he was falling in love with Bacall.[14] Did Faulkner know about this off-screen drama—one that paralleled what he had gone through with Estelle and Meta? Bogart and Faulkner drank together, but "there was no meeting of minds," Stephen Longstreet asserted. "Bogart was just an actor who imagined he was a Hemingway character, and about as bright as any actor which doesn't say much. Bill would drink with almost anyone at the studio, but hardly ever got to a personal level with them."[15] But Faulkner did write to Estelle: "Tell Missy [Jill] I am becoming good friends with Humphrey Bogart, the star."[16] How personal did you have to get with William Faulkner in order for him to read you?

Just as absorbing was the developing character of Eddie, the "rummy" (another Jiggs), played brilliantly by Walter Brennan with an extraordinary array of tics and staggers and frailties that the actor exploits and yet overcomes in a relentlessly cheerful performance.[17] No matter how harshly Harry speaks to him, Eddie returns for more, knowing about Harry's better self. For all Eddie's failings, he believes that Harry needs him. Why? Because Eddie trusts in Harry's goodness. To keep Eddie aboard Harry's boat is a vindication of Harry's own humanity. When Harry's fascist-like client Mr. Johnson wonders why Harry keeps the feckless Eddie as a crew member, Harry responds that Eddie thinks he is taking care of Harry. And more than Harry is ever willing to acknowledge, Eddie does just that. Eddie is *always there* when Harry needs him. Eddie is, in the parlance of Faulkner's South, Harry's "nigger." The role Eddie plays is the role black people played in Faulkner's life. They were always *there,* loyal and reliable, no matter their foibles. In fact, their foibles were essential to a man who wanted to believe in himself as the master, the patriarch, the hero of his own domain. The paradoxical nature of Eddie's appeal—he is a dependent who is not really subservient, insofar as he has his own personality to express, which is never suppressed in his service to Harry—is the same that obtained among the black people in the Faulkner household.

Fascists do not understand—such is the message of *To Have and Have Not*—that the world is not divided between the strong and the weak. There is an interdependency in human affairs that cannot be summed up in a survival-of-the-fittest ideology. The strong are strong only inasmuch as they take everyone on board—not just those who don't drink or have no disabilities. Eddie helps Harry do the right thing. Even though Harry sends Eddie away, Eddie sneaks aboard the boat. And the same is true for Marie; she fails to take off, and Harry is the better for her decision. Meta never emphasized those aspects of Faulkner that were off-putting—not just his drinking but his desire, always, to have his own way. She did more than cope. She brought out his desire to help her and respect her rights, even as he knew he was bound to disappoint her. Like Eddie's faith in Harry, she never gave up on Bill. Furthman's Eddie dies; Faulkner not only keeps Eddie alive, but he softens Harry's treatment of him. Making Eddie integral to the plot also fit right in with the director's deployment of Brennan in supporting roles in several successful movies from *Barbary Coast* (1935) to *Rio Bravo* (1959).

Bruce Kawin succinctly describes the different Harrys that went into the making of *To Have and Have Not:* "Furthman's was a tough adventurer, Faulkner's a sometime misogynist on the verge of political commitment, and Hawks's a witty and self-confident professional." All were different from Hemingway's hero: "a family man, an ex-cop, a desperate planner, an unsentimental killer, an individualist ground to death by giant forces, a loser."[18] Furthman's Harry hits Eddie hard and slaps Marie, a brutality removed from the final screenplay since the distinction between Harry's violence in the service of a good cause and that of the fascists cannot be diluted. In Harry, Faulkner had also found a character who suited his own fantasies about working with a bootlegger in New Orleans. Faulkner as "tough guy, one who was aware of evil in the world, even intimate with evil, and cynical—a semi-saint, semi-sinner who was somehow still a good man."[19] Robert Jordan, the antifascist, pro–Spanish Republic hero of *For Whom the Bell Tolls,* also inspired Faulkner's treatment of Harry. In "Battle Cry," a French resistance fighter names "an American book written by a Mr. Hemingway" that is read aloud as a refusal to accept fascism.

Few reviewers understood the full import of the film, regarding it as a knockoff of *Casablanca*—primarily because Bogart as tough-guy reluctant hero seemed similar in both films, as did the anti-Vichy politics, although Hawks actually toned down some of Faulkner's strident propaganda passages reminiscent of "Battle Cry." Other reviewers thought the romance detracted from the serious politics. "*To Have and Have Not* has a healthy democratic flesh tone," John T. McManus observed in *PM* (October 12, 1944), "and it is only skin deep." In the *New York Times* Bosley Crowther remarked that

Walter Brennan's Eddie is "affecting" but "pointless."[20] The distinguished film critic Manny Farber did not care for the film, "even though one of its screen authors is William Faulkner." Why? Because of the "unbelievable and irritating" effort to change the "most determined kind of asocial man into a French patriot."[21] Yet that is close to what happened to William Faulkner during his Hollywood war years.

11

Hollywoodism

May–December 1944

Fitful Family Man

Bill broke it to Meta that Estelle and Jill would be coming west for the summer. His daughter missed him and wanted to see Hollywood. He didn't want Jill around her mother's drinking now that school was out. Evidently, Meta did not think to ask, "What about Jill around you when you're drinking?" He had already rented a house. "For the first time," Meta felt "put upon cruelly." Wife and family belonged in Oxford, not in Meta's province: "I had the short end of the stick, the sweepings, the leavings. His wife and daughter had everything." He tried to assure her nothing had changed. For Meta, everything had changed. It had been humiliating to share him with Estelle eight years earlier. Nothing he could say mollified her. She had finally made him choose, and he had chosen his family. She cut him off, refusing even to go out for drinks or dinner. Apparently he did not tell her that Estelle had gotten quite used to the idea of Meta.

To Buzz Bezzerides, Faulkner had simply used Meta, and he did not believe she ever understood that side of his nature: "He was a very selfish fellow and didn't seem to be aware of the demands he was making, the burdens he was putting on people." It could seem otherwise because Faulkner never asked for help: "You found yourself inviting him to do something because he needed it. You were very aware of his needs." But then, Bezzerides seemed to take it back: "I didn't feel used. I was glad to do what I did, and I don't think Meta felt used. She was glad to do what she did because she loved him. I was very fond of Faulkner and I liked him very much." How to reconcile two seemingly contradictory attitudes? Naturally enough, Bezzerides, like Meta, wanted more from Faulkner than he was willing to give, and more, perhaps, than he knew how to give. An aggrieved Bezzerides added: "I had contempt for his inability to recognize that one has responsibility when he accepts this kind of responsibility from others, but he showed no signs of recognizing it." Why not? Bezzerides's own explanation traced Faulkner's inability to the example of his great-grandfather, a man who was forgiven much because he had been a writer and brought a certain glory to his family. Faulkner "took it as his privilege as a great writer to make demands on people, get what he wanted, what he needed." Writing, in sum, was its own realm and made of Faulkner a sovereign. Bezzerides believed that Faulkner hated Hollywood and would never have returned if not for the income it provided. Maybe so. But the desire to escape home for *somewhere else* never abated.[1] This counter-pull made Faulkner, as a result, a fitful family man.

To Cho-Cho, Faulkner wrote that "after years of Rowan Oak and trees and grounds, maybe Big and Little Miss will enjoy living in a city apartment, with nothing to break the silence but the shriek of brakes and the crash of colliding automobiles, and police car and fire wagon sirens, and the sounds of other tenants in the building who are not quite ready to lay down and hush at 1 or 2 a.m. They may like it. At least we will be together." They would enjoy music, riding horses—and he wanted Jill to take fencing lessons. He told Cho-Cho to tell her husband, Bill Fielden, "not to talk to me about gardening. I'm homesick enough without any nudging from him on the subject."[2]

Estelle wrote to Malcolm to tell him what it was like that summer in Southern California. On Saturdays after lunch they went to a bookshop to pick up what they needed for the week's reading, then did some food shopping: "Billy is really enjoying having a home, even if it *is* a small apartment, and it is a pleasure for me to cook all the things he is fond of because he eats with such evident relish." For Sunday breakfast Estelle set out a huge spread: fresh figs, sausage, eggs, toast, coffee, and cake. After eating out (noontime sandwiches and Coca-Colas), they returned home for a hot supper.

Mrs. House, owner of a horse ranch, became a family friend. She had a large family, and the children were always underfoot, and that made it all seem "homelike." Jill was "supremely happy" horseback riding. Fathers and daughters and horses were a natural combination. Toluca Lake was stocked with bass, and Estelle had been "invited to fish in it—hurrah!" When a boat slid up to a landing, who should emerge but "the Sinatra himself!" A thrilled Jill now had something to write home about. "Hope all this Hollywoodism doesn't bore you," she told Malcolm.[3]

That Malcolm would want to hear all this is obvious from his own detailed letters about his daily doings in New York, which included just then reading *The Wild Palms* and remarking that "Bill is truly a student of human behavior patterns." But you had to stay awake to understand his prose, Malcolm said, and that's why some people did not like to read him.[4] In May 1944, now overseas, Malcolm wrote to his mother: "For some reason this country [England] reminds me of Billy. I think back over my years with him and realize how fortunate I have been in having him in my younger years. Now that I am becoming mature in my thoughts I realize that he has shaped my character & mode of thinking greatly. He is truly a great man, not because of his writings but because of his knowledge, his kindness and his understanding. I long for the day that you all can really settle down at Roanoak & Billy can start his great writing period which is yet to come."[5] Faulkner sometimes gave the impression that his family did not appreciate him. Their correspondence, at any rate, suggests otherwise—and also why he wanted them with him. "My own precious son," Estelle wrote to Malcolm on July 11: "Your letters are the very breath of life to me. . . . Billy, Jill, and I read them avidly before I send them home. Bless your heart!"

Faulkner did not hesitate to take Estelle and Jill to Musso & Frank's. "The 'hoi polloi' sit up in front, but Jean, the head waiter, greets us very grandly at the door, and ushers Jill and me back to holy-of-holies where the regular crowd meets," Estelle reported to Malcolm. She reveled in meeting many fascinating and charming people, while Jill (the only child present) behaved so well that she seemed quite at home, although she was amazed that the patrons treated her father as a celebrity. Her mother had to explain to Jill that Pappy was equivalent to a movie star.[6] Some of these people, for sure, knew about Meta, but evidently that did not trouble Faulkner, or he did not let on.

Eleven-year-old Jill swam and rode horses with Zoe Bezzerides, Buzz's daughter. Jill wrote home about her "dearest little fox terrier puppy" and wanted to share every new experience with Vicki (Cho-Cho's daughter): "I love you so much that if you tried to pick it up you would go through the ground. So *please* don't try to pick it up." Like her father, she missed home and family and sometimes complained about "nothing to do." She wanted regular reports, she instructed Vicki: "tell Bro. Bill [William Fielden] if he doesn't write me I'm going up there and tickle him good." This was a family joke—about how ticklish Jill and Bill Fielden were. When he first arrived at Rowan Oak from the Far East in 1941, Jill had announced: "Brother Bill, I'm Sister Jill. If you don't tickle me, I won't tickle you." Fielden got down on the floor and hugged Jill. He was part of what Jill and her father thought of as home. "Pappy and my father were immediate friends," Fielden's daughter Vicki recalled. The handsome Bill Fielden fit right in.[7] Jill had a "nice time" at a Saturday-night dance and "danced with every boy but four." She often added a P.S. like this one: "If the world was full of the Fieldens, the Faulkners and the Franklins everything would be just fine. I love all of you more than I can tell."

Something about Buzz's concern for Estelle touched a nerve. "Something went wrong," she told Buzz, breaking down in tears about her marriage to Bill. "I don't know what went wrong. We used to go fishing together. We loved each other." At the end of September, after she returned to Rowan Oak, Buzz wrote her an extraordinary letter: "Nothing is wrong. You know I love you, always have, always will, you know I miss you, stay awake at night, dreaming of you. The only reason I have not written is because the things I want to say to you must be breathed, whispered, how I wish I were there. I would look at you mooneyed, hold your hand, besides I am lazy, negligent, careless, and slightly busy. Forgive me for not writing sooner." This love letter—what else can you call it?—Estelle preserved, and it became part of her son Malcolm's papers. Buzz felt Estelle had made him a better man, more courteous and thoughtful. Buzz had formed a fierce attachment to Estelle in such a short time. It was unusual, Buzz wrote. His daughter felt it too, and it moved Buzz that Jill had written to say she loved him and his family.

The summer of 1944, even with Faulkner's family beside him, had sometimes been a trial. He worked indifferently and for brief periods on several films, including a vehicle for Errol Flynn, released in 1948 as *Adventures of Don Juan*. Assigned to rewrite the first draft, this "cut and polish job" yielded, in producer Jerry Wald's words, a script that was not "quite right," but good for "budgeting purposes." He needed a writer with "experience doing this kind of costume picture." Steve Trilling revised Faulkner's script, but neither he nor Faulkner received any credit for the finished product.[8] Other short-term projects also yielded no credits: "God Is My Co-Pilot" (the story of the Flying Tigers who fought the Japanese in China), "Fog over London" (a psychiatrist becomes involved with criminals), "Strangers in Our Midst," also titled "Escape into the Desert," about Nazis escaping from an internment camp. Bezzerides, a cowriter on this project, remembered they had trouble taking it seriously.[9] Actress Jean Sullivan befriended Faulkner during the shoot and learned that he liked to ride horses, which they did two or three times a week. "What am I doing in Hollywood?," he asked her. "They've messed up the script so badly. The only time I feel free is when I'm riding." He later invited her to Jill's wedding.[10] But Faulkner's efforts did not go unappreciated. When Wald had trouble with *Background to Danger*, he showed it to Faulkner, who diagnosed the problem: "too much running around." He straightened out several scenes, Wald recalled: "He really did a magnificent job."[11]

After Estelle and Jill left for home, "Billy had a mild bout," Buzz confided to Estelle, "but we got him out of it in short order. I think this time he senses my outrage and impatience and anger because he has been apologetic . . . and a trifle worried. It pleases me to think that he values my friendship enough to be concerned about losing it." Not to worry, Buzz assured her: "I like the guy, even with his faults, I don't think I'd ever let him down, he gets pretty dependent and helpless. But he is fine now, the picture he is writing is to be shot very soon, and he is feeling tiptop."[12] And no wonder, since the picture would prove to contain so many of the elements that made up his own character and career—a project handed to him by the redoubtable Howard Hawks.

Faulkner had another reason to recover: the return of Meta Carpenter. Henriette Martin, Meta's friend and a screenwriter, ran into Faulkner, who said he was looking for a place to stay—perhaps realizing he had overstayed his welcome at the Bezzerides household. He accepted her immediate offer of a room with its own bath and entrance. Meta, who had remained estranged from Faulkner, asked, "How does he look?" Henriette answered: "The way some boozers do. Absolutely marvelous. Your average teetotaler should look so good." Meta began to get reports from Henriette, who told her that so far as she knew Faulkner never brought anyone to his private room. "Does he ever ask about me," Meta wanted to know. "Always." Then she heard from actor Victor Killian that a drunken Faulkner had told him: "Meta doesn't love me anymore. . . . Tell me what to do, Victor. Tell me how to get her back." She showed up at his apartment, offering to give him a lift to work. She remembered his voice breaking as he said her name. "And so we resumed," she remembered, spending time alone but also with Henriette, the Crowns, the Paganos, and other friends.

THE FAULKNER MYSTIQUE

Buzz Bezzerides: "I remember one day walking with Faulkner over to the drugstore where he was going to exchange a stack of mystery stories for a new stack. I asked him, 'Why do you read all of these damn mysteries?' and he said, 'Bud, no matter what you write, it's a mystery of one kind or another.'"[13] Detectives solve mysteries, but sometimes, as in the case of Philip Marlowe, the detective is the mystery and develops a mystique that enveloped William Faulkner for the whole of his working life.

It seems that nearly every screenwriter had some version of the Faulkner mystery to tell. It usually involved wanting to know how Faulkner wrote some story or character. So writer Elik Moll asked Buzz to introduce him to William Faulkner. Moll promised Bezzerides not to ask Faulkner about his writing. In the Warner writers' building, Bezzerides introduced Moll: "This is a friend of mine, Elik Moll, this is William Faulkner." Faulkner had only two words to offer: "Yes, sir"—which he said without even taking his hand off his pipe to shake hands. He walked away as Moll began discussing *Go Down, Moses,* climaxing his onslaught with, "How did you do that?" Faulkner acted as though he had not heard the question. Moll repeated the question to no effect and then "dropped back." Bezzerides caught up with Faulkner:

> "Bill."
> "Bud."
> "You know, Elik Moll."
> "Who?"
> "The fellow I introduced you to; he asked you a question, and you did not answer. Why didn't you answer?"[14]

Such a question deserved no answer, Bill told Buzz. Such a question that got no answer could also have been put to Philip Marlowe. Howard Hawks and William Faulkner had talked about working together on Raymond Chandler's novel *The Big Sleep.* Hawks told Jack Warner he could produce a screenplay in less than a month[15]—a boast he probably would not have made if he had not counted upon Faulkner, who could produce thirty pages in a day to the typical screenwriter's three. Hawks, impressed with Leigh Brackett's hardboiled dialogue in *No Good for a Corpse,* teamed her with Faulkner, famous for breaking down a novel into filmable segments. She remembered his elaborate courtesy: "a parody of the way in which a Southern gentleman might treat a nice young lady on her very first job."[16]

Marlowe does not smoke a pipe like the taciturn Faulkner, but he smokes his cigarettes quietly and rarely gives away much to his interlocutors. Marlowe seethes with "repressed anger," as the screenplay puts it, confining himself to two words: "Get out"—said to Carmen Sternwood, one of two sisters (the other is Vivian) who make a play for him while he investigates what happened to Shawn Regan, the man whom both women loved and, it turns out, Carmen murdered. Regan, a good man Marlowe knew and admired, was also loved by General Sternwood, the sisters' father, who is attracted to the straight-shooting Marlowe. In short, Shawn Regan, who for much of film is merely missing—supposedly having run away with a casino owner's wife—fills a need in the dying general's life that is the same need his two daughters have to remedy their "rotting blood"—as Vivian acknowledges. Regan has been the general's new blood he has lost even as he sits blanketed in a hot house, decaying with cold, no longer the whole man depicted in the portrait with "battle-torn pennons" in the noir decadence of this mansion and family.

Could Faulkner have wished for a better project? Like Faulkner, Marlowe never telegraphs what he thinks. By the time he does explain himself, what he has been thinking all along is becoming plain to everyone else in the plot.

No actor could have played Marlowe better than Bogart, who began in *Casablanca* and continued in *To Have and Have Not* to withhold what he thinks and what makes him mad. Gary Cooper also knew how to underplay, but he was too tall and just too loftily attractive. Clark Gable was too bluff, too extroverted to keep so much of himself repressed. Jimmy Stewart did not have enough grooves in his face to play the battered but handsome detective. In *The Big Sleep*, Marlowe might as well be Faulkner walking into a room: "You're not very tall are you?," Carmen Sternwood says when she first meets Marlowe. Bogart was five feet, ten inches (five inches taller than Faulkner) but not an overwhelming physical presence, and not the husky fellow described in the shooting script. Bogart-Marlowe's reply to Carmen applies as well to Faulkner: "I try to be." No one tried to walk taller than William Faulkner. He stood up so straight while walking that Buzz Bezzerides wondered why Bill did not fall over. For all his tough-guy, understated style, Marlowe, like Faulkner, is a romantic, and in the shooting script he even gives his hard-boiled version of a Nobel Prize speech: "Pride is a great thing, isn't it? And courage—and honor—and love. All the things you read about in the copybooks—only in copybooks nothing ever gets tangled. The road always lies so straight, and clear, and signs say to love and honor and be brave." Marlowe might as well be a writer, with a sense of narrative pace, since he saves what is for him a long speech until near the end of his story—for it is his story, one that he makes the other characters tell to him.

What happens in *The Big Sleep* is confusing and subject to much critical discussion—"figuring it out makes you faint," Manny Farber remarked.[17] James Agee called it "wakeful fare for folks who don't care what is going on, or why, so long as the talk is hard and the action harder."[18] Herbert Cohn in the *Brooklyn Daily Eagle* (August 24, 1946) spoke for many reviewers when he concluded that he did not understand any more about the film than if it had been written by Gertrude Stein. Here is the shortest version of the plot: "[The screwy behavior of] Carmen Sternwood, daughter of a retired general, brings forth a blackmailer. This brings Philip Marlowe . . . private dick into the scene. And this in turn causes Vivian Sternwood . . . Carmen's somewhat predatory but smart sister to step in and try to close the case in an effort to protect Carmen" (*Big Spring [TX] Herald,* October 6, 1946). What matters is Marlowe's strength of character, admired again and again by everyone—including the police who resent his scoops, the women who try to manipulate him, and even the men who try to kill him. Eddie Mars, the casino owner who wants Marlowe killed, calls him a "soldier"—as do others because Marlowe is so committed to doing his duty. Mars is sarcastic, and yet he is respectful, realizing that Marlowe will not be deterred from finding out what happened to Shawn Regan, and Marlowe, like Faulkner, treats his case as a kind of trade secret he won't share with anyone until he figures out what happened to Regan. Soldiers do their duty and follow orders—except when they don't because they have an even higher sense of duty to the truth. Marlowe ultimately figures out that the Sternwood sisters have collaborated with Eddie Mars in covering up a crime because he understands the passions of love—of Eddie's wife, for example, who perpetuates the ruse that she ran off with Regan in order to help Eddie cover up a crime. The only honorable thing for Marlowe to do is to sort out these conflicting passions, even after General Sternwood has paid him off.

Marlowe becomes what the war was about: courage and honor and love. He becomes, as a result, yet another way for Faulkner to express the values that inspired "The De Gaulle Story" and "Battle Cry." Marlowe gives no speech about honor and pride and love in Chandler's novel. The Hollywood Faulkner signed on to write such speeches as a testament to what soldiers like Marlowe believed could be restored in postwar society. The Sternwoods allude to a decline in their line that fits Faulkner's conception of the Compsons and Sartorises. General Sternwood, for all his hard, bitter demeanor, wants to believe in love—that Shawn Regan has not abandoned him—and Marlowe allows the general to believe that Regan has only gone away and wishes the general well, rather than stating the truth: Carmen killed Regan in a fit of jealousy. Marlowe's gift to a dying man is also the hope that men like Regan and Marlowe inspire. The gentleman-hero survives in Marlowe for all his tough monosyllabic talk and his silences. In effect, Marlowe becomes a family man, when Norris, the family butler cum all-purpose servant, "takes the liberty" of moving Marlowe's car into the driveway and expresses "our gratitude" for what Marlowe has done for the Sternwoods—much as a black servant might do in a Faulkner novel. Marlowe inherits, like an eldest son, the Sternwood mythos. At the end of the film, Marlowe, who hardly ever has time to even sleep in his apartment, says to the arriving cops that they will have no trouble catching up with him: "I've decided already myself to stay." Hardly ever at home in Hollywood, Marlowe, whose office has been everywhere, like the displaced Faulkner,[19] has finally found a refuge. Although Jules Furthman rewrote the picture's final scenes, they depend on Faulkner's and Brackett's opening sequence: "The mutual affection and respect that develop so naturally between Marlowe and General Sternwood . . . is barely hinted at in the book."[20]

Leigh Brackett disparaged Faulkner's unwieldy dialogue but delighted in his story construction, which makes the shooting script a marvel of interlocking scenes featuring a moving in and out and returning to several interiors similar to the opening and closing of doors in *To Have and Have Not*, creating the effect of following the characters into scenes in the most natural, fluid way. In *The Big Sleep*, we become a part of Marlowe's itinerary—visiting the Sternwood mansion, the orchid house, various Sternwood bedrooms, the Geiger bookshop (the blackmailer's lair), Geiger's house, Marlowe's living room, Marlowe's bedroom, Marlowe's car, Marlowe's office, Joe Brody's apartment (another blackmailer's lair), the district attorney's office, Eddie Mars's casino, Mars's private office, the automobile shop where Marlowe is roughed up. Very few scenes occur outside: on a few streets, a fishing pier, and a highway. All this coming and going in "transitory spaces"[21] is the point of the film as Marlowe's wit and strength are tested from every conceivable angle in a film of "hopeless enclosure within an ominous universe."[22] Losing a grip on exactly what is happening and who is guilty has never seemed to bother many viewers because Bogart's Marlowe is so resilient and so much his own man, impregnable in many of the same ways as William Faulkner even as it is apparent that beneath that impervious mien is a smoldering fury.

Marlowe has been a hired hand. "I try to do my job," he says, as Faulkner did. But what a job in this case, since the novelist cum screenwriter did not so much adapt another writer's novel for a screenplay as participate in a screenplay that worked out the existential dimension of his own Hollywood career: the detective story as displaced autobiography. Faulkner rarely had much to say about a finished script, but after doing his final rewrites he told James Geller, head of the story department, he had worked on them, even after receiving final payment, "in respectful joy and happy admiration. WITH LOVE, WILLIAM FAULKNER."[23]

12

Hollywood and Horror, Home and Horses

December 1944–September 1945

BUSINESSWOMEN, BROTHELS, AND VAMPIRE LESBIANS

Before securing a six-month reprieve from his Warner Brothers contract, Faulkner rewrote one of several screenplays for Jerry Wald's production of *Mildred Pierce.* How seriously he took the project is in doubt. He introduced a new character, a black maid who soothes a distraught Mildred by singing "Steal Away." In the margin, Faulkner wrote, "God damn! How's that for a scene?" And yet he produced a sequence (never filmed) reminiscent of Thomas Sutpen's rebuff at the white planter's front door. A proud Mildred Pierce experiences a similar rebuff at the front door of a Beverly Hills mansion, and like Sutpen, she is galvanized into creating her own establishment, a successful restaurant—her all-consuming design—only to come to grief when her daughter, Veda, murders Mildred's husband, who has been having an affair with Veda. The violence and quasi-incest, the flashbacks and retrospective point of view—all in the James M. Cain 1941 novel—have led to speculation that Cain had rewritten Faulkner who rewrote Cain for the screen.[1]

Mildred Pierce, only one of the women's films of the 1940s that revived Joan Crawford's career, is reminiscent of a treatment Faulkner wrote in 1941, an adaptation of a novel, *The Damned Don't Cry,* that he worked on again in May and June of 1944. Not yet under contract to Warner in 1941 but hoping to secure one, he sent to the studio a commentary on a previous writer's treatment as well as supplying one of his own that actually presaged the decade in film to come. His treatment rectified what he diagnosed as the main character's problem: Zelda was passive, a victim of circumstance, and as such lacked any vital interest for moviegoers. He made her a poor white southern woman, bold enough to want more from life even when it seemed to make her conventionally immoral. As if to progress beyond *Sanctuary,* Faulkner not only put his heroine in a brothel, he made her the owner—once again portraying a strong woman, like Mildred Pierce, establishing her own business. Like Temple Drake, Zelda is involved with a southern aristocrat, Dan Carter, weak in the manner of Gowan Stevens, with a "lack of ambition," a "willingness to condone injustice rather than struggle against it, his backward-looking toward the dead past and veneration of family merely because it is old. She sets out to buck him up, make him ambitious to improve himself and the world, too." This turn in the plot anticipates both *Intruder in the Dust* and *Requiem for a Nun* and the social-justice pictures that Twentieth Century-Fox would produce after the war in that Zelda persuades Carter to "take without pay the case of a falsely accused, dissolute and penniless Negro," a case that Carter wins. Faulkner included plenty of melodrama—several rapes and Zelda's illegitimate child—that made his treatment unfilmable,[2] although *The Damned Don't Cry,* released in 1950, retained Faulkner's basic conception of Zelda, now named Ethel, whose ambition and desire to surmount her poor white background bolsters the strong, if morally compromised heroine Joan Crawford personified. Faulkner's treatment served his own purposes, part of a process that turned his fiction inside out, exploring in great detail the social and political implications of his characters' private dramas.

In November 1944, Howard Hawks purchased the film rights to Irina Karlova's *Dreadful Hollow* and turned the project over to William Faulkner. The surviving first-draft screenplay, all in Faulkner's words, does not include a date, and it is not mentioned in his extant correspondence. On January 25, 1951, Hawks was trying to get Darryl Zanuck to approve production of the film. The producer declined, saying he had nothing against the picture, but it seemed formulaic. He had "'seen it all before' in one form or another."[3] What was he thinking? How could a lesbian vampire movie by William Faulkner seem prosaic? Three years later, Jack Warner also passed on the project.[4] The *Oxford American* (Winter 2002) announced that "Dreadful Hollow" would be produced by Lee Caplin's Picture Entertainment Corporation, although no film has so far appeared. Caplin assured me the "book is under development as a feature film."[5]

Jillian Dare arrives at Rotherham Halt, 204 miles from London, to take up employment at the Grange (remember *Wuthering Heights*), a country estate inhabited by "two furriners and a loon," as an old yokel calls them. That word, "furriners," first used in *The Sound and the Fury,* evokes the anxieties about the alien that marks *Absalom, Absalom!* as well—only in this case it is not

Sutpen or mixed-blood Bon who disturbs a homogeneous and xenophobic community but a countess from the continent. Zanuck saw only a formula and not the use to which Faulkner put it—the way he capitalizes on suspicions of "race and nationality that emerge in classic vampire cinema."[6]

Dare's family desperately needs her income, and the independent Jillian sets off to walk to work, refusing the offer of a lift from Larry Clyde, who motors by and tries to pick her up. "Nonsense, my dear child," he says to her condescendingly. "Be sensible, Miss Muffet, and take advantage of providence." His words conjure up the fairy-tale atmosphere of the movie and also the formulaic aspect that Zanuck spotted. Vampire movies often have young doctors as heroes and sometimes intrepid females like Jillian who dare. But here the formulaic is playful. After all, Clyde calls Rotherham Halt "Little Rotting-off-the map." The persistent, jocular Clyde finally succeeds in driving her to the Grange and on their arrival says: "Here we are. Are you still sure this is where you want to go"—even after the "loon," Jacob Lee, menaces her with gardening shears, saying: "Go way! Nobbut ain't allowed here!" The redoubtable Jillian—she may have appealed to Hawks's penchant for strong women—answers: "Nonsense. I'm expected. Go back to your work."

Jillian rings an "old fashioned bell. It BOOMS hollowly in the depths of the house—a deep portentous sound in keeping with the grim exterior." The quite slow buildup to the occult is reminiscent of *Curse of the Demon,* which director Jacques Tourneur would turn into a classic a little more than a decade later. The lady-in-waiting to the countess has the manner of Mrs. Danvers in *Rebecca.* Jillian stands at the door: "A face is looking out at her from around a parted curtain in a window—a grim, harsh woman's face. The curtain falls back, after a moment the door opens with a slow grinding of heavy bolts and the same woman stands in it. She is SARI. She is gaunt, spare, forbidding, in severe black with a maid's cap and apron. She has a harsh, yellow face. She gives Jillian a swift up-and-down examination but says nothing." Jillian is standing in a hall that has "an air of wealth and decayed splendor with a faint foreign flavor. Jillian, still carrying the suitcase, looks about curiously. Then she hears the heavy bolts grinding again and looks around to see Sari holding the door again as if the house were a fortress with an enemy just outside." Jillian is the outside world. She is us, come to call—except that she shows no fear and, unlike us, is equal to the situation. Or so it seems. The decayed splendor is not all that different from the house haunted by memories in *Flags in the Dust* or the house disquieted by an idiot in *The Sound and the Fury.* As in a Faulkner novel or in *The Big Sleep*, Jillian enters a degenerated world in need of new blood.

Jillian now meets her employer, the countess. Jillian feels a sudden inexplicable reluctance as the Countess Czerner with "clawlike hands" caresses

Jillian's hand. Sari intervenes: "If my lady begins to fondle and make a fuss over you, *you must let me know at once. AT ONCE,* do you hear?" Sari's concern seems genuine, but Jillian as the younger woman also seems to excite Sari's jealousy, suggesting that Sari sees a sexual rival that will consume the countess's attention. Is Jillian also a reminder of Sari's earlier, uncorrupted self? Hard to say, but it is a possibility, one that a director and actress might exploit. Sari and the countess are not sisters, but they act like the Sternwood sisters in *The Big Sleep,* seemingly devoted to one another but also pursuing their passions.

Rejuvenation, as in *The Big Sleep,* becomes a major theme, with the countess, like General Sternwood fixing on Marlowe, seeking a substitute in Jillian for her own failing powers. Like Sternwood, the countess cannot get warm enough. She sits "in a high-backed chair almost like a throne, close to the hearth on which a fire burns even though it is June." Death is the big sleep the countess has tried to delay, and her saying "no to death" is the phrase that comes to haunt *Requiem for a Nun.* The countess and Sari seek to freeze time and remain in the kind of stasis that is familiar to readers of *A Rose for Emily* and of Miss Rosa's time-stopping narrative in *Absalom, Absalom!*[7]

It is tempting to see in the countess the southern lady defined in *Absalom, Absalom!* in the figure of Miss Rosa, feeding off her family: "it is as though she were living on the actual blood itself like a vampire, not with insatiability, certainly not with voracity, but with that serene and idle splendor of flowers arrogating to herself, because it fills her veins also, nourishment from the old blood that crossed uncharted seas and continents." Miss Rosa, remember, has Quentin in her clutches in the expectancy that he will perpetuate her story, which is her will to dominate, which is what the "Southern woman, gentlewoman" arrogated to herself, taking over the household, dispossessing the cook and seasoning the food, and taking "command of the servants" as a blood rite, so to speak. She will live through Quentin, as the countess, both aged and almost childlike—like Miss Rosa—will renew herself through Jillian.[8]

The countess is perched between youth and age in a strange way: "At first glance, she appears to be an old woman. But something is wrong and strange. She was beautiful once. She looks frail and wrinkled, her face is lined and the hand which she holds out to the fire looks like a claw. Yet her hair is raven black, her eyes and teeth are those of a young woman. Even her voice is young in pitch, with only a slight crack in it." She explains that she is a Transylvanian blue blood, saying it all in the passive voice, which emphasizes her debility, admitting that, as with Faulkner's blue bloods, there is a taint, a "tiny drop of black gypsy blood," a drop that is "all the fire and fury of a volcano." In short, the edifice of superiority is corrupt, and only the outsider can reverse the rot that subdues the Sternwoods in the *Big Sleep* and the Compsons in *The Sound and the Fury*. The "tiny drop" of black blood is of course what makes someone black in southern white mythology, the drop that the white Falkners never acknowledged—a horror to them that could be explored only in fiction and in the form of a vampire film.

Garlic wreaths adorn the doors of the Grange, which any horror-movie addict recognizes as a prophylactic measure against the intrusions and attacks of the undead. No odor of verbena—only the stalwart Jillian, who desperately needs the job and braves all without any outward sign of foreboding, even though as she watches from a window "a dark shape" runs out of a copse and Larry Clyde shows up to ask Jillian, "Little Muffet, are you all right?" His concern only annoys her—as does Sari, who, notwithstanding Jillian's protests, locks her in for the night, supposedly to prevent an attack from the prowling loony Jacob Lee.

The next morning in the kitchen Jillian sees a large bowl "half filled with a dark liquid" that looks like blood. Clyde comes calling again (like her alter ego alerting her to the danger). He got a look at that dark shape: "big, black. It looked like it had wings and was about to fly." Jillian says he is foolish: "I saw nothing. And I don't think you did either." Still she shivers when Clyde recites Tennyson's *Maud:*

> I hate the dreadful hollow behind the little wood,
> Its lips in the field are dabbled with blood-red heath,
> The red-ribbed ledges drip with a silent horror of blood,
> And Echo there, whatever is ask'd her, answers "Death."

Although Clyde is a doctor, like his father, his aspiration has been to be a poet, and it is his imaginative perceptions that Jillian dares to deny at her own peril. She is a staunch British empiricist, not an unfamiliar figure in horror film, but here presented with a certain poignancy, given Clyde's romantic inclinations. In effect, Jillian tells Clyde that she is being paid to overlook what might seem strange, and Clyde riles her up by treating her like a child afraid of spiders: "Leave this place of the dreadful hollow, Miss Muffet."

Sari, who seems even more forbidding than the countess, locks her mistress in her room—as Jillian, outside, sees when looking through the room's window. Even though the countess is in bed looking like a corpse, suddenly she rises and runs with "amazing agility and speed" to the windows, beseeching Jillian to unlock the door, which Jillian does as the countess draws blood: "It is my finger nail. Do forgive me, child," the countess says. In effect, the countess has arisen out of her own past, as Jillian can see when she examines a photograph of the countess "with a wild strange look, slender, in the riding habit of a bygone day, posed, slim-waisted, in a full skirt and a hat with sweeping plumes." Jillian is nineteen confronting the nineteenth century. When she finds a book with Tennyson's lines about the dreadful hollow, she shivers and shuts it, and then sees a stuffed but lifelike wolf in a closet. She gives out a prolonged scream, as though the literature she reads has come to life. The power of words, of rhetoric, is so Faulknerian. No wonder Hawks wanted him to work on this film.

As Jillian begins to realize her harrowing plight, Larry Clyde searches through his father's journal for an account of a trip to Transylvania that might reveal what is happening at the Grange. Vera, the countess's niece, shows up, seeking the same revival of the "old past, when life was worth living."[9] She is accompanied by a doctor, Vostok—Clyde's coeval—who tells her that the "beauty you believe you see is a mirage, the deceitful colors that merely tint and hide corruption." The peasant blood that enlivened the Czerners has also crazed them, Vostok explains. When Clyde learns of Vostok's presence, he notes that the doctor is "quite famous—in his way. Does things with corpses. . . . He's trying to bring people back to life. He's pulled it off once or twice, I understand. But they are sensible corpses and go back to sleep." Clyde, like his father, is intrigued with this vampiric experience and even drawn to it when he hears Vera singing: "He looks at Jillian, sees her succumbing to it, as if it were to Jillian that Vera directed all its force, even while she struggles against it"—the "it" inherent in the power of the words, of literature to animate desire and a longing Faulkner was drawn to all his life in the language he created. Jillian's susceptibility is reminiscent of vulnerable Miriam in "Revolt in the Earth," a victim of the voodoo spell.

But the lust for young blood becomes a threat to the community when a young boy goes missing, with the clear implication that he has become the countess's victim. The child is, in effect, Jillian herself, as the dialogue makes clear:

Clyde: You must leave here. Don't you see you must?
Jillian: They will find the child.
Clyde: What makes you think something has happened to the child (as she stares at him staring, he grips her arm). Jillian have you seen or heard anything suspicious while you've been here?
Jillian: (almost violently) No! No!

Jillian begins to tremble and cannot stop. Clyde holds on to her, asking her to marry him, but she only wants him to let her go. This moment, one of the most powerful in the script, portrays a young woman who is youth and what everyone wants at the price of surrendering her own will, which she refuses to do no matter how much she is frightened. The lesbian vectors of the plot converge in a crescendo as Jillian reenters the house with Vera "singing in a triumphant peal."

When Jillian answers the plaintive call that the ailing countess is worse, she is accosted by a swooping bat-like creature that is only deterred by a garlic wreath she holds under her arm. Jillian wonders if she is going mad but is prevented from leaving the Grange because of the police investigation of the missing boy. In her next encounter with Vera, Jillian is amazed at how old she looks in her "dull black cloth" robe that "clings to her as if it were wet, folding about her like folded wings." Vera, like the countess, moves swiftly toward Jillian, toward youth, become "brilliant, vital, eager." Vera, like nearly everyone else, calls Jillian her "dear child" and tries to coax her to abandon the wreath.

Clyde, reading his father's journal, gradually works out what is happening at the Grange. The count, a man of "contemptuous pride" like Colonel Sartoris, introduces Clyde's father to his wife, "descendant of the gypsy Magda who lies at the crossroads with a stake through her heart. . . . She is a vampire, as Magda was. The curse has fallen upon her, she cannot escape nor be saved. Unless you do as I ask," the count tells Dr. Clyde, "every child, every young creature in this district walks under the shadow of death. Without human blood she cannot live. Draw her vampire teeth—and let her die mercifully in peace." If Clyde's father refuses, "then the peasants will destroy her, as they did the gypsy Magda." The teeth are extracted, and she fades away, but her progeny have survived.

In the denouement Larry Clyde and Inspector Gregory, informed of what is really happening at the Grange, combine to rescue Jillian as the Grange goes up in flames. There is a lot of running around involving Sari "heavily panting" and Jillian "stumbling up the drive, almost spent." Faulkner, keenly aware of the ludicrous, put in a note to Hawks: "One modern woman running is ridiculous, comic; one chasing another doesn't help it much. Am trying to tell this in more or less static shots."

Sari prevents the countess from pursuing Jillian. Sari confronts the countess with "despairing grief" and kills her with an axe, chopping her head off, and then Sari dies of a heart attack. Vostok's motivations, which have been occluded—he seems to want to save the countess and Vera but also realizes they cannot continue to murder for blood—are finally explained by Sari, before she dies, who reveals that the old count made a gentleman of Vostok and made Vostok's medical fame possible. The very idea of a gentleman—so precious to Faulkner's own sense of himself—becomes in "Dreadful Hollow" a source of fealty to the past but also a propelling force for change. The gentleman has a duty to revere tradition, especially one's ancestors, and yet to change that tradition if it is to survive. Vostok has set fire to the Grange (it is hard not to think of Sutpen's Hundred in flames) to "make a clean sweep," Clyde surmises: "house, policemen, witnesses, body, evidence—all. Then he would take her [Vera] and clear off," allowing Jillian to supply the countess's needed blood.

A lesbian vampire film—what else can be made of the countess and Vera vying for Jillian?—would hardly seem a fitting subject for William Faulkner and Howard Hawks, and yet the brooding on doom and family disintegration, the hold of the past that must be acknowledged but also broken, the power of these female characters, their down-to-earth indomitability, and the role of the gentleman hero as exemplified in the two Clydes and Vostok reflect much of the ethic that the gentleman-director and his gentleman-screenwriter exemplified. And not to be discounted is the sheer brio of their encounter with a genre they sought to parody and to transform.[10] Can't you just hear Hawks say, "Bill, see what you can do with this"?

With the major effort on "Dreadful Hollow" resulting in no production, and Faulkner's patience for rewriting scripts exhausted, he departed Hollywood. "We'll think of you Bill," Jerry Wald said. The producer thought he saw a twinkle in the writer's eye, "I'll think of you too," Faulkner said in his characteristic slow drawl, "in the middle of the night."[11]

HOME

In mid-December, on his return home, Faulkner worked on his fable, which itself had been inspired in Hollywood. By January 24, he had completed sixty pages of the novel.[12] He had established a rhythm: six months in Hollywood, six months off, staying home with "movie work locked off into another room."[13] But he also felt different now—no longer so young and full of rhetoric that gave him "personal pleasure. . . . I'm doing something different now, so different that I am writing and rewriting, weighing every word, which I never did before. I used to bang it on like an apprentice paper hanger and never look back." Consequently, it was "going to take longer than I thought." He had a "rough outline" in place and could go at it for another six months before heading back to the California salt mines—his own term for his indentured servitude.

While some books had not required much revision, others went through long gestation periods and much reworking—but not paragraph by paragraph and page by page as Faulkner wrote his drafts of *A Fable*. What was different now is how much, all along the way, he returned to earlier drafts rather than moving ahead. He was writing retroactively, reading what he had done as if teaming up against himself, like Hollywood writers did with one another as Furthman had rewritten Faulkner and Faulkner had rewritten Cain in a collaborative chain reaction that made writing itself more of a back-and-forth process than Faulkner had experienced at home alone. Faulkner kept wanting to show what he had written of his fable to Random House, to his agent Harold Ober, and to Malcolm Cowley, who began writing him about an anthology that was to become *The Portable Faulkner*. Writing the fable seemed less of a private, personal matter and more of a testament he wanted to share. To be sure, part of his eagerness to send out his fable had to do with money—an advance from Random House, perhaps a magazine sale Ober could engineer, or an option payment for a treatment based on the novel.[14]

Early in the year, Joe C. Brown, a local African American schoolteacher, visited Rowan Oak to talk about his poetry. Three years earlier, on the street in front of Neilson's Department Store on the square, they had talked about Brown's writing. "I thought then," Faulkner wrote to Brown on January 25, "you were going to let me see it, and when I didn't hear from you anymore, I was disappointed. The invitation I offered then still holds. . . . I will expect to hear from you soon. I will read the work, then we can have a talk about it." He even gave Brown his telephone number. Less than a week later Brown showed up, and Faulkner had not only read but also edited one of the poems. He had cut back on the rhetoric so that the passion came through cleanly, Faulkner explained. He called it sitting on the passion. Brown's cry for freedom and opportunity had to come from the reader's response: "make him say it to himself *for* you."

Whatever Brown made of Faulkner's encouragement and criticism, Faulkner did not forget him when he wrote to fellow Mississippian Richard Wright: "A friend of yours lives in my town, Joe Brown. . . . I have (I hope) helped him to learn what you learned yourself: that to feel and believe is not enough to write from." Brown needed to read more (Keats, Shelley, and Whitman), Faulkner said, but Brown was improving, and Faulkner intended to see him again.[15]

Faulkner had written to Wright to say that his autobiography, *Black Boy*, "needed to be said, and you said it well." But he thought nonfiction could not have the impact of *Native Son*, since "only they will be moved and grieved by it who already know and grieve over this situation." The novel was "lasting stuff" because it came out of "one individual's imagination and density to and comprehension of others suffering of Everyman, Anyman, not out of the memory of his own grief." The novel, in short, did not focus on the writer but the story, which is why Faulkner rejected a proposal from a publisher to write about Mississippi—even though such a book appealed to him and would have yielded a much-needed advance. Doing a nonfiction book had never occurred to him, which meant he did not know where to begin and did not have the spark that would ignite his effort. He estimated he had another three books in him that he wanted to write: "I am like an aging mare, who has say three more gestations in her before her time is over, and doesn't want to spend one of them breeding what she considers (wrongly perhaps) a mule." If he took fire, he would reconsider, and he wanted Ober to hang on a month before letting go of the offer. To do anything less than his best would put him "morally and spiritually in Hollywood."[16] At home, he had to keep that Hollywood room locked. At home, he was still sovereign. About a hundred thousand words of the fable had been amassed by the middle of March—"my epic poem. Good story: the crucifixion and the resurrection," Faulkner told Ober. And then it had all been rewritten down to fifteen thousand words: "I had my usual vague foundationless idea of getting enough money to live on out of it while I wrote and finished it. But I ought to know now I dont sell and never will earn enough outside of pictures to stay out of debt."[17]

Such comments suggest a Faulkner bound to the studio regimen, which he wanted to modify to suit the rhythms of his own life. On March 8, he wrote to James Geller: "It's been a wet winter here. I've got little done except cleaning ditches, fixing fences, repairing houses, etc. hope to start breaking ground this month to get some early corn planted. Dammit, I wish I could have a different system: be at the studio working Jan.-Feb.-March, be here farming April-May-June, at the studio July-Aug.-Sept., then back here for rest of the year to gather and sell crop."[18]

Spring weather returned in late January, and a delighted Estelle wrote to Malcolm about how much she enjoyed her long walks with Billy. Jill—"my little Puritan sister," as Malcolm called her—wrote to Malcolm about picnicking with friends on their mounts. With Jill singing in the choir, Faulkner even went to church. Estelle's reports from the home front to "homesick" Malcolm, now stationed in Europe, brought back his "beautiful memories" of family outings.[19] "Spring was a time of great beauty at Rowan Oak," Malcolm remembered, with daffodils and iris appearing first in "violet and yellow patches along the driveway beneath the cedars." Then came the pink and white peonies on the eastern edges of the lawn and yellow roses by Easter. Estelle made a celebration of the season on April 1 with a sumptuous dinner, sometimes including a huge chocolate pie, presenting Pappy with the largest piece. He had been known to remark, "Quite good 'Stelle—as you know, I never turn chocolate down." He said it without letting on about the cotton wool laced through the chocolate.

On the Rowan Oak lawn the blooming jonquils, peonies, and Lady Banks roses, tall and thornless climbers flowering early in the spring, made perfect hiding places for the traditional Easter egg hunt. Faulkner gathered Vicki and Jill and their friends on the verandah, lined them up, gave the signal to start, and watched the laughing, chattering, and shoving—the girls stooping over and showing off their laced-edge petticoats. Afterward, as Malcolm remembered it, they let loose the hunting dogs, who found what the children had overlooked.[20]

Faulkner kept hoping Hollywood would tear up his contract, but instead it had granted leaves of absence and in May issued a June call-up with a salary of five hundred dollars per week.[21]

THE SALT MINES

By the end of June, Faulkner wrote to Estelle's mother, "Miss Lida," about the wet spring in Hollywood that had been "good for blooming. . . . There is a hedge-plant here which looks like our laurel." Much has been made of the tensions between the Oldhams and Faulkner, and yet this letter shows how important family was to him, as he described the plant's "four-petaled white bloom about the size of a dollar" resembling an

> enlarged Confederate jasmine. . . . I intend to see if it will transplant to Miss. Also a geranium which I never saw before, which blooms from scarlet through pink and on to pure white and then with a faint bluish tinge. I wish we had that too. Bougainvilleas everywhere as usual, much lantana, ranging from yellow through the normal orange with red center which I know at home, to solid deep maroon-magenta, and a lot of blue plumbago which I like. It all looks pretty fine, a lot of magnolia blooms but the magnolia leaves are a lighter shade of green, almost sickly, not like our strong deep green.

Everyone had a garden, but they looked "amateurish" to him: "Gardening people miss the Japanese, who used to do all that around private homes. They made a bad mistake in not watching their Japanese gardeners and learning something while they had a chance." No mention of the detention camps, but Faulkner had a keen eye for what was missing and what made life worth living.

Faulkner still fretted about the Warner Brothers contract and about the agent, William Herndon, who would not let go of a client who no longer wanted his services. In an arrangement similar to the one he had with Bacher and Hathaway regarding his fable, Faulkner worked on the side, operating as an independent contractor, with neither agent nor studio involved. He had returned to living with Buzz Bezzerides, with whom he collaborated on a spec script, "Angel's Flight," which they were unable to sell to Howard Hawks, or anyone else. Vera Morgan holds out as the only juror who thinks the accused, Joe Trotter, is innocent of murder: "There is nothing in her background that would make her read social values and implications into the life of Joe Trotter . . . but for this strange, formless doubt." Trotter had been found drunk in a room next to a man bludgeoned to death. He has no alibi except for drinking companions who have not turned up to defend him. Vera is coerced into voting guilty, having to admit all the evidence points to Trotter's guilt. He is a "rugged, hard-looking young man," but with "something introverted, vexed about him; the look of a man who is accustomed to abuse, has given up fighting it, but does not yield without an element of cynicism." Vera, approached by another juror with doubts, is so upset she goes to the district attorney, who scornfully turns her away, saying justice was done. In church a rector tries to suggest it is her conscience that is troubling her. He tells Vera to visit the condemned man and take a good look at him: "This, together with the facts of the trial, might convince her of his guilt and her conscience could be eased." Her doubt that Joe is guilty increases when she sees his face close up—that of a "whipped man and hopeless." Joe is fascinated with Vera: "The guard laughs . . . a hell of a time for him to be getting a case on a dame." The rector warns that her effort to exonerate Joe may invite an attack by the real murderer. She should go to the police. But Vera knows the police are not interested in Joe's story. After much trouble, Vera is able to find the flophouse where the murdered man lived and the bag he left behind that has his name and address on it. But in fact it was a bag sold to the dead man, so again Vera is stymied, although the original owner of the bag remembers the murdered man had come from a mining camp. She discovers the identity of the dead man by playing the concertina in the camp. Two men recognize the instrument Fred Evans used to play and report that he had ten thousand dollars in a money belt around his waist (the motive Vera has been seeking that could exonerate Joe). Joe escapes while being transported to San Quentin, hitches a ride, and sees Vera, telling her he loves her but to stop trying to prove he is innocent. She confesses she has fallen in love with him. After almost being caught by the police, Joe surrenders voluntarily, and Vera tells her family she has married him. They are at first aghast, but then her father examines his own conscience and supports his daughter. Vera tracks down the killer, Lacer, who tries to throw her into traffic. But she escapes. The murderer turns out to be one of the miners she questioned earlier who knew about the ten thousand dollars. The murderer then kills the drunk who witnessed the murder, and so again Vera is stymied as she has been at every turn. After many more plot complications, Vera remembers the name of the woman (Gladys Fields) on the registration certificate for the jalopy parked outside the flophouse where the murdered man stayed. That name may be the key to someone who knew the murdered man and also knew he had that money belt, the new evidence Vera needs to convince the district attorney to reopen the case. It turns out that Gladys Fields is hiding in an abandoned oil-pumping station. Gladys shoots at Vera, thinking she is the man who tried to murder Gladys earlier that night. As Vera gets in her car to tell the police about Gladys, Lacer, the murderer, grabs her. He tells her she has figured it out, "how he and Jack Fields murdered Fred Evans in Trotter's room." She barely manages to escape the blow of Lacer's wrench and runs away from her car onto the beach. In the struggle near a well, she manages to throw him off, and he perishes in the well. Gladys arrives in time to identify Lacer as her attempted murderer. The last scene shows Vera at Joe's release from prison.[22]

The script is reminiscent of *Intruder in the Dust* and the stories Faulkner would collect in *Knight's Gambit,* in which a character sets out to rectify an injustice and exonerate a man accused of murder. Vera generates the evidence based on nothing but an inarticulate feeling about the accused. The power of the interpreter, as in so much of Faulkner's work, is on display. The script occupied two weekends of Faulkner's time, he told Estelle, so that he could "make enough money to get the hell out of this place and come back home and fix Missy's room and paint the house and do the other things we need." To make matters worse, he was spending three hours a day on busses going back and forth to work now that Buzz was without a car. "I try to write either to you or Missy at least once every week, no matter how 'written-out' I feel. I try to write to mother at least once a week ditto."[23]

Somehow Faulkner also found time for some off-the-books work for Jean Renoir. At their first meeting, Faulkner spoke in French and moved the director to later say the writer had *"la galanterie."* Their mutual respect resulted in Faulkner's work on a few scenes in *The Southerner,* which became Renoir's favorite American film. Zachary Scott, who later appeared in *Requiem for a Nun* with his wife, Ruth Ford, a Faulkner favorite, recalled the scene when he catches "Lead Pencil," the big catfish, and also the scene when Scott's wife lights the stove, reminiscent of the fire and the hearth in *Go Down, Moses.* But the film, as a whole, is Faulknerian in spirit, showing the indomitability of country folk, the power of nature as it inundates a cotton field with ruinous rain, the parties with corn liquor and the singing of songs like "Beulah-land," which Faulkner could have written, although they owe their authenticity to fellow southerner Nunnally Johnson.[24] It would be good to know if Faulkner contributed any dialogue to the film's final scene, in which the merits of urban and rural life, farming and factory work are debated in a very Faulknerian way, showing both how important it is to remain close to the land and yet recognizing change, the exchange of mules for tractors, the making of the equipment that enhances the farmer's desire to improve on nature. Faulkner told Malcolm Cowley that he was prouder of his work on *The Southerner* than on any other film.[25]

Stallion Road, an adaptation of Stephen Longstreet's novel, took up much of the summer. By July 28, Faulkner had a complete screenplay, revised and turned in on September 1, jettisoning the novel's focus on Henry Purcell, an eastern novelist who comes to California to write for the movies.[26] In the novel, Purcell makes friends with Larry Hanrahan, a rancher and veterinarian, learns a lot about horse breeding, and gets involved in a romantic triangle with Larry and Fleece Teller, a handsome horsewoman. Learning so much about love and horses, Hanrahan decides to stay horse-bound. Experimenting with a cure for anthrax, he succumbs when he infects himself.

Judging by Faulkner's adaptation, he loved the horses and did not much care for the characters. He makes Larry a drunk and a gambler who gets in fights with a rival, Rick Mallard, the casino owner, over the fetching Fleece. Larry strokes a mare's hair as if it were Fleece's. His idea of romance is grabbing and kissing her without warning. Fleece has a competitor, Daisy, and the two women come to blows over Larry. He strikes his Mexican hostler, Pelon, although he has the grace to apologize to Pelon, a fully realized, sensitive character in the script. Although Faulkner mentions in his character synopsis that Larry has returned from overseas service "moody," this fact is never worked into the script, making his truculence mystifying. Larry does get the girl in the end—but only by way of melodramatic manipulation: Daisy, the femme fatale, stabs Larry with an anthrax-laden needle. He is saved with an application of his anthrax antidote. In the end, Larry proposes to Fleece as she sits atop a horse, so that standing by her side he has to draw her face toward his to propose.

Did Faulkner really think the studio would settle for such an aggravating set of characters who carry on quarreling in several scenes? If his plan was to wring out some of the sentiment in Longstreet's novel, he succeeded. Disgust with doing this sort of adaptation may also have been a factor. Even after the Breen office objected to the adulterous affair between Daisy and Larry, Daisy remains an example of what Faulkner calls "nympholepsy" and flaunts her affair in public. Faulkner's script, Longstreet commented, was "a little strong for then."[27]

Eventually Longstreet himself was called in to write a movie that starred the anodyne Ronald Reagan (Hanrahan) and the suave Zachary Scott (Purcell) as friendly rivals. Longstreet restored the emphasis on Scott's character as a cynical writer redeemed by his contacts with honest horse people. This time Rory (no longer Fleece) gives Hanrahan the anthrax antidote. Purcell knows enough not to pasture any longer on the range. He drives off, telling Hanrahan that he has enough material to write another novel.

As a well-constructed screenplay, *Stallion Road* is serviceable and reflects several of Faulkner's interests in the land, the horses, and country people. But if Larry Hanrahan is heroic in his efforts to rid his land and animals of anthrax, he nevertheless lacks the rooting interest in the hero that Hollywood expected—except for the final scenes where the scientist/vet's life is at stake. A hero did not need to be as bland and likeable as Ronald Reagan, to be sure, but he did need to have some kind of mystique or romantic aura to succeed on studio terms. Longstreet called Faulkner's screenplay "wild, wonderful, mad."[28]

"THE PLASTIC ASSHOLE OF THE WORLD"

Faulkner had still not been able to rid himself of his agent, William Herndon, who threatened legal action if Faulkner actually broke their contract. On July 31, Finlay McDermid, who had succeeded James Geller as head of the Warner Brothers story department, worried that Faulkner might be "contemplating the idea of taking a walk rather than face the general unpleasantness." Did McDermid know about Faulkner's legendary Death Valley walk? At any rate, he noted, "Will have to be a little careful handling him, I imagine, during the next few weeks." McDermid correctly read the signs. On August 20, Faulkner told Harold Ober: "I think I have had about all of Hollywood I can stand. I feel black, depressed, dreadful sense of wasting time, I imagine most of the symptoms of some kind of blow-up or collapse. I may be able to come back later, but I think I will finish this present job [*Stallion Road*] and return home. Feeling as I do, I am actually becoming afraid to stay here much longer." Even hack writing at home or editorial work seemed a better alternative than Hollywood. He had lost weight and did not feel well. To stay and run the risk of collapse might make it impossible for him to return.

Like Geller, McDermid seemed solicitous. He had gone out of his way to help arrange Faulkner's travel from Oxford to the West Coast at the beginning of June when cross-country rail travel was still unpredictable because of the war. McDermid had introduced himself by letter: "you may remember me as the almost bald-headed guy who occasionally popped out of the Story Department door as you were on your way from the writers' building to the commissary."[29]

By the end of August, McDermid knew the "quietly unhappy" writer wanted OUT: "he asked me if there would be a chance of getting a release from his contract." The relationship with Faulkner had been "pleasant," McDermid reported, and Faulkner had been "uncomplainingly turning out scripts which nearly any Hollywood writer could have written." McDermid proposed to his boss a liberalized contract giving Faulkner much more leeway: "I feel that if Faulkner could really cut loose on a story in which he was terrifically interested that we might get something pretty spectacular, but it seems a shame to waste one of the country's top novelists on routine melodrama." His boss simply noted on the letter, "Suspend & extend when returns." In short, the indentured servitude would continue.[30]

McDermid's assessment of Faulkner's prowess was seconded by Stephen Longstreet: "By the time he left Hollywood in September, 1945, he had become capable of writing with the best of his lot, the few real talents who were here then."[31] He had produced significant treatments and scripts: "The De Gaulle Story," "Battle Cry," "Country Lawyer," *Stallion Road*, "Dreadful Hollow," *To Have and Have Not*, and *The Big Sleep*—not to mention many of the films he had doctored into life such as *Air Force* and *The Southerner*. But he told Longstreet, "Artistically, Southern California is the plastic asshole of the world."[32]

On September 8, McDermid reported, "I have been informed by William Faulkner—in a very mild and friendly manner—that he will not this time sign the usual extension and suspension papers." Faulkner said he only wanted to write fiction. He had no interest in writing for another studio. McDermid, for all his sensitivity to Faulkner's concerns, did not quite get how disaffected the writer had become: "It is my feeling Bill will retire to his native haunts, come what may, unless we can hold out a more tempting bid to him than his present deal offers."[33] Certainly Faulkner hated his contract, but he did not want a better contract. The studio agreed to a six-month suspension, provided that it had the right of first refusal for any story material Faulkner produced during that period.

Meta realized that Faulkner was "unable to summon the purpose that had carried him through in Hollywood in past years. He rarely smiled or chuckled. He was downcast." She sensed he would not remain in Hollywood until the end of year. He broke it to her that *Stallion Road* would be his last project for Warner Brothers. He had earlier promised to leave Estelle as soon as Jill turned twelve. Now that was forgotten, and Meta was angry. By her own account, she pushed him away. But afterward he wrote her a letter saying, "this bloke in question really means better than he does, how's for seeing your face before I leave." She forgave him, and he left her on his way to pick up the horse trailer that would bring home a horse for Jill.

Faulkner's farewell to Stephen Longstreet occurred on a "wonderful sunny" September day. They were standing at the studio gate, which perhaps reinforced Faulkner's feeling of incarceration. Longstreet remembered him scowling: "What a god damn place. One leaf falls in one of those god damn canyons, and they tell you it's winter." A week later Faulkner was gone.[34]

13

"A Golden Book"

The Portable Faulkner,
September 1945–April 1946

NATIVE HAUNTS

Faulkner arrived home having missed the suffocatingly hot weather and went to work on his fable. He often did significant writing in the hottest periods, when even taking a long walk seemed unwise. He would sit at a window and look out at the pasture. He could see his nephew Jimmy and other boys playing. Sometimes he joined them.[1] Other times, he'd bolt out of a chair and go out shirtless to chop down the bitterweed. After an hour, he would return to his typewriter. Then he would shower, put on a coat and tie, and sit on the east verandah in the evening sipping a gin and tonic.

Missing July Fourth did not matter so much. It was not a holiday for Mississippians in those days—too many memories of Grant's occupying army. July 14, Bastille Day, on the other hand, became an opportunity for him to wear his RAF uniform on a walk into town to pick up his mail. In the evening, again on the east verandah, he would uncork the champagne and toast France.

On Halloween, children gathered to hear ghost stories. Dorothy Oldham, in a sheet, made an impressive ghost descending the Rowan Oak steps. Malcolm remembered a Halloween when Faulkner scared the younger ones so much with ghost stories that he had to drive them home. His favorite was about Judith Sheegog, daughter of Rowan Oak's first owner, who had fallen in love with a Yankee soldier. He sneaked over to Judith's window, threw her a rope, and she descended, breaking her neck when the rope broke.[2] Faulkner described the awful silence as her lover listened for a heartbeat but heard only

276

the sounds of night birds. They buried Judith beneath the magnolia at the far end of the cedar walk. Sometimes a piano could be heard playing. "That has to be Judith," Pappy said. He did a hauntingly beautiful portrait in charcoal of Judith that entranced his step-granddaughter, Vicki, who wondered what happened to it after his death.[3]

One Halloween night when, as usual, Faulkner had extinguished most of the lights, Cho-Cho saw a "filmy swirl" of the gown of a woman with "dark hair and exquisite features"—it had to be Judith. Cho-Cho arose from bed to follow the departing figure onto the balcony when the ghost just drifted away to the arching cedars and the magnolia tree.[4] Such stories suited the nostalgic side of Faulkner's fealty to the past and his desire to keep it alive in the minds of children. Every time he returned home from Hollywood, he found something new. "The place is changing fast," he said.[5]

Pappy took Jill, Vicki, and Dean for hayrides along Old Taylor Road, with more ghost stories at night. During a tea dance at the Oldhams, Faulkner played Prince Charming to Dean, the damsel in distress when she became confused and took both lemon and milk in her tea, which curdled. Asked for his preference, Pappy said he would take his tea with both too. He amused Dean at a dinner party when a lady, a bit drunk, missed her chair and fell on the floor. He sat down next to her and offered her a drink from his glass saying, "You know, I've always wondered what it was like to have dinner on the floor."[6]

Dean remembered that he could go for long periods as a social drinker and then lapse into a binge—sometimes stopping himself by "digging up bitterweeds in the pasture. He used a hand spade and worked steadily to keep the demons at bay." That he worked at home puzzled the children. They could have ridden horses through the house, and he would not have noticed while he was writing.

To Dean, Jill was as reticent as her father: "Even as a little girl Jill had donned her invisible armor, her protection from the pressures she would endure for a lifetime: too much to live up to, too much to live down, and no means of escape. We never shared a secret." What secrets? Once, when Jill was twelve or thirteen, she overheard her parents arguing upstairs at the stair landing by her father's room. Estelle "didn't want him to go out, said he wasn't going out, and he took her by both arms and pushed her down the stairs, breaking her collar bone."[7] Only once at the onset of an alcoholic binge did Jill dare to entreat her father, "Please don't start drinking." He was walking away from her but turned and said, "You know, no one remembers Shakespeare's child." She never again asked him to stop.[8] Jill said her father "didn't really care about people. I think he cared about me. But, I also think I could have gotten in his way and he would have walked on me."[9] Jill was old enough to realize her family did not quite fit in. She "was made to feel unwelcome at some friends' homes," she later admitted to an interviewer. "No one took her to church or Sunday School, but she went with friends to different churches. She 'ached for mediocrity.' . . . What she wanted more than anything else was to be just like the others, to be accepted."[10]

Perhaps with her mother prone to debilitating periods, Jill seemed to her cousin Dean like the lady of house, perfect in every way, a straight-A student, and an accomplished horsewoman—her father's pride. She played the piano and spoke with an adult vocabulary. At twelve she was editor of her school newspaper. Dean admired her exquisite taste in clothes and welcomed Jill's hand-me-downs. Faulkner's archive at the University of Virginia includes doll cutouts that show Jill's interest in ensembles, cultivated by her mother.

November was hog-killing time. After a big breakfast of meat, grits, eggs, and toast with Dundee marmalade and hot, black Louisiana coffee, Faulkner set out with his black neighbor Wallace. Fifty-gallon oil drums placed on sandstones and filled with water to boil over roaring fires awaited the hog Faulkner shot with his rifle while Wallace slit its throat, and then with block and tackle suspended it from an oak tree, swinging it over the blackened drums for scalding, then scraping it with butcher knives and rinsing it with a garden hose, readying the carcass for butchering. Various cuts were placed in a salt bin for a week before transfer to the smokehouse. Bourbon and fresh meat also made up a meal right then. Even in November, with the sun out, "you were almost hot," Malcolm remembered.

Next: the Thanksgiving bird hunt with Colonel Hugh Evans, Bill Fielden, Faulkner, and Dorothy Oldham in the old Ford he had driven to California twice—now with a leaky canvas top—followed by Malcolm with more gear in a jeep. Home with the day's shoot piled up on the kitchen table, they enjoyed a drink, a crackling fire in the library, welcoming neighbors Kate and Bill Baker for dinner, at a table with a holly centerpiece. Norfleet in a starched white coat entered with roast duck on a silver platter, followed by Boojack with a platter of squirrel and dumplings, and then collard greens, cornbread, and butter. Cognac was served in the library, with Norfleet bringing in the delicate little glasses.[11]

Right after Thanksgiving, Faulkner embarked on a two-week deer hunt. He spotted seven deer, all does, and did not shoot them. Every day they ran the dogs and rode their horses, at one point tracking an old buck almost fifty miles from seven in the morning until three, when the dogs "gave out," and the buck, even with three bullets in him, got away, Faulkner was "glad to know." He didn't seem to care about killing animals but only the sport of tracking them. Usually a quiet man in camp, he did not indulge in "hoorahing and storming and all that." He enjoyed a laugh and liked to tell stories.[12] Hawks, who hunted with both Faulkner and Hemingway, said: "Ernest was always trying to prove what a man he was. Bill didn't give a damn about proving that—just enjoying himself and being with people that he liked."[13] A letter to Jill illustrates what Hawks meant:

Mr and Mrs Hawks, Clark Gable and I went to Calexico and shot doves, came back that Sunday night with 120 doves among us. Mrs Hawks is a good shot, a good hunter, cleans everybody's game that will let her. Mr Gable is a fine shot but lazy, he sits under a tree to hunt. Mr. Hawks hunts like I do, early and late, dont mind walking in the sun, is a fine shot. I used his 20 gauge gun, like Buddy's [Malcolm's] then I used Mr Gable's hand-made 410 gauge, almost as a small and light as my pistol. I sure wish I could get one now like it for Missy to start on. Mr Gable said he thought he could find me one. He is a good fellow, not conceited at all, anybody can come up and talk to him and get an autograph. Not at all a swell-headed matinee idol but more like a university senior.[14]

Faulkner seldom brought home game from his hunts. He "liked to watch the dogs work" but did not like killing things, Jill said.[15] He liked to watch Jill and her dogs and published in the *Oxford Eagle* an obituary for one of them, "His Name was Pete": "He was standing on the road waiting for his little mistress on the horse to catch up, to squire her safely home." A hit-and-run driver in a hurry could not have heard "only a dog flung broken and crying into a roadside ditch. . . . But Pete has forgiven him. In his year and a quarter of life he never had anything but kindness from human beings; he would gladly give the other six or eight or ten of it rather than make one late for supper."[16]

Most of the time that fall of 1945 had been spent getting "Malcolm Cowley's Viking Faulkner into shape. It is going to be a good book," Faulkner told Robert Haas. He had produced a new work for Cowley's anthology, the "Compson Appendix." He had also produced sixty-five pages of his fable, rewritten and edited three times and "pretty good"—maybe even "good enough for me to quit writing books on, though I probably won't quit yet."[17] He still had Warner Brothers insisting he return to fulfill his contract, his "biblical seven year servitude."[18] He knew his own value: "In France, I am the father of a literary movement. In Europe, I am considered the best modern American and among the first of all writers. In America, I eke out a hack's motion picture wages by winning second prize in a manufactured mystery story contest ["An Error in Chemistry" for *Ellery Queen's Mystery Magazine*]."[19]

Running out of money again, Faulkner nevertheless remained at home. "I hope the soil of Mississippi has acted as a tonic and that you are feeling tip-top," Finlay McDermid wrote on January 24.[20] Faulkner appreciated McDermid's efforts to rid him of William Herndon, the agent who kept asserting a claim on Faulkner's Hollywood earnings: "I thank you for having a shot at Herndon. He wants his pound of flesh, no matter how much blood and skin come off with it. It's a curious situation to me. It's like having a woman fasten onto you for alimony for the rest of your life: not like a man. I am well, doing some quail shooting, training a pointer pup, a good deal of resting and reading, waiting for spring."[21] McDermid's interoffice correspondence reflects the efforts of an executive who deeply respected Faulkner but expressed some futility about the failure to secure a better contract for the writer. McDermid even considered abandoning the contract altogether.[22] In March, Faulkner sent the studio sixty-four pages of his fable, asking for more time to finish it rather than report for more screenwriting. Warner agreed but expected him to report for work as soon as he finished his own book. "Random House and Ober lit a fire under Warner, I dont know how," Faulkner told Malcolm Cowley, "and I am here until September anyway, on a dole from Random House, working on what seems now to me to be my magnum o."[23]

SUCCESS

Most of Faulkner's novels were out of print when Malcolm Cowley first wrote to him in January 1944 in a letter addressed to Oxford. Three months later, in Hollywood, Faulkner replied, saying he would "like very much" for Cowley to write the long essay rectifying what the critic saw as an imbalance between the writer's worth and his reputation. After so much hard work, a dismayed Faulkner regretted that he seemed to leave "no better mark on this our pointless chronicle than I seem to be about to leave." So, in fact, he did not feel he could afford to wait. He approved the project, except for the biography part, which seemed to him nugatory: "if what one has thought and hoped and endeavored and failed at is not enough, if it must be explained and excused by what he has experienced, done or suffered, while he was not being an artist, then he and the one making the evaluation have both failed."[24]

After completing work on *The Portable Hemingway,* Cowley wrote again in July 1944 to say he was shopping his proposed essay to various magazines and could give Faulkner a market report on his standing as a literary figure. His name was "mud" in publishing circles because he did not sell, and the critics "did a swell job of uncomprehending and unselling you." Writers, on the other hand, had nothing but admiration for him. All this meant that Cowley saw a wide-open opportunity for a new approach. But before embarking on his work, he wanted to settle a basic point. Had Faulkner intended to write a kind of allegory or legend about the South?

By the time Faulkner replied in November 1944, he had read Cowley's essay "William Faulkner's Human Comedy" in the *New York Times Book Review* (October 29): "It was all right." His so-called "formless 'style'" had to do with his trying to "say it all in one sentence," putting it all, so to speak, on "one pinhead." And to do that, each time he had a try at "new way." As to the South, he was "inclined to think that my material . . . is not very important to me." It is just what he knew, and he didn't have the time to "learn another one [new material] and write at the same time." Life was the same "frantic steeple-chase toward nothing everywhere and man stinks the same stink no matter where in time." As to his characters, he left them to their own devices that were not his own. Quentin brooded, not Faulkner. To make that distance even greater between author and character, Faulkner resorted to speculation: "Quentin probably contemplated Sutpen as the hyper-sensitive, already self-crucified cadet of an old long-time Republican Philistine house contemplated the ruin of Samson's portico. He grieved and was moved by it but he was still saying 'I told you so' even while he hated himself for saying it." Faulkner did not take full ownership of his own work: "I accept gratefully all your implications, even though I didn't carry them consciously and simultaneously in the writing of it. In principle I'd like to think I could have."[25] It apparently did not occur to Faulkner, or he did not want to admit the possibility, that an understanding of his own biography might reveal what he had hidden from himself.

Over the next nine months Cowley published his long essay in sections, feeding the market with enough material to attract the interest of Viking Press. On August 9, 1945, he announced the good news to Faulkner. A *Portable* would mean the opportunity to present a full selection of work—about two hundred thousand words. From the start, Cowley proposed a chronological scheme rather than just a "best of Faulkner" anthology. He presented various choices for Faulkner's consideration, noting, however, that they had to be complete units even if they were excerpts from novels. Fortunately, the Mississippi work hung together: "there is nothing like it in American literature." Cowley would not go ahead without Faulkner's say-so. The critic knew his man, for he ended the letter with what Jean-Paul Sartre had said: "Pour les jeunes en France, Faulkner c'est un dieu." To which Cowley added, "Roll that over on your tongue."

A week later, Faulkner, again in Hollywood, replied: "The idea is very fine. . . . By all means let us make a Golden Book of my apocryphal county." He had expected to do as much in his old age. Now he relished the idea of sorting out what should go where. He accepted many of Cowley's suggestions but also thought the Jason section of *The Sound and the Fury* would work as a representation of the New South. "Write me any way I can help," Faulkner concluded.[26]

The back-and-forth of the correspondence reflects Faulkner's deep commitment to the project, even though he ignored many of Cowley's obtuse remarks, such as that *Absalom, Absalom!* "would be better if cut by about a third, maybe all the early parts of it omitted, leaving only Quentin's story to his roommate."[27] But Cowley had stimulated in Faulkner another way of looking at his own work, and the result was the "Compson Appendix," which put not only *The Sound and the Fury* but nearly all that had gone before in Faulkner's work into a new historical perspective—one that came, as he wrote from Oxford on October 18, at a telling moment in his career: "I think it [the "Appendix"] is really pretty good, to stand as it is, a piece without implications. Maybe I am just happy that that damned west coast place has not cheapened my work as much as I probably believed it was going to do."[28]

Cowley fretted about inconsistencies and puzzling details, and Faulkner provided some clarifications, including dates for the excerpts, although he was not overly concerned, since the differences in details reflected different points of view and an evolving conception of the characters. "I never made a genealogical or chronological chart, perhaps because I knew I would take liberties with both—which I have," Faulkner wrote on November 7. As Cowley later realized, "the true Compson story was the one that lived and grew in his imagination."[29] Or, as Faulkner said, his work kept "growing, changing" as he understood more about his people.[30]

To a remarkable degree, Faulkner permitted Cowley to do as he wished. When Cowley decided to include "Raid" from *The Unvanquished* because without those "black people tramping the road to Jordan, it wouldn't be the book I want it to be," Faulkner wrote in the margin "GOOD!!! Would have done so myself to begin with." Cowley wanted to excise Faulkner's reference in the "Appendix" to T.P. wearing clothes manufactured by "Jew owners of Chicago and New York sweatshops," noting, "I'd rather not see a false argument over anti-Semitism injected into the reviews." Faulkner wrote in the margin, "all right."[31] In Hollywood, a Jewish writer had once accused him of not liking Jews. And Faulkner had said, "You're right," and then paused before saying, "But I don't like gentiles either."[32]

When Cowley presented copy ready to be printed, Faulkner replied on December 8: "It's not a new work by Faulkner. It's a new work by Cowley all right though." He still insisted on as little biography as possible and provided the critic with a few paragraphs, eliding exactly what he did in uniform and still pretending he had injured himself in a crash. Was it for his own amusement that he included at the very end of his sketch: "Oh yes, was a scout master for two years, was fired for moral reasons."[33] He did not seem at all troubled by the faults Cowley and others found in his work, many of which he attributed to the solitude in which he worked and the lack of a significant literary tradition in the South. "I am not always conscious of bad taste myself," he confessed to Cowley, "but I am pretty sensitive to what others will call bad taste. I think I have written a lot and sent it off to print before I actually realized strangers might read it."[34] As the book neared publication, Faulkner, who had addressed the critic as "Cowley" or occasionally "Maitre," now wrote "Dear Brother."[35] Faulkner asked for a dozen copies and inscribed one, "Mother with love Billy."[36]

On April 29, 1946, Viking Press published *The Portable Faulkner*, an anthology almost two years in the making. A week earlier, Faulkner had written to Malcolm Cowley: "The job is splendid. Damn you to hell anyway. But even if I had beat you to the idea, mine wouldn't have been this good. By God, I didn't know myself what I had tried to do, and how much I had succeeded."[37]

The headline for Caroline Gordon's front-page assessment in the *New York Times Book Review* (May 5, 1946) established the importance of *The Portable Faulkner:* "Mr. Faulkner's Southern Saga: Revealing His Fictional World and the Unity of Its Patterns." The O'Donnell thesis propounded in 1939 of a clash between the old and the new order, represented by the Sartoris, Millard, and Compson families versus the Snopes clan, had been subsumed in Cowley's portrayal of an epic poet of Balzacian proportions. For Gordon, Faulkner could be divided in cycles and phases in the lives of the planters and their descendants, the townspeople of Jefferson, the poor white people, black people, and Indians. In effect, Cowley argued the whole of the Yoknapatawpha saga, as he termed it, was greater than its parts, as presented in the novels and stories, which were, in Gordon's words, like the limbs of one great tree. Cowley's chronological, decade-by-decade approach meant much rearrangement of the Yoknapatawpha fiction to justify calling it a "saga." The *Portable* excerpts did not do justice to the full scope of Faulkner's talent, Gordon emphasized, to the "brooding intensity" of the full-length novels "moving backward and forward in time," hovering over characters from "every conceivable angle."

The Portable Faulkner received few reviews, but it drew the attention of significant critics and novelists like Gordon, Robert Penn Warren, and Edmund Wilson. "A new kind of Faulkner book," wrote Wilson in a one-paragraph *New Yorker* notice (July 27), "a real contribution to the study of Faulkner's work." Cowley had "unscrambled" Faulkner, Wilson observed, presenting

Yoknapatawpha's phases from 1820 to 1945. "An original approach," declared the *Nashville Tennessean* (May 12). Other brief mentions in newspapers recognized that the *Portable* signaled Faulkner's growing reputation "nationally and internationally."[38] In the *Chicago Tribune* (May 26), Will Davidson endorsed Cowley's argument that the saga, not the novels (problematic in structural terms), constituted Faulkner's highest achievement. The *Winnipeg Tribune* (August 4) suggested that the *Portable* portrayed an America that is "far different to the loud optimism and easy confidence which the American mind fondly believes its own," and possibly served as "a more reliable guide to the extremes of which it is capable."

In the most lengthy and insightful review, Robert Penn Warren in the *New Republic* (August 26) praised Cowley's selections that show the "principles of integration in the work." But he also cautioned that while "no writer is more deeply committed to a locality than Faulkner, the emphasis on the southern elements may blind us to other elements, or at least other applications of deep significance." Cowley's legend-of-the-South approach should not obscure that Faulkner's fiction constituted a "legend of our general plight and problem. The modern world is in moral confusion. It does suffer from a lack of discipline, of sanctions, of community, of values, of a sense of a mission." Such words hit hard after victory in World War II. If the traditional order did not prevent the world from ruin, it offered, in Faulkner's fiction, a "notion of truth, even if man in the flow of things did not succeed in realizing that truth."

To illustrate his point, Warren selected the passage in *Go Down, Moses* in which Ike invokes Keats's "Ode on a Grecian Urn." The lines, "She cannot fade, though thou has not thy bliss" and "Forever will thou love, and she be fair," are Ike's belief that "truth is one" and "doesn't change. It covers all things which touch the heart—honor and pride and pity and justice and courage and love." For Warren, Faulkner via Keats contended that "human effort is what is important, the capacity to make the effort to rise above the mechanical process of life, the pride to endure, for in endurance there is a kind of self-conquest." This notion of self-conquest led Warren to the deepest reading so far of Faulkner's view of nature as expressed in "The Bear," the beast "pursued for years" that is also "an object of love and veneration, and the symbol of virtue" that is part of a "ritual of renewal" during the deer hunt, which expresses the paradoxical closeness of man to the nature that he masters and kills.

Faulkner's humor, Warren pointed out, cut across class lines from the Jason section of *The Sound and the Fury* to Miss Reba's scenes in *Sanctuary* to the frontier humor of "Spotted Horses"—all designed not merely to be amusing in their own right but also to provide an ironic perspective. Although Faulkner's treatment of poor white people was so often connected to the Snopeses,

Warren noted that *As I Lay Dying* portrayed this class with "sympathy and poetry." Similarly, Warren saw "pathos or heroism" in figures like the runaway black man in "Red Leaves" and Dilsey in *The Sound and the Fury*. Joe Christmas, in Warren's view, is a "mixture of heroism and pathos." Most telling, he cited the passage in *Go Down, Moses* when Ike says to McCaslin Edmonds that blacks have got their virtues "not even despite white people because they had it already from the old free fathers a longer time free than us because we have never been free." Even works that Cowley viewed as disjointed had, in Warren's estimation, a thematic and symbolic unity.

Warren's effort to distinguish different kinds of technique from the objective presentation of character and scene to the dramatic (using the characters' own voices), to the episodic with a narrative voice providing a sense of unity, had the effect of shifting attention away from subject matter per se and on to polarities and paradoxes that were part of a dialectical principle in Faulkner's fiction. Warren presented Faulkner's importance in terms that went considerably beyond Cowley's: "The study of Faulkner is the most challenging single task in contemporary American literature for criticism to undertake. Here is a novelist who, in mass of work, in scope of material, in range of effect, in reportorial accuracy and symbolic subtlety, in philosophical weight, can be put beside the masters of our own past literature." Cowley's work might well mark a turning point in the appreciation of Faulkner, but Warren was so confident as to imply that Faulkner ultimately had no need of Cowley's assistance.

The "Compson Appendix"

Reviewers did not reckon with the significance of the "Appendix," "done at the same heat as the book," Faulkner assured Cowley.[39] It also constituted the only work Faulkner had written exclusively for the *Portable*. The "Appendix" differs markedly from *The Sound and the Fury* in that it approaches the form of a chronicle. It specifically dates the period of time it covers (1699–1945), and it includes accounts of Ikkemotubbe ("A dispossessed American king"), of Jackson ("A Great White Father with a sword"), and of the generations of Compsons who precede the Compsons of the novel. By opening his "chronicle" just before the beginning of the eighteenth century and carrying it down to the middle of the twentieth (exactly two hundred years after Quentin MacLachan "fled to Carolina from Culloden Moor"), Faulkner reverses the method of *The Sound and the Fury* in which the family's history is discovered and interpreted solely from the family's point of view. That history is now seen as a larger process out of which the family has developed (or failed to develop) as one particular unit.

Mr. Compson's fatalism, for example, has its historical place in an "Appendix" that recounts the family's penchant for lost causes, which seem to a latter-day Compson an illusion revelatory of man's "folly and despair." Mrs. Compson's fatalism, her "dreading to see this Compson blood beginning to show" in her favorite, her second son, the fourth Jason, is reified in the "Appendix." "Who can fight against bad blood," she wonders as she dwells on Caddy's misbehavior and looks for a way to help Jason escape "this curse." All the children absorb the mother's hapless surrender to fate even as they try to resist it. "There's a curse on us its not our fault is it our fault," Quentin says to Caddy. "I'm bad anyway you can't help it," she resignedly confides to Quentin. Jason, who feels the least like a Compson, nevertheless acts cornered and cramped by time and expresses a sense of futility that links him to the time-obsessed Compsons.

Quentin has evolved not only out of the Compson saga but out of the national history evoked in the "Appendix," for his obsession with Caddy has its historical analogue in the portrayal of Andrew Jackson, a "rough-edged-soldier with a chivalric streak," determined to protect his wife and "the principle that honor must be defended whether it was or not because defended it was whether or not." Similarly, Jason Compson is defined in the "Appendix" in relation to an actual historical event. He is described as "the first sane Compson since before Culloden and (a childless bachelor) hence the last." He is the "first sane Compson" because he accepts what is inevitable and refuses to keep fighting the lost battle of Culloden—standing for all doomed romantic causes—and in so doing partially frees himself from the fatality and helplessness of the latter-day Compsons. Having abandoned principle and tradition in the interest of "practicality," he is able to compete and hold his own with the Snopeses, the new economic men. But Jason's selling of the Compson house and property not only characterizes his attitude toward the past; it also marks the culmination of a historical process of which the Compsons are only a part.

The "Appendix" also deals with the dispossession of the Indians and portrays all of the manifold yet interrelated changes that occurred as a result of that dispossession: the successive transformation of the "solid square mile" of land from the time when Ikkemotubbe swapped the land for the racehorse belonging to Jason Lycurgus Compson, "the grandson of a Scottish refugee who had lost his own birthright by casting his lot with a king who himself had been dispossessed." Then the mile was almost in the center of the town of Jefferson" when Brigadier Jason Lycurgus II put the "first mortgage on the still intact square mile to a New England carpetbagger in '66," which deteriorates into the "weedchoked traces of the old ruined lawns and promenades, the house which had needed painting too long already." Finally, Quentin's father sells part of the mile to pay for Caddy's wedding and Quentin's last year at Harvard, and Quentin's brother Jason sells the remainder. Nevertheless the square mile is still "intact again in row after row of small crowded jerrybuilt individuallyowned demiurban bungalows," still identifiable as the land Jason Lycurgus Compson obtained through a horse trade. Indeed the fate of the Compson house itself as a "boardinghouse for juries and horse- and mule-traders" recalls, in an ironic way, that first horse trade. Notwithstanding all the changes, the Compson mile retains its basic shape as a physical reminder of the past. Even after Ikkemotubbe's "lost domain" has become the "Compson Domain" and then been divided into even smaller units, Jason IV still retains his own "particular domain," a "railed enclosure" in the farmers' supply store. In Jason's arrogation of his own "domain"—no matter how small or insignificant it might seem—the historical process obtains: though Jason rejects the past, the very form of his rejection fits ironically into the pattern of history as it unfolds in the "Appendix."

In the Quentin section of the "Appendix," his intense sense of dislocation from the mainstream of history is exacerbated by his family's loss of land, which is tantamount to its loss of honor it created by acquiring, holding, and defending its land. Caddy stands as Quentin's substitute for land, for the locus of his identity. She is "a miniature replica" of Compson land, honor, and identity—a compact symbol for the overwhelming history of defeats that Quentin cannot reverse. She is Quentin's virgin wilderness, like the one out of which the family fashioned the Compson mile, and she is just as fragile, just as prone to violation as the land and the Compsons have been all along. Quentin has tried to center all of Compson history into the figure of his sister and perpetuates the family's doom.

The "Appendix" is an inquiry into the structure of history out of which the novel emerged. For not only does Faulkner continue Caddy's biography by connecting her to a German staff general, he also links the Compson family history to the Nazi endeavor to purify history. Serene in her prolonged beauty, Caddy also knows she is damned. In ranging so far beyond Yoknapatawpha, Faulkner confirms the universality of its history and shows that his county is a part of a greater history that Yoknapatawpha—that "keystone in the universe"—has helped to shape.

The pattern of history in the "Appendix," however, is not the same as Malcolm Cowley's idea of a "saga of Yoknapatawpha County." The "Appendix" does not derive from a preconceived history of Yoknapatawpha but is an independent work in which the author creates new "facts" and sometimes contradicts old ones. Faulkner seems to have regarded Yoknapatawpha's past, present, and future as continually developing out of each new act of creation: "I would have preferred nothing at all prior to the instant I began to write, as though Faulkner and Typewriter were concomitant, coadjutant and without past on the moment they first faced each other at the suitable (nameless) table."[40] No doubt Cowley's "saga of Yoknapatawpha County" stimulated Faulkner to reflect upon the historical process portrayed in his fiction. Certainly the "Appendix" and the novels following it, especially *Requiem for a Nun,* deal with that process in a much more explicit way than *The Sound and the Fury* and other early novels. But the historical process presented in the "Appendix" is not specifically southern, and Faulkner never acceded to the proposition that he was recording or creating a "legend of the South."

14

Impasse

June 1946–December 1947

INTERRUPTIONS

On June 7, at a little after 7:00 p.m., Madeleine Simons showed up at Rowan Oak's front door. A boy [perhaps Malcolm] greeted her, and she told him she was writing a study of William Faulkner's work. "Oh, come in," he said. "Come on in." He went into another room and told two giggling girls [Jill and Dean?] that a French girl had arrived. They greeted her with a "good evening" and departed, followed shortly by William Faulkner, dressed in torn pants that he had evidently just worn on a fishing trip. He seemed shy and apologized for not answering her letter. He complimented her on her English, asked a few questions about her background, and wanted to know what had attracted her to his work. It was the scene in *The Hamlet* between Ike and the cow—so poetic—she said. He smiled and said, "I am pretty well satisfied with that chapter." He told her he was not a literary man but would do his best to answer her questions—and she had lots of them. He had not based Thomas Sutpen on anyone, he said in answer to one of her queries. The character stood for "a state of mind," the desire for a son. "To have a son," Faulkner said, was "the most modest ambition you can think of. Almost anybody can have a son. But this was the thing he devoted his whole life to and was never able to achieve." He told Simons that with Sutpen he was reaching for some "larger human truth." Much of what he told her would be familiar to any student of Faulkner's life and work, and she did most of the talking, which was fine with him. When she told him that "there is often more in what is written than the author realizes," he replied: "Yes how true."[1]

Musings on how such moments seemed to Faulkner are part of the inescapably wistful record of biography. A character shows up at an antebellum mansion's front door and is not rebuffed but welcomed inside, and then is accorded the respect of its owner, who has no son but instead a devoted reader. What he tells her about not having a son is not like what he says elsewhere about his greatest novel.[2] Such fleeting moments are accidentally memorialized, fixed in writing, at the solicitation of a biographer interested not only in the great achievements of the writer's life but in his quotidian existence. Simons would go on to write a master's thesis about William Faulkner's work, one of several theses that students were beginning to write even before Malcolm Cowley produced his *Portable Faulkner*.[3]

A few weeks earlier Faulkner had thanked Malcolm Cowley for warning him about a proposed visit from Russian writer Ilya Ehrenburg, who said he had several questions for Faulkner, including, "How did he stand on the Negro question?" Faulkner had not given a significant interview for more than six years, and the times had changed. He would now be asked about social justice issues that by and large he had been able to avoid before the war. "What the hell can I do?," Faulkner asked Cowley: "Last month two damned Swedes, two days ago a confounded Chicago reporter, and now this one that cant even speak english. As if anything he or I either know, or both of us together know, is worth being said once, let alone twice through an interpreter. I swear to Christ being in Hollywood was better than this where nobody knew me or cared a damn." When a State Department official called to arrange a meeting, Faulkner said he could give Ehrenburg an hour, and that apparently was enough to prevent the encounter.[4] Cowley later learned that the two Swedes had shown up in Oxford because of a rumor that Faulkner might be awarded the Nobel Prize.[5]

WORK IN PROGRESS

Faulkner said he hated the interruptions from people who wanted to see where he kept his tail or his other head. "I am busy on this new book [*A Fable*], it is hot now," he told Random House editor Robert Linscott. Faulkner had much more to write and couldn't say "where it's going because that's what I'm trying to do by writing it," but he thought the book might be not just his best but "perhaps the best of my time." He needed more than the usual six-month break in his contract with Warner Brothers. So far he had subsisted on the five hundred dollars per month Random House sent him, and the publisher agreed to continue the payments so that he would not have to return to Hollywood. Faulkner touted the book as a *War and Peace*, "close enough to home, our times, language, for Americans to really buy it." He sent along several sections, some of which might stand alone that Harold Ober could sell.[6] In July, Ober sold the film rights for "Death Drag" and "Honor" to RKO for $6,600, easing, somewhat, the pressure to return to Hollywood, although Faulkner was on suspension and the studio added on to the contract the time he was away—a practice that would soon be outlawed by a Supreme Court decision.

Faulkner reported to Robert Haas that work on the novel slowed in August for farming, and then again in October for harvesting. Faulkner now estimated it would take at least another year to finish his fable, especially since he had stopped work on it to earn $3,500 for doctoring a movie script. What it was he did not say, but he returned to his novel in December, after deer hunting at the end of November. Hunting, it seems, was a kind of reprieve from the rest of life. John Cullen, one of Faulkner's hunting companions, said he was "always cheerful, quiet, and willing to do his part of the hardest, dirtiest work in camp. I have never heard him grumble about any hardship we ever had, and sometimes it has been pretty rough in the Delta." Faulkner did not bring books along with him or talk about his work. At most he would read a newspaper. Cullen could remember only a few occasions when his friend got drunk. Most of the time, he was just a sociable camp drinker. Faulkner had never stood out in camp and always did what Ike Roberts, the leader of the hunt, told him to do. Bill kept quiet most of the time, but Ike did remember one story. A northern senator, partial to southern women, told one that he liked their "wonderfully slow speech." She said: "You'd love my sister. She certainly speaks slowly. One time on a date the man asked her whether she had ever had any and before she said no she had."[7]

Faulkner had "missed a magnificent stag twice," a "beautiful creature," running at something like thirty miles per hour like a horse, coming into full view, he told Haas: "I picked two perfect openings in trees and shot twice. I left my customary 30–30 carbine at home for my boy to use and was shooting a .270 bolt action. I think the first bullet hit a twig and blew up. The second one missed him clean, over or maybe behind him; he was just running too fast. He was a beautiful sight. I'm glad now he got away from me though I would have liked his head."[8] His account suggests that when his blood was up he would shoot, no matter how ambivalent he felt about killing.

The thrilling adventure came even as Faulkner told Cowley: "It's a dull life here. I need some new people, above all probably a new woman." Faulkner admitted he had become a slave to his possessions, even though, in truth, he really did not want the encumbrances. At thirty he thought he might somehow escape them, but now, nearing fifty, he knew that he never would.[9] But this was not the whole story. On January 25, 1947, he made the final payment on Rowan Oak. Will Bryant had died, and Faulkner now dealt with Bryant's daughter, Maggie Lea Stone, who also tolerated his late payments but appreciated his scrupulous efforts to catch up. He told her that "throughout the whole transaction between Mr Will and myself while I was buying this property, the relationship was not that of two men doing business with one another, but rather that of a young man with an older man for whom he had a considerable respect and admiration and who, the young man believed, held for him a warmer feeling than mere acquaintanceship." But it was more than Will Bryant who mattered: "I will never again find such nice creditors as you and your mother and father have been," he assured Maggie Lea. All paid up, he wrote, "I hope some day to be able to call on you all, but it will be for the pleasure of seeing you again." His last letter enclosed a blank check, since the final interest payment had to be calculated, and he trusted Maggie Lea and her husband, Ike Stone, to fill in the proper amount. "This concludes the matter," Faulkner added. "In a way, I am a little sorry to sever at last even this slight thread with the memory of one for whom I could have felt no more warmth and admiration if I had been kin in blood." The memory of Will Bryant, so rooted in Rowan Oak, abided, no matter what William Faulkner said about his boredom and his responsibilities.[10]

Another Faulkner admitted to Harold Ober that he did not write as fast as he used to. It might take two more years to complete his fable.[11] He had three hundred pages, but by the spring of 1947, he considered taking a break and visiting New York. He seemed to want to allay any concerns Random House might have, so he proposed to Robert Haas a rendezvous so he could tell him the whole story.[12] While Ober fended off Warner Brothers, Faulkner found "another serious bug in the ms." He blamed Hollywood for the "trash and junk writing" that he now had to clean out, and he still thought of visiting New York since he felt "a little stale."[13]

Between April 14 and 17, Faulkner met with six Ole Miss literature classes in informal question-and-answer sessions for an honorarium of $250. As usual he treated his film work as insignificant, but some of his answers were surprising. In his depiction of his native land he said he used "imagination when I have to and cruelty as a last resort. The area is incidental. That's just all I know." When a student asked if, then, Faulkner gave a "wrong impression" of the South, he answered: "Yes, and I'm sorry. I feel I'm written out. I don't think I'll write much more. You have only so much steam and if you don't use it up on writing it'll get off by itself."[14]

Two faculty members remembered how he had excused himself: "I must go home and let the cow out." They said his appearances left him "a little tired but also quite refreshed."[15] He discovered that his usual reluctance to talk about his work and about literature abated. He even enjoyed himself.[16] But his appearances had unfortunate consequences in write-ups that quoted him as saying Hemingway had no courage. An incensed Hemingway had his friend General Buck Lanham write to Faulkner, attesting to the novelist's bravery in both world wars and the Spanish Civil War. On June 28, Faulkner replied, saying he had not commented on Hemingway as a man but on his "craftsmanship as a writer." Faulkner explained his ranking of writers, which he would repeat in several variations for the rest of his life. All of the writers named—Hemingway, Wolfe, Dos Passos, Caldwell, and Faulkner too—had failed, with Wolfe the "best failure because he had the most courage," risking "bad taste, clumsiness, mawkishness, dullness, to shoot the works win or lose and damn the torpedoes." Faulkner's correspondence had often included comments about his own bad taste, which he deemed a consequence of his experiments with language. In this context, Hemingway had not dared to "risk bad taste." Faulkner wrote to Hemingway, "I'm sorry of this damn stupid thing." If he had known his remarks would be published, he would have insisted on looking them over before they were made public. He hoped it did not matter a damn to Hemingway. But if it did, "please accept another squirm from yours truly."[17] A mollified Hemingway cheerfully accepted Faulkner's apology and threw some compliments his way and wanted, it seemed, to continue the correspondence.[18] But Faulkner did not reply.

By mid-July, Faulkner had accumulated more than four hundred pages of his fable and projected that it would run to at least one thousand. Again he thought he might have to return to Warner. Otherwise he did not see how he could pay his tax bill, now that the IRS had rejected his exemption claims for his 1944 residence in California. But on a summer visit Buzz Bezzerides laughed about the income tax problem and called Faulkner a "sap." Buzz's tax consultant, specializing in movie writers' tax returns, could save Faulkner a lot of money. "I have graduated from trying to make my own returns now," Faulkner reported to Harold Ober.[19]

Bezzerides, working on a script in Florida about sponge fishermen, had contacted Faulkner, who insisted on a visit before Buzz returned to California. Faulkner picked him up at the train depot in a dilapidated car that had no floorboards. Bezzerides had to sit with his feet propped up on the dashboard. It seemed to take hours driving in the dark to Oxford. Estelle served marvelous meals, part of the payback, Buzz thought, for the times he had put up Faulkner in Hollywood. It was all a little ramshackle, almost a parody of the master and the big house and the black attendants—so it seemed to Bezzerides, who noticed, he thought, how people said "Good morning, Bill," with "an air of contempt." Others treated Faulkner's farming as a big joke. A few years later Phil Stone told Carvel Collins that Faulkner had "enough resentment of the town's early attitude toward him to say that he'd like to be a Prussian officer & put his foot on some of their necks."[20]

Cho-Cho's daughter, Vicki, confirmed that the Faulkners were "a constant source of ridicule and slander." She "never knew quite why we were treated differently." To her, Faulkner was not a famous writer; "he was simply Pappy." She heard his typewriter in the mornings, but "it just didn't register." While Faulkner typed, Estelle read Dostoevsky, Gogol, Henry James, and H. P. Lovecraft. She liked to build a fire in her bedroom on cold winter nights and read while, at a card table in the same room, Jill, Vicki, and an animated Pappy played "cutthroat Hearts." "He wanted to dump the lady on us every time," Vicki said. "Oh he loved getting that Queen of Spades."[21] It was fun at home. In town, she felt "a subtle shunning."[22] But what did it matter? "To me, as a young child, Rowan Oak was an enchanted place, a cocoon that protected us all, thanks to Pappy," Vicki said. When her parents returned home from the Far East in 1941, they lived at Rowan Oak until Bill Fielden found a job. "There was never any question that my family would share living quarters at Rowan Oak until we could get our lives in order."[23]

Vicki was not the only one who viewed Rowan Oak as a place of enchantment. William Lewis Jr., the son of one of the town's merchant princes, remembered Estelle at the piano, playing, it seemed, every show tune of the 1920s and 1930s from Sigmund Romberg to George Gershwin. He was one of Dean's school friends and just one of many children who used to congregate at Rowan Oak and play in Bailey's Woods. Faulkner was "Pappy" to all children, as they sat to hear stories that kept them on edge. Just when he would get to the climax and say, "And then," he would pause, examine his pipe, take out a pipe cleaner, puff on his pipe, and with the children just about ready to wet their pants in anticipation, he would say, "Now where was I?" Estelle would break in and say, "Now Bill, go on." Pappy was such a tease. Estelle remained in the background, but she was welcoming to the children, greeting them sometimes with a hug, always with an exclamation of pleasure. Sandra Baker Moore remembered Estelle's bedroom, where she had an easel set up at just the right window to catch the light. For Sandra, Rowan Oak exuded the nimbus of family, including "Aunt Dot," Estelle's sister Dorothy. Only years later did Sandra realize they were not actually related.

For Faulkner this realm stood against the change taking place in town. Kate Baker, who had spent four years in Fort Smith, Arkansas, had returned to run her dress shop on the square, and she wrote in her letters about postwar Oxford, "a different town, crowded and busy." Soldiers were returning to the university under the GI Bill and looking for rooms to rent. Postwar shortages meant she had trouble stocking enough lingerie for their wives.

Some things had not changed: Faulkner would show up outside the dress shop and call to Ruth Mullet, the black woman who worked for Miss Kate. He would hand her a note, and Kate Baker would come out in her riding habit to accept Faulkner's invitation. "Men, you know, did not like to enter women's shops," Kate's daughter Sandra said.[24]

Saturdays on the square were the same, too, with the "colored folk," as they were called then, coming into town. They bought secondhand clothes in an open-air market on a corner of the square close to Phil Stone's law office. Stone, too, seemed the same, carrying around Juicy Fruit gum for children and smelling of cigars.[25]

Faulkner drove Buzz around the countryside complaining about the changes: A stream had been dammed up to make a lake stocked with fish for tourists. "Faulkner fulminated about how they had destroyed a natural stream that was a beauty in the area." He predicted the lake would silt up and become polluted. Buzz had trouble downing the local corn liquor—"like drinking fire!" Bill drank and drank without any apparent impact. Estelle also seemed a target of veiled ridicule because of her drinking.

On one of the early mornings of their weeklong stay, Buzz and his wife were startled to hear, coming from Estelle's bedroom, her "vicious whisper": "Don't you touch me." Then they heard a sound, a "sharp, intense striking of a hand against flesh." Buzz assumed Bill had slapped Estelle, but who is to say it was not Estelle who landed the blow? What really happened? "Shortly after that, we became aware of a sexual encounter on the other side of the door." The next morning a cheerful Estelle served breakfast. To Buzz, the incident reflected what he knew of the unhappy marriage. Bill needed sex and love, Buzz said, but Estelle's angry response showed that she "didn't want to be taken advantage of."[26] It was a lot to assume, even in such proximity to this complicated couple. Buzz saw her as frail, the weaker partner in this marriage, and he had sought to comfort her, but was she showing him something quite different at breakfast?

Vicki suggested that her grandmother feared having another child. She wanted separate bedrooms. "Contraceptives were largely unknown then, and I think Grandmama probably said, at the age thirty-six or so, 'Enough is enough.' . . . She was a tired, sick lady by then." Not too sick or tired, though: "Grandmama ran the place. And she did a damn good job of it!," Vicki insisted. "Almost single-handedly she maintained Rowan Oak. She made repairs, grew and [during the war] worked the 'Victory garden,' made it produce; she canned vegetables and made jams and jellies."[27]

Estelle, whatever her lapses and troubles, carried on, sounding exuberant, as usual, in her letters. "We are the busiest family imaginable," she had written to her daughter Cho-Cho, living in China with her husband, Bill Fielden, before the beginning of the war. Their daughter, Vicki, stayed at Rowan Oak. Shanghai, where the Fieldens lived, seemed a dangerous place for a child. "Mama & Daddy, PLEASE don't let those people (the communists) get you, and come on home," Vicki wrote to her parents.[28]

"School, of course, comes first—but the children's extra-curricular activities keep pappy and me up and (often times) out, all hours of the day & night," Estelle wrote: "Vicki looks positively *lovely* with her hair short and we think she has gained a bit too—very popular at school Jill says, and she is definitely proud enough to want to stand pretty high in her class." Estelle did not reveal her feelings when she reported that "Uncle Ned died in Ripley yesterday—with his burial tomorrow. Billy & I will go over of course."[29] Ned Barnett, the crusty family retainer who had worn the old Colonel's clothes and slaughtered Black Buster, reminded the Faulkners every day of their heritage. Ned could have lived rent-free at Greenfield Farm but had wanted to return to Ripley and a place of his own, just like independent Lucas Beauchamp in *Go Down, Moses*. Both Faulkners had cried as they sorted through Ned's possessions, one of the few times Malcolm had ever seen his stepfather in tears.[30]

Throughout the summer and into the fall, Faulkner continued work on what might be a masterpiece—or might be no good. It worried him, but he wanted to press on. Random House continued to back him, sending monthly checks and covering his back taxes.[31] He seemed to lack confidence. *Partisan Review* rejected an excerpt from the novel. Why?, Faulkner asked Ober. "Did they find it dull as written?" Random House had never given him an opinion, "other than to go ahead." Faulkner wanted Ober's opinion. "Dull? Too prolix? Diffuse?" He sought some explanation for his impasse, declaring that

> man is in a state of spiritual cowardice: all his bottom, reserve, strength has to go into physical stamina and there is nothing left to be concerned with art. That magazine does not exist now which would have printed sections from Ulysses as in the 1920's. And that the man crouching in a Mississippi hole trying to shape into some form of art his summation and conception of the human heart and spirit in terms of the cerebral, the simple imagination, is as out of place and in the way as a man trying to make an Egyptian water wheel in the middle of the Bessemer foundry would be.

Partisan Review editor Philip Rahv had rejected the fable fragment, saying "it read like a first draft—it just wasn't ready for publication." Faulkner, refusing to believe he had wasted his time, supposed that it would be "50 years before the world can stop to read it. It's too long, too deliberate."[32]

What to do? The same as he had done with *Absalom, Absalom!:* write another novel.

15

New Audiences

Intruder in the Dust,
January 1948–October 1949

OFF THE CUFF

On January 15, Faulkner put his fable aside and turned to a short novel, one that had been percolating in his imagination for more than a decade as he avidly read mysteries. Eric Devine remembered a visit to Rowan Oak in 1937 when Faulkner talked about a mystery novel he was reading. Faulkner had laughed out loud at the digging up of a body—the only time Devine had ever heard his friend do so.[1] Now Faulkner wrote his own murder mystery probing the "relationship between Negro and white, specifically or rather the premise being that the white people in the south, before the North or the govt, or anyone else, owe and must pay a responsibility to the Negro. But it's a story; nobody preaches in it. I may have told you the idea," he wrote Harold Ober, "which I have had for some time—a Negro in jail accused of murder and waiting for the white folks to drag him out and pour gasoline over him and set him on fire, is the detective, solves the crime because he goddamn has to to keep from being lynched, by asking people to go somewhere and look at something and then come back and tell him what they found."[2] The black man in question is the independent Lucas Beauchamp, featured earlier in *Go Down, Moses,* a black aristocrat of sorts because of his descent from white masters whom he regards as his coevals. In effect, Beauchamp is Faulkner's innovative variation of the gentleman-hero armchair detective, an Auguste Dupin in black, forcing white people to detect a white criminal hiding in plain sight.

Lucas Beauchamp exerts a tremendous sense of authority, like Uncle Ned Barnett, who had served the old Colonel and could, in effect, pull rank on the old Colonel's great-grandson. After all, Faulkner had deferred to Ned as the authority on the old Colonel when Robert Cantwell came calling. Like Callie Barr, Ned knew things, had seen things, before William Faulkner was born. Ned served without being servile and had experienced the history that Faulkner sought to master in his fiction. And rather than staying on Faulkner's farm, he had returned to Ripley, remaining his own man.

In about six weeks Faulkner had a first draft, which he began to revise and expand in late February. By April 20, he had finished the novel in time for the fall list. It had now become as much about Chick Mallison, "a 16 year old boy who overnight became a man,"[3] as about his black detective. In fiction, Chick would prevent the Nelse Patton lynching that Billy Falkner, as witness or not, had nevertheless lived with for forty years. He was always a Falkner, part of that family, even when he declared his independence and added that *u* to his name. Estelle called him Billy even into their adult years. He was always that boy she fell in love with; he was always that boy who identified with other boys having to reckon with their fraught heritage.

This new novel came as a tremendous relief. "Please tell Bob [Robert Haas] about it," Faulkner instructed Ober; "it might make him feel better about me.... I've been on Random H's cuff a long time now."[4] The wording is significant, as though Faulkner had to prove his worth to his publisher just as, in the company of Uncle Ned, the great-grandson had to pay his respects to Falkner family history. Writing *Intruder in the Dust* became in both personal and professional terms a work of redemption. On July 11, MGM bought the motion picture rights for fifty thousand dollars, 20 percent of which went to Random House, which had continued to provide Faulkner with a monthly stipend.

At the same time, *The Portable Faulkner* had done its work. "When you get North," Malcolm Cowley wrote, "you'll find that you're not a neglected author any longer, that they're studying you in the colleges, including Yale, where lots of the kids think that 'The Bear' is the greatest story ever written."[5] Carvel Collins came to Oxford that summer as part of his planning to teach the first graduate seminar on Faulkner at Harvard. There he met Peggy Park, on the faculty at Ole Miss, and learned that she had invited a reluctant Faulkner to her classroom, telling him her students did not understand his work very well. Half of them were Naval Reserve trainees. Although Faulkner doubted he could say much, perhaps he agreed to come because of the military connection and because she promised that no other faculty would be present. Faulkner had grumbled he did not want to be exhibited like a "two-headed calf." He consented to appear for about fifteen minutes but stayed an hour.

Park followed up with several visits to Rowan Oak, even getting him to appraise the writing of a pharmacist friend of hers. She called Faulkner's comments "gentle, compassionate, and very nearly clairvoyant." In her company, Collins met and interviewed a "gracious and polite" author who showed him Jill's new horse. Collins left elated.[6] "I have seen Bill several times lately and he seemed to like you because he strained himself enough to volunteer some oral remark as about you," Phil Stone wrote to Collins.[7] Stone's disaffection is apparent, although Faulkner continued to see him. Sometimes Faulkner would show up at Stone's law office, and Stone would not come out to see him, irked that in his view he had not been given enough credit for Faulkner's success and that Faulkner had not turned out to be quite the writer Stone had hoped for. That more callers like Collins began to talk to Stone did not, it seems, gratify Stone so much as it showed him that he had lost Faulkner to the world, which could not possibly understand Bill the way Phil did.

That summer Faulkner sailed on Sardis Reservoir, created by a government flood-control dam. Retired colonel Hugh Evans, local doctor Ashford Little, and Ross Brown, a Faulkner friend and fellow hunter, had built a houseboat under Faulkner's supervision. Working on this barge, more than forty feet long, became a sort of community event, and Faulkner's own description of the work recalls the hauling of Ikkemotubbe's steamboat: "Out of Confusion by Boundless Hope: Conceived in a Canadian Club bottle She was born A.D. 15th August 1947 by uproarious Caesarian Section in prone position with her bottom upward in Evans's back yard eleven miles from the nearest water deeper than a half inch kitchen tap and waxed and grew daily there beneath the whole town's enrapt cynosure." The boat, towed by truck, made a circuit around the courthouse square. It was called the *Minmagary* after the wives of its builders: Minnie Ruth Little, Maggie Brown, and Mary Evans. Pappy drew up papers for the ship, his niece Dean recalled, invoking "whatever authority I may have inherited from my Great Grandfather William C. Falkner Colonel (paroled) Second Mississippi Infantry Provisional Army Confederate States of America." He commissioned the *Minmagary* as a "Ship of the Line in the Confederate Navy given under my Great Grandfather's sword this Twenty Fourth July 1948 at Oxford Mississippi. William C. Falkner II." At a party he hosted aboard ship, Faulkner "presided in captain's cap, bathing suit, deck shoes, and blue work shirt with sleeves rolled up." Ole Miss dean Estella Hefley showed up, protesting the presence of coeds, who were not supposed to be near Sardis Reservoir let alone aboard a ship during the school term. Faulkner greeted Hefley, one of his mother's friends: "Estella, what a pleasant surprise, please join us." He could "charm a cobra out of a basket" when he chose to, his niece said. On this occasion, with the coeds hiding in the cabin, pleasantries were exchanged about Maud before the dean expressed her concerns, which Faulkner listened to sympathetically, lamenting how standards had fallen since the war. But several students aboard were veterans and gentlemen, he pointed out, and so he and Dean Hefley parted on amicable terms, with rebel yells coming from the cabin only after she had left the boat.[8]

In September, Random House planned to publish a collection of Faulkner's short stories, and Bennett Cerf invited him for a New York stay. He looked forward to time with the Cerfs, but he preferred a hotel since "my expedition is vacation from the nest-and-hearth business."[9] To Hamilton Basso's query about doing a profile, Faulkner wrote on September 23: "Oh hell no. Come down and visit whenever you can, but no piece in any paper about me as I am working tooth and nail at my lifetime ambition to be the last private individual on earth & expect every success since apparently there is no competition for the place."[10]

Faulkner arrived in New York on Monday, October 18, a few days after he finished with squirrel and dove hunting. The next day Malcolm Cowley got his first close-up look at Robert Haas's Park Avenue apartment during a dinner with two hired butlers and lots of cognac. Cowley observed a short, "neatly put together, slim and muscular" figure with "beautifully shaped hands," a low forehead, deeply set eyes, a Roman nose, and gray hair around his head like a wreath. The drooping mustache reminded him of the melancholy Poe. Cowley took notes for his editor at *Life,* Robert Coughlan, who wanted Cowley to write a profile, which the critic would not do without Faulkner's consent. Present also—as they almost always were on such occasions—were Hal Smith and Eric Devine, who left with Faulkner at two in the morning for Smith's apartment.

The next day, Wednesday, Faulkner gave two interviews, saying to John K. Hutchins of the *New York Herald Tribune,* "I think of myself as a farmer, not a writer." But he did relent insofar as he mentioned his fable, "based on the story of the Crucifixion and the Resurrection." Referring to the presidential election, in which the Democrats split, with the "Dixiecrats" opting for their own segregationist candidate, Strom Thurmond, Faulkner said: "I'd be a Dixiecrat myself if they hadn't hollered 'nigger.' I'm a States' Rights man. Hodding Carter's a good man, and he's right when he says the solution of the Negro problem belongs to the South." Such statements would inevitably have an impact on the reviews of *Intruder in the Dust.* Hutchins wrote that Faulkner then paused and "added, with mild irony: 'There isn't a Southerner alive who doesn't curse the day the first Northern ship captain landed a Negro slave in this country.'" It was a telling remark, and one that southerners often made about the northern complicity in the slave trade that had propelled the country's economy.

Like Hutchins, Ralph Thompson of the *New York Times* described Faulkner as shy. Asked about the increasing academic interest in his work, Faulkner remained silent. Apparently the pressure began to build. In such situations, he felt cornered. "Look," he finally said, "I'm just a writer. Not a literary man." The reporter watched him shift uncomfortably in his chair. He did not deny the symbols and patterns others found in his work, but he was like a "good carpenter," putting the nails "where they belong." Uncharacteristically, he revealed some of what he felt about his place in Oxford. Most people did not care much about his books or that his picture appeared in a New York newspaper, except to ask him for a loan, "figuring I've made a million dollars. Or else they look twice and figure I couldn't make a thousand." He just did not want to talk about his writing career, making out that it had all been an accident, a lark that only turned serious when Sherwood Anderson encouraged him.[11]

These two interviews, done presumably to promote *Intruder in the Dust* and to fulfill his deep regard for all Random House had done for him— this author who had made very little money for them—drove Faulkner to continue the drinking that had begun at the Haas party and the late night with Smith and Devine. After the interviews, he went off by himself to the Algonquin. A worried Malcolm Cowley, whose lunch appointment had been canceled because Faulkner was too drunk, showed up at the Algonquin on Friday, October 22. In Faulkner's room, Cowley observed the whiskey and beer bottles on the dresser, and the writer on his back "naked and uncovered except for a silk pajama top." Faulkner, grunting and muttering, couldn't seem to say an audible word. "Can't I do something for you," Cowley asked. "What'n you do?," Faulkner managed to ask. "I could cover you. I could get you a drink." "Drink," Faulkner said. Cowley poured one and had to hold Faulkner while he got it down. The critic sat by the bed but could think of nothing else to do. Later Cowley kept seeing the scene: "on the hotel twin bed, his very small penis exposed unless he covered it with his hands. Sometimes he moaned in his alcoholic sleep."

Blotner did not include this scene in his biography, but spoke to Bill Fielden, who said: "He would trick you, bargain with you, humiliate you, anything to get a drink when you were trying to get him to quit, nursing him. It would be hard to keep him upstairs." Fielden would hear him come "stumbling, falling, downstairs." Once Fielden grabbed him and actually got into a cold shower with Faulkner, who said that was "no way to treat kinfolks." Other family members, like Faulkner's brother John, sometimes would watch over him during these bouts, but then John, too, would sometimes get drunk. Weak and debilitated, Faulkner would taper off with beer.[12]

In New York, Cowley and others had Faulkner put into the Fieldstone Sanitarium, where he spent only a day, showing, once again, extraordinary recuperative powers. The next day, Cowley took Faulkner home to Sherman, Connecticut. Cowley's vigilant wife, Muriel, monitored Faulkner, feeding him and spacing out and watering down his drinks and coping with his withdrawal symptoms: the shakes and the sweats.[13] Cowley listened to Faulkner talk about the projected collection of short stories. The critic suggested the work should appear in one big volume arranged by subject matter and with a foreword by Faulkner. "He promised to think about it," Cowley noted as he listened to an account of the fable: "Christ in the French army, a corporal with a squad of 12 men—and a general who is Antichrist and takes him up on a hill and offers him the world. Symbolic and unreal, except for 300 wild pages about a three-legged racehorse in Tennessee. Mary Magdalen and the other two Marys. There is a strange mutiny in which the soldiers on both sides simply refuse to fight. The corporal's body is chosen for that of the Unknown Soldier. Christ (or his disciple) lives again in the crowd."

They moved on to Faulkner's account of his time in Hollywood and then to stories about Callie Barr. This was about as much as Cowley could get out of Faulkner, who resisted—but did not actually reject—the idea of an article with biographical material. And yet, on a beautiful autumn day with oaks that "wore an imperial purple," as they drove across the foothills of the Taconic Range, Faulkner kept talking about his life—from the postwar period in New Orleans to travels in Europe, how his conception of Yoknapatawpha developed, his notion of the South as a frontier society, Falkner family lore, hunting, his farm, run by "three Negro tenant families," and about writing, usually in the morning but sometimes afternoons and evenings too. Gavin Stevens, Faulkner insisted, was no mouthpiece. He stated what would soon become evident to readers of *Intruder in the Dust:* "If the race problems were just left to the children, they'd be solved soon enough. It's the grown-ups and especially the women who keep the prejudice alive." At the end of the day, still wanting to talk, he paced back and forth in Cowley's living room, a combination, somehow, of humility and "something close to Napoleonic pride." He had more yet to say about his "prodigious sentences" conveying a "sense of simultaneity, not only giving what happened in the shifting moment but suggesting everything that went before and made the quality of that moment." Faulkner left Cowley with a copy of Charles Jackson's *The Lost Weekend,* the famous story of an alcoholic writer played by Ray Milland in Billy Wilder's film. On the way back to Oxford, Faulkner sent Mrs. Cowley a dozen long-stemmed roses.[14]

At home in early November, he wrote Cowley about the structure of *Collected Stories* that laid out a geographical Yoknapatawpha and the world beyond it—just as the critic had suggested. Faulkner followed Cowley in another matter too: He wanted a corduroy coat "like yours, white or near-white corduroy, bellows pockets and a loose belt and a vent in the back so I can ride a horse in it." Brooks Brothers had nothing like that in stock, and so he asked Cowley if he could get them to "make me one like yours."[15]

"An Event in American Literature"

In the *Dallas Morning News* (September 26), John Chapman observed that "it should not seem particularly strange that Faulkner, having dealt with the displacement of people from war and poverty, should finally come to deal explicitly with the most dispossessed and displaced of all, the Negro."[16] Horace Gregory in the *New York Herald Tribune* (September 26) called Lucas Beauchamp a new kind of black man in American fiction: "no mere 'Uncle Tom,' that Pantaloon of sentimental abolitionist literature, but one of the most convincing Negro characters in American fiction, a rare figure of unmarred dignity, and it is one of the marks of Faulkner's genius that he can write of the Negro without false pity, without the usual haze of shallow sentiment in which so many 'men of good will' scatter patronage, and the sweet, slightly rotted fruits of 'good intentions.'"

Between Edmund Wilson and Eudora Welty stretched the literary and political ground on which Faulkner's novel was appraised. Wilson complained about "snarled-up," tract-like prose.[17] The critic presumed the novel derived from a response to the civil rights plank at the Democratic National Convention and to an antilynching bill in Congress, unaware that Faulkner had conceived the novel nearly a decade earlier and had been exploring the race issue in his wartime screenplays. When Wilson said that "it is difficult to reduce what is said to definite propositions," he contradicted his own argument that Faulkner had written a tract. As Harvey Breit observed in the *New York Times Book Review* (September 26), Stevens's speeches are "non-paraphrasable because they have not been conceived in political terms nor are they expressed in ready formulas. They are individual notions, expressed with utmost particularisation, and no camp or faction will find them readily usable."

Eudora Welty read a different novel from Wilson's. "*Intruder* is marvelously funny," she wrote in the *Hudson Review* (Winter 1949). "The complicated intricate thing is that his stories are not decked out in humor, but the humor is born in them, as much their blood and bones as the passion and poetry." Welty, a master of comic prose and scene setting, noticed sentences like this one: "Miss Habersham's round hat on the exact top of her head such as few people had seen in fifty years and probably no one at any time looked up out of a halfway rifled grave." This old lady is helping sixteen-year-old Chick Mallison to dig up a body as part of the proof that Lucas Beauchamp is innocent. A bullet will prove Lucas's gun was not involved in the murder. Faulkner attends to the incongruity of the characters, the setting, and the time—the past (the old hat) impinging upon the present, the living upon the dead. A crime has been covered up, literally buried. Ultimately the novel is not simply a murder mystery—that is its casing, Welty noted—or a response to social issues (although those are *there*). "What goes on here?," Welty began her review: "Grave digging. 'Digging and undiggin.' What's in the grave? One body or maybe another, maybe nothing at all—except human shame, something we've done to ourselves." Perhaps not wanting to give the ending away, Welty does not add that the solution of the crime leads to the discovery of fratricide, a family crime of a white man killing his twin brother, so that consciousness of race, so keenly a part of the community's desire to punish a victim with death, becomes a blow against itself for wanting the proud Lucas to "be a nigger first," like Charles Bon and Joe Christmas. "The concepts of justice and tolerance are themselves brought under examination," wrote the reviewer in the *Irish Times* (October 1, 1949), in a novel that probes and evaluates the "dialectics of individual and communal responsibility."

Several reviewers noted that *Intruder in the Dust* was Faulkner's first novel in eight years (most did not count *Go Down, Moses* as a novel), and their enthusiasm suggests the pent-up demand that triggered sales and tributes. But they were also puzzled. In the *New Statesman and Nation* (October 15, 1949), Walter Allen called Faulkner's novel "inspiring . . . scarcely the adjective one would have applied to his work in the past." Lucas Beauchamp, unlike Joe Christmas, is not lynched but saved and emerges triumphant. As the anonymous reviewer put it in *TLS* (October 7, 1949), the novel had no "figure of doom comparable with Popeye or Joe Christmas." Yet what had changed was more a matter of emphasis, since the elements of inspiration surely suffuse *The Sound and the Fury, Light in August, Absalom, Absalom!, The Hamlet,* and *Go Down, Moses* in the persistence and even triumphs of Dilsey, Byron Bunch and Lena Grove, the French architect, Ratliff, and Lucas Beauchamp. The boy-man reckoning with his heritage in *The Unvanquished* reaches his fulfillment in Chick Mallison.

Nathan Glick in *Commentary* (May 1949) provided a remarkable paragraph of biographical criticism:

It is as if Faulkner were trying to formulate his feeling toward a special branch of his family, with which his parents have had some vague but rankling quarrel, but whose individual members he has come to like. His book *Go Down, Moses* is dedicated to "Mammy" and indeed in much of his fiction the mother image is a black woman. His black and white boys hunt, sleep, and eat together as brothers (or cousins) until the adult's race pride seeps down and destroys their ease, as it complicates the white boy's feeling toward the Negro mother. A sense of his own complicity in this estrangement from one's earliest companions motivates Faulkner's attempt to project himself wholly into the Negro's mind and feeling. Whatever we may think of the tribal, superstitious elements in his statement of the racial situation, Faulkner's involved affection and respect for the Negro may indeed be a profounder sense of fraternity than the Northerner's easy, and impersonal, liberalism.

This passage hits full force when it is remembered that the poor white Vincent Gowrie is murdered by his white brother, an event that surely reflects Faulkner's understanding that in the effort to lynch Lucas white people have tried to revenge themselves on the wrong brother. When Gavin Stevens calls the South homogeneous, he is referring to black and white people alike and the brotherhood that lynchings have sought to deny. As to the "special branch of his family," the reviewer came close to recognizing that *Intruder in the Dust* is a tribute to Uncle Ned.

In the *Sewanee Review* (Winter 1949), Andrew Lytle argued that no matter Faulkner's motivations in addressing a contemporary issue, as an artist a literary truth, as in Dickens, had to prevail. For Lytle, Chick Mallison, troubled by his debt to Lucas Beauchamp, who had rescued him from drowning, and by the shame he feels about the effort to lynch Lucas, is the moral center of novel, making it dramatic, not didactic. He is, in the words of Morton Fineman (*Philadelphia Inquirer,* September 26, 1948), "all impassioned awareness" set against his uncle, the "oracular and patient" Gavin Stevens. It is Chick's "moral destiny," Lytle affirms, that is at stake as well as Lucas's life. Chick cannot redeem himself without rescuing Lucas as well. But Chick cannot do it alone, which is why Miss Habersham is called up to direct the unearthing of the crime and the culprit. Curiously, Lytle does not mention Aleck Sander, Chick's black counterpart, who performs, as Ringo does for Bayard in *The Unvanquished,* the role of sidekick and teammate, and without whom Chick, like Bayard, could not measure the degree of his commitment to moral action.

Like Bayard's, only more so, Chick's consciousness is part black: "Because he [Chick] knew Lucas Beauchamp too—as well that is as any white person knew him. Better than any maybe." Chick has been inside Lucas's home, eaten at his table, and been cared for by Lucas's wife. He is like the barber in "Dry September," knowing the black man to be lynched in ways that the rest of white community does not. Lucas, as much as Thomas Sutpen or his white ancestors, has his own domain, a ten-acre patch deeded to him by his white first cousin, McCaslin Edmonds. Lucas, Aleck Sander, and their black families are "a rich part of his heritage as a Southerner." Faulkner never quite put it this way in previous novels—this explicit acknowledgment that southern white identity *depends* on its black counterpart, as it did for Faulkner himself. Lucas wears his "fine old hat" with a "swaggering rake," reminiscent of a Sutpen-like flamboyance but also of Uncle Ned in the old Colonel's clothing.

While Chick tries to work out the fate of Lucas Beauchamp, Gavin Stevens pontificates about the state of the South: "We are defending not actually our politics or beliefs or even our way of life, but simply our homogeneity from a federal government to which in simple desperation the rest of this country has had to surrender voluntarily more and more of its personal and private liberty in order to continue to afford the United States. And of course we will continue to defend it." Faulkner said such speeches were characteristic of southern liberals, a term he never used for himself, but one that seemed to fit in a University of Virginia classroom: "no one can be saved by an outsider. He must be saved from inside himself. That is, the South must correct that evil, as it applies to the South, ourselves, that it can't be done by—by laws or philosophical or political theories compelled on us from the outside." But to Faulkner, at least, his sharing an opinion with Gavin Stevens did not mean the character was there to support Faulkner: "The writer is too busy writing about people struggling with their own hearts, with others, or with environment, that his own convictions and opinions about injustices come out, but he's not, at that moment, concerned in telling the reader, 'This is what I think about injustice or morality.'"[18]

The failure of Reconstruction and the subsequent efforts to redeem that failure through legislation seem evident to Stevens, as they seemed to Faulkner. The character can be separated from the author, to be sure, but nevertheless they share many of the same opinions, including a deep and abiding belief that changes of heart cannot be coerced by legislation. What could, then, produce a change of heart? Isn't that one important reason why Faulkner wrote novels? The loquacious Stevens seems there in the novel to keep in play the argument between the South and the North that Faulkner stubbornly would not relinquish, for he believed that to capitulate to northern liberal opinion would be to abnegate the anguish and triumph that Chick is able to experience on his own terms. To accept the North as an intervening agent would mean to take away the story Faulkner felt compelled to tell.

Chick's terms, Faulkner's terms, included insisting on the hegemony of his own fiction. In the *Partisan Review* (October 1948), Elizabeth Hardwick declared: "There are probably very few novelists in America who have not in some depressed, sterile hour wished for Faulkner's madness. He is authentically, romantically possessed by his genius; he can lose himself not only in the act of writing but in the world his imagination has created and populated." She referred to his map of Yoknapatawpha and the "Compson Appendix," which suggested a world intact, sufficient to itself: "And he is so beautifully our young writer's image of the artist: he has done it by himself, in solitude, far from New York, in spite of critics, little magazines, fads, and professors— our natural genius, isolated, sure of himself, magnificently hallucinated as we feel the artist ought to be." Perhaps not quite so isolated as she supposed, as she left Hollywood out of her myth of the solitary great American novelist, and she did not seem to realize that some of that inspired writing occurred in the offices of Random House. Having created this myth of the "possessed, legendary writer," she was dismayed to find he had written a polemic, "even in its odd way a 'novel of ideas,'" as if he "ran down from the hills to make a speech in the public square." Her attitude reflects a desire to set Faulkner aside and immunize him from social and political pressures.

Hardwick's Faulkner is a segregationist in a different sense of the word:

> The sickness of *Intruder in the Dust,* the fear and despair, are intimately connected with the future of Faulkner's career, a career which demands that there be a South, not just a geographical section and an accent, but a reasonably autonomous unit, a kind of family ready, and even with a measure of geniality, to admit the existence of the people next door and to cooperate in the necessary civic responsibilities, such as the removal of garbage and the maintenance of highways, but beyond that unique and separate, not to be reproached, advised, or mourned for the goings on behind the door.

In short, the world had finally gotten to William Faulkner. Drenched in her thesis, Hardwick misread the novel, actually saying that Lucas wanted to be lynched, to "add his own blood to the South's dishonor, as his last act of contempt for his oppressors." But Lucas, notwithstanding Hardwick's contention, does not want to become a martyr. He might seem passive by not professing his innocence, but he realizes that only through Chick, through a sensibility uncluttered with adult notions of "Negroes," can he possibly be saved.

Lucas Beauchamp's courage and intelligence have been insufficiently accounted for in many readings of the novel. In effect, he is the detective, not the white people. He tells them where to look for the evidence. He is the Dupin who solves a crime without leaving the confines of his own mind. It is not just that he does not act like a frightened "nigger." He does not act as a frightened man at all. Lucas is proud of his aristocratic heritage, his descent from a plantation owner, but his superiority is not really race-based. He does not see white people as superior, and he does not identify with black people. He is that remarkable specimen in a racist society, one who is race neutral: "What makes Faulkner's casting of the problem so original and astute in *Intruder* involves his refusal to represent the question of black enfranchisement as it was usually posed: what to do with the negro? Faulkner's ultimate answer seems to be: abolish 'negro.' Also abolish 'white,' along with the entire figment of race."[19]

Lucas trusts Chick because the boy has shown himself to be observant and self-reliant. He does not defer to adult authority, and he has shed many of the conceptions of race that hinder white people, even the liberal ones like those of his Uncle Gavin. Chick may be daunted by what Lucas asks him to do, but he does not think it impossible. He is not old enough to accept the limits of the possible. This faith in youth, this reverence for the honest reactions of children, is a very Faulknerian conceit. Lucas is not presented as *"the Negro."* He does not believe he represents anyone other than himself, and that is how Chick also responds to him. If Lucas had accepted his status as "nigger," then, certainly, he might become *"the Negro."* Gavin Stevens, prone to palaver, transforms Lucas's case into one of "Sambo," the lawyer's term that allows him to make sweeping generalizations about race and also to express a "self-consciously arrogant" attitude, since the term itself cannot be anodized simply because Stevens uses it.[20] He is not equipped to understand Lucas's motivations, and yet he is the one who has to champion Lucas's right to a defense, just as he is there when Butch Beauchamp's body returns to Yoknapatawpha.

Hardwick calls Stevens "absurd" and "strident," and his speeches "written with frantic bad taste." But is the bad taste Faulkner's? Isn't Stevens's florid defensiveness risible? Faulkner disarmed the proponent of some of his own ideas by making him so hortatory. After all, this is the well-meaning but baffled character in the last story of *Go Down, Moses* who cannot really come to terms with the black community he wants to serve. And this is also the Gavin Stevens who bloviates on the white blood–black blood complex in *Light in August,* and the Stevens to come in *Requiem for a Nun* who behaves like a moralistic hound. He does plenty of good in *Knight's Gambit* solving crimes, but there he is more concerned with the clues to human character and the logic of events. In *Intruder in the Dust,* Stevens "talks about everything but his own failure." He cannot "see past the persiflage of his own words."[21] Stevens, after all, believed Lucas was guilty until Chick, Aleck Sander, and Miss Habersham proved otherwise. Stevens, prone to tangents, is often brought back into focus by Chick and Miss Habersham, both of whom speak in "short, simple declarative sentences."[22]

Reviewers treated *Intruder in the Dust* all by itself and with no reference to Stevens's other appearances in Yoknapatawpha. Fair enough. But a reader of the Faulkner canon can approach the good lawyer with some skepticism. Similarly, the biographer cannot help but see Phil Stone somewhere there in the background—not as a lawyer who professes Stevens's views (in fact Stone was much more of a hard-line segregationist), but as a hapless, garrulous figure with some talent and generosity but without the wherewithal to do that much for himself or his family. Faulkner did not imitate Stone's style, but reading through Stone's letters results in an impression of a pontifical, ideological, and ineffectual person as frustrated as Stevens is in his inability to connect with others.

SUPPRESSED FAULKNER

Several reviewers complained about Faulkner's lack of sentence structure—how his sentences went on and on—and presumed the "faults" were the result of laziness and lack of discipline. A study of his manuscripts and typescripts shows, however, that the famous Faulknerian sentences were the result of much revision that occurred six weeks after he wrote his initial short draft of the novel and went on for at least another six weeks. The published Faulkner, in other words, is rewritten Faulkner. The published Faulkner was also an act of suppression.

Although Faulkner told Harold Ober that "nobody preaches" in *Intruder in the Dust,*[23] the novelist had to work hard to prohibit the preaching. In an omitted preface, he declared: "These characters and incidents are fictional, imaginative, and—some will say—impossible. In which case let them be accepted not as the puppet-play of a whodunit but as the protagonist-pattern of a belief that not government first but the white man of the South owes a responsibility to the Negro." To say as much before the novel began allied the author to Gavin Stevens. Faulkner drafted and then discarded a reference to himself and *Absalom, Absalom!:* "so that in five hundred years all America can paraphrase the tag line of a book a novel of about twenty years ago by another Mississippian, a mild retiring little man over yonder at Oxford, in which a fictitious Canadian said to a fictitious self-lacerated Southerner in a dormitory room in a not too authentic Harvard: 'I who regard you will also have sprung from the loins of African kings.'" Faulkner had typed "self-lacerated Mississippian" and crossed out the word and wrote in "Southerner" to expand the import of his prophecy.[24] Not since *Mosquitoes* had he dared to refer to himself in a work of fiction, which he would not do ever again, except for his later semi-fictional essay "Mississippi."

In his fiction, Faulkner suppressed something else: the reality of lynching in his own time and what it would have taken to stop it. By 1948, lynchings were rare, as Rebecca West noted in her famous reportage "Opera in Greenville." In that piece, much admired in the South, she took essentially Faulkner's approach, believing that southerners were on the way to eradicating lynching, that in fact the lynching trial she covered was an anomaly in a rapidly changing South.[25] If so much else around him was changing so fast, it did not seem unreasonable to Faulkner to suppose that segregation, too, would seem outmoded as well as immoral. But he also knew that his fellow Mississippians would recognize, even in 1948, that his characters were Faulknerian—that, in fact, no one like Lucas Beauchamp could survive—not then anyway, as John Cullen said to his interviewer Floyd Watkins: "Lucas Beauchamp was more independent than he could actually get away with as a real person in Oxford."[26]

What would it take to stop a lynch mob? It is as if Faulkner asked himself that question. In *Intruder in the Dust,* he supplied the answer: Miss Habersham. Without her, Lucas Beauchamp, Chick Mallison, Aleck Sander, and Gavin Stevens, who combine to see that justice is done, could not prevail. The film adaptation makes the point even more strongly, and while Faulkner did not write the script, he read Ben Maddow's version and revised parts of it.[27] He coached Juano Hernandez, who played Lucas, as well as giving every indication that he approved of the film, which is itself an interpretation of the novel that makes Miss Habersham even more crucial to the action. When Crawford Gowrie approaches the jail spilling gas from his can along the way and onto the floor where Miss Habersham sits, barring his way to Lucas Beauchamp, she does not flinch when he lights a match, which he has to extinguish when he realizes he cannot frighten her. As he retreats, she gets out of her chair and confronts the lynch mob, telling them they should be ashamed of themselves. They should go away. They do not. Instead they stand, with several of them bowing their heads or looking away. It is, in effect, a stalemate until the sheriff arrives with the real murderer and the mob disperses. That stalemated moment, by design or happenstance, revealed a South stuck in its old ways and yet unable to perpetuate the past without some encouragement.

Instead the mob is witness to an old lady, who should herself be the embodiment of those women who erected monuments to the Confederate dead, telling them to move on.

There is no evidence that Faulkner wrote that scene, but he sure saw it before it was filmed. He knew nothing like it could happen except in Jefferson, not Oxford. But the world would have to change even as Jefferson was changing in the last decade of his work on the Yoknapatawpha fiction.

HOLLYWOOD COMES TO OXFORD

MGM chose Clarence Brown, educated in Georgia, and involved in filmmaking since 1920, to direct *Intruder in the Dust* at a time when only one other picture dealing with race issues, *Lost Boundaries* (1949), was in production. That film dealt with a light-skinned African American doctor who passed for white when he could not find employment in the South. Brown regarded filming Faulkner's novel as a "payment of his conscience," according to screenwriter Ben Maddow. The director had witnessed black people shot down during an Atlanta race riot.[28] He wanted to adapt Faulkner's novel even before it went into galleys.

Brown had a daring plan: to shoot on location in Oxford and use the local people in bit roles and in mob scenes. Studios were wary of location shoots, which often ran over budget. But Brown convinced MGM it would be cheaper to film on-site. He had the fortunate backing of Dore Schary, a liberal producer who believed in Brown's mission. The director wanted to show the South how to see itself as Faulkner saw it: capable of resolving its own problems. "The thinking must come from within," he argued. He turned the filming into a community event, recruiting college professors, bankers, barbers, truck drivers, and workers from a local creamery. The whole film, Brown said, was "shot within a radius of three blocks," except for a cemetery scene, but that, too, was in Oxford. It took a week, Brown admitted, for the community to adjust to filming, but then they were enthusiastic supporters.[29] More people came to church during the filming of scenes there than Emily Stone, Phil's wife, had ever seen attend a service.[30] Phil appeared briefly in the church scene.[31]

At first, many in Oxford were uneasy when they heard an MGM film crew of fifty would be coming to town. The "worst side would be presented and the community held up to shame and ridicule." Many believed Faulkner only showed the "sordid" side of life. But others welcomed the business. At least one Mississippi paper deplored such mercenary motives.[32] But Brown had the winning argument: making the film in Hollywood would mean Oxford would have no say in how it was depicted.[33]

Brown also had a certain cachet as the director of the popular *National Velvet* (1944), starring Elizabeth Taylor, and *The Yearling* (1946), set on a Florida farm and based on Marjorie Kinnan Rawlings's celebrated bestseller. Claude Jarman Jr., who played Jody Baxter, the boy who adopts an orphaned fawn in *The Yearling,* now arrived in town to play Chick Mallison. Jarman and Elizabeth Patterson (Miss Habersham) were both southerners. Brown's own southern background may have helped his case. So, too, did the excitement of making a motion picture that even had some suggesting to Brown ways to make the lynch mob more authentic, including those who argued that a knotted rope ought to be in the scene.[34] Brown opted for a more subtle approach. Perhaps, also, he told the town some version of what he said to the press: "Our picture is merely a good whodunit. It concerns three people who save a man from a lynching. The man could be a Negro or he could be white. It makes no difference to the story."[35] Of course, race did make a difference, but MGM had done an earlier lynching film, *Fury* (1936), starring Spencer Tracy, whose character narrowly escapes a lynching in California, so Brown could have made the most of his studio's bona fides. None of Stevens's long speeches appeared in the film, much to Phil Stone's dismay, because he wanted audiences to see what a "tolerant, educated white Southerner thinks about the race issue."[36]

Faulkner kept watch over the director, or so Brown claimed, calling the author an "elusive little devil." In a store window reflection, Brown saw Faulkner peering at him, but when the director turned around, Faulkner had vanished. He always seemed to be just gliding out of view. Robert Surtees, the cinematographer, described Faulkner as the most reticent man he had ever met, who did not repair the ruts in his driveway, hoping to discourage intruders. Occasionally, Surtees saw Faulkner slip in to watch the rushes, the printed results of a day's shooting.[37]

Faulkner suggested shooting locations and rewrote certain scenes, Brown said: "He's interested in motion picture technique." What techniques Brown did not say. Faulkner later said he "liked the way Mr. Brown used bird calls and saddle squeaks and footsteps in place of a lot of loud music telling you what emotion you should be experiencing."[38] Did Faulkner also notice the film's careful use of low-angle shots to depict Lucas Beauchamp? Such shots place the audience at ground level with Chick looking up at Lucas, making Beauchamp a towering figure next to the story of a boy's dealings with the adult white world that tries to diminish Beauchamp's humanity, separating him out from the community as the news reports had done to Nelse Patton. In the film adaptation, Stevens is never allowed to dilute the rapport between Chick and Lucas.

Faulkner watched, fascinated, even spellbound, as one of Jill's classmates, a stand-in for Claude Jarman, fell into an icy stream created by pouring paraffin into the water. Lucas rescues Chick from the icy stream in an immersion/baptism scene that begins Chick's rebirth and Lucas's role as his savior. Faulkner even socialized with the crew to an extent that surprised Vicki Fielden, who said he adored Elizabeth Patterson (Miss Habersham), who had also played Aunt Jenny in *The Story of Temple Drake*. Faulkner was also very much "taken by Juano Hernandez who was a fine gentleman," playing Lucas Beauchamp.[39] Faulkner did not let on to his mother. On set, as they sat in canvas chairs next to the director, he turned to her during a series of retakes and said, "I told you it was boring."[40] Phil Stone showed up for the filming of a jail scene, and Claude Jarman Jr. signed an autograph for him.[41] To Eric Devine, Faulkner wrote: "Much excitement here, since they are making a movie of my book in Oxford. It's too bad I'm no longer young enough to cope with all the local girls who are ready and eager to glide into camera focus on their backs."[42] The filming stirred other memories, and he wrote to Meta a love letter, which she concealed from Wolfgang Rebner, whom she had remarried. "He wanted me to know that he dreamed of me often, even too often," she wrote in her memoir, "but that now it was so 'grievesome.'"

Faulkner also took Dean to watch the filming, and the Faulkners hosted a party for Claude Jarman Jr., who played Chick, and danced with Jill. Jarman remembered Faulkner as a "very quiet, quiet guy," smoking his pipe and observing. He "never talked to you until you talked to him first."[43]

Maud Falkner struck up a lasting friendship with Elizabeth Patterson, who bought one of Maud's paintings. Rotary, the Chamber of Commerce, and Mayor Bob Williams organized festivities, a special invited luncheon, and other events over two days honoring the filmmakers. Estelle hosted a party, organized by seventy-six-year-old Aunt Bama, wearing her customary large hat and beads, an imperial presence (she had the Falkner Roman nose) who selected the vintage wine and catered the fish fry.[44] Conspicuously absent from the party at Rowan Oak was Juano Hernandez. A highly respected stage actor, he had to stay with a local black undertaker. To invite Hernandez required the Faulkners to invite Hernandez's black hosts as well. The Faulkners had wanted to invite Hernandez, but Mayor Williams "begged Pappy not to do it for the sake of peace in the town," Dean said.[45] A furious Faulkner acquiesced. Neither Brown nor Faulkner dared to break the racial barriers the film and novel exposed. Hernandez, observing the conventions of a segregated society, said "nothing goes on in Oxford that doesn't go on in New York City. I didn't have to play at being Lucas Beauchamp. I've been him too many times. When I tried to buy a home in Hempstead, Long Island, I was mobbed and so was my family."[46]

On the square, on the film's opening night, three marching bands and three floats paraded through the streets, taxis threaded through traffic arriving with celebrities stepping out into the congested streets and into an Oxford lit up with MGM klieg lights. "I mean everybody really put on the dog!," Vicki Fielden remembered. "Grandmama made a dress for me with taffeta I'd brought back from Hong Kong."[47] Vicki and Dean wore hose for the first time.[48] More than five hundred Oxford residents had been used in the movie production. Eight hundred moviegoers now showed up to see the result. Ticket prices were $2.60, a hike from the usual sixty cents, and as a result the theater was not completely full, with some theatergoers waiting until the price dropped.[49]

Phil Stone attended the premiere. A few weeks earlier, Faulkner had inscribed a copy of the novel "To Phil from Bill," and Stone had dropped Faulkner a note, calling the book "a skillful job" but too tricky and too talky. Stone claimed the novel grew out of his suggestion that Faulkner write something for the slicks to make money.[50] Stone grumbled that he had to pay for his own tickets. Faulkner had been offered some but did not want to bother handing them out. Bess Condon, Stone's secretary, also expected tickets, but she didn't have enough "pull." She later said she should have talked to Bill and "reminded him that he owed me a big typing bill that he could pay off with two tickets." But she had doubted Bill and Estelle would attend the premiere. Going to the show would be too much for them: "They are both alcoholics and the least thing out of the ordinary is sufficient for them to make them take up a bottle, so that they can brace themselves for the occasion." She was amazed, she told her son, that the Faulkners had appeared and made it through the show.[51] Mayor Williams had a batch of tickets but did not want to play favorites and just gave them out on a first-come, first-served basis.

Faulkner seemed unmoved by the moment when the worlds of Hollywood and home coalesced. He was not happy about the fuss and about who would sit where and what they would do.[52] He was also still angry about the Hernandez incident.[53] On the day of the premiere, he remained in pajamas in his room. The women, all dressed up, could not budge him. Then Aunt Bama arrived and said to him, "We need an escort, Billy, and you're going to be it." He had once joked to a cousin, "she owns us."[54] He could not refuse, and in fact, as Vicki Fielden put it, "he got all gussied up, like a peacock strutting around, almost." The family drove over in two cars, and Faulkner made a grand entrance with the six women in his life: Estelle, Jill, Dean, Aunt Bama, his mother, and Vicki, as they entered what she called the "dingy, rat-ridden" Lyric Theater[55]—freshly painted, remodeled, and with a new screen.[56]

Faulkner rose to acknowledge audience applause. He bowed and then sat down. Dean remembered that the crowd kept applauding, forcing him to rise again: "I held my breath, hoping that he would say something, anything, so that people would keep looking at us in our new dresses." But he only nodded and sat down again. Watching the film, Dean and Vicki cheered Miss Habersham, who reminded them of Maud.[57]

Faulkner spoke briefly at a press conference, along with Brown and the cast. According to a newspaper account, he did not "primp for the occasion," showing up unshaven and wearing casual clothing, including a sport coat and a tee shirt. He answered some questions, said he liked the movie, but that his favorite was still Mickey Mouse. He took up writing when he got tired of hunting and fishing.[58]

In the *New York Times* (November 23, 1949), Bosley Crowther hailed *Intruder in the Dust* as "one of the great cinema dramas of our times." Other reviewers offered similar superlatives, although the film had its critics who suggested it did not present a coherent attack on racism. Memphis censors approved the film for exhibition but said it didn't "live up to Southern ideals" and that "No Southern Negro would act the way the one in the picture does."[59]

Walter White of the NAACP called the film "magnificent," noting it did not repeat Faulkner's argument against outside intervention or his "claptrap about distinctive Negro odor."[60] That odor, however, is, as Chick realizes, "an idea"—part of a mental process, not just a physical one.[61] Blacks in an integrated audience in Detroit laughed at the film, puzzling a white reporter, who was unable to determine why, except for a scene with Aleck Sander (Elzie Emmanuel), who came close to the stereotypical eye-rolling black man of Hollywood films.[62] Emmanuel had protested but was forced to play the scene.[63] Perhaps the very idea of a white boy and an old white lady working for, so to speak, an incarcerated black man amused them. Wasn't the humor, the very comicality of the plot, bred into the novel, as Eudora Welty contended? Novelist Ralph Ellison said it was the only film dealing with the race issue that could be exhibited in Harlem "without arousing unintentional laughter." His comments were generally in line with the positive comments in the black press.[64]

What Faulkner thought of the movie can be surmised from his short note to Sam Marx, the story editor who had supervised him at MGM. Referring to their "mild fiasco of twenty years ago," Faulkner said his conscience had troubled him at times. But the MGM production of *Intruder in the Dust* had allayed his qualms "some. I may still be on MGM's cuff, but at least I am not quite so far up the sleeve."[65]

None of the reviewers quite said it, but with *Intruder in the Dust,* novel and movie, Faulkner entered the mainstream of American culture. The novel sold fifteen thousand copies in the trade edition, better than any other title heretofore. The well-received movie, if not a huge hit and excoriated by some southern newspapers, remains the high point of films adapted from his work.

Two signs of his emerging popularity are apparent in Bernadine Kielty's review in the *Ladies' Home Journal* (October 1948) and in the paperback reprints of his work. Kielty compared Faulkner, "our foremost living novelist," to Balzac. Faulkner focused on a small southern town, but his canvas of human character rivaled the French author's and the "emotions run if anything deeper." Mississippi, a state whose economy bloomed with slavery, suffered a tragic downfall. Stories of mixed blood and miscegenation made for melodrama. If Kielty said nothing new, she nevertheless emphasized, for a broad audience, Faulkner's varied work, including stories where "people talk straight." Certain reviewers still deplored the violence and so-called sordid aspects of his work, as well as his convoluted style, but Kielty finessed those issues in prose that counseled a measure of patience and appreciation: "Sentences are sometimes two pages long with practically no punctuation. At first the unbroken vista of words seems insurmountable. But then as you read on, you get used to it, and in retrospect you see that the style serves its purpose." Absent is the usual querulous attack, the plaintive regrets about his faulty grammar, and his refusal to square himself with conventional storytelling. This was a new kind of tone in the mainstream press, portraying Faulkner without any special pleading, taking him on his own terms, and showing why he mattered.

Paperbacks—starting with the Avon Pocket Size edition of *Mosquitoes* (1941); the Armed Forces collection *A Rose for Emily And Other Stories* (1945), not much bigger in dimensions than a three-by-five index card; and then cheap Signet Book editions of *Sanctuary* (1947), *Intruder in the Dust* (1949), *The Wild Palms* (1950), and *Pylon* (1950)—put Faulkner in the hands of three million readers at approximately one hundred thousand outlets— newsstands and drugstores,[66] and wherever a shop, bus depot, and train station had a revolving rack of paperbacks. Readers could pick up a Faulkner novel and put it into their pockets and purses next to their favorite romance, mystery, or science fiction authors. They did not have to walk into the nine hundred bookstores to find him in hard cover, which is where critics like Malcolm Cowley went looking.

Cheap paperbacks, the province of pulp fiction, now also featured classic authors. Later Billy Wilder's *The Seven Year Itch* (1956) made fun of this paperback revolution that could even tout Freudian books as long as they had lurid, bodice-ripping cover illustrations. No matter. Faulkner could hardly be deemed abnormal where the ladies bought their cosmetics and the gentlemen their papers and cigarettes. If such unprestigious paperbacks stayed at the bottom of the pecking order in publishing, Faulkner's characters had long appreciated them, including Dr. Peabody's taste for "lurid, paper-covered nickel novels," and Miss Jenny's partiality for the tabloids. Joe Christmas reads pulp fiction "of the type whose covers bear either pictures of young women in underclothes or pictures of men in the act of shooting one another with pistols."[67] The Gathright-Reed Drugstore would have provided Faulkner with the expertise to assess paperbacks published as he scanned the racks for mysteries to read. One of his own stories, soon to be included in *Knight's Gambit,* had been published in *Ellery Queen's Mystery Magazine.* By May 1948, the Signet *Sanctuary* and *The Wild Palms* had sold close to a half million copies, earning Faulkner more than twelve thousand dollars.[68] Signet publisher Victor Weybright not only touted Faulkner titles, but he also defended the author when distributors complained about what they considered his sensationalistic fiction and treatments of race and sex.

Like Clarence Brown, and before him Howard Hawks, Signet's cover artist James Avati became an important mediating force that helped to sell Faulkner to a broader audience. The artist's first Faulkner cover not only dramatized the central dynamic of the novel—Lucas Beauchamp's word against a white mob—it also created an air of menace and anticipation: the black man is identified as such by his black head bent downward as he picks up his hat.[69] His back is to the crowd, which, by synecdoche, is reduced to seven representative figures (farmers and workmen) turned toward Lucas and one another as if to reinforce their common hostility against him, emphasized by the sheriff, who holds on to Lucas as he eyes the assemblage. All are wearing hats or caps—they retain their dignity even as Lucas has temporarily lost his. The scene, in its own way, is as effective as Brown's tracking shot of the mob's faces as they watch Lucas emerge from the sheriff's car, bending over to pick up his hat, which has fallen in the street. Both film and paperback cover create a man-against-the-crowd tension, abetted by placing the sheriff's car on the diagonal, between Lucas and the swarming white throng. Avati did not simply design four-color covers as promotional pieces. The artist's work served as commentary that led readers directly into the book.[70]

Pulping Faulkner brought him out of a literary isolation that neither Hollywood nor Random House had overcome, and provided him with a widespread impact on American sensitivities. Faulkner's decision to follow up *Intruder in the Dust,* which had brought in an unprecedented ten thousand dollars in royalties, with a collection of detective stories, *Knight's Gambit,* reveals a desire to capitalize on popular taste.

16

Coded Autobiography

Knight's Gambit,
November 1948–November 1949

FAULKNER THE FOREIGNER

Something went wrong with Phil Stone. He missed out. And it had happened to William Faulkner, too, although it would take the writing of a novella for Faulkner to figure it out. Stone never did. Faulkner's mentor had started out as the gentleman hero, the knight, whom William Faulkner followed around, listening to his stories the way Chick audited Uncle Gavin. Stone did make his contribution to the law, arguing important cases, but gradually, under mounting family debts, anxieties over a wife, Emily, who could not produce the fiction that would enlist Faulkner's favor, grief over a precocious son whose literary ambitions were never fully realized, and a changing South that embittered him, Stone ossified and became a crank—a fate that Gavin Stevens barely escapes himself. But Faulkner kept Stevens going. The code of the gentleman—so important in Faulkner's upbringing—confronted a modernizing world that Stone despised and Stevens sought to comprehend fitfully and with mixed results. Stevens became increasingly important to Faulkner not as an alter ego but as a worrisome proponent of the gentlemanly ideal. The author and his lawyer-character converged at several points and also diverged at others as Faulkner worked out his complicated view of where the world was headed.

In November 1948, Faulkner wrote to his editor, Saxe Commins, about a collection of stories in which Stevens "solves or prevents crime to protect the weak, right injustice, or punish evil."[1] Faulkner wanted to collect five Stevens published stories as well as a published novella. Working on *Knight's Gambit* meant putting off the edition of *Collected Stories,* well along in the planning stages, for a less distinguished volume. Faulkner called the novella the "story I seem to be hottest to write now." Like "An Odor of Verbena," which is a coda to the stories in *The Unvanquished,* the novella reflected on the earlier Stevens stories—"Smoke" (*Harper's,* April 1932), "Monk" (*Scribner's,* May 1937), "Hand upon the Waters" (*Saturday Evening Post,* November 4, 1939), "Tomorrow" (*Saturday Evening Post,* November 23, 1940), and "An Error in Chemistry" (*Ellery Queen's Mystery Magazine,* June 1946). They had seemed complete in themselves, and yet, on second thought, this work needed a denouement that brought together their history in a new way. In "Smoke," Stevens traps a murderer into revealing himself. In "Monk," he exonerates the falsely accused Monk, too retarded to mount his own defense against a murder charge, but Stevens is thwarted when Monk is again conned by another murderer into committing murder and this time is hung. In "Hand upon the Waters," Stevens proves that Lonnie Grinnup, seemingly the victim of an accident, has been murdered, a victim, actually, of his mental incapacity and the mendacity of others. In "Tomorrow," Stevens solves another murder case that involves his own past and a previous legal case. "An Error in Chemistry" exposes a murderer in disguise, impersonating the man he has killed. In "Knight's Gambit," Stevens foils a murder plot that, in the end, is inextricably linked to his own romantic past, which he is called upon to rectify. In all these cases, Stevens's deep immersion in his own community, his sensitivity to human character and circumstance, and his self-reflection account for his crime-solving success. But underlying these stories, especially the novella, is a concern with change in the lives of individuals and their community, and the responsibility Stevens feels to himself and to others.

In June 1949, just as Faulkner was completing work on *Knight's Gambit,* Stone, then president of the Mississippi bar, delivered a powerful address full of ideas promulgated by Gavin Stevens in *Intruder in the Dust.* Of course, for years Faulkner had heard Stone fulminate against the centralized state. Stone advocated a liberalism that took back responsibility for the public good in defiance of federalism: "we have indolently sprawled supine while money was wasted by our own people, and education languished, and roads were quagmires, and individual rights denied."[2] Stone called his community to account, asking it do better and to acknowledge its failings. What could one man do? Stevens did not say. Faulkner's answer: *Knight's Gambit.*

Not that Stevens would be presented as a paragon. "As I understand chess," Faulkner told Saxe, "the knight's gambit is an opening which involves the knight's pawn one or two squares forward in the first movement. It's an unorthodox opening."[3] It could even be called a reckless maneuver expressive of Stevens's eccentricity. What is a detective without quirks, who does not take risks, contravening conventions? Stevens as detective relies on his intellect and his understanding of human character, which he uses not so much to collect evidence as to generate it. He is more of a Platonist than an Aristotelian, often intuiting the nature of a crime and the identity of the criminal before assembling his case. Stevens, in short, is an a priori detective. The empirical proof comes later.

Stevens is also a throwback: "Mr. Stevens, you are what my grandpap would have called a gentleman," the governor tells him: "And you are trying to bring the notions of 1860 into the politics of the nineteen hundreds. And politics in the twentieth century is a sorry thing. In fact, I sometimes think that the whole twentieth century is a sorry thing, smelling to high heaven in somebody's nose." Faulkner's family had been steeped in politics. His great-grandfather had run for office, and others in the clan had been judges and public officials—don't forget the Butler side—so that Faulkner just absorbed it without having to make it a study or to dwell on its particulars. And then, too, the affiliation with the Stones and other important political families, like the Oldhams, gave Faulkner his fill.

Phil Stone held office too as head of the state bar association and staunchly stood by principles, honoring his father's debts and otherwise upholding the old order, as does Gavin Stevens. In "Hand upon the Waters," when Stevens identifies the man who murdered the retarded Lonnie Grinnup, the descendant of Louis Grenier, a founding father of Yoknapatawpha, the lawyer is doing more than solving a crime; he is honoring history: "Actually his [Lonnie's] hut and trotline and fish trap were in almost the exact center of the thousand and more acres his ancestors had once owned. But he never knew it." Grinnup had been found caught in his own fish trap—an accident, it had been supposed, until Stevens begins to inquire. Besides his natural curiosity, Stevens's interest is aroused *because* he knows about Grinnup's ancestry—a heritage that is fast becoming not even a memory. Like Stone, Stevens is a kind of community historian whose knowledge is an inheritance no longer valued but which Stevens insists on living by.

It is as if Faulkner decided that with an intricate novel like *Absalom, Absalom!* behind him, and with a larger audience now available, he could introduce the layering of history and why it was important in the guise of a more accessible genre: the detective story. When Stevens looks at the present, he sees the past: "Louis Grenier, whose dead face Stevens was driving eight miles in the heat of a July afternoon to look at, had never even known he was Louis Grenier." When Stevens first examines the murder scene, he thinks: *And it's not right.... It don't add. Something more that I missed, didn't see. Or something that hasn't happened yet.*" What makes him think so is a Faulknerian aware-ness of time—that what has happened, the crime, continues to reverberate and will only be solved by looking forward, in this instance, to those in prox-imity to the murder scene and concocting, in his mind, like Poe's Dupin, the criminals' movements and motivations, by looking backward.

The formulaic stories in *Knight's Gambit* all contain within them convolu-tions of plot and interpretation familiar to Faulkner readers, but they cannot compete with the sinuosity of the concluding novella, which recasts virtually every aspect of Faulkner's life and work from his experience in World War I, to his separation from Estelle, to the sojourn in Hollywood, to his frustra-tions over his failure to serve in World War II. It is all *there* and *not there*—like the reflection of Faulkner looking at Clarence Brown in the window, like the wistful letter to Meta grieving over their lost love. Something about the making of *Intruder in the Dust* inspired and unnerved William Faulkner. He could not utter that something in so many words, except through the figure of Gavin Stevens. The character is not Faulkner's spokesman but, like Phil Stone, Faulkner's aristarch.

By the late 1940s, Malcolm Cowley, Carvel Collins, Glenn O. Carey, and many others wrote and came to call on Phil Stone as the man best equipped to explain, as Stone himself had done in the *Saturday Review of Literature* (Sep-tember 1942), "William Faulkner and His Neighbors." Stone came closest to the voice of a community that had, by turns, fostered and forsaken William Faulkner. Approaching Stone involved listening to a man as circumloqua-cious as Gavin Stevens, who made of the elusive Faulkner a mystery requir-ing considerable elucidation. Stone told Carey that if Faulkner "answered all the letters he receives and all of the people who want to see him, he would never have time to do anything else and would have to employ about two secretaries. As it is, my relationship with him causes me to have a great deal of my time taken up by people who can't get in touch with him." Stone went on to summarize Faulkner's April 1918 trip to Yale, the periods in Toronto, New Orleans (referring Carey to *Double Dealer* editor John McClure), the trip to Europe, the Ole Miss experience and the post office, and a few com-ments on Faulkner's abortive education. "You have probably surmised this by such things as appear all through his work, especially . . . in KNIGHT'S GAMBIT." What biography Stone imparted to Carey had to be written with-out acknowledging Stone. Discreet about his indiscretions, Stone, like Ste-vens, liked to work under cover. He would, though, from time to time, engage Faulkner on Collins's behalf, even as he reiterated: "What I mean is that you can use anything I have told you without quoting me as authority. Of course I shall not leave you out on a limb: if anyone should challenge your facts I shall write you a letter backing you up." Stone was referring to a *Life* magazine profile that Collins had been encouraged to write. When Faulkner issued his veto, Collins backed off, even while continuing his collaboration with Stone.

Stone enjoyed his authoritative role, welcoming the opportunity to critique Carey's thesis on Faulkner as Stone had done earlier with Louis Cochran's profile. Much of what Faulkner knew about the Civil War came from Stone, the lawyer assured Carey. Others in Oxford who claimed to know Faulkner were late arrivals and not present at the creation: "You must beware of these people, especially people in the English Department of the University of Mississippi here, who tend to romanticize Faulkner. . . . [T]hey just don't know what they are talking about." Stone wanted Carvel Collins to filter all biographical material through him, "so I can check it for you." Stone commandeered the field, so to speak, in a very Gavin Stevens–like way.

As to Faulkner's work, Stone took no credit, except for the humor. "At the beginning he was a very humorless person," Stone told Carey. But those early days had not fulfilled their promise. As to Collins's enthusiasm for *Absalom, Absalom!,* Stone said: "You are a better man than I am. The neglect of great possibilities annoyed me so that I could not finish reading the manuscript." Stone, like Stevens, was hard to pin down: "For God's sake don't always take my suggestions at face value," he told Collins. "My tragedy seems to be that people either ignore my suggestions completely or take a casual suggestion as gospel. Almost never do they take the middle ground." In the aftermath of *Knight's Gambit* Stone could still say, "I am fonder of Bill than I am of anybody in the world," so that any effort on Stone's part to capitalize on their friendship would be a very "saddening shock to Bill, even more than he realizes, because I think that, of all the people in the world that he knows, he has a profound faith in my integrity and in my personal loyalty to him. If I should destroy this (although maybe I am now being vain) I don't know just how severe a shock it would be to him."[4]

Gavin Stevens in "Knight's Gambit" is the pillar of integrity that Stone still strained to embody, the authority Faulkner would call on to discuss a point of law. In Yoknapatawpha, that Stone is transmogrified into a cynosure, a figure whose own biography—and Faulkner's—becomes the fulfillment of what is missing in the preceding detective stories. Gavin Stevens is actually at his chessboard, playing with his nephew Chick just as Faulkner played with his stepson Malcolm. All along, playing the game is meant to emphasize, on the one hand, Stevens's adept moves as detective, and yet, on the other hand, his rejection of reality for the more abstract pleasure of chess. The Harrisses, brother and sister, come knocking at his door. Their last name sounds like a form of harassment, which, in effect, it is. Stone will confront, as in chess, a move that will result in recognizing a loss even as he also achieves a gain. They live in "a once-simple country house transmogrified now into something a little smaller than a Before-the-War Hollywood set." It is a curious way to identify them as coming from wealth, in an establishment that has obliterated the past even as that past will be called up in the story. The brother is attached to his sister—as attached, it seems, as Quentin is to Caddy—and yet he manhandles her in a way no gentleman could abide: "the boy held his sister, not by the arm or elbow, but by the forearm above the wrist like in the old lithographs of the policeman with his cringing captive or the victory-flushed soldier with his shrinking Sabine prey." What they want is a mystery to Chick, but his Uncle Gavin, Chick realizes in retrospect, "knew already more than the boy or the girl either intended to say yet; perhaps, even then, all of it. But it would be a little while yet before he would realise that last. And the reason he was so slow about it was his uncle himself." In short, the story is not so much their own as it is Gavin Stevens's to divulge. At first what the boy wants is the law (Stevens) to stop Captain Gualdres, a foreigner, an Argentinian, "a fortune-hunting Spick," from marrying their mother instead of honoring his engagement to her daughter, who admits to Stevens that she loves Gualdres. When Stevens does nothing, the boy tells him he has been "warned." Chick is astonished at his uncle's immobility, a man in constant physical or mental motion, who in this case just turns his attention back to the chessboard. Yet to Chick the incident is like part of a "slick magazine serial, even to the foreign fortune-hunter." The world of movies and the pulps—one part of Faulkner's world—intrudes upon a Gavin Stevens whose unreal talk is described as listening to literature, to what Stone talked to Faulkner, when, like Stevens, he was the aesthete, not the lawyer who was real and "walked and breathed and displaced air."

The county (Yoknapatawpha) watches what happens next, like it watches in "A Rose for Emily," or in *Absalom, Absalom!* Events "unfold as the subscribers read and wait and watch for the serial's next installment," the appearance of the "stranger . . . without warning out of nowhere," marrying the woman who will become the mother of the son and daughter who accost Stevens. The nebulous father, like Charles Bon, "had no past, no yesterday; protagonist of a young girl's ephemeris: a shade, a shadow." He is the other, the foreigner, whom Captain Gualdres now personifies.

How all this relates to Stevens is the point, although no one, other than Stevens, can say—and he isn't talking. Only in retrospect, after "Knight's Gambit" concludes, can it be made out that the "shadow," the Harriss who marries the children's mother, is, in effect, Stevens's shadow, the suitor (Stevens) no one knew about because Stevens had departed for Europe in 1918 without having become engaged, as Faulkner himself had departed when his shadow, Cornell Franklin, married Estelle and fathered a boy and a girl with her. All of the Gavin Stevens mysteries are coded affairs that only he can decipher, and the same can be said of William Faulkner's. Gavin Stevens, the story relates, earns his Ph.D. in Heidelberg, whereas William Faulkner earned quite another education in Europe, but still one that took him, like Stone and Stevens, back home. When Stone mentioned *Knight's Gambit* in his letter to Glenn O. Carey, he was dropping another clue, expecting the neophyte student to summon his own surmises.

To the community's "spinster aunts," the Harriss husband (never given a full name) and his bride (not named until the end of the novella) became a melodrama: "watched . . . as you watch the unfolding story in the magazine installments." The to-and-fro—so much the pattern of Faulkner's own life—is replicated in the Harriss serial: "Then it—the victoria—was seen occasionally in the Square for another month with just the bride in it before the town found out that the husband was gone, back to New Orleans, to his business: which was the first anybody knew that he had a business and where it was. But even then, and for the next five years too, they wouldn't know what it was." The carriage is a sign of the exclusivity of wealth, since it seats two, with an elevated driver's seat in front. The elegance is achieved, it is later learned, through bootlegging, an illicit occupation that Faulkner claimed to have practiced in New Orleans, giving a raffish air to his reputation and career evidently sustained by unlicensed behavior.

What is at stake in the story is the changing identity of a community, which Stevens monitors and which Faulkner observed every time he returned from his stays in Hollywood and every time he thought about his own childhood and how technological progress had altered a way of life. The turn into the twentieth century is announced when Harriss's " big business" results in his return home from New Orleans "in the biggest and shiniest car that had ever stayed overnight within the county's boundaries, with a strange Negro in a uniform who did nothing but drive and wash and polish it." And then in the mechanization of daily life in the "electric lights and running water in the house, and the day-long night-long thump and hum of the pump and dynamo were the mechanical sounds where there used to be the creak of the hand-turned well-pulley and of the ice-cream freezer on Sunday." The past that remains only in traces of itself is precisely what Stevens has yet to confront in his own biography, kept hidden from Chick and everyone else. Stevens's history, at this point, seems almost obliterated, a palimpsest of the past: "now there was nothing left of the old man who had sat on the front gallery with his weak toddy and Ovid and Horace and Catullus for almost fifty years, except his home-made hickory rocking chair and the finger-prints on the calf bind-ings of his books and the silver goblet he drank from, and the old setter bitch which had dozed at his feet." Stevens is not that old man, and yet he spends his evenings translating the Bible into Greek.

The progress that seems to vitiate the past, however, cannot prevail against history, which is to say that what seemed like progress is actually retrograde. When the mysterious Mr. Harriss disappears, leaving his wife behind, their home becomes a "mausoleum of electric wires and water pipes and automatic cooking and washing machines and synthetic pictures and furniture." Then he reappears, as in a melodrama, with a difference: "in an aeroplane; they said it was the same aeroplane which ran the whiskey up from the Gulf to New Orleans." He rebuilds his house so that "it looked like the Southern mansion in the moving picture, only about five times as big and ten times as South-ern." The grandiosity—so Sutpen-like—is also just another makeover that occludes but cannot annihilate the past that Stevens and his community have yet to account for.

Most outlandish of all is the Harriss polo field and steeplechasing grounds, which will become the plaything of Captain Gualdres, although he does not appear on the scene until after the Harrisses do their European tour, and the widowed Mrs. Harriss returns home, looking no different from her former country self, even though she is thirty-five, "constant against all change and alteration," except for the addition of her two children and the Argentine cavalry captain, who now is the new stranger, the new foreigner, whose moti-vations are suspect. He is the "dark romantic knight" opposed by the Harriss boy, the ineffectual "young earl," a Quentin Compson figure who plots the knight's death by purchasing a wild horse said to have killed a man and sta-bling him where the knight trains his own horse at night. What troubles the "young earl" is Gualdres's capability. He is better at everything, the image of the equestrian gentleman that the Harriss boy cannot rival. Gualdres is the foreign body the community would like to expel, which is perhaps why Rafe McCallum sells the murderous horse to the Harriss boy.

Captain Gualdres is the heroic figure that Stevens, Chick (who is in ROTC during the war), and the boy Harriss cannot become, and Gualdres understands, saying he knows that Stevens does not like him. Gualdres is the cynosure—what Mrs. Harriss, her daughter, and all those male competitors want. He is the dashing figure that William Faulkner could not cut—his uni-form notwithstanding. Gualdres represents the "heart's thirst for glory and renown." Imagine Phil Stone reading sixteen-year-old Chick's words to an RAF recruiter: "If I could get to England some way, they would take me, wouldn't they?" Stone made a point of telling Carey that Faulkner never got off the ground in Canada. Gualdres soars on his horses; he does not fall off as Faulkner did in trial after trial.

Stevens, having missed out on his suit to Mrs. Harriss, having missed out on the war, is at last compelled to confess to Chick: "A knight comes suddenly out of nowhere—out of the west, if you like—and checks the queen and the castle all in that same one move. What do you do?" They are talking about chess but also about Stevens's own experience, which Stevens, like Stone, was most reluctant to fully disclose. Chick says: "You save the queen and let the castle go." Chick suddenly understands the contest is not just between Gualdres and the Harriss boy but between Stevens and Gualdres, whom Stevens has warned about the wild horse. What is at stake is the daughter of the mother Stevens had not won in marriage. "It was that girl. The Harriss girl. You bet him the girl. That he didn't want to cross that lot and open that stable door. And he lost," Chick concludes. "Lost?" Stevens asks. Chick explains: "A princess and half a castle, against some of his bones and maybe his brains too?" Still puzzled, Stevens asks, "Lost?" Chick repeats, "He lost the queen." "The queen?," Stevens asks. "What queen? Oh, you mean Mrs Harriss. Maybe he realised that queen had been moved the same instant he realised he would have to call the bet. Maybe he realised that queen and the castle both had been gone ever since the moment he disarmed the prince with that hearth-broom. If he ever wanted her." The prince disabled with the hearth broom is the boy Harris, who had tried to attack Gualdres while they were fencing. Stevens's apparent puzzlement during the exchange with Chick is surprising for such an agile disputant, detective, and chess player. Is he, as mentor, purposefully allowing Chick to work out the truth, or is he stalling for time to make his confession? Either way, the result is revelation—the kind that Faulkner himself backed away from and that Stone alternately advanced and reneged on when Faulkner followers came calling.

The story, set around Pearl Harbor Day, fuses Stevens and Chick together as they confront past and present, going backward and going forward. As they travel backward on an old, unpaved country road, Stevens asks Chick, who is driving slowly, "Are you afraid of motion?" They are driving out to Mrs. Harriss's house. It is a journey, as well, into the past, the horses and mules and the "creak of harness," and also, in the spring of 1919, "the end of a four-year tunnel of blood and excrement," as Stevens thinks of a generation's sacrifice and their courage and faith. He is going to see the Mrs. Harriss, his childhood sweetheart, whom he had failed to win at thirty, leaving her behind when he went to Europe, fell in love with another woman, and then ruined his chances with both of them by mixing up the envelopes and letters so that each woman received the other's mail. In Europe, Stevens had felt estranged from home, he tells Chick: "You must bear in mind my age. I was a European then. I was in that menopause of every sensitive American when he believes that what (if any) future Americans' claim not even to human spirit but to simple civilization has, lies in Europe." Returning to Mrs. Hariss, he announces on December 7, 1941: "I'm Gavin Stevens and now I'm almost fifty." This time he goes through with his proposal and marries. Gualdres, the foreigner, has married the daughter, and the son, like Chick, goes off to war, as Benbow Sartoris and Gualdres do, the latter enlisting with American forces. Chick rehearses all the ironies involved in this war effort, this commingling of such different motivations and personalities and nationalities:

> One night an American acquaintance tried to kill him with a horse. The next day he married the American's sister. The day after that a Jap dropped a bomb on another American on a little island two thousand miles away. So on the third day he enlisted, not into his own army in which he already held a reserve commission, but into the foreign one, renouncing not only his commission to do so but his citizenship too, using an interpreter without doubt to explain both to his bride and to his adopted government what he was trying to do.

Chick knows all this because Gualdres has come to tell him so and to say that he hopes Stevens is satisfied. What that satisfaction means is never explained, although in terms of the novella itself, Gualdres has reversed Stevens's claim to have once been a European. Gualdres, apparently no longer wishing to be a foreigner, accepts by marriage what Stevens had rejected twenty years earlier—that is, returning home to claim his other identity.

The Second World War that seemed like a palimpsest of the First, the inroads of progress, the picture shows that intruded into Oxford, the time spent away from home, the returns, the lost and recovered sweetheart, the heroic role that his nephew Jimmy, Faulkner's Chick, now assumed as an aviator, a feat that Faulkner had wanted for himself—all get spread across "Knight's Gambit" in the coded autobiography that perhaps only Phil Stone was prepared to understand and to keep secret until another Chick came along. On his copy of *Knight's Gambit*, Stone noted, on the concluding page of the novella: "A damned good job, Bill. Far and away the best thing in the book."[5]

"TALES OF CRIME, GUILT, AND LOVE"

In the *Milwaukee Journal* (November 6, 1949), Christopher Matthew made the inevitable comparison between Sherlock Holmes and Watson and Stevens and Chick, with the usual description of Faulkner dealing in "substandard folks" and "animalistic bayou billies, naive and ferocious by turns."[6] Donald Heritage (*Newark [NJ] Sunday Star-Ledger,* December 4) sounded the common note: "If this is not Faulkner's best work, it still is Faulkner and even not-so-good Faulkner is so very much better than the best of many another."

Lawrance Thompson (*Louisville Courier Journal,* December 11) asked: "Has Faulkner just turned a corner, in his career as storyteller? . . . Is the mellowing Gavin Stevens the tip-off, with his utopian sermonizings at the end of *Intruder in the Dust,* and with his symbolically hopeful surrender to love, in 'Knight's Gambit'? If so, those of us who are his cautious admirers must brace ourselves." Two decades earlier Horace Benbow had tried to make things right and been held back, a futile handservant to Belle Mitchell, a belabored brother to his sister Narcissa, and a lawyer who could not manage his own community.[7] *That* was the kind of character associated with Faulkner: an alienated native returnee from World War I. The ascetic Stevens constantly holds on to his cob pipe, as if to get a grip on himself and his emotions, employing a soothing tool that Faulkner carried with him everywhere, perhaps feeling a little lost when he mislaid it. His letters include drawings of pipes, queries about what happened to them, reflecting the importance of a prop that gave him something to do in uncomfortable exchanges with others or a topic of conversation with those who shared his habit. Stevens comes into his own in "Knight's Gambit," no longer making do with tobacco and chessboards and finally making good on his romantic promise twenty years after World War I. His marriage makes him a fully engaged member of his community. His detective work in story after story has had a therapeutic impact by isolating the "cause of communal disease and instability" and restoring the "body politic."[8] His last task in "Knight's Gambit" is to restore his own well-being.

But Ruth Chaplin in the *Christian Science Monitor* (December 8) detected the trouble with Gavin Stevens that most reviewers had not noticed: "For the benevolent paternalism which Gavin embodies in such a fresh and attractive form is, as surely Faulkner knows, a familiar serpent in the southern Eden, with a long history of luring men to surrender individual responsibility for a partial good—which almost inevitably degenerates into a consuming evil." *That* Gavin Stevens would soon make his appearance in *Requiem for a Nun* as a character who moves from representing a community's standard of morality to one who dictates it through his pontifications. Faulkner, too, would begin to have his say outside the margins of Yoknapatawpha, and beyond his remit, certain critics would begin to grumble.

When the first reviews of *Knight's Gambit* began to appear, Faulkner had been hunting and sailing his new boat, named the *Ring Dove*. Sixteen-year-old Jill and two neighbor boys served as crew. She didn't relish roughing it, but her father ignored her complaints. He had been out in a "dozen different weathers" and seemed to welcome these adventures. Nevertheless, he confessed to the kind of boredom that often presaged work on a new book, or his yearning for a new woman.[9]

17

Acclaim and Fame and Love

1950–1955

"The First Great American Writer"

On August 21, 1950, Random House published forty-two stories divided into six sections: "The Country," "The Village," "The Wilderness," "The Wasteland," "The Middle Ground," and "Beyond." This retrospective, in the planning stages since 1948, did not select simply the best stories or present a chronological order but featured, instead, the Balzacian range of Faulkner's work in all of its pastoral, provincial, modern, and even supernatural forms. He designed the book to be "an entity of its own, single, set for one pitch, contrapuntal in integration, toward one end, one finale"—which, in this case, was "Carcassonne," his credo as an artist: "I want to perform something bold and tragic and austere. . . . Me on a buckskin pony with eyes like blue electricity and mane like tangled fire, galloping up the hill and right off into the high heaven of the world."

Although urged to write a foreword, Faulkner resisted, perhaps not wanting to spoil his composition with commentary.[1] Even though he judged certain stories like "Shall Not Perish" as "not too good,"[2] he realized that for the sake of his writing about his homeland and war, the story belonged in the first section of *Collected Stories*. Nor did it bother him that some of his earliest uneven work appeared in the last section, since part of his mission included, as the section's title intimated, transcending his own time and place. "It's all right," he wrote to Saxe Commins, "the stuff stands up amazingly well after a few years, 10 or 20."[3] Why so amazed? Forty-two of the forty-six stories had appeared in magazines, beginning in 1930, and

Faulkner, often writing for the market, had not, perhaps, valued the work as highly as it deserved.

On August 20, on the front page of the *New York Times Book Review*, Harry Sylvester proclaimed that "for the reader not yet lost from the world of literature, Faulkner can be a deep and continuous source of wisdom. For this kind of reader Faulkner reveals the laws of existence and the conditions of survival—and how people behave under them." Unlike previous books, *Collected Stories* received no negative reviews and won the National Book Award in March 1951.[4] For the first time, the Book of the Month Club had made a Faulkner book an alternate selection, bringing to him "a brand-new layer of U.S. readers," *Time* (August 28) noted: "The stories are also pretty sure to bring a spate of re-estimates by the critics themselves." The anonymous *Time* reviewer concluded that the collection "has the excitement that comes from never knowing when, amidst pages of failure, there will come a masterpiece." Edward Parone (*Hartford Courant,* September 3, 1950) said Faulkner's difficulty, his unruliness, was "part of his genius, part of his originality, this illusion of order rising out of chaos right before your eyes. It gives him a bardic quality. And these things, together with his subjects, his conception and his accomplishment make him the first great American writer." Parone concluded: "There are no extrinsic trappings, no introduction, only intelligent grouping which ends the book wisely with the voluptuous death dream 'Carcassonne.'"

Horace Gregory (*New York Herald Tribune,* August 20) extolled the volume's "Elizabethan richness . . . [i]ts humors, its ironies, its ancient tempers, its latest fashions, its masks of horror, its violence, its comedy, its pathos." This was the book's purpose, so that it was "gratuitous to say that the stories are uneven in depth, quality and interest." Although the critic could not resist pointing out that the Mississippi material remained the strongest, he emphasized that the "idea of honor, however thinly worn, however gray it may appear, floats behind the panorama of Faulkner's writings: his people, rich or poor, red-skinned, or black or white, carry that idea as though it were an unnamed element of blood within their veins." Gregory did not use the word "nobility," but it is the term that applies to so many of his characters, whatever their failings or crimes.

In a widely syndicated review, Hodding Carter (*Delta Democrat-Times,* Greenville, SC, August 27) read the stories set in the 1920s and 1930s from the perspective of *Intruder in the Dust,* remarking on how much the South and Faulkner had changed, as reflected in stories like "Dry September" that did not yield the hope that the later novel projected. Unlike most reviewers, Carter did not view Faulkner's Mississippi, or his South, as all of a piece untouched by time. Neither did Faulkner, as evidenced in the contrasting sections "The Country" and "The Village," the former featuring later World War II fiction that provides a positive contrast to earlier, bleaker, post–World War I stories.[5] The Hollywood work during World War II forced upon Faulkner, or at the very least accelerated, a desire to sync the South into the national psyche.

Given the exigencies of reviewing, it is not surprising that the volume's structure, and the interaction between the stories, received little attention.[6] Most treated the collection as a menu from which they savored the choicest items and shunned others. They did not appreciate *Collected Stories* as the embodiment of a career that had always juxtaposed "tales of his apocryphal county with stories set elsewhere." The volume was his microcosm, which was also a microcosm of "existence itself."[7] *Collected Stories* can also be regarded as a counterpoint to *The Portable Faulkner*, which concentrated exclusively on Yoknapatawpha. In his imagination, Faulkner seemed to suggest, the world beyond the one he had mapped was also his concern, and, in fact, in the section "Beyond" he seems to be leading the reader right out of any confining sense of the Faulkner canon. This urge to extrapolate beyond the borders of Yoknapatawpha had been building as he continued to work on *A Fable,* his book on the fate of civilization, his *War and Peace.*

Collected Stories is perhaps Faulkner's bravest book, in which he encountered his failures at a time when he knew about the possibility of a Nobel. Throughout his career even his greatest novels had been called uneven, and critics had deplored his lapses. Yet he created an omnibus not to please the prize givers but to ponder his own achievement, declaring, once again, his independence. "Been hearing rumors for about three years, have been a little fearful," he reported on February 22, 1950. "It's not the sort of thing to decline; a gratuitous insult to do so but I dont want it. I had rather be in the same pigeon hole with Dreiser and Sherwood Anderson, than with Sinclair Lewis and Mrs. Chinahand Buck."[8] To Meta, he said the prize was an "affront to literature."[9] If he sometimes bemoaned the neglect of his work, he was also proud to stand alone, not wishing to be part of any group of writers that would put him in another Ward—no matter how gilded. *Collected Stories,* a transgressive work, crosses all sorts of boundaries, as its six sections show.

THE NOBEL

In March 1946, the Swedish journalist Thorsten Jonsson, author of *Sex amerikaner: Hemingway, Faulkner, Steinbeck, Caldwell, Farrell, Saroyan* (1942), had visited Rowan Oak and predicted, "Someday you will receive the Nobel Prize." Others made similar predictions, and by early November 1950, newspapers began to feature Faulkner as a leading contender. He told a friend he thought he was "being considered for something because he was being looked over the way the University of Mississippi looks over people who are prospective football players."[10] Yet when the call came, on November 10, 1950, he admitted to Mac Reed, "I can't believe it."[11] Already fending off Malcolm Cowley and Carvel Collins, who wanted to do personal profiles, Faulkner told the Swedish journalist who had called him announcing the prize that he would not receive the award in person: "I hold that the award was made, not to me, but to my works—crown to thirty years of the agony and sweat of a human spirit, to make something that was not here before me, to lift up or maybe comfort or anyway at least entertain, in its turn, man's heart." Divesting himself of the award also meant contributing the thirty-thousand-dollar award to scholarships for black students and to various charities.

But the world and his family went to work on William Faulkner. The Swedish ambassador asked him to reconsider. Estelle was quoted as saying: "I'm glad Bill is getting recognition while he is still alive. I've always known that he is a great writer, and I am glad the world is recognizing it."[12] She wondered why Bill would deprive Jill of such an important opportunity to see the world. He went hunting. In camp, they had "a coon collard supper to celebrate the Nobel Prize. We was proud that William won that. He was just old William Faulkner," John Cullen said.[13] Ike Roberts, president of the hunt, was there to join the party for "old Bill. I hunted with his daddy." You could not have a better friend, Ike said, although he added, "Bill is a peculiar boy." Ike told Bill "the boys" had supposed that winning that prize money meant he would not join them that year. "There's no deer meat in that money, is there?," Faulkner replied. An enterprising reporter from the *Deer Creek Pilot* tried to interview a reticent Faulkner during the hunt. Asked which of his books was his favorite, Faulkner replied, "I'd have to say that was *Lanterns on the Levee*." Too late, as the paper went to press, the reporter realized the book had been written by William Alexander Percy, not exactly one of Faulkner's favorites.[14]

Phil Stone joined the circle around Faulkner, reminding him of what he owed to Jill. For all his latter-day carping about Faulkner, Stone provided a public tribute that turned his friend into a Christ-like figure, a symbol of decency, honor, and loyalty: "If you are his friend and if the mob should choose to crucify you, Bill would be there without summons. He would carry your cross up the hill for you."[15] But Stone could not resist hectoring: "Now, Bill, you do right." Faulkner replied that he was sick and tired of everyone from the Swedish ambassador to his "Negro houseboy" telling him to do right. But he did, taking Stone's advice to write a short speech. "I never heard a bad short speech in my life," Phil told Bill. After several drafts Faulkner produced 550 words. Later Stone deemed the Nobel Prize address "the best damn thing Bill ever wrote."[16] Charles Nelson Sr., principal of Oxford's University High School, noted that beginning with the filming of *Intruder in the Dust* and now the Nobel Prize, the town's attitude toward Faulkner began to change in his favor.[17]

On November 27, Faulkner wired the Swedish ambassador: "RETURNED HUNTING TRIP TODAY. RECEIVED YOUR LETTER NOV 21ST. WILL BE PLEASED TO JOURNEY TO STOCKHOLM. APPRECIATE VERY MUCH YOUR UNDERSTANDING." The hunting party, however, had led to more drinking and the grippe. Phil Stone, called in to help, described the effort to sober up the prize winner as "quite a saga . . . like one of his Snopes tales."[18] Yet Faulkner managed, along with Jill, the trip to New York on December 6. On his departure from Oxford, he was quoted as saying he had a "monkey suit and a plug hat" awaiting him.[19] Random House supplied a tuxedo with tails for the Nobel ceremony. Faulkner asked Bennett Cerf if he could keep the ensemble. The publisher wanted to know what Bill would do with it: "Well, I might stuff it. And charge people to come and look at it in the parlor. Or . . . I might rent it out."[20] He did not say that he liked to dress up. And, after all, he was going to meet a king. He couldn't wear, he said, the suit he had on hand for funerals. "Three cheers for Faulkner," an editorial proclaimed in the *Southern Illinoisan*. "Three cheers for all men who recognize the sartorial requirements for certain occasions and conform." This "nonconformist in social use and custom," the paper speculated, "may have liked the feel of formal attire."[21]

The Faulkners flew to Stockholm on December 8. At the airport, Faulkner said: "This is the top. After that, there is nothing for a writer to live for, to wait for any longer. I am proud and flattered."[22] On December 10, William Faulkner delivered his address. Few members could hear the soft-voiced writer, but his dignified presence impressed the press. "We had a wonderful time in Stockholm," Jill wrote to Aunt Bama; "Pappy looked so very nice at the presentation ceremony and I was so proud of him and all the ambassadors said what a fine stroke he had made for America in Sweden."[23] Faulkner did draw the line, though, when it came to eating reindeer meat, telling a friend that eating it would be "a little like eating Santa Claus."[24]

For all his qualms, Faulkner took on the role of a diplomat, writing to the Swedish ambassador: "I hope that it was within my power, and that mine and my daughter's conduct was such, to leave as high an opinion of America in Sweden as the regard and respect for Sweden which we brought away." Such words, of course, can be regarded as a formality, but they also came to play an important role in Faulkner's own sense of himself and his connection to the world. When Meta heard about the Nobel, she realized she could never again be on the same intimate terms with her lover. Orin Borsten said to her, "It's as though history had claimed him, instead of a woman." Meta agreed: "There was also some subconscious preknowledge that Bill was destined for great things."[25]

Faulkner did not regret his trip, admitting to Robert Haas that "it was the only thing to do; you can commit a mistake and only feel regret, but when you commit bad taste, what you feel is shame. Anyway, I went, and did the best I knew to behave like a Swedish gentleman, and leave the best taste possible on the Swedish palate for Americans and Random House."[26] The code of the gentleman prevailed in a man who wanted to believe he was raised right. Aunt Bama concurred, reporting to her nephew Vance Broach: "At air port so many recognized him & came up to say 'Isnt this Mr Wm Faulkner' & he would smile graciously & say 'Yes.'"[27]

A part of the gentleman's obligation was the Nobel address. Taken as his writer's testament, it was also his coming out as a world citizen on a stage he had not sought but that now had found him. He confronted his responsibility head-on, addressing the "universal fear" in an atomic age: "When will I be blown up." Not we, for as in the Pine Manor Junior College address, he spoke to individuals, to writers, in this case, who must learn again the "problems of the human heart in conflict with itself." Only the "old universal truths" counted: "love and honor and pity and pride and compassion and sacrifice." These words about human persistence can be found in his letters as well as in his "Battle Cry" screenplay and appeared in his speech as he evoked an image right out of *Absalom, Absalom!*, saying that after "the last ding-dong of doom has clanged and faded from the last worthless rock hanging tideless in the last red and dying evening, that even then there will still be one more sound: that of his puny inexhaustible voice, still talking." Was he thinking of the French architect, cornered by Sutpen and seemingly defeated, who goes on talking, and with a gesture that seems to fling away the failure of his own puny resistance, overcoming his own defeat? Such moments, to be sure, are sporadic in Faulkner's early fiction, but their latency emerges in the Nobel address. When Faulkner spoke of lifting man's heart, did he have in mind Joe Christmas's last tormented moments, which nevertheless, like Christ's, are a kind of triumph, ennobling him even as Percy Grimm cuts away at his manhood? And did Faulkner think of his own beginnings when he chose the word "poet," not "writer" or "novelist," when he concluded: "The poet's voice need not merely be the record of man, it can be one of the props, the pillars to help him endure and prevail"? Faulkner summed up his own opinion of the address a month later: "The piece was what I believe and wanted to say, though I might have said it better with more time to compose it. But then, maybe not; I might have lost the thread in trying to make literature out of it."[28]

Syndicated columnist Dorothy Thompson noted the "many voices perpetually talking gobbledegook at the top of their corporate lungs that the still small voices of truth are drowned out. . . . Mr. Faulkner had something to say. Put that on the air.[29] Newspapers across the country repeated his belief that nuclear war would not annihilate the human race and his portrayal of man still talking after the last "ding-dong of doom." The man who said he only wrote stories, that he was not a "literary man," not a sociologist, the one who called himself a farmer, now commented on nothing less than the fate of civilization. He was taking a great risk, opening himself up to public scrutiny in a way his novels alone, or even the Nobel Prize, did not invite.[30] As a result, he alternately exerted his new authority—the perfect right of a gentleman—and retreated from his newfound fame.

One reporter noted his shy, embarrassed manner, his soft and patient voice, as he sat stiffly in his high-ceilinged living room at Rowan Oak. He seemed actually in pain, saying, "My soul is not my own until this mess is over." Pressed to comment on a student editorial in the Ole Miss newspaper advocating the admission of black students to the graduate school, Faulkner replied, "I think that young man stated something that sooner or later his papa will have to accept." He supposed the older generation would have to die out before the changes that would surely come.[31]

Press reaction to the award varied—from "William Faulkner is the father of the outhouse school of American literature and he has consistently defamed the south as inhabited principally by decadents, degenerates, perverts, and all other malodorous types"[32] to "a serious artist of force and penetration."[33] Syndicated columnist Ralph McGill seconded the award citation for Faulkner's "forceful and independent artistic contribution to modern American fiction." He noted that Faulkner had not, like Hemingway, promoted himself as a legend. The Nobel Prize winner had simply done his work—at home and in Hollywood—to the best of his ability. "Faulkner's triumph is one we can all share."[34] Faulkner wasn't so sure: "I fear some of my fellow Mississippians will never forgive that 30,000$ that durn foreign country gave me for just sitting on my ass and writing stuff that makes my own state ashamed to own me."[35]

ELSE

At a banquet the night before the Nobel ceremony, Faulkner met Else Jonsson, the thirty-nine-year-old widow of the Swedish journalist who had first announced to Faulkner that he would someday win the Nobel Prize. She was fluent in English and well informed about his country. At the dinner, Faulkner's Swedish publisher toasted Thorsten Jonsson, "the man most responsible for our dinner tonight."

When Joseph Blotner met Else fourteen years later, he recorded his impressions: "A tall woman with finely-chiseled features, smart and very well turned-out, now perhaps 50. . . . Else's hair is glossy auburn or light chestnut, with some red in it, obviously helped out, as with most Scandinavian women, but very attractive. She has bright blue eyes & fine skin that must have been beautiful in 1950. Nice teeth, small, well-shaped nose & ears. A photo of Else taken in NY shows her tall, statuesque, full-face & vivacious—a beauty." Faulkner inscribed several books for her, including *The Town*: "For Else. Love & tenderness."[36]

After the Nobel ceremony, Jonsson remembered a friend saying, "What a gentleman of the old school Mr. F. is like a perfect cavalier to his daughter, never have I seen a Swedish father with such courtesy." Jonsson and Faulkner quickly began to converse, perhaps because he had known her husband and knew that she had just been widowed. "I have known you all my life," he told her, and she just nodded in agreement. "It did not surprise me a bit," she said. "After dinner I went and sat down next to Bill on a sofa as naturally as if we had been friends for life."

The usually reserved Faulkner, seemingly so self-contained, wanted Jonsson to tell him he had "behaved all right." She had a calming effect, telling him he had "behaved beautifully." She watched him receive the prize from the king and called Faulkner the most "elegant of them all, very graceful indeed, almost pirouetting while making several elegant bows." She watched him from far away, an unforgettable appearance.[37] He asked her to lunch the next day. She wanted to meet Jill, but he wanted Jonsson to himself. She recalled that they "tried breathlessly to keep up to our life-long friendship, but the time was so heartbreakingly short. My apartment was nearby, we walked through a grey winter day. Soon Helen [Jonsson's four-year-old daughter] came home from school."[38] The next morning Faulkner left for Paris, where a delighted Jill enjoyed the car and driver put at their disposal.

Faulkner saw Else Jonsson intermittently over the next four years. Perhaps with the somewhat older Else, Faulkner formed a kind of marriage that he could no longer share with Estelle, when he wrote about his work and farm and of a Europe with her that was a home away from home.[39] He saw her in Paris in the spring of 1951 and 1952. In London, in June 1952, in agony over a back complaint, he called Jonsson, and she immediately booked a hotel in Oslo and hired a masseur who relaxed the muscle cramps. He spent Christmas of 1954 with her in Stockholm. In April 1954, she hospitalized him in Paris during another drinking bout.

Faulkner never asked Jonsson to wait for him. He never promised her anything, although he said, "Some day tell Helen about us." It was Jonsson's own decision, she said, to "take this unhappy genius . . . as a lover."[40] He could confide in Else, telling her that he drank from fear.[41] He told her that after completing *A Fable*, "I shall be through, can break the pencil and cast it all away, that I have spent 30 years anguishing and sweating over, never to trouble me again."[42]

Raising crops and cattle, training horses and riding with Jill helped, he wrote Else, to relieve the pressures of his work.[43] He watched the weather, hoping to get the hay in before it became too wet. Baling hay in humid Mississippi, full of dust and sweat, he would come home to Rowan Oak, shower, and have a drink in the twilight before supper, and then to bed listening to bugs and then waking to another day and more baling. Afterward, he told Else, the plowed earth and sown seed ensured the cattle could graze in winter. In November, more of the same, although this time with corn, a gathering and sowing and vaccinating of cattle.[44] He also dreamed up excuses to come to Europe so that he could see her.[45] He spoke of his unhappiness and his "natural nervousness." He spoke of a "stupid existence," with "parasites who do not even have the grace to be sycophants." He was just plain tired of it all.[46] More drinking, more collapses—he did not hide any of it from Else. His back hurt like hell.[47] "Always write to me," he enjoined her.[48] But by the mid-1950s, he wrote her less, saying he was saving all his energy for the few remaining years of productivity as a writer.

But he always wrote to her—at one point saying that the Nobel Prize was nothing compared to spending an afternoon with her. He was still writing her at the end of 1960.[49] He had Mac Reed send an inscribed copy of *The Reivers*, "To Else and Helen, with love," that reached her two days after his death.[50] Faulkner destroyed her letters to him, but perhaps someday the letters she preserved will show how passionately he wanted her, and how good she was for his soul.

Meta Carpenter, a Mississippi native and Faulkner's beloved.

Faulkner and Meta Carpenter in the Hollywood Hills.

Howard Hawks and Fredric March on the set of *The Road to Glory,*
one of Faulkner's many depictions of World War I.

Malcolm Franklin, Faulkner's stepson,
who adored his stepfather and left a
moving record of their relationship.

Faulkner's drawing of two-headed Warner Brothers for his daughter Jill, whom he missed while working on *To Have and Have Not* and *The Big Sleep*.

William and Estelle Faulkner standing beside Jill Faulkner on a horse.

William and Estelle at Rowan Oak.

Earnest McEwen, ca. 1943–44. Faulkner helped to pay for his college education.

Faulkner receives the Nobel Prize in Literature from King Gustav of Sweden, 1949.

Faulkner in the 1950s.

Faulkner horse-jumping at Rowan Oak, ca. 1954.

Faulkner on the Lawn at the University of Virginia
with the Rotunda in the background, 1957.

Automobile stuck in muddy water, reminiscent of the scene in *The Reivers*.

18
What Mad Pursuit
August 1949–March 1954

JOAN

What happened to the fable? It had stalled, although work on it continued fitfully. Faulkner seemed to be looking for a revival of spirit. Gavin Stevens, also in his fifties, found fulfillment in marriage. Phil Stone, similarly stymied, had temporarily found a reprieve when he married a younger woman by whom he had two children. But Stone had done more than that: he had championed his wife's work, finding in her another protégé to promote. Whom did Faulkner have? Estelle had long ago abandoned her own fiction. Jill showed no sign of wanting to be a writer. Other family members, like his stepson Malcolm, upset by the war and having trouble settling down, were no help—or like his nephew Jimmy just did not have the literary or emotional depth that Faulkner craved to share with someone. When he found Joan, he proposed two extraordinary projects: they should write a play together, and she should write an epistolary novel about their "affair."[1] The word has to be put in quotation marks because it was so sporadic and hardly consummated at all—lots of driving around looking for a place to land—and yet Joan Williams remained for four years one of the constant sources of Faulkner's inspiration and frustration. Once upon a time, Estelle had been his be-all—deeply read and articulate and a writer. He had turned away from that part of her even as she seemed to have turned away from that part of herself. In a subordinate role, Estelle had diminished herself and seemed to him beyond recovery.

In August 1949 Joan Williams, an attractive, trim, twenty-one-year-old aspiring writer, first met an ornery William Faulkner, who regarded her as another intruder on his property and turned her away from the gates of Rowan Oak, so to speak. He had been warned in advance of her proposed visit and had grumbled, "Does she want to see if I have two heads?" Did he recall that drawing he had done for Jill during an incarceration in planet Hollywood, showing the two-headed moguls (labeled Warner Bros.) in one body, clubs in their hands, in prison-guard uniform, looking like aliens, towering over Faulkner stooped over his typewriter, pounding away at the keys, while smoke rises from his pipe, powering the studio's products? So often he had been turned into an object, a means of production. He resented this aspect of his bondage like an inmate pining for home, sending Jill "love and kisses." Those who came calling no doubt wanted their look at a freak of nature.

When it occurred to him that Joan might also alleviate his writer's agony, he responded to her letter apologizing for her intrusion. He wanted to make love to her, and his writing, as in his earliest days, became suffused with the wooing of a woman, beginning with his first letter to her: "The discovered flower is already doomed for the first frost; until 30 years later a soiled battered bloke aged 50 years smells or remembers it, and at once he is 21 again and brave and clean and durable. I think you know enough now, already have enough; nothing to lack which a middle-aged writer could supply." But if she would send him questions, he would answer them. When she did send questions, he answered, "A woman must ask them of a man while they are lying in bed together." Taken aback, she later said she never had an affair in mind, but she continued to write to him. Shy and independent and persistent, she addressed him as an acolyte, hoping for advice about how to pursue a writing career.

He became the postulant, seeking entrance into her world even as he put himself first, never quite capitulating to her desire for not a lover but a mentor, a guiding spirit and supporter who devoted himself to her genius. The more she later learned about Faulkner from biographer Fred Karl, the more she began to distrust what Faulkner had told her: "Learning so much in more recent years about how Phil Stone really tutored Faulkner in the beginning makes me more than mystified and also miffed that Bill did not do anything of the sort for me. His mind grows more and more curious." She wondered about the stories he told, the "untruths: did he believe them?"[2] What untruths? He said that Estelle had tricked him into marriage after Cornell Franklin had thrown her out for drinking. Faulkner even claimed that Jill was not his biological daughter.[3]

Perhaps Faulkner did not see the genius in Williams that Stone had seen in him. But then how was Faulkner to know what Williams might do, any more than Stone could know what Faulkner would ultimately make of himself?

Williams had won a *Mademoiselle* prize for a story, marking a beginning not much different from her contemporary Sylvia Plath. For more than four years, Faulkner did try to help Williams. "She has been my pupil 3 years now, when nobody else, her people, believed in her," he wrote to his agent Harold Ober, perhaps thinking of his own family, except for his mother. "I am happy to know my judgment was right," Faulkner wrote, alluding to a piece she had published in the *Atlantic Monthly*. "She is shy and independent, will ask no help. But for my sake, do whatever you can for her."[4] The description could fit the young Faulkner, who did not ask for help but knew how to take advantage of it when offered. Ober replied: "Miss Williams came into the office and seems happy about the Atlantic sale. She is a nice, bright girl, and I hope that she will write other stories that we can handle successfully for her."[5]

Faulkner seems to have believed she filled a lack. He had been looking for her, and she had found him. When he thanked a scholar for an article in *College English,* he noted: "I agree with it; I mean re Faulkner's aim. You and Cowley have both seen it, along with Prof. Warren Beck of Wisconsin and one twenty-one-year-old Tennessee school girl." She was then a Bard undergraduate, but his turn of phrase suited a man who believed in the percipience of young people. Never one to expatiate on the process of writing, with Joan he opened up and confided in her—not so much about his fiction as what it felt like to write and rewrite, revise and reject draft after draft as the world around him went on without much concern for his success or failure. As a writer, and often simply as a man, he had felt inconsolably lonely. He sought to share the writer's singular plight and glory with an acolyte and lover. He believed they could become one in the suspension of life that art provided.

Faulkner's letters to Williams were about solitude, suffering, and worry—all of which took time to work through until the "passion, the controlled heat" of writing would emerge. She could expect much unhappiness, forsaking "peace, money, duty too, if you are so unlucky." The words seem meant to assuage himself as much as to comfort her. In retrospect, Williams came to believe that Faulkner wanted more than her: "He cared about young people wanting to follow the craft and once wanted to set up a colony for them himself."[6]

When he met her in New York in February 1950, he proposed they collaborate on what would become the play *Requiem for a Nun.* Was he hoping to spare her some of that solitude even as he revved up his own hopes in her as the new woman he craved? He gave her specific scenes to work on, almost as he might have done in a writers' workshop or in the Ward at Warner Brothers. He would send her a few pages, urging her to rewrite them, suggesting that first drafts often did not resemble the finished work. Pulling apart what was on paper was just part of the process. Williams made notes—astutely questioning the undeveloped character of Nancy Mannigoe—but did not write much of the play, even though Faulkner insisted it was hers. He even said that he would not continue work on it without her. But in fact he continued with the play and gradually realized it had become "some kind of novel."

Faulkner continued to hope, even suggesting more sexual experience might heal the hurt he detected in her, the result of a narrow, middle-class upbringing in a home of stifled feelings. Her vivid words put her right beside him at Rowan Oak: "the two rows of trees and the house and the left-over rain and that was summer and now the leaves snow, so circling slowly they loosen from the trees and fall when the wind blows, only the dried brown ones are left and a few yellow, they rustle when you walk." Whatever she meant, such passages excite. Later she would write: "To have found someone, embodying so many things I've looked for, in so strange a way, under strange circumstances. I guess I have felt I wanted to cry because it was all so wonderful and means so much to me; that is why it is hard to tell you about because it is so close to me and means so much. Bill, I do love you." Sometimes she seemed about to surrender: "Oh hell, Bill, hell hell hell—I want to see you too. I want to somehow reach you, lose my restraint, timidity—all the things that keep us from being close."[7]

The differences in their ages bothered her. She treated him like a father confessor, a role her own father had not fulfilled. Faulkner tried another tack—"an idea for you"—this time in the form of a letter that reads like a film treatment: A famous man of fifty spends a day with a college senior. They have an instant rapport and talk about everything. She is flattered and thinks "maybe he will of a sudden talk of love to her." But the meeting is unresolved, and she is troubled by the meaning of it all. The next day a telegram arrives with the announcement that he is dead from a heart attack. She realizes that "he knew it was going to happen and that what he wanted was to walk in April again for a day, an hour." She represents, in other words, his youth, his love. Faulkner may well have been reading Hemingway's *Across the River and into the Trees,* in which Colonel Cantwell develops just this kind of attachment to the young Renata. "You can do it," Faulkner urged Williams. She rejected the idea as "gimmicky."[8] It sounded like the kind of movie an aging, still handsome Gary Cooper could do with the youthful Patricia Neal. Joan felt Faulkner wanted her to do it all his way, and for her to be forever in love with him, although his letters to her do not rival the passion he expressed for Meta. It had been Joan's first letter to him, not her face, that had stirred him. He knew that Joan was not exclusively his—that she saw other men. But the "patterns of erotic longing" established in his pursuit of Helen Baird and Meta recurred with Joan, including his penchant for quoting from *Cyrano*,[9] the lover by letter. Later Faulkner took her to a performance of *Cyrano* starring Jose Ferrer.

Joan became a rendezvous point for him in New York. She remembered how much he liked his getaways from Oxford, playing the literary lion and introducing her to writers and editors and publishers. But for nearly three years she put him off. She would not sleep with him, and he then resorted to drinking—blaming her for lapses that resulted in more Algonquin Hotel overdoses that came perilously close to finality since he also took Seconal to put himself to sleep and had to be hospitalized. Joan had coped with such episodes in her father's life and knew what to expect. She still wanted Faulkner's approval, seeking his comments on her stories, which he supplied, saying: "I am only trying to help you become an artist. You owe me nothing in return for what I try to do or succeed in doing for you." But he did want more, as he told her while saying that he wrote *The Wild Palms* "in order to try to stave off what I thought was heart-break too. And it didn't break then and so maybe it wont now, maybe it wont even have to break for a while yet, since the heart is a very tough and durable substance or thing or whatever you want to call it."

Involved in the romance with Joan was Faulkner's love of intrigue, of finding ways to meet her that evaded Estelle's suspicions. At some point they collaborated on a script, "Innocent's Return," perhaps meant for television. Henry Morgan, in his mid-forties, a member of a prosperous publishing house, is dominated by his forceful wife but contented in his marriage. He is caught in compromising circumstances with Jackie Gordon, "successful nightclub singer, making good money, good looking in a hard metropolitan way, about 25." During a hotel fire he is seen coming down in the elevator with Jackie in his bathrobe. Nothing has actually happened, but his wife accuses him of infidelity. He then pursues an affair with Jackie, who leads him on but only to arouse her husband, the agent Tony Minetti, "big, handsome, in Madison Avenue clothes." The story ends with Tony spanking Jackie and Jackie telling Henry to respect her privacy.[10] Nothing came of this effort, but Faulkner seemed fascinated with the idea of being found out in his own pursuits, if not his pajamas. He even proposed a meeting between Estelle and Joan reminiscent of the Estelle-Meta engagement.[11] Joan did visit Rowan Oak in the company of a boyfriend, just as Meta had been escorted to the Estelle encounter. In this theater of duplicity Faulkner seemed subdued and Estelle even quieter and not very attractive, remembered Joan's date, who found the Faulkners an "odd match." But then Joan's mother had seemed to him much the same, a lonely woman lost in her marriage.[12]

When Joan had initiated lovemaking in her car after a return trip from Europe, her momentary, spontaneous, and passionate pursuit was baffling, especially since she almost immediately drew away, although they resumed, at intervals, their sexual intimacy.

Faulkner advised her to jettison her middle-class morality and risk everything on becoming an artist, which also meant his lover. Yet he talked about "Mrs. Faulkner." His marriage made a huge difference to Joan; she could not overlook it. He claimed Estelle did not respect his life as an artist, but Estelle spoke otherwise to Saxe Commins: "Truly, he has too much to do here—It is bad, I know, for an artist to undertake all Bill does—but how to circumvent it? I am at a loss."[13] Estelle added that she had done all she could for "Billy's comfort and well being—Keeping an even keel mostly!" Four days earlier, on October 25, 1952, he told Saxe a different story: "Hell's to pay here now. While I was hors de combat, E. opened and read Joan Williams's letters to me. Now E. is drunk, and I am trying to nurse her before Malcolm sends her to a hospital, which costs like fury and does no good unless you make an effort yourself. I cant really blame her, certainly I cant criticize her. I am even sorry for her, even if people who will open and read another's private and personal letters, do deserve exactly what they get." He wanted to get to New York but could not leave so long as Estelle continued to drink and suspect his motives: "nothing would ever convince her that it was not only to be near Joan, since she (E.) has never had any regard or respect for my work, has always looked on it as a hobby, like collecting stamps." What Estelle thought of his work, other than her expressions of pride, remains a mystery. She did sometimes venture an opinion. She didn't care for Chick Mallison in *Intruder in the Dust* and told her husband so. "That was the end of that & they never talked about the book again," Joseph Blotner's notes record Estelle saying: "He was very sensitive to any kind of criticism."[14] This family man lamented: "I used to be the cat who walked by himself, and wanted, needed nothing from anyone. But not any more." Like Estelle, he solicited Commins's advice, adding: "I probably wont take it, but it should comfort me."[15]

ESTELLE

"Estelle Faulkner, without Bill & Jill, *would* be a total nonentity," she had written to Saxe Commins.[16] She went to Memphis, accompanied by Dean's widow, Louise, and a close friend and neighbor, Kate Baker, to confront Joan.[17] Estelle wanted to know Joan's intentions: "Do you want to marry my husband?" The question astounded Joan, who would not have considered such a proposal until Faulkner had divorced Estelle.[18] Mrs. Faulkner's foray had its intended impact. Joan, more than ever, worried over her involvement with a married man, although she continued to see Faulkner, seek his advice, and unburden herself to him.

A concerned but confident Estelle stood her ground, writing to Saxe: "Unfortunately, a man in Bill's position is an object of envy and an awful lot of malice—A friend? of mine from Shanghai days delights in sending me accounts that could be disturbing. Luckily I have managed a stiff upper lip & retained my dignity."[19] She did not believe her husband's claim that Joan was his student or that they were seriously collaborating on a play. Estelle let the drama play out while enlisting the sympathy of Faulkner's editor. Faulkner often portrayed his wife as pitiable, a weak person in her cups. But she had begun to attend Alcoholics Anonymous meetings and would manage eventually, in 1955, to stop drinking, abetted by the painting her granddaughter watched as part of Estelle's recovery of herself as an artist.[20] In her forthright correspondence she seems a very different person from the wife he denigrated. Estelle, upset, to be sure, persevered and remained, to use a Faulkner word, indomitable, even though she sometimes seemed on the verge of giving up on her husband. In such moments she counted on Commins, who had stood by Faulkner during his worst alcoholic bouts in New York: "Your letter Saxe gave me pause. I was just on the verge of writing Bill that I was suing for divorce. I still believe it the only wise thing to do—on his account, as well as Jill's & mine." During the four-year period of his involvement with Joan he had been away from home frequently—the Nobel trip, a stint in Hollywood to work on a script, time in Europe scouting locations for *A Fable,* various trips to New York to see his editors and pick up awards, and then an excursion to Egypt to work on yet another film. Stays at home had become a "nightmare of drunkenness. He must be very unhappy—so the only cure I know of is to help him get free—legally—Heaven only knows he has been free in every other sense." She wanted Saxe's advice: "Please believe that I'm only endeavoring to make everyone concerned a little happier."[21] "*Nothing* can alter my love & devotion—nor upset my faith in Bill's actual love for me. Though right now, he swears he doesn't care," Estelle confessed.[22] She told Saxe he could tell Bill whatever Saxe thought he should hear about her letter.

While Estelle held on, Faulkner seemed to be looking for a way out in the fall of 1953. Estelle told Saxe: "*Bill had Malcolm open and read her* [Joan's] *letters to him* & Mac, shocked, gave them to me."[23] Malcolm described to southern historian Jim Silver a scene during which a drunken, naked Faulkner on his bed listened to a Negro family servant reading, with difficulty, one of Joan's love letters as Estelle entered the room, sat on the bed's edge, and took the letter, "dramatically rendering it for her husband." Malcolm and his sister also copied one of Joan's letters they thought might be useful if the Faulkners divorced.[24]

The role-playing that Jill had often observed in her parents' exchanges and their desire to have others participate in the theatrics of their marriage reached a climax in scenes worthy of Edward Albee—not to mention *Knight's Gambit,* where Gavin Stevens mixes up the letters to his two beloveds so that they discover his divided passions. Faulkner resumed his liaison with Meta when he returned to Hollywood in early 1951 for work on *The Left Hand of God.* On his return home, he shared the family romance with Phil Stone, who served as the recipient of Meta's letters, so that she did not have to use a Rowan Oak address.

Estelle's remarkable letters to Saxe Commins described her husband's behavior but did not air her personal grievances as the put-upon wife fending off the "other woman." A divorce on the grounds of incompatibility seemed ridiculous to her after twenty-five years of marriage. She seemed buoyed by Saxe's supportive, uplifting letters, and disavowed jealousy: "I certainly don't blame Joan. In all probability had *I* been an aspiring young writer and an elderly celebrity had fallen in love with me—I would have accepted him as avidly as Joan did Bill—Who am I, to judge her? I dont— And, in a way, I feel sorry for Bill—He *is* in a mess."[25] Elderly? Faulkner, approaching his mid-fifties, did write about himself as old. He had allowed Malcolm to read Joan's letters around the time she said she intended to marry. Why he chose that moment to confide in Malcolm, who was exceptionally close to his mother, is a mystery. Faulkner had written to Joan in October 1953, declining to "stop in": "If this is the end, and I assume it is, I think the two people drawn together as we were and held together for four years by whatever it was we had, knew—love, sympathy, understanding, trust, belief—deserve a better period than a cup of coffee—not to end like two high school sweethearts breaking up over a Coca Cola in the corner drugstore."

By March 1954, Faulkner had dismissed Joan Williams as a worthy mate, telling Saxe Commins: "We knew a year ago that her life was not right, she was not demon-driven enough for art, writing, to suffice, too much middle class background. . . . I was not free to marry her, even if I had not been too old."[26] She had failed to become the "daughter of his mind."[27] But Faulkner, who loved to celebrate birthdays, would continue to send Joan telegrams remembering hers, which came the day after his: "Many happy returns on your birthday and love."[28]

Jill came of age during the Joan Williams affair. She had graduated from high school in May 1951 listening to her father's warning words about "forces in the world today" that were using "man's fear to rob him of his individuality, his soul, trying to reduce him to an unthinking mass by fear and bribery—giving him free food which he has not earned, easy and valueless money which he has not worked for." It did not matter what the government called itself— "communist, socialist, or democratic"—he summoned Jill's generation to "never be afraid to raise your voice for honesty and truth and compassion, against injustice and lying and greed. If you, not just you in this room tonight, but in all the thousands of other rooms like this one about the world today and tomorrow and next week, will do this, not as a class or classes, but as individuals, men and women, you will change the earth."[29]

How many actually heard the speech? Or wanted to listen? When Jill's friends heard her father would address them, they said, "Aw, Jill, let's get somebody important." But then they had grown up with her and perhaps remembered what she said when children were asked in school what their fathers did. Jill said, "Pappy doesn't do anything."[30] Faulkner spoke, according to the school principal, "like a man who is seventy years old. He seemed frightened and was inaudible."[31] But he did better backstage. "Mr. Faulkner pretty well ruined his reputation as a recluse and as being uncooperative with the press and the general public," reported Phil Mullen in the *Oxford Eagle* (May 31, 1951). "A chunky teenage girl, obviously a visitor, said timidly, 'Mr. Faulkner, would you shake hands with me.' He said certainly and he talked for several minutes with her and a young lad."

In the fall of 1951, Jill enrolled in Pine Manor Junior College, a two-year junior college for women in Chestnut Hill, Massachusetts. She was still "Missy" to Faulkner's "Pappy," as he put it in many letters to her: "Pappy loves [her] more than even his soul" (October 15, 1951).[32] He often referred to himself in the third person, as if examining his role as a father, which sometimes he failed to fulfill, apologizing to Jill, for example, for the insobriety that hurt her. This "dreadful behavior" (September 20, 1953) appalled him. But if fatherhood functioned as a role he struggled to perform, so, too, daughterhood served as a projection of his own concerns. As with Joan Williams, Faulkner provided Jill with guidance, if not an attentiveness to Jill's own concerns. He told her he was proud of her, encouraged her to study well, and wanted to hear from her, but he never inquired about what life was like at college.

Faulkner wrote Jill most often from Rowan Oak, providing reports on the days there, especially his experiences with horses, which were important to

Jill. He did not ask about her social life, her dates, or do more than, in a general sense, say much about her maturation, other than to provide her with an allowance and stipulate that she could now learn to manage her own money. What mattered is that she become her own person, the theme of a graduation speech that revived what he had said two years earlier: "It is us, we, not as groups or classes but as individuals, simple men and women individually free and capable of freedom and decision, who must decide, affirm simply and firmly and forever never to be led like sheep into peace and security." Even within a normal life, with no ambition to be another Joan of Arc, a person could make a difference. "Because it begins at home."[33]

What did Jill think about her own home and her parents' marriage then, as she listened to her father say that home meant "love and fidelity and respect to who is worthy of it, someone to be compatible with, whose dreams and hopes are your dreams and hopes, who wants and will work and sacrifice also that the thing which the two of you have together shall last forever; someone whom you not only love but like too, which is more, since it must outlast what when we are young we mean by love because without the liking and the respect, the love itself will not last."[34] Like her father, she remained, in important respects, opaque. Even family members were wary of the formidable Jill—which made her parents' worries a wonder. They made her part of their equation, a factor in their own complex calculations vis-à-vis Joan Williams. In the fall of 1952, Estelle wrote to Saxe Commins about her husband's deepening involvement with Joan: "I am worried—almost to the point of desperation—but mostly about Jill and her future—Unless it's the *only* way to save Billy—I *must* put Jill and her happiness first."[35] Ten days later Bill wrote to Saxe: "I am fearful about Jill. I mean, to disrupt her in the middle of her senior year at school." He feared that his daughter, at Pine Manor Junior College, might have to deal with her mother's demand for a "formal separation and so forth." He worried about Jill doing something desperate in reaction to the school gossip, putting in italics the kind of sentence found in a Faulkner novel: *"All these people know that my parents have separated."* He owed his "first responsibility" to himself as an artist, but "there is a responsibility too to the female child whose presence in the world I am accountable for."[36]

Estelle described her husband's unhappy summer in a late-July 1953 letter to Saxe and Dorothy Commins: "Jill and I will be relieved and glad when he decides to 'take off' again," although Joan, living in New York, had apparently come home, "so perhaps Jill and I will leave *first* after all."[37] By early February 1954, Estelle reported to Saxe: "Jill (she will tell you this very frankly) and I are happier and *more at ease* when Bill is away—Since his unfortunate disclosure to Jill about his current affair—she hasn't felt too secure around him."[38]

According to Estelle, Bill "chided Jill for not having ambition like Joan, and several other comparisons that aren't worth mentioning. . . . He is afraid to face reality because of Jill—Jill worshipped him—still does—youth is resilient and she'll forget soon that Pappy hurt her—*if* he will permit it. . . . The only thing that I shudder at and might try to evade, is a divorce—and *that* only on Jill's account."[39] Estelle set forth her mission in a following letter: "My one thought was *really* to get all three of us, Bill, Jill and me, out of a tragic—and in some ways—comic—situation, in as dignified a manner as possible."[40] By March 12, 1954, the drama was over: "Jill showed me the announcement of Joan's wedding," Estelle reported to Saxe.[41]

Joan Williams was only four years older than Jill and very aware of Jill's plight, which Faulkner made palpable for Joan when he had her read one of Jill's letters, beseeching him to be "nicer to Momma." Joan was familiar with the routine—her father's long absences from home and her mother's drinking. Jill's letter, Joan said, was "exactly what I was escaping from with my own parents, and what I wanted to say to them."[42]

Neither Jill nor Joan seemed to have had any illusions about parents who believed they were protecting their children. Unlike Meta, who accepted Faulkner's accounts, Joan scoffed at Faulkner's attacks on Estelle's competence. That was typical of Joan's own father's attitude toward her mother and also typical, Joan believed, of southern men at that time, who had a compulsion to chase after women and talk about their unhappy marriages.[43] Joan marveled at Faulkner telling her "what a terrible childhood I had and feeling so sorry for me, and he's doing the same thing to his own daughter."[44] Williams may have overlooked, however, a crucial difference between her father and Faulkner. Making sure that both Estelle and Jill knew about his attachment to Joan made them, in some paradoxical fashion, a part of the Faulkner team. Many years later, Jill said: "Pappy liked ladies, liked women, you know, plain and simple. I think that Joan was important because she was writing and it appealed to something in Pappy to have a protégé."[45] He seemed to want Jill and Estelle to understand as much.

The ladies? Not Joan alone, but Ruth Ford and Else Jonsson and Jean Stein deserve their own chapters. Their stories form erotic enterprises that intersected and counterpointed one another in ways worthy of a Faulkner novel.

JOAN

The Wintering (1971) resembles the epistolary novel Faulkner wanted Joan Williams to write about their love affair. Sometimes his letters appear almost verbatim, or altered just enough to make the novel a little more pointed and to incorporate what he said as well as what he wrote. Joan met Estelle on only a few occasions but managed to evoke the pathos of a fading belle (renamed Inga) as she appeared to Faulkner (renamed Jeffrey Almoner):

> She came totteringly on the weak heels of the aged silver dancing shoes.
> God, Almoner thought, she had done it all in exact sequence, the sweetly seductive bath, then her hair and her make-up and a nap in her robe; her dress had been donned a moment before the beau's arrival. Now, she held out a hand. For the corsage? Almoner anguished over life itself as much as over what it had done to Inga.

There are moments when Inga commands the house and Almoner is over-ridden. Just as fascinating are glimpses of the black people, like Jessie, who attend Almoner, trying to read his moods, giving a sense of him that is missing in Faulkner biographies. Here is Jessie watching Inga when she discovers Almoner's obsession with Amy (Joan): "Miss Inga's shadow was going all over the room and she walking up and down telling him she wasn't going to put up with it and he not saying nothing. Usually he say something make her just shut up. Some reason he ain't saying nothing. Then I thought, Mister Jeff care. He ain't taking no chances on saying nothing because this time, Mister Jeff care." Almoner presses his suit, as Faulkner did with Joan, making Amy feel that "in trying to help her, Jeff was about to take over what belonged to her." Faulkner's patient, even humble courtship sometimes turned her toward resentment, which is shown in Amy's cornered observations: "Jeff, by waiting to see what she was going to decide, made her often feel put on a spot." Fiction and fact blend when Amy, like Joan, a woman of silences and stubborn independence, is a match for Almoner/Faulkner, who says, "I like to think I made you, as you made me over."

When Almoner dies, Amy hears the news from Jessie, sent to Amy by the dying man. Amy asks Jessie if anyone else knows about Jessie's mission to Amy. "What?," Jessie asks, with "a practiced dumb look, for white people." Amy says, "Nothing," and takes the cue from the black woman who knows better than to admit everything she knows. It is hard not to believe Faulkner would have liked such a scene.

Faulkner's romance with Williams occurred during a time when the South was just entering the modern civil rights era, and she captures that, too, in scenes with a young black man who cannot sit at a drugstore counter but who boldly has Amy sit beside him in his car. She asks him, "Things are changing, aren't they?" He agrees: "Yes . . . I would have to say that they are better."

Nine years after the novel's publication, Williams published in the *Atlantic Monthly* (May 1980) a memoir, "Twenty Will Not Come Again," a line from

Housman, whom Faulkner urged her to read.[46] The memoir adds to the poignancy of their story: "In time, Faulkner would say, I don't know anything else to do with the rest of my life but put it into your hands." Williams wanted to emphasize that their romance occurred during a more formal time with a sense of propriety and decency that was also changing but still held in their culture. At Rowan Oak on her first visit a "grown man in shorts and wearing no shirt was a surprise to me." Going into the city always meant putting on hats and gloves.

She wondered why he needed her: "Once, in New York, we were going to a party given by a Random House editor and Faulkner said he was so much more comfortable going with me. I was surprised because he had known these people a long time. But you are my countryman, he said." He had said the same to Meta. He did not take out other women in New York. He was alone much of the time, and, she could have added, he liked to drink alone, like many alcoholics do, like Don Birnam in *The Lost Weekend,* which Faulkner read and rewrote in "Weekend Revisited," published as "Mr. Acarius."

She reported on the reasons for Faulkner's drinking: "Writing, he told me, was the only thing he ever found to alleviate the boredom of living. And I believe he drank to help pass time. All writers know the feeling: what to do with time left over when the day's writing is done." He could not handle pressure, so he turned to alcohol and to art: "He contended that art is a little stronger than any human passion for thwarting it."

Williams wrote her memoir as she was turning fifty—about the same age as Faulkner when she met him. "Someday, Joan," he told her, "you will know that no one will ever love you as I have." She knew that now and also realized, "I was taking care of him for the whole world, remember."

THE END OF THE AFFAIR

During his agonizing affair with Joan Williams, Faulkner read Graham Greene's *The End of the Affair* (1951), "for me," he wrote, "one of the best, most true and moving novels of my time, in anybody's language."[47] He did not often, at this point, read the work of his contemporaries, and Greene's Roman Catholicism would not seem to have had any special appeal, although the religious-like intensity of Faulkner's quest for meaning was akin to Greene's, and in later interviews Faulkner's invocation of God as vital to his understanding of man accorded with the English novelist's belief. The writer/protagonist in *The End of the Affair,* Maurice Bendrix, is full of Faulknerian doubts. When asked about one of his novels—if he believes it is a failure—Bendrix replies, as Faulkner would, "I feel that way about all of my books."

It is said of Bendrix, as it could be said of Faulkner, "you can hear the nerves twitch through his sentences." But it is not so much Bendrix as writer, but Bendrix as lover, who resembles Faulkner and Faulkner's characters. Bendrix mourns and rages over the loss of his lover, Sarah Miles, married to a dull civil servant, just as Harry Wilbourne grieves over Charlotte Rittenmeyer, who jettisons her middle-class life for her lover. It would not be out of character for Bendrix to declare, as Faulkner had, "Between grief and nothing, I will take grief." Unlike Charlotte, Sarah remains with her husband, unwilling to shatter his life in order to fulfill hers. Her pain over her marriage, over staying with a man who cannot speak to her dreams while he provides for her comfort, resembles Faulkner's own disappointment with Estelle. Greene's powerful romantic and religious novel struck home.

19

Two Lives/Two Faulkners

1949–1951

BLACK AGAINST A WHITE BACKGROUND

"William Faulkner took us sailing on his sailboat on a big inland lake they've cut out of the woods there—waves and everything, big," wrote Eudora Welty on September 2, 1949. She called him "a wonderful person" with "the most profound face, something that nearly breaks your heart though, just in the clasp of his hand—a strange kind of life he leads in Oxford, two lives really." Strange, perhaps, because there was nothing bookish about it and literature never entered her conversation with him. "He can do or make anything, and can sail beautifully," Welty noted. "We got in his 20 year old Ford touring car which he hunts and fishes and goes over the farm in, with holes in the floor ('well, I know where all the holes are') and when we couldn't open a back door he said, 'There's a cupboard latch on it,' you ought to see that car."

Welty did not mention anyone else at the party. Stuart Purser (1907–1986), the new chairman of the Department of Art at Ole Miss, came aboard on sketching trips. The two had first met in an unusual encounter on the square. Purser heard a voice over his shoulder asking the artist about his preference for drawing black people against white backgrounds. Purser, engaged in his drawing and unaware that the voice behind him was William Faulkner's, did not say much, but the questioner persisted: "Did you give my brother John Faulkner the graphic award because you thought the drawing had merit?" What was Faulkner really asking?, Purser wondered. Did John have talent, or was he chosen because of his last name? Purser explained that the drawing of a possum hunt had been submitted anonymously. Thereafter Purser watched

Faulkner talking with country people, black and white, not in groups but as individuals. "You get your ideas and inspiration from observing these people, while I get mine through talk with them," Faulkner told him.

The remarkable aspect of the Faulkner-Purser colloquies is that Faulkner took the initiative. About a local black artist Purser had championed, Faulkner asked, "Does Mayfield have real talent, or is his work getting attention because he is black?" Both, Purser answered. M. B. Mayfield (1923–2005) with a seventh-grade education, painted and wrote poetry without any formal instruction, making him a fitting contemporary for William Faulkner. Purser had discovered Mayfield's roadside art work in Ercu, Mississippi, and had found Mayfield a job as a janitor at the University of Mississippi. The job was just a cover for Mayfield, whom Purser installed in a broom closet of a classroom, where Mayfield could observe, through his "narrow opening," classes devoted to art. Did Purser share with Faulkner this secret worthy of a Faulkner novel?[1]

Purser objected to an Ole Miss librarian's comment about an unfriendly Faulkner, and she replied, "Oh yes, he loves to talk to Negroes and poor white trash." Purser felt he learned from Faulkner. The artist liked to quote Dr. Robert Coles's comment in the *Christian Science Monitor*: "Here in the United States William Faulkner made it his business to spend hours with his townsmen in Mississippi—he made brilliant use of his dreams and fantasies—but he also knew that his understanding of others made him a rich man. He was willing to be taught by his neighbors."[2]

Black against a white background is what Faulkner seemed to have in mind when he wrote Hal Smith in October 1933 about a novel, *Requiem for a Nun*, "about a nigger woman. It will be a little on the esoteric side, like As I Lay Dying." But then he put it aside, for no reason, except that *Absalom, Absalom!* began to press upon him, although he considered returning to *Requiem for a Nun* the following year.[3] Sixteen years later, in an Algonquin Hotel room, he was hard at work on the first act of a play, returning to the "nigger"—a word he put between quotation marks:

a known drunkard and dope user, a whore with a jail record in the little town, always in trouble. Some time back she seemed to have reformed, got a job as nurse to a child in the home of a prominent young couple. Then one day suddenly and for no reason, she murdered the child. And now she doesn't even seem sorry. She seems to be making it impossible for the lawyer to save her.

So at the end of this act, everybody, sympathy is against her. She deserves to hang, a sentiment which reflects even on the lawyer defending her.[4]

This time, unlike *Intruder in the Dust,* the accused black person has committed murder. The remaining question is why, and what role these white people will have in her story. Faulkner seemed to want to know himself when he asked Joan Williams to write the play with him.

Did the response to *Intruder in the Dust,* the novel and the film, rouse Faulkner to resurrect *Requiem for a Nun*? And why a play? Early on, before he had written his first novel, the theater of Eugene O'Neill had fascinated Faulkner, especially the playwright's exploration of dualism in the form of the masks that his characters wore to occlude seething passions that threatened to overwhelm them. In 1933, just as the idea of *Requiem for a Nun* occurred to him, he met Ruth Ford, a philosophy graduate student at Ole Miss, whom Dean Faulkner brought to Rowan Oak. Ten years later, Ford met Faulkner again at Warner Brothers, where she was under contract. "The one thing I want most in the world is for you to write me a play," she told him. She was a striking, dark-haired beauty—the photographs of her as Temple Drake are mesmerizing. She had a commanding presence that made her courtier politely propose: "Ruth, I've been your gentleman friend for quite a while now. Ain't it time I was promoted?" She laughed and brushed him off with, "Oh, Bill!" She steadfastly denied a romance and emphasized, instead, their deep friendship and their bond as southerners. She called him "the perfect gentleman."[5]

Ford wanted a professional relationship, not a romance, and Faulkner seems to have respected her all the more for it. In New York in October 1948, she had been one of his friends who had found him almost unconscious in his Algonquin Hotel room and arranged for his hospitalization. He had seen her again, along with his Random House editors, in February 1950 on a trip to New York to consult about *Collected Stories.* Ford knew a lot of writers and took Faulkner to their parties—all part of her determination to snag him and of his desire to please her. If this was not *All about Eve,* it was pretty close to being all about Ruth Ford, although William Faulkner, so bent on his promotion, was not deceived. In November, he did more New York party-hopping with Ford. If he still did not talk much, he listened "avidly," observed reporter Rhea Talley, who also said "his companions had little trouble getting him away to the next party." She watched him ask questions about an eccentric painter who had become the object of discussion. Then he turned to Talley and said, "This is what I come to New York for—gossip." Ruth Ford admitted she had coaxed him onto this social tour by saying they would "drop in on some people."

By May 1950, he had written two acts of the play but realized "more than ever that I cant write a play," although he hoped someone could rewrite it. The someone, Joan Williams to begin with, had neither the time nor the heart to make William Faulkner playable. And that's when Faulkner thought of how what he had already written might get onto the page, if not the stage. Before the month was over he had written a third act but was calling it a novel, with "three introductory chapters which hold the 3 acts together." He had not given up on a producible play, but concentrated, for now, on the project as a book, while he still sought contributions from Joan Williams. By January 1951, after the Nobel trip, he returned to his novel/play, expecting to publish it in the fall of 1951.[6]

Then Howard Hawks called and called and called.

COLLABORATING WITH THE ENEMY

A Hawks biographer boils down the director's pitch: A picture based on William E. Barrett's "timely and inspirational novel, *The Left Hand of God,* about an American flier trying to escape the embattled China of 1947 disguised as a priest. The trappings of the story—the resourceful pilot hero, a gorgeous young nurse, the endangered outpost of humanity [a Catholic mission] trying to stave off violent and unpredictable forces—had obvious appeal to Hawks, who certainly would have played up the adventure and romance angles."[7] But what was the appeal to Faulkner? Hawks telephoned eight times in one evening from Hollywood, and before the eighth time, Faulkner told Aunt Bama, "I hope he doesn't phone me again because I will have to give in."[8]

The money was good: two thousand dollars per week and a bonus if Faulkner finished the work in a month. But did Faulkner need the money after the thirty-thousand-dollar Nobel award? In fact, he did, because he had set up a twenty-five-thousand-dollar trust fund. Much of the Nobel wealth would go to doing good works so that Faulkner would become the benefactor of his community—just like his great-grandfather. Phil Stone advised him on his will, his trust, and the impact on his taxes. "Best of luck, and let me know if there is anything I can do for you," Stone wrote in a letter sent care of Charles Feldman, now handling Faulkner's Hollywood contracts.[9]

But would money alone be enough to entice a Nobel Prize winner to return to the site of the Hollywood horror show and memories of the Ward, where he bent over his typewriter turning out products like a machine for the two-headed Warner Brothers monster? In a handwritten discarded draft of his Nobel Prize address on Algonquin Hotel stationery, he had recorded his humiliation and outrage: "A few years ago I was taken on as a script writer at a Hollywood studio. At once I began to hear the man in charge talking of 'angles', story 'angles', and then I realized that they were not even interested in truth, the old universal truths of the human heart without which any story is ephemeral—the universal truths of love and honor and pride and pity and compassion and sacrifice."[10] Why collaborate with the enemy? What could Hawks have said that would have moved Faulkner to return? Well, it was Howard Hawks, and Faulkner believed he owed a man whose work Faulkner respected and learned from. As a deeply loyal man—Faulkner had held on to Hal Smith even after the publisher's bankruptcy had meant the loss of *Sanctuary*'s royalties—how could he deny Hawks, the director who had been responsible for two of Faulkner's most important screenwriting credits, for *To Have and Have Not* and *The Big Sleep*? He had another reason, as his letter to Meta on August 8, 1951, reveals: he wanted to see her again, and working on a film would be his excuse to leave home.[11]

And what if *The Left Hand of God* abetted Faulkner's own life and work? What if Faulkner's adaptation of this "inspirational novel" fulfilled the work on "The De Gaulle Story," "Battle Cry," and *Requiem for a Nun,* all of which dealt with the theme of redemption and of individuals asserting a newfound integrity in the midst of history? Faulkner's first draft screenplay has been called "craftsmanlike" but "rather dull and sincere, with an abundance of narration," which is why Hawks did not produce the film, according to one of his biographers.[12] But Faulkner's work is neither perfunctory nor boring and is superior to the film eventually released starring Humphrey Bogart and Gene Tierney.

Like so much of William Faulkner's life, what was deeply personal and what motivated his writing remain mysterious, one of those "trade secrets" he begrudgingly confided just once in a letter to his mother way back in those heady New Orleans days in 1925. "He lived in a world that we did not enter," his niece Dean said: "My grandmother was the only person with whom he shared those brilliant people he created. . . . They would go into a bedroom and close the door. He shared the stuff he loved with her."[13] What Faulkner gave to his work he wanted to stay there, as if to share too much of himself even with his intimates would have robbed him of his powers—forces that had to be kept inside. At all costs, he had to avoid spillage, the leaking out of energies that more properly belonged in the books. Consequently, the biographer, like one of Faulkner's own characters, has to, at some points, speculate in order to complete the story of that character, William Faulkner. With Faulkner, one detects, surmises, infers, imagines, and ratiocinates.

Faulkner wasn't just the writer and the sailor/farmer/carpenter/painter/hunter/novelist. He was also the lover/screenwriter/playwright. Between 1949 and 1954, Faulkner worked away at *A Fable,* started a play, turned the play into a novel, turned the novel back into a play, went to Hollywood, and wrote and carried on with Joan Williams, Meta Carpenter, and Else Jonsson, traveling to Memphis, Hollywood, New York, London, Paris, Stockholm, and Oslo before meeting Jean Stein in St. Moritz. Each of these women enjoyed a part of the man, and each of them also built him up into a character of their imagining, one who could now deploy himself surreptitiously across continents. "This is in most complete confidence," he wrote to Saxe Commins from Hollywood in February 1951. "The principal reason is, I dont want my family in Oxford to learn about it until I decide to tell them myself. If it works out that way, I will let them think that I am merely in New York finishing my play-novel." What was "it"? Faulkner wanted to go to Europe in mid-April for two weeks, and he wanted to travel via "Betty Haas's aeroplane."[14] The old spelling for airplane, more British than American, defined Faulkner's vintage, the young man on the loose in the 1920s, who now had it in mind to visit Else Jonsson, although he did not say as much to Saxe, who, along with Robert Haas, was expected to collaborate in their author's machinations—in this case employing Haas's daughter to pilot Faulkner to his tryst.

Faulkner wrote this letter during his reunion with Meta Carpenter. During their separation, she had read "everything that came my way about Faulkner—book reviews, interviews, evaluations of his body of work, squibs in *Time* magazine." She rejoiced when he wrote her that MGM had bought the movie rights to *Intruder in the Dust*. His correspondence, she admitted, often treated her as his own, not the woman remarried to Wolfgang Rebner. She was still Faulkner's "sweet love," as he signed one of his letters to her. Rumors about her involvement with Faulkner had spread, and she became an object of "awakened interest." Only then, more than a decade after their first assignation, had she realized she had been "loved by a man for the ages." But she could only imagine what the Nobel celebration at Rowan Oak was like. Then the powerful agent Charles Feldman had finally broken the Warner Brothers contract, and Faulkner was free to accept Howard Hawks's offer.

He called her from the plush Beverly Carlton on Olympic Boulevard, and she arrived to see him looking like his recent photographs: "august, bonier and more severe of mien, somewhat professorial" but still the man she loved with the crinkling eyes. But did he still love her? She suspected he had become involved with a secretary, and when she confronted him, he broke down, lamenting the ten years they been away from one another.[15] For the first time in five years they made love, but this time a "grave and sweet ardor" replaced their earlier unbridled passion. He seemed remorseful: "Why did we let it happen? I, more than you. This long, agonizing time away from each other. Foolish. Senseless waste. No warrant to it." His regrets included Estelle: "I've been hard on her in many ways, some of them, I now realize, without justification." He surprised Meta by not saying much about Jill, now eighteen. She said Faulkner did not share Hawks's belief in *The Left Hand of God* as the "basis for a successful motion picture, but he said nothing." It is hard to believe this was his last word on the project.

On February 11, Faulkner wrote to Joan Williams, who had declined to join him at the Beverly Carlton, "Fantastic place, fantastic work." That's not much to hang a story on, but with Faulkner it has to serve. He followed the spirit and often the letter of Barrett's novel, but with an added value. By happenstance, Hawks had found a property worthy of a Nobel Prize winner, and Faulkner went at the screenplay in what looks like a Hollywood-be-damned mood even as Faulkner, an old Hollywood hand of nearly twenty years standing, perfected certain Hollywood/Hawksian conventions.[16]

To begin with, Faulkner conceived of the film, although set in China, as a Hollywood western. Here is how his film opens: "Evening after sunset. A small gorge or mountain pass, barren solitary. A rough trail along which pass a column of mounted men and heavy though crudely laden packanimals with their drivers." The studios almost always wanted their audience to identify with foreign characters and situations as though the world abroad was American. So in the released version of the film, Lee J. Cobb plays a Chinese warlord. Faulkner did not suggest actors for the roles, but in creating Hank, it is hard to believe he did not have Walter Brennan in mind, one of the stars of *Banjo on My Knee* and *To Have and Have Not*. Hank is not in Barrett's novel. He is a singular Faulkner creation but also a Hollywood creature. He is the wisecracking sidekick so often employed in the Brennan-Cooper films and, even more notably, for Faulkner's purposes, in the Brennan-Wayne collaboration in *Red River* (1948). After the first appearance of Jim Carmody (Humphrey Bogart) comes the "second white man," Hank, subordinate to Carmody but also his critic, functioning as Brennan does in *Red River* as Wayne's conscience. In one version of the film, Brennan also narrated the story, providing a perspective—by turns serious and comic—on the hero just as Hank does, who supports Carmody but also questions his decisions. As for the Chinese, well, they are make-do American Indians and even sometimes sound like refugees from *Drums along the Mohawk*.

Without Hank, the released film lacks humor and tension, so that even an actor as great as Humphrey Bogart can seem if not exactly boring, then without enough to do, since he has no one, really, to answer to.[17] Listen to Hank narrate the story and you can hear Walter Brennan: "China, 1951 right under the edge of Tibet a thousand miles from nowhere and for my nickel you could have had the country and the job both two years ago, and by now even Jim too was going around to that idea." The hard-boiled, apolitical language—right out of *The Big Sleep*—is applied to history. Soon the

Communists would take over this part of the country, but their encroaching power is only an off-camera phenomenon alluded to in the dialogue.[18]

Hank's voice-overs, it is true, are uncommonly long for the screen, but they could have been compressed while retaining his mordant humor. His narrative interludes function like the introductory sections of *Requiem for a Nun,* a draft of which Faulkner was writing on the reverse side of the *Left Hand of God* script.[19] Without narrative, the released version of the film lacks the background necessary to savor Carmody's developing moral consciousness, which he works out under Hank's intense scrutiny.

Jim and Hank are downed pilots now working for a Chinese warlord, Yang, their rescuer who will not let them go. They are also in the midst of a civil war trying to avoid "soviet gangs" who are moving across Yang's territory. When one of Yang's men kills a traveling priest, Carmody whips the murderer across the face—assuming an authority that Yang accords to himself. When Yang orders Carmody to do the same to Hank, the two white men escape, knowing full well that Yang, not daring to lose face, will come after them.

Carmody, wearing the dead priest's clothes, and Hank, dressed as a servant, find refuge in a Catholic mission, which has been expecting the arrival of a priest. Carmody, who has said, "Religion is for children," is called upon to perform mass, hear confession, administer communion, attend to the dying, and, in general, take care of the mission, which becomes his mission—at first only as an effort to save himself but, in the end, to serve humanity, the "Chinks," as Hank calls them. Carmody, for all his reluctance, performs well as a priest, inspiring reverence among his congregation—rather like the recalcitrant Nobel laureate who found, perhaps to his surprise, that he could fulfill his public responsibilities with considerable success. It had not been easy. "Billy has gotten so touchy we don't dare mention his fame, and believe me, we edge off. He is so very proud and happy over winning the prize, but is his own shy self about publicity," his mother explained.[20]

Faulkner had insisted in his graduation speeches that the world could change only if individuals, one by one, changed themselves and protested injustice. Carmody mentions he was an altar boy but is now a lapsed Catholic, and the dying priest replies, "There is no such thing." He might as well say, as Gavin Stevens does, "The past is never dead. It's not even past." Later Carmody says, "there is no such thing as was." Although Carmody jokes when he calls himself "an American white devil" when rejecting the attentions of a courtesan, he regards himself as unredeemed.

Faulkner's serious moral purpose as well as his enmity toward Hollywood and his own dealings with popular culture erupt as he pictures Hank lying in bed reading a "movie magazine or detective story of True Confessions, or maybe a battered Saturday Evening Post two years old"—none of which prepare him for the hazardous and morally complex sojourn in the Chinese mission, which includes encountering Dr. Sigman, a disaffected radical who has fled Europe to this poor village of people "not even valuable as political material." Carmody states his fear of the "Soviets" and shies away from political talk. What matters, in Faulkner's screenplay, is Carmody's courage and loyalty to Hank and Hank's self-sacrifice. Carmody explains what happened after their plane crashed: "It must have taken him [Hank] days to keep me alive and still get me down that mountain to where he could find help. I don't know how he did it." Carmody tells the hero's story just as Faulkner spoke of a crash landing that entitled him to his cane and head wound plate.[21]

Hank has saved Carmody, but the hero has not yet figured out how to save himself. That the mission welcomes Carmody as a priest becomes less significant, ultimately, than his understanding that their faith in God and humanity is what will redeem him. His qualities as a man, not just a priest, invite the attention of Dr. Sigman, his wife, and Anne, the wife of a lost American pilot (presumed dead). Anne, a devout Catholic, is troubled by her romantic attachment to Carmody, who does not tell her he is not actually a priest. He is susceptible to her as succor to his soul. Faulkner plays down their sexual attraction as he concentrates on Carmody's spiritual revival. He has been a man who figured all the angles, a soldier of fortune, who gradually renounces his own ambitions.

Dr. Sigman suspects Carmody is hiding a secret and jokes with his wife, who also finds Carmody attractive: "Go on. Be a papist. Defend him." Faulkner's Dr. Sigman relinquishes the stereotypical role that Hollywood usually assigns to well-meaning white people. His hospital has failed to attract patients until Carmody shows up. Sigman laments that "we—the white men—have lost face." They have run out of supplies: "What else can these people think of a foreign god who cannot even keep aspirin in his dispensary." They have to leave, Sigman says, before the "communist troops" start "hammering at the gates." His wife, like Anne, refuses to leave. "Then I am," Sigman answers. "We went through that once"—that is, running from the Communists in Europe. Dr. Sigman, like "Father" Carmody, says, "there are no miracles," and yet almost in the same breath he practically quotes from Faulkner's Nobel Prize address about the "human race, which, for all its baseness and folly, is still capable of fidelity and sacrifice for the sake of love." For all Hollywood's corrupt dealings, Faulkner was still trying to redeem it in this script.

When the villagers come to Carmody he is so moved that he kneels to them—a spontaneous gesture that Hank is sure came as a surprise: "I don't guess he knew why, either. But it was the right thing to do. It was exactly right.

It was as if the Lord himself was taking care of him—of us—." The "us" is everyone, white and Chinese alike, and Carmody's spontaneous submission to his fate, to saving the village, seems like a gift of grace, not an action of his own volition. Without Hank, how could the power of this salvation have been conveyed? It certainly does not occur in the released film. Was Faulkner also thinking of the grace he had shown in the Nobel ceremony, the pirouetting that Else Jonsson noticed—not aware that this was the same man who had doused himself with liquor in the days approaching the Nobel event? When Faulkner said the award was not just to him, he meant it. Accepting the prize meant he could no longer go it alone, as he had done so often in Hollywood, in New York, at home, acting as his own soldier of fortune.

By all accounts, Faulkner's presence at Stockholm, notwithstanding his virtually inaudible voice, inspired awe. Anne, watching Carmody perform as Father O'Shea, exults: "Never in my life did a Mass move me as that one did. He was so deliberate—so reverent—so sincere. It was as though it could go on forever, and I wanted it to go on forever—none of us ever to leave the church again—." She is speaking of a moment but also of eternity and universality, the very terms of Faulkner's Nobel sermon. The Communists in the film are described as godless—not only in the disbelieving sense but in their obliteration of individuality. No wonder, then, that the Nobel declaration of faith is a key Cold War document reified by this film. Such moments sound preachy, but Hank is always there to be earthy—this time at a baptism to say he can assist Carmody: "I can co-pilot on that. (*Carmody reacts*) The baptizing. I can hold a Texas yearling while they notch its ear. I guess I can hold a Chink kid while you sprinkle it.—Okay, okay, just say I'm bored." How Walter Brennan, a devout Catholic and Oregon rancher who loved using racial epithets, would have relished saying the lines William Faulkner had written for him.

Carmody is Faulkner in character: "The whole Chinese family is watching him with the same air of complete trust. He sees the family and speaks to them in the hill dialect, indicating that he is learning even something of that." That Faulkner had a similar impact is undeniable. Perrin H. Lowrey Jr., writing to Phil Stone while Faulkner was in Hollywood working on *The Left Hand of God*, testified that "as a young writer, I wanted to tell someone close to him how much his speech of acceptance in Stockholm meant to those of us who are trying to turn out something good. The dignity and selflessness and awareness of that speech must have been particularly meaningful and encouraging to all the young writers of my generation. . . . So I wanted him to know . . . I simply wanted to thank him for doing so generous and so fine a thing."[22] Even if Stone never forwarded this letter, Faulkner had to know through Joan Williams, Shelby Foote, Eudora Welty, and many others that his words inspired generations of writers.

Hank, who has kidded Carmody all along, calling him "Father," admits, "something has happened to you." Hank does not have to spell it out. Nor does Carmody: "something happened to me. I don't even know myself what it was. Yes, I do know—an old Buddhist priest—a man dying of leprosy—a woman dying in childbirth who held my hand and believed in me while she died—the patience, the suffering, the hope, but above all the trust—You see, I can't tell you," he says to Dr. Marvin, the priest who comes to relieve Carmody after he has saved the mission. Like the marshal (Gary Cooper) in *High Noon*, one of Faulkner's favorite pictures,[23] or the sheriff (John Wayne) in *Rio Bravo* (1959), everyone awaits the appearance of the head villain. "What are you going to do when this—Mieh Yang?—finally arrives?" Full of Gary Cooper doubt, Carmody replies, "I don't know." In the end, Carmody relies on himself, in his reading of Yang, but also on the faith the mission has instilled in him.

What Carmody does know is that he can only save the mission by dealing with Yang one-to-one. It is a literal gamble. They will throw dice. If Carmody wins, the mission is saved. If Carmody loses, Yang may still withdraw from the village, but at the price of enslaving Carmody. Even before the dice have rolled, though, Carmody tells Yang why he cannot win, even though he threatens Carmody with torture: "if I stood the torture well, people would say that I was stronger than Mieh Yang, since he could not break me. And if I stood it badly, they would marvel that such a weak man commanded your troops. They would wonder if maybe you too were not weak." In short, Yang's putative victory over Carmody and the mission would result in the warlord's ultimate defeat.

William Faulkner's *Left Hand of God* never got made because of Production Code violations and the Catholic Church's opposition.[24] Even with his redemption, Carmody, in Faulkner's script, was too unsavory for the Production Code, which forbid, for example, scenes with a character pretending to be a priest and actually performing holy services. The absurdity of this prohibition is apparent: This is a motion picture. Any actor playing a priest would be bogus. Words like "papist" would have been excised. And the cynical Dr. Sigman, clearly an atheist who attacks the Church, required a Production Code anathema. When he touches Carmody's cassock, the doctor thinks of "all the bloody history of this cloth—the fanaticism, the injustice which has been committed in its name."

After two decades in Hollywood Faulkner knew that his mixture of the profane and the sacred could never be approved. Perhaps he thought Hawks could finesse the censors, as he had done in previous pictures. Or perhaps writing a screenplay drawing on both an understanding of Hollywood limits and a wish to transgress those limits was enough compensation. Or he knew that his script, like all Hollywood products, would be rewritten, and he might as well have his say—as he did, for example, with *Sutter's Gold* and *Drums along the Mohawk,* films rewritten and released, but not nearly as powerful or as honest as his scripts.

STAGING HISTORY

On the flip side of those *Left Hand of God* pages, Faulkner went back to work on *Requiem for a Nun,* another work of redemption ramified through a succession of pasts—not only the various stages of Temple Drake's life but also those of Jefferson, her community, and its extension to the world. Faulkner's work on women's films, *The Damned Don't Cry* and *Mildred Pierce,* which created strong, if morally compromised women, broke new ground in his fiction.[25] As he worked on *Requiem for a Nun,* his sense of the historical became more pronounced, stimulated by his acute consciousness of change, and of the need to interpret and to live with that change, which included new roles for women.

Eight years after the ending of *Sanctuary,* Temple has married Gowan Stevens and acquiesced to a conventional life with two children, until Pete, brother of Red, the lover Popeye murdered in Memphis, blackmails her with letters she sent to Red. Her dealings with Pete arouse in Temple a passionate desire to forsake all for an affair with her blackmailer, who resembles her former lover. She can no longer abide her husband's sufferance of her past. He, in turn, endures the guilt of not having defended her honor. For him the marriage is a kind of atonement, but husband and wife, trying to forgive one another, have been tormented by their bad faith. Nancy, the family's black nursemaid, a reformed prostitute and drug addict, and now a devout Christian, is the only one Temple can talk to without apology or explanation. Nancy has failed by every means she knows to keep Temple at home. In desperation, Nancy, willing to do anything to prevent Temple's departure and the breakup of the family, kills the youngest child. Sentenced to hang, Nancy becomes the burden Temple bears for her own infidelity. Gowan's uncle, Gavin Stevens, puts Temple on trial, in effect, seeking to compel her to reckon with the chain of events that have resulted in her child's murder. Realizing that Temple will do anything to save Nancy, Gavin Stevens persuades her to make a plea in person to the governor to prevent Nancy's death, although Stevens's larger mission is to get Temple to reckon with her past and to reconcile herself to her present marriage.

Temple has been viewed as a "transitional figure . . . representing both the breakdown of the icon of the southern white lady and her reinvention as a moral agent."[26] Temple suffers, in part, because she is expected to be wife and mother exclusively and to settle down, as Estelle did, after returning from her misadventure abroad. Then the death of their first child had troubled their marriage, and Estelle's fragile condition meant extra care and concerns about her stability. The prolonged tensions between husband and wife also filtered through his affairs with other women, especially now with Joan Williams, whom he encouraged to abandon her middle-class restraints. She was nothing like Temple Drake, but her desire to break from convention made her an ally in his effort to probe Temple's divided psyche. Temple's impressive vocabulary troubles one biographer,[27] but it would not be amiss in a characterization of the well-read Estelle Faulkner, or Joan Williams.

Gavin Stevens construes a narrative of events that also constrains Temple's effort to escape the conventions that William Faulkner felt bound both to honor and to break. Like Faulkner's fraught marriage, Temple's holds, even though it is a kind of "horror fantasy about marriage and an heroic affirmation of marriage's capacity to endure."[28] Faulkner may not have seen the play in such stark terms, but Temple can seem caught, "as Faulkner was . . . between the erotic promise of a new young mate—the possibility of repeating earlier sexual adventures—and the more mundane task of struggling to make a marriage survive."[29] Stevens hovers over the Temple-Gowan marriage—like Phil Stone did in wry comments about the Faulkners to Carvel Collins and others. Stone told Stark Young that *Requiem* was a "shoddy job."[30] If Faulkner was exploring his own guilt, as one biographer has suggested, with Stevens/Stone as his conscience, he found an odd way to dramatize it by making the wife, not the husband, unfaithful.[31]

Given Faulkner's previous portrayals of religious fanaticism in *Light in August,* his portrayal of Nancy's stolid faith, her repeated "Just believe," uttered in her jail cell as she awaited her execution, is surprising. The rousing role faith can exert, which is captured in Carmody's transformation in *The Left Hand of God,* perhaps reinforced the depiction of Nancy's repose after her own history of sin. She regards herself as an instrument of the Lord, like Doc Hines, but she is curiously underdeveloped, a deux ex machina more than a fully developed character, forcing Temple to confront her derelictions. "What about me?," the doubting Temple asks Nancy in her jail cell. If there is no heaven, how will she be forgiven? Nancy, if not a fully realized character, is a startling rebuke to the stereotypical black woman-in-waiting, the sentimentalized moral instructress in the *Gone with the Wind* school of southern literature. If her uncompromising rectitude is murderous, it also calls into question the compromised motivations that trouble Temple's marriage.

Requiem for a Nun brings to the highest pitch Faulkner's re-creation of history as a contemporary event, occurring now, as the author, the characters, and all of us probe a problematic past in the three prologues and the three acts of the play. The novel emphasizes the interdependence of fiction and fact by including both Jefferson and Mississippi's actual capital, Jackson, in presenting the geographical and historical development of the state, even though Faulkner's stage directions refrain from identifying the state with the setting of the play in which only his fictional characters appear: "On the wall behind and above the chair, is the emblem, official badge, of the State, sovereignty (a mythical one, since this is rather the State of which Yoknapatawpha County is a unit)." In *Requiem's* play, Temple Drake and Gavin Stevens debate and define a range of responses to the past and to the present that make up the historical process in the prologues.

Requiem expands the method of the "Compson Appendix" by simultaneously updating the lives of characters who appear in earlier novels and extending the historical reach of the narrative to a remote past until the very beginnings of the county are revealed. In the "Appendix," Jefferson begins as "one long rambling onestory mudchinked log building housing the Chickasaw Agent and his tradingpost store"; in *Requiem* the town is at first hardly more than a "postoffice—tradingpost-store." In the "Appendix," as soon as Jason Lycurgus Compson obtains possession of the land, that "square mile" begins to go through increasingly radical transformations; in *Requiem,* as soon as the people of Jefferson begin to think of themselves as inhabiting a town that requires a number of separate and progressively larger institutions, both the rate and the complexity of change are so great that "overnight it would become a town without having been a village; one day in about a hundred years it would wake frantically from its communal slumber into a rash of Rotary and Lion Clubs and Chambers of Commerce and City Beautifuls . . . a fever, a delirium in which it would confound forever seething with motion and motion with progress."

Not just Jefferson but the world itself begins in an extremely chaotic form: "the steamy chiaroscuro, untimed unseasoned winterless miasma not any one of water or earth or life yet all of each, inextricable and indivisible." Just as Jefferson must have its courthouse and jail, then a school, and then its "rash" of organizations, so the world itself becomes cluttered with more and more agencies and institutions, "changing the face of the earth." As the prologues approach the present time of the play, dates begin to proliferate and become more specific. In particular, the second prologue ends with a comprehensive list of names, a roster of cities, lists of forms of transportation, accommodation, and diversion—all of which emphasize the multiplication of man's activities and the acceleration of his motion through time. That Faulkner obtained his statistics from the WPA guide to Mississippi reveals his understanding of a state now opened up to the modern world—no matter how much it held on to its traditions. The changes are so swiftly accomplished a hundred years after its foundation that the members of the town "no longer even knew" who Doctor Habersham and old Alec Holston and Louis Grenier, the founders of the town, were. The original character of the land, forested in the "old days," is replaced by "formal synthetic shrubs contrived and schooled in Wisconsin greenhouses."

In the third prologue, Faulkner switches to the second person, suddenly addressing "you, a stranger, an outlander say from the East or the North or the Far West." "Outlander" is a term frequently used in *Intruder in the Dust,* signifying Faulkner's increasing awareness of how the world elsewhere had now come home, to him and to his characters. Between 1942 and 1948, he had rued but also relished the world's neglect that allowed him his own preserve, invaded only intermittently by visitors. During this reclusive period, even while he resided in Hollywood, no interviews were published, and he did his best to scale back Malcolm Cowley's efforts to profile William Faulkner of Oxford. Gavin Stevens's long monologues in *Intruder* are a lost cause, insofar as the South will not be let alone to seek its own justice. Stevens cannot override the outlanders with words any more than Phil Stone could in his increasing diatribes against northern interference in southern affairs.

Faulkner decided, in *Requiem,* to meet the world head-on, acknowledging "you" as someone trying "to learn, comprehend, understand what had brought specifically your cousin or friend or acquaintance to elect to live here—not specifically here, of course, not specifically Jefferson, but such as here, such as Jefferson." What you observe in Jefferson is a phenomenon occurring everywhere in a changing world. In Jefferson, and in all towns such as Jefferson, an awareness of the past increases at the same rapid rate as the changes that efface its traces. Those who hold on to the past find it in the objects that do survive, such as "one small rectangle of wavy, crudely-pressed, almost opaque glass, bearing a few faint scratches apparently no more durable than the thin dried slime left by the passage of a snail," but that "you will descry to be a name and a date." The scratches, like the cryptic notes in the commissary books, are the tracings of "that tender ownerless obsolete girl's name [Cecilia Farmer] and the old dead date in April almost a century ago—speaking, murmuring, back from, out of, across from, a time as old as lavender, older than album or stereopticon, as old as daguerreotype itself." The pane of glass commemorates the girl's glimpse of the soldier whom "she had not known or even spoken to long enough to have learned his middle name or his preference in food, or told him hers." Farmer would be no more than a ghost of the past—a Judith Sheegog that Faulkner re-created for his children—if not for the human desire to record a name and a life. Unlike Judith Sheegog, Cecilia Farmer rides off with her beloved and becomes an outlander. So history circles back and comes home in *Requiem for a Nun,* even as Temple tries to escape her past and, in the play, is forced to return after Nancy kills her child.

The past is gone and yet forever present in this paradoxical novel. Temple can no more escape her past than Carmody can really renounce Catholicism or Judith Sutpen retreat to England in "Revolt in the Earth." At the end of *The Left Hand of God,* Carmody puts himself under the discipline of the church and awaits his punishment for impersonating a priest. He has not become a believer, exactly, any more than Temple will become a model wife and mother at the end of the play, but the desire to redeem the past, to fix what went wrong, fuels the theological thrust of *Requiem for a Nun* and *The Left Hand of God.*

Although Cecilia Farmer's scratches can seem pathetic, they are really no more so than the labors of the settlers as they "clawed punily" a "tiny clearing" out of the "pathless wilderness," or than the very creation of the "broad blank mid-continental page for the first scratch of orderly recording." All attempts at communication, at defining the world and its history, begin in a seemingly feeble way. Nevertheless, the girl has made her own "scratch of orderly recording," and we are made to feel it, in all of its tangibility, as the message of one human being to all human beings who will follow her: "Listen, stranger; this was myself: this was I." Earlier in the novel the narrator says we want to say "no to death" and to project ourselves into history, back into the past of 1865 and forward into the future of 1965, the last date mentioned in *Requiem for a Nun.* This is our mission, Faulkner implies.

Near the end of the novel the narrator, who has become "the culture itself, relating its collective and imperfectly synthesized memories of its own beginnings,"[32] says that "all you had to do was look at it [the pane of glass] a while; all you have to do now is remember it," and then "you" will hear the "clear distanced voice as though out of the delicate antenna-skeins of radio," the modern mode of communication that Faulkner abhorred in his own home. The radio tended to drown out the artist's voice, but in *Requiem* radio is paradoxically, metaphorically, used to suggest that the lines of communication are still open, still continuous, like the fragile thread of Cecilia Farmer's signature.

The narrator can operate with a degree of flexibility that Faulkner tried to work into Hank's voice-overs, making film at least an approximation of *Requiem*'s eyewitness reporter, speculator, and synthesizer, condensing and dramatizing different rhythms of past and present—and differing points of view. The present overcomes the past, the prologue announces, like the "next act and scene" of a play, "itself clearing its own stage without waiting for propertymen; or rather, not even bothering to clear the stage but commencing the new act and scene right in the midst of the phantoms, the fading wraiths of that old time which had been exhausted, used up, to be no more and never return."

The play joins the historical process of the prologues in the argument between Temple Drake and Gavin Stevens: She insists that her life now is what constitutes her identity, and he counters that her life must now be viewed within the context of her past. The very absoluteness of Stevens's statement—"The past is never dead. It's not even past"—has to be set against the narrator's evocation of life as motion, with a succession of pasts that are left behind in the tremendous velocity of human energy. Not only is each successive moment superseded, the past lives only to the extent that in living in the here and now we can imagine what it was like to live there and then.

And yet the relentless Stevens has a point that is made in the narrative prologues. As soon as the people of the Chickasaw trading post decide to name their place of habitation Jefferson and call it a town, they hitch themselves to the racing engine of history. The analogue in Temple's life to Jefferson's development, to the sense that the present emerges out of the past, is her belief that her child's death has been caused by her involvement eight years before the present time of *Requiem* with the gangster Popeye, and a lover, Red, in a Memphis whorehouse, after her boyfriend Gowan, now her husband, got drunk and passed out. Of course the events of *Sanctuary* are not the precise and the immediate cause of Nancy's killing of Temple's six-month-old child any more than the decision of the men at the Chickasaw trading post to call themselves a town is the precise and immediate cause of the modern city of Jefferson. But each of these initial events sets in motion a train of cause and effect leading to the present. To that extent Temple is neither more nor less responsible for Nancy's actions than the founding fathers of Jefferson are responsible for its present state.

Instead of admitting Temple's right to exist as Mrs. Gowan Stevens, Stevens insists on referring to her as Temple Drake, which is tantamount to thinking of the town of Jefferson as no different from the Chickasaw trading post. Eight years have elapsed in which Temple has tried to be a good wife, to raise a family, to live with her guilt feelings concerning her own past and with her husband's constantly forgiving her for that past. But Nancy killed Temple's child in order to prevent Temple from returning to her past even as Temple's attachment to Nancy, a reformed whore and dope fiend, suggests that Temple has never been willing to abandon that past entirely. Stevens, then, is carrying on Nancy's left-handed work of redemption by putting Temple on trial, so to speak, in their appearance before the state's governor—ostensibly so that Temple can plead for Nancy's life.

Stevens's attempt to uncover the sequence of events that led to the death of Temple's child places a greater burden on Temple than is necessary or wise for a human being who must go on living after a terrible tragedy. In Stevens's view the past completely eclipses the present, and Temple's obsessively repeated question as to whether she will have to reveal all of her past merits sympathy for her and suspicion of Stevens's moralism. His obstinate refusal to set aside any part of her past is as unrealistic and self-defeating as Drusilla Hawk's rigid unwillingness in *The Unvanquished* to set aside any part of Bayard's past. Yet without Stevens's persistence, it is doubtful Temple could surmount the past that she is too quick to say she jettisons. For all their antagonism, the two function together to provide a comprehensive reading of historical continuity.

That continuity seems the point of introducing Sutpen's French architect. In *Absalom, Absalom!* he is created as an adjunct of Sutpen's demonizing in Miss Rosa's account, and in Mr. Compson's as a complex abettor and obstructor of Sutpen's outrageous design. In *Requiem,* he is first introduced as Sutpen's "tame Parisian architect—or captive rather." But the "settlement had only to see him once to know that he was no dociler than his captor." Not a mythological figure but a man, the architect speaks to a community's desire to build an edifice of itself: "You do not need advice. You are too poor. You have only your hands, and clay to make good brick. You dont have any money. You dont even have anything to copy: how can you go wrong?" Jefferson takes its shape from his molds and kilns. Even the destructiveness of war fails to disturb "one hair even out of the Paris architect's almost forgotten plumb." The architect's imprint remains, more than a hundred years later, "not on just the courthouse and the jail, but on the whole town," for he has built and made possible the community's own drive to preserve and perpetuate itself, a drive more narrowly conceived in *Absalom, Absalom!* in relation to Sutpen's ambitions. In *Requiem,* even after the community apparently loses much of its historical identity—"gone now from the fronts of the stores are the old brick made of native clay in Sutpen's architect's old molds"—still there is a surviving remnant of memory and of place found in the "thin durable continuity" of the jail itself and what it stands for.

The analogue in the play is Temple's account of Rider's lonely despair, which is very much like her own. Temple's memory of Rider reveals an awareness that her suffering is not unprecedented in her community; and to that extent the drama of her life is simultaneously a part of her people's history—white and black—entangling all of them, as Nancy tried to demonstrate in her demented murder of Temple's child. It is significant that Rider's name is not mentioned, since Temple is recalling a past separate from her own but similar enough to stimulate a communal consciousness the narrator exhibits in the prologues. Temple's struggle to recall Rider's story becomes particularly poignant when one reflects on the white deputy in "Pantaloon in Black" who missed the meaning of the black man's hysteria. By making Temple a witness to Rider's suffering, Faulkner finds yet another way of making Yoknapatawpha morally and historically coherent. But Temple herself, like her author, does not feel redeemed. She remains in her marriage, answering her husband's call at the end of the play, but her fate (she is still in her twenties) remains undecided. "Temple cannot resee her past so as to begin anew. Nor could her author, with respect to his own life,"[33] as he headed into one of his most demoralizing periods.

The reviews did not help. In the *New Yorker* (September 22, 1951), Anthony West considered the play preposterous and the product of a writer working in the wrong genre, consoling himself with the thought that "Henry James, too, wrote plays, and that Shaw wrote novels." In the *New York Post* (September 23), Maxwell Geismar, never very friendly to Faulkner's art, called *Requiem* "absolutely worthless." He wondered what Faulkner actually made of this trite, sophomoric, and pretentious book. Sterling North's review in the *New York World-Telegram and Sun* (September 24) perpetuated the portrayal of an author wallowing in the "sensational and melodramatic" in "ungrammatical, clumsy prose."

In the *Hudson Review* (Spring 1952), Frederick Morgan argued that the play actually resembled a movie scenario, citing Temple's hard-boiled retorts:

> TEMPLE (crushes cigarette into tray) Then listen. Listen carefully. (She stands, tense, rigid, facing him, staring at him) Temple Drake is dead. Temple Drake will have been dead six years longer than Nancy Mannigoe will ever be. If all Nancy Mannigoe has to save her is Temple Drake, then God help Nancy Mannigoe. Now get out of here. She stares at him [Stevens]; another moment. Then he rises, still watching her; she stares steadily and implacably back. Then he moves.

Line up Lauren Bacall, Morgan suggested. Without a camera close-up to make gestures like crushing the cigarette pop out while understating the passion, the scene seemed too remote for stage work.

Many reviewers did not know what to make of the three prose narratives, but there were exceptions. Milton James Ferguson in the *Brooklyn Daily Eagle* (October 7) declared the novel a "Greek tragedy, in three acts, with the public and the history of the county taking the part of the chorus." Louis

Rubin in the *Richmond News Leader* (September 24) regarded the Jefferson jail as the meeting point of history, where Temple joins Nancy, where the prologues join the play in the awareness of evil and the moral purpose of civilization. In the *Delta Democrat-Times* (September 30), Carvel Collins suggested the "major change from the earlier Faulkner being that he now chooses to write about the struggle for affirmation of belief rather than about the outrage felt by the potential believer. This is not a new coin: it is the other side to the old, the best montage in twentieth century American letters." Rubin considered *Requiem* one of Faulkner's "strongest novels," whereas others, like Irving Howe in the *Nation* (September 29), called it an "ambitious failure," reflecting Faulkner's unceasing experimentation, seeking "new forms and widening the bounds of his subject matter." He lauded Faulkner's rehabilitation of Temple, now a morally complex character, but regretted the play's lack of action. Nancy troubled him, as she did many reviewers: "Her murder of the white child is hard to take in terms of ordinary human motivation," especially since Nancy's action is viewed as the impetus for Temple's salvation. Few critics commented on the novel's title, but in the September 23 *Arizona Republic,* the reviewer said it was a "song for the dead Nancy, who has taken the veil in spirit and has been purified from sin." Granville Hicks (*New Leader,* October 22) regarded Nancy's smothering of Temple's child as an existentialist *acte gratuit,* a sudden disruption, a rebellion against the course of events that she is otherwise unable to stop. In the *New York Times Book Review* (September 30), Robert Penn Warren observed that we accept Nancy, "if we accept her, because we know the world she came from, the world of old Yoknapatawpha." In effect, the review declared Warren's loyalty to a body of work that overrode certain qualms about the play, as though the history presented in the prologues sanctioned the play.

Howe marveled at what he called the prose interludes—the rhapsodic, elegiac, and "humorous recall of the Yoknapatawpha past." For Malcolm Cowley (*New York Herald Tribune,* September 30), the prologues provided a necessary context for the play but also an overview of Yoknapatawpha itself, as if Faulkner's whole body of work is brought to bear on the actions of his dramatis personae. The prologues brought history itself to the subjectivity of his characters, providing a new objective voice to his fiction. This new novel replaced the "unregenerate author of novels about incest, rape, arson, and miscegenation" with a "reformed Faulkner, conscious of his public duties, who has become the spokesman for the human spirit in its painful aspirations toward 'love and honor and pity and pride and compassion and sacrifice.' . . . Soon his readers on the five continents will have to decide which of the two authors they prefer."[34]

20
In and Out of Phase
August 1951–January 1953

HANGING FIRE

In early August Meta Carpenter wrote to Faulkner asking when he would return to Hollywood, and three days later he replied: "I cant now. The Hawks matter is still hanging." *The Left Hand of God* needed more work, but Faulkner had no idea when he might be recalled, and in the meantime he worked on his play.[1] In June, Ruth Ford had found a producer, and Faulkner hoped to have the play ready for the fall theatrical season. He concentrated on act 2, breaking up several long speeches.[2] By the end of the summer he expected to be in New York doing more rewrites during rehearsals. If he knew that a fall premiere was out, he would shelve the play for now and join Meta. Hawks remained the priority, and Faulkner would return to Hollywood if the director wanted him, he assured her: "I am financially 'hot' now, which wont last forever; I'm 53 and wont write good stuff much longer, cant afford to waste what is left writing trash, which will hurt my value, for a temporary sum, most of which taxes will take up." The play would be "good stuff," even if it closed, and he would draw two thousand dollars per week from it while it ran, the same amount as for his Hollywood work.[3] In all, Faulkner produced three *The Left Hand of God* scripts, none of which were produced.[4] But his status in Hollywood had risen. In February 1951, even a Hollywood god like the arrogant Preston Sturges, an Academy Award winner and director of several classics, including *The Lady Eve* (1941), *Sullivan's Travels* (1941), and *The Miracle of Morgan's Creek* (1944), approached Faulkner in awe. Edmund Kohn, a Faulkner friend sitting at a restaurant table, watched Sturges, entering with his entourage, come over: "I never saw a man more meek and humble than Sturges with William Faulkner."[5]

Aunt Bama watched her prize-winning William and detected no difference. She told Carvel Collins that on his last trip home from Hollywood, he exhibited the same kindness that she considered part of his personality. He had told his family he would arrive in Memphis on the 10:00 a.m. plane. But it landed at 8:00 a.m., and he just waited at the airport so that the family would not have to get up too early in Oxford for the drive to Memphis. Faulkner's return reminded her of the family's former glory: When her father returned from Europe, the whole town of Ripley turned out welcoming the hero home from his long trip. Faulkner had, "in a sense, skipped over the generations and had so many of the characteristics of his great-grandfather: literary work, fame, and great leverage on the world," Collins wrote to her.[6] Any number of editors at Random House could have seconded Aunt Bama, as did his agent, Harold Ober, who wrote, "William Faulkner is one of the finest writers alive today and one of the sweetest and gentlest of men."[7]

And one who said he wanted to be left alone: "I have deliberately buried myself in this little lost almost illiterate town, to keep out of the way so that news people won't notice and remember me." He had no intention of cooperating with *Life* magazine reporter Robert Coughlan, who wanted to do a biographical profile. "I will probably do whatever I can to impede and frustrate it," he told Robert Haas. He sent a telegram to Hal Smith, asking him to deter Coughlan. Perhaps that is why Faulkner told Haas about writing his memoirs, "a book in the shape of a biography but actually about half fiction, chapters resembling essays about dogs and horses and family niggers and kin, chapters based on actual happenings but 'improved' where fiction would help." He might even put some of his own drawings into the book. He wanted Haas's reaction.[8] This ploy, sometimes taken by writers to head off biographers, did not jell.

In September, the Faulkners took Jill to enroll in Pine Manor Junior College, in Wellesley, Massachusetts. Leaving home was a relief. Her adolescence had been a trying time—in part because her father had trouble accepting her maturation. Malcolm Franklin's first wife said that a jealous Faulkner, threatened by Jill's boyfriends, appeared naked when one of her boyfriends arrived at Rowan Oak. "Excuse me please," Faulkner said, "it's hot." Jill's anger at both parents came out in a documentary done under the auspices of the University of Mississippi, and she told another Faulkner scholar about a "recurring dream": "in twenty-four hours her legs were going to give out, or be cut off. She would never be able to walk again, and she had to determine how she would spend the time with her parents. She suddenly realized that neither of them cared."[9] Neither of them ever seems to have realized the depth of Jill's estrangement—at least judging by the letters they wrote to Saxe Commins, in which, by turns, mother and father worried about the negative impact the other was having on their daughter.

In parts of October and November Faulkner worked on the play in nearby Cambridge, for a trial two-week run, but that production, as well as one in Paris, was delayed. The problem was not Faulkner's script, but Ruth Ford. Lemuel Ayers, the producer, told Harold Ober he could not finance the play with her in the lead. Ayers liked her and did not want to hurt her feelings, but the difficult lead part required a "really great actress." Ober, knowing that Faulkner had entrusted the play to Ford, patiently waited to see if she could sell herself.[10]

During Faulkner's time in Cambridge, Arthur Kaledin, a Harvard junior, spotted the great man walking along the Charles River and started to walk along in his wake. Faulkner stopped to watch some ducks "washing and strutting." On this autumn day, under a heavy gray sky and a cold wind driving the yellow leaves down to the river, the impetuous Kaledin approached Faulkner. "I quickly explained that I knew him well," Kaledin remembered. "I felt we were already friends." Would it be all right if Kaledin walked beside him? "He shook my hand firmly and said, 'Yes, I am William Faulkner.' I had not mentioned his name." This dapper author, dressed in a tweed jacket and a green corduroy hat, pants a little short, and black shoes, seemed quite old and wrinkled to Kaledin, but also very warm, asking the young man about crew as the shells "slid up and down the river." Kaledin asked him what he was writing, and Faulkner explained his work on a play. But mostly they talked about Harvard: "If he had a son, he said, he would have sent him here. When he mentioned Yale and Princeton, his voice, for the only time, sounded angry. He said they were snobbish, shallow and visceral, adding that only Harvard is capable of producing worthwhile men."[11] Faulkner said he enjoyed Kaledin's company and told him he had recently visited Concord and Lexington and wanted to see Salem soon before he returned to Mississippi. After an hour they parted, and Faulkner thanked him for his company, expressing the hope they would meet again and saying that he liked to walk along the river in the afternoons.

Two days later Kaledin fell in step with Faulkner again in silence. Faulkner had a hypnotizing presence but seemed awkward with someone who wanted to exchange "pointless poetic observations." Faulkner just looked straight ahead as Kaledin complimented him on his work. Ashamed at trying to draw the writer out, Kaledin sensed that writing was a very private experience, a sanctuary that Faulkner did not want to violate. For the rest of their time together, they just walked. There was no more to it than that. Neither one, evidently, had a word to say about Quentin Compson.[12]

INVITATIONS, VISITATIONS, AND HONORS

On October 26, 1951, the renowned author received the award of the Legion of Honor from the French consul in New Orleans. This honor, the highest of five orders, made him a Chevalier, the equivalent in English of a Knight, for twenty-five years of eminent merit in his profession. This honor followed his election to the American Academy of Arts and Letters (September 27, 1948) and his acceptance of the William Dean Howells Medal for Fiction (1950). Often stiff during interviews, the smiling Sir William held up his bourbon as if to study its color and answered a New Orleans interviewer's question: "If I had my life to live over again." He couldn't decide. Maybe as a "woman or a tramp. They don't have to work so hard." Or "a rich orphan—with a trust company instead of kinfolks." Writing was work, of course, but "what else are you going to do?," he asked. "You can't drink eight hours a day. Or make love. Work's about the only thing a fellow has to do to keep from being bored." But then, he followed up with what had become his stock persona: "I ain't a writer. Why, I don't even know any writers, I don't pay no attention to publishers either. They write me a letter—if it don't have a royalty check in it, I throw it away." He preferred silence and horses and trees. Hollywood? "Sunshine all the time," he said, looking to the interviewer like a gloomy tragedian "confronted by a monotony of stormless days." Drinking occupied a good deal of the talk, including references to his grandfather's drying out, part of the puritanical drive of his ancestors that he had rebutted with his beer broadside, advocating the legalization of the drink in Lafayette County. He had a characteristic comment about football: "Why, it's like a musical comedy dance-line now. Everybody in place and kicking on the beat. The old flux and excitement of individual effort is lost in the precision team."[13]

In late November, Faulkner joined the annual hunt. Carvel Collins, in Oxford in August to interview Ike Roberts, heard about a dedicated hunter—going at it for three-day stretches tracking deer all day and coon at night until Ike told him to "ease up."[14] At fifty-three, whatever Faulkner said, he seemed to have plenty of energy—continuing his correspondence with Meta, writing to Joan Williams and Else Jonsson, whom he spent time with in May and June 1952, while ostensibly visiting World War I battlefields for his work on *A Fable.*

In Oxford, Faulkner continued to see his mother every day. His granddaughter and niece remembered his gentle voice: "Mother, we're going to have lemonade now." Like her son, Maud was no joiner, rebuffing invitations to join the Daughters of the American Revolution. During one visit, the DAR ladies came upon Faulkner stripped to his shorts and fled screaming. Maud, an adventurous reader, took *Catcher in the Rye* (1951) in her stride. She thought "For Esme" was the second-best short story in the world—"A Rose for Emily" was the best. Maud had a shoe bag inside her closet with compartments used as a filing case for her son's manuscripts. On the street, she often passed him by, not wanting to interrupt his concentration. Christine Drake, who lived with Maud during this period, remembered that his visits usually lasted about a half hour, after which he would tip his hat and say, "I've enjoyed this conversation with you two ladies." But sometimes mother and son would sit on their rockers, "rocking out of phase with each other by the hour."[15]

In late December, Faulkner wrote Saxe Commins, "I am getting bored, and shall get to work on something soon now."[16] The something was *A Fable,* as refractory as ever while he awaited news of a play production in Paris. He farmed, sailed, and fell off horses, claiming not to have hurt himself but in fact suffering back pain that would soon become excruciating. In June 1952, in Paris, X-rays revealed compression fractures. "I have a broken back," he told Saxe Commins.[17]

Faulkner welcomed the idea of cooperating with a Ford Foundation film about him shot in his hometown, regarding the documentary as "a history of my apocryphal county."[18] He seemed to accept such invitations and visitations—like his appearance at an Ole Miss class—when he did not see a way forward in his writing. It had been a long time since he had "anguished over putting words together, as though I had forgotten that form of anguishment." Was he storing up energy, he wondered, to "start again"?[19] When Pinckney Keel, a young journalist just starting to write, knocked on Rowan Oak's front door, blurting out: "I want to see you. I want to write," Faulkner said, "Well you come on in and we'll see what we can do to help." In shorts and tee shirt, smoking a pipe and speaking low, Faulkner advised: "Then go plow a while until a thought comes. Then sit under a tree and write it down." No need for fancy equipment, Faulkner said, pointing to his aged typewriter. "It will last as long as I need it, I guess." Keel had the nerve to say, "People around here think you are different." With a slight smile, he said: "In Mississippi the people work for their money and you can understand how they feel about writing, why it puzzles them. In Mississippi, a man goes out in the sun and sweats for his dollars." Pinckney came away inspired, even though Faulkner had said no more than "Just keep writing."[20]

On May 15, 1952, Faulkner turned directly toward his fellow Mississippians, addressing an audience of five thousand at the Delta Council meeting in Cleveland, Mississippi. It was a strange appearance for him and for his audience, used to hearing from businessmen and politicians. "When I hear of Delta manners," historian Jim Silver said, "I am reminded of the incident when Faulkner was speaking to the Delta Council. Someone grabbed the microphone, pushed Faulkner aside, and announced that Senator Byrd had entered the hall. The planter audience rose and cheered."[21]

Faulkner had been invited by W. T. Wynn, whom Faulkner called Billy, a former president of this organization founded to address the economy of the Delta. Obviously pleased by Wynn's unexpected compliment, Faulkner repeated it: "We not only want to honor this particular fellow-Mississippian, we want him to honor us." Such a generous gesture called upon Faulkner to summon his own form of crowd-pleasing compliment: "You can't beat that. To reverse a metaphor, that is a sword with not only two edges, but with both edges on the same side; the receiver is accoladed twice with one stroke: He is honored again in honoring them who proffered the original honor. Which is exactly the sort of gesture which we Southerners like to believe that only another Southerner could have thought of, invented. And, sure enough, it happens so often as to convince us that we were right."

He began by mentioning his "fan mail" from "another Mississippi gentleman, who takes a very dim view of my writing ability and my ideas both. He is a Deltan, he may be here today, and can ratify this. In one of his last letters, having reviewed again his opinion of a Mississippian who could debase and defile his native state and people as I have done, he said he not only didn't believe I could write, he didn't even believe I knew anything about farming, either." Faulkner replied that he had never touted himself as a writer and that "after fifteen years of trying to cope not only with the Lord but with the federal government too to make something grow at a profit out of the ground, I was willing to agree with him on both of them."

Could any polished Rotarian speaker have opened with a better gambit? After this jibe at the New Deal, he followed up by keeping his audience in suspense as to the topic of his talk while playing still more with his putative lack of qualifications: "So I shan't talk about either writing or farming. I have another subject. And, having thought about it, maybe I don't know very much about this one either, for the reason that none of us seem to know much about it any more, that all of us may have forgotten one of the primary things on which this country was founded." So there they were: All southerners and also remiss, in some fundamental way, about the Founders' principles: life, liberty, and the pursuit of happiness, which meant not chasing happiness but working for it, which, in turn, meant "not just pleasure, idleness, but peace, dignity, independence and self-respect." The first Americans had risked everything, including their lives, to secure liberty for themselves and for succeeding generations, but then "something happened to us." The fate of the nation seemed more secure, and subsequent generations did not feel the same urgent sense of responsibility for the freedom the Founders had achieved. And "now, in 1952, when we talk of security, we don't even mean for the rest of our own lives, let alone that of our and our wife's children, but only for so long as we ourselves can hold our individual place on a public relief roll or at a bureaucratic or political or any other organization's gravy-trough." Faulkner stood up as a conservative Southern Democrat speaking to his cohort. At the same time scenes of Sam Fathers in *Go Down, Moses,* bequeathing a heritage to Ike McCaslin, sidled into the talk when he spoke of the "responsibility, not only the desire and the will to be responsible, but the remembrance from the old fathers of the need to be responsible." It was quite a moment, enveloping a man who had written more than a few letters complaining about his responsibilities even as he accepted his obligation to assume them. Here was the paradox: a man had to be himself, complete and sovereign, and yet forge his integrity by fealty to family and community. He deplored the "radio, newspapers, pamphlets, tracts, the voices of politicians" talking about rights, not responsibilities, obligations, and duties. But he spoke of "we," including himself and all present as part of the problem.

Americans had allowed themselves to forget the fight for freedom by accepting the welfare state. Faulkner was not blaming anyone, believing that "we" had all been seduced by an enemy within that we did not recognize as such because:

> He faces us now from beneath the eagle-perched domes of our capitols and from behind the alphabetical splatters on the doors of welfare and other bureaus of economic or industrial regimentation, dressed not in martial brass but in the habiliments of what the enemy himself has taught us to call peace and progress, a civilization and plenty where we never before had it as good, let alone better; his artillery is a debased and respectless currency which has emasculated the initiative for independence by robbing initiative of the only mutual scale it knew to measure independence by.

John Kenneth Galbraith would later call this state of affairs "the affluent society," although his New Frontier remedies were far different from Faulkner's. In this too comfortable time, as Faulkner saw it, he issued a contrarian call to action, based on his own brand of individualism. Citing George Washington and Booker T. Washington in the same phrase, as well as other American heroes—Jefferson and Lincoln, Robert E. Lee, Helen Keller, and even the fictional Paul Bunyan—Faulkner delivered his peroration: "I believe that the true heirs of the old tough durable fathers are still capable of responsibility and self-respect, if only they can remember them again." His speech, received with loud applause, was part of the remembering he had now taken up as part of his public role that contributed, as well, to the final two volumes of the Snopes trilogy.

"Another Collapse"

Faulkner worked fitfully, announcing on August 12, "The big book going well," and on August 20: "I seem to have lost heart for working. I cant find anything to work, write, *for*."[22] On September 18, he was admitted to the Gartly-Ramsay Hospital in Memphis. His doctor's notes explain what happened:

5:45pm

WF brought in because of a convulsive seizure, probably due to alcohol.

Had terrible nights. He continued to complain of pain in his back and was given pain pills.

25th WF felt better for the second day in a row. He was better in the morning. Had a convulsion, presumably later in the day, cause unknown.

26th AM Dr. suggested spinal fluid test. WF refused and insisted on leaving in spite of his being fidgety.

This was just the beginning. Answering a frantic call from Estelle, Saxe Commins arrived at Rowan Oak on October 7. His diary describes a scene of desolation: "Bill is completely deteriorated. The mind is gone, the pride is gone, even the gallantry is gone. He mumbles incoherently and can only manage a plea for more beer. . . . His pajama trousers were down and what could be seen of them was streaked with fecal stains and his genitals were exposed." Norfleet, "a giant Negro," and Malcolm carried an enfeebled Faulkner, every fifteen minutes or so, to the bathroom. The editor heard a barely audible "warm and affectionate" greeting from his author. A shocked Saxe described a "bruised and battered" body, a leg "covered by dried feces" that left its "imprint on the toilet seat." The "malty odor" of Faulkner's breath filled the room. Saxe came near a breaking point: "The appeal in his teary eyes almost made me give in. But I had to be stern." Faulkner wanted more beer. In this "shabby, bare, rambling house," deprived of his dignity, Faulkner could not be helped and was in desperate need of professional care that Saxe would arrange even as another crisis ensued:

Just now I was startled by a cry and I got to the stairway just in time to prevent a head over heels tumble from the second to the first floor. Once more the obnoxious note of setting the lord on the throne and carrying him back to bed. This time I was really tough and refused his crying appeal for beer, threatening to go back to New York tomorrow and, even worse, fighting him with the prospect of his being sent back to the hospital in Memphis. At last my sternness was understood. He is quiet now.

I wrote too soon. Again the frantic cries of more beer. Again the support to the bathroom. This time I submitted and gave him another one, and now he is wailing for more. What can I do? . . . This is a nightmare!

Cleaned up, Faulkner looked better the next day, but the family physician, Dr. Culley, delivered the grim diagnosis and recommendation to Commins: Faulkner had to be committed, "in a straitjacket if necessary," although he might become violent and blame Commins for abducting him. The patient had a sound heart, but his kidney and liver were likely to give out.

At Rowan Oak, Commins promised a drink on the way to Gartly-Ramsay, and that got Faulkner going. He drank six cans of beer. Malcolm had to pull over to get Faulkner out of the car, and Commins undid Faulkner's fly so he could relieve his bladder. At the hospital, Malcolm, Saxe, and an orderly undressed Faulkner, who had blacked out. Then Malcolm drove the editor to the airport. The doctors took over:

WF back with more back pain after more falls in past 2 weeks.

[Dr. Adler]: Patient tries hard to cooperate for an alcoholic. Paraldehyde substituted for alcohol. The patient was on a beer kick. He had bad nights and . . . had to increase sedation.

He is not sleeping more than 2 to 4 hours a night due to pain and fidgetyness.

10 Oct: Very shaky today . . . dt's.

Gradually he recovered, taking walks around the hospital grounds. The hospital discharged him on October 21. A grateful Estelle wrote to Saxe: "Just a note with my love enclosed & a word about Billy. His nurse reports this morning that he had a good night last night, ate a splendid breakfast, & was *very* cooperative. That means a lot." They could not thank him enough "for, in your gentle way, taking charge of the situation and getting our 'Pappy' back to the hospital. I am optimistic about him for the first time in many fearful weeks—and you turned the trick."[23]

On October 24, Faulkner wrote to Else Jonsson: "I have been sick. Another collapse, this one pretty bad," but he expected to be "less nervous and depressed by next week, and will write you a better letter then."[24] By the end of the month, he was much stronger but still vulnerable, Estelle wrote Saxe: "The Ford Foundation people are coming . . . but now that is a bother to him. He is afraid his voice is bad & that perhaps it is the wrong time of year. Ordinarily all this would have been done with Billy's usual detachment & ease. But now, he seems actually to worry what people might think— something so foreign to his nature." The documentary filmed a somewhat stiff Faulkner and Stone talking in Stone's law office. "Bill was just as gracious and patient about this as possible, and I am quite alarmed about him," Stone wrote to Carvel Collins. "I want to get him to a doctor soon to be sure he is not developing a split personality. I am telling all this to you because I wish you would get your book on Bill out as soon as possible."[25]

In November, Faulkner was in Princeton, staying with Saxe and Dorothy Commins at their invitation and doing some work on *A Fable*. This was, in part, a Random House rescue-and-relief operation. "A thousand thanks to you," Robert Haas wrote to his colleague, about his "miraculous" rehabilitation of their prized author.[26] In Princeton, Faulkner met a young Frenchman, Loïc Bouvard, and told him: "I love France and the French people very much. I feel at ease in France; it is so lovely." Bouvard began the interview by telling Faulkner that in France "we regarded him as one of the writers of our generation who has contributed most to an understanding of man." Man, not God, had been their focus, led by Sartre and Camus. Faulkner believed that doing away with God, forsaking the idea of a higher power, was a mistake. Bouvard said they had reached this level of conversation quickly—exploring the very themes that Faulkner had written into *The Left Hand of God* and *Requiem for a Nun*. When Faulkner called God "the most complete expression of mankind," he agreed with Bouvard that he was thinking of Henri Bergson's God and of the philosopher's "theory of the fluidity of time. There is only the present moment, in which I include both the past and the future, and that is eternity. In my opinion time can be shaped quite a bit by the artist; after all, man is never time's slave." Faulkner had never said anything like this in an interview, never wanted to discuss ideas at all. Here he seemed to be arguing with Camus: "I don't hold with the myth of Sisyphus. Man is important because he possesses a moral sense. I have tremendous faith in man, in spite of all his faults and his limitations. Man will overcome all the horrors of an atomic war; he will never destroy mankind." In words familiar from the Nobel Prize speech, Faulkner insisted that "art is not only man's most supreme expression; it is also the salvation of mankind," even though each artist "speaks only for himself," and in that speaking creates his own language. Then he quoted Valéry and Gide on the hardship of art and expressed his affinity for Flaubert, Balzac, and Proust, although he claimed not to have read Sartre or Camus. The Bouvard interview is startling because Faulkner, for only the second time, openly acknowledged his worldwide importance and his wide-ranging intellectual interests. Only in the Nobel speech had he heretofore dared to directly address the world beyond the covers of his books.

Faulkner visited Joan Williams in New York, and she spent Thanksgiving with him at the Commins home. She gave herself to him, but he sensed that for her it was not enough, and he began to drink again, which led to another stay in a Bronx sanitarium for several days. They did some writing together for television, a new source of revenue, Faulkner hoped.

In December, he was home again and on Christmas Eve reported to Saxe Commins about doing a "daily stint" on *A Fable:* "Things are calm here yet, due to Jill's presence. But it will probably blow up as soon as she is gone [to college]; already, after a few drinks in her [Estelle], the lightning flicks a little. Hope to God I can keep J out of it, but dont know of course."[27]

By the end of the year he had "run dry" on *A Fable,* he announced to Joan Williams. Three days later, just after New Year's, he wrote her again: "I was wrong. The work, the mss. is going again."[28]

21

Steal Away

January–December 1953

INTO THE NIGHT

Going again, yes, but not in a "fine ecstatic rush like the orgasm we spoke of at Hal's that night," Faulkner wrote to Joan Williams. "This is done by simple will power; I doubt if I can keep it up too long. But it's nice to know that I still can do that: can write anything I want to, whenever I want to, by simple will, concentration, that I can still do that." It was no longer the same sort of fun, though—more like proving to himself that he still could.[1] He worked on *A Fable* every day, he told Saxe Commins, repeating what he said to Williams, but adding, "I must get away as soon as I can." He hoped to be in Princeton by February 1.[2]

Estelle's cataracts had worsened. Malcolm, always close to his mother, took her to the hospital on January 14 for an operation. A week later she had the other cataract removed and recovered quickly. Faulkner feared she would want to accompany him east, but Malcolm alone drove Faulkner to the bus station on January 26. Malcolm's diary reveals that the family depended on him to watch over his mother.[3] Faulkner often portrayed Estelle as the problem, but his mid-February letter from New York to Malcolm suggests otherwise. After a rough two weeks in New York, hospitalized twice because of more problems with his back and self-medication with alcohol, he confessed: "I am distressed at heart very much to have caused all this worry. I know that I have not been quite myself since last spring. I mean, those spells of complete forgetting. I have had three of them, one in Paris for two days last spring, two here. The idea has occurred to me that maybe, when Tempy

386

snatched me off Sunny last March, that when I hit the ground so hard on my back, that I might have struck my head too." He didn't want Malcolm to say anything about these blackouts, assuring his stepson that "Mr. Saxe" had found a good doctor. "Tell Mamma I am all right," he instructed a concerned Malcolm, who had called Commins. "I will take better care of myself. I want you to be fond of me always, but I dont want you to worry, to let worry over me interfere with your work. *Don't worry.* Am glad you called Saxe. Reassure Mamma, as he has tried to do. Remember, he will not lie to you about me. When anything serious happens, he will tell you."

Faulkner's letter to Malcolm suggests that he had brooded some on his drinking, although he never made excuses for his drunks even if he apologized for them. He also did not rationalize his periodic alcoholism, which would soon become public knowledge in Robert Coughlan's "The Private World of William Faulkner."[4] The trouble in New York started when he discovered a bottle of forty-year-old applejack in Hal Smith's sideboard. Perhaps that discovery triggered his memory of Charles Jackson's *The Lost Weekend,* which includes a memorable episode about alcoholic writer Don Birnam's craving for applejack that is locked in a farmhouse closet.

On February 19, Faulkner delivered a nineteen-page typescript of "Weekend Revisited," a story the *New Yorker* rejected but that the *Saturday Evening Post* retitled as "Mr. Acarius" and published after Faulkner's death.[5] Faulkner later called it "funny but true." Before the atom bomb blows everything up, fifty-year-old Mr. Acarius wants to experience the "opium of escaping" and to anticipate the luxury of recovery: "with a butler to pour your drink when you reach that stage and to pour you into the bed when you reach that stage, and to bring you the aspirin and the bromide after the three days or the four or whenever it will be that you will allow yourself to hold them absolved who set you in the world." In Oxford, in Hollywood, in New York, in Paris, and on later trips abroad, Faulkner perfected this periodic alcoholism and recuperation, which in his story becomes Mr. Acarius's effort to "be one with man, victim of his own base appetites and now struggling to extricate himself from that debasement."

Faulkner's story makes a paradox out of periodic alcoholism, which is an acknowledgment of the doom of being human and the equally human, if futile, desire to escape that doom. Mr. Acarius realizes that "in the last analysis there is no escape, that you can never escape and, whether you will or not, you must reenter the world and bear yourself in it and its lacerations and all its anguish of breathing, to support and comfort one another in that knowledge and that attempt." Supposing that he should join other alcoholics institutionalized in a posh hotel, Mr. Acarius, a dilettante who has done nothing, it seems, except collect art, is undone by their constant, frantic schemes to bootleg drinks in a comedy of craving that drives him to flee down a fire escape, saved from an arrest by his rescuing doctor. They rush home, where Mr. Acarius smashes all his liquor in a bathtub as his doctor comments: "So you entered mankind, and found the place already occupied." Mr. Acarius agrees, "Yes," and cries out: "You can't beat him. You cannot. You never will. Never."

Throughout the story, Watkins, one of the alcoholics, keeps repeating the lyric, "Did you ever see a dream walking?" Faulkner told Joan Williams that the character had been based on a hospital experience in which an old man would sing the line all night. Faulkner thought it was funny.[6] Watkins never finishes the song, although its final words, "was you," tell the whole story for those who know how the song ends: "Well, the dream that was walking and the dream that was talking / And the heaven in my arms was you." Watkins wants his girl, Judy, who is kept away by the nurse, but Watkins addresses the lyric to Mr. Acarius, who is another dream walking, a deluded soul. The song seems to sum up a kind of romantic quest in the very dregs of human waste, a wistful, almost beatific vision of the kind that Don Birnam conjures while drinking that sooner or later subsides into ridicule of his own delusions. Mr. Acarius supposes he can escape and also experience the suffering and recovery of mankind, but he finds himself unequal to the occasion. Neither escape nor recovery suffices any more than the alcohol that he annihilates. For Faulkner, such abstinence was as periodic as his alcoholism. He seemed to have no interest at all in psychological explanations of his drinking. He saw it as a manifestation of his anguish and anxiety, not his psyche.[7] In spite of the smashed liquor bottles at the end of the story, "Mr. Acarius" is not the work of a man who wanted to stop drinking.

Robert Linscott, an editor at Random House, had the rare privilege of hearing Faulkner talk about his drinking—"a matter of chemistry." For weeks or months he drank sociably, "then the craving would come," and he would fight it off, or "something would happen that would 'get me all of a turmoil inside,'" and he would escape into liquor. Linscott learned to read the signs: "drumming fingers, evasive looks, monosyllabic replies to questions," and Faulkner would disappear and be discovered "out cold."[8]

Recovery

Faulkner liked working in Saxe's New York office, where he had his own typewriter and desk, but he needed a quieter routine in Princeton, where in mid-February he worked on *A Fable* in the morning, took walks with the Comminses' dog in the afternoon, and then resumed work until tea time, then more work, and a relaxed dinner at seven.[9] Sometimes he accompanied his editor into the city.

Near the end of the month Faulkner submitted to a *New Yorker* interview—more like an observation—in Commins's office as the author "typed very, *very* slowly, mostly with the middle finger of his right hand, but with an occasional assist from the index finger of his left." The keyboard work continued as the phone rang, Faulkner coughed, and his editor worried about a cold. "Isn't anythin' Ah got whiskey won't cure," Faulkner said, getting up and stretching: "Work hurts mah back. Ah think Ah'm goin' to invent somethin' like an ironin' board, so Ah can lie flat on mah back while Ah type." After some talk of Jill and jumping horses and falling off them, Faulkner said, "Ah have a feelin' of doom hangin' over me today," as he returned to his tepid typewriting. Then he began to red-pencil a pile of pages with *X*'s, saying, "Ah wish mah doom would lift or come on. Ah got work to do." To his editor's worried words, Faulkner replied, "Ah can bear anythin'." This routine went on for another half hour until he departed for a lunch date. How much of this was for show is hard to say.

"Not much happier here but am working, busy," Faulkner wrote Else Jonsson on February 22. Even though his back continued to hurt, and he continued to worry that he might have a brain injury resulting from his fall from a horse, he had produced "Weekend Revisited," a reminiscence about Sherwood Anderson, worked on a television adaptation of the "Old Man" section of *The Wild Palms,* and on "Mississippi," his semi-autobiographical essay that continued the movement in *Requiem for a Nun* to explicitly juxtapose his creation of Yoknapatawpha against the state's actual history. All this work helped to cover significant medical expenses and hospitalization and tests, which showed he did not have a skull injury, although a doctor advised him that "a lobe or part of my brain is hypersensitive to intoxication. I said, 'Alcohol?' He said, 'Alcohol is one of them.' The other was worry, unhappiness, any form of mental unease, which produced less resistance to the alcohol." The doctor did not say to quit drinking forever, but he did advise a three- or four-month respite and then more tests. "He said my brain is still normal, but it is near the borderline of abnormality. Which I knew myself, this behavior is not like me."

What behavior? Hal Smith had told Faulkner he could no longer use his apartment. Apparently Faulkner had misbehaved to such an extent that even an old and close friend could no longer tolerate his stays. Faulkner had usually been a sweet drunk, but his alcoholic lapses had become ugly, and that is what Smith found so disturbing. Now sober, Faulkner worked steadily, and planned to stay in New York until June, when he would give the graduation address at Pine Manor Junior College and then take Jill home to Rowan Oak.[10]

Then on Friday, April 10, Malcolm wrote in his diary: "Mama had gastric hemorrhage." The next day, at the hospital, Malcolm noted her condition was fair as he lined up blood donors. She returned home on April 12, still only in fair condition. On Saturday, April 18: "Mama started hemorrhaging again—rounding up donors. P.M. called Pappy. Went to meet P & Jill at airport & picked up 5 pints blood!" Estelle began to recover almost immediately, and by April 25, she was home and, on May 4, part of an outing to see *High Noon*.[11]

During this worrisome period, Faulkner continued to work on the "big book," calling it the last ambitious effort of his career. "I know now that I am getting toward the end, the bottom of the barrel," he wrote to Joan Williams. "The stuff is still good," but now he had to sift out the "little trash" that constantly came up. Did he mean the mannerisms that infect mature writers? Now that he had to labor so long to achieve his best he realized "for the first time what an amazing gift I had: uneducated in every formal sense, without even very literate, let alone literary, companions, yet to have made the things I made. I dont know where it came from." How to reconcile the man Joan knew as Bill Faulkner and the man who wrote those books? He seemed to see "little connection" between them. Perhaps this is why he never bothered much to deal with himself. In his mind, the work stood alone "apart from what I am."[12]

By mid-May, Faulkner had returned to New York, evidently still convinced that he worked better there. He wrote to Meta about her troubled marriage to Wolfgang Rebner. He had seen Wolfie recently. "Write me here [Random House]," he directed her: "tell me your problems, if I can help with them." He seemed in a melancholy mood, telling her he still saw Hal Smith and Eric Devine, though "not as much as I would like. Devine and I liked each other well in the old days. Change in people: the saddest thing of all, division, separation, all left is the rememberings, the dream, until you almost believe that anything beautiful is nothing else but dream."[13] He sounded the refrain of Watkins in "Weekend Revisited": "Did you ever see a dream walking?" The same day he wrote Else Jonsson that Estelle was "better now" and that after Jill's graduation in June he would "go away somewhere to have peace and quiet to work in; I hope it might possibly be Europe for the time or at least some of it, but still I cannot say yet."[14]

On June 18, an exuberant Estelle wrote to Saxe Commins: "What a lovely trip I had & how good it is to be Home once more. The very nicest & best part of my little vacation was the three days spent with you." She hoped that Saxe would visit Rowan Oak. It would "please Pappy no end!" The proud mother and wife announced that Jill had the "highest scholastic record in her class. Bill's address was perfect. He looked very handsome and distinguished in his cap and gown. . . . Remembered Saxe's injunction—say every word as clearly as possible—hence the message was plainly understood." She enjoyed having all of her family at home. "I was so long without them."[15] Did Estelle's happiness mean anything to Faulkner at this point? Still obsessed with Joan Williams, he did not say.[16] But Jill, in a note to Dorothy Commins, certainly put her mother's happiness first: "To these poor thanks let me add my deepest for all you did to make Mama's visit with you wonderful—wonderful for her."[17]

Writing to Joan Williams in early July, Faulkner "ran dry" on *A Fable*: "I would destroy it every night and still try again tomorrow, very bad two weeks." By early August, however, he was so "near the end of the big one that I am frightened, that lightning might strike me before I can finish it. It is either nothing and I am blind in my dotage, or it is the best of my time. Damn it, I did have genius, Saxe." He estimated they would need a few weeks to go over the book (sometime in September, he expected) and do some cutting of the projected seven hundred typed pages.[18] But then Commins had a heart attack, and Faulkner, after hearing Commins was making a recovery, wired: "GLAD TO HEAR IT. BEGGED YOU LAST SPRING TO REST AND LET JOINT EXPLODE. MAYBE YOU WILL NOW. LOVE TO DOROTHY. BILL."

On September 1, Phil Stone, a Carvel Collins informant, announced: "Bill stopped me on the street the other day and told me that he had just finished the best thing that he had ever written and probably . . . the best thing anybody had ever written, and yet there are still people who believe in Faulkner modesty." A week later, Faulkner was not so sure. His mood swings, and what he told Phil Stone, Ben Wasson, and Joan Williams, widened as he alternated between euphoria and depression. On September 8, he checked into the Gartly-Ramsay Hospital for three days, according to the doctor's notes:

Patient is intoxicated from drugs as he was on previous admission. (Had been dosing self?) Asked for paraldehyde constantly. Appetite good but looked dilapidated. Dr. Adler saw him.

9 Sept. Patient complained of vague abdominal distress. The liver was palpable below the costal margin [lower edge of the chest]. There was tenderness on palpating in the right upper quadrant.

10 Sept. Patient left before treatment could be completed. Impossible to reason with him. Called family, but patient left. An acute and chronic alcoholic.

Faulkner seemed to allude to this periodic alcoholic episode in a letter sent later from New York to Malcolm: "Am feeling fine, working again on my mss. which ran dry on me at home in August, which may have been partly responsible for my—and your—trouble. It's going all right now though."[19] Malcolm continued to clean up after Faulkner's lapses.

Then this: On September 28 and October 5, 1953, *Life* published Robert Coughlan's profile, "The Private World of William Faulkner." The piece contained some errors but was the work of a diligent researcher and writer who admired his subject's work. Coughlan had shown up at Rowan Oak, startling Estelle and angering her husband, who then relented and allowed the reporter to ask questions as long as they were not personal. Phil Stone, one of Coughlan's informants, wrote him on September 30: "the article is extremely good and has in it some splendid phrasing. . . . You emphasize too much that Bill occasionally, very occasionally, throws a drunk. . . . On the whole he drinks very little."[20] The next day, Stone reported, "Your article, I think, has the whole town stewing." He promised to collect the gossip and pass it on to Coughlan.[21] A week later he added: "We thought you would also like to know that almost all the grand old ladies around Oxford think your article is very fair and very accurate. . . . I don't know whether Bill is drunk or not, but I haven't seen him for two weeks."[22]

Mac Reed ordered thirty copies of the *Life* issues and showed one to Faulkner when he came into the drugstore. Mac thought Faulkner would be "interested in seeing it." Mac was taken aback when Faulkner asked, "Aren't you ashamed of yourself?" Mac protested: "But people have been requesting it." A furious Maud Falkner canceled her subscription to *Life* and asked Reed to burn his stock. Reed refused. She said interest in the articles was "malicious." He disagreed: "people were interested in her son and admired his ability to write."[23] An outraged Faulkner declared: "There seems to be in this the same spirit which permits strangers to drive into my yard and pick up books or pipes I left in the chair where I had been sitting, as souvenirs." Sweden and France had honored him, but his native land had invaded his privacy "over my protest and my plea. No wonder people in the rest of the world dont like us, since we seem to have neither taste nor courtesy, and know and believe in nothing but money and it doesn't much matter how you get it."[24] Gloria Franklin, Malcolm's second wife, said Faulkner had taken an axe to his driveway to make holes to deter visitors. Lamar Stevens, who sometimes took care of Rowan Oak when the Faulkners were away, claimed that Faulkner "urinated systematically in the flower beds off the front porch when he was menaced by tourists."[25] Locals splattered paint on his "private property" sign, and two teenagers stole it.[26] Such incidents revealed a lingering feeling among some in Oxford that Faulkner was a "character," a neighbor out of place, and, to some, a phony. You never knew what you would meet, how he would be dressed, whether he would have anything to say or pass you by without a word. Such erratic and unpredictable behavior meant people could not place this performance artist—a term that no one then would have used.[27]

In mid-October, Faulkner returned to Princeton and New York to complete the final revisions of *A Fable*. He had written to Saxe: "I will be frank: I would like to stay in Princeton with Dorothy and you, not only because it will be good to work in the quiet and you and I can unravel the manuscript, but because of money." A crop failure had been costly, and working on his book at home gave him no peace. "I have almost got to teach myself again to believe in it. I seem to have reached a point I never believed I ever would: where I need to have someone read it and tell me. Yes, it's all right. You must go ahead with it."[28] Estelle could not be that person. As she told Joseph Blotner, she never did understand why her husband wrote a book so far away from Yoknapatawpha County. And he had tried—reading whole chapters to Estelle and Jill.[29]

Random House rallied around editor and author. "I think Bill's book is simply tremendous. To my mind it's one of the greatest novels that I've read, and I use the word 'greatest' advisedly," Robert Haas wrote to Saxe Commins. Even so, he found parts of it confusing and suggested the "structure and sequences are sometimes harder to follow than need be."[30] "It's great," was Donald Klopfer's succinct verdict on *A Fable*.[31] On November 5, Commins announced to Klopfer: "With this letter Bill is bringing the final, complete, ready-for-the press manuscript of *A Fable*. Both of us feel, in the excitement and lift of working so steadily and to such wonderful purpose, that the script is as near perfection as we can make it."[32] "Random House thinks it's 'a masterpiece.' I'm afraid I think it's a flop," Robert Coughlan wrote to Phil Stone.[33]

Mississippi on the Nile via the Alps

During this final work on *A Fable*'s structure and style, stretching to the end of November, Howard Hawks wrote, cabled, and called Faulkner about a new film project, *Land of the Pharaohs*. He made it sound a lot like *The Wild Palms, Banjo on My Knee*, and "Louisiana Lou" aka *Lazy River*, a New Orleans/Delta medley, with Pharaoh as the original slavemaster:

Egypt is great, perfectly beautiful and very interesting. This can be an amazing picture. Here's a little description which you probably already know.

Egypt is a river, outside of the land alongside of the river it's a desert and all life is centered around the river. Old days the Nile used to overflow and the land was inundated except for the villages which are always built on higher ground, naturally or artificially. During flood times the people worked for the Pharaoh. The Pharaoh was God, he controlled all the people, fed them, and according to his nature, ruled them. If he were warlike they fought, if he were artistic the arts became worth while.

Did Hawks's account of dragging pyramid stones to the Nile remind Faulkner of the Indians rolling that riverboat home to their plantation?

At any rate it was enough for Bill Faulkner, who took off on December 1 to join Hawks in Paris with no word to Estelle. "Did he get away?," she asked Saxe and Dorothy Commins, nine days later.[34] He would not be home for Christmas, a holiday at Rowan Oak he had rarely missed. The job would bring in fifteen thousand dollars plus expenses. To his mother he claimed he did not want a movie job, but "Mr Hawks has been too good to me."[35] His letters home to Maud are reminiscent of his European hegira in 1925, although Hawks put him up in hotels and palaces in Stresa (Italy) and St. Moritz (the Swiss Alps). It was all very beautiful, with stars like Gregory Peck and powerful agents like Charles Feldman, and writers galore, but he said he did not like it and preferred to be home with "Missy and little Jimmy and Dean and Vicki and all my children."[36] He had no word for Estelle. She claimed that "both Jill and I have the happy faculty of never becoming lonely even in this big untenanted house."[37] No one back home heard about his first meeting with Jean Stein in St. Moritz on December 25, or his stopover in Stockholm the next day to see Else.

22

Civilization and Its Discontents

December 1953–January 1955

AFFAIRS

Jean Stein quoting Gore Vidal talking to Jean Stein:

> You were around and somewhat unfocused, not terribly interested in the academic world to which you had been committed at Wellesley, like a nunnery. There you were in your nun's gown. I said, "Meet some more interesting people." So I took you to one or two literary things. I don't usually recommend anybody to go to such things, but if you haven't seen one, you have no idea. And as I've told everybody, I didn't see her for six months, and the next time I did, she was with Faulkner.[1]

William Faulkner:

> Incidentally, a queer thing has happened to me, almost a repetition; this one is even named Jean. She is 19, daughter of the M.C.A. [Music Corporation of America] cap [Jules Stein] living in Paris in the house of her bachelor uncle, the European representative. She came to me in St Moritz almost exactly as Joan did in Oxford. But she has none of the emotional conventional confusions which poor Joan had. This one is so uninhibited that she frightens me a little. . . . She came to Rome when we moved there, and stayed there until her momma found out where she was, and ordered her back to Paris by telephone. I expect any day now for her to come to Cairo. She is charming, delightful, completely transparent, completely trustful. I will not hurt her for any price. She doesn't want anything of me—only to love me, be in love.[2]

It might as well have been Gary Cooper and Patricia Neal in *The Fountainhead* or Cooper and Audrey Hepburn in *Love in the Afternoon*. The Steins wanted their daughter to marry a prince, but she wanted an affair with another kind of aristocrat. She was not like the rich American expatriates Faulkner despised, "who have moved intact their entire Hollywood lives to Europe."[3] To Jean Stein, Faulkner seemed uncomfortable in the midst of this European hotel luxury. "He told me that he liked young people because he felt that they hadn't been corrupted yet.... As we started talking, he felt more at ease with me.... I hadn't read much of his work." That seemed to please him. He did say he thought *A Fable* was his greatest work. She remembered him looking for a location near the Arc de Triomphe, where the runner in his book had "insulted the Generalissimo and then been attacked by the mob.... He took lots of photographs of the street from different angles. I think he always wanted to believe it was his greatest novel." She called him

> the most important person in my life really. I always thought there must be something more in life than what I was growing up in but I was a very scared, shy person, and wasn't able to do it by myself and when I met him he, he became that person that really changed the whole direction of my life. He was a very honorable man, a man of great integrity.... He believed that you are to do something with your life that will have meaning.... He had terrible times of depression.... Very fragile and that had to do with the greatness, you know he was so sensitive.[4]

What she shared with Faulkner, she could not bear to share with others, except to say that his "sense of values" impressed her. That set of principles she always carried with her. "She hated real society types. She was suspicious of wealthy people and social climbers. She was game, adventuresome,"[5] and only much later seemed to suffer from a remorse that she was too young to fully appreciate him. Around him she built a kind of shrine. Twenty years later, when Meta and Joan came up in discussion, Stein commanded, "Don't mention the others."[6]

Faulkner was not alone in his attraction to this "charming, delightful, completely transparent, completely trustful" ingénue, called by another observer "a shy, intelligent young beauty with a breathy, Marilyn Monroe-like way of speaking; a slender, curvy figure; and dazzling smile." Her "tentative, self-effacing manner made people want to protect her,"[7] which also made her a good listener, which she put to good use when she later opened up Faulkner in her *Paris Review* interview, which began her own career that resulted in *American Journey: The Times of Robert Kennedy, Edie: American Girl,* and *West of Eden: An American Place.* She developed, in the words of one of her friends, "a savage view . . . of society and its effects on the sensitive." Right from the beginning she "sought out independent, radical, and ungovernable people."[8] She knew how to cosset the people she liked and remained fiercely loyal to them, revealing remarkably little about her affair with Faulkner.

"I like this city," Faulkner wrote to Joan Williams without mentioning Jean. "It is full of the sound of water, fountains everywhere, amazing and beautiful—big things full of marble fixtures—gods and animals, naked girls wrestling with horses and swans with tons of water cascading over them." The marble faun had been released from his bondage. Back home Phil Stone wrote to Judge Edwin R. Holmes: "It was in 1925 that I sent you the copy of THE MARBLE FAUN and I hope you still have it because the last I heard it is worth from $75.00 to $100.00 as a collector's item." You can pick one up now for around $22,500.[9]

"Bill's letters (three so far)," Estelle told Saxe Commins, "have been notes—mostly business, about taxes etc. Not even the cold comfort of a formal salutation—just plain statements and instructions." He seemed determined, she supposed, to drive her away. "I'd rather not be driven—still it's hard to be completely indifferent and ignore him—I am far from callous—worse luck."[10] She was not the only one. Phil Stone told Carvel Collins he did not see why Faulkner had to go to Egypt to do a script "because any Faulkner can tell you everything about Egypt even though he has never been there. Strictly between us and completely off the record, I am just about fed up with Bill and as far as I am concerned I don't care much if he never comes back."[11]

Estelle called Saxe, a soothing listener, and felt a little better.[12] In March, she did some entertaining, enjoying her guest, Supreme Court justice Felix Frankfurter. "I completely lost my heart to him." She seemed cheerful—or was she just resigned when she said to Saxe: "Bill F. writes that he will be away until June at least—Am glad for him that he can stay away awhile"? She added a postscript: "Did you like Bill's Mississippi?" He had just published a semi-autobiographical piece in *Holiday* magazine, treating himself in the third person, which is perhaps why she referred to Bill F. as though he were a character. "The mother of the 'son-of-the-absconded-banker' cut me dead in our local super-market!," Estelle confided to Commins.

What did Faulkner do in Egypt? He couldn't remember much, Jean Stein said.[13] Faulkner said he hadn't done much. The project had not begun well since he showed up with a bleeding head wound from some misadventure in a bar and then asked Hawks if they were going to do *Red River* "all over again." Later Faulkner said it was the same picture Hawks always made, and made well: "The Pharaoh is the cattle baron, his jewels are the cattle, and the Nile is the Red River."[14] He might have added that the driving of the slaves was akin to the cattle drive in a Hawks western. The other two writers, Harold Jack Bloom and

Harry Kurnitz, like Faulkner, knew almost nothing about Egypt. Bloom found Faulkner irritable and taciturn—no longer the sweet drunk so many other screenwriters had previously encountered. To his mother, Faulkner wrote: "I don't like Egypt—have had stomach trouble ever since I got here—the food, water, sandals— . . . Unpleasant."[15] He had not really wanted to go to Egypt, saying beforehand to Saxe Commins that his back hurt and he was not well.[16]

Hawks wanted them to focus on a Pharaoh obsessed with building a pyramid with legions of slave labor—not so different from a grandiose Hollywood studio mogul (Jack Warner was bankrolling the picture) or Hawks himself, according to his biographer writing about the fifty-six-year-old director's recent marriage to a twenty-four-year-old. Did Hawks, after meeting Jean Stein in St. Moritz, also see parallels with Faulkner, the creator of Sutpen's Hundred, with a penchant for rebirth via young women? Other than polishing some scenes, Faulkner mostly talked out his sequences, and Kurnitz rewrote them and later claimed that only one of Faulkner's Pharaoh lines survived, "So . . . how is the job getting along?" Faulkner wrote Jean Stein on March 14: "Worked very hard this past week. . . . Finished script again, for the second time. . . . He [Hawks] can tear the script up again. . . . But just maybe, maybe, he wont." He did. Faulkner completed his work by the end of March, just before principal photography began.[17]

The film seems Faulknerian, even though he did not write it. The Pharaoh means to make his mark on time with a burial edifice that is impregnable and that will endure, and he hires a foreign architect just as the slave-driving Sutpen does to create his own dynasty, which, like the Pharaoh's, fails. Jokes aside about Faulkner asking if he could make the Pharaoh talk like a Kentucky colonel, he apparently understood why Hawks had chosen him for the project. Hawks wanted more than the prestige of hiring a Nobel Prize winner. The director insisted on Faulkner's important contribution to the film,[18] and who knows what they might have said to one another or intuited during the stages of working on the film when Hawks rewrote what his writers wrote. Faulkner's collaboration with Hawks, begun two decades earlier, remained symbiotic. Concerns about Faulkner's exact contribution to certain films are, to a certain extent, misguided, since the importance of his work consists of precisely his effort to apply his genius even to projects that seemed to affront his intense individualistic mentality.

YOU CAN'T GO HOME AGAIN?

Estelle was not the only one who realized William Faulkner did not want to come home. "I was talking with his publisher the other day. . . . [H]e has a hunch that Bill will never go back to live in Mississippi: that Bill believes he can't write there anymore," Robert Coughlan wrote to Phil Stone, who replied, "I also think that Bill is never coming back to Mississippi and, just between us, I don't care personally whether he does nor not." Stone supposed Faulkner preferred the company of "idolaters" to those who "knew him when." Without doubt, Random House had become a source of support that he now relied on implicitly not just for publication but for many of the necessities of life. "Another reason (strictly off the record) that Bill is not likely to come back here," Stone added, "is that I think he is permanently getting rid of Estelle."[19]

"Bill communicates with us so seldom," Estelle wrote to Saxe Commins on April 19. She may not even have known that he had spent two days in the American Hospital recovering from another binge. Perhaps through Commins, Faulkner found out that Jill wanted to get married to Paul Summers, a West Point graduate and Korean War veteran, since Estelle told Saxe she was "only waiting for Bill's consent."[20] Jill wrote to her father asking him to return home because she wanted to get married. He made it to Rowan Oak by the end of April and announced to his editor that Jill would be married in August. He decided to dedicate *A Fable* to her as a way of saying "Good-bye to your childhood, you are grown now and you are on your own."[21]

Faulkner hoped that Saxe and Dorothy could come down for it. "This business is going to cost, so I will need money probably. . . . Jill and her mother seem bent on making a production out of this, and her trousseau, wedding stuff, bridesmaid's dresses, champagne etc will run to quite a piece of jack I fear."[22] He sounded begrudging, but he was the kind of man who liked to dress up and put on a show. On June 24, 1954, William Faulkner and Estelle Oldham Faulkner signed a "Warranty deed": "In consideration of the love and affection we hold for our daughter, Jill Faulkner, and One dollar cash in hand paid, We CONVEY AND WARRANT TO Jill Faulkner that land as described. . . . This is our homestead, known and comprised under the designation 'Rowan Oak.'"[23]

WAR AND PEACE

Just then politics obtruded. Faulkner never seemed that interested, but he read the papers and had opinions. After signing 1,100 copies of a limited edition, he told Jean Stein, "I hate Wmfaulkner almost as much as mccarthy."[24] After a June party hosted by Paul Summers and his parents, Faulkner wrote his editor about the "damndest collection of prosperous concerned stuff-shirt republican senators and military brass hats and their beupholstered and becoiffed beldames. . . . Fortunately hardly any of them ever heard of me, so I was let alone."[25] Faulkner told the press that politics for Republicans was a "form of behavior" whereas for Democrats it was an "activity. Like poker or raccoon hunting, it's a game you play and have fun at."[26] A journalist at the party heard Faulkner say pointedly, "Nobody should be afraid to say what he thinks." He did not have to add that this was exactly what people feared to do because of McCarthy's anti-Communist smears. Asked about the reaction to the senator's hearings in Mississippi, Faulkner said, "We feel shame down there just as you do here." He feared the rise of autocracy since "man doesn't produce a benevolent autocrat." He understood that politics ought to be taken more seriously, and he would have more to say on the subject in *The Mansion*. "It's something to do when you have failed in something else. We ought to train people for government." When the reporter commented that the "Negro comes out best" in Faulkner's work, he replied: "Maybe the Negro is the best. He does more with less than anybody else."[27] That remark had political implications that Faulkner would be called upon to explain in due course.

His *Holiday* magazine essay "Mississippi," quoted in the state's newspapers such as the *Jackson Clarion-Ledger* (March 18) and the *Hattiesburg American* (March 20), highlighted his ambivalence, his love for the land "not for the virtues, but despite the faults." His inclination to make comments of political significance signaled his emerging role as a public figure. In 1950, he had declined to write an introduction to *Collected Stories*, believing his work should stand on its own, and yet for *The Faulkner Reader*, published on April 1, 1954, he provided an autobiographical introduction that went beyond his semi-fictional reminiscences in "Mississippi." He describes an education acquired in his grandfather's "diffuse and catholic library." He generally skipped forewords and prefaces, "too eager to get on to what the people themselves were doing and anguishing and triumphing over." Yet he had read the preface to a Henryk Sienkiewicz novel about how the Poles had turned back the Turks and saved central Europe. Faulkner quoted from memory: "This book was written at the expense of considerable effort, to uplift men's hearts." Faulkner thought it a "nice thing to say," although then, in 1915 or 1916, he wanted to fly aeroplanes and do glorious deeds, not write books. Maybe, although he was already writing poetry and reading all sorts of things and then publishing his first book that turned him into a demon-driven writer.

The Nobel Prize notwithstanding, Faulkner did not care to make invidious distinctions: "To uplift man's heart; the same for all of us: for the ones who are trying to be artists, the ones who are trying to write simple entertainment, the ones who write to shock, and the ones who are simply escaping themselves and their own private anguishes." Writing was saying "No to death." The words were a triumph over the "dead and fading name." An urge to say as much, outside the realm of fiction, had been carefully controlled after the publication of the notorious introduction to *Sanctuary.* He insisted that Bennett Cerf quash a proposed *Time* cover story in connection with the imminent publication of *A Fable,* eliciting the publisher's awe: "I'll bet you're the only man alive today who ever voluntarily turned down a cover story in Time Magazine!"[28] Even as Faulkner resisted queries and stories about his life, he became more visible, more photographed, more reviewed, more interviewed than ever before. By including his Nobel Prize address, and *The Sound and the Fury* intact, as well as excerpts from his novels and his most popular short stories, *The Faulkner Reader* exhibited a range that exceeded *The Portable Faulkner.*

In a review of *The Faulkner Reader,* Charles Poore in the *New York Times* (April 1) refuted the notion that this supposedly "difficult writer" appealed mostly to cultists and obscurantists. Random House had sold more than a half million copies of his books, and paperback editions approached five million copies. He pushed his point, claiming, "Anyone who can follow the punctuationless cadence of a telephone conversation can follow Faulkner." Dissenters recapitulated attacks on his sordid and ungrammatical fiction, but in the main the rebuttals read like William Schott's in the *Kansas City Star* (July 24): "The harshness and evil Faulkner explores are no more harsh or evil than that of classic Greek or English tragedy."

On August 2, the publication of *A Fable* commanded more than two hundred reviews, the most Faulkner had ever received—many of them by the foremost critics. Their response reflected not only his importance but the long-awaited delivery of his putative masterpiece. Warren Beck in the *Milwaukee Journal* (August 1) hailed a "tremendous venture in symbolic composition," demanding the attention given to a "fugue or symphony" that should be "viewed both closely and in perspective, like great architecture." The book coalesces around a central event in May 1918: "a French regiment's refusal to attack, and the consequent lull at the front, both sides sensing that men might will peace." The Christian parallels are suggestive: the thirty-three-year-old corporal (Christ) leading the mutiny is betrayed by twelve followers and taken to "a high place and offered worldly power." The entire Passion Week story ends in an Easter Sunday denouement.

Beck explained the central digression, a story published separately as "Notes on a Horse Thief." This stand-alone story troubled some reviewers, who did not see its relevance, although Faulkner was using a story-within-a-story maneuver favored by eighteenth-century and early nineteenth-century novelists such as Henry Fielding and Sir Walter Scott. The point of the story is how a black preacher-hostler helps an English groom to steal a millionaire's injured horse, restore it to health, and profit from the winnings in races, but then they abandon themselves to the sheer glory of watching the horse run. Beck called it a story of "spiritual conversion" and an affirmation of "men's recurrent idealism and susceptibility to grace" in a corrupt and hard-hearted world. Beck might have added that the story commented on the paradox of war, in which nobility and ignobility coexisted. War had inspired William Faulkner, and it had also disgusted him, and the characters in his novel exhibit a similar range of reactions.

World War I, Faulkner understood, became a meaningless war begun in the human desire to find meaning in it. Delmore Schwartz (*Perspectives,* Winter 1955) argued that *A Fable,* ultimately, is about the necessity of belief. Schwartz's review is remarkable because he was given the time to absorb and rebut many misguided reviews. He cited the misunderstood example of the English battalion runner, a war dropout who responds to the racehorse story, which inspires in the horse thieves, Schwartz points out, "a renewed belief in mankind: convinced that they have come upon a love and nobility which transcend the enforcement of law, they are transformed into fanatical protectors of the horse's cause and his keeper's safety." Inspired by the story, the runner, another racer, exclaims: "Maybe what I need is . . . to believe. Not in anything: just to believe." As with Nancy's puzzling injunction in *Requiem for a Nun* to "believe," it is not religious faith that is recommended but, in Schwartz's words, the "cause of belief and nobility in other human beings." The agonizing absence of belief, not the war, not the murder of a child, is Faulkner's fundamental subject, to which his books are meant to minister.

Here Faulkner's quarrel with the existentialists is dramatized in the insistence on a concept of God that subjects mankind to a higher authority. The corporal's commander in chief, the marshal, is also his indulgent father, another paradoxical figure who enforces military discipline but also acknowledges his son's claims to spiritual ascendancy. For Beck, the various levels of symbolism, and the characters who represent the "irreconcilable conflict between the expedient world of affairs and the realm of absolute spirit," make Faulkner "more than ever our greatest novelist." Beck's phrasing is telling: Here was a writer who had spent a lifetime wishing he could just be left alone to write but who, again and again, compromised with the "expedient world of affairs," preferring, he said, to be known only by his work, an unknown soldier in the cause of literature. This is one reason why he has the corporal's body blown up and then buried again as the unknown soldier. This is why the English groom, now a soldier, throws the corporal's medal at the commander in chief's state funeral coffin. Faulkner wore his military uniform proudly on many special occasions. But he wanted more—and less. On his discharge papers, under "Casualties, Wounds, Campaigns, Medals, Clasps, Decorations, Mentions, Etc." "NIL" is stamped. When Jimmy Faulkner had won his medal, a frustrated Faulkner could not get him to tell the story. Faulkner had won the Howells Medal, but he did not show up to claim it and said he doubted he had anything worth talking about for two minutes. But the Nobel medal was met with a credo. Then he almost lost the medal on his way out of Sweden. It was found in one of the Nobel House's potted palms. And there would be more medal presentations to come in world acclaim that sometimes meant a good deal and sometimes nothing at all. All the ambivalence of a lifetime fractured *A Fable*. Faulkner wanted to believe he had written his magnum opus because he felt its tensions and paradoxes in his own person. Just before *A Fable* appeared, he accepted another honor: the State Department's offer to attend an international writers' conference in Brazil.

Malcolm Cowley in the *New York Herald Tribune* (August 1) provided a reverential reading of many scenes but still felt Faulkner was caught in a contradiction: "The feeling of the novel is deeply pacifist. It says that war is wrong and that men who refuse to have any part in it are saints or even incarnations of Christ. Faulkner's logic, on the other hand, says that some wars are right, or at least necessary, and that men who refuse to have any part in them are fools. If the corporal is a fool, he cannot be truly Christlike." Is this the passage that provoked Faulkner to tell a friend, "Dr. Busby, outside of Malcolm Cowley, is the greatest living jackass."[29] Or was it this one berating Faulkner's "murky theology":

> But we don't know what to think of the marshal either. He plays a double and even a triple role. He is the judge, or Pontius Pilate, and he is also the tempter, or Anti-Christ, but he is something more than either of these. In this great scene he speaks with such foreknowledge of the future, and with so much loving pity for the sinful and foolish but enduring race of man, that he seems to embody something of the divine." No man, perhaps Faulkner would have replied, can be more than the left hand of God. Like Beck, however, Cowley saw the book as an edifice: "It is likely to stand above other novels of the year like a cathedral, if an imperfect and unfinished one, above a group of well built cottages.

Granville Hicks believed the book explored human redemption:

> Rather than being a book about the evils of war, *A Fable* is about the qualities in man that make for survival and victory. And, as one looks back,

one can see that this has always been Faulkner's theme. He is constantly amazed at what human beings are capable of.

Think how many arduous pilgrimages there are in his books, from Lena Grove's in *Light in August* to the tall convict's in *The Wild Palms,* how many Herculean labors, from Sutpen's in *Absalom, Absalom!* to Chick's and Aleck's and Miss Habersham's in *Intruder in the Dust.*

This was nothing less than a heroic book befitting a heroic writer's career.

Some reviewers, like Maxwell Geismar in the *Chicago Sunday Tribune* (August 1), regarded the solemn and earnest book as an ambitious exemplification of the Nobel Prize speech, and as such too abstract, allegorical, polemical rather than dramatic, and weighted with an "empty moralism." *A Fable* lacked Faulkner's customary "demonic power," complained Orville Prescott in the *New York Times* (August 2). Even at this late date, James Aswell in the *Houston Chronicle* (August 8) wrote a recidivist review calling Faulkner a "loony" who wrote "goo" that would reward only "real esthetic hep-cats." In the *New Republic* (August 23), Leslie Fiedler employed a Faulknerian oxymoron to decry the "furious immobility" of a style that had become "rigidified."

Fiedler stood out for calling *A Fable* a political book—one that was naive, a "Poor Man's Dictionary of Received Ideas." Only such a naïf could have contrived a scene in which generals on opposing sides met in a conspiracy to perpetuate war. Norman Podhoretz (*Commentary,* September 1924) made a similar point about the conference of generals, saying Faulkner saw only "silliness in the machinations of the political mind." But was he so simplistic? What if the scene is not taken literally but rather as a symbolic representation of how civilization had, in fact, collaborated on all sides to continue military conflict? The broader political point is that even generals, like the corporal's father, go to war despite knowing better. And isn't that in fact what historians often discover when they write the history of wars? Faulkner, who had stood aside from the hurly-burly of politics, had over a nine-year period in Hollywood and travels abroad incorporated into his fiction a historiographical perspective, emerging first in the "Compson Appendix" and then in *Requiem for a Nun* as he worked on *A Fable.* It may be, too, that the stalemated Korean War contributed to the book's portrayal of futility.

For Fiedler, only the "Notes on a Horsethief" section represented authentic Faulkner, in which the Reverend Tobe Sutterfield, the black preacher-hostler, called by the French "Toolyman" (*tout le monde*), is a "real rather than a literary Christ adequate to Faulkner's obsessions rather than his ambitions; and where the Negro touches the book it comes most alive; for it is the Negro who must save Faulkner, whoever else is to be the savior of the rest of us." This prophetic passage comes just on the cusp of Faulkner's public statements on race, when it proved impossible for him not to comment on politics beyond the boundaries of his fiction, even as his fiction brought him to that public forum.

Biographers have lamented the book's grandiloquence, lack of psychological complexity, its "unmastered ambivalence," sighed over its "brilliant scenes and many obscure, abstract passages," and called it "flawed in a new adventurous way." But they have also admired it as "magical and fabulous," a "prose poem" that should not be measured by the standards of a realistic novel. Faulkner was interested less in war than the "myth of war."[30] In fact, in his correspondence Faulkner usually referred to his "fable," not his novel.[31] On the front page of the *New York Times Book Review* (August 1) Carvel Collins suggested the book should be ranked with Kafka's parables—in this case about "opposition between nationalism and brotherhood, between force and love."

This fable of fascism, as another biographer suggests, centers on the encounter between father and son, the marshal and the corporal.[32] The corporal is offered absolute power—in effect, inheriting his father's role. But the bequest is renounced, although the renunciation is, in effect, unknown, and in all likelihood, another soldier will confront the same fascist temptation, which perhaps Faulkner recognized in the advent of McCarthyism and in the perennial return of demagoguery, which had been so much a part of the southern politics that governed his life. The issues of human rights that World War II and the American Civil War should have settled remain to be decided, *A Fable* affirms.

On January 25, 1955, the National Book Award judges chose *A Fable* "for its moments of powerful and profound insight, the bold scope of its imagination, and its creation of a varied, many-leveled background of human experience for the legend of Christian sacrifice which it undertakes to tell. Despite its imperfections, the heights it attains make it the most distinguished novel of 1954." Malcolm Cowley, Wallace Stegner, and Robert Penn Warren, all longtime discerning critics of Faulkner's career, were on the panel that provided this mixed tribute to a work that remains one of the most problematic texts in the Faulkner canon. Faulkner himself predicted that "it may take 50 years before the world can stop to read it. It's too long, too deliberate."[33]

CROSSOVERS

Faulkner fought the war before in Hollywood, and *A Fable* was more than a little indebted to his service there.[34] Not only did Faulkner storyboard *A Fable* by posting sequences on his home office walls, in *Today We Live*, "War

Birds," and in *The Road to Glory*, an adaptation of a French film and novel, *Wooden Crosses*, he worked on panoramic scenes that foreshadowed *A Fable* (with a cross on its cover, as the author requested). The concatenation of sounds and sights, near the beginning of the book, resembles a Faulknerian screen treatment:

> [A car] came fast, so fast that the shouts of the section leaders and the clash of rifles as each section presented arms and then clashed back to "at ease," were not only continuous but overlapping, so that the car seemed to progress on one prolonged crash of iron as on invisible wings with steel feathers,—a long, dusty open car painted like a destroyer and flying the pennon of the supreme commander of all the allied armies, the three generals sitting side by side in the tonneau amid a rigid glitter of aides,— the three old men who held individual command over each of the three individual armies, and the one of that three who, by mutual consent and accord, held supreme command over all.

The aural montage that amalgamates the soldiers, their weapons, and the machines of war, the car that moves through the action like a ship that also flies—all in the service of an unholy trinity with aides in glitter given off, most likely, by their medals, and all amalgamated into the one figure who is the supreme commander, superseding the authority of the other two generals and their "individual armies," is the perfect tableau of fascism, or at least of a uniform military condition that paraded itself in Faulkner's imagination as a spectacle that both aroused and appalled him. Such passages seem a kind of Hollywoodism turned against itself, a big scene that inspires awe and ends in anguish at the mobilization of mass and the denudation of individuality.

A Hollywood costumer would have been delighted at the attention to military dress that reflected style and authority, the aesthetics of power that so appeals to fascists: the striking red and blue designs, beautifully polished leather putties, "four different tones of leather," "flareless breeches," the "prim piping of linen collar," the Bedford cords, the "plain G.I. tunic and trousers," an "ill-fitting" private's tunic, the "horizon-blue of an infantry corporal's uni-form," an officer's stick, a sergeant's chevrons, the differences between French, English, and American uniforms—a "German general standing rigid . . . his close uniform as unwrinkleable as mail against the easy coat of the Briton like the comfortable jacket of a game-keeper, and the American's like a tailor-made costume for a masquerade in which he would represent the soldier of fifty years ago," a soldier who had once looked forward to nothing more than a Boy Scout's uniform, "generals in their panoply and regalia and tools of glory," a "pole-thin Negro youth in the uniform and badges of a French sub-lieutenant," Senegalese soldiers "lounging haughtily overhead along the catwalks and lending a gaudy, theatrical insouciance to the raffish shabbiness of their uniforms like that of an American blackface minstrel troupe dressed hurriedly out of pawnshops." Sometimes the uniforms take on a life of their own, as individuals become objectified in war: "there were American uniforms in France, not as combat units yet but singly, still learning: they had a captain and two subalterns posted to the battalion, to blood themselves on the old Somme names, preparatory to, qualifying themselves to, lead their own kind into the ancient familiar abbatoir." And yet, the uniform is also a distinction, an honor, and award, especially to the initiated, to those who wear the uniform as part of their identity so that "all who knew the old marshal's name believed: that the old man remembered the name and face of every man in uniform whom he had ever seen." Uniforms signify the "braided inviolate hierarchate" juxtaposed against the "platoon or section leaders and company commanders and battalion seconds stained with the filth of front lines,"[35] the grime and grind that the fastidious Faulkner wanted to avoid in his aerial pursuits. The uniforms have individual, national, and collective stories to tell, just as Faulkner used his to fashion his own fiction, as he came home to show that he had distinguished himself by becoming part of a larger cause and a world beyond the boundaries of his native reputation.

In *The Road to Glory,* the contest between the French officers La Roche and Denet, which becomes, as well, a friendship, Faulkner began to explore his conflicted and sometimes celebratory vision of war dramatized in the dialogue between the marshal and the corporal. War is not all vainglory, or certainly all heroics. Neither pacifism nor militarism dominates. In the *Road to Glory,* the men just go on, with Denet, in the end, giving the same speech as his commanding officer, La Roche, urging his men to do their duty, as it had been done first in Napoleon's time. But Denet, however much he admires La Roche and talks like La Roche, knows the human cost of such sacrifice, which the film is not prepared to explore. Such endings, devolved from his work with Howard Hawks, left Faulkner with more to say than Hollywood could accommodate. Early on, years before *A Fable* became a book, Hawks, Henry Hathaway, and Faulkner agreed to produce an independent film that they knew had no place in Hollywood.

Did Faulkner conceive then of a "cross-over hit, the text that would bring modernism to the masses by rigging out a well-known 'uplifting story with the abstruse tackle of modernist literary technique'"?[36] To Robert Haas, Faulkner predicted a "rosy future for this book. I mean it may sell, it will be a War and Peace close enough to home, our times, language, for Americans to really buy it."[37] The book has been called an example of "sentimental modernism," an "engagement with the manipulations of American mass cultural entertainment."[38] Personal and family dramas are a staple of sentimental fiction and film, sometimes with religious, especially Christian, connotations. In this respect, Faulkner chose to make his hero more recognizably a Christian martyr of the kind that could be broadly accepted by filmgoers and readers than could, say, Joe Christmas. Remember, this is the writer who would have preferred to write for Mickey Mouse, and who knows what meaning he might have been able to bootleg into cartoons, which, after all, often have a fable-like quality.

The corporal's followers are his band of brothers, a family broken up by war. They become in Hollywood parlance part of what Darryl Zanuck called the "rooting interest" audiences wanted to take in a movie. Faulkner's brotherhood is the opposite of the Dirty Dozen, yet he acknowledged mixing the profane and the sacred, Hollywood and his art, in acknowledging the novel's origins as a "basic idea" suggested to him by Henry Hathaway and William Bacher, although the book subverted studio conventions as much as it adopted them. Hathaway later said he did not recognize much of what he had proposed in *A Fable,* and the flaw from a Hollywood point of view is that the corporal is not built up into a role fit for a star in a commanding central action. As Hawks might have reminded Faulkner: no digressions, no flashbacks.

In movies, men fought, no matter what. Hollywood could show cowardice, as does the Lionel Barrymore character in *The Road to Glory,* and the horror of war—as in *All Quiet on the Western Front* (1930), but no studio product could show the glory of refusing, on principle, to fight. To do anything less than soldier on, in Hollywood, would have been declared a mutiny. When Henry Hathaway first pitched his fable in 1943, Faulkner went for it as for no other scenario during his Hollywood enlistment, developing a fifty-page treatment, "Who?," which, he thought, could be a film, a story, a novel—he wasn't yet sure which.[39] His openness seems of a piece with his work on "Battle Cry," which had incorporated a variety of magazine articles and stories in segments that included the familiar flashbacks and digressions in his novels. The corporal in *A Fable* seems to owe something to Corporal Battson in "Battle Cry," an orphan who does not see himself as northerner or southerner, who believes in the birth of a new nation, begun not in 1776 but in 1861–65, out of Lincoln's own words: "the suffering, the agony, the blood and grief and travails out of which rose a nation which can become in reality the shape of man's eternal hope and which, for that reason, must not and shall not perish from the earth." The long gestation of *A Fable* included separating out that original scenario from the evolving novel. If *A Fable* does not read like a scenario, which suggests Faulkner's successful disambiguation of the screenplay/novel "Who?," *A Fable* nonetheless reflects his work on "The De Gaulle Story" and "Battle Cry" insofar as he explicitly shifts his attention to war as a field of human effort occurring on several fronts at once, between and around the German and Allied entrenchments, with certain allegorical figures, similar to the Hollywood studio approach, emphasizing "collective efforts and the setting aside of individual egos."[40]

On May 2, *A Fable* won the Pulitzer Prize for fiction. Another kind of award was in order for the best work of fiction based on a screenplay.

23

Ambassador Faulkner

June 1954–January 1955

On June 29, Faulkner accepted an invitation from Muna Lee to attend a writers' conference in Brazil: "Can there be more than one Muna Lee? More than the one whose verse I have known since a long time?"[1] Born and educated in Mississippi, she had first been published in *Poetry* in 1925 and beginning in 1941 had worked for the State Department on cultural affairs in Latin America. He told Saxe Commins of his mission: "to strike a blow of some sort for hemispheric solidarity." He expected his editor to suit him up for the trip, specifying a dinner jacket and pants, English shoes ("Church is the maker"), and even directing Saxe to a shop on Madison Avenue where Faulkner had seen the shoes in a display window. He needed a size 6½ B or C width, although he could also wear a 6D. But even that did not suffice: "Not pumps, lace shoes, patent leather evening shoes, with lace-up fronts." This kind of detail reveals how Random House catered to William Faulkner but also how William Faulkner perfected his appearance with a meticulousness worthy of a film star. He did not say if he knew about the growing cult of Latin American writers like Gabriel García Márquez who followed him.

Estelle watched her husband's preparation for departure and could see that he was happy.[2] Two bottles of Peruvian brandy waylaid him, resulting in a two-day debacle and the attendance of a doctor. He recovered, did a public reading of the Nobel Prize speech, and spoke about the vital issue of race—signaling his increasing desire to have his say now that, in effect, the world was watching him. Interviewed by the press from Brazil, Peru, and Venezuela, he performed as the perfect diplomat, declaring he had been "deeply impressed by the intellectual energy of the youth of South America." *Time* caught up with him, reporting his remark that failure "brings me stimulation to try to do better in each new book. . . . I confess honestly that *A Fable* does not please me. It took nine years to write that book and I once tore up its first version."[3] Was this his settled opinion? Did Saxe Commins share critic Lawrance Thompson's long, confidential letter to the editor declaring Random House was "stuck with a dud"?[4] In all likelihood, Commins spared his author that blunt judgment. Random House, especially Bennett Cerf, remained bullish on the book, writing to Faulkner on July 26: "The front-page review in next Sunday's *New York Times Book Review* is wonderful and I am enclosing advance galleys thereof for you. I know you don't care about critics in general, but this piece is so good that I beg you to read it."[5] What Faulkner ultimately thought of the book cannot be ascertained. He gave various versions of this answer: "The work never matches the dream of perfection the artist had to start with."[6]

In Brazil Faulkner had what amounted to a conversion experience, as he explained to Harold E. Howland of the State Department: "I became suddenly interested in what I was trying to do, once I reached the scene and learned exactly what was hoped from this plan of which I was a part." He wanted to do more—not just give an oral report when he was next in New York but to call on Howland to "discuss what further possibilities, situations, capacities, etc. in which I might do what I can to help give people of other countries a truer idea than they sometimes have, of what the U.S. actually is." Faulkner had been impressed with the "high type of men and women" who ran the Foreign Service, and singled them out by name to convey his gratitude. He commended their "tact and dignity and good taste"—all in terms befitting the gentleman diplomat. It had come as a revelation—this new opportunity to spread a code of conduct. Aunt Bama, who liked to point out the physical resemblances between her father, the old Colonel, and her nephew William, might well have been heartened by this latter-day Faulkner who was doing much more than just rambling in Europe. In Brazil, he had lamented: "We Americans once had the beautiful dream of every man's being free. What happened to that dream? . . . We failed in that we forgot the needs of the rest of mankind, perhaps we are too self contented and too rich."[7] By going abroad, he was calling on Americans to return to first principles because nothing less than the entire world depended on it. He wasn't built for this kind of work, which vexed and weakened him, but he would not relinquish this new role, and he would triumph over his setbacks by calling on his sense of duty and obligation.

Howland replied enthusiastically to Faulkner's offer of service, saying, "Reports from Peru and Brazil have been most glowing."[8] Muna Lee told

Saxe Commins that the Faulkner visit had inspired several favorable articles and described how the reticent writer had opened up, impressing everyone with his "high idea of the purpose of writing and his deep faith in humanity." In Peru, he withstood an onslaught of questions for two hours with an aplomb that made the time go quickly. In Brazil, Faulkner spoke impromptu to a capacity audience who listened to him speak about his books, including *A Fable*—"good work although weak in spots." He thought more highly of *Light in August*. Lee relayed the opinion of the secretary general of the Organization of American States that Faulkner and Robert Frost, who had also appeared under State Department auspices, had been "immensely valuable . . . in counteracting international communist propaganda attempts to depict the United States as not only lacking culture but inimical to it."[9]

"THE PERFECT VIRGIN"

Faulkner returned to Oxford a week before Jill's wedding on August 21. Saxe and Dorothy Commins attended, making the "event perfect and complete," Jill wrote to them, knowing full well how often they had comforted, encouraged, and rescued her father. Ben Wasson acted as Faulkner's dresser, helping him put on a wing collar, studs, and cuff links. In a double-breasted waistcoat and striped trousers, he gave his daughter away in a "big and beautiful" ceremony at "quaint red brick" St. Peter's Episcopal Church, with his niece Dean and step-granddaughter Vicki attending as bridesmaids behind Jill in her white satin wedding dress, a sheer white veil, a pearl necklace, heavy lace around her wrists, and with "lace panels inset in the cathedral-length train"— the very cynosure of a traditional wedding as the church's century-old bell rang out. Dean remembered that there were "so many satin-covered buttons at the wrists and from the neckline to below the waistline that Miss Kate Baker had to use an old-fashioned buttonhook to get Jill into the gown, which showed off her eighteen-inch waist to perfection."[10] At the reception Estelle appeared in a "stunning marionette blue taffeta gown fashioned by Triana-Norell of New York," reported Jane Sanderson of the *Memphis Commercial Appeal*. Guests spread out over the lawn decorated with Chinese lanterns Estelle had purchased in Peiping (Beijing).

Shelby Foote remembered a euphoric Faulkner who said in front of his daughter: "Isn't Jill the perfect virgin?" She wouldn't look at her father.[11] Bern Keating, who photographed the wedding, found Faulkner an impressive physical specimen. He was extremely strong with the "kind of muscle on his back that farmers have."[12] Faulkner invited Carvel Collins and his wife and daughter to the wedding. Collins noted to another member of the family that

Faulkner's "mother and his brother John were, through the years, most supportive of my attempts to get at least some of the facts straight about William Faulkner's life and works."[13]

Upset over the printing of family photographs in Robert Coughlan's *Life* magazine articles, Faulkner forbid press coverage of the wedding. The *Memphis Commercial Appeal*, which ran an interview with Estelle years earlier, assigned Sanderson to infiltrate the event. She called Estelle, thinking "mothers are sympathetic." Sanderson supposed Estelle would want a record of the wedding to "cherish for a lifetime." Sanderson arrived at Rowan Oak properly dressed in a "luscious raspberry organza." She had brought a photographer with her, and both quietly went about their business, insinuating themselves into the event. Sanderson did not see a euphoric father. He was "sulking under a mammoth magnolia tree." He looked "resplendent" in tails, "gazing pensively at absolutely nothing." Sanderson, mission accomplished, decided to accost Faulkner and tell him about her assignment. She described him as standing back and taking a good look at her. He seemed amused and said, "Now they're coming in disguise."[14]

Faulkner seemed to like Paul Summers, described by Faulkner friend Jim Silver as "an extremely pleasant guy, wonderfully outgoing, extroverted . . . and a nice man." Silver told Carvel Collins that he had once heard Faulkner "make a very quiet remark which struck Silver as an extremely damaging one." Faulkner, musing, said, "'I have never seen Paul pick up a book.' This was not said with great hostility but with a kind of judgment on the kind of person he [Paul] was."[15]

For both mother and father, their daughter's wedding proved a joy and a woe. Estelle's granddaughter Vicki remembered that after Jill's wedding, her grandmother's drinking rapidly got out of control: "Dorothy and Saxe left, and my parents had to go on elsewhere. I was left after the wedding at Rowan Oak with Grandmama and Pappy. I had just learned to drive that summer, and I didn't drive too well, and I didn't have a license yet. Grandmama went off the deep end and was in bed, immobile, out! She had lost her baby. Her Jill was gone!"[16]

Ella Somerville, a family friend who had been part of the drama group at Ole Miss when Faulkner wrote *The Marionettes*, explained what it was like when Estelle drank. She would come over to Ella's and say she was out of gin because her guests drank so much. Ella would play along with this "ladylike fiction" and say that she, too, had guests, but they had not been drinkers. Ella would produce a bottle and offer a few drinks to Estelle—but not enough to get her drunk. During one of Estelle's boozy bouts, Faulkner interceded, calling Ella and pleading with her to take Estelle with her on a planned trip to New York. A reluctant Ella said she already had her plane reservations and theater tickets.

In truth, she did not want Estelle to ruin her trip. An insistent Faulkner said he would arrange with Random House to supply more theater tickets and cover expenses. Ella relented, and to her surprise Estelle came through the New York excursion without causing trouble. This example of how Faulkner looked out for his wife impressed Collins, who had heard so many stories to the contrary.[17]

Weddings in Faulkner's fiction (think of *The Sound and the Fury* and *Absalom, Absalom!*) are fraught affairs. Ella Somerville said husband and wife were in their bedrooms passed out.[18] Then Faulkner went on a "binge of binges," with only young Vicki to take care of him. After two days of trying to "keep at least the beds clean of vomit and excrement and everything else, Pappy somehow, in his drunken stupor, realized I couldn't take it anymore, couldn't handle it. I was too immature." He mumbled, "Get Malcolm to take me to Byhalia." He spent a few days at Wright's Sanatorium in Byhalia and then, on his return home to Rowan Oak, greeted Vicki with, "I knew you were in trouble."[19] He could never relinquish the idea that even while drenched in drink he was in control.

Then he departed for New York in early September, leaving Estelle stranded, and Jill upset, trying to reassure her father of her happy marriage but also suggesting that it partly depended on her mother's well-being. "Dear Pappy," she wrote on September 20: "You've always scrupulously kept your word to me—so there's really no reason I should mention this, but for the record, you have opened an account for Mama at the Oxford bank so she will feel free to do as she wishes? (& be able to do so). We agreed that was the best solution—remember?" Jill wanted his help "in making Mama happy. Please, Pappy, I'm depending on you to do every thing possible to give Mama happiness. I'm afraid she feels I'm more or less lost to her."[20]

In New York, in the early fall, Faulkner worked on short stories and recorded work for Caedmon Publishers in that soft breathless voice that glided over the long sentences, keeping inflections to a minimum. He recited but did not dramatize his work. In addition to selecting excerpts from *As I Lay Dying* and "Old Man," he included his Nobel Prize address and parts of *A Fable,* suggesting that whatever his misgivings, he saw this later work as central to his achievement. He asked Random House to keep the recording and to send a copy to Jean Stein, who remained much on his mind.[21]

HOME ALONE

On his return home in mid-October, Estelle, for once, would not be there to back him. On October 4, she had visited Phil Stone's office, asking him to help her with a passport application. She was going to visit Cho-Cho, then living in the Philippines with her husband, Bill Fielden. Estelle told Phil that she wanted to get away "before Bill got back." Stone did not know what this meant and told Robert Coughlan, "it probably means nothing, as most of what Estelle says means." He had never accepted her as a worthy wife to his friend, and in this instance his disgust prevented him from even imagining she was about to make some momentous changes that would in the years to come mark a recovery of an artist's identity and independence.

Faulkner did not see this coming change. Apparently no one did, perhaps not even Estelle. "E leaves for Manila Friday [October 29]," he told Saxe Commins, "still says she does not want to go, but ticket bought, trunk shipped, and apparently she is. Nice to be able to spend 3000 bucks doing something you constantly remind the owner of the 3000 bucks you dont really want to do."[22] Estelle did balk. She wasn't eating, and Gloria and Malcolm Franklin found her constant requests for them to eat with her tiresome, but "anything to keep peace and get her on her way," Gloria said. But she understood what Estelle had had to put up with. "I don't know how long Pappy will be able to stand it alone in the house—with no one to cook for him etc. . . . I sort of wish he would go back to N.Y. . . . Pappy is doing fine, so far, he has been in good spirits & I think utterly amazed that Mama really left him," Gloria Franklin wrote to Saxe and Dorothy Commins. "Perhaps a taste of being alone in that house would serve him right & do him good. I hope when he finds that no one is going to entertain him, he will return. That would be just one more thing off of our minds to worry about."[23]

Estelle Faulkner had returned to the environs of her first marriage and to the grounds of her fiction. She enjoyed the Fieldens' "charming home on the Bay," a lovely garden adjacent to the beach, with "interesting neighbors" and "splendid servants." She confessed to homesickness.[24] She also revealed a sensibility that had not changed, and an imagination like her husband's that transcended the confines of her time and place: "The artificially induced gaiety of the Far East is very pronounced here—a feverish clutching at nothing that is a little short of terrifying," she wrote to Saxe and Dorothy Commins. She sat "looking out on Manila Bay with its warships & carriers . . . ready for instant action." She felt "an insecurity verging on panic. But in a little while I'll go on out to tea, cocktails, dinner & what have you, and join in all the inconsequential chatter of the internationals."[25] William Faulkner was not the only one dining with diplomats.

"THE DREAM OF PERFECTION"

In November, Faulkner went on the annual hunt, but his heart, he told Jean Stein, was not in it. "I began to discover several years ago that I dont want to shoot deer, just to pursue them on a horse like in the story." He referred to "Race at Morning," which he had finished in September and the *Saturday Evening Post* would publish on March 5, 1955. The story features a twelve-year-old adopted by Mr. Ernest, who teaches the boy how to hunt while showing that the chase is more important than the kill. Mr. Ernest lets the twelve-point buck survive another year. The life shared between the boy and the buck is the point, Faulkner realized, just as Jean Stein's youth revived for him his own youth. He had had enough of killing: "Because every time I see anything timeless and passionate with motion, speed, life, being alive, I see a young passionate beautiful living shape.[26] Did writing *A Fable* also have an impact on how he now felt about the hunt? He had written a note (unpublished) insisting it was not a pacifist book, but the power of pacifism is evident, especially in his depiction of war's futility, although the mood that prevails in "An Odor of Verbena" is pacific as well.

Faulkner spent Christmas with Jean Stein at the Comminses' Princeton home, while Estelle wrote to Saxe and Dorothy to say: "What a treat for him [Bill]—You are so wonderfully kind and generous to us." Jean accompanied Faulkner to receive the National Book Award on January 25, 1955. His brief speech announced a theme he would often repeat about the artist's struggle "to create something which was not here before him," and the failure to match the "dream of perfection." The award stood out in a culture that went on its way avoiding artists most of the time, he said. The award was like writing on the wall of existence: "'Man was here also A.D. 1953 or '54 or '55', and so go on record like this this afternoon." He gave the award a kind ambassadorial purpose: "To tell not the individual artist but the world, the time itself, that what he did is valid." The failure that he earlier spoke of had to be "splendid," a quest for "unattainable" perfection. Success had not come easily to him, and perhaps that is why he distrusted it in a country, he said, where success is "too easy." He ended his speech with what amounted to a proposal: "Perhaps what we need is a dedicated handful of pioneer-martyrs who, between success and humility, are capable of choosing the second one."

The very way Faulkner walked along Park Avenue near Grand Central Station in his trench coat and Alpine hat, looking into shop windows impassively, bespoke a man "contained and unhurried, in the madding crowd," said interviewer Harvey Brett, who accompanied him. Faulkner's words came right out of the National Book Award address: "The writer in America isn't part of the culture of this country. He's like a fine dog. People like him around but he's of no use." But then he mentioned the possibility of doing more work for the State Department, prompting Brett to suppose writers might yet have their uses in the Cold War competition with the

Soviet Union. Faulkner seemed doubtful and yet counted on writers to show a "side of our country" that people abroad did not know. It would never be easy, though, for Faulkner to believe in this new role: "The artist is a little like the old court jester. He's supposed to speak his vicious paradoxes with some sense in them, but he isn't part of whatever the fabric is that makes a nation."[27]

24

Past and Present

February–August 1955

The Old Hunter and the Artist

In February, Faulkner worked on the dummy for *Big Woods,* published on October 14, in time for hunting season. This collection included what he called "interrupted catalysts."[1] Set in italics, the interpolations between stories give the book a historical heft similar to *Go Down, Moses* and *Requiem for a Nun.* In the first catalyst, Faulkner portrays the "thrusting back" of the wilderness by *"one vast single net of commerce"* that *"webbed and veined the midcontinent's fluvial embracement; New Orleans, Pittsburgh, and Fort Bridger, Wyoming . . ."* before presenting "The Bear," Ike's initiation into the premodern wilderness. An excerpt from "Red Leaves" that precedes the second story, "The Old People," depicts the Indians hunting a slave, another way of reifying the italicized history of dispossession described at the beginning of *Big Woods.* In "The Old People," featuring mixed-raced Sam Fathers (Indian, black, and white), Ike is told: "Think of all that has happened here, on this earth. All the blood hot and strong for living, pleasuring, that has soaked back into it. For grieving and suffering too, of course, but still getting something out of it for all that, getting a lot out of it, because after all you don't have to continue to bear what you believe is suffering; you can always choose to stop that, put an end to that. And even suffering and grieving is better than nothing." The "blood hot and strong for living," which Faulkner sought again and again in his affairs, realizing how they would end, and his willingness to suffer the consequences, made the stories about much more than hunting. Even the third story, the slight, comical "A Bear Hunt," is given a historical frame by the italicized passage from another Indian story, "A Justice," about the logrolling of Doom's steamboat to his plantation, exploiting his people and ruining the wilderness as the trees are cut down for the potentate's pleasure procession. The values Ike learns in "The Bear" and "The Old People" are overrun by the railroads driving into the wilderness, the paved roads, the economic enterprises of the Snopeses while *the Big Woods themselves being shoved, pushed just as inexorably further and further on.* Something of Faulkner's own ambivalence, reflected in his diminishing appetite for the hunt, seems to counter the nobility of the last story, "Race at Morning," which is preceded with semi-autobiographical passages from the essay "Mississippi" and followed by an italicized excerpt from "Delta Autumn" that ends the book: *"This land, said the old hunter. No wonder the ruined woods I used to know don't cry for retribution. The very people who destroyed them will accomplish their revenge."*

Faulkner devoted meticulous care not only to the stories but also to Edward Shenton's drawings for *Big Woods*.[2] On a double-page spread, he noted: "The foliage is right, most of the leaves still on. Yes, live- and pin-oaks, many. Yes, moss. Cypresses too. Contents page. I like the sumac, myself. To Mr Shenton: yes, this is right." The observations were precise—on Lion, the dog that helps to bring down "Old Ben": "It is the bony ridge of his brow which gives him a look of concern which seems to me a little wrong." The history had to be right: "This was roughly about 1880. He [Ike] could have worn either hat or cap, I think. The cap makes him look more like the boy he was. I think the muffler and coat are right. He could have worn a Confederate private's jacket, as you see country people now in 1945 battle jackets." The interplay between the drawings and the words reveal the sophistication of an often overlooked Faulkner volume: "To Mr. Shenton: would you risk suggesting Sam Fathers is an Indian to this extent? He is bare-headed, his hair a little long, a narrow band of cloth bound or twisted around his head? Or maybe definitely long hair showing below a battered hat? Since you are not illustrating, but illuminating (in the old sense) you could have any liberty you like. I realise the figures must be too small for much detail." Faulkner had profound respect for a fellow artist: "Mr Shenton is doing so well, I am extremely timid about getting in the way," Faulkner said to Saxe Commins.[3]

Lewis Garnett in the *New York Herald Tribune* (October 14) called the book "something new . . . Mr. Faulkner's fabulous Old Testament." Carlos Baker (*Nation,* October 29) concluded: "Faulkner and his editor have achieved a real unity, both of theme and development." Baker took the book's dedication to Saxe Commins seriously: "We never always saw eye to eye but we were always looking at the same thing." He noted the "slow swing of the seasons from November round to November, the deliberate spiral down the years from reconstruction to modern times," the very arc and tempo of Faulkner's own life. Baker referred to the "old ghosts of the Chickasaws" never forgotten in the book's forward motion, the very natives that Faulkner had so enjoyed talking about with Will Bryant while shoring up Rowan Oak and making it inhabitable for another generation.

Most reviews were decidedly short, implying Faulkner had produced a minor work, or simply a rehearsal of previously published pieces, and did not even note, as Dayton Kohler did in the *Louisville (KY) Courier-Journal* (October 23) that the stories coalesced around the "theme of the passing of the wilderness, which for most Americans in our century is little more than a region of myth under the sunset, a symbol of man's lost happiness and freedom." That one sentence alludes to the volume's wistful quality and humor that brought back that happiness and freedom. The book was an elegy, the "struggle to accept loss" and to restore in memory at least the virtues of a bygone time.[4] Reviewers occasionally mentioned Shenton but apparently did not see, as Faulkner did, how much the illustrations—like the one of the fleet deer emerging from the woods—make this lost world magical and palpable.

Hal Smith, staunch friend of William Faulkner and his publisher, reckoned in the *Saturday Review* (October 29) with the book's pessimism: "In the prefaces to each of these stories and in the epilogue to 'Race at Morning' he infers that while man is doubtless endurable he can also look forward to an existence that may not be worth living." Smith might have added that the very hunters Faulkner honored had been responsible for the demise of their happiness—or perhaps Smith did say as much by quoting Faulkner's evocation of a time when unthinking men went about "changing the face of the earth, felling a tree which took two hundred years to grow, in order to extract from it a bear or a capful of wild honey."

FOOLS RUSH IN

William Faulkner had known for several years that the United States Supreme Court would strike down segregation. Robert Farley, a childhood friend, and dean of the Ole Miss law school (1946–63), had told him so.[5] The issue of race and civil rights, muted in *Big Woods,* became a focal point of Faulkner's engagement with history in the spring of 1955. On March 20, ten months after the Supreme Court declared segregation unconstitutional, the *Memphis Commercial Appeal* published his letter, which began, "We Mississippians already know that our present schools are not good enough." White students went out of state to obtain their education in the humanities, law, engineering, and medicine. Phil Stone, although a staunch segregationist, had done as much. Mississippi had failed to "assuage the thirst of even our white young men and women. In which case, how can it possibly assuage the thirst and need of the Negro, who obviously is thirstier, needs it worse, else the Federal Government would not have had to pass a law compelling Mississippi (among others of course) to make the best of our education available to him." He did not just blame the state. He made it more personal and uncompromising:

> So what do we do? make them [the schools] good enough, improve them to the best possible? No. We beat the bushes, rake and scrape to raise additional taxes to establish another system at best only equal to that one which is already not good enough, which therefore wont be good enough for Negroes either; we will have two identical systems neither of which are good enough for anybody. The question is not how foolish can people get because apparently there is no limit to that. The question is, how foolish in simple dollars and cents, let alone in wasted men and women, can we afford to be?

On April 3, he made clear the damage segregation had done at home and abroad: "What we need is more Americans on our side. If all Americans were on the same side, we wouldn't need to try to bribe foreign countries which dont always stay bought, to support us." The world, he realized, was watching, and now adjusting to his role as diplomat he wanted America to set the right example to itself as well as to others. If *Brown v. Board of Education* had been the catalyst for Faulkner's controversial letters, his work abroad, which he intended to continue, also made it imperative that he speak up. To a letter writer who had challenged Faulkner's qualifications to speak on education, he replied: "I have no degrees nor diplomas from any school. I am an old veteran sixth-grader. Maybe that's why I have so much respect for education that I seem unable to sit quiet and watch it held subordinate in importance to an emotional state concerning the color of human skin."

On April 17, Faulkner commended an anonymous letter from a student supporting integration and pointedly placed his faith in the younger generation, implying that he knew full well that many of his own contemporaries did not share their children's sense of fair play and tolerance. "And what a commentary," he concluded, "that is on us: that in Mississippi communal adult opinion can reach such a general emotional pitch that our young sons and daughters dare not, from probably a very justified physical fear, sign their names to an opinion adverse to it." In his speeches at Jill's graduation from high school and college, he had called on students to assert their individuality, which now meant, he admitted, taking the risk not only of disapproval but even of violence.[6]

AN EDUCATION

What had Faulkner learned?—not only from Mammy Callie, Uncle Ned, many other family black people, the workmen who had helped him to restore Rowan Oak, and all the others he saw around the square and talked to, but also from Earnest McEwen Jr.? Two years earlier, sometime in the spring of 1953, Faulkner met McEwen for the first time. Born in Oxford, Mississippi, in 1931, McEwan grew up wanting two things: a house with running water and a college education. He read everything he could find—not an easy task in a community without a bookstore and where black people could not check out books from a library. Only half the state was literate, and of that 50 percent, only half were literate enough to read a book; among the African American population that figure was surely lower. But Earnie, his friends said, was the kind of person who could see the other side of the mountain—a man ahead of his time, although they wouldn't put it that way.

No one in Earnie's family served as a model for his aspirations. With the exception of his father, who bought some land from a friendly white man, Earnie knew about only two kinds of black families: those who were share-croppers and those who were not. Both his parents had eighth-grade educations. Unlike his light-skinned father, McEwen looked quite black. His family, a mixture of African American, Native American, and white—every range of color—picked cotton from sunrise to sunset. They could not afford books. He liked to read the books borrowed from his teachers; others he retrieved from the trash. He sold packets of seeds to buy books. He was the first in his family to make it through high school. Then a janitor's job opened up on the Ole Miss campus, and Earnie was hired. After work, he would read the newspapers, books, and magazines wherever he could find them. A black janitor reading on a segregated campus excited attention. A faculty member let Earnie use his office as a quiet place to read.

If you were black and had dreams of bettering yourself, you kept it to yourself. To do otherwise could lead to trouble and worse. True enough, the old Colonel had financed an African American's education, but such support remained an anomaly in the Jim Crow South that hemmed in Earnie and his contemporaries. To speak up about his dreams, as Earnie did, to any-one—white or black—would invite attacks for not knowing his place in a segregated and oppressive economy of human relations that restrained, when it did not crush, a black young man's ambitions. But Earnie was magnetic, and he persisted, talking to anyone, white or black, on the Oxford square or on campus, expressing himself with a natural spontaneity that seemed to charm, when it did not overwhelm, his auditors. Logically, someone like Earnie should not have existed. Writing him into fiction as a character might well have elicited cries of "improbable!" William Faulkner might conceive of a character like Lucas Beauchamp, proud and independent, acting like the equal of the white people who tried to subdue him and even lynch him, if necessary, but to imagine, let alone to actually find, a man like Earnest McEwen Jr. in the environs of Oxford, Mississippi, would have seemed unlikely. But what could not be imagined happened. Sooner or later, it is apparent now, Earnie would tell his story to someone who would not only want to help him but would find a way to do so.

In 1953, on the campus of Oxford, Mississippi, an Ole Miss student introduced Earnie to Dean L. L. Love, who had heard the janitor's story. Love had been raised in Oregon and educated at Ohio State, where he received his Ph.D. and served as a dean. He had family in Kentucky and Tennessee and considered himself partly southern. Earnie was not an activist. He was not a member of the NAACP and did not advocate integration. Love saw him as the type of black leader the state needed.[7] But Earnie wanted to study engineering at a northern college. Love initially thought of Howard University but then persuaded Earnie to consider Alcorn A&M College, the nation's first public historically black land-grant institution, founded in 1871 in Lorman, Mississippi.[8] Love told him, "Mr. McEwen, I think I know someone who can help you." When Earnie's daughter, Gloria Burgess, later recalled this moment, she marveled at "Mr." Who called a young man like Earnie "Mr." in the Jim Crow South? Dean Love handed over a piece of paper with the name William Faulkner written on it. "Tell him I sent you," Dean Love said. Earnie had heard about this aloof author who lived on the edge of town but could not imagine why William Faulkner would take an interest in him.

When Earnie arrived at Rowan Oak in his Sunday best, walking down that long corridor flanked by cedar trees and approaching the front steps of this restored antebellum home with the pillars that are so much a part of a southern white hegemonic world, no one can say what he was thinking, but Earnie did not break stride as he walked into his future. Awaiting him was William Faulkner, who already knew his visitor's story and had decided on what was needed. They spoke for hours in the shade of old oak trees. Earnie talked about his reading. Already married with two daughters, he wanted a better future for them. "Mr. McEwen, do you have a college in mind?," Faulkner asked. He approved of Earnie's choice of Alcorn. The segregated University of Mississippi would not enroll its first black student, James Meredith, until 1962—and then only with the support of federal troops.

Faulkner said he would pay for Earnie's college education. When Earnie, who had always been his own man and always supposed that somehow he would fund his own dreams, told his benefactor that he could not accept his offer, William Faulkner, in effect, told him: "You do not understand. I do not expect you to pay me back. All I ask is that someday, when you can, do for someone else what I have done for you." Every month Faulkner sent money to Alcorn, arranging for Earnie and his wife to get jobs too so that they could live near school. Dean Love also sent food and clothes.

So began a lifelong friendship. Earnie moved away to Michigan but brought his family home to Oxford, usually at Easter, and, as his daughter Gloria remembered, they would sit on Rowan Oak's side porch sipping lemonade as their father paid his respects to Mr. Faulkner. No one in the McEwen family ever said much about these visits, and Earnie made no special effort to tell this remarkable story, which probably would not have become part of William Faulkner's biography without Gloria's efforts. Over more than a decade she sought to learn more details about her father's story. She made calls to William Faulkner's family, but they rebuffed her. No one came forward, which may not have surprised William Faulkner, because he had cautioned Earnie: "Even with a college education, you may find that the world has not changed that much for you." But Earnie persisted, becoming a lab technician and then beginning a career in engineering; his daughters pursued careers in education and social work.

The world did change for the McEwen family. A whole row of McEwens came to hear Gloria Burgess tell the story of her father at a congregation of Faulkner readers on the Ole Miss campus, sharing with the assembly what a difference his friendship with William Faulkner had made in all their lives. As she told a part of the story related here, the family responded, as they would in church, with the familiar call-and-response in a rising crescendo of affirmation reminiscent of the Reverend Shegog's sermon in *The Sound and the Fury*. Gloria Burgess, an inspirational speaker, was just as moving as Shegog and with the same mission, as though she arose out of the pages of a William Faulkner novel, with her family whom she called out by name, giving a voice and a character to the history that William Faulkner had helped to foster.[9]

"THE EMPTY MOUTHSOUND OF FREEDOM"

Quite aside from helping a deserving black man, Faulkner saw in Earnest McEwen Jr. "hope for the individual man," the bedrock conviction on which

America had been founded, audiences at the University of Oregon and the University of Montana were told in April 1955. The speech, later published as "On Privacy" in *Harper's* (July 1955), had been occasioned by Robert Coughlan's biographical profile. To inhabitants of the "old nations," the new land had proclaimed, Faulkner wrote: "There is room for you here from about the earth, for all ye individually homeless, individually oppressed, individually unindividualised." Civil rights, and the right to an education, derived from this promise of a relief from oppression. Embodied in every American, in short, was the nation itself. To tyrannize over any individual in effect meant violating the nation as well. That American dream of the sovereign individual "is gone now," he asserted: "We dozed, slept, and it abandoned us. And in that vacuum now there sound no longer the strong loud voices not merely unafraid but not even aware that fear existed, speaking in mutual unification of one mutual hope and will. Because now what we hear is a cacophony of terror and conciliation and compromise babbling only the mouthsounds; the loud and empty words which we have emasculated of all meaning whatever—freedom, democracy, patriotism—with which, awakened at last, we try in desperation to hide from ourselves that loss." Upset over McCarthyism and over the invasion of his own privacy, Faulkner lamented the loss of a core belief, that the writer—apart from his work—could be free from public scrutiny, that "his private life was his own; and not only had he the right to defend his privacy, but the public had the duty to do so since one man's liberty must stop at exactly the point where the next one's begins; and that I believed that anyone of taste and responsibility would agree with me." But Faulkner had discovered that the public not only wanted a piece of that privacy, it kept in business the publications that catered to their tastes for such personal exposure. Thinking of Coughlan, Faulkner said, "It's not what the writer said, but that he said it." The writer now became part of the market for bad taste: "The point is that in America today any organization or group, simply by functioning under a phrase like Freedom of the Press or National Security or League Against Subversion, can postulate to itself complete immunity to violate the individualness—the individual privacy lacking which he cannot be an individual and lacking which individuality he is not anything at all worth the having or keeping—of anyone who is not himself a member of some organization or group numerous enough or rich enough to frighten them off." Faulkner cited other examples—Lindbergh and Oppenheimer—stripped of their privacy so that they became "one more identityless integer in that identityless anonymous unprivacied mass which seems to be our goal." This de-individualization had been carried out in the name "of the empty mouthsound of freedom." The erosion of privacy he equated with the eradication of individuality. He cited instances of people who had perished in press campaigns that took away their sense of themselves as individuals. A special anger seethed through the speech, emanating from Faulkner's belief that in America the artist did not count—unless his fame could be used to sell something.[10]

In Oregon, the speech earned Faulkner a thousand dollars and a little peace of mind. He was driven to the Mackenzie River, a great fishing spot. He didn't say much but offered that the scene was "even more beautiful than I thought." Over an enjoyable dinner, especially two drinks, he conceded, "This type of thing could get to be a habit—people listening and such a substantial check."[11]

For the brief stopover in Montana, where critic Leslie Fiedler headed the English department, Robert Linscott passed on this advice: "As you can imagine, Bill doesn't enjoy lecturing and does it, frankly, for the money. . . . He doesn't like crowds, receptions and chit chat. You'd get along with him just fine and he'd love to see the Montana country but inquisitive females and fancy cocktail parties make him nervous. . . . Bill likes a Martini at lunch, one or two Bourbons (preferably Old Grandad) and water before dinner. . . . Bill is a good guy and a gentleman in the absolute sense of the word."[12]

What to make of Faulkner's dour necropsy of the American Dream while he enjoyed himself on various jaunts? Was it enough to have his say and move on? "I do a lot of moving about these days," he wrote to Else Jonsson, "doing jobs for magazines in New York, and international relations jobs for the State Department, have been in South America and there is a possibility of Europe some time soon I understand." He did not sound upset over these assignments: to cover a hockey game and the Kentucky Derby for *Sports Illustrated*,[13] but then he seemed between novels, or perhaps even wondering if he would write another one. Sailing on the Sardis Reservoir in his sloop occupied part of his time. Another offer came from Hollywood, but he thought not—"I dont think I need the money at present," he told Saxe Commins.[14]

But he still considered escaping from home—now a troubling place, he wrote to Else Jonsson on June 12, because "there are many people in Mississippi who will go to any length, even violence," to prevent integration and full voting rights for the Negro. "I am doing what I can. I can see the possible time when I shall have to leave my native state, something as the Jew had to flee from Germany during Hitler."[15] Surrounded by family and friends who remained arch segregationists, Faulkner felt cornered and alienated. "Apparently what has happened to Bill is that the Nobel Prize has completely turned his head and has convinced him that he is now a world authority on every subject including education and law," Phil Stone wrote to their old friend

Hubert Starr. "He has been writing a lot of letters to the Memphis paper about the situation. Also, as you know, glorifying the nigger is now one of the leading fads in New York City and that is where Bill sells his product. I am still bewildered that glorifying the nigger should be popular in New York and at the same time glorifying the Confederacy is too. I can't figure that one out. Perhaps you can."[16]

On July 5, Faulkner responded promptly to Harold Howland at the State Department: "Yours of July 1st at hand. I will be prepared to leave here at any date you set." By July 29, he was on his way to Japan, desperately drinking and worried about how well he could perform abroad but determined to do his duty anyway.

25

East and West

August–October 1955

In February 1954, Marilyn Monroe visited Japan and Korea on a two-week tour that electrified the troops and excited worldwide press coverage that far exceeded the reception accorded to any other American public figure traveling abroad. It seemed that no moment of her public appearances remained unrecorded in photographs and on film. The recently established United States Information Service (USIS; later renamed the United States Information Agency, or USIA), dedicated to public diplomacy, decided to give William Faulkner the star treatment, creating a thirteen-minute documentary, *Impressions of Japan: William Faulkner,* about his three-week visit. It did not include, of course, his staggered start, when he missed a reception, complained of a bad back, and in general seemed so out of sorts that Leon Picon and his USIS staff dreaded a disaster. The ambassador wanted Faulkner gone, but Picon offered to resign if he could not rectify the visit. A grateful Faulkner promised to do better, and he did.

The film begins with a Northwest Airlines plane landing in Tokyo, shots of Faulkner disembarking, looking surprisingly fresh in a neat white jacket and dark trousers, with close-cropped hair, carrying a briefcase, walking into the terminal, where he is met by reporters to the accompaniment of a voice-over narrator: "This is how it began, the probing questions and bright lights, the posings and signings." They want to know about his trip, what he thinks of Japanese culture, man's soul, and Ernest Hemingway.

What was he thinking? Did he remember Estelle's return with a Japanese nurse in a traditional dress that wowed Oxford, and Ben Wasson, who listened to Faulkner say Japanese women were sexually different and made on the bias? Or that scene in *Today We Live* when Claude sends Bogard a Japanese parasol? Or the Japanese detention camps that are just beyond the boundaries of "Golden Land" in that story's references to the way Angelenos miss their Japanese gardeners? Or the attack on Pearl Harbor in "Two Soldiers" and the talk of "whupping the Japanese," or Major de Spain's boy, who runs his plane into a Japanese battleship in "Shall Not Perish," or the work in "Battle Cry" on Mama Mosquito, the old Chinese woman who miraculously outwitted the Japanese invaders, and his work on *God Is My Co-Pilot,* the story of the Flying Tigers who fought the Japanese in China?

Faulkner had some practice at handling a press scrum on his earlier trip to South America but also in a Ford Foundation seventeen-minute feature that had followed him around Oxford talking to friends and posing in the square. Howard T. Magwood, the director of that film, had called Faulkner an "interested actor," willing to restage scenes like his graduation speech to Jill's high school class. "He's very good," Magwood said. In fact, Faulkner now had a persona, what is now loosely called an icon, that he had perfected.

The film cuts to shots of a locomotive traveling from Tokyo to Nagano and then to a contemplative Faulkner in a Japanese robe seated beside a koi pond reading and puffing on his pipe: "a peaceful, pleasant place, a nice place to live," he is quoted as saying. Then several shots show him visiting ancient temples "containing the secret of man's salvation." He meets with a Buddhist abbess and is shown answering students' questions, articulating his faith in the individual. He is quoted as saying the Japanese wanted to meet a person, not an intellectual, a writer whose books spoke the "simple language of humanity." Over several shots of people of different ages the narrator reports Faulkner's wish just to look at the faces Manet and Van Gogh would have loved. One fleeting shot of a child and a toy boat in a pond recalls—at least to a Faulkner biographer—his delight in watching children and adults float their boats in Paris. A pilgrim praying segues to a geisha performing a ritualistic series of gestures that seem, the narrator quotes Faulkner: "elfin: puckish: or more than puckish even: sardonic and quizzical, a gift for comedy, and more: for burlesque and caricature: for a sly and vicious revenge on the race of men." We see what Faulkner watched, and we wonder what he thought of the painted face, the mask not so different from the masks of *The Marionettes.* As we see Faulkner's kimono-wrapped servant set the table, the narrator supplies what Faulkner says:

She does not speak my language nor I hers, yet in two days she knows my countryman's habit of waking soon after first light so that each morning when I open my eyes a coffee tray is already on the balcony table; she knows I like a fresh room to breakfast in when I return from walking, and it is so: the room done for the day and the table set and the morning paper ready; she asks without words why I have no clothes to be laundered today, and without words asks permission to sew the buttons and darn the socks; she calls me wise man and teacher, who am neither, when speaking of me to others; she is proud to have me for her client and, I hope, pleased that I try to deserve that pride and match with courtesy that loyalty.

She bows as if to acknowledge the voice-over tribute.

Next, shots of Faulkner in a car, pipe in hand, gazing at and praising the countryside, the impressive mountains and rich rice-growing land. He thinks of the rice paddies at home—larger and worked by machines and not as intensively cultivated by Japanese hands. He is shown talking to farmers—telling them about his farm and saying he is really just a farmer. He walks in an orchard and comments on how the apples are covered in paper in ornamental displays reminiscent of Christmas trees, but here they are integral to the everyday culture of these people. Among various water features he extols a culture's oblations to water itself. He is shown hefting various house-making tools of ancient origins. Did he say anything at all about his own craftsmanship in wood and words? He observes a house built without nails. He sits on a floor watching an archer. The film does not show his own attempts at archery, which were wide of the mark. Taking up the challenge, though, was part of his characteristic openness to this new culture. The film does not disclose what Faulkner later confessed: He often felt awkward and out of place. The archery exhibition puzzled him. The archer had been knighted by the emperor and performed a kind of ritual, shooting at a target at a short distance. Faulkner said the archer would "get up, and go through certain motions to free . . . his forearm from his kimono, and then he would pace forward so many paces and bow to where the Emperor would be. Then he would get up and go through some more ritual and fit the arrow to the string, and then he would pace towards the target and stop and turn and do a sort of a—a ballet almost and draw the arrow back and let it go, and sometimes it hit the target but that didn't matter. Nobody cared, you see. . . . It was no trouble to hit it." What Faulkner did at this point is not clear, but he realized that he had "committed a—a fearful—it was more than a *faux pas*. It was *lese majesty* somehow. I—I had made a—a dreadful social error, and that is the Japanese—we simply could not communicate."[1]

The film suggests otherwise with a closing low-angle shot of Faulkner gazing out over a Japanese vista of land and village, similar to his sketch in "The Hill" and to a passage of perspective he had yet to write about Yoknapatawpha in *The Town.* The film ends with a testimonial: "Something fragile contained in the mountains, but something supple and sturdy and enduring, a place of beauty worked wisely by such kind people." Not a word of Faulkner's fiction is quoted in the film. His own voice is never heard. But in his silence and composure he seems the wise man and teacher he denies himself to be.[2]

In *To the Youth of Japan,* a USIS pamphlet, he presented a harsher view of Reconstruction than appears in his fiction, a view that historians of Reconstruction would now reject, especially his description of "the conqueror [who] spent the next ten years after our defeat and surrender despoiling us of what little war had left. The victors in our war made no effort to rehabilitate and reestablish us in any community of men or of nations. . . . But all this is past; our country is one now. . . . I mention it only to explain and show that Americans from my part of America at least can understand the feeling of the Japanese young people of today that the future offers him nothing but hopelessness, with nothing anymore to hold to or believe in." To rebuild required faith in man, "in his own toughness and endurance." Faulkner extolled art as the "strongest and most durable force man has invented or discovered with which to record the history of his invincible durability and courage beneath disaster, and to postulate the validity of his hope." Good writing had fueled the southern resurgence, he claimed—an idea that twenty-five years earlier he would have scoffed at. He predicted the same renaissance for Japan and its writers as they responded to war and defeat—although he tactfully never applied the word "defeat" to the Japanese. The only worthwhile struggle was for freedom and the consent of the governed—and not for an ideology or race.

Over three weeks Faulkner gave ten interviews, meeting with fifty Japanese professors of American literature, giving press conferences and talks—enough to fill a book—with a degree of courtesy and unprecedented patience. He remained "genial and informal."[3] He knew how to entertain, delighting the Japanese when he told them he wrote *Sanctuary* in order to buy a horse. The film and photographs and transcripts do not reveal his long silences, which made his utterances all the more dramatic, even when they were not otherwise remarkable. He loved talking to children, who did not ask him about Ernest Hemingway. This grueling schedule tired him, and he wanted to drink. Picon told him, "You are under contract to the U.S. government," and Faulkner came through—doing better, Picon noticed, if he included young pretty women in the audience. Faulkner soon had his own young attendant: Midori Sasaki, who shaded him with an umbrella and blushed behind her fan when he flirted with her. She reminded him of Jean Stein, he said. He had it in his plan to join Jean in Italy after his Japanese assignment. As for Sasaki, she later received $490 from a fund Faulkner set up for worthy students. She attended the University of North Carolina at Chapel Hill.

Asked about the "Negro," Faulkner predicted the coming of "complete equality," but it would take time ("maybe in three hundred years") and patience, especially on the part of black people because of white people's fears of economic competition. He was between novels, he explained, and would continue to write.[4] Many of his answers were restatements of the Nobel Prize address. Where he could, he mentioned Japanese literature—mainly as he understood it through Ezra Pound's translations.[5] When he said that "every young man should know one old woman . . . an old aunt . . . just to listen to," readers of his work and his biography might think of Aunt Jenny or Aunt Bama. The posture of young Japanese females pleased him, although he did not elaborate.[6] As to the South, he maintained the same ambivalence he had acknowledged in his essay "Mississippi," declaring, "I was born there, and that's my home, and I will still defend it even if I hate it."[7] But another part of his reasoning suggested he could not stand with the South alone since the development of rapid communications and travel meant a country could not "conduct its affairs without much regard for other countries. . . . [O]ne nation's trouble now is everybody's trouble. One nation's freedom is every man's freedom."[8]

The professors wanted to know what he read and what influenced him. His remarks on the Old and New Testaments had a bearing on *A Fable,* although no one, including Faulkner, made the connection. He read the Old Testament for its stories about people and the New for "philosophy and ideals" with "something of the quality of poetry" that dealt with the "aspiration of man within a more or less rigid pattern, such as the pattern of the art formed by philosophy." Critics had complained about the rather abstract, allegorical characters in *A Fable,* treating it as a New Testament that lacked the rich storytelling of the Old Faulkner.

Asked about Rousseau, Faulkner maintained the same position he adopted in *Sutter's Gold.* There was no going back to a state of nature, no return to recover humanity—only "advancement. . . . We must take the trouble and sin along with us, and we must cure that trouble and sin as we go."[9] He spoke simply and directly, striking one American professor as the "least affected and most genuinely modest man I ever met."[10]

Faulkner patiently and diplomatically answered every question and explained why he had decided to do so. As a young man he was "busy . . .

[d]oing the work. Later on, when the blood gets slower, just like the athlete that can't move as fast as he could once, he has more time to become aware of what people think, and then it becomes more important to him what people thought because that is the only measure of whether he has wasted his time or not, is what people think. And if what he has said caused people to want to talk to him, to ask him questions, if young people are interested enough to come where he is and want to know what his experiences were, then that is a reward for what he did."[11] That attention paid mitigated his frequent remark that in America writers did not count for much in a moneymaking economy.

The polite question-and-answer sessions rarely touched on personal matters, but Faulkner was asked about drinking. "I consider drinking a normal instinct . . . [a] normal and healthy instinct."[12] Faulkner was good with chopsticks,[13] seemed to fit in for all his Western ways, and the State Department staff considered his visit the high point in Japanese-American relations. For many Japanese, the encounter with Faulkner was memorable and powerful, as one American witness told Joseph Blotner. And yet Faulkner had his doubts. At Mary Washington University a questioner remarked that he seemed to have touched the Japanese. "Well, I hope so," he responded, "but I wasn't aware of it at the time. They would ask me the same questions over and over and then answer them themselves."[14]

On August 23, Faulkner left Japan for Manila, spending two days there with Bill and Victoria (Cho-Cho) Fielden and somehow managing to fit in some sailing. To Leon Picon, Faulkner wrote he was already missing Japanese food and sake. He had taken to Japanese ways, wearing a kimono. Whitman biographer Gay Wilson Allen had watched Faulkner imbibe considerable quantities of the local brew but never saw him drunk.[15] To Picon, Faulkner wrote, "I hope things will go well here, to match our good Japanese record." He was meeting with the press and various literary groups.[16] He reiterated much of what he said in Japan, emphasizing what had brought him to the public stage. It was not the Nobel Prize per se but to see "these many people, some of them young people, coming to hear him because they believe that he knows something of the truth. That is better than the Nobel Prize."[17] He had always had a special feeling for young people. They were the unspoiled ones who could change the world. At the University of the Philippines he said: "I saw more people listening to me than I ever saw before in my life. And I do hope that what little I may give you, tell you, you will remember after I am gone." How much of a diplomat he had become is evident in his saying, "When I leave your country I will leave something of me behind, that someday I will be forced to come back here to recover it."[18] He made a good impression. He seemed the antithesis of the so-called Ugly American second-raters depicted in a novel with that title three years later. He was, paradoxically, humbly proud about America's contribution to the world and not at all defensive when criticism of it came up in conversation. And of course as a southerner he had his own complaints that he aired in Japan that put him on their side, and in the Philippines as well, with its history of brutal and patronizing American interventions. He was good listener, often giving answers that were shorter than the questions and comments put to him.

A STAR TURN WEST

Word had been sent ahead, and on August 28, Jean Stein met William Faulkner at the Rome airport for a ten-day amour. Did Stein offer him her little bag of chocolates that she often produced for friends at the theater? She adored art, had an affair with sculptor Alberto Giacometti before she met Faulkner, and she would later start an important literary magazine, *Grand Street,* fund aesthetic endeavors, and produce three important oral histories. Artists wanted to be with her, attend her parties, and meet one another. "She was interested in their minds and imaginations," as a friend of hers put it. As the daughter of a powerful Hollywood agent, she had learned early to size people up and had a toughness that allowed Faulkner not to worry, as he did with Joan, about what pain or confusion his interest in her might cause. Not since Meta had he found a woman so given over to him, and yet, even at twenty, Jean was more worldly than any woman he had ever wooed, except for Else Jonsson. At the same time—and this was part of Jean's paradoxical appeal—she had a "fluttery vulnerability" to go along with that breathy Marilyn Monroe voice. She was "gamine and bird-like, a determined waif," a figure very like Audrey Hepburn and the epicene women of William Faulkner's fiction. This was no cheerleader or gushing William Faulkner fan. When they discussed his work, she opened him up—a rare experience for a man who kept his process of creation so private. Sharing himself with her was also a way of opening up to a world that he felt all too often was closing in upon him. Decades later, her friend John Heilpern teased her: "'Terrific start. Faulkner yet . . .' She looked surprised. 'But he was really interesting,' she protested, and meant it."[19] She was a Hollywood princess and would have known exactly what it was like for William Faulkner to be at the mercy of agents and studio heads. She watched countless actors and Hollywood's power elite cater to her father. Like Faulkner, she went out of her way to be herself. Her daughter said, "She loved quirky people and misfits . . . whistle blowers and trouble-makers." Hilton Als said, shortly after Jean committed suicide: "She really was a teenager in spirit. She never became jaded and never forgot the feeling of what it is like to feel like to be new in a place."[20] She appealed to William Faulkner's powerful feeling for the young and stimulated his reckoning with the world-shattering changes he was about to write about in *The Town* and *The Mansion.*

A taciturn Faulkner proved a disappointment to Italian writers Alberto Moravia and Ignacio Silone. After his Asian tour he seemed all talked out. On his visits to three cities, he did manage to revive and deliver a characteristic salvo: "The people in our State Department in Europe are intelligent people. They have learned by hard experience that the enemy, the opponent, is not the foreigner, it's in the State Department in Washington, the bureaucrats in Washington." Feted by his Italian publisher, Alberto Mondadori, Faulkner loosened up, writing an appreciative thank-you note for "your kindness and courtesy," and for a "happy and memorable" visit. He then resorted to a diplomatic formula he had worked out in Japan: "They say to part is to die a little or if not to die, at least one leaves some part of oneself behind, which I have done in Milano and Italy, so that I shall not be complete until I have returned to Italy and Milano and joined myself whole again."

In Paris by September 19, after a brief visit to Munich for a performance of *Requiem for a Nun,* Faulkner departed from routine by consenting to more than just a diplomatic interview for Cynthia Grenier, the young, attractive wife of a Foreign Service officer. The setting helped. On an Indian summer day, he stretched out on the "broad green lawn at the back of the U.S. Information Service building." As one of his Oxford acquaintances put it, "in the out-of-doors he seemed to open up."[21] Perhaps it helped too that her last name was the same as one of the founders of Jefferson, Mississippi. She sat beside Faulkner, looking into his "very alert black-brown eyes under epicanthic lids." He may have admired her vocabulary as well. She seemed smitten with this well-turned-out "handsome man, with a well-brushed head of white hair" and "tanned face." Perhaps the secret of drawing William Faulkner out had to do not with the questions but with the quality of attention—what the interviewer could give to him by way of a relationship. This romantic portrayal included a close-up: "His chin juts up and out meeting the world directly and defiantly. He speaks in a soft, slow voice with what could be called an educated Southern accent." Educated—as in practiced, refined? She caught the stops and starts that now were part of his persona: "Sometimes his sentences are short—'cause I do'—and other times when he is speaking of his craft or his beliefs fine long involved rhetorical sentences roll out, as they do in his prose." Interviewer and author shared an intermediate realm—somewhere between the everyday and the effigy of a writer he had now perfected. Did she understand that he was responding to *her* when she commented on his "considerable engaging quiet charm which succeeds in being courtly and puckish at the same time"? Puckish—the very word he had used for that geisha. It also helped that he felt at home in Paris, which he called a second home: "There's the liberty here to be an artist. It's in the air." A different air, and a different reception, awaited him back home.

To her question about whether he could write in Paris, he responded with a "little side grin" to her: "Oh, I couldn't. I'd have too much fun here to ever work." She did not ask him, or at least did not record, what he meant by "fun." Instead of just cataloguing the writers he liked to read, which meant in most cases reread, he actually explained why Balzac, for example, mattered to Yoknapatawpha: "His people don't just move from page one to page 320 of one book. There is continuity between them all like a blood-stream which flows from page one through to page 20,000 of one book. The same blood, muscle and tissue binds the characters together." Faulkner's last three novels would prove more Balzacian than ever.

Unlike most interviewers, Grenier made herself into a character, eyeing her subject even as he scrutinized her. Something was in play here that did not often get into other interviews precisely because most interviewers were not playful. When Faulkner said Simenon's stories were like Chekhov, Grenier said, "I guess maybe I'd better read Chekhov again." This made Faulkner pause, perhaps because he was not used to this kind of banter that broke through his facade. Of course he did fall back on old chestnuts when he summed up his days with Sherwood Anderson or his piloting. Was he thinking of Estelle and Helen Baird when he said: "Success is feminine. It's like a woman. You treat her with contempt and she'll come after you, all fawning and eager, but chase after her and she'll scorn you"? He shared with Grenier his fantasy about establishing a house for artists similar to the writers' colony he told Joan Williams he wanted to organize, providing the room, the paper, and the equipment to create. But this was not about sharing ideas. They should work—not talk too much. He did not mention *Mosquitoes* or that New Orleans had wrung that kind of talk out of his system.

If Faulkner had no time for critics of his work, he also admitted: "I doubt if an author knows what he puts in a story. All he is trying to do is tell what he knows about his environment and the people around him in the most moving way possible. He writes like a carpenter uses his tools." That his characters often succumbed to their fate did not bother him. Someone always survived, he pointed out—and what mattered, anyway, is *"how* they go under." Which meant?, she wanted to know: "It's to go under when trying to do more than you know how to do. It's trying to defy defeat even if it's inevitable." Too bad they did not make a list, putting the French architect and the Bundrens perhaps first. Like his own work, man's was a record of failure, but: "He wants to have more compassion than he has. Suddenly, sometimes, he finds to his surprise he *is* more and more honest." All through this interview Faulkner smoked his pipe, which he seemed to employ as a kind of punctuation, a prop in an actor's hands. Just at this point Grenier intervened: "Faulkner holds interviewer with long firm look, then tamps down pipe."

Faulkner got off that wonderful phrase about his work "being a kind of keystone in the universe." It also became obvious why he had spent so much time away from home: "If they believed in my world in America the way they do abroad, I could probably run one of my characters for President . . . (studiously tamping his pipe) maybe [F]Lem Snopes." He gave her a keen look when she said, "I see you got some of us Greniers living in a shack as half-wits down in Yoknapatawpha County." She was referring of course to Louis Grenier, the retarded descendent of one of the county's founders. Cynthia Grenier, like Joan Williams, found a wordless Faulkner companionable: "One of the most agreeable qualities about Faulkner is his capacity for being silent in a natural, easy way." Throughout the interview, she mentions his smiling and watching her, reading her every move, it seems.

Grenier got a rise out of him when she said she admired Ike McCaslin for repudiating a tainted inheritance. Faulkner demurred: "I think a man ought to do more than just repudiate. He should have been more affirmative instead of shunning people." Faulkner, often described as an Oxford recluse by many of its residents who were polled by scholar Robert H. Moore, might have been surprised at his neighbors' answer. Many of them treated Faulkner as standing apart from them, like Ike, and even as inimical to their town. You can spend your life in Oxford, one of them said, and never see, let alone meet, William Faulkner. But they did not consider that keystone, or know him as Mac Reed, Phil Stone, Kate Baker, and many, many children did, or even as a newspaper editor like Walter G. Anderson, who said: "I thought the world of Mr. Faulkner and visited with him on my regular trips to Oxford which were once a month."[22]

Faulkner was heading in the direction of *The Town* when he described Ratliff, Gavin Stevens, and Chick Mallison as his affirmative characters—antidotes to the isolated Ike McCaslin, and perhaps to the Faulkner who used to be. They would form a triumvirate that took over Jefferson's history from the narrative voices of *Requiem for a Nun* and the essay "Mississippi." Their deep engagement with community lore and the rise of the Snopeses would constitute Faulkner's move toward voices joined together in a cross-generational, democratic continuum. None of them could outmatch the character-narrators of earlier work, but their Yoknapatawpha triptych brought a new dimension, a new kind of history to fiction. Gavin Stevens might not "succeed in living up to his ideal. But his nephew the boy, I think he may grow up to be a better man than his uncle. I think he may succeed as a human being."[23]

The interview ended as Faulkner announced he had an appointment on the Left Bank. Perhaps it was that event hosted by his French publishers, Gallimard, at which he no longer appeared so relaxed, after that interlude on the grass. Madeleine Chapsal, a French journalist who observed him, called it his "most grueling ordeal," a cocktail party. This Faulkner appeared stiff, "unbending and strong, peasantlike. . . . He looks like the kind of man who gets along well with animals and children." Even Albert Camus, at work on an adaptation of *Requiem for a Nun,* received no more than a handshake. Talking to Faulkner was like scaling a wall. In response to each question, he took a step backward. The trouble was they wanted to get a story out of him—Faulkner as fodder for print. He softened up some with a bourbon and a young woman. "Women," Chapsal suggested, are "like Faulkner . . . [m]ore inclined to feel like displaced persons." By the end of the evening in a party that eventually included four hundred people, Faulkner had bivouacked at the "far end of the garden, beneath the tree with the heaviest foliage, backed up against the wrought-iron barrier." Detachments would be sent out to reconnoiter and would return to say: "It's appalling! I can't watch it; it's like seeing someone being tortured." One lady, determined to bag her man, returned saying, "It's cold out there beneath the trees." She no longer sounded so confident. What he had to give was in his books, Chapsal concluded.[24] Usually yes, but not always, as Jean Stein or Cynthia Grenier could have told her.

Stein arranged parties for him in Paris, where he had a reunion with Anita Loos. Tennessee Williams appeared and depicted a haunted Faulkner who belonged in a Tennessee Williams play: "Those terrible, distraught eyes. They moved me to tears."[25] When Faulkner did not enjoy himself and felt cornered—he refused to talk about black people with Williams—he sometimes turned surly and insulting. When a French friend wanted to excuse herself to attend another party, Faulkner laughed and said, "Go with your queers."[26] It is hard to gauge what came over him at such moments, when, for example, over a case of corn liquor, he said to a fellow farmer that black people were the ruination of the country,[27] or expressed similar racist comments to a screenwriter working on *Land of the Pharaohs.*[28] This recidivist Faulkner erupted to do what? One Oxford resident who knew Faulkner's family and observed him as a boy said, "He delighted in being different—being a little shocking."[29]

On the way back to the United States, Faulkner, the hardened Cold Warrior, visited Iceland for five days of public receptions and press conferences.

At one of the receptions, Donald Nuechterlein, a Foreign Service officer, told the taciturn, uncomfortable Faulkner about his two-year-old daughter named Jill asleep in an adjoining room. "He seemed pleased to be diverted from the party and spend a few minutes in a dark bedroom leaning over the crib of our sleeping beauty. He even smiled when we exited the room."[30] Back to business, he was asked about the presence of American troops and answered, "Is it not better to have American forces here in the name of freedom than a Russian one in the name of aggression and violence, as in the Baltic states?" A U.S. Legation member noted in a report, "Just what the doctor ordered." Brad Wallace, a political affairs officer at the Iceland embassy, remarked that Faulkner was "so different from so many intellectuals at home who think the Cold War is an American invention."[31]

Faulkner understood the game—that the Soviet Union did not want a united Europe any more than it wanted a united Germany since whole nations would not turn Communist. So confident was he that communism could not rule over Europe that he proposed the following to Harold Howland at the State Department: "I wonder what would happen if we took publicly a high moral plane and said that a un-unified nation is such a crime against nature and morality both that, rather than be a party to it, we will allow Germany to withdraw from promise of NATO troops, and be unified under any conditions they wish."[32] Faulkner would elaborate his "high moral plane" argument in a forthcoming speech to the Southern Historical Association. It seems doubtful that the State Department considered his proposal. There is no record of Howland's reply.[33]

From New York on October 20, Faulkner wrote to Else Jonsson: "I will go back to Mississippi soon and get to work again. I know I wont live long enough to write all I need to write about my imaginary country and county, so I must not waste what I have left."[34]

26

North and South

September 1955–Spring 1957

MURDER

On September 6, William Faulkner released, at the request of the United Press, his response to the murder of Emmett Till, a fourteen-year-old African American, a Chicago native visiting family in Greenwood, Mississippi, about eighty miles from Oxford. It was said he had flirted with—perhaps even whistled at and made an obscene remark to—Carolyn Bryant, a white woman, who much later recanted her accusation that he had done so. Such incidents were common enough. Faulkner had written about one in "Dry September"—even suggesting, as in this case, that the violation of white womanhood was imaginary. Perhaps Till did no more than look directly at Bryant, transgressing a southern code that forbid such spontaneous eye contact. Bryant's husband and a family accomplice abducted Till, tortured him, and threw his body in the river. In Chicago, thousands attended Till's open-casket funeral that revealed his bloated and bludgeoned body. Both white men were acquitted by a white jury.

When William Faulkner now reacted to such a crime against humanity he thought in terms of a new sense of history, no longer the man who had written so callously about lynching to a newspaper in 1931. That new sense of history included the whole world, in which, as he wrote, three-quarters of the human race was not white. In Italy, having just arrived from Japan, he asked:

> Have we, the white Americans who can commit or condone such acts, forgotten already how only 15 years ago, what only the Japanese—a mere

eighty million inhabitants of an island already insolvent and bankrupt—did to us?

How then can we hope to survive the next Pearl Harbor, if there should be one, with not only all peoples who are not white, but all peoples with political ideologies different from ours arrayed against us—after we have taught them (as we are doing) that when we talk of freedom and liberty, we not only mean neither, we don't even mean security and justice and even the preservation of life for people whose pigmentation is not the same as ours.

A disunited America would perish:

Perhaps the purpose of this sorry and tragic error committed in my native Mississippi by two white adults on an afflicted Negro child is to prove to us whether or not we deserve to survive.

Because if we in America have reached that point in our desperate culture when we must murder children, no matter for what reason or what color, we don't deserve to survive, and probably won't.[1]

Faulkner had typed up his statement in a USIS office and had, like a good diplomat, asked for suggestions. As so often, however, he would lapse back into undiplomatic but encrusted and retrograde attitudes, saying a year later in a radio interview: "The Till boy got himself into a fix, and he almost got what he deserved. But even so you don't murder a child."[2]

A New Confederation

On November 10, William Faulkner addressed the twenty-first annual meeting of the Southern Historical Association at the Peabody Hotel in Memphis. James Silver, an Ole Miss history professor and friend of Faulkner's, invited him to address an integrated audience of five hundred or so history teachers. By Faulkner's side, Benjamin Mays (president of Atlanta's Morehouse College) became, after much cajoling from Silver, the first black person to address the association, or even to be allowed into the hotel at a white gathering. Mays gave the best speech Silver had ever heard: "great intellect, real fervor, and an old-time evangelical ministerial delivery which were a magnificent combination."[3]

Silver and Faulkner had known one another ever since Silver had taught Cho-Cho in a class in 1936. Before the friendship deepened, Silver regarded Faulkner as an "amorphous" and "awesome figure," appearing in town, sometimes, barefooted in torn and tattered clothing, but at Rowan Oak as the country squire, elegant and meticulously dressed, with Estelle, "an aging belle," presiding at the table as an "agreeable and remarkable hostess because she liked people." After dinner, Faulkner retired to the library, smoked his pipe with a brandy, and conversed with Dutch, Silver's wife, while Jim kept Estelle company at the dinner table. Dutch remembered helping Faulkner prepare for a party and asking him, "Is there anything I can do for you?" Faulkner replied, "What could any tall good-looking brunette do for a man?"[4]

During one memorable evening at Rowan Oak, Ashford Little and Hugh Evans, Faulkner's houseboat buddies, brought their wives to dinner. Mrs. Evans, "a short lady," somehow missed her chair and slid under the table. She wasn't hurt but considerably embarrassed. "So just about the time we got her over the shock," Little recalled, "Bill just with a straight face slid right under the table, deliberately pulled his chair back and just slid (laughing) under the table."[5]

Silver remembered Faulkner's "obsession with Ole Miss baseball" and other times when he appeared to socialize after football games. The Silvers drove Cho-Cho to the hospital for the birth of her only child. Silver knew the details of the extended family's life—for example, about Bill Fielden, a New Yorker who set up cigarette factories in the Third World. The Silvers and Fieldens became close friends when Bill and Cho-Cho returned during the war to stay in Oxford. The two Bills played baseball with Jill's playmates, pitching on opposite sides. When Malcolm returned from the war, Silver and Faulkner heard the horror stories. The Silvers knew about Faulkner's attachment to Joan Williams just as the historian began, during the filming of *Intruder in the Dust,* to engage Faulkner in serious discussions of civil rights. Silver was an activist, and his friendship with Faulkner, along with Faulkner's trips abroad, had made the novelist keenly aware that Mississippi could not go it alone in opposition not only to the federal government but to the world at large. But the rest of his family, including Estelle, kept pulling him back from Silver's outspoken brand of public protest, which risked for Faulkner not merely peace of mind but his very safety. Estelle's attitude toward political activism is apparent in her letter to Silver, thanking him for a copy of his book *Mississippi: The Closed Society:* "Though we differ in some of our convictions, nevertheless I sincerely admire you for taking a positive stand on what you believe to be right. Personally, I have the nightly problem of keeping myself in tune & and am hardly a fit person to . . . judge the acts of others. . . . All of which may mean that I am a moral coward. I'm certainly no crusader!"[6]

That Faulkner consented to address a room full of historians on the issue of race seemed an especially fraught experience—one that perhaps only became possible because of his proximity to James Silver, who every day, at considerable risk to himself and his family, proclaimed his liberal views on race. If Jim Silver could do that much, surely William Faulkner could give a speech. Faulkner began his address by saying, "To live anywhere in the world of A.D. 1955 and be against equality because of race or color, is like living in Alaska and being against snow." He explained that his trips abroad had shown him that America's "idea of individual human freedom and liberty and equality" was its most potent weapon against communism, which threatened, he believed, to encircle the United States in Asia and in Europe. The American devotion to freedom for all remained the "strongest force in the world." He chose a word, "confederate," that had a certain resonance in the room, and he used it to suggest that "all of us who are still free had better confederate, and confederate fast, with all others who still have a choice to be free— confederate not as black people nor white people nor pink nor blue nor green people, but as people who still are free with all other people who still are free; confederate together and stick together too, if we want a world or even a part of a world in which individual man can be free, to continue to endure." Responding to a postcolonial world in Africa and Asia, he advocated aligning with nonwhite people so that they did not choose a new slavemaster, one that sought to discredit democracy by pointing to its failure in the West. Americans could win the competition with Communists by ensuring equality at home for a nonwhite population already sold on American values in spite of their treatment as inferiors.

Faulkner's early education that justified slavery as an improvement over the supposed savagery and backwardness of Africa emerged when he suggested that "only three hundred years ago" black people were "eating rotten elephant and hippo meat in African rain-forests." They lived "beside one of the biggest bodies of inland water on earth and never thought of a sail." They moved from year to year to avoid "famine and pestilence and human enemies without once thinking of a wheel, yet in only three hundred years America produced Ralph Bunche and George Washington Carver and Booker T. Washington." "Nonwhites," to use Faulkner's term, had yet to produce someone like Klaus Fuchs, a German scientist, and the American couple, the Rosenbergs, who gave secret intelligence on the atomic bomb to the Soviets, or like the Cambridge spies Guy Burgess and Donald Maclean in England, not to mention the blueblood Alger Hiss, a State Department official convicted of conspiracy to commit espionage. For "every prominent communist or fellow-traveler like [Paul] Robeson, there are a thousand white ones," Faulkner contended.

He made a distinction between integration and equality, arguing that the "Negro" was more interested in the latter. He did not use the word, but he had miscegenation in mind when he chastised his fellow southerners for their obsession with the purity of their white blood. The choice, he insisted, was not between colors but between "being slaves and being free." The time was past for choosing "freedom established on a hierarchy of degrees of freedom, on a caste system of equality like military rank." Freedom was homogeneous and could not depend on color. To make it plain, he told these teachers of history: "The question is no longer of white against black. It is no longer whether or not white blood shall remain pure, it is whether or not white people shall remain free." In their own self-interest, in other words, white people could not expect to maintain their liberty without according the same to nonwhites.

J. Merton England, editor of *Journal of Southern History,* an organ of the Southern Historical Association, called the program on which Faulkner appeared "the best we have ever had." And yet his membership complained that it wasn't history but "propaganda" and "crusading," and "rubbing salt on some pretty sore hides."[7] Faulkner seemed undeterred, hosting several meetings at Rowan Oak to confer with Silver and others about combatting the efforts of the White Citizens' Councils, who defended segregation. But Silver saw his friend waver, wanting to remain in the good graces of his family and native region.[8]

"I get so much threatening fan mail," Faulkner wrote to Jean Stein two weeks after his Southern Historical Association talk, "so many nut angry telephone calls at 2 and 3 am. . . . I don't like to not know just how serious they are. I wish I had Ben's [Wasson] complacent view that only sporadic incidents will happen in Mississippi."[9] Conservative black people, however, seconded his position, opposing complete integration, as one black correspondent told him: "She says my stand does harm to her people, keeps the bad ones in her race stirred up, that what the Negro really wants is to be let alone in segregation as it is, that the Negroes are against NAACP." At the same time, another influence was at work—a State Department that wanted to accede in a "limited manner" to African American demands for equal rights so as to mollify international opinion without disrupting American society. Thus the *Brown v. Board of Education* decision, in the State Department's lexicon, stood not for some radical departure, an overturning of past practice, but an "achievement of the U.S. status quo."[10] To the diplomats, in other words, Faulkner was speaking their language. Rather than regarding him as a renegade southerner, they saw him as advancing the State Department line. The slow progress of racial equality suited the Foreign Service just fine. Better Faulkner's cautionary words than radical integration and race riots. The experimental, innovative novelist proved to be quite an establishment stalwart, taking a paradoxical position that few of his fellow writers understood or appreciated.

But at home, in his family, Faulkner had to contend with brother John writing in the *Memphis Commercial Appeal* (December 4, 1955): "Communist gold supports the NAACP. This is of record. Our Supreme Court hands down decisions based not on precedent which is the basis of our system of justice but on the policies of the NAACP, which is communist-supported." The white man, in John's view, was now treated as subversive if he joined other white men opposing integration. But integration, he declared, was the "credo" of Communists and was part of the "final step" to destroy religion. "I have noticed this: Of those white men of the South who mount the platform to speak in favor of integration, I know a small few personally. Of those I do know, not a single one is a member or active communicant of any church." One of those he knew was his brother William Faulkner.

The next day Faulkner drafted three letters in reply. They were not published and probably not sent to the *Commercial Appeal.* "I see in your correspondence of last Sunday that the threat of communism and of atheism (agnosticism) are being used to defend status quo segregation," one draft began. He did not mention his brother in any of the drafts. To John's concern about communism, Faulkner countered: "All that's lacking of the old Hitler formula is the threat of Semitism." Having established the link between southern racism and fascism, he noted that no proponent of segregation had addressed the following: Christianity recognized no distinctions "among men since whosoever believeth in Me shall never die"; the Golden Rule; the Constitution that declared, "there shall be no artificial inequality—creed race or money—among citizens of the United States." If there were an agreement to abide by these principles and beliefs, "maybe all of us would be on one side." Other drafts provided more historical context to his position and were later incorporated into his essay "On Fear," which he would publish in June 1956.[11] The pressures in the family were mounting and were about to erupt in an interview Faulkner would shortly grant to journalist Russell Howe.

Then, in February 1956, Autherine Lucy attempted to enroll in the University of Alabama.

"Go Slow Now"

On June 29, 1955, the NAACP secured a court order preventing the University of Alabama from denying Lucy's admissions application. More than two years earlier she had been admitted and then rejected when the school discovered she was black. On February 3, 1956, she enrolled as a graduate student in library science, becoming the first African American to be admitted to a white school in Alabama. Three days later rioting broke out, the university president's home was stoned, and threats were made against Lucy's life. William Faulkner thought she would be killed. For her own safety, the school suspended Lucy's enrollment. By the end of March the university had expelled her, claiming she had defamed the school. The NAACP, which had brought her case to court, decided not to pursue further legal action on her behalf.

The danger had been defused, but everyone understood that other African Americans would soon seek admission to white schools. During this tense period—before Lucy's case had been resolved—Faulkner wrote his "Letter to a Northern Editor," published in *Life* on March 5, hoping, as he later said, to "save the South and the whole United States too from the blot of Miss Autherine Lucy's death."[12] He still hoped his letter would serve should another similar crisis ensue. It began: "I was against compulsory segregation. I am just as strongly against compulsory integration. Firstly of course from principle. Secondly because I dont believe it will work." The extremes on both sides (the White Citizens' Councils and the NAACP) were crowding out the middle, which is where he put himself. A federal government–enforced integration would remove the African American from underdog status and turn Faulkner and other moderates like him back to the "white embattled minority who are our blood and kin," removing him and others like him as agents of change. He did not want to be forced to choose between his principles and his family. Then Faulkner made his controversial plea to the NAACP and other organizations pressing for integration: "Go slow now. Stop now for a time, a moment. You have the power now; you can afford to withhold for a moment the use of it as a force. You have done a good job, you have jolted your opponent off-balance and he is now vulnerable. But stop there for a moment; dont give him the advantage of a chance to cloud the issue by that purely automatic sentimental appeal to that same universal human instinct for automatic sympathy for the underdog simply because he is under." In short, don't allow the reactionary forces of the South to feel like the aggrieved party. To make his argument work, Faulkner had to believe that the pressure to change could come from within, as Gavin Stevens had contended in *Intruder in the Dust*. The North, in short, was forcing upon Faulkner the same decision that Robert E. Lee had made when he sided with his home state, the choice Faulkner had read about as a schoolboy.

Faulkner's references to "blood and kin" arose out of an exchange with his brother John, who had declared that he would oppose any effort in Oxford to enroll a black person in a white school, and John would do it with a gun. Over dinner in an Oxford restaurant, one of Maud's friends told Faulkner that he had upset his mother by stirring people up. He flushed and banged the table, but said nothing. This was a topic the Falkners almost never discussed, and for William Faulkner to have done so publicly had violated a taboo. Yet the restraint he showed with his own family seems to have driven him to say more, on the record, of what he could not say to his blood and kin.

What, then, would William Faulkner do? The question drove him to drink, paralyzing him with a fear for all—black and white—that would line up with him somewhere in the middle. Would he really have to take a side? The problem, he believed, was not only his own. He saw the civil rights struggle in conservative terms, as did some black people, who wrote to him fearing for themselves because of the militancy of civil rights organizations like the NAACP, and many white people, who wrote to vilify him for supporting integration. The northern liberal did not "know the South," Faulkner insisted. "He cant know it from his distance. He assumes that he is dealing with a simple legal theory and a simple moral idea. He is not. He is dealing with a fact: the fact of an emotional condition of such fierce unanimity as to scorn the fact that it is a minority and which will go to any length and against any odds at this moment to justify and, if necessary, defend that condition and its right to it."

Faulkner kept some of the responses to his *Life* article, and they reveal the range of opinion he had to confront. "Your Negroes come to New York, just as the Irish came after the potato blight, and the East-European Jews after the pograms [*sic*]. Your Negroes come for similar reasons: to find decency and build a better life," wrote a City College of New York lecturer. "There is a saying in Harlem: 'better a lamp post on Lenox Avenue, than the governor of Georgia.'"[13] Another reader thought otherwise: "Last week while waiting in a doctors office I came across your artical [*sic*] in a magazine about segregation which I most heartily agree with and I know thousand of others up north do likewise. It makes you sick at some of the remarks and talks of the Politicians around New York City where they are only looking for the negro vote."[14]

Before Autherine Lucy's case had been resolved, Russell Howe interviewed William Faulkner for the London Sunday *Times* on February 21,[15] when Lucy decided not to pursue her admission to the university. Faulkner was in New York at the time, continuing to see Jean Stein. In fact, before the Howe interview, she had poured out the liquor he had been drinking, which was like "burning books," he told her. Perhaps she understood that the drinking would loosen certain inhibitions, providing a release from the unbearable tension of a man caught between his convictions, his family, and his heritage.[16] Howe, like a good journalist, went right to the heart of the matter: "Wouldn't a 'go slow' strategy lose some of the ground already gained?" Faulkner said: "I don't know. I try to think of this in the long term view." He believed that in three hundred years intermarriage would obliterate the

"Negro" race: "It has happened to every racial minority everywhere, and it will happen here." And yet Faulkner also said the black man did not really want to consort with white people: "He likes his own school, his own church. Segregation doesn't have to imply inferiority."

Faulkner thought the NAACP should continue its fight to enroll students in southern white schools until the "people of the South get so sick and tired of being harassed and worried they will have to do something about it." His reference to the people of the South perhaps reflected his distrust of staunchly segregationist southern governments. But right now he feared an armed insurrection—even another Civil War. He regarded the *Brown v. Board of Education* decision as an extension of the Emancipation Proclamation, but that did not mean immediate progress. Instead, Faulkner advocated a kind of time-out, to let the white man "see that people laugh at him. Just let him see how silly and foolish he looks. Give him time—don't force us."

Faulkner almost seemed to be commenting on Shreve's prediction in the last paragraph of *Absalom, Absalom!*—except that Faulkner turned that prediction into a political point: "This whole thing is not a confrontation of ideologies but of white folks against folks not white. It is world-wide. We must win the Indian, the Malayan, the sixteen million Negro Americans and the rest to the white camp, make it worth their while." The remarks could certainly be interpreted as patronizing. And yet "go slow" was not code for "give up." He supported the Montgomery bus boycott as a demonstration of how interdependent the races had become: "Today the white women of Montgomery have to go and fetch their Negro cooks by car. It is a good step, to let the white folks see that the world is looking on and laughing at them."

But then came his most controversial comments: "If I have to choose between the United States government and Mississippi, then I'll choose Mississippi. What I'm trying to do now is not have to make that decision. But if it came to fighting I'd fight for Mississippi against the United States even if it means going out into the street and shooting Negroes. After all, I'm not going to shoot Mississippians." He believed, in fact, that most black Mississippians would also be on the white side even at the cost of their own equality. He did not disavow the NAACP, but he rejected what he considered as militant tactics, which did not allow white southeners to feel generous that they were doing right by reversing nine decades of segregation. Black people had the moral case, Faulkner said, "but there is something stronger in man than a moral condition." Those in the wrong would still resort to their guns, feeling the majority of the country was against them.

Faulkner's use of "must have" when referring to his own family heritage suggests how unexamined the issue had remained over several generations:

"My [great-]grandfather had slaves and he must have known that it was wrong, but he fought in one of the first regiments raised by the Confederate Army, not in the defense of his ethical position but to protect his native land from being invaded." He even went so far as to say, "My Negro boys down on the plantation would fight against the North with me." Perhaps some would, but others, like Loosh in *The Unvanquished,* probably would not. Perhaps his belief that racist ideology had been grafted onto an economy of "peonage" explained his conviction that *his* "boys" would fight beside him because their economic survival was at stake. This was the paternalistic mind-set of a farmer with three black tenant families. "He lets them have the profits, if any," Malcolm Cowley reported, because the "Negroes don't always get a square deal in Mississippi."[17] But the very word "plantation" was odd, since he had only a farm, and not even his great-grandfather could have been said to have been master of a plantation. This southern fantasy still had a grip: "remnants of antebellum identity remain embedded, shard-like, in this anguished southerner caught up in mid-1950s racial turmoil."[18]

At the same time Faulkner paid tribute to black people who were more interested in education than white people. The black man's tolerance showed a "sort of greatness": "He's calmer, wiser, more stable than the white man." Black people rose above their anger, he said. Did he think of Charles Bon at that moment? Black people had done well with far less than white people. He even attributed black vices to white hegemony.

With all the talk of violence Howe wanted to know if Faulkner carried a gun. Faulkner said his friends had encouraged him to do so. But the author of "An Odor of Verbena," a story that renounced violence even as Bayard Sartoris took up the cause of his violent father, explained: "I don't think anyone will shoot me, it would cause too much of a stink. But the other liberals in my part of the country carry guns all the time."

The Howe interview caused an uproar, which Faulkner acknowledged in a letter to the *Reporter.* He would have corrected some of the inflammatory remarks if he had seen the piece before it was printed: "They are statements which no sober man would make, nor, it seems to me, any sane man believe." This seemed to be an admission that he had been drinking at the time of the interview. During the Autherine Lucy period he had been beside himself— the cliché seems unavoidable for a man who seemed to be outside himself looking in, seeing himself as a character in one of his own fateful scenes, cornered with no way out. His sober judgment: "The South is not armed to resist the United States that I know of, because the United States is neither going to force the South nor permit the South to resist or secede either." He repudiated the foolish and dangerous statement that he or anyone else would side with a state against the Union: "A hundred years ago, yes. But not in 1956."

In Howe's reply, he stood by his "verbatim shorthand notes," adding that if the "more Dixiecrat remarks misconstrue his thoughts, I, as an admirer of Mr. Faulkner's, am glad to know it. But what I set down is what he said."[19] The Howe interview remained a disturbing departure from Faulkner's more reasoned public pronouncements, but it was not so much an aberration as, again, a kind of recidivist reaction. To W. C. Neill, who had called Faulkner "Weeping Willie" in the *Memphis Commercial Appeal,* Faulkner wrote: "I doubt if we can afford to waste even on Congress, let alone on one another, that wit which we will sorely need when again, for the second time in a hundred years, we Southerners will have destroyed our native land just because of niggers."[20]

On March 1, David Kirk, a white University of Alabama student, troubled by the Autherine Lucy controversy on his campus, wrote to William Faulkner. Kirk had studied Faulkner with O. B. Emerson, an authority on Faulkner's early reputation, and Kirk had a brother on the Ole Miss campus who had seen the Nobel Prize winner, a moderate on race so far as Kirk was concerned. "I was very alone and secretive about it, because knowing him was a danger for me, even a little more than I realized," Kirk later said: "At that time the whole campus was racist—professors, students and chaplains." Kirk had been beaten for setting up a barricade to protect Lucy.[21] Faulkner wrote to assure Kirk that segregation could not continue and the South should abolish it, "if for no other reason than, by voluntarily giving the Negro the chance for whatever equality he is capable of, we will stay on top; he will owe us gratitude; where, if his equality is forced on us by law, compulsion from outside, he will be on top from being the victor, the winner against opposition. And no tyrant is more ruthless than he who was only yesterday the oppressed, the slave." This thinking seems another holdover from the southern view of Reconstruction, in which black people were pictured in *Birth of a Nation* as shouldering white people aside and terrorizing them. He encouraged Kirk to confederate with the *Tar Heel,* the student newspaper at the University of North Carolina. An "inter-State University organization" would promote "integrity and decency and sanity in this matter." Perhaps that confederation could be extended across the South. "And remember this too," Faulkner concluded: "you will be dealing with cowards. Most segregationists are afraid of something, possibly Negroes; I dont know. But they seem to function only as mobs, and mobs are always afraid of something, of something they doubt their ability to cope with single and in daylight."

In April W. E. B. Du Bois challenged Faulkner to a debate, which he declined by telegram: "I DO NOT BELIEVE THERE IS A DEBATABLE POINT

BETWEEN US. WE BOTH AGREE IN ADVANCE THE POSITION YOU WILL TAKE IS RIGHT MORALLY LEGALLY AND ETHICALLY. IF IT IS NOT EVIDENT TO YOU THAT THE POSITION I TAKE IN ASKING FOR MODERATION AND PATIENCE IS RIGHT PRACTICALLY THEN WE WILL BOTH WASTE OUR BREATH IN DEBATE."[22] Faulkner was just then recuperating from the stress of his pronouncements on race. On March 18, hemorrhaging and unconscious, he had been rushed to a Memphis hospital. The doctor told his brother Jack, the one male member of the family who had stopped drinking, that Faulkner's alcoholism would end in his death. When told of the doctor's prognosis, Faulkner only smiled. He said to a cousin, "If I can't lead a normal life I'd just as soon be dead." To him, it was normal to go on, as both his father and grandfather had done.

Drinking, for all its deleterious consequences, remained a coping mechanism—even if it provided only temporary relief, since it was impossible to go anywhere now without confronting race. In Bailey's Woods, Faulkner encountered two boys playing. One of them asked what made him so different. Faulkner suggested they ask around and tell him the answer. One of the boys returned to say two people told him Faulkner was a "nigger lover." Well, it was better than being a fascist, he said.[23] He persisted, teaming up with Jim Silver and others in meetings at Rowan Oak for a one-issue satire, the *Southern Reposure,* taking aim at a segregationist stalwart, Mississippi senator James Eastland.[24] Faulkner sent copies to friends in New York.[25]

In the June *Harper's,* he tried again, suggesting in "On Fear: Deep South in Labor: Mississippi" that the South contained "rational, cultured, gentle, generous and kindly" people who would fight for segregation. It was those southerners he did not want to see sidelined because of their fear of change, which he knew was coming. They knew better, knew that segregation created an economy that benefited white people at the expense of black people, and the real threat to white hegemony would be the economic rise of black people.

Faulkner's views on race derived, in part, from a deep distrust of the New Deal federal government: "We—Mississippi—sold our states' rights back to the Federal Government when we accepted the first cotton price-support subsidy twenty years ago. . . . Our economy is the Federal Government. We no longer farm in Mississippi cotton-fields. We farm now in Washington corridors and Congressional committee-rooms." But if he had no faith in the federal government, he seemed to have less in the silent southern churches, who did not speak on behalf of equality, of the Golden Rule, or support equal protection and rights under the U.S. Constitution. In private correspondence he also spoke negatively about the NAACP. To Harold Ober, Faulkner emphasized, "I am not trying to sell a point of view, scratch anybody's back, NAACP or liberals or anybody else."[26] To Jean Stein, he noted, "You can see . . . the mistakes the NAACP makes in this country, since they don't understand it either."[27] His "distrust of group action and behavior sabotaged his lifelong attempts to describe group behavior: he was often a clumsy commentator on cultural phenomena because he believed, at base, only in individual reality."[28]

Then Faulkner turned toward his fellow Mississippians and excoriated them for their fears:

> Why do we have so low an opinion of ourselves that we are afraid of people who by all our standards are our inferiors?—economically: i.e., they have so much less than we have that they must work for us not on their terms but on ours; educationally: i.e., their schools are so much worse than ours that the Federal Government has to threaten to intervene to give them equal conditions; politically: i.e., they have no recourse in law for protection from nor restitution for injustice and violence.

> Why do we have so low an opinion of our blood and traditions as to fear that, as soon as the Negro enters our house by the front door, he will propose marriage to our daughter and she will immediately accept him?

What had turned Faulkner into a Jeremiah? His travel had not been only for the purposes of recreation and remuneration. And he seemed surprised: "Suddenly about five years ago and with no warning to myself, I adopted the habit of travel. Since then I have seen (a little of some, a little more of others) the Far and Middle East, North Africa, Europe and Scandinavia." He had discovered that the American dream lived abroad. People believed in "the idea of individual human freedom and liberty and equality on which our nation was founded, which our founding fathers postulated the word 'America' to mean." In view of this global perspective, Americans at home had better unite and "take in with us as many as we can get of the nonwhite peoples of the earth who are not completely free yet but who want and intend to be, before that other force which is opposed to individual freedom, befools and gets them." Ultimately, he implied, the victorious desire to enforce racial prejudice would result in the enslavement of all. One of the letters attacking Faulkner had called him "Weeping Willie."[29] In this, his most prophetic piece, he sounded indeed like that other weeping prophet, warning his people to reform their ways before it was too late.

GANDHI'S WAY

In September, in *Ebony*, Faulkner published "A Letter to the Leaders in the Negro Race," repudiating once again the incendiary remarks in the Howe review and reiterating his "go slow" doctrine. This time he added, "be flexible." He had been relieved when Autherine Lucy had withdrawn from additional legal action: "I want to believe that the forces supporting Miss Lucy were wise enough themselves not to send her back—not merely wise enough to save her life, but wise enough to foresee that even her martyrdom would in the long run be less effective than the simple, prolonged, endless nuisance-value of her threat." He wanted to see other Lucys persist in applying to white schools until white people realized that black people would not abandon the cause of equality. In effect, he argued for pursuing civil rights on a case-by-case basis, taking into account local conditions and adopting nonviolence, "Gandhi's way." He never mentioned Martin Luther King Jr. but claimed he would join the NAACP if he were a black man. He was not against collective action, but he did not think it should be mandated: "I would say that all the Negroes in Montgomery should support the bus-line boycott, but never that all of them must, since by that must, we will descend to the same methods which those opposing us are using to oppress us, and our victory will be worth nothing until it is willed and not compelled." Faulkner rarely addressed his own presumptions, but perhaps given his audience, he had to change course: "It is easy enough to say glibly, 'If I were a Negro, I would do this or that.' But a white man can only imagine himself for the moment a Negro; he cannot be that man of another race and griefs and problems." Faulkner urged, nevertheless, that black people handle themselves with grace and dignity. Then he quoted Booker T. Washington: "I will let no man, no matter what his color, ever make me hate him." Turn patience and dignity against the impetuous and unruly white man. Some of the wording remained patronizing, as in his injunction to accept "the responsibilities of physical cleanliness and of moral rectitude." Earlier he had said that black people had already exhibited such virtues. His closing words, spoken in the "if I were a Negro" mode, crossed a line he had maintained in his fiction: never speaking directly for black people in any of his characters.

"The Far Side of the Moon"

In the fall of 1956, Dean enrolled at Ole Miss, and by spring she had become politically active through the influence of her next-door neighbor Sandra Baker Moore, whose friends were "so radical compared to my usual circle that they might have come from the far side of the moon." Soon she became involved in publishing an underground newspaper attacking white supremacists. Meeting in secrecy in the university's YMCA building, they posted lookouts while mimeographing broadsides, sent runners into dorms, fraternity and sorority houses, and dispersed one by one so as not to attract attention. Even so, they were called "nigger lovers" in the university cafeteria. No Falkner had ever actually engaged in public protests. But who had paid for the press effort, including repair of the mimeograph machine? They speculated it might be that notorious liberal James Silver. She had never considered that her Pappy had funded the paper until years later Silver told her so.

Why had it not occurred to Dean that her own uncle stood by her? Perhaps because no one in the Falkner family ever supported integration—even if William Faulkner had put himself on record as doing so. What could he have said to his own mother, who instructed Dean that all men were created equal "with the exceptions of nigrahs, foreigners, Catholics, and Jews."[30]

27

Going On

January 1956–May 1957

THE ACTUAL AND APOCRYPHAL

Near the beginning of the year, Faulkner wrote to Saxe Commins: "Doing a little work on the next Snopes book. Have not taken fire in the old way yet, but unless I am burned out, I will heat up soon and go right on with it. Miss. such an unhappy state to live in now, that I need something like a book to get lost in."[1] What he needed, as with Joan Williams, was more than an editor. "I feel pretty good over your reaction to the new Snopes stuff," he wrote to Jean Stein. "I still feel, as I did last year, that perhaps I have written myself out and all that remains now is the empty craftsmanship—no fire, force, passion anymore in words and sentences. But as long as it pleases you, I will have to go on; I want to believe I am wrong you see."[2] Much more than Joan, Jean was a galvanizing force, sexually and aesthetically. As one of her editors wrote: "Her voice was alluring. Her manners were impeccable."[3] That combination pleased and thrilled William Faulkner. By January 28, he wrote her: "The book is going too good. I am afraid; my judgement may be dead and it is no good."[4] Why should her opinion matter that much? She was not only his lover but also, to use Alfred Hitchcock's word for her, a "litterateur."[5]

Faulkner had once said to Joan Williams that he had placed his life in her hands. Now he did as much and more for Jean Stein, collaborating with her on an interview for the spring issue of the *Paris Review*. Considered something like a writer's testament, the "Art of Fiction" series usually granted the interviewee the opportunity to edit and even rewrite the record. There is no reason to think it was otherwise for William Faulkner. They began with his comment on the unreliability of his interviews, especially concerning his private life. He reacted violently to "personal questions. . . . I may answer or I may not, but even if I do, if the same question is asked tomorrow, the answer may be different." He regarded himself as a kind of vessel of literature, taking an approach similar to T. S. Eliot's in "Tradition and the Individual Talent." "If I had not existed, someone else would have written me," Faulkner asserted. "The artist is of no importance."

Some of his answers were routine: He reiterated his belief that "All of us failed to match our dream of perfection." If he still kept writing, it was in the hope that he could do it better. He disliked the idea of literary competition: "Try to be better than yourself." He adopted a Wildean view of the literary enterprise, declaring the writer is a "creature driven by demons" and is amoral and prepared to "rob, borrow, beg, or steal from anybody and everybody to get the work done." And that included family: "the 'Ode on a Grecian Urn' is worth any number of old ladies." Environment didn't matter, although he preferred brothels, which provided shelter and were quiet in the morning when he wanted to write. The business side of life was simple and consisted mainly of a once-a-month payment to the police. And plenty of social life in the evening with females to defer to him as "sir" and friendship with police he could call by their first names. Faulkner described an environment quite different from the role and responsibility of Rowan Oak as he indulged his fantasies about a life without a family.

He listed the tools of his trade: "paper, tobacco, food and a little whisky." Writers did not need foundations. Such support ran counter to his staunch individualism. "Nothing can destroy the good writer," he maintained, perhaps thinking of Hollywood and everything else that could have gotten in his way. Hollywood became the next question. He still got offers to write for the movies. He expressed an interest Orwell's *1984:* "I have an idea for an ending which would prove the thesis which I'm always hammering at: that man is indestructible because of his simple will to freedom." He mentioned Humphrey Bogart and said, "the moving picture work of my own which seemed best to me was done by the actors and the writer throwing the script away and inventing the scene in actual rehearsal just before the camera turned." He did not rate himself highly as a screenwriter, but he had taken the work seriously. His stories about his Hollywood adventures suggested they provided a welcome diversion.

His only advice to writers was to write and learn from mistakes and judge yourself by your own standards. He could not discuss technique as something separate from the writing itself. He did not deny the importance of technique but regarded it as simply arising out of the material at hand, not something imposed on the work. The characters took charge and told him what to do.

This had happened with *The Sound and the Fury,* with each part compelled by the previous one. As to *A Fable* and its Christian allegory: it was one of those "charts against which he [man] measures himself and learns to know what he is." For him the trinity of the young Jewish pilot officer, the old French quartermaster general, and the English battalion runner represented the "trinity of conscience": "knowing nothing, knowing but not caring, knowing and caring." The options were: "This is terrible. I refuse to accept it, even if I must refuse life to do so. . . . This is terrible, but we can weep and bear it. . . . This is terrible, I'm going to do something about it."

He seemed to want to settle certain matters, like the organic nature of *The Wild Palms:* one story had grown out of the other. That answer seemed to provoke a discourse on how stories came to him as "a single idea or memory or mental picture. The writing of the story is simply a matter of working up to that moment, to explain why it happened or what it caused to follow." When asked about the origins of this story making, he returned to his old stories about Sherwood Anderson and New Orleans, his growing up on the Old Testament—all of which seemed more important to him than his predecessors, contemporaries, Freud, or critics: "The critic is writing something which will move everybody but the artist." To Malcolm Cowley's observation that "your characters carry a sense of submission to their fate," Faulkner responded, "That is his opinion" and then went on to provide counterexamples in Lena Grove, Lucas Burch, and the Bundrens.

The Yoknapatawpha saga had resulted from his realization that not only each book but his entire output had to have a design. Here he came closest to that one sentence he was always trying to write that would encapsulate all he had to say: "Beginning with *Sartoris* I discovered that my own little postage stamp of native soil was worth writing about and that I would never live long enough to exhaust it, and by sublimating the actual into apocryphal I would have complete liberty to use whatever talent I might have to its absolute top."[6] Faulkner called the interview Stein's "stoutest effort."[7]

MR. JEFFERSON'S UNIVERSITY

On April 15, Jill gave birth to her first child, a son. "Both fine," Faulkner wrote to Stein. "Am drinking milk every 2 hours, eating my infant rations, going to bed at 10 o'clock." Even with his back hurting, he progressed on the next Snopes novel, *The Town.* Then Frederick Gwynn of the University of Virginia English department came calling on the Faulkners at Jill's Charlottesville home. She had signaled to Gwynn, who regarded her father as the greatest American novelist, that Pappy might be interested in a writer-in-residence appointment. Indeed he was, dismissing Gwynn's concerns about proper remuneration by saying in the spirit of the *Paris Review* interview that a little whiskey and tobacco would complete the deal. They agreed on a ten-week-or-so trial period over the late winter and early spring of 1957.

Estelle stayed with Jill in Charlottesville while her husband returned to Rowan Oak in early May 1956. He worked fitfully on *The Town*, interrupted by his statements about race and the back-and-forth correspondence supporting and attacking his articles. He also spent time "remaking his sail boat," his mother reported. "Every time he leaves it on the Reservoir, some one deliberately sinks it. The last time, it was a year before they located & raised it." He was awaiting a visit from his son-in-law, Paul, who helped to restore the wreck.[8]

"Dear Mr. Faulkner," the June letter began, "I am writing to ask your help." President Eisenhower spoke of the "great struggle being waged between the two opposing ways of life," a struggle the United States could not win with diplomats and information officers alone but only through the "support of thousands of independent private groups and institutions and of millions of individual Americans acting through person-to-person communication in foreign lands." He wanted Faulkner to chair a group of writers, which would demand "some time and effort on your part to make it successful." This "patriotic work" was of "vital importance to our national interest."[9] Faulkner could, in short, lead his fellow writers by personal example.

How could he refuse? The pre-Nobel Faulkner might have, but now, nearing the completion of his second Snopes novel, and with no work expected on the Eisenhower program until September, he accepted his commission. Toward the end of August, he wrote to Jean Stein: "Just finishing the book. It breaks my heart. I wrote one scene and almost cried. I thought it was just a funny book but I was wrong."[10]

In late September, Faulkner sent out invitations: "The President has asked me to organize American writers to see what we can do to give a true picture of our country to other people. Will you join such an organization?" He enclosed some sample ideas, including anesthetizing "for one year, American vocal chords," abolishing, for one year, American passports, and establishing a government fund to bring young Communists to "this country and let them see America as it is." The letter went on in a similar facetious tone, ending with a postscript: "In a more serious vein, please read the enclosed one-page description of Mr. Eisenhower's purpose." The letter reflected considerable ambivalence and seemed designed to entertain and to disarm the alienated writer's belief (Faulkner's own) that writers did not count for much and had no impact on the government or the economy.

Rejecting Faulkner's invitation to attend a meeting, several writers noted on a questionnaire their objections:

[Conrad Aiken:] unworkable, drop it.

[Edna Feber:] shocked by your letter; will come to meeting out of curiosity; writers shouldn't be organized—must be free.

[Katherine Anne Porter:] no. Expedient political device.

[Lewis Mumford:] no: Such an organization would be automatically suspect as being government-sponsored.

[Edmund Wilson:] No: Author's works are best propaganda.

[Shelby Foote:] No, Writers should stay at home, unorganized, and work.

Others asked how writers could, in good conscience, join such a group while others were blacklisted in Hollywood? Waldo Frank suggested examining the discrepancy between what the "President says he wants and State Department's refusal to grant passports for cultural missions to such places as China." Some were Democrats and wanted nothing to do with a Republican administration. The poet Donald Hall, helping Faulkner to organize a meeting, wrote to him on October 14: "There seems to be a general recalcitrance against joint action, some of which sounds vain, megalomaniac (imagine thinking that this committee would help Eisenhower be elected!) and exhibitionist to me. The man who says 'writers shouldn't be organized—must be free' is not reading your letter."

Several writers said yes to Faulkner, including John Steinbeck, Truman Capote, Erskine Caldwell, James T. Farrell, Marianne Moore, Malcolm Cowley, E. B. White, and Allen Tate. Gore Vidal sent a characteristic reply: "Of course I would be interested in joining such a group as you propose: it has a fine vagueness, a sense of good will." Robert Lowell, who had gone through a period of anti-Communist mania, responded: "Of course you can see deeper into us and our country than I can. Long ago, I wrote you a long fan letter. I never dared to mail it, but I think I said (as the Democrats say of themselves) that you were our writer with style and a heart. You are. What a joy that this business has allowed me to say so." Paul Green, who had given Faulkner a lift to New York after the Virginia writers' conference in 1931, replied: "Your impish and kiss-my-behind letter about organizing American writers has reached me here. Such gleeful prickings of American self-esteem and pinching of the aged ghost of our founding fathers presages well for the work to be undertaken." To Harvey Breit, helping Faulkner to get it all started, Lionel Trilling wrote that he was skeptical but willing to go along "since it is Faulkner who puts the question."[11]

At the September 11 meeting of the People-to-People Program, Faulkner appeared paradoxically delicate and stony-looking, according to Donald Hall. He drank from a tall glass of bourbon and did not say much. Hall described the meeting as "generous with sincerity, silliness, booze, and posturing." Faulkner, Steinbeck, and Hall were designated as a subcommittee that met the next morning at Random House. Faulkner and Steinbeck talked about rifles, agreeing the Springfield was the best. They came up with some suggestions about changing immigration laws and following up on Faulkner's idea of inviting Soviet citizens to the United States. Steinbeck was against Hall's suggestion that they recommend freeing Ezra Pound from his detention at St. Elizabeth's Hospital. "Sudden enthusiasm illuminated Faulkner's eyes," Hall recalled. "He said yes, we should free Ezra Pound, and addressing the note taker, remarked that the chairman of this committee, appointed by the president, had been awarded a prize by the government of Sweden, but America locked its best poet in jail."[12] Faulkner's involvement, assisted by Random House, lasted three months, and then he resigned. Had all this been just to placate a president? The state did not enter into much of Faulkner's thinking, although he was patriotic, and communism's hegemonic ambitions, its destruction of individuality, troubled him.

A CONFESSION

For many years now, the lives of William and Estelle Faulkner seemed to run on parallel tracks that sometimes veered toward junctions that just as soon split off again. For Estelle, this troubling bifurcation had finally brought about a need to explain and share her burden. On November 5, she began her dramatic confession to Saxe Commins: "Here is a letter I've intended writing for some time." She had wanted to tell him sooner, but they never seemed to find the time for a "quiet talk." Her letter now served that purpose: "You must have been aware in the past, (or maybe Bill told you) that I drank a lot at times—in fact a most unpleasant alcoholic I was—Especially, when I got upset over unfortunate occurrences etc—drink seemed to me an ideal escape."[13] According to Vicki, Estelle's granddaughter, her grandmother was "the classic alcoholic—a glass of wine at dinner was enough to set her off. Once she started, she couldn't stop and wouldn't until she passed out. . . . On the other hand, Pappy could drink socially and not get drunk." He could not understand why Estelle could not control herself. His binges were deliberate decisions, taken "consciously and soberly." He was like a child, Vicki said, who "merely wants his own way."[14]

Faulkner's belief in his own self-control seems to be the reason why he never seriously tried to stop drinking or even regarded it as a problem, other than as a lapse in manners and respect for others that he would admit and regret. But in Estelle's case, she viewed her compulsive drinking as a sickness she finally had to treat: "I still don't know just *when* it became a *necessity* beyond my personal feelings, to stop drinking—but I got in touch with Alcoholics Anonymous in Memphis, and by the grace of God, and A.A.—I stopped—and have reason to believe for good."

In command of her own emotions, she treated her husband as the weaker one deserving compassion. She described their drive to Sardis Reservoir, twenty miles from Rowan Oak, when Bill disclosed his affair with Jean Stein. Eighteen months sober, Estelle seemed to have surprised herself in taking the news calmly, with resignation: "I know, as you must, that Bill feels some sort of compulsion to be attached to some young woman at all times—it's Bill—At long last I am sensible enough to concede him the right to do as he pleases, and without recrimination—It's not that I don't care—(I wish it were not so)—but all of a sudden [I] feel sorry for him—wish he could know without words between us, that it's not important after all." Her newfound peace and confidence resulted in their living "more amicably, and with better understanding the past year than ever before."

The Faulkners seemed to be nearing a period—the Charlottesville years—when, in Vicki's words, they "became very close friends again. At times they even looked and seemed like they were a newly married couple. There was a joy they shared, and Pappy took pride in Grandmama's having licked her alcoholism. He was very proud of her. I don't think he felt she ever would have had the guts to do it, but she did quit and without too damn much help from him, either."[15] Estelle depended on her husband's discretion not to embarrass her or Jill, and he let her down one more time.

A FAUSTIAN TIME OF TRIAL

In early January 1957, someone calling himself A. B. Stein telephoned Estelle, saying, "I'm no kin to her, but for $500.00 I can tell you something about a Miss Stein and your husband." Estelle told the caller she already had that information and hung up. "She was startled, off balance, because, for all our faults, people here in the south dont do things like that," Faulkner told Saxe Commins, imploring him: "Do anything you can, I will pay, find who this is . . . I will attend to him." Faulkner even considered hiring a private detective. There were three more calls—one from another party and all about Jean Stein. "If another call comes," Faulkner told Commins, "and I am away and cant take it myself, Estelle will try to get more details. This is an outrage, persecution, not of me but of Estelle."[16] Apparently the calls stopped, and Faulkner took no action.

Then Jean Stein ended the affair (she planned to get married and would do so in a year, to a diplomat), and the stress of Faulkner's back-and-forth life resulted in another breakdown. Truman Capote claimed to have seen Faulkner sobbing over Stein in Robert Linscott's Random House office.[17] On Monday, February 5, Saxe Commins arrived in the afternoon at the Hotel Berkshire on Madison Avenue at Fifty-Second Street. He substituted milk and ice cream for the beer Bill demanded in his despondency over losing Jean and the bootless People-to-People Program. Why would the failure of a State Department program so upset him? At the University of Virginia he haltingly told students why. He had wanted to show that America was about more than business:

> It is the reason for sending people like Louis Armstrong that—that blow horns and—just for the sheer pleasure of blowing horns and writers and people that are interested in something else besides success, interested in things of the human spirit rather than in things on—in—the black ink on the ledger. It was interesting work. I myself of course can't see just how much good it does. The report from it is that it does a lot of good, but I—I don't—am not aware of it myself. I do know that—that the—the foreign people I have—have visited have—have seemed quite anxious to—to learn things about our country, which I would have thought they could have known easily. Then I realized that the usual travelled American is not interested in these things and had no reason to tell them, and they were too timid to ask. But to someone who approaches them in their own cultural terms of believing that things of the spirit are important, they have less shyness about asking these questions.[18]

The failure of so many of his fellow writers to see the point of such a program hurt him more than he let on. And his presence as writer-in-residence on the University of Virginia grounds would later rectify, in part, this failure to reach out to the world through the government program.

Right now, however, Saxe Commins discovered William Faulkner in all of his solitary despair, completely undone: "I found Bill stark naked, his clothes scattered all over the floor and an empty gin bottle, an empty whiskey flask and an empty wine bottle. He began at once to plead with me for a drink and

I became adamant. He said, 'I warn you. If you dont get me a drink it will be the end of our friendship.'" Three hours later Commins was still holding out, administering Seconal to keep Faulkner sleeping. Otherwise he kept up a "whimpering cry for drink." In just five days, Faulkner was supposed to be in Charlottesville to begin his writer-in-residence semester.

The strain on Commins, who had already suffered one heart attack, was terrific: "Worried about the erratic behavior of my heart," he noted in his diary. Dr. Benjamin Gilbert arrived and gave Faulkner injections of a liver extract and vitamins. He recommended giving Faulkner an ounce of whiskey every three hours, which posed less risk than Seconal. Then Gilbert took Saxe's pulse and warned him about the "dangers of too much tension." It all seemed so Faustian to Saxe: "A creative man, getting old, needs his young Marguerite. He can't devour her and still have her. To get her partially he makes a deal with his own demon and in the end the demon extracts his price." Disregarding the doctor, Faulkner drank more beer while Commins tried to distract him with dinner, managing to "get some soup down him." When Saxe turned his back to fill his pipe, he heard a loud crash: "It was Bill's head landing on the table which he missed for the pillow and right in the middle of the food debris." Commins washed off Faulkner's face the remains of dinner, including melted chocolate ice cream. "He is too anesthetized to feel any pain," Commins noted.

Two days later, Commins, still at the hotel, reported that Faulkner had fallen into a snore at 9:00 p.m. the night before after consuming most of a whiskey bottle. Saxe had taken a Seconal to fall asleep but had been awakened at 10:40 p.m. when Faulkner fell out of bed, saying he had to go to the bathroom. "Half supporting, half carrying him, myself in a drug daze, I managed to get him seated on the pot." Much of the same routine continued that afternoon.[19]

And yet by February 10, Faulkner had made it by train to Charlottesville, reporting for duty at the university. Commins relayed the good news to Dr. Gilbert: "You will be pleased to learn that Bill telephoned me and reported that he was in fine shape. This, I believe, he owes in large measure to you. Certainly you were wonderful to him as doctor and friend. I need not tell you how much I appreciate it." After a weeklong visit to Charlottesville in March, Commins told Gilbert: "Bill was in grand shape, the best of hosts and friends. He spoke glowingly of you and asked especially that I tell you how much he appreciates you."[20]

It had not been so grand for Estelle. On February 15, she had written to Saxe and Dorothy that she had reached a breaking point. She wanted a divorce. Bill had not agreed because, in her view, he had his freedom already.

"I would like to be free," she announced, "not from Bill for once . . . but from the utterly false undignified position I've occupied the past six years. I am tired of being the poor deceived wife." He had admitted the affair, and she had tried to excuse it, but now the calls revealed he had been indiscreet. Everyone in New York probably knew about the affair, Estelle surmised. That would have included Saxe and Dorothy, but Estelle did not say so. They remained a sort of lifeline for her: "As you see by now—with me it is not a question of a hurt heart, but of an affront to what little dignity I have to salvage. In short, I'm sick of it & would welcome a clear decisive end. I refuse to tear myself to pieces emotionally over things, people & circumstances over which I have no control." Still, she held on, soliciting their advice.[21] What advice the Comminses offered is not on the record, but they would hardly have suggested leaving Faulkner since the import of all their surviving correspondence sought reconciliation between the couple, even though both Saxe and Dorothy tacitly condoned Faulkner's affairs.

Jim Silver thought husband and wife had reached the point of such hate that if "either one could have killed the other without being punished for it they would have done so."[22] And yet they both showed up in Charlottesville, ready to put on a good performance, and with a renewed effort at reconciliation.

28

Writer-in-Residence

October 1956–January 1959

THE PROFESSOR

On October 10, 1956, Maud Falkner announced: "Billy & Estelle are going to Charlottesville in February where he will be writer in residence for the second semester—which means he will use the University as a peg to hang his baby-sittin' on. Jill lives there & her baby is precious & Billy is crazy about him."[1] Jill noticed that her father seemed, gradually, to mellow. He was now a professor, he proudly told James Silver. Coming from the Deep South, and from a state that remained a frontier when Virginia led the South into a new nation, it remained the pinnacle of southern pride that had its atavistic grip even on an adamant individualist like William Faulkner, whose code of the gentleman had been fostered by books like Owen Wister's *The Virginian*. He provoked some amused amazement, and perhaps some offense, when he called Virginians snobs—after all, this was the creator of that gentleman-drunkard Gowan Stevens—but he liked snobs, he said at a February 15 hour-long press conference: "A snob has to spend so much time being a snob that he has little left to meddle with you, and so it's very pleasant here." He put it more graciously in a courtly handwritten letter to Annie Churchill Berkeley: "You have shamed me. I meant a compliment. I meant my own definition of snob: one so assured of his or her position as to not need envy nor want anything of anyone else, so that when an outsider is lucky enough to be offered that friendship, he does not have to worry lest anything more than reciprocal courtesy will be expected or demanded of him. That's why I like Virginians, especially Virginia ladies. I wish Virginians might like me half as well." She responded in kind: "Thank you for your charming letter—and may I say, here is a Virginian who likes you 'more than half as well' as you like us."[2]

Faulkner said in his letter of acceptance to Floyd Stovall, the English department chair, that he hoped the university would "gain as much in benefit from the plan as I expect to gain in pleasure by sojourning in your country." The reference to "your country" suggests just how much of a diplomat Faulkner had become, and how much he had changed from the young writer who wrote on September 24, 1931, to Professor James Southall Wilson, comparing himself to the "hound dog under the wagon" who had to be cajoled to come out.[3] Now he was not hiding out or playing the truant but submitting to a press conference. Asked about the southern heritage his grandson would bear, Faulkner answered: "I hope of course that he will cope with his environment as it changes. And, I hope that his mother and father will try to raise him without bigotry as much as can be done. He can have a Confederate battleflag if he wants it but he shouldn't take it too seriously."

President Colgate Darden did not really want Faulkner on the university grounds. Faulkner's comments on race and integration made him controversial and a target of segregationist ire—not what Virginia, then an all-white, all-male school, wanted. Students by and large were not interested in politics, and such a patrician institution did not harbor radicals or protestors. Segregation was simply a way of life, one that most students passively accepted. Professor Robert Scholes remembered that, at University of Virginia football games, black people sat in the end zone and white people along the sides of the field. Scholes, a Brooklyn Yankee, got into an exchange in a local newspaper when told that black people sat in the local theater balcony because they smelled bad.

Faulkner's only appearance on university grounds in 1931 had been widely covered, including his drinking and apparent indifference to social and intellectual discussion. A university president did not think that this writer, even with a Nobel Prize, would be a welcome presence. Did Darden speak with James Southall Wilson about Faulkner's visit? Wilson confided to a colleague that Faulkner had "said and done a lot of foolish things" and later wrote a note of apology: "If I hurt anyone while I was in Charlottesville, will you please make my apologies?"[4] Not until the 1960s did writers become a firm feature of academic life, teaching courses in creative writing and literature. The idea of letting loose this unpredictable writer on the university grounds upset academic administrators. "The University of Virginia," President Darden declared, "had sufficient prestige without William Faulkner."[5]

What William Faulkner needed was blockers, some faculty members who could run interference, so to speak, to relieve the skittish author from demands on his time that were beyond the bounds of his classroom commitments. Floyd Stovall could not have chosen the key members of his offensive line better. Frederick L. Gwynn and Joseph Blotner, both World War II veterans who had been in combat, coached Faulkner and accompanied him to meetings and events, catering to his tastes and winning his confidence and admiration.

At a press conference on February 15, reported the next day in the school newspaper, the *Cavalier Daily,* he explained that he hoped to help creative writing students "out of my experience as a writer, and to help create an atmosphere." He realized that it was his precedent-setting presence, as much as anything he said, that counted. He called himself "lazy. . . . [W]riting is work, but simply will not let me rest in peace. It worries me sometimes." Did he write more easily now?, a reporter asked. "I fumble less now, but put (working) off more. I'm convinced that I'll live to be 100." Then came the inevitable question about integration, which began with a routine answer and ended with a startling windup: "The schools are poor, and should be improved to the standards of the best students, no matter what color. The negro must earn the responsibility to be equal. There is more to a right than just the gift of it. We should not bother keeping the negro out, but should raise the standards and possibly keep some of the whites out."

Faulkner saw the humor of his appointment, February to May 1957. When Blotner showed his chief (that is what he often called him) a student caricature of Faulkner, "long-nosed and spindly, cuff over his knuckles, a book under his arm, and one hand resting on a broken column," he flushed with soundless laughter that led to a coughing fit.[6] At a track meet, where Faulkner helped out by getting the names of the first three finishers in the 440-yard race, one of the officials said to him, "Well, Mr. Faulkner, I see they've put you to work." He replied: "Yes. Blotner and I are workin' for our letter. When we get it, we're going to put it on a sweater. I get to wear it on Saturdays."[7] At another sporting event a Richmond journalist got to talking with a short man in a trench coat, not immediately recognizing Faulkner. "And what do you do?," the reporter asked. "I write," Faulkner said.[8]

Nancy Hale, the wife of an English department professor, watched Faulkner walk the university grounds like "an actor in a trench coat." He never seems to have walked with his wife. But Estelle appeared at formal functions, looking "girlish," Hale said, "with the famous Southern waist a man's hands can span." At a reception she appeared in a "delightfully dippy hat" with her hair trained into "tiny grey snail-shell curls," and a face "piquant behind a pair of very dark glasses." Like others in the know, Hale had been prepped by Gwynn and Blotner not to ask literary questions, so she mentioned a few mutual friends in New York, and he nodded without a comment. At another gathering, she hit on the right topic: drinking. As soon as she said how good that first sip of whiskey was, he lighted up, talking about nocturnal tree toads, the smell of waking up to the first snow, and then how surprised and pleased he had been to learn that students really wanted to hear from him. When Gwynn or Blotner would suggest they had taken enough of Faulkner's time, he said: "Well, I've told you, this is a dreadful habit to get into, where you can stand up in front of people and nobody can say, 'Shut up and sit down.'" He seemed to enjoy reading from his own work, amusing himself, although the audience found it hard to follow his soft-spoken delivery. He probably did not mind, for all his fame, that most Charlottesville residents paid him no mind and in many cases did not even know about the man or his work.[9]

Never comfortable with lectures, Faulkner adopted the question-and-answer format that had become his staple in Japan. Even so, he admitted to a reporter from the *Charlottesville Daily Progress* (February 15): "I'm terrified at first because I'm afraid it (class discussion) won't move." Would it be a waste of time, he wondered, but discovered that "once it begins to move it's all right." He would be satisfied if in a hundred students one of them found his presence of "some value." Occasionally he read from his work, but in the main he wanted to hear from students, many of whom were women, then only admitted into the nursing and education schools of the university. One female graduate student (a high school science teacher) saturated herself in his writing and attended all of his public classroom sessions, which included members of the Charlottesville community as well. Faulkner also met with the English club, law school wives, and the Jefferson Society; appeared on a university radio program to discuss the different dialects in his fiction; and gave readings at various public events.

In his classes, Blotner prescreened questions and would approve some, discard others. On the first day of class, February 15, Faulkner sat serenely in silence for a long time until Gwynn broke in with a question about *The Sound and the Fury*. Then others followed—most of them dealing with that novel. In coats and ties, the men asked polite questions; the women seemed to speak up without hesitation. Faulkner's direct and casual manner often surprised his audiences. His frank answers amused them. His down-to-earth manner, unexpected in a university setting, delighted them, especially when he said he had failed a fourth time in the last section, which got several laughs. He sometimes gave inaccurate answers about his own work. He usually relied on memory and had no interest in rereading his stories and novels or preparing in other ways for his encounters with students. Although the recordings of his sessions reveal that he rarely changed the even tone of his voice, sounding deadpan all the way, he could sparkle with spontaneity and get a rise—often more laughter—out of his audience. When a student asked if he had made an assessment of his own writings, the sixty-year-old Faulkner replied: "No, I still haven't done it, but I intend to live to be about a hundred years old, so I've got forty more years yet. By that time I'll answer your question, if you're still around."

He did quicken his response a bit when asked why Caddy did not have her own section. That was a good question, Faulkner said, which revealed his thinking. He didn't want her to tell the story because then it would be less passionate. After the "Appendix," in which she is seen in the company of a German staff officer, he could not imagine bringing her back, he told Gwynn. It would have made her seem shabby, Faulkner said. Asked about the snake in "Red Leaves," Faulkner referred to him as the "old fallen angel"—then added, drawing laughs, "the bright shinin' angel ain't very interesting." At the first session, he thanked all the students for listening, "because I know you're hungry." At other sessions, other Faulkners appeared. Lloyd Smith recalled that when a student wondered how Faulkner could justify writing "The Bear" since it glorified the slaughter of animals, Faulkner called the question stupid and said no more.

Sometimes, quite by accident, questioners cued up Faulkner's most hilarious tales. Asked about "Spotted Horses"—"Have you ever seen such an auction taking place?"—he said, "Yes'm. I bought one of these horses once," provoking loud laughs and yet still more laughs as he recounted his adventures. He did not mention that his father, a good storyteller, had his own tale to tell.[10] Asked a question about technique, he demurred, saying, as he often did, he was not a literary man and just wrote about people and characters who came to him. Calling himself a veteran sixth-grader, and therefore unqualified to give an academic answer, he then added—to great laughter—that perhaps he could now pass freshman English after his experience at the university. Faulkner favored these kinds of exchanges for the same reasons they appear in his novels: only the dialectical dynamic of human interaction approached the possibilities of entertaining truth emerging out of a sense of community, as it does in *The Town*. These shared moments at the university, when Faulkner scored, were akin to the setups Gavin Stevens provides for Ratliff and Charles Mallison, and they provide for Stevens.

Contrary to his usual practice, Faulkner showed up at Robert Scholes's class on *Absalom, Absalom!* saying he had reread the novel in order to answer the students' questions. When they had satisfied themselves, Scholes offered his own observation that the "further away we got from the eye-witnesses and the deeper we got into the imaginative reconstruction of events by those who were never near them, the closer we were coming to the truth. All I remember is that he confirmed my view, or seemed to. And it is a literary view, the view of an artist not a country gentleman."

Faulkner was in fine form when he spent a day at Mary Washington University, an all-women's college. Before reading one of his stories, he said, "I've already found out that the only way to hold an audience is to be a little higher than it is, and for a short man like me it's impossible to do it unless you are higher, so if it's all right, I'm going to stand up." During a long pause in the question-and-answer session, he aroused laughter when he encouraged them to ask questions, "whether you think it's silly or not, ask it."[11]

Faulkner saved some of his best lines for his office hours from 11:00 to 12:00 on Tuesdays and Thursdays. The *Cavalier Daily* announced he would be available to talk to faculty and students but would not read manuscripts. A small group of students, some of them wishing to be writers, would try to pry wisdom out of him. He left his door open and would sit reading the paper or in front of a big typewriter. He seemed more approachable than during his solitary excursions on the university grounds, although one student remembered spotting Faulkner walking and pulled up in a car and introduced the two excited co-eds who wanted to meet him. "He was very sweet with those girls. The four of us had such a lovely experience that I was glad we had stopped to talk," Jack Docherty remembered. One student, William Lecky, who liked to stop by the office when no one else was around, got to talking with Faulkner, and soon they would go together to university baseball games. Faulkner went to Lecky's apartment to see Lecky's charcoal drawing of a scene from a Faulkner novel. Another student, Joe Carroll, spotted Faulkner, and they nodded to one another in a Charlottesville theater while watching *The Long Hot Summer*, based on *The Hamlet* and other stories.

Ken Ringle recalled an especially insightful office colloquy:

"Mr. Faulkner," I asked him, "In your book *As I Lay Dying*, most of the characters are socially pretty reprehensible. The only one with any kind of sensitivity or nobility is Addie Bundren, the schoolteacher. Yet you have her marry Anse Bundren, absolutely the most dreadful of the whole lot. How can you justify that?" Faulkner rubbed his mustache and re-lit his pipe, then looked at me a long, long time.

"My boy," he finally said in his slow drawl. "Haven't you ever heard the story of the beautiful butterfly? That flitted from flower to flower? And lit at last on a horse turd?"

Most students found it difficult to approach the reserved Faulkner—treated with awe even if they had not read him. But Ringle recalled that a brash undergraduate, Zeke Waters, an English major, worried about passing his comprehensives, spotted a strolling William Faulkner and decided this was the help he needed. Zeke knew enough not to begin with a literary quiz. Talk turned to sports, the weather, where Zeke was from, and soon they were walking—the tall Zeke with his arm around the esteemed author—toward Faulkner's home. Faulkner invited him in for a drink, then another drink, and perhaps a third. Now the serious talk turned to horses. Next came dinner laid out in spectacular fashion—fine crystal, a vase of flowers, and so on. Losing his balance, Zeke grabbed on to the tablecloth, taking down with him the whole splendid display. He had done Gowan Stevens proud. Faulkner seemed only concerned that Zeke had hurt himself. The embarrassed but unharmed undergraduate excused himself, never getting to the questions and answers that would help him with his exams.

Waters was not alone. Another hard-drinking student, called only "Henry" in Jack Docherty's account, charged with escorting Faulkner to an awards ceremony, showed up with an arm around "Bill," as he called Faulkner, to the consternation of an English department member, Professor John Coleman. But Faulkner seemed to enjoy the whole affair. To Docherty, Faulkner seemed to be the very walking symbol of the Virginia gentleman they were taught to revere.

"Mr. Faulkner seems to be enjoying himself here a great deal," Charlotte Kohler, editor of the *Virginia Quarterly Review,* reported to Carvel Collins: "He certainly adds a note of color to the community as he walks along Rugby Road in his amber-colored Bavarian hat and heavy tan walking gloves, with his pipe directly at a right angle to him. He has been very agreeable to the students here and I think they appreciate it."[12]

Bess Lyon Eager, who first met Faulkner in 1933 or 1934 while teaching at Ole Miss, renewed her acquaintance in Charlottesville. In the company of Emily Whitehurst (who married Phil Stone), she visited Rowan Oak on several occasions to see the shy and gracious author of the shocking *Sanctuary.* Now she often passed him during his walks on the university grounds and heard about the packed audiences who came to hear him. "They simply adored him," she recalled. On the way to the library one day she encountered a very large portrait of him, placed on the lawn by some students. Under it they had written, "Genius at Work." Faulkner had told her that "he loved to be left alone and *we left him alone.* Therefore he learned to love us. . . . It is so satisfying to think of him as being happy with us, for (to me) there seemed to be a sort of sadness about him, in addition to that Mark Twainish humor he undoubtedly had!"[13]

R. C. Greene, driving on the university grounds, stopped for a "mustached Southern Gentleman in a white linen suit and blue-and-orange tie, with an umbrella hooked over his left arm, [who] had his right hand and thumb out seeking a ride." The man gave no name but said he was a university professor going downtown. Would it be possible for the driver to pick him up the next week at the same spot? Greene agreed and was chagrined to learn from a friend that William Faulkner had been Greene's passenger. On their next trip together, Greene apologized to Faulkner for not recognizing him: "Putting me fully at ease," Greene recounted, "he said that he had to admit that he did not recognize me either, and we shook hands, acknowledging one another with a laugh. He was fun and easy to talk with—a bit 'crusty' and I liked that." When Greene tried to ask Faulkner about the "hidden meaning" of a certain passage, he replied, "I wrote what I meant, and I meant what I wrote."

Toward the end of the semester, Faulkner reflected on his writer-in-residence role, having realized "more and more . . . how pleasant it was . . . the young people that have come into my office with their carefully rehearsed literary questions, [*audience laughter*] and once we get past them we just talk, and that's interesting." They told him what they wanted to do and what they thought of the race issue and "what we should do about it. Almost every day one comes in, and once we get past the stiffness of that first question which—which they have rehearsed because they're seeing me, then you get down to—to a human being . . . that's better. I went out to Albemarle School one morning, and it—it took a little thawing but after a while, it became quite well. By the end of it, there was a young man trying to sell me some cattle. Another man wanted to swap horses with me." He had everyone laughing.

He now seemed ready, as well, to speak his mind on race. He told the *Charlottesville Daily Progress* (May 11) that Virginia needed to take the lead: "He mentioned as an example 'the unhappy business' of last Friday night's State Chamber of Commerce banquet for distinguished Virginians and the furor that arose when it was discovered six Negroes had been invited through error. 'That's the sort of thing you'd expect Mississippi to do, but not Virginia. . . . Virginia to the rest of the South must be like Caesar's wife (above reproach).'" He had some hope for progress in his own state. To much audience laughter, he said that Governor James Coleman was "a better man than anybody in Mississippi expected. I imagine if they had known his true sentiments, they would never have elected him in Mississippi." For a writer who often said the writer counted for nothing in American life, Faulkner sounded gratified: "I have had some correspondence with him since he was elected, and every now and then he sends me copies of letters he writes to his legislature, and every now and then he quotes me, things that I have said on the subject of segregation."[14]

In the *Cavalier Daily* (May 22) he refuted rumors that the English department had "hampered his activities in Charlottesville." On the contrary, he said

"I have them [Blotner and Gwynn] trained to fetch and carry." Some changes would be made for a second semester, beginning in February 1958. He had grown tired of answering the same questions, which is perhaps another reason why Joseph Blotner screened the questions his students asked. Faulkner was not even sure he wanted to try another semester. He would think about it during the summer of 1957.

FROM JEFFERSON TO THE WORLD AND BACK

Published on May 1, 1957, *The Town,* the second novel in the Snopes trilogy, reflected Faulkner's travels from home that stimulated him to link Yoknapatawpha to a larger world. It is telling that in the midst of a comfortable semester at Virginia, he tore off for two weeks in Greece to do more work for the State Department in the usual round of talks and interviews, visiting the land of the polis, where small-town democracy was born. He also attended the opening performance of *Requiem for a Nun,* after which he smiled and embraced the director-producer and said, in tears: "It touched me here," pointing to his heart. He went backstage to congratulate the actors and gave a short curtain speech.[15] The play, performed in several European venues, including Camus's celebrated production in Paris, put Yoknapatawpha on a world stage. He now seemed almost comfortable as a public man, drinking plenty of ouzo as he sailed for a few days around the Greek islands, avoiding the collapses of earlier expeditions abroad. Even during a stormy patch, he seemed to settle down as he sailed deep into the ancient past, impressed with an immersion in Homer's "wine-dark sea."[16]

The Town opens with an amusing account of another trip abroad—how Gavin Stevens, a reader of ancient Greek, took a Snopes to war with him and ended up importing to Jefferson that same Snopes, who opens up a photography studio, calling it an atelier, that is actually a front for the dark room where his business is showing pornographic French postcards. What had America done by venturing to Europe? Stevens thought, like Woodrow Wilson, that Americans could rehabilitate Europe, but what actually happened is European corruption came home to the States. In an earlier novel, the political implications of such an episode would not be quite so knowingly set out. Writing *The Town,* teaching at Virginia, and representing his country abroad were now all central to William Faulkner's identity in a way that the Charlottesville Faulkner of 1931 could not have imagined.

The change is noticeable by his making Gavin Stevens the "looming presence . . . in the representative ordeal of his engagement as witness, devotee, interventionist, and elegist."[17] Often mistaken as Faulkner's spokesman,

Stevens, for all his centrality, is not always a sound authority. He regards Flem's quest to supplant Mayor de Spain as president of the bank simply as a reflection of Flem's greedy moneymaking ethos, his rapacity, which is why Ratliff says in his two-sentence chapter, referring to Stevens: "Because he missed it. He missed it completely." Stevens misses Flem's drive for respectability, what Ratliff obliquely refers to as Flem's emergence into a "clearing" where his motivations are now plainly visible. Behind-the-scenes maneuvering will no longer suffice. Flem requires that his success be shown—in a mansion with "colyums," as Ratliff pronounces the word so as to maintain his folksy Greek chorus persona and a way of speaking that sets him apart from the lawyer's rhetoric. Ratliff's interpretations, at many crucial points, supersede Stevens's.[18] And when Flem becomes a bank president and wears a respectable public face—that's when the real threat to everyone emerges. If Stevens "missed it completely," what about everyone else? Flem's elevation to higher office signals the "failure of an entire society, willing its own crash."[19] If Faulkner declared his faith that man would prevail, that did not mean his own society would not fail.

The long-delayed sequel to *The Hamlet* is also suffused with Faulkner's yearning for youth, the angst of middle age, and a troubled awareness of the role sex has played not only in his life and community but in the larger polity. Just about every significant clan and race and family in Yoknapatawpha from the Chickasaw to the Sartorises is mentioned in *The Town,* as Faulkner recapitulates the history of his own creation. By one measure, *The Town* outdoes *Absalom, Absalom!* and *Go Down, Moses,* novels similarly concerned with history but more narrowly grounded in the lives of Thomas Sutpen and his progeny, and in Isaac McCaslin as the embodiment of a heritage. In focusing on the disruptive presence of the Snopes clan and Eula Varner in Jefferson, the narrators of *The Town*—Charles Mallison, Gavin Stevens, and V. K. Ratliff—also present their understanding of how their world is structured. Their interplay is political, insofar as they are concerned with how the town's life is managed. Stevens is a county attorney who has trouble separating his romantic feelings from his official role, although his private passions also contribute positively to his performance as a public servant. Faulkner's erotic and chivalrous sensibility suffused his activities as a public man and saturate Gavin Stevens's conduct in *The Town.* Although set in the 1920s, the novel exudes the sensuosity of the 1950s in its evocation of Major de Spain, the dashing romantic leading man, the rooster in a red roadster, who brings the allure of the automobile to Jefferson. His advent is explicitly linked to the decade in which Faulkner wrote his novel, when Charles Mallison, writing in retrospect, supposes that Major de Spain "would have been by acclamation ordained a high priest in that new national religious cult of Cheesecake as it translated still alive the Harlows and Grables and Monroes into the hierarchy of American cherubim."

Faulkner had watched Jean Harlow on a film set and was quite aware of what Monroe signified: "She's something of the new age," he remarked to Blotner, "wiggling even while she's standing still."[20] She suggested motion and sexual arousal simply by being present. In the new age of the 1920s, another kind of motion (progress) is associated with the automobile that Major de Spain, aka Mayor de Spain, runs rampant in his taunting of Gavin Stevens, who lusts after Eula Varner, although it is not Stevens alone, as Charles Mallison confirms: "So when we first saw Mrs Snopes walking in the Square giving off that terrifying impression that in another second her flesh itself would burn her garments off, leaving not even a veil of ashes between her and the light of day, it seemed to us that we were watching Fate, a fate of which both she and Mayor de Spain were victims." Did Faulkner see Marilyn Monroe in *Niagara* (1953), the film noir directed by Henry Hathaway, who had pitched the plot of *A Fable* to Faulkner more than a decade earlier? In that film, Monroe walks down a cobblestone street near Niagara Falls in a scene that caused a riot of fan mail and much outrage in the public prints that deplored her disruptive sashay. Publicity stills put her against a stone wall with the Falls in the background, touting her as yet another wonder of nature. And so is Eula: a "woman who shapes, fits herself to no environment, scorns the fixitude of environment and all the behavior patterns which had been mutually agreed on as being best for the greatest number; but on the contrary just by breathing, just by the mere presence of that fragile and delicate flesh, warps and wrenches milieu itself to those soft unangled rounds and curves and planes." The town is for naught when Eula arrives—the mayor forgets his responsibilities and pride of position. Eula, like Marilyn, can be set against Niagara Falls, and you will look at her.

In that unusual film noir in color, Monroe plays an adulteress whose magnetizing presence dominates the attention of all—male and female—in precisely the way that Eula Varner does in *The Town*. The outrage is that society gathers itself around Monroe, not around the respectable and those who conform to propriety. And Eula, like Marilyn, does not for a moment stop to reflect about her own power, which is what makes her so infuriating for those who play by the rules and control their appetites. Eula/Marilyn are dispositive of a sexuality that unsettles the law (Stevens), the government (De Spain), and youth itself (Mallison), who is born into Eula's eighteen-year reign and does not know of a world without her. He is twelve for much of the novel and just learning to gird his loins.

Like Darryl Zanuck saying the audience had to have a rooting interest in the characters, Mallison remembers: "We were simply in favor of De

Spain and Eula Snopes, for what Uncle Gavin called the divinity of simple unadulterated uninhibited immortal lust which they represented." Mallison's mother puts it on the line: "The ladies of Jefferson dont care what she does. What they will never forgive is the way she looks. No: the way the Jefferson gentlemen look at her." Eula is not a lady, and gentleman are not supposed to look at her that way. Mrs. Mallison is herself too much of a lady to specify exactly what way that is.

For Faulkner the issue had been joined in his own life: in their turn, Meta, Joan, and Jean—his Harlow, Grable, and Monroe—had almost ruined the regime of Rowan Oak. Gavin Stevens embodies the tensions in Faulkner himself, but the lawyer, who never leaves home except to serve in war and study in Heidelberg, does not satisfy his lust for Eula. It is as though she is on a Grecian urn, more valuable as the image of his unconquerable desire than she could ever be in his bed. He cannot lose her so long as he does not have her. That he cannot put even this much in words, however, means he must displace his yearning to go after her by confining himself to a rivalry with Major de Spain and a campaign against the devious pécuniaire Flem Snopes. Stevens must maintain his honor, never getting his hands dirty, even though he resorts to childish plots, enlisting Charles and his companion Aleck Sander in waylaying the red roadster with a sharpened rake that punctures a tire as De Spain roars past the Mallison residence, where Stevens dines. Stevens's relish for intrigue is very Faulknerian. Just how childish the competition between De Spain and Stevens becomes is evident in the rake with flowers bound by "thin rubber" that De Spain sends to Stevens, which Chick later realizes is a used condom.

Like Faulkner, Stevens's romantic affairs cross generations—in this case including sixteen-year-old Linda, Eula's daughter, the infatuation of a "county attorney [who] must not be actually seen running down his office stairs and across the street into a drugstore where a sixteen-year-old high school junior waited." Was Faulkner thinking at such moments of how Joan carefully parked her car in Oxford so that Faulkner could slip into it? Or their aimless trips around the countryside—not knowing where to land and what to do? "Gavin Stevens metamorphoses from a caricature of Phil Stone into a caricature of Faulkner himself, always eager and always thwarted."[21]

Stevens is weaning Linda away from the stultifying home of Flem Snopes just as Faulkner preached the writer's gospel to Joan, disparaging her parents' middle-class lives. But Stevens remains celibate, refusing the opportunity to marry Linda, and preserves a kind of purity of motive that Faulkner could never maintain. He brought fine wine to his romances, whereas Stevens buys Linda ice cream cones and supplies her with books. Stevens—by turns noble and foolish—is a role Faulkner played intermittently with Joan Williams and could not quite relinquish. He had tried to see her in New York City a little more than a week before publication of *The Town* and wrote about missing her: "I haven't got over you yet and you probably know it, women are usually quite aware of the men who love them, so I thought maybe you were dodging me."[22] With no Joan or Jean, he did the next best thing, writing to Else Jonsson about "training a young jumping mare."[23] Just so Stevens trains Linda to want more than Jefferson, sending her, ultimately, to Greenwich Village, where Faulkner had spent some of his own youth, and where Joan Williams got a job. By the time Linda is ready to leave Jefferson she is nineteen—just about Jean Stein's age when she met Faulkner. Flem has wanted to keep Linda in a local academy, just as Jules Stein wanted to ensconce his daughter at Wellesley, which seemed a lot safer than St. Moritz. Linda is described as a "pointer," because she walks like she knows where she is going, but "not like a pointer about to make game, but like water moves somehow." Linda, in short, is a force of nature, setting up her own current—a Jean Stein with a sense of direction. And, remember, Faulkner said he wrote *The Town*, in part, for the pleasure of sending it to Jean for her delectation.

The inimitable Eula Varner Snopes commits suicide before her husband, Flem, can tell Linda that she is the product of Eula's coupling with Hoke McCarron,[24] who departs the scene as soon as he has had his way. The daughter is spared the sordid story Flem will make of it, but Eula's reasons for committing suicide do not satisfy anyone, really. Charles Mallison's tribute to her seems an almost prophetic forecast of a death like Marilyn Monroe's and its aftermath: "my bet is there was more than me in Jefferson that even just remembering her could feel it still and grieve. I mean, grieve because her daughter didn't have whatever it was that she had; until you realised that what you grieved for wasn't that the daughter didn't have it too; grieved not that we didn't have it anymore, but that we couldn't have it anymore: that even a whole Jefferson full of little weak puny frightened men couldn't have stood more than one Mrs Snopes inside of just one one-hundred years." Mythically speaking, Eula cannot have a daughter like herself. There can be no next Eula any more than a next Marilyn simply because, as Charles says, "she was alive and not ashamed of it like maybe right now or even for the last two weeks Mr de Spain and Uncle Gavin had been ashamed." Eula Varner is the one thing that no man—not even Flem Snopes—can possess, but the paradox is she has to die in order to maintain that possession of herself, that identity that so many men have desired to defile in their "male hunger which she blazed into anguish just by being, existing, breathing; having been born, becoming born, becoming a part of Motion;—that hunger which she herself could never assuage since there was but one of her to match with all that hungering." The sui generis Eula "no more had friends than man or woman either would have called them that Messalina and Helen had." Was Eula lonely? She never says so, but she seems, at the end, as forlorn as Marilyn Monroe.

Gavin Stevens wanted Eula to remain the "perfect virgin": "What he was doing was simply defending forever with his blood the principle that chastity and virtue in women shall be defended whether they exist or not." So Stevens puts up no fight against Major de Spain or Hoke McCarron. Faulkner said he almost cried when he wrote up Eula's death—and no wonder, since she represented the purity of a principle he revered in his own daughter and that Quentin Compson went to so much trouble to defend.

Although Faulkner opposed Rousseau, there is something of that state of nature in Eula. She tells Gavin: "Dont expect. You just are, and you need, and you must, and so you do. That's all. Dont waste time expecting." She rightly observes that he is a gentleman, and that inhibits him with all sorts of prohibitions. Much of original man is also invested in Charles Mallison, "Chick," who is, as V. K. Ratliff observes, a "boy . . . that hadn't been spoiled and corrupted yet by the world of growed-up men into being his enemies." Ratliff, by the way, turns out to be of Russian descent, a fact that slips out when Eula refers to him as Vladimir, surprising Stevens, who thinks he knows his friend so well. This outing of V. K. (the second initial stands for Kyrilytch) is another way for Faulkner to bring the world to Jefferson, just as the joking about the country way Ratliff talks reveals a ruse: he talks that way to remain on terms with his fellow man as Faulkner did himself when he was most at home. Ratliff offers a performance, but the performance is his way of remaining genuine and rooted. Chick will learn to do the same, but Faulkner needs him as the undefiled self that Eula in death will perpetuate, no matter how many times she has sinned with sex. That paradox, that gravitation toward sexuality and innocence that prevailed in the cheesecake era of the 1950s, had its counterpart in the man and his work.

There is a joking moment in *The Town* that suggests the tempering of sex and passion in society that Eula Varner agitates. It occurs when Chick's mother heads off for the Wednesday meeting of the Byron Society, which has long since lost its purpose. No one "read anything because they played bridge now but at least she said that when it met with Miss Jenny Du Pre they had toddies or juleps instead of just coffee or coca colas." This is the Miss Jenny in *Flags in the Dust* who had that passion for reading about crime in the papers. Even Byron, the poet mad, bad, and dangerous to know, has now become part of the conformist party that has no place for Eula and that Linda will abandon by setting off for New York.

And yet for all his travels and lovers Faulkner still faced homeward, turning toward his character Gavin Stevens, standing upon a ridge as Stevens addresses himself: "you, the old man, already white-headed," surveying the scene below and the "main highway leading from Jefferson to the world." This romantic passage near the end of *The Town* brings Faulkner back to his first sketch, "The Hill," and to the USIS documentary that showed him on a hill looking down on a Japanese settlement, musing on how a civilization is formed. Recalling again the Chickasaw and Doom, who plundered his way to respectability, and not mentioning but alluding to Flem Snopes (there in his rapacity and newfound desire for respectability as president of a bank), Faulkner surveys a creation that comes out of and yet is detachable from himself:

And you stand suzerain and solitary above the whole sum of your life beneath that incessant ephemeral spangling. First is Jefferson, the center, radiating weakly its puny glow into space; beyond it, enclosing it, spreads the County, tied by the diverging roads to that center as is the rim to the hub by its spokes, yourself detached as God himself for this moment above the cradle of your nativity and of the men and women who made you, the record and annal of your native land proffered for your perusal in ring by concentric ring like the ripples on living water above the dreamless slumber of your past; you to preside unanguished and immune above this miniature of man's passions and hopes and disasters—ambition and fear and lust and courage and abnegation and pity and honor and sin and pride—all bound, precarious and ramshackle held together, by the web, the iron-thin warp and woof of his rapacity but withal yet dedicated to his dreams.[25]

Faulkner's ambition, a subsequent passage seems to imply, has been as rapacious and ruthless as "Sutpen and Sartoris and Compson and Edmonds and McCaslin and Beauchamp and Grenier and Habersham" and all the snatchers and grabbers. But he is there, as well, on the hill with Stevens, and with Quentin and Shreve, part of that rippling water and the wheel of history they half-observe and half-create.

As in the essay "Mississippi," Jefferson and Oxford are overlayed. Flem's will is drawn up by a Mr. Stone in Oxford. "I know him," Stevens says. "Even if he did go to New Haven." And this exchange between Stevens and Ratliff about why Stevens is sending Linda to Greenwich Village puts paid to Faulkner's own peripateticism:

"It's a place with a few unimportant boundaries but no limitations where young people of any age go to seek dreams."

"I never knowed before that place had no particular geography," I says. "I thought that-ere was a varmint you hunted anywhere."

"Not always. Not for her, anyway. Sometimes you need a favorable scope of woods to hunt, a place where folks have already successfully hunted and found the same game you want. Sometimes, some people, even need help in finding it."

What was Faulkner doing, after all, with those students at the University of Virginia? Providing "help in finding it."

Two Towns

"In many ways, *The Town* is one of Faulkner's strongest novels," Louis Dollar-hide concluded in the *Jackson (MS) Clarion-Ledger* (April 28): "*The Hamlet* is more directly told and is less complex. But what *The Town* may lose in direct-ness of narrative it gains in richness of detail, energy and variety of character." Arthur MacGillivray (*Best Sellers*, May 1) called the novel "picaresque" with no overall unified theme, except for the ascent of the Snopeses. Murray Kempton, a journalist with a literary flair usually saved for the political beat, saw the wider implications of *The Town* and of Faulkner's other work, noting: "It was impos-sible to look at the Till trial without seeing a Sartoris in the judge, a Snopes in one of the defense attorneys, a Lucas Beauchamp in Moses Wright, the Till boy's uncle, although none were entirely recognizable as Faulkner's since they had not been transformed by his heightened sensibility, any more than a piece of stone is recognizable as a final work of Phidias to anyone but Phidias" (*New York Post*, May 5). Kempton saw the frontier humor that other reviewers rel-ished, but he added an important proviso: "Told any other way, these scenes would break the heart; they come close enough to doing so anyway." He did not say it, but certainly Eula's suicide suggested an aspect of the spirit that soci-ety had no way to honor as Flem Snopes triumphed, ridding himself, also, of the disreputable members of his clan. His triumph, Kempton observed, was ours—that is the triumph of business that so depressed Faulkner. "We are all of us in this fight Snopeses," Kempton declared, thinking about how we all go about our business while others suffer. "It is a terrible thought, and I'm afraid the next and final volume will be unbearable." What is so moving about *The Town*, Kempton might have added, is that the three narrators do care about the suffering and are watchful and proactive, if not always practical and effective.

More than the Snopeses, though, are involved in Faulkner's desire to show how a polity is created. His work on programs like People-to-People, even though a failure, signaled his deep interest in how a society is organized. The

Snopeses do it one way; the narrators of the novel in another. Faulkner, so individualistic, had trouble belonging to any sort of group and was wary of bureaucracy. In *The Town,* the "Snopeses' processes of organizing offer both the ideal model for scaling representation from the individual to the social, and a vision of the gothically terrifying consequences that may result."[26] No matter how difficult Faulkner found it to function within institutions, he understood their claim upon him, and what it meant not to pay attention when syndicates like the Snopeses take power.

Some reviewers, like Granville Hicks (*New Leader,* May 6), were disappointed because *The Town* did not have the intensity of *The Hamlet* and because Eula, a goddess in *The Hamlet,* now seemed mundane, wordy, and unworthy. Several reviewers quoted Alfred Kazin's *New York Times* review (May 5): "Tired, drummed-up, boring, often merely frivolous." Malcolm Cowley in the *New Republic* (May 27) regretted characters that "communicate chiefly by striking attitudes at one another." Gavin Stevens came in for a drubbing: excessive, foolish, old-fashioned, romantic, and unrealistic in Joseph Longley Jr.'s compendium in the *Virginia Quarterly Review* (Autumn 1957). Longley had a succinct rebuttal: *Don Quixote,* which, as it happens, was a book Faulkner reread every year. There was a lot of Don Quixote in William Faulkner, his wife pointed out.[27]

Ben Wasson (*Delta Democrat-Times,* May 5) was one of the few reviewers who noted the political dimensions of the novel—that it was not just about how Snopeses take over Jefferson, or even just about Flem's own chicanery, but instead about how a community, the South, and the "country as a whole" had been corrupted. "We have only to look at such people as Senator Joseph McCarthy . . . [a]nd you'll see a fine example of Snopesism." He also understood the dimensions of Eula's Marilyn Monroe–like significance, of how Eula's death gave her life. Faulkner had "created a lasting vital and beautiful woman and anyone so terrifically alive can never seem dead." Richard Ellmann (*Chicago Sunday Sun-Times,* May 5) summed up the novel's bifurcated dynamic forces: "One is Flem's stunted but unarrested mind. The other, painted more gaudily, is his wife Eula's irresistible body. The battle lines are drawn: she has the indifferent purity of instinct, and he has the scheming intensity of greed. Flem achieves respectability and Eula loses it. But her only sins are generosity and abundance, while Flem's new morality is reptilian. The passionate, Faulkner tells us, are the honorable. Eula wins whatever is worth winning."

By the time reviews of *The Town* appeared in the spring of 1957, Faulkner was at work on *The Mansion.* He almost never looked back or read reviews. The new work, as he told his University of Virginia audiences, was all that mattered since he could do nothing about what had already been published.

He also had family troubles. Malcolm, who had never recovered from his World War II experience, was, as his mother said, "in a very bad condition both mentally and physically." He had been part of the medical corps that had cleaned up at Buchenwald and the horrors of coming right after Patton's advance into Germany shattered Malcolm. He screamed and had nightmares as Cho-Cho watched her mother hold her brother to comfort him. Faulkner, too, stood by Buddy, as he often called Malcolm, and even inscribed one of his books to "my son."[28]

The war had been only part of the problem. He suffered from devastating insecurity. He never really knew his father, Cornell, and he spent his growing-up years living with and spoiled by his grandparents, the Oldhams. But he kept coming to Rowan Oak seeking his stepfather's acceptance. "He didn't know where he belonged, which father was really his," said his niece Vicki. The gap between the two residences was there: even at Christmas Faulkner would not enter the Oldham home, although Vicki pleaded with him to accompany her.[29]

Malcolm had been partially restored in a Richmond sanitarium—at Faulkner's urging and to Estelle's relief. Faulkner's intervention had been crucial: "Malcolm adores Bill—always has—and has proven his devotion though the years, especially when Bill had been drinking," Estelle confided to Dorothy Commins. Malcolm had also learned to drink like his stepfather, staying in bed and then roused into sullen action by his mother. "Sometimes I wonder whether or not I'll ever lead a sane, normal life—Doubt it—involved as I am," Estelle lamented. Joan Williams, another vexation, had been writing Faulkner for help with her work. "I would still feel clear—rid of it all—Bill included," Estelle ventured, hoping to spend a few days in New York with Dorothy.[30]

In late May, it was Faulkner who headed to New York to present the Gold Medal for fiction to John Dos Passos, an ordeal performed at the urgent request of Malcolm Cowley, who said only two hundred words or so would be needed. During the event, Faulkner left the stage twice to smoke, saying, "How long does *this* go on?" When his turn finally came, he could not manage even two hundred words and said hardly more than "No man deserves it more."[31] The two had met in New Orleans and perhaps on a few other occasions, including on the University of Virginia grounds, when they encountered one another unexpectedly and produced this riveting exchange: "Hello Bill." "Hello Dos."[32]

On June 10, he was again in New York helping his niece Dean prepare for her study-abroad year. She understood his unhappiness even as she empathized with Estelle:

As I met each of Pappy's women over a twenty-year period, my first reaction was instinctive: I simply hoped they made him happy. William Faulkner—this man of many faces, literary genius, desperate alcoholic subject to severe bouts of depression, driven early on by the unassuaged fear of failure—was my Pappy, not only the sole owner and proprietor of Yoknapatawpha, but the sole means of support, financial and emotional, off and on, of our family. We took so much and gave so little in return. No wonder he looked elsewhere for solace, and how could one woman have possibly filled the void? My meetings with the women in his life were easy and cordial, accidental in some cases, arranged by mutual friends at other times. Any animosity I might have felt was tempered by feelings of gratitude for what they had meant to him. I wished the same peace and joy for Aunt Estelle in whatever form it took.

I agree with Jill's comment "Pappy liked the ladies." Having personally known five of the women Pappy loved, I must say that he had great taste in women.

Though none of them resembled one another physically—some were dark-haired, others blond—all were graceful, charming conversationalists, sophisticated, quick-witted, and well-read, with a subtle vulnerability that drew people to them. This description also fits Aunt Estelle, who was a consummate hostess, gourmet cook, master gardener, and lady of the house when she chose to be.[33]

And none of these women were Faulkner's dependents, waiting for him at home. But they were also not the reigning Mrs. Faulkner.

On the return to Charlottesville, Faulkner stopped off at Rockville, Maryland, for a big party the Summers family had planned to celebrate their son Paul's graduation from the University of Virginia law school. Faulkner detested these kinds of social events and did not like Paul's parents and their friends, who arranged for a reporter to be present. In a bad mood when Betty Beale interviewed him for the *Washington Star,* he told her he did not expect to return as writer-in-residence for a second semester: "I sat in an office and answered questions from students, questions that either a priest or a veterinarian could have answered." He was thinking about his dog and farm and not about writing. Yet he assured a Charlottesville party guest that he would return. So which was it, Betty Beale wanted to know. "I never tell the truth to reporters," Faulkner said. This was such a hostile performance that Beale went away disenchanted, unable to square this man with the one she had liked so much in an interview with him three years earlier.[34]

Faulkner spent the summer of 1957 at Rowan Oak. Martha Carol White, an Ole Miss undergraduate, remembered wheeling around the Oxford square and coming to "a screeching halt because a little red-faced man in a white suit and hat stepped off the curb into my path. Yes, it was Mr. Faulkner," she wrote, shaken by the thought of almost running over him.[35] On July 6, Maud Falkner reported: "Bill and Estelle are home. He says he has not decided whether he will go back to the University of Virginia next year, but I think his little grandson will decide it for him. The baby is walking, is extremely good, loud, noisy & happy natured."[36]

After the disturbing phone calls about Jean Stein, after she had broken off the affair, the Faulkner marriage seemed to simmer and then—as Dean observed—transform itself into something "tender. They shared a gentle respect for each other, a pleasure in being together, a tacit closeness that comes only from a lifetime of shared memories. It was a joy to be with them. I cannot imagine either of them being married to anyone else."[37]

"THE WRITER-IN-RESIDENCE"

On September 9, Faulkner wrote to the English department chair, Floyd Stovall, seeking to secure his status as "THE writer-in-residence of the University." He did not want to be displaced, but he had certain "conditions which may not be acceptable." As before, he wanted a February start, with a break so he could see to his farm and other matters. It all worked out.

During the summer and early fall Faulkner continued to work on *The Mansion,* but he could not ignore the Little Rock, Arkansas, school integration crisis, when federal troops were called in to prevent violence at Central High School. Although Faulkner sometimes gave way to despair, thinking the races could never get along, and that equality between them remained a distant goal, he also believed the nation had to go forward, no matter what. America did not live only "among a continent of nations nor even in a hemisphere of nations, but as the last people unified nationally for liberty in an inimical world which already outnumbers us." He still thought his country stood for the individual against the "monolithic mass of a state dedicated to the premise that the state alone shall prevail"—a theme he was exploring just then in *The Mansion.* His trip to Greece and his palpable sense of an ancient past seem to have heightened his notion of America's uniqueness: "We because of the good luck of our still unspent and yet unexhausted past, may have to be the rallying point for all men, no matter what color they are or what tongue they speak, willing to federate into a community dedicated to the proposition that a community of individual free men not merely must endure, but can endure." That last sentence of his letter to the *New York Times* (October 13), suffused with the words of Jefferson and Lincoln, sounded a note he would carry into the very heart and head of the former Confederacy.[38]

On February 20, 1958, Faulkner addressed an invitation-only meeting of the Raven, Jefferson, and ODK Societies of the University of Virginia. The state's governor had vowed a massive resistance to integration. Some Charlottesville schools had been closed in 1958–59 to prevent black people from enrolling. In many respects regarding race, Charlottesville was no different from Oxford. Sam Oglesby, a student and, later, Foreign Service officer, recalled the visit of Ralph Bunche, winner of the 1950 Nobel Peace Prize: "The touchy matter of Virginia's segregation laws and how they would affect Dr. Bunche were side-stepped when he was offered overnight accommodations in the president's house and entertained on campus, saving this world-renowned figure the humiliation of being refused service in one of the local greasy spoons."[39]

Anything Faulkner said about race could involve President Darden in controversy, but Faulkner went ahead anyway after showing his text to Gwynn and an enthusiastic Blotner. Faulkner wanted to reconcile Virginians to the inevitable move toward integration, but he did so in his usual paradoxical fashion, speaking as a conservative southerner when he speculated: "Perhaps the Negro is not yet capable of more than second class citizenship. His tragedy may be that so far he is competent for equality only in the ratio of his white blood." Since he had said all along that fear of integration had to do with economics, not race, this emphasis on blood is puzzling, not to say retrograde. Such comments can only be understood as those of a man deeply involved in his own community. He was trying appease Virginians even as he was alienating certain northerners by supposing that in the North "by ratio of Negro to white in population, there is probably more of inequality and injustice there than with us." "Us" is the operative word with a man who still thought of northerners as Yankees.

Sounding as paternalistic as his great-grandfather, Faulkner spoke of taking the black man "in hand" and teaching him the "responsibilities of equality." This is what he meant by the South's obligation to clean up its own mess, although his words were much more polite and deferential to his audience. Moral principle and practical common sense demanded equality. But white people could not, by themselves, uplift a race, and here is where Booker T. Washington's *Up from Slavery* made its mark. Faulkner's words sound condescending, even racist, when he argued that black people must demonstrate they were worthy of equality and behave better than the best white people: "He must learn to cease forever more thinking like a Negro and acting like a Negro." What did that mean? He could not see, or at least could not acknowledge, that in the civil rights movement and elsewhere black people had already established both the principle and practice of equality.

The novelist who had read Ralph Ellison's *Invisible Man* emerged in this admission: "The white man can never really know the Negro, because the white man has forced the Negro to be always a Negro rather than another human being in their dealings, and therefore the Negro cannot afford, does not dare, to be open with the white man and let the white man know what he, the Negro, thinks." Even Lucas Beauchamp, sitting in his jail cell, and at the risk of a lynching, cannot tell Gavin Stevens what he is thinking. Stevens cannot really see Beauchamp as an individual. Stevens makes all sorts of assumptions about Beauchamp's behavior that Beauchamp knows he is powerless to refute. Lucas Beauchamp's power, in the novel and in the movie, is derived from his silence and from his pointed but terse comments to Chick Mallison, who has to think hard about what Beauchamp does not tell him but what needs to be said. Chick is Lucas's only hope because the boy has not yet obfuscated his imagination with abstractions like "Sambo"—Stevens's offensive term for black people. And yet Faulkner could imagine an understanding of black people only in white southern terms, arguing that white people "are capable in individual cases of liking and trusting individual Negroes, which the North can never do because the northerner only fears him."

Faulkner did not provide solutions, except to pointedly say that black people had to be included in white schools or white teachers had to be assigned to black schools—presumably as a temporary measure on the way to integration. More than any particular answer to the race problem was the role Virginia could play as "the mother of all the rest of us of the South. Compared to you, my country—Mississippi, Alabama, Arkansas—is still frontier, still wilderness. Yet even in our wilderness we look back to that mother-stock as though it were not really so distant and so far removed." He returned to the attachment to blood, "Virginia blood," that had populated that frontier. Faulkner did not refer to his own university appointment, to his pride in being one of the chosen, but there it was, even if unstated in his closing appeal to those "worthy to be trained to the old pattern in the University established by Mr Jefferson to be not just a dead monument to, but the enduring fountain of his principles of order within the human condition and the relationship of man with man—the messenger, the mouthpiece of all, saying to the mother of us all: Show us the way and lead us in it. I believe we will follow you."

Afterward, in an hour of questions and answers, he seemed, if anything, even more conservative, conceding a willingness to improve black schools rather than push for integration. Apparently no one mentioned miscegenation, although it was there in the subtext of his frequently repeated statements that the races did not want to mix. He drew laughs when he said the black man's "attitude toward the white man is something like the white man's toward him. He likes a few of them, but he don't think much of all of them."[40] The last questioner wanted to know if "race assimilation" would solve the problem between white and black people. Faulkner doubted it. People were people, as far as he was concerned, and they would continue to "bicker."

Asked about miscegenation in a University of Virginia class, he saw it as an error—not a moral one but simply one that society, so far, could not tolerate. When asked by publisher Lyle Stuart to comment on Norman Mailer's assertion that the white man feared the black man's sexual potency and preferred the status quo—the black man's sexual supremacy—Faulkner replied: "I have heard this idea expressed several times during the last twenty years, though not before by a man. The others were ladies, northern or middle western ladies, usually around 40 or 50 years of age. I dont know what a psychiatrist would find in this."[41]

When asked about the Ku Klux Klan, Faulkner said that mainly poor, unsuccessful whites, full of resentment, became members. He could have been describing Mink Snopes's white sharecropper hostility to the black man who works for Jack Houston in *The Mansion:* "He hates the Negro because the Negro is beating him at his own poor game. . . . His only superiority over that Negro is—is not economic any longer. It's because he's white, and that Negro's not white, and so he's going to do everything he can to keep that Negro black, because it makes him feel good. That's the only thing, the only edge he has."

The *Cavalier Daily* endorsed Faulkner's word to Virginians: "Faulkner's proposals were based on his observations of Negroes from Mississippi to Virginia. Considering his insight into human nature as evidenced in his novels, and his acquaintance with Negroes and their problems (we have heard that he sits on a nail keg down by the liquor store on Vinegar Hill observing and taking notes) we feel that his proposals have much merit and are worthy of review." The paper evidently did not ask President Darden to comment. Faulkner seems to have amassed so much goodwill in his first semester that the segregationist contingent left him alone—not what he would have encountered back home, he told his Virginia audience, where he faced threats from those who would just as soon burn his barn down. He would say such things without rancor and sometimes even provoked laughs. He urged people to put their battle flags away.

"Moby Mule"

Faulkner met only a few classes in February—mainly concerned with the problems of writing—before departing for Princeton. Leslie Aldridge, then the wife of literary critic John Aldridge, spotted an almost shabby-looking Faulkner on the Princeton Junction train platform. He was part of her conception of a literary Valhalla, but instead of rushing him, she hit upon a clever maneuver, turning to Faulkner's companion, Saxe Commins, and talking to him. She was sure the editor would have to introduce her to this awesome figure, which he did, of course. Even better, Saxe was only seeing Faulkner off. So she seated herself close to Faulkner on the train, and then at Pennsylvania Station she offered him a ride in her taxi, which he declined by offering her his. Exactly what she wanted, sitting beside a man so susceptible to young women and ready to open up, talking about the work he would do on *The Mansion* at Random House. They parted then, but some days later, there he was: walking down Nassau Street, Princeton's main corridor. She stopped her car and nabbed her literary prize, luring him off the street with the offer of a drink, although it was 10:30 a.m.

At home she called out to her husband, who came into the room, speechless at the sight of this literary monument, which his wife had brought home "like a prize cabbage from the supermarket." Now Aldridge was an elegant man, comfortable in the company of writers like William Styron, Norman Mailer, and Ralph Ellison, but it took the literary critic a few minutes to compose himself. It was the closest he had ever come to fainting, Aldridge recalled. The drinks helped and led to lunch and more drinks, with Faulkner's "terrifying silences" stonewalling literary discussion. But Leslie got on well with a writer who liked to flirt. John noticed she was already calling him Bill. John did better as soon as he brought up his childhood on a Tennessee farm and his mule Nancy. Faulkner had written an ode to the mule in *Flags in the Dust* and raised them on Greenfield Farm and told the Aldridges all about it and how important *Moby Dick* was to him, concluding, "I think one day I might write a novel called 'Moby Mule.'"[42]

An elated Saxe Commins wrote to Ruth Ford about the "two exciting weeks" of the "visit . . . exciting certainly for the students and faculty of Princeton and, I believe, rewarding for Bill. We managed to get in a few licks on the new manuscript [*The Mansion*], about one-third of which is finished, and a great work it promises to be."[43] It is remarkable that after so many talks in University of Virginia classrooms this reticent writer would want to do more. Perhaps he did so because he was meeting in one-on-one sessions with students who wanted to be writers. Ace Barber met Faulkner in Firestone Library for what turned out to be, in Barber's words, "something of a religious initiation." Barber did not show Faulkner any of his writing and came, in effect, for inspiration, and somehow Faulkner realized what was at stake, saying in words that Barber would never forget: "You will write. I'm not going to say how good it will be, but you will write." Faulkner seemed more than kind. To Barber, it felt like he had been given a blessing. You can read the transcripts of what Faulkner said in classes and public events and never realize what his presence, his tone of mild and yet absolute authority, conveyed to those seeking his counsel. This was the man who had been an excellent scout-master, a coach who bonded with the company of youth.

A few days later Barber saw Faulkner again with Saxe Commins and a group of about twenty students at Professor Willard Thorp's home. He remembered Faulkner refusing a second bourbon and seeming uncomfortable with so many people in the room and with all the literary talk. Near the end of the evening Barber tried to resume a conversation with Faulkner, who no longer seemed interested: "It wasn't, to me, a rebuff. It was just sort of a signal that I'd better get to work and stop talking." Later Faulkner mentioned Barber to a literary agent who agreed to represent Barber, who sold a story to the *Transatlantic Review*. Barber wanted to think his experience had been unique—like one in Faulkner's fiction: "as surely as Sam Fathers smeared blood on the boy's forehead, Mr. Faulkner gave me permission to work in his religion."[44] Barber (1936–2003) went on to a successful career as a writer and university professor.

One of the students talking to Faulkner provided an account in the *Daily Princetonian* (March 19, 1958) that coincided with his University of Virginia advice: Start writing, stop thinking about it. Write for pleasure and do it with passion and not for money. Don't be a "writer." Just write. Read other writers to see how they write about people as characters. Don't think in terms of ideas. Write an action that defines a character not only now but in terms of what he will become. Stop while you are still hot. Leave something for the next day. Leave talk of symbolism and style to the literary folk and the professors. In the end, you may make money anyway.

THE OXFORD-CHARLOTTESVILLE-PRINCETON AXIS

Estelle joined her husband in late March for a return to Rowan Oak to take care of some business and to attend to her son Malcolm, who remained disconsolate and listless. Husband and wife were now drawn more and more to Virginia, where Jill was expecting a second child. Estelle made her preferences plain to Dorothy Commins: "I'm hoping and *praying* that Bill will see his way clear to buy a place up here. Where you can come if you wish & stay and stay and stay. How I'd love that!" They had found an "ideal house. . . . But of course I realize how serious a move it will be, for Bill—and say little—I've sort of trained myself to be reasonably satisfied anywhere—but to be near

Jill and her little family means a great deal."[45] In both Princeton, where the university fended off press requests for interviews, and in Charlottesville, the Faulkners seemed refreshed and glad to be where they were treated as people of importance and actually let alone.

In April and May, Faulkner met with more classes in literature and one in psychology as well as giving public readings from *The Town* and *The Sound and the Fury*. He was now an accomplished public interlocutor. He had told an English department member that he had first arrived not knowing what he could do and nervously confronted his first class conference. But he settled down quickly, and in May 1958 his ease and humor made his appearances delightful and even playful. Asked by Joseph Blotner, "Could the title [*Pylon*] refer to the girl Laverne, the marker or beacon around which all the other, all the men gravitate?," Faulkner replied: "Now, there's some more of this erudite, professorial symbolism. . . . I'm sure that you're quite right, I just hadn't thought of that. I'm—I'm glad to know it. I'll remember that. I'll use that sometime probably." Blotner had become a confidant, and Faulkner knew that his friend would be amused. Always courteous and respectful, Faulkner had been restrained in earlier appearances. He had been asked several times about the reasons for the Southern Renaissance and usually disavowed any expertise in handling such a question. But this time, when he was asked, "Why is it that Mississippi seems so very active in a literary way, and yet we don't find the same phenomenon in New Jersey?," Faulkner said, "Well, that's—that's because Mississippi is in the South and New Jersey's in the North." As the laughter settled down, he added: "I think that the wisest thing any nation can do when it gets itself into any sort of a economic muddle is to pick out some rich nation and declare war on it, and get licked and then be supported. The folks in the South write because the North has supported us ever since 1865. We had plenty of time to write." The laughter reached a crescendo. He had anticipated, by the way, the plot of a Peter Sellers film, *The Mouse That Roared* (1959).[46] Sometimes the comedy came in very short bursts:

> What do you think of the dramatizations that have been made of your
> work for the movies and for the play coming out next year?
> [William Faulkner]: I saw *Intruder in the Dust*. I thought that was a—a
> pretty good picture. It was a good deal like my book.

These interactions were part of Faulkner on duty. As usual, he drew a line when not on the University of Virginia clock. "WF was in a very mellow mood when they came to dinner—too mellow in fact, for he resolutely declined to answer yours or any other questions that evening having to do with his work," Linton Massey reported to Carvel Collins.[47]

By mid-June, again at Rowan Oak, Faulkner settled down to work on *The Mansion,* rejecting a State Department invitation to visit the Soviet Union: "If I, who have had the freedom all my life in which to write truth exactly as I saw it, visited Russia now, the fact of even the outward appearance of condoning the condition which the present Russian government has established, would be a betrayal, not of the giants: nothing can harm them, but of their spiritual heirs who risk their lives with every page they write; and a lie in that it would condone the shame of them who might have been their heirs who have lost more than life: who have had their souls destroyed for the privilege of writing in public."[48]

Faulkner's letters during this period often mention his working with horses, training and showing them off, riding them and falling off in a pattern that would continue—no matter what bone he broke. He even admitted to fearing horses, which is why he said he had to conquer them. He withdrew into familiar routines, rejected offers to lecture elsewhere, and did not want to have anything to do with film adaptations of his novels, except to collect the money for them. He was looking forward to another Princeton trip, seeing more students, and staying with Saxe and Dorothy Commins.

Then Saxe died:

July 17

DEAREST DOROTHY WE ARE SHOCKED AND HEART BROKEN. JILL AND BABY ARE HERE. JILL IS CRUSHED AS WE ARE. BILL OR I WILL COME IMMEDIATELY IF IN ANY WAY OUR PHYSICAL PRESENCE WILL HELP KNOW THAT WE IN MISSISSIPPI MOURN TOO OUR LOVE

ESTELLE JILL BILL

July 18

THE FINEST EPITAPH EVERYONE WHO EVER KNEW SAXE WILL HAVE TO SUBSCRIBE TO WHETHER HE WILL OR NOT QUOTE HE LOVED ME UNQUOTE

BILL FAULKNER

Saxe was sixty-six, and his weak heart had done him in. He had been much more than an editor—more like a body servant. "I think I will give Bill a warm alcohol rubdown. It always helped that sore spot before," he told his wife. This was just after one of Faulkner's drunks. A horrified Dorothy said: "A rubdown with alcohol! . . . I think a couple of aspirins and some hot lemonade might be better." She liked to remember the two men studying pages on the floor, "on their knees, moving from one page to another, marking, delet-ing, transferring passages here and there!" Faulkner never seemed to object to Saxe's comments: "'Bill,' he would say, 'this won't do! You've said it before!'" The revised pages would come, overnight, to the editor's delight.[49]

The Princeton Affair

The Faulkners did not make it in time for the funeral, but Bill Faulkner did return in November to meet students and to see Leslie Aldridge. At Dorothy Commins's urging he reluctantly attended a party to introduce him to mem-bers of Princeton's Institute for Advanced Study. "I don't understand their world," he told her. He remained monosyllabic during the evening, at one point shutting up Robert Oppenheimer, who wanted to talk about a tele-vision program, by saying, "Television is for niggers." At such affairs, he had always counted on Saxe Commins as a buffer. "We all miss Saxe," he wrote to Harold Ober, another Faulkner stalwart: "I will have to hunt up somebody else now who will stop anybody making the Wm Faulkner story the moment I have breathed my last."[50]

He took Leslie Aldridge to Lahiere, then Princeton's only French restau-rant, a venerable establishment that had served every sort of famous person from Albert Einstein to Bob Hope.[51] Over white wine they discussed whom he might choose to be his biographer. Aldridge did not mention names but noted that Faulkner did not want to leave the selection to his publishers. The name Faulkner, he told her, derived from falconer, a man who trained falcons to hunt small game. They had a long lunch as Faulkner began to explain the sex habits of falcons. After lunch they went to the Aldridge home and sat on the lawn. As Faulkner lit up his pipe he propositioned her. She mulled over her "patriotic duty." Would his lovemaking match his exquisite, sensitive prose? Reluctantly, she decided to remain faithful to her husband, and Faulk-ner, a good sport, continued to sun himself in her garden. He told her she was beautiful and that he loved her. They both laughed. Soon he was giving her his recipe for hush puppies. She asked if she might take a photograph—but not one of those dour "palm-under-the-chin" poses. She had an idea: Why didn't he pretend to be drinking champagne out of her shoe? He smiled and removed her foot from her old black pump and she snapped her picture. Did he recall those happy, playful days with Meta, and his own pornographic drawings? Then she wanted one of him clasping his hands together and pray-ing. Sure thing. She snapped away at his greatness. The next day he sent her a dozen roses with the message: "You still are. I still do." They exchanged let-ters. "Dear, I don't know what to say here," he began. "I am old enough to be your uncle but I don't feel much like it." She wondered why he had not said "father." Did it make him feel even older, incestuous? She sent him a photo of herself in bare feet. He responded: The photograph revealed her character. She undressed "from the feet up: the last to come off will be the brassiere, unless you have on ear-drops or a locket? Right?" Writing from Charlottesville, he regretted he could not come to see her. She was going away with her husband, who had a Fulbright to Munich. She had predicted it would take four years before Faulkner would reach "that stage when I cannot bear the anguish except to go all the way from Va. to Princeton just to look into your eyes for ten minutes." Then he closed by saying, "Incidentally, did I ever tell you about the two falcons who didn't wait 4 years?" They exchanged a few more letters for a year or so, with Faulkner still writing about falcons, but they never met again. In his last letter, he urged her: "Do come on home. In 2 and 1/2 years more my white beard may be so long I shant be able to see you through it."

AT THE ALGONQUIN

By the end of November, he had checked into the Algonquin, his favorite hotel. The manager remembered this "distinguished white-haired Southern gentleman in impeccable attire. I always assumed that some English tailor must have custom made his clothes. . . . He was very reserved. He would talk to the staff. He knew all of us. Seemed to be in a private world of his own."[52] Harry Celetano, head bellman, was there to greet Faulkner when he arrived, quiet and courteous, going immediately to his room, carrying a small bag but never a typewriter. He never went to the bar, but he had a favorite green sofa in the lobby, where he would meet people. The furniture was positioned away from the entrance behind a barrier, allowing for some relief from the traffic. Celetano and Faulkner talked sports, especially horse racing. The coral in Florida soil made for strong-boned racehorses, Faulkner told Celetano, just like the limestone in Kentucky. Faulkner had done his research, Carvel Collins discovered, and realized that the soil on Greenfield Farm lacked the limestone that would produce big-boned mules. Faulkner talked about other sports as well, especially sailing, about which he knew a great deal, including crew races and rowing. But steeplechases and jumping horses were his favorite topics, and sometimes the news of the day. Celetano recalled Faulkner's animated talk about the Kentucky Derby and a hockey game he reported on for *Sports Illustrated*. Celetano knew all about Faulkner's drinking and reluctantly mentioned an incident when a maid had complained to the bellman about the bottles piled up in Faulkner's room. Celetano said Faulkner drank quietly, alone, and was never troublesome or noisy. For some alcoholics, as Leslie Jamison notes in her memoir, drinking alone is a tremendous comfort and a way to shut out the world. Celetano remembered that penetrating gaze, that reading of people. Staying usually no more than four days at a time, Faulkner would give Celetano a generous tip and say, "now you will share this with the boys." Another bellman, Earl Miller, had similar impressions, especially of a "self-contained" Faulkner, friendly but without small talk, and always a quiet drinker.[53]

AT THE HUNT

Faulkner, now far from the frontier, spent time in the homes of Virginia aristocrats, dressing up in their riding habits. He sent a polite thank-you to Mrs. Julio S. Galban for the "pleasure and honor" of riding with the Farmington Hunt on New Year's Day. There had been a mishap: "I got separated and still thought I was following the hounds until Mrs Cochran and Hyers told me we were on the way home."[54] He returned to Mississippi in early January for some quail shooting too, but where was his home now? "AM HOMESICK FOR EVERYBODY ... VALENTINE'S LOVE," he wired Estelle in Charlottesville.[55] By mid-February, he returned to full membership in the Farmington Hunt and bragged about taking four-foot walls and fences mounted on a horse called Powerhouse: "Good fun, also pleases my vanity to still be able for it at 61 years old." And more mishaps: "Excuse this typing," he wrote Muna Lee at the State Department. "Was fox hunting today and the horse and I went through a thicket in high gear and a twig caught me in the left eye and it's watering and sight not too good."[56] This was apparently no exaggeration. One of his fellow hunters called Faulkner "extremely game" and a "true sportsman" who "absolutely would not stop in his pursuit of the fox."[57] At Lee's urging, he agreed to attend a UNESCO conference in Denver (October 2) and after much coaxing delivered a short address, concluding, "The last sound on the worthless earth will be two human beings trying to launch a homemade space ship and already quarreling about where they are going next."[58]

Meta Carpenter wondered what William Faulkner in his hunting club finery had to do with the marginalized writer she had adored as they walked along Hollywood Boulevard.[59] He did not seem to be the same man. But in fundamental respects he remained the same. "He was an unenthusiastic socialite," said Salley Knight, whose parents, the Heywards, horse people, hosted a Faulkner visit. They were part of one of the largest slave-owning families in South Carolina and also related to the playwright DuBose Heyward, author of *Porgy and Bess*. She grew up hearing about the "War between the States."

"There was nothing 'civil' about it," her father would say. Salley said: "The story was he [Faulkner] would disappear." Like his poet persona in "Artist at Home," he was much more comfortable in the kitchen or out in the stables. He did not have much use for dinner party conversation. The Heywards understood. That's just how Faulkner behaved. "This was a world where there was more acceptance of oddities. Everyone had their place," Knight recalled: "The redneck worked on the farm, the black people were in the kitchen, Cecil who did the horses, Mary who cooked the food." Whoever was there had a story to tell, and they were there with the white family right to their dying days. Like Faulkner, Salley grew up with "the help," black people to whom she was much closer than to her parents. It seemed like "there was a black person for every kind of task. I feel I am the person I am because of the care I got from these wonderful black people. But it is hard to talk about that now. The emotional warmth I got was certainly not from my parents." Salley lived in the kitchen because upstairs was a bore. "It was a tough two worlds to put together."

If Meta had sat beside Faulkner during those hours and hours in university classrooms and at Charlottesville public events, he would not have seemed so different. He steadfastly refused to say that anything mattered more than the writing, than being a writer, dealing with people, characters—not plot, not ideas, not themes or messages. When *Faulkner in the University: Class Conferences at the University of Virginia* appeared at the end of the year, Faulkner wrote to Albert Erskine, Saxe Commins's successor, that Saxe, defending his author's dignity, did not want the book published, "saying it would inevitably be taken as Faulkner's definitive opinion on Faulkner. I didn't quite see this, or didn't think it mattered, and was ready to agree to the publishing of it, but submitted to Saxe since he was my literary wet-nurse, etc. He finally agreed. . . . I didn't think it was all that important, myself. It was done impromptu, off the cuff, ad lib, no rehearsal; I just answered what sounded right and interesting, to the best of my recollection after elapsed years, at the moment."[60]

He was working again on *The Mansion* for a few days before returning to Charlottesville, where Jill's son, William, was born on December 2. Faulkner had found a new circle of friends, including the wealthy Faulkner collector Linton Massey. Riding to the hounds at the Keswick and Farmington Hunt Clubs now substituted for the Mississippi Delta hunts. He rode with what passed for Virginia gentry. On January 23, 1959, he finished a complete draft of *The Mansion,* concluding Flem Snopes's quest for respectability.

29

Full Circle

January–November 1959

FAULKNER ON STAGE

On January 30, *Requiem for a Nun,* starring Ruth Ford and her husband, Zachary Scott, finally premiered on Broadway. Estelle wired Mr. and Mrs. Zachary Scott: "AM DISTRESSED OVER MISSING YOUR TRIUMPH TONIGHT. STOP. CONFIDENT THE ACCLAIM WILL BE OVERWHELMING. REGARDS ESTELLE FAULKNER."[1] Both play and novel had been conceived decades earlier, encompassing Yoknapatawpha—from the courtroom to the countryside, from the gentry to the peasants (sharecroppers), with the townsmen in the middle. This world was changing, as Faulkner often pointed out in his University of Virginia talks. He no longer observed a stable middle class, he said, and that troubled him because he saw an erosion of standards. Snopeses were not the cause of this corruption but rather a symptom. Gavin Stevens, for all his faults—his high-handed pursuit of justice, his foolish romanticism—was trying to hold the world together against forces that sought to abolish all distinctions in a quest for money and respectability.

Zachary Scott, a Texan, had worked with Faulkner on *The Southerner.* In periodic meetings over several years as *Requiem for a Nun* went through several European productions, with notable successes in Paris and London until Ruth Ford was finally able to secure a U.S. run, Scott observed a Faulkner who in some respects resembled Quentin Compson, "constantly in search of reasons for the behavior of Southerners, why they left the South, and what happened to them." It is not too much to say that Faulkner treated Ford and Scott as family. He called the couple whenever he knew they were in New

York and went to see them. "He and Ruth were very simpatico," Scott said. "It was a pleasure, a joy to see them together." They did not have to say much; not much needed saying. All three could sit "easily in silence" for a half hour. Scott remembered walking into a room with Ruth and Bill on the sofa, saying nothing. "What are you doing, Bill?," Scott asked. "I'm just sitting here loving Ruth," was the reply. Estelle believed it had all begun when Ruth dated Dean Faulkner at Ole Miss. That is why Ford had the irrevocable stage rights to *Requiem* and why Faulkner stood by her when at least one producer wanted to replace her, and why he essentially turned the play over to her so that it could become more playable.

Scott noted that Faulkner had an actor's keen awareness of self-presentation: "one of the most camera conscious men I ever knew. In pictures taken he was always a little apart from the rest, looking away. It might be the same way in conversation. He might seem apart from it, not hearing it, but he was still a close person, he had the heart of the conversation, the soul. . . . [H]e never imposed himself in any way." Scott described Faulkner as a character, a creation, and a force of nature: "He looked like he should have looked. . . . He attracted children, birds, and animals. His mind was both sensitive and wicked. Yet he was sweet. He was naive and sophisticated at the same time. He radiated charm and wisdom."[2]

Nearly all reviewers agreed that Ford and Scott were virtually perfect as Temple Drake and Gavin Stevens, yet the play never caught on. Faulkner had waived two weeks of royalties hoping to extend the play's run, but it closed in March just as he completed his revised typescript of *The Mansion*.[3] While praising several powerful scenes, critics deemed the play devoid of action with too much talking, elliptical and repetitious. Kenneth Tynan, who saw productions in Berlin, Madrid, Paris, and London, called the text "intoned rather than embodied."[4] Faulkner thought the play worked best as a closet drama with a small audience. That seems to be what Brooks Atkinson had in mind when he said the play belonged to "art theater."[5]

COMING HOME

No longer tied to a university calendar, Faulkner went riding, fracturing his collarbone in a fall, and in June, just as he finished working through *The Mansion* galleys, he found a Charlottesville home, 917 Rugby Road. He resumed riding as often as four or five times a week.[6] His new editor, Albert Erskine, urged him to reconcile the discrepancies in the Snopes trilogy. Faulkner tolerated some changes but preferred, in the end, to include this prefatory statement to *The Mansion:* "there will be found discrepancies

and contradictions in the thirty-four-year progress of this particular chronicle; the purpose of this note is simply to notify the reader that the author
has already found more discrepancies and contradictions than he hopes the
reader will—contradictions and discrepancies due to the fact that the author
has learned, he believes, more about the human heart and its dilemma than he
knew thirty-four years ago; and is sure that, having lived with them that long
time, he knows the characters in this chronicle better than he did then." *The
Mansion* retold stories familiar to readers of *The Hamlet* and *The Town,* but
the reiteration was not so much an effort to unify the trilogy as to reinforce
the obsessive nature of storytelling, and of the stories a community tells to
itself across generations and in different circumstances, making discrepancies
a part of the nature of history itself.

Settling into the Rugby Road home made the contrast between past and
present all the more palpable. Faulkner now lived in town, not adjacent to it.
He had become a fixture in a community that had invited him to reside there
in a home now "furnished in at least a livable fashion," Estelle reported to her
sister Dorothy. Faulkner liked to walk in the city, visiting a saddle shop, where
he bought tack or had it repaired. He sat in one of two chairs smoking his
pipe, returning the greetings of people who knew him. Sometimes he would
talk about horses, but just as often he would remain quiet, saying nothing.[7]

The first reviews of *The Mansion,* dedicated to Phil Stone, appeared.[8] While
still in Oxford Faulkner had dropped off a copy of the book at his friend's law
office, and Stone sent him a note: "Don't think I am not interested by the
fact that I have not yet had time to read it. [Hal] Freeland [Stone's law part-
ner] and I have been working four nights a week and I work every Sunday,
so I don't have much time to read a book, but I do hope to get this one read
during the holidays."[9] Freeland, on the other hand, always had plenty of time
for Faulkner, answering his questions about the law and learning much from
the nature of this genius's interests.[10]

Stone, the man who recognized himself in Gavin Stevens and claimed the
conception of the Snopeses as his own,[11] now working so hard to discharge
his debts, watched Faulkner finesse his way from one home to another, and
from one honor to another. A Stone law clerk remembered Faulkner coming
into the outer office "hungry to see Mr. Phil," and Stone would duck out the
back door, dreading that Faulkner might demand the money he had lent to
his mentor.[12] What Faulkner thought of Stone's cold note is not known, but
the long-delayed denouement of the trilogy, and the story of Mink's abiding
his long-contemplated revenge against Flem, has to be factored into Stone's
own resentments as he saw his erstwhile protégé ensconced in the mansion of
Virginian ascension that neither one of them had foretold.

Some reviewers treated *The Mansion* as a career-ending novel of a writer in decline: "Mr. Faulkner, as it has become painfully evident in recent years, is not the writer he once was," concluded R. E. L. Master in the *Shreveport Times* (November 1). The prose lacked intensity; the telling was typically confused and repetitious and undramatic. "An intolerable bore," declared Orville Prescott in the *New York Times* (November 13). Already, Granville Hicks (*Saturday Review,* November 14) propounded what became the customary view that Faulkner had reached his peak between 1929 and 1942.

Perhaps the oddest criticisms were also the oldest, dating back to his first reviews—that Faulkner's characters were depraved. None of the negative notices contemplated for a moment that *The Mansion,* like *The Town,* had three ethically inspired narrators: Gavin Stevens, Charles Mallison, and V. K. Ratliff, who do not merely try to do good but are committed to monitoring—and are implicated in—what happens in their world, both good and evil. The moral compass of the trilogy is hard earned through the narrators' complex examination of themselves and the Snopeses, Varners, Sartorises, and those who come into contact with them. What the narrators know, or suppose they know, depends on who they are and what they do. Their world and their characters cannot exist outside of their own creation and interpretation, which means that the straightforward telling of a story, as if that story is somehow a fact, is precisely what Faulkner could not endorse but that his detractors desired.

Even the negative reviews praised the story of Mink Snopes, "one of Faulkner's driven men," Hicks proclaimed, nursing a thirty-eight-year-old grudge in Parchman prison against Flem, who did not save his relative from serving a life sentence for murdering Jack Houston. Mink Snopes exemplifies Faulkner's practice, enunciated at the University of Virginia, of not judging his characters but understanding them—in this case, Mink's grandiose sense of his own dignity and how it has been violated first by Jack Houston and then by Flem Snopes. Mink, a small, scrawny man of no accomplishment, is never patronized in Faulkner's prose. The unapologetic Mink, confirmed in his own probity, is magnificent, if deluded and determined and nearly ridiculous in his belief that he has been cheated out of what is owed to him: the cow he has conveniently wintered over on Jack Houston's property and that he has then to buy back when Houston refuses to return the cow, now much more valuable since it has been fattened up. Mink turns the situation completely around until he regards himself as the wronged party. His logic seems sound to him, and Faulkner endows him with a powerful self-deceiving imagination. Objectively, Mink is a fool and one of Faulkner's "depraved" characters, and yet, by his own lights, Mink has stood up for his own humanity. He has to be included in what Faulkner constantly called the verities at the University of Virginia. Mink is, for all his faults, an individual supreme, and as such he too is an example of why Faulkner thought man would not only endure but prevail. Mink's tenacity and dedication, over decades in prison, mirrors Faulkner's own sense of mission. Hicks calls Mink an "ugly little man, bestial in appearance and manner" but "heroic in his pursuit of his evil ends." True, but hardly enough to explain Faulkner's commitment to his character. James Meriwether insisted in the *Houston Post* (November 15) that *The Mansion* is Mink's book. He is the one to bring Flem down because Flem has, above all, dehumanized so many people, including himself.

Another favorite of reviewers: Senator Clarence Eggleston Snopes, who haunts whorehouses and is described as the "apostolic venereal ambassador." The epitome of the corrupt and irredeemable, he is the gravamen of the charge sheet that can be drawn up against humankind. He relishes his salacious repasts and is the very antithesis of that anomalous Wall Snopes, who pursues his grocery chain business with integrity and independence and with an energy very like what Montgomery Ward Snopes puts into his pornographic enterprise. The clever Clarence almost gets away with becoming a U.S. senator by turning his World War II hero opponent into a "nigger lover" because he has commanded black troops. But Ratliff engineers a humiliation for Clarence—making a pack dog urinate on the politician's surreptitiously scented pants—so that a disgusted Will Varner, Snopes's political boss, makes him withdraw from the race. Although Stevens finds Ratliff's ploy too simple to believe, the point, really, is that Clarence has not been paying attention, like the acute Flem Snopes, and is bound, one way or another, to fail.

Linda Snopes, whom Gavin successfully spirits out of Jefferson, comes home the widow of a Jewish, Communist sculptor-husband named Barton Kohl. He dies during their mission to save the Spanish republic. Some reviewers deemed her unconvincing and an example of Faulkner's faulty understanding of post–World War II America. That Faulkner had seriously come to terms with his travels abroad and with the national security state never seems to have penetrated their mind-sets. What role an individual can still play in a centralizing and collectivist world—Faulkner's constant concern—was not even dimly discerned. Linda represents the return of the native, the next generation not bound by the perfidy of her clan or the racism of her fellow southerners, and as such hers is a very American story of the progress, however fitful, that Faulkner thought possible. But her story, like the others, is not without irony, since it is Linda who works to get Mink out of prison and into Flem's sitting room for Mink to kill him.

As in *The Town,* where Stevens does not act upon his love for Eula—even when she offers herself to him—so in *The Mansion* he deflects Linda's love, wishing to make their bond more selfless than Faulkner ever achieved with the young women he pursued. It might be, though, that Linda, deafened by war and speaking in a quacking voice—no match for the beauty Ruth Ford—nevertheless owes something to Ford, who did not want to trouble her friendship with Faulkner by promoting him to a romance. His loyalty to Ford, dating from his first meeting with her in Oxford and continuing in Hollywood and New York, seems to inform Gavin Stevens's devotion to Linda, who has to make a world for herself, which has included working in a wartime factory, unencumbered even by the man who has done so much to advance her dreams.

Eula remains an abiding presence in *The Mansion* as its Helen of Troy. The references to her as Helen, as the woman who got away from Gavin, call to mind Helen Baird. Gavin and Linda even rendezvous in Pascagoula, where Linda works in a war plant. Physically Helen Baird is no match for Eula Varner Snopes, but Helen Baird's reserved and even aloof response to Faulkner, whose poems to her, however impassioned, came nowhere near to winning her, still stimulated him to think of her as the very embodiment of desire. Like Faulkner, Stevens has to live with the grief of never having consummated a love that once meant everything to him.

Jean Stein witnessed Faulkner's experience of prolonged grief on a deserted Pascagoula beach at sunset: He saw "a woman in the distance and as we got closer he realized that it was someone he had known and he went over and talked to her for a few minutes and then we walked on and that was it. And only years later did I find out from someone else, a biographer or someone, that it was a woman that he had been very much in love with in about 1926 when he was writing I believe *Mosquitoes.* But he never told me. He never said anything." That kind of grief he shared with no one but vouchsafed in his fiction. The trajectory from Helen Baird to Jean Stein was akin to that from Eula Varner Snopes to Linda Snopes Kohl and her avatars: Ruth Ford, Joan Williams, and perhaps even his date Leane Zugsmith, the politically engaged proletarian writer, friend of Lillian Hellman and Dashiell Hammett, whose brother Albert produced *The Tarnished Angels* (1957), an adaptation of *Pylon.*

The Mansion is a brooding political novel. Not only Flem Snopes has to be watched. As Gavin Stevens puts it: "That one in Italy and one a damned sight more dangerous in Germany because all Mussolini has to work with is Italians while this other man has Germans. And the one in Spain that all he needs is to be let alone a little longer by the rest of us who still believe that if we just keep our eyes closed long enough it will all go away." The rest of us is not just Gavin, Chick, and Ratliff and not just Jefferson, but us—everyone. In *The Mansion,* Yoknapatawpha is a geopolitical creation, reflecting, in Warren Beck's words, the "ubiquity and persistence of evil, and the innate tendency in many men to resist it." As essential to the global Faulkner is Ratliff inasmuch as his "magnificently vernacular accent" reflects a "point of view that is anything but local."[13] Ratliff is, paradoxically, the international voice, seeking to make sure that the Snopeses are not appeased. Faulkner's first short stories about fascism that derived from his 1925 walking tour of Italy and the inception of the Snopeses are in close proximity. That Linda Snopes is an antifascist is a fulfillment, not a factitious outcome, of the Snopes trilogy.

In the *Delta Democrat-Times* (November 22), Ben Wasson understood that the trilogy had become in its final iteration a world-historical saga, moving from the strictly southern locale of *Sartoris,* which Wasson had edited, to New York and London and Paris, with Snopeses "burrowed into the nooks and crannies of all the world: cheap, shoddy, sleazy, vicious, uncaring, unmoral." "Snopes" is a word for "corporate man," J. Robert Barth suggested in *America* (February 27, 1960): "A Snopes is any materialist, any opportunist, any man who has allowed greed to triumph over love in his life. It is the curse of the South, Faulkner says; it is the curse of modern society; it is the curse of fallen man."

Even reviewers well read in the trilogy did not have the space to consider the shifts in point of view—for example: Jack Houston's grief over his wife's death in *The Hamlet* mitigates what Ratliff calls in *The Town* Houston's "overbearing" nature, which becomes in *The Mansion* his mean-spirited treatment of Mink—demanding a "pound fee" in addition to the increased price of the cow. Mink's own degradation now becomes the focus of Faulkner's compassion, as Mink finds it hard to relinquish his belief in clan solidarity, his hope that Flem would bail him out. Mink's murder of Flem is not simply revenge but a recognition that blood ties do not matter. He can dispose of a Snopes just as Flem has discarded Mink, Montgomery Ward, and any other Snopes who gets in his way. The fading, isolated Flem, inside a mansion no one has entered except for Linda and the help, has nowhere to go, no further goal to achieve now that he is a bank president. When the lethal Mink, now an old man, shows up, Flem remains seated, awaiting Mink's second and successful effort to get him with a rusty gun. The length of Mink's twenty-year sentence, doubled when the Flem-directed Montgomery Ward tricks Mink into a doomed attempt to escape prison, is also the length of Flem's own incarceration in his senescent dream of success. In the *Columbia Spectator* (November 20), Luciano Rebay observed that Flem, "an elemental force in conflict with the world," joins the civilization he sought to undermine and is ironically brought down by the man who once thought President Flem was omnipotent.

RACE AND POLITICS AND SEX

Faulkner's consciousness of race and politics—how they shapes Mink's behavior, for example—is evident in the very grain of the novel's sentences. We watch him watch his adversary: "Houston ordered whoever was on the front gallery to step inside and fetch him out whatever it was he had come for like they were Negroes." Mink does not have to say it: Houston has treated him like a "nigger," which is particularly galling since Houston has a black employee who, Mink thinks, condescends to him. Later Mink's racism is on display when he has to work for a black man, picking cotton to earn enough to get to Jefferson for the kill. It is the black man, in fact, who refutes Mink's scornful comment that Linda is faking her deafness: "A woman in a war. She must have ever body fooled good. I've knowed them like that myself. She jest makes claims." The black man, offended at such ignorance and sexism, rejoins: "Whoever it was told you she is fooling is the one that's lying. There are folks in more places than right there in Jefferson that know the truth about her." Linda's work, it seems, has had more of an impact than Stevens or Ratliff or Chick could possibly realize. The black man can see and hear precisely what eludes Mink's consciousness. Mink understands nothing about oppression— other than personal slights—whereas the black man is politically aware and understands his place in the world. Mink encounters another example of a changing South and is clearly puzzled when a soldier turned preacher has a congregation that includes black people. The war, as Faulkner foresaw in "Battle Cry," would produce characters like the soldier/preacher and the war hero leader of black troops who runs against Clarence Snopes.

Mink's resentment of Linda, whom he has never seen and only heard about, is not simply the product of his own psychology. She seems to virtually everyone an anomaly. She has grown up a Snopes, although her birth father is Hoke McCarron, whom Stevens later arranges for her to meet in New York. She does not really need this meeting, which is more for Stevens's sake as part of his anti-Snopes crusade. She is sui generis, which means she is a challenge for everyone in Yoknapatawpha, as such women were for William Faulkner when he went to New York and met southern-bred women like Leane Zug-smith, who operated beyond the boundaries of southern womanhood and history in ways that Estelle Faulkner could not contemplate or that Joan Williams could not quite transcend—notwithstanding Faulkner's urging her to jettison her family's middle-classism. Later Williams would say that she never conceived of acting like the free-spirited Jean Stein. Linda is closest to Stein, bred by a powerful Hollywood family fortune and industry force but rebellious and her own person. Linda, like Stein, is a culturally transformative figure, a bank president's daughter fighting for the new aesthetics and politics. Marrying a Greenwich Village sculptor means that her devotion is to principle, to the work itself, not to the way a society requires her to behave. She is, as Ratliff remarks, "the first female girl soldier we ever had, not to mention one actually wounded by the enemy." With eardrums blown out by a bomb, she has become deaf to the talk that would try to turn her away from her conscience. Faulkner had traveled quite a distance in time and space from Drusilla Hawk.

Linda's independence owes something to the changing position of women in the Faulkner family. College-educated Dean, whom he had watched mature in Mississippi and then in a year abroad, and his step-granddaughter, Vicki, made him look at this new generation "with a new respect."[14] Linda Snopes is conceived five years before Susan Sontag—born the same year as Jill, and three years before Dean—disrupted the modern scene. Linda à la Sontag enters *The Mansion* with "a fine, a really splendid dramatic white streak in her hair running along the top of her skull almost like a plume." The straight-up-and-down Linda, like the tall Sontag, flies under her own flag, a cause in herself—served by Gavin Stevens, Ratliff, and Charles (Chick) Mallison, her court, but as a sovereign who keeps her own counsel. Faulkner makes her a Hollywood tough guy who don't say much: "Because Linda didn't talk now any more than she ever had: just sitting there with that white streak along the top of her head like a collapsed plume, eating like a man."[15]

Linda is so far out ahead of everyone else that even Chick, six years younger, is baffled and supposes the way to get at her is in bed. He even asks his Uncle Gavin for permission! Even with the go-ahead, however, Chick retreats. And here is why: "it wasn't his uncle he was jealous of over Linda Snopes: he was jealous of Linda over his uncle." Gavin Stevens has been Chick's mentor, but the stodgy Stevens will not do. Only Linda can bring the world home to Yoknapatawpha. But that is why she is so scary to Chick. She defines the shifting ground on which all of them try to stand. She waits for no man, telling Gavin she loves him in as bold and unembarrassed manner as her mother, so that Stevens, once again, passive and fearful, demurs and marries, instead, a more docile woman.

Linda does not look like Eula. Linda is straight where her mother was curved. And yet Chick cannot resist imagining Linda undressed because he is sure this surprising woman would surprise him yet again. But like Sontag, busting out of Southern California and Chicago and arriving in New York via

London and Paris in 1959, Linda is just too big for these men, and Yoknapa-tawpha cannot hold her for long. Her mission is to eliminate Flem via Mink, a mission of which she tells no one but that becomes obvious at the end of the novel as she leaves town. All along, Stevens has denied the truth that Ratliff has tried to tell him: Linda has engineered all of it—getting Stevens to petition for Mink's release and then providing Mink with getaway money so that he can return to Jefferson to murder Flem Snopes.

Linda's father, Hoke McCarron, it becomes clear, has contributed significantly to her genetic independence. His invasion of Yoknapatawpha upset all the rules—you might even say the laws—of courtship by which Stevens and everyone else has abided: "Because this here was a different kind of a buck," Ratliff observes:

> coming without warning right off the big mountain itself and doing what Lawyer [Stevens] would call arrogating to his-self what had been the gyne-cological cynosure of a whole section of north Missippi for going on a year or two now. Not ravishing Eula away: not riding up on his horse and snatching her up behind him and galloping off, but jest simply moving in and dispossessing them; not even evicting them but like he was keeping them on hand for a chorus you might say, or maybe jest for spice, like you keep five or six cellars of salt setting handy while you are eating the water-melon, until it was already too late, until likely as not, as fur as they or Frenchman's Bend either knowed, Eula was already pregnant with Linda.

When Linda meets McCarron in New York, he does not tell her he is her father, and she does not need anyone else to tell her so. It is obvious. And she doesn't need him precisely because she is so like him. It is the other men who need to talk it out, not Linda. No one knows what it was like for Faulkner to create such a magnificent character, but it is hard to believe he was not as thrilled to discover Linda as he was when he met Jean Stein.

Linda erupts out of all those trips to New York City, where Faulkner felt out of place so often and yet sometimes in place. On the trip to New York with Linda and Stevens, Ratliff has an ur-Faulkner experience:

> And I remember how he [Stevens] told me once how maybe New York wasn't made for no climate known to man but at least some weather was jest made for New York. In which case, this was sholy some of it: one of them soft blue drowsy days in the early fall when the sky itself seems like it was resting on the earth like a soft blue mist, with the tall buildings rushing up into it and then stopping, the sharp edges fading like the sunshine wasn't jest shining on them but kind of humming, like

wires singing. Then I seen it: a store, with a show-window, a entire show-window with not nothing in it but one necktie.

The ties in the shop are expensive—no less than seventy-five dollars apiece, and the frugal Ratliff cannot bear the thought of wearing one back home, even though they are handmade by a Russian woman who learns what V. K. stands for. To do a Hoke McCarron, to dress in such a way as to violate community conventions, is anathema to Ratliff, who for all his singularity wants to fit in—as, in important ways, Faulkner did too. You cannot take New York home with you. Only Linda Snopes can do that, but Faulkner could not resist making his own kind of left-handed homage to the city, where a significant portion of the trilogy was written and revised. No more than Ratliff was he actually going to wear his Nobel Prize getup or talk about that store on Madison Avenue where he had spotted the shoes he wanted to wear away from home. He might joke about putting the Nobel suit on display in Rowan Oak, but all that, as with Ratliff, had to be tucked away.

As long as Linda is there, the men can hit the hot spots—the Stork Club and Twenty-One—and they can talk a brand of politics that otherwise does not get into the Yoknapatawpha novels: "the war, about Spain and Ethiopia and how this was the beginning: the lights was going off all over Europe soon and maybe in this country too." Spain, World War II, drives part of the narrative in *The Mansion* as in no other Faulkner fiction. Similarly, Chick Mallison reflects on his uncle's generation and the World War I experience: "young men or even boys most of whom had only the vaguest or completely erroneous idea of where and what Europe was, and none at all about armies, let alone about war, snatched up by lot overnight and regimented into an expeditionary force, to survive (if they could) before they were twenty-five years old what they would not even recognise at the time to be the biggest experience of their lives." These men return home thinking nothing has changed. But the world they left no longer exists. Twenty-five years after the war's end, Chick Mallison refers to young Bayard's twin, John, as the "last Sartoris Mohican"—the last one to believe World War I could perpetuate the glory and martial values of the Civil War.

The world that has changed is what Linda Snopes helps to define. She is named the "inviolate bride of silence" because she cannot be possessed or manipulated to be other than what she is. She can be invoked, like Keats's urn, but not captured. She is the epitome of all Faulkner's nonfiction talk about individuality. She may also be the "new and final woman of his heart."[16] She brings with her connections not only to communism but the National Recovery Act, Harry Hopkins (Roosevelt's righthand man), John

L. Lewis (head of the mine workers' union), and the FBI. She stands for and is investigated for her solidarity with the Left that Faulkner did not share and yet supported when it came to the Spanish Civil War and the intrusiveness of the federal government. Linda and her husband, Barton Kohl, for those who know their history, served alongside "35,000 anti-fascists of fifty-two different nationalities" in the Spanish Civil War. When she enters Yoknapatawpha again, she brings with her a world of experience. The Lincoln Brigade the Kohls served in suffered more than seven hundred casualties, "a higher rate than the casualties sustained by the U.S. in WWII."[17] She is the survivor of a defeated and decimated remnant, and she is determined not to lose again.

In Linda Snopes, Faulkner provided a gloss on his controversial "go slow" admonition to the civil rights movement. At the University of Virginia he had reiterated that while southerners had to resolve the race issue themselves, that did not mean they should be entirely left to themselves: "the outsider who is doing it because he's a do-gooder serves some purpose in keeping a certain pressure on. But nobody knows when to let well enough alone, and if he could just keep the constant, faint pressure and let it be at that, he would serve his purpose, but he gets too enthusiastic with changing overnight a—a condition which is emotional according to a pattern of morality which he can't do." Yet Linda, not exactly an outsider, persists: "Apparently she went without invitation or warning, into the different classrooms of the Negro grammar and high school," Chick reports. Linda contacts the teacher and principal, who are wary of her activism and more comfortable with the gradualism of Booker T. Washington and George Washington Carver, Faulkner's own favorites. Linda takes on the school board and then the Board of Supervisors and is called a "nigger lover," although she still has, as far as the community is concerned, cover as a banker's daughter. Not even blazing crosses deter her or signs that call her a Jew and Communist. Being married to a Jew is enough to marginalize her and make groups like the Ku Klux Klan a constituent part of the American fascism she has been called home to combat.

Only Munich and the advent of World War II cause Linda to scale down her activities, so that she now meets black children in churches on Sundays while the FBI investigates her. "Then Poland," Chick announces in a two-word sentence like no other in Faulkner's previous fiction. Heretofore public history had not been the driver of events; it followed in the train of his characters' doings. The Faulkner who worked on "Battle Cry," on the Soviet segments, the episodes of the French woman giving herself to the occupiers, and who had written to Churchill praising his wartime speeches, now enters 1940 Yoknapatawpha: "The Nibelung maniac had destroyed Poland and turned back west where Paris, the civilised world's eternal and splendid courtesan, had been sold to him like any whore and only the English national character turned him east again; another year and Lenin's frankenstein would be our ally but too late for her; too late for us too, the western world's peace for the next hundred years, as a tubby little giant of a man in England was already saying in private, but needs must when the devil etcetera." The wartime alliance that saved the Soviet Union also promulgated the Cold War, which makes its way into Yoknapatawpha just as Faulkner moved out of it on his State Department missions. Tellingly, though, he had rejected the invitation to tour the Soviet Union, not wishing to do the devil's work, even as he was approaching the trilogy's denouement.

What must his FBI brother have made of Stevens's principled anti-McCarthy stand against a government agent?: "'I see,' I said. 'You offer a swap. You will trade her [Linda's] immunity for names. Your bureau will whitewash her from an enemy into a simple stool-pigeon. Have you a warrant of any sort?'" Linda solves her security problem by going to work in a defense plant, which is her antifascist contribution. "Oh, she was still doing her Negro Sunday school classes," Stevens reports, "still 'meddling' as the town called it, but after a fashion condoned now, perhaps by familiarity and also that no one had discovered yet any way to stop her." Not a revolution but a nudge, the kind of insistent but low-key pressure Faulkner endorsed.

Stevens, Faulkner's flawed knight, seeker of truth and justice, now resembles a "Hollywood Cadillac agent," settling into marriage with a woman his own age—as Faulkner now seemed to do with Estelle—and the life of a squire, although without the "boots and breeks" that Faulkner now wore for fox hunting, which at West Point he would soon say he "liked best." If he tacitly admitted to himself that he had in some respects retired, he still had Linda streaking ahead of him. Whatever misgivings he might have about her activism, he recognized that, like the Freedom Riders, she is a "part of the change." Asked about student riots and protests, Faulkner responded that they demonstrated "a perfectly normal impulse to revolt."[18] Even Chick is not young and bold enough for Linda. He has trouble keeping up. He has to run after her, so that she is "startled—not alarmed: just startled; merely what Hollywood called a double-take, still not so far dis-severed from her Southern heritage but to recall that he, Charles, dared not risk some casual passerby reporting to his uncle that his nephew permitted the female he was seeing home to walk at least forty feet unaccompanied to her front door."[19] It is a constant scramble to keep up with Linda, with what is truly young and fresh. Faulkner never forgot this, constantly asking Joan when they were together, Am I too old for you?

Stevens's devotion to Linda is all-consuming, but he remains a high-minded Humbert Humbert.[20] His nephew Chick is almost as besotted but explains his uncle's celibacy as the cagey old "spider-lover" wise enough to realize "that initial tender caressing probe of the proboscis or suction tube or whatever it is his gal uses to empty him of his blood too while all he thinks he is risking is his semen" while he loses his "insides too in the same what he thought at first was just peaceful orgasm." Linda is too powerful for these males and is beyond the reach of Stevens's chivalric code and Chick's romantic and their mythological illusions. Ratliff is not as beclouded by male fantasies and shares a secret bond with Linda. His Russian ancestry—never really discussed—is nonetheless enough to make him appear suspect and an alien if, like Linda, he spent more time in New York and came home wearing the expensive tie Stevens offers to purchase for him. In a sense, Ratliff's very identity has made him a potential subversive—not such an absurd notion in McCarthyite America, which is why he is so careful to speak the dialect of his neighbors even when he knows what is grammatically correct. Ratliff is bound by the town. Only Linda can seize a place on a world stage, representing Faulkner's response to the "cold war and the racial struggle more radical than in his interviews, letters, and speeches."[21] Is she also an "immoral character"—as ruthless as Flem in her premeditated plan of assassination, driving off in a Jaguar, ordered to coincide with his death and departure?[22] She has the luxury of revenge, having turned Stevens, Ratliff, and Mallison into her accomplices. Her departure is stylish, like a scene in a film noir, with Linda as the femme fatale[23] in an international car, a world motor sport winner, advertised for its "Grace, Space, Pace."[24] She is a character who could easily fit into *Mildred Pierce* and other women's films of the 1940s, like *Johnny Belinda* (1948), featuring Jane Wyman as a deaf mute protected by a doctor (Lew Ayres, a Gavin Stevens figure) who guides her to a sense of her own worth. Linda outdoes Manfred de Spain's "swaggeringly sexual roadster,"[25] and Stevens's own Cadillac roadster that he has garaged rather than showing it off.

What exactly Linda is revenging she does not say, but her retaliation seems overdetermined and involves her mother's isolation and suicide; Snopesism's perversion of community values into a form of fascism valuing only winners that her husband fought against; and her disgust with a society in which Flem's criminal activity goes unpunished while the poor suffer the harshest punishments of the law. She opposes, in short, "undue process."[26] Although Flem does not involve himself in politics and is not a member of the Ku Klux Klan that Clarence Snopes tries to use to his advantage, Flem profits from a society lacking in social justice that links him to demagogues abroad.[27] Linda is that "rare thing in Faulkner: a *political person*."[28] She is not, however, without precedent. Remember Maria Rojas in the "Mythical Latin-American Kingdom Story"? Linda's meetings with Jefferson's two Finnish Communists in her father's parlor, not to mention her community organizing among black people, has brought her to strike a blow at the man who pretends to be her father and who is, in that respect, a fake. In existentialist terms, she has struck a blow at the inauthentic.

There is one more motive for revenge that cannot be proved but should not be discounted: self-defense. Linda gets her father before he gets her. Flem had duped a younger, more naive Linda into making him the beneficiary of her will. She never discloses how she later reacts to his connivery, but after she meets her birth father, Flem's trading on his bogus blood tie to Linda, it can be imagined, outrages her as much as Mink is maddened by Flem's refusal to aid a kinsman. Stevens surmises that Flem himself has scrawled "nigger lover on the sidewalk" so as to *"bank a reserve of Jefferson sympathy against the day he would be compelled to commit his only child to the insane asylum."* Far-fetched? It does not matter because this is the kind of duplicitous world that Linda has learned to navigate. She dare not remain exposed to Flem's nefarious schemes. Fascists can be overcome only by deadly force. In this respect, it is difficult not to see Stevens as the ineffective liberal attempting to ameliorate Flem-fascism rather than to eradicate it. Early on, as soon as she leaves Jefferson for the first time, Linda chooses the radical option: to root out evil. To Linda, apparently, the Stevens way would only isolate her even more from the world and perpetuate evil.[29]

The impotent Flem Snopes ends up a burnt-out case, facing "a cold empty fireplace" just like played-out old Bayard in *Flags in the Dust*. The generational changes that Faulkner kept forecasting in his interviews and essays begin to emerge in *The Mansion*. She is the change that is coming for the black people she tutors. Mink, so scornful of her, is the unwitting executioner of her plan.[30] Mink, like all males in Yoknapatawpha, regards Linda as one of the weaker sex. His attitudes also fit the fascist model that Faulkner exposed when he created another disabled character, Eddie, in *To Have and Have Not*. A homegrown fascism that believes that it shows strength by preying on the weak eventually weakens itself by not perceiving there are many different ways to be strong.

Mink, now sixty-three, near Faulkner's age when the novel was published, tries to sleep anywhere but on the ground as a result of thinking, in the narrator's words, "The very moment you were born out of your mother's body, the power and drag of the earth was already at work on you." Mink is fighting not only his age but, in a sense, life itself, which has tried to down him. It is every man's purpose, the novel implies, to elevate himself above the earth even as he knows it will claim him someday. What Mink wants is what Charles Bon wanted, what everyone wants: to be acknowledged. Mink imagines the death scene with his nemesis: "Look at me Flem." In the end, Mink does not have to say the words because Flem turns to look at him, staring his own death in the face in a fulfillment of Mink's destiny. All along, Mink has expressed his faith in "Old Moster," his way of believing that his revenge has divine sanction notwithstanding the weak weapon he has brought to this reckoning.

Free of his mission to murder Flem, Mink finally feels he can risk resting on and in the earth. His revery, one of the most remarkable passages Faulkner ever wrote, is, ultimately, about the journey from life to death, the nearing of an end that he could imagine approaching, freed from "bother and trouble":

> following all the little grass blades and tiny roots, the little holes the worms made, down and down into the ground already full of the folks that had the trouble but were free now, so that it was just the ground and the dirt that had to bother and worry and anguish with the passions and hopes and skeers, the justice and the injustice and the griefs, leaving the folks themselves easy now, all mixed and jumbled up comfortable and easy so wouldn't nobody even know or even care who was which anymore, himself among them, equal to any, good as any, brave as any, being inextricable from, anonymous with all of them: the beautiful, the splendid, the proud and the brave, right on up to the very top itself among the shining phantoms and dreams which are the milestones of the long human recording—Helen and the bishops, the kings and the unhomed angels, the scornful and graceless seraphim.

Like all of Faulkner's other characters—none of whom he wanted to judge—Mink joins the hallowed history of humanity. He, too, gets his salute in a grand ending that can be set beside the tribute to his "betters," the Sartorises of *Flags in the Dust,* with Mink's "Old Moster" the equivalent of "the Player" that has a hand in the first family's outmoded game.

At the end of *The Mansion,* which might have marked the end of Faulkner's career, since he spoke of breaking the pencil as often as he said he had more to write, the last words are "Charlottesville, Virginia 9 March, 1959," appending yet another bit of history—even autobiography—to his fiction.

"An 'Interview' with 'Pappy' Faulkner"

In the summer of 1959, Hollywood columnist Joe Hyams, visiting Oxford to report on the filming of MGM's *Home from the Hill,* starring Robert Mitchum, decided to tree the elusive William Faulkner. He asked around and was advised that the usual forms of communication—a letter, a phone call, or just showing up at Rowan Oak—would result in a rebuff. The redoubtable Hyams, a World War II veteran and Bronze Star winner, persisted, taking up his post between 2:30 and 3:30 across from Mac Reed's drugstore—where local intelligence had it his prey would show up to talk with friends and acquaintances. Wait fifteen minutes, he was told, and then introduce yourself. If, however, Faulkner did not show up, then Hyams was directed to visit Miss Maud and say he wanted to buy one of her paintings, which he should admire in the hope of getting her to loosen up about her son. If Hyams's prize showed up, the reporter would try to get his drive-by interview. But then Hyams would need to go slow, trying to make out Faulkner's soft voice while *never* asking Faulkner to repeat himself. But even that much seemed doubtful, since Faulkner, Hyams heard, was drying out and "testier than usual, which is pretty damn ornery." Several topics could not be discussed: Faulkner's private life, his work, and, "under no circumstances," reviews of his play *Requiem for a Nun*. Hyams might be able to engage Faulkner on his early days in Hollywood, a friend suggested, or segregation. After getting drenched on the square, the impatient and pugnacious Hyams took a taxi out to Rowan Oak. A servant let Hyams into the house, and after about ten minutes, to the accompaniment of creaking floors and slamming doors, Faulkner, in the "shabbiest tweed jacket" the reporter had ever seen, "slipped" into the room. "What do you want?," Faulkner asked. "An interview," Hyams replied. Faulkner said he did not like to answer questions and was not one of those people who wanted to see his name in the papers, "but you have a job to do." Hyams described Faulkner as then closing his mouth on his pipe "like a ten cent mousetrap." The two men stared at one another in a twenty-second standoff as Hyams took in his subject's "grey flannels, sturdy shoes, and regimental tie," looking like a "dehydrated movie version of a college professor with short, cropped white hair and a military mustache." Faulkner advised the reporter to give up. Then an "irate" Estelle entered and asked, "How did you get in here?"—adding that "Mr. Faulkner doesn't see people, but since you're here, sit down." More staring between Faulkner and Hyams, who tried to relieve the silence by saying Faulkner had granted a "superb interview" with a reporter in Japan. Faulkner countered: But that was on the State Department's time and he had been paid for his services. Then Hyams mentioned Jerry Wald. Faulkner said he liked Jerry, although they were in different rackets. Wald had produced two film adaptations of Faulkner's work. Faulkner understood Wald, but Wald did not understand Faulkner, Hyams was told. Faulkner supposed Wald had done the best he could with Faulkner's work, although Faulkner said he had not seen the films. Talk of the films shown in the local theater did not interest Faulkner, who did not go to see films that appealed to kids and college students, who went to see anything that moved. After a little more desultory talk, Hyams decided it was time to move on. A relieved Faulkner said to say hello to Wald and to Harry Kurnitz, if Hyams saw him: "They're nice fellows." Perhaps Faulkner was responding to what Hyams said of his departure: It had been a kindness to leave.

30

Renascence

1960–1962

So with my eyes I traced the line
Of the horizon, thin and fine,
Straight around till I was come
Back to where I'd started from.

—Edna St. Vincent Millay

BETWEEN HOMES

In mid-January, William Faulkner wrote a long, unusual letter to his wife. It resembled the exuberant notes he wrote to her when he first came to New York and told her about his adventures. This renewed correspondence is the surest sign of his mellowing and his revived interest in sharing his life with her. During certain periods in Hollywood, he had felt a similar tenderness about her and home. Now he was home, and she was not there. She had committed herself to a new life in Charlottesville, where in her last years, near her daughter and grandchildren, Estelle's efflorescence would appear on her shimmering canvases, which she would sign E. O., emphasizing, her granddaughter Vicki said, independence from the Faulkner name.[1] She was the one away from home—a separation her husband sought to slacken with a tall tale. The letter's comic tone is reminiscent of the Snopes trilogy, with his brother John as his foil, playing the fool, to Faulkner's Ratliff. The brothers looked alike, which only heightened the irony for William Faulkner. These brothers in estrangement, these Faulkners (John had added the *u* to his name and on his novels, which irritated Brother Bill)[2] were no Snopeses, but the fictional and factional families shared some of the same tensions.

It all began when Miss Maud bilked herself into believing she had bought a bargain: a twenty-cent-per-month insurance policy that would cover all her hospital bills. When her son John told her that Dr. Holley demanded payment, she responded, as usual, that "somebody was cheating her." First, Faulkner had to calm his mother down (he had been paying her medical bills for years), and second, enjoin John, "don't do it again." Let her think she had taken care of her own medical expenses. But then Faulkner came down with pleurisy and treated his heaves and high fever with penicillin and whiskey. He drank himself into a delirium and passed out. The next thing he knew, John had arrived in an ambulance and they were on the way to the Byhalia sanatorium. Folks who saw the brothers were not sure which was which: "people are always mixing us up." When Faulkner woke up the next day, he asked for a drink and was promptly served, while John, in the other bed, was refused: "he had only paid for one." The outraged John called a cab and left, stopping in Holly Springs to purchase two cases of beer. Or so Faulkner had gathered, like Ratliff, from community intelligence. Somehow Jim Silver also joined the cast, and then Dean's mother, Louise, then Silver's wife, Dutch, and John's wife, Lucille. They were worried about John's whereabouts, but Miss Maud, still in the hospital, assured them he was probably just riding around in the ambulance. Lucille said: "Where is John? Not that I care." Louise assured Lucille that John would be home by night. Then John walked in with his beer. It took Faulkner himself two days to come to, and he spent the next two "getting built up." He was home Sunday but thought if he had stayed in Byhalia a week he would have won enough to pay John's sanatorium bill since Faulkner had already taken thirty-five dollars off of a young doctor in a poker game. That's why, Faulkner figured, he had been discharged early—so as not to clean out the young doctor. It was funny but not so funny: "I crossed Lucille at the hospital," Faulkner told Estelle, "she never said beans: just beamed at me, a really good beam of four or five seconds—you know, like a tiger." Faulkner was not exaggerating, according to Estelle's granddaughter Vicki: "Lucille hated Bill and Estelle. John was her life, and she was totally jealous of anything that Billy did."[3]

As for mother, she had been becalmed with a "stack of reading matter" but fell out of bed trying to arrange her stack. She had broken nothing this time. As for Faulkner, he was "feeling pretty fair, nothing to brag about but well enough." This comedy had to be shared: "Let Miss [Jill] and Paul read this, and Linton might enjoy it. Certain Blotner would whoop over it." He could not resist one final dig at John, who had "sold another book or something, and is going to be a nuisance and a menace until he has drunk it up."

The letter reveals how much Charlottesville had become a second home, with a cadre of followers not available in Oxford, and who would not mix him up with his brother or beam its hostility at him. Between October 1 and December 23, 1959, the University of Virginia's Alderman Library had run an exhibition, *William Faulkner: "Man Working," 1919–1959*, organized by Linton Massey. Walking around the Oxford square was one thing; strolling on the University of Virginia grounds, quite another. He had set up a Faulkner foundation and was now the community's benefactor as well as its honored citizen. He was no longer that hound dog under the spring wagon, the southern refugee beating it back home. On August 25, 1960, Faulkner accepted the position of Balch Lecturer in American Literature at the University of Virginia. Essentially an honorary appointment (renewable each year), he would give one public reading a year, meet a class for questions and answers once or twice a year, and (if he liked) meet students informally from time to time. He would have no other official duties, and that suited him just fine.[4] He was now asked to wear the colors of the Farmington Hunt Club. "I have been awarded a pink coat," he wrote to Albert Erskine, "a splendor worthy of being photographed in."[5] To his nephew Jimmy he wrote asking him to send the black boots with tan tops to complete his ensemble for the fox hunt, and mind: get the right ones—not Jack Beauchamp's but the *"newer* pair with *newspapers* rolled in them" to serve as boot trees. Below his signature, Faulkner even included a sketch of the boots.[6]

Faulkner continued to split his time between Charlottesville and Oxford. Family, whatever its troubles, meant as much as ever to him. He still went bird hunting with Jimmy, who always called him "Brother Will." When Jimmy became a colonel in July 1960, he told his uncle that very day, who said "he was prouder of that than anything else I've ever done." Jimmy thought it was because of the old Colonel: "Somebody in the family had to do it. Every time he had a chance after that he introduced me as Col. Falkner."[7]

Maud Falkner remained an audience of one for her eldest son. Ratliff had become a family friend for the both of them. She never tired of her son's tales about him. As she neared the end, dying on October 18, 1960, at eighty-eight, she latched on to her son's comment that "most people died of boredom." "I'm bored enough and tired enough," she replied. He gave her a good look: "I won't let you die on me." Then he "changed the subject to the latest whodunit they had read."[8] He always thought he could keep life going with another story. Her three boys were at her bedside and kissed her good-bye. What Faulkner felt, he kept to himself. Not even his brothers record his reaction in their memoirs. He picked out the casket, a simple wooden box, as she requested. She wanted no embalming and said she wanted to "get back to earth as fast as I can." She was a bit like Addie Bundren with a son like Jewel who did not care to share his feelings with others but would just as soon expend them upon a horse. The Faulkners, Bundren-like, were the only ones to handle the casket on its way to St. Peter's Cemetery. Maud Falkner left behind something like six hundred paintings, some of which can still be seen in her home on Lamar Avenue.

In a March 1961 letter to Muna Lee, discussing another trip to Venezuela for the State Department, Faulkner said he did not want to be "shielded from tiredness and boredom and annoyance." He considered his mission a job and would do his best, even though he still feared "I am the wrong bloke for this," since he was not the literary man people expected, and even as a writer he had run dry: "I am not even interested in writing anymore: only in reading for pleasure in the old books I discovered when I was 18 years old." He would sign autographs for Venezuelans and other Latin Americans but preferred not to deal with Anglo-Americans, "since the addition of my signature to a book is part of my daily bread."[9] He confided to Bill Fielden, then in the tobacco business in Caracas, that he had been reluctant to undertake the trip because it was sponsored by a "group of North Americans who found they could make more net money living in Venezuela than anywhere else." He doubted they had any interest in him, but he had capitulated to the State Department's pleadings. The week (April 3–10) in Venezuela went well, and Faulkner seems to have enjoyed himself more than he expected, since Bill Fielden "through his connections was able to take Pappy into the interior," Vicki recalled, and "showed him some of the horse farms there, and Pappy rode some of the horseflesh. . . . He had quite a good time. It was not the sophisticated cocktail party scene."[10]

In Charlottesville that spring Elliott Chaze, a Hattiesburg, Mississippi, native, did another one of those annoying impromptu doorstep interviews that sometimes worked if, as Jill said, her father was in the mood. Chaze interrupted Faulkner's two-finger typing, announcing, "I drove a thousand miles to see you." Chaze had tried to call but was told Faulkner did not answer the phone. "That's right, sir," said Faulkner in a barely audible voice; he was "composed and motionless as a photograph." Faulkner stared: "What is it you want from me?" Chaze chattered about stories he found more exciting than Hemingway's. Faulkner sighed. He did a lot of sighing and just looking at Chaze before saying, "You come on in and we'll see what we can do to help you." Those were the exact words he seemed to use for such intrusions whenever he decided to relent. Faulkner had a "controlled glitter," which brings to mind Edwin Arlington Robinson's "Richard Corey," the masterwork of a poet Faulkner had spied in a New York City bookshop so long ago. Although

Chaze did not refer to the poem, his awestruck impressions accord with that evocation of a community's worship of elegance and grace. Faulkner seemed to know it, explaining his writer-in-residence role: "you walk around and people see you and say, well, there he is, there he goes." Faulkner would give them that much—but not much more. He did not like talking about writing even when he talked about writing. How he worked—the specifics—he would not supply. He changed the subject: "There is something about jumping a horse over a fence, something that makes you feel good. Perhaps it's the risk, the gamble. In any event it's a thing I need." For the rest, Chaze got boilerplate, and left after hearing Faulkner raise his voice only once to say, "Good luck to you."[11]

He felt fit, rising at daylight on most mornings and riding until about ten. He had three horses he could rely on for hunting four days a week. Then the unexpected happened. He began another novel, *The Horse Stealers: A Reminiscence,* later retitled *The Reivers.* He showed three chapters to Joseph Blotner, who noted on July 9: "Strikes me as mellow & funny." Certainly it put Faulkner in a good mood. Nine days later he had more pages to read to Blotner. "Most laughing & eye contact I can remember with him ever," Blotner recorded. "WF convulsed & red with his silent laughter. 'This book gets funnier all the time,' he says."

The novel began, "Grandfather said:" and was as much a book for the grandchildren as for himself. His step-granddaughter Vicki remembered sharing a tender moment with him and her grandmother when he announced with a smile that he had dedicated the book to her and his other grandchildren. Vicki remained convinced that Estelle's sobriety had turned around the Faulkner marriage, helping Faulkner to "right his ship" and produce some of his best work in years, starting with Saxe Commins's sudden death. Albert Erskine, a fine editor, nevertheless could not do all that Commins had done for Faulkner, and so he turned increasingly to his wife. Their life in Charlottesville had become quite social. "He was easier with people," Vicki observed. "He wasn't so isolated."[12] "I intend to be in Charlottesville every winter for the hunting," he wrote to Alexander Rives, a fellow horseman. Rives and his wife visited the Faulkners for drinks, and their son Billy received a copy of *Requiem for a Nun* after Faulkner spotted the nine-year-old on a shaggy pony at a fox hunt and became fond of him, perhaps remembering that pony he rode when he was a boy.[13]

It took Faulkner hardly more than two months to complete *The Reivers* during another hot Mississippi summer. On August 21, he finished a draft of a work first described in May 1940 in a letter to Robert Haas: "a sort of Huck Finn—a normal boy of about twelve or thirteen, a big, warmhearted, courageous, honest, utterly unreliable white man with the mentality of a child, an old negro family servant, opinioned, querulous, selfish, fairly unscrupulous and in his second childhood, and a prostitute not very young anymore and with a great deal of character and generosity and common sense, and a stolen race horse which none of them actually intended to steal." This picaresque novel, to which Faulkner later added a stolen car, led to an adventure lasting a "matter of weeks," written, in a sense, in real time, when he went at it twenty years later. The story had a sort of moral, with the boy learning from "experiences which in his middle class parents' eyes stand for debauchery and degeneracy and actually criminality; through them he learned courage and honor and generosity and pride and pity." The last words with their coordinating conjunctions show how the Faulkner of 1940 was on his way to the Faulkner of the Nobel Prize address and the fiction of the 1950s and early 1960s. And that jibe at parents suggests he saw himself as a sort of middle man between parent and child, a role he now played with relish as a grandparent.

It took another month to clean up the first draft, and by the end of November he was in New York working at Random House with Albert Erskine, readying the book for publication in June 1962.

Grandfather Faulkner

The novel was something special. It delivered what its subtitle promised: a reminiscence. It came close to the memoir Faulkner would never write. "Dear Bill," his brother Jack wrote: "We are pleased with the book and proud that you sent it to us. I recognize most of the folks in it, the others I never met or they exist only in your imagination. It brings back Dad to where I can almost see him again."[14] Earl Wortham, the Oxford blacksmith, remembered, "The Colonel [Faulkner's grandfather] had him a man named Chester Carruthers" who drove the Faulkner car: "I can still sees them two tearing across these old gullies—the old Colonel sittin' back there, staring straight ahead, and Chester just a glowing 'cause he was chasing all them white folks off the street."[15]

Murry Falkner finally had a place in his son's fiction. Faulkner's affection for his father had always been muted, if not entirely absent from his recorded comments. Thanks to his father, Faulkner had never been a "starving artist." He did not trouble his son "about the need for sweat to earn your daily bread."[16] Faulkner told Malcolm Franklin that Murry was "a kind and gentle man who always made sure I had two feet under the table."[17] Murry also came off well when Faulkner told University of Virginia students about the origins of "Spotted Horses." In *The Reivers*, Maury, like Murry, is the owner of a livery stable. He has three sons. Like Faulkner, Lucius is the oldest. Like Murry and his father, Maury remains a diminished figure compared to Lucius's grandfather, Boss Priest. Maury, unlike Murry, is not so much checked by his powerful father as he is an extension of his father's authority. When Maury gets out his razor strop to punish Lucius for his reiving, Boss Priest stops him, and Maury objects: "'No,' Father said. 'This is what you would have done to me twenty years ago.' 'Maybe I have more sense now,' Grandfather said." The brutal days of the frontier justice and family discipline give way to Grandfather's more modern approach concerning old-school values: a conversation with Lucius about the obligations of a gentleman that makes the boy feel more chastened than any beating could accomplish. In such scenes, Faulkner brought his awareness of the past into the present, making his heritage function all the same in a changing world that Boss Priest has prophesied:

> "Twenty-five years from now there wont be a road in the county you cant drive an automobile on in any weather," Grandfather said.
> "Wont that cost a lot of money, Papa?" Mother said.
> "It will cost a great deal of money," Grandfather said. "The road builders will issue bonds. The bank will buy them."
> "Our bank?" Mother said. "Buy bonds for automobiles?"
> "Yes," Grandfather said. "We will buy them."
> "But what about us?—I mean, Maury."
> "He will still be in the livery business," Grandfather said. "He will just have a new name for it. Priest's Garage maybe, or the Priest Motor Company. People will pay any price for motion. They will even work for it. Look at bicycles. Look at Boon. We dont know why."

Like horse races, the racing automobile rouses the community out of the "fatigue and the inertia of everyday life" and fosters a "communal solidarity," so that "motion unifies the whole novel."[18] It also brought Faulkner home, so to speak, to a family that had not always welcomed him. He stood apart, like the "I" who narrates *The Reivers,* but in the same novel he became "we" when Lucius celebrates his brotherhood in the comedy of crime and the solidarity of family, to whom he must account.

Here, finally, was a novel that all the family members could rejoice in. Faulkner had always resisted pleas to write in a crowd-pleasing way, and this novel served that purpose, as Bennett Cerf quickly realized even before the book went into production: "I read your novel over the weekend and think it's one of the funniest books I have ever read. I can't tell you how fine I think it is, and I have great hopes for a big best seller, believe it or not."[19] *The Reivers* became a Book of the Month Club main selection.

The novel came right out of family lore about Judge J. W. T. Falkner's stolen automobile. "Somebody did actually take his car to Memphis without his permission," said a friend of Faulkner's uncle. The judge preferred reading novels like *Ben-Hur* and *The Clansman*. A few years before the judge's death on January 20, 1962, he said to his nephew in front of Mac Reed's drugstore: "You're one of the finest writers. Why don't you write something . . . your friends here would really appreciate?" Faulkner "dropped his head, smiled and said, 'I may do that.'"[20]

The Reivers, dedicated to Faulkner's grandchildren, uses the Scottish ancestral word for thieves, recalling all those earlier Faulkners or perhaps Falconers, as Faulkner liked to believe, who had stolen away to a new world. The novel casts a retrospective and ruminative eye on the history of Yoknapatawpha in the mellow tones of a grandfather, Lucius Priest, telling his grandchildren about the Mississippi of 1905 and focusing on a seemingly simpler era, when an automobile was a work of wonder, and when a trip from Jefferson to Memphis could seem like an epic adventure. In fact, Lucius says, the car made only one such trip—the one he is about to recount. The human scale of this world, when Faulkner was eight, had to be recovered for a generation that never knew it.

It is the biographer's temptation to see Lucius as the author's self-portrait,[21] but the differences between the creator and his character stand out: Lucius does not have Faulkner's early aesthetic bent, or an encouraging artistic mother, or a precocious female playmate like Estelle. Lucius has to be lured into trouble; young Billy Falkner had no trouble stirring up his own. Where author and character coincide is in a love of horses and an education in the gentleman's code—their standard of measurement in a changing world. Like Faulkner's other characters, Lucius is true to some particulars of the world William Faulkner grew up in but also fictionalized out of Faulkner's own biography, although sometimes the parallels are tight: Mammy Callie becomes Aunt Callie.

Lucius recounts the time he and Boon Hoggenbeck, a family retainer, become reivers[22] when they "borrowed" the Winton Flyer belonging to Boss Priest and set off for the big city. Boon is in love with a car that has to be hand-cranked—perhaps the same way Boon treats his whores—and can perform at night with kerosene lamps. This open touring car has curtains that could be put up to convert the vehicle into a boudoir. But in the open air it became part of a special outing: "all of us, grandparents, parents, aunts, cousins and children, had special costumes for riding in it, consisting of veils, caps, goggles, gauntlet gloves and long shapeless throat-close neutral-colored garments called dusters." The almost ceremonial, formal feel of life then, Faulkner knew, would seem a novelty to his younger readers not schooled in the decorum and manners of north Mississippi way back when.

Boon wants to visit Miss Corrie in a Memphis cathouse and introduce eleven-year-old Lucius to a world that (Boon assures him) Lucius will one day understand and avail himself of. Boon is not exaggerating. Many young boys then did go to Memphis brothels for their sexual initiation, and Faulkner himself would turn his own time in bawdy houses into both horrifying and humorous fiction ending in this PG-13 performance, with Grandfather Lucius doing the guidance. It might have occurred to Faulkner—at the advent of the 1960s, and after the lubricious talk of semen in *The Mansion*—that the times for a wholesome whorehouse tale were just right.

Boon's employer, Boss Priest, has put the noisy, noxious conveyance out of circulation. Grandmother can't stand the smell of gasoline. Boon is a fool to think that he can make it all the way to Memphis in anything like good time and get back undiscovered. The car comes with "a new axe and a small coil of barbed wire attached to a light block and tackle for driving beyond the town limits." In other words, these "flyers" often broke down, especially on muddy, unpaved roads. In 1903, one enterprising motorist took more than sixty-three days to travel from San Francisco to Manhattan, trying to find decent roads, using block and tackle to get out of mud holes and horse teams to get pulled out of sand.[23]

Lucius's escapade with Boon is made possible by Boss Priest having taken the train to attend the funeral of his wife's father, Lucius's other grandfather. Boon is supposed to lock up the automobile and not use it while Boss is away. The meaning of "gentleman," which involves taking responsibility for one's actions and abiding by a code of honor, is developed in references to Yoknapatawpha history in the first chapters of the novel, in which descriptions of the Sutpens, the Compsons, the McCaslins, and all the county's important families impinge on Lucius's consciousness. What he does, in other words, will be measured against what his forebears and predecessors have done. Lucius's decision to leave home is a declaration of independence, but it is also another act in the drama of his community's history. In effect, Lucius as "grandfather" is telling his children their history, showing how the individual has to understand it in order to come to terms with himself.

Calling *The Reivers* nostalgic and a summation of Faulkner's Yoknapatawpha saga is understandable but also misleading, since doing so suggests that the novel is not in the same class as his earlier and presumably greater novels. In just this way many critics and biographers have discounted *The Reivers,* taking the narrator's relaxed tone as a sign of the author's more indulgent and less complex art. This assumption ignores the circumstances of the telling: a grandfather addressing his grandchildren. His narration is all about the child's discovery of the adult world as told by an adult to his own kin, who will, in turn, discover the world in their way. To confuse Faulkner with his narrator—no matter how many similarities between them can be assembled—is to wreck the fiction and to deny Lucius Priest his independent existence as a character. His word, as he admits, is not the last word: "I'm sure you have often noticed how ignorant people beyond thirty or forty are."[24]

Certainly the darker events of Faulkner's earlier novels—the suicide of Quentin Compson, the castration of Joe Christmas, and revelations about the evils of slavery—are not explored. But their consequences are—especially in the figure of Ned McCaslin, Boss Priest's coachman, who stows away in the automobile and declares he also wants his fun in Memphis. He has been called "a black man of inexhaustible vitality and well-forged folk wisdom"[25]—and as such he is an alternative authority even if he is bound to white power. His insubordination and wiliness, including a certain minstrel "Uncle Remus" behavior, has been attributed to Faulkner's atavistic view of race,[26] but this seems a misguided perception in view of Ned's ability to subvert the status quo even as he appears to serve it. His own stature and family identification is reflected in the way he speaks: "What Boss likes is a *horse*—and I dont mean none of these high-named harness plugs you and Mr Maury has in that livery stable: but a *horse*"—horse, not hawse, or any variant on that word that would make Ned simply a dialect character, part of the black chorus that appeared in Hollywood films as racist variants on Sir Walter Scott's or Thomas Hardy's rustics. Ned does have his origins partly in the comedy of subordination, but he is also, like Lucas Beauchamp, a proud clan member. He is also one of Faulkner's "avatars of motion," one of those individuals using horses, airplanes, automobiles, and horses that engage in the "comedy of motion" conveying the "pure sense of being alive" while providing in their races in *Pylon, The Unvanquished, The Hamlet,* and *A Fable* a "pure sense of being alive."[27]

Lucius refers to Ned as "our family skeleton." He was born in 1860 and claims that his mother "had been the natural daughter of old Lucius Quintus Carothers himself," the original progenitor of the clan. In other words, Ned claims direct descent from a founding father, whereas Lucius's line "were mere diminishing connections and hangers-on." He is reminiscent of Uncle Ned Barnett, born in 1865, who not only served the old Colonel but in Faulkner's day wore his master's clothes. To readers of Faulkner's other novels—especially *Go Down, Moses,* which explores the McCaslin genealogy and the white family's inextricable connections with the lives of the McCaslin slaves—Ned's pride and self-assurance are all the more appreciated. Boon cannot gainsay Ned's presence, even though as a white man Boon ought to be able to master his so-called inferior in this highly segregated society.

The Ned of *The Reivers,* like Uncle Ned, affects an air of authority based on his proximity to the family's "boss." This kind of consanguinity between black and white, and the idea of a black man as both authority figure and servant, seemed so alien in 1969 that the producers of the film adaptation made Boon and Ned rivals, completely distorting the complex nature of race that Faulkner tried to show Cantwell by introducing him to Uncle Ned and that pervades *The Reivers.*

Segregation and racial distinctions keep breaking down in the world of Faulkner's fiction. Ned McCaslin represents a deft way of showing that dissolution even in an adventure story intended to entertain children. Compared to the crafty Ned, Boon and Lucius are innocents abroad. Lucius has been rightly called a "motorized Huck Finn,"[28] and yet it is as if Faulkner takes Jim off the raft and puts him in control of the story that becomes *The Reivers.* Ned turns the seemingly simple road trip that Boon and Lucius have planned into a rococo plot that involves getting his kinsman Bobo Beauchamp out of trouble by trading the Winton Flyer for a racehorse, which Ned will then put up in a race against another horse, with the prize being the automobile and other winnings that will pay off Bobo's debts and return the vehicle to Boss Priest. So devious is Ned's strategy that it is not revealed until near the end of the novel, which becomes the denouement of a mystery of Ned's devising. In fact, only after the race is won does Ned divulge to Boss Priest the intricate series of events and developments that neither Lucius nor Boon has been able to explain. Without Ned as the mastermind, the novel has no engine, no way to proceed or to resolve itself.

Because Lucius is telling the story, remembering his childhood even as he invokes his status as a grandfather, *The Reivers* has a double perspective: Lucius then, Lucius now; the world then, the world now. Although a good deal has changed since 1905, the moral values Lucius seeks to impart remain the same and belong to the historical continuum that the novel itself enacts. And Ned is the conduit of that continuum. He is forty-five years old in 1905, Lucius reports. Ned will live to the age of seventy-four, "just living long enough for the fringe of hair embracing his bald skull to begin to turn gray, let alone white (it never did. I mean, his hair: turn white nor even gray. . . .)." Although Ned responds to change, represented by the automobile, he has no interest in driving it or learning about the new technology. And yet his very steadfastness in the midst of change, his knowledge of his own mind and his place in the world, renders him able to adapt to every new and unforeseeable situation on the ride to Memphis and in its aftermath. In short, he cannot be distracted by novelty or deflected from his purpose.

On the other hand, the slow-witted Boon (he failed the third grade twice) is impulsive, a man who acts in the moment without taking aim. His poor shooting is legendary. He is all id to Ned's ego, with Lucius trying to manage his own superego and inclinations and adhere to his upbringing while coping with the behavior of the shrewd black man born into slavery and the excitable white man saved from undoing himself by the grace of his gentlemen employers, beginning with old General Compson. Boon may be six feet four and weigh 240 pounds, but he has the "mentality of a child." He is a rough-hewn woodsman, with a "big ugly florid walnut-tough walnut-hard face." This physical description suggests an impermeable quality in Boon, who cannot learn from experience as Lucius does, or profit from it as Ned can. Boon can drive the action forward, just as he drives the Winton Flyer, but he cannot plot his adventures or predict their pitfalls.

A case in point is Boon's confident belief that he can drive the automobile through Hell Creek bottom, a treacherous bog maintained that way by a farmer who makes his living dragging vehicles out of the mud. Even though Boon paid the man two dollars the summer before to pull out the Winton Flyer, he thinks that this time, with Ned and Lucius helping, he can use block and tackle to move the car through the sludge. After several efforts that saturate Boon and Ned with muck, Boon pays the man with the mules two dollars per passenger to rescue them from the mire. This episode is a perfect example of Boon's self-defeating actions, which tend to make his dilemmas worse than they were to begin with. In short, Lucius's up-to-now pristine existence, guided by the courtly examples of his father and grandfather, is enveloped in the mess Boon makes.

Arriving in Memphis, the action shifts to the brothel and to its madam, Miss Reba—last seen accommodating Clarence and Virgil Snopes in *The Mansion*. She is enchanted with Lucius's manners—such a contrast to the conniving Otis, a young nephew Miss Corrie is trying to reform. Lucius is smitten with Miss Corrie, whom he describes as a "big girl. I don't mean fat: just big, like Boon was big, but still a girl, young too, with dark hair and blue eyes and at first I thought her face was plain. But she came into the room already looking at me, and I knew it didn't matter what her face was." She may be a whore, but there is an innocence in her that Lucius connects with, and they quickly form a bond that leads to Lucius being cut by Otis's knife in a fight that starts when Lucius strikes out at Otis for denigrating Miss Corrie. She, in turn, decides to reform herself in order to be worthy of Lucius's devotion. Set against her sincerity is Mr. Binford's cynicism. He turns a critical eye on Lucius and tries to corrupt him, offering beer even though Lucius steadfastly refuses the drink, announcing that he has promised his mother that he will not imbibe until he is of age.

Then Ned shows up with a horse he has named Lightning, informing Boon that the Winton Flyer can only be recovered by winning a horse race. On the way to the race site, Ned, Boon, and Lucius encounter the sadistic deputy sheriff Butch Lovemaiden, who arrests Boon and Ned for possessing a horse that is stolen property. The price of their release, Butch informs them, is a night with Miss Corrie. Seeing no way out, she complies and is later assaulted by Boon, who thus loses Lucius's respect.

The novel's exciting denouement centers on the horse race. Ned admits to Lucius that he believes he can make their horse a winner (Lightning has lost races against his rival, Acheron), but the neck-and-neck heats in which the neophyte jockey Lucius rides make the result anything but certain. After their triumph, Ned explains that he has studied the psychology of his horse and discovered its liking for sardines, which Ned carries with him at the finish line in sight of the galloping Lightning, who vindicates Ned's prediction.

In the novel's coda, when Lucius is spared the beating his father is prepared to give him, Boss Priest intervenes and suggests that it is punishment enough for Lucius to live with a sense of his transgressions. "A gentleman accepts the responsibilities of his actions and bears the burden of their consequences, even when he did not himself instigate them but only acquiesced to them, didn't say No though he knew he should." To the young Lucius, expecting corporal punishment, the psychological and moral burden his grandfather places on him seems overwhelming. But Boss tells him, "A gentleman can live through anything." And this is surely what Lucius, as narrator, is telling his grandchildren without actually saying so directly. Lucius has lived to tell the tale and is the better for it.

All along, Ned has been preparing Lucius for the moment when he will have to confront Boss. Ned has known from the start that they could not get away with their adventure, or even just accept their punishment and be done with it. Instead, as in all of Faulkner's fiction, the past is never past. It has to be borne and contended with as an inextricable part of a community's and an individual's history.

FOOL ABOUT A HORSE

During the summer of 1961 in Oxford, Jack Cheatham, from a Florida racetrack family, and a devotee of fox hunts and a polo player, began pestering an Ole Miss law school classmate, William Lewis Jr., for an introduction to William Faulkner. "Oh, no, Jack, I don't think I can do that. I can't take you there," Lewis told him. Lewis's father ran Neilson's Department Store on the square, and Lewis Jr., the same age as Faulkner's niece Dean, had grown up in and around Rowan Oak and saw a good deal of William Faulkner. They were by no means close friends, but Lewis knew how Faulkner guarded his privacy. Lewis also believed that, contrary to lots of stories about Oxford's neglect of their famous author, those who knew about Faulkner's writing respected his right to be let alone. At a dinner in the Lewis home, Jack asked Lewis's father about meeting Faulkner. Lewis Sr., well read in Faulkner, called Rowan Oak and said: "Bill, I've got a man here interested in a lot of the things you are. He'd like to see if you could meet him." Faulkner said, "Send him right on out." Jack went that night and thereafter they became riding companions—in Virginia as well, where Jack later saw displayed in the University of Virginia library, the wok he had used to make meals when out on expeditions with Faulkner. Jack remembered Faulkner always brought a bottle along and would say, "Jack, would you like a little tug?" Jack could see that Faulkner's horses were too strong for him.[29]

On December 24, 1961, William Faulkner was admitted to Tucker Hospital in Richmond, suffering from an acutely painful back and a respiratory infection. Five days later he was back home and on a horse by January 3, and off again—he could not remember how—coming home with a black eye, a bruised forehead, and a broken tooth. A Demerol shot did not deaden the pain, and he turned to drink, checking into Tucker once again on January 8. The doctors examined a man in good shape for a sixty-four-year-old. X-rays revealed ribs that had been broken quite some time ago—the aftermath of his riding accidents. Tests showed a normal heart, normal blood pressure and liver. They treated him for pleurisy. Faulkner seemed unconcerned. He behaved the perfect gentleman, if unwilling to do much about his health. He did what he pleased. He seemed to have a feeling nothing would happen to him. Yet he did tell Dr. Asa Shield: "I'm going to stop being a damn fool and acting like a 45-year-old and start living as a 65-year-old and perhaps live to be 85 years old."[30]

Like Robert E. Lee on his favorite horse, the intrepid Traveller, charging into many battles Billy Falkner had read about as a boy, one horse, Tempy, came to epitomize all the others William Faulkner rode, throwing her rider regularly and refusing jumps over fences even as he continued to train her and sorely savage his own body. "Faulkner's men of action ride horses—Jewel Bundren, John Sartoris, Thomas Sutpen, Roth Edmonds, Jack Houston," symbols of masculinity, control, and power.[31] But horses ultimately meant something more, which is why Faulkner had to remount after a fall. They recaptured his youth on that pony his father bought for him, and the pony he bought for himself, and the art he always described as a "splendid failure," and memorialized in the poet's revery in "Carcassonne": *on a buckskin pony with eyes like blue electricity and a mane like tangled fire, galloping up the hill and right off into the high heaven of the world."*

And yet Faulkner, off the horse, and off the page, often struck interviewers as "utterly still . . . composed and motionless—almost to an inhuman extent," as Simon Claxton, an English visitor to Rowan Oak, noted in March 1962. Faulkner's "glittering hooded eyes" held him, as they had Elliott Chaze a year earlier in Charlottesville. Claxton generated no news, except for Faulkner's comment that he was not then working on a book, but even that, given Faulkner's admitted inclination to give different answers at different times, cannot be taken as definitive. "I am not working on anything at all now," he had told Bennett Cerf. "I wont work until I get hot on something; too many writing blokes think they have got to show something on book stalls. I will wait until the stuff is ready, until I can follow instead of trying to drive it."[32] He was still riding every morning and fox hunting in Virginia, he told his foreign visitor. Although taciturn, Faulkner seemed to relent, talking to Claxton about the Lake District and saying that "he hoped I was enjoying his country as much as he had enjoyed mine."[33]

PRESIDENT FAULKNER

On April 19, Mr. and Mrs. William Faulkner, accompanied by Jill and Paul Summers, arrived at the Presidential Suite of Hotel Thayer on the West Point campus, where Faulkner had been invited to speak and to meet with students. It was almost like an official state visit, with Henri Cartier-Bresson assigned to take the photographs. Although Faulkner had been offered a car, he preferred to walk along the banks of the Hudson River on the nearly mile-long ascension to Thayer Hall, where he met his host, Colonel Alspach, and drank coffee with members of the English department, telling them: "I make my coffee at home in an old lard bucket that I haven't cleaned for twenty years. I put some coffee and water in, boil it for a while, and that's coffee." The Faulkners dined with West Point commandant William Westmoreland and his wife, and then Faulkner read from *The Reivers* to an audience of 1,400, including a thousand cadets.[34]

In the question-and-answer period, he addressed the familiar questions, occasionally adding variations. How had he succeeded in lifting man's heart? "It's possible that I haven't," Faulkner replied, although "that is the writer's dedication." He was asked about Ernest Hemingway's suicide, which had occurred on July 2, 1961. In private, Faulkner had been quite critical. Even if Hemingway had been sick, he had done something unmanly. But in public, perhaps after reconsidering, Faulkner said: "I'm inclined to think that Ernest felt that at this time, this was the right thing, in grace and dignity, to do. I don't agree with him. I think that no man can say until the end of his life whether he's written out or not." Faulkner seemed to have himself in mind. The two writers had never met, and yet Faulkner used Hemingway's first name twice, the second time later in a classroom making it sound as if they had known one another: "The last time I saw him he was a sick man. But I prefer to believe that he had reached that point that the writer must reach— Shakespeare reached it in *The Tempest*—he said 'I don't know the answer either,' and wrote *The Tempest* and broke the pencil. But he didn't commit suicide. Hemingway broke the pencil and shot himself."[35]

After bowing in his courtly manner to audience applause, Faulkner submitted to a press conference. Asked about his impressions of West Point cadets, he observed: "In Princeton and Virginia there is something a little sloppy which is not here." Not a surprising comment from this erect, stately man, with his love of uniforms and even the discipline they commanded. He appeared to connect his own idea of the writer's service and even subordination to literature to martial virtue. One journalist expressed his surprise at the cadet response to Faulkner's declaration, "If a spirit of nationalism gets into literature, it stops being literature." Certain "predecessors from this institution," the questioner observed, "think nationalism is a great virtue." Faulkner shot back: "Well, they didn't believe nationalism was a great virtue while they were here. It's only after they got out that they become Edwin Walkers—years after here."[36] President Kennedy had accepted General Walker's resignation after he had persisted in right-wing politicking among the troops under his command. Lee Harvey Oswald would later shoot at and slightly wound Walker, an anti-Communist zealot and racist who would later become involved, after Faulkner's death, in the 1962 Ole Miss riot over the admission of African American James Meredith.

The next day in an American literature class, the author of *A Fable* made himself felt: "War is a shabby, really impractical thing anyway, and it takes a genius to conduct it with any sort of economy and efficiency." He was explaining the ending of "Turnabout," when the dive-bombing pilot curses "all the higher echelons that got all of us into this to kill some of us." But it was a dramatic moment in a story, not an "idea," Faulkner emphasized: "That was something that at that moment he could feel, but it would not be a conviction of his that he would keep always—just at that moment."[37]

Asked about student riots, Faulkner mused: "It could be a perfectly normal impulse to revolt," although he thought it "a force of youth that is misdirected." He did not want to condemn protest. "I am not sure it does any harm. But it's a force that, if it could be directed into another channel, it could do something a little more—well, I don't like the word productive either." As always, he was open to change, whatever his regrets and criticisms, and responded sympathetically to a student questioner who asked if youth rebelled as a result of "not living what our hearts would have us live? In other words, the conformity of today? . . . Do you feel that the outbursts of youth are the result of this sort of constriction or restrictions?" Faulkner acknowledged such pressures and attributed them to an overpopulated world trying to order and regiment itself.[38] It had all been different once upon a time, his public reading of *The Reivers* seemed to imply.

On race, Faulkner had not changed, still supposing "the Negro has got to be better than the white man" so that the latter would be compelled to say, "Please join us." But he also blamed political leaders and wished they had been "trained for leadership coming up as a constant new crop of military officers coming up all the time; instead of using government as a refuge for your indigent kinfolks as we are prone to do in this country. A man can't make a living any other way, we elect him to something."[39] Global Faulkner rejected the implication of a question that consigned democracy to western Europe and the Americas: "I would not like to believe that certain people are ethnologically incapable of democracy." But democracy was a matter of education and leadership. "I don't believe that we are any wiser or more sensible than Russians or Chinese."[40]

Faulkner admitted that at West Point he had "expected a certain rigidity of—not thinking—but of the sort of questions I would get. And I was pleasantly astonished to find that the questions I got came from human beings, not from third class men or second class men or first class men" who had honored him with the idea that he might have some answers. Shortly afterward his comments on the old Colonel—that he was a "martinet"—raised again the responsibilities of leadership in a changing world that his own forebears had not adjusted to very well.[41]

Two days at West Point seemed enough. Major Fant, one of Faulkner's hosts, asked him if "there was anything else he'd like to see." Faulkner said: "No sir. I think I've seen enough. I'll just let it gestate for a while."[42] Estelle had enjoyed the generals who squired her around. The trip had been fine but exhausting.[43] Faulkner wrote to General Westmoreland expressing his "pleasure and pride" at seeing his name recorded in the Academy's "handsome log book." The honor was all the more memorable in the company of his wife, son, and daughter. "Our pleasure was of course a private one. That was watching our youngest daughter being fetched back to visit his alma mater by her husband (Paul Summers, class of '51), not as a guest of the class of '51 but among the very top brass hats themselves."[44]

A New Home

At the end of June, Faulkner announced his desire to purchase a $200,000 property in Albemarle County. The Red Acres estate included a 250-acre farm not far from Farmington and the posh set, so different from the setup at Rowan Oak that Faulkner had worked so hard to hold on to. It would stretch his finances to acquire the property, but he counted on Random House and Linton Massey, whose Faulkner collection was now housed at the University of Virginia, to advance some of the funding, or at least guarantee it if necessary.[45] The land alone, not to mention its various old buildings and pristine landscape, would become the citadel to which Joseph Blotner would later repair for his circumspect interviews with Estelle Faulkner.

On April 20, President Kennedy invited William Faulkner to the White House. Blotner laughed when he heard Faulkner say, "I'm too old at my age to travel that far to eat with strangers." Those strangers were the fifty-one American Nobel laureates. The snub is puzzling. To be sure, Faulkner disliked such large social gatherings that put him on display with nothing to say. But he had never refused an American president—in this case a Democrat, the head of Faulkner's party. He had voted for Stevenson in 1956. One biographer calls Faulkner's response "sanctioned by that inner ethical gauge."[46] How was it unethical to accept such an honor from his president? Another supposes he no longer needed the recognition of the outside world.[47] More likely is Fred Karl's view that Faulkner felt used by a president who liked the "patina of culture."[48] Whatever the honor, Faulkner still believed the writer's place in America was marginal. President Kennedy would get no help from William Faulkner, who had Lucius Priest sum up the political landscape: "a Republican is a man who made his money; a Liberal is a man who inherited his; a Democrat is a barefooted Liberal in a cross-country race; a Conservative is a Republican who has learned to read and write."

On May 6, in his last recorded interview in Charlottesville, with a visiting Yugoslav academic, Faulkner recalled his youth and "restless life," rushing "all over America and the world. I took an interest in everything. And now I prefer to be here." His answers were curt and formulaic. He remained a believer in change, even if he preferred nature and no longer cared for "the hustle and bustle." Toward the end he acknowledged his recalcitrance: "I don't know whether you have got what you expected of this interview. I am sorry. I am not a conversationalist."

On May 24, Faulkner reluctantly left home for New York to accept the Gold Medal for Fiction, presented to him by Eudora Welty, a fellow Mississippian and no stranger. He met, as well, old friends like Lillian Hellman and Conrad Aiken, reciting one of the poet's poems. To Malcolm Cowley, Faulkner just wanted to talk about his grandsons and his desire for a granddaughter. He looked like a countryman, "his face bronzed under the white hair and apparently glowing with health."[49]

This most marginal of writers, so often treated in reviews as a perversion of literature, had at last found a way to integrate himself into the mainstream—not by attending White House dinners but by associating himself with the "individuality of excellence," as he put it in his acceptance speech, drafted by Joseph Blotner: "I think that those gold medals, royal and unique above the myriad spawn of their progeny which were the shining ribbons fluttering and flashing among the booths and stalls of forgotten county fairs in recognition and accolade of a piece of tatting or an apple pie, did much more than record a victory. They affirmed the premise that there are no degrees of best; that one man's best is the equal of any other best, no matter how asunder in time or space or comparison, and should be honored as such."[50]

31

End of Days

June–July 1962

BEFORE THE FALL

Several reviewers praised *The Reivers* but considered it off-speed Faulkner: funny and exciting, if not exactly profound and sometimes sententious. The novel had "none of the demonic power and little of the dazzling originality of the half dozen great books that appeared between 1929 to 1943," concluded Granville Hicks in the *Saturday Review* (June 2). Others were dismissive: "a boy's book, and not even a superior specimen of that genre," declared Stanley Edgar Hyman in the *New Leader* (July 9). Winfield Townley Scott's review in the *Santa Fe New Mexican* (June 3) stood out: "I can only, however awkwardly, record my curious sensation that I was reading a book which had long been classic American literature. I dare say that's what's going to happen to it."

Even the many good reviews calling the novel "truly fine" (*Miami Herald,* June 3) and a "small, fresh masterpiece" (*Atlanta Journal,* June 3) and noting that "Faulkner's Tall Tale Tops Mark Twain's" (*Denver Post,* May 27) would not have mattered much to Faulkner. He revealed his deep satisfaction with *The Reivers* at the West Point press conference: "It's one of the funniest books I ever read. . . . I wish I hadn't written it so I could do it again."[1]

By early June, the Faulkners had returned to Rowan Oak. Phil Stone spotted him on the street and reported to Carvel Collins: "I have never seen him look so old before. It is not the eyes, but the skin around the eyes; looks like that of an old man, and he looks to me like he has aged about five years since I saw him a few months ago." Two others, Dr. Chester McLarty and Joan Williams, on a brief visit to Rowan Oak, also noticed the pallor—unusual in

McLarty's observations of his patient. Emily Stone saw him around this time and recalled, "The fire had gone out of his eyes."[2]

THE FALL

Phil Stone still seemed to be avoiding Faulkner, and apparently at his wife's urging, he wrote a note thanking Faulkner for dropping off an autographed copy of *The Reivers,* although Stone once again said there would be some delay in his reading it since "all I have time to read is law books."[3] Stone and Faulkner did meet. "Bill got thrown by another horse and is having trouble with his back again. I told him he was going to break his neck one of these days," Stone reported to James B. Meriwether.[4] A few years earlier Maud Falkner had mentioned seeing a man on a beautiful horse pass by her house. She could not tell who it was. "Did he fall off?," her eldest son asked. "No," she said. "It wasn't me then," he said with a laugh.[5]

The fall had occurred on June 10, and for three weeks the excruciating pain did not let up. Faulkner's niece Dean remembered visiting him near the end of the month. He could not get out of bed. But he promised to be better for the July Fourth celebration picnic. Apparently he had no reason to think he would not recover, as he had always done before. Around June 24, Meta wrote him a letter, and he responded that he expected to come out to her in September.[6]

On July 3, Faulkner managed to walk into town. He stopped by Gathright-Reed to pick up a copy of the *Memphis Commercial Appeal* and speak with Mac, who estimated that over four decades Faulkner made something like 120 trips to the drugstore, standing outside the front door visiting with old friends for a half hour and more, talking about how the town was changing. Mac noticed a copy of *The Reivers* in Faulkner's hand. He said it was for a Swedish friend (Else Jonsson). Mac filled out the postal form since Faulkner had left his glasses at home and put the book in a carton. Faulkner's last words to Mac: "I been aimin' to quit all this."[7]

Faulkner took Estelle out for their usual filet mignon dinner. He complained that "things hadn't tasted right. 'The meat and bread tasted alike.'"[8] That night Jimmy Faulkner visited Rowan Oak and found his uncle in bed in his office, drinking gin and taking prescription painkillers. By the next day he was on his second bottle. He agreed with Jimmy that later in the day they would go to Wright's Sanatorium in Byhalia. But because of the intense heat they agreed to postpone the trip until the next day, by which time Faulkner had deteriorated. He seemed delusional, talking about sergeants and captains and saying he wanted to go home, although he was at Rowan Oak. But

Chrissie Price, who helped out in the Rowan Oak kitchen, thought Mr. Bill meant something else by home. He had been behaving "differently." Late that afternoon (July 5) Estelle and Jimmy checked William Faulkner into the Byhalia "drying out hospital," his sixth stay since September 1953.[9] By Faulkner's standards, this time was unusual, occurring much earlier than in previous drinking cycles.

Jimmy and a young black orderly helped Faulkner down the corridor, where Dr. Wright examined him. Faulkner seemed to have roused himself. All vital signs were normal, although he complained of heart and back pain. As usual in such examinations, he was "quiet, tractable, humble," and even joked. The black orderly then assisted Faulkner into bed, undressing him and putting him into pajamas. The on-duty nurse called him a "delightful person," a remarkable thing to say since she believed he knew he was dying.

Vitamin injections were followed with a half ounce of alcohol every hour until 10:45. This treatment, standard at the time, concentrated on preventing delirium tremens and other adverse reactions to alcohol withdrawal. He also received an "egg flip," a mixture of eggs, cream, and perhaps alcohol too. By 10:00 p.m., after two more egg flips and an antinausea medication, Faulkner seemed relaxed and sleepy. Estelle bent over his bed and said something Jimmy could not hear and then went out into the hall. Jimmy said, "Brother Will, when you are ready to come home, call me, and I'll come and get you." Jimmy remembered his uncle looking up at him, eyes "bright and sharp," saying in a clear, unslurred voice, "Yes, Jim, I will."

Near 11:00 p.m., after his last half ounce of alcohol, more antinausea medication, a muscle relaxant, and a sedative, the nurse told him, "I'll see you in the morning." He replied, "I don't think so." At 12:40 a.m. he awoke with acute intestinal distress and was given a paregoric mixture and a dose of alcohol. Some time after 1:00 a.m. Faulkner sat up on his bed, groaned, fell over, and died of a heart attack.[10]

An hour later John Faulkner showed up at Rowan Oak and went upstairs to Estelle's room. Dr. McLarty had given her a sedative, but she paced back and forth clenching her hands. John embraced her. "I can't believe it," she said. "I can't believe it. He's not gone. He's not gone."[11] She pushed John away and resumed her pacing. Estelle and her sister Dorothy had another concern. They did not want the press to report that Faulkner had died in Byhalia and disclose his treatment for alcoholism. So the first notices of the death placed him at home.

Jimmy Faulkner called his uncle Jack in Mobile, Alabama. Jack had not seen his brother Bill since their mother had died. The brothers were not close, and Jack, like John, had been upset by Bill's belief in integration. Jack spoke for the family when he acknowledged their puzzlement. Bill lived just like they did, with black servants, and except for his public statements, never gave a sign that he did not share their segregationist beliefs. "I never knew him to say anything he didn't mean," Jack said, but he never heard his brother "say anything to indicate that he wanted or expected the two races to associate otherwise." Jack still loved his big brother, but race had divided the family in ways that even his brother's death could not obliterate.[12]

A FABLED END

Faulkner's life had stopped as abruptly as old Bayard's in *Flags in the Dust*. When Dean learned of her uncle's death on July 6, she recalled this was the old Colonel's birthday.[13] A reader of *Flags in the Dust* might think the Player had planned it. So much of these last days seemed of a piece, including *The Reivers,* which for many readers, and for his family, brought a fitting closure to William Faulkner and his fictional world.

The Faulkners buried their dead quickly, putting them back into the earth as soon as possible—in a plain wooden coffin, as Maud had requested for herself and that was good enough for her son, who, like her, wanted an inexpensive funeral. But Dorothy Oldham and Ella Somerville objected, complaining that Faulkner looked cramped in the cheap-looking box. Back William Faulkner went to the funeral home—this time arriving at Rowan Oak in a more substantial cypress casket, felt-lined and with silver-plated handles.

His black friends, dressed for the occasion, gathered in the kitchen while the closed casket rested in the room where Faulkner had delivered a funeral elegy for Callie Barr. They wanted one last look at him, and Estelle agreed to allow the funeral director to open the casket. They stood looking at him in silence, some in tears, and then the casket was closed again, forever.[14]

In hundred-degree heat and no air-conditioning—just the way Faulkner, for all his complaints, always wanted it—the funeral in the front parlor of Rowan Oak ended with the Lord's Prayer. Shelby Foote also seemed a part of the Faulkner plan. "His hoarse, whispery voice with southern rhythms was familiar and reassuring," Dean said. "It was as if Pappy had sent him." Businesses on the square, with a few Snopes holdouts, closed for fifteen minutes "in memory of William Faulkner." A funeral procession went past the Confederate soldier on the square.

Jimmy described Estelle as "shaken," but, as Dean said, "the Faulkners do not cry in public." That included Jill, who had held back graveside tears by concentrating on the "most garish wreath" she had ever seen. "Ever. Gold and purple plastic grapes sprinkled with gold glitter and tied together with yards and yards of gold ribbon. Pappy would have found it patently absurd." Estelle sat next to her son Malcolm, who held her right hand, encased in a long black glove, in both of his, her face obscured by a large black hat and her bowed head. She did break down at one point. Phil Stone, never fond of Estelle, commented: "Stelle and Bill loved one another in spite of their difficulties their whole lives."[15] In 1972, she came to rest beside him.

A solemn John Faulkner sat right behind Estelle and Malcolm. Phil Stone and Mac Reed were among the pallbearers who brought William Faulkner to his grave. Novelist William Styron, there to cover the funeral for *Life,* felt like an interloper, knowing full well how William Faulkner detested invasions of his privacy. Donald Klopfer had suggested Styron for the assignment. The family welcomed the novelist, whose books were in the Rowan Oak library. The heat made it seem to him that everyone was moving in slow motion. This was the "unholy weather" of Faulkner's novels, Styron thought, as he listened to Shelby Foote's advice to move sideways in the heat. It was Saturday afternoon on the Oxford square, the time for farmers and townsmen to mix, just like all those Saturdays that Faulkner relished by watching and talking to so many who never read a word of his writing, if they even knew that he wrote. To Styron, John Faulkner looked like the ghost of his brother, and Murry (Jack) "sad-eyed" and, like brother Bill, soft-spoken. Bennett Cerf and Donald Klopfer were there to represent Random House. Ben Wasson and Linton Massey rounded out the gathering of his first and last friends.

Cerf really didn't know Faulkner very well. Jim Silver liked to tell the story about the time Faulkner autographed a book for Bennett Surf. When Cerf tore out the page, on the next one Faulkner misspelled the publisher's first name.[16] But Klopfer was another story. He called Faulkner "a marvelous man. Strange, involuted, but a great, great human being." The publisher often saw Faulkner in New York. Over the years the drinking and drying-out cycles became less frequent. He spent weekends at Klopfer's farm in Hunterdon County, New Jersey. Next to Faulkner's guest room, the library had a bar table, well stocked, including one of Faulkner's favorites, Jack Daniels. Klopfer never mentioned the bar, and during his stays Faulkner never got drunk. "Ever," Klopfer emphasized. Faulkner enjoyed wine at dinner, a cognac afterward, and then he would walk right past the bar to his room at the other end of the house, where he certainly could have liquored up alone. This was the same man who in the city drank himself silly, becoming an incomprehensible idiot, Klopfer remembered. A vivid moment Klopfer declined to have recorded was Faulkner's upset over a young lover who had married. Whether it was Joan or Jean, Klopfer did not know or did not want to say. Another time Faulkner came on crutches after a fall from a horse. He said to Klopfer's wife, Pat, "You're always sympathetic to me, whether I've been thrown by a dame or a horse." Later, after reading Faulkner's biography, a dismayed Klopfer said: "The way we treated him—oh well. His books were out of print and we couldn't send him more money. We didn't have it and he didn't have it. I feel ashamed of myself." Not even with his publisher would Faulkner talk about literature. "He was the only author I've known who didn't give a damn what anybody said about his books. He didn't read the reviews," Klopfer said. "He knew what he wanted to do."[17] Estelle Faulkner called him "the one man I've ever known who dared to be himself."[18]

Earl Wortham, the blacksmith who had shod Faulkner's horses, was there to see him off. Earl had been there from the beginning, delivering wood to the Oldham house with a "little pair of oxen" yoked to a wagon. Estelle and her sister Dorothy would hop on as Earl assured their mother they would not get hurt. He had watched Callie Barr walking with little William on the plank sidewalks before the streets were paved. He would break away and run into the square. Later Earl asked him why he did that. "I like to be in the dust," William told him. Earl thought it a mistake for Faulkner to ride "that big grey horse Stonewall"—the last horse to throw him to the ground. Earl had told him, "You don't need this horse." The horse startled easily and reared up at unpredictable times when he seemed quite still. But Stonewall was a good jumper, and Faulkner could not bear to part with him. Perhaps in memory of those livery stable days, Faulkner always stopped and spoke with Earl, who said, "I suppose it is not very common for one man to love another one, but I loved William Faulkner."[19]

Notes

ABBREVIATIONS

B	Malcolm Franklin, *Bitterweeds*
CCP	Carvel Collins Papers, Harry Ransom Humanities Research Center, University of Texas
CGBC	Louis Daniel Brodsky and Robert W. Hamblin, eds., *Faulkner: A Comprehensive Guide to the Brodsky Collection*
CWF	M. Thomas Inge, *Conversations with William Faulkner*
"DSF"	Dean Faulkner Wells, "Dean Swift Faulkner: A Biographical Study"
EDBS	Dean Faulkner Wells, *Every Day by the Sun: A Memoir of the Faulkners of Mississippi*
ESPL	William Faulkner, *Essays, Speeches, and Public Letters*
FAWP	Joseph L. Fant and Robert Ashley, *Faulkner at West Point*
FB (1974)	Joseph Blotner, *Faulkner: A Biography* (1974)
FB (1984)	Joseph Blotner, *Faulkner: A Biography* (1984)
FC	Malcolm Cowley, *The Faulkner-Cowley File*
FL	Judith Sensibar, *Faulkner and Love*
FWP	Floyd Watkins Papers, Emory University
JBP	Joseph Blotner Papers, Louis Daniel Brodsky Collection, Center for Faulkner Studies, Southeast Missouri State University
LDBP	Louis Daniel Brodsky Papers, Center for Faulkner Studies, Southeast Missouri State University
LG	Louis Daniel Brodsky, *Life Glimpses*
LITG	James B. Meriwether and Michael Millgate, eds., *Lion in the Garden*
MBB	John Faulkner, *My Brother Bill*
MCR	Meta Carpenter recordings, UM
MFP	Malcolm Franklin Papers, Special Collections, Thomas Cooper Library, University of South Carolina
NYPL	Berg Collection, New York Public Library
RHMP	Robert H. Moore Papers, University of North Carolina, Special Collections.
SL	*Selected Letters of William Faulkner*
UM	Archives and Special Collections, University of Mississippi
UVA	William Faulkner archive, Albert and Shirley Small Special Collections Library, University of Virginia

VJR	Recording of Louis Daniel Brodsky interview with Victoria Johnson, LDBP
WFCR	M. Thomas Inge, *William Faulkner: The Contemporary Reviews*
WFTF	William Faulkner, *William Faulkner at Twentieth Century-Fox: The Annotated Screenplays,* edited by Sarah Gleeson-White

1. Faulkner's Shadow

1. Paddock, *Contrapuntal in Integration,* 111.
2. Qtd. in *FB* (1974), 418.
3. Interview with Mrs. Vernon Omlie, November 24, 1963, CCP.
4. Gresset, *Fascination,* 240.
5. *SL,* 239.
6. See Millgate, 140–41, for details about the Shushan air show.
7. Gwynn and Blotner, eds., 36.
8. Hamblin, "Faulkner and Hollywood: A Call for Reassessment," 19–20.
9. McBride, ed., *Hawks on Hawks,* 57.
10. Yonce, "'Shot Down Last Spring': The Wounded Aviators of Faulkner's Wasteland," 206, cites Keats in her description of the narrator in "The Lilacs," the first poem in *A Green Bough,* but the phrase seems applicable to the reporter as well.
11. Interview with Hermann Deutsch, February 1965, JBP.
12. Brooks, *William Faulkner: Toward Yoknapatawpha,* 183. See also 399, 402, for Brooks's identification of Deutsch as the model for the reporter.
13. Interview with Murray Spain, early June 1960, CCP.
14. Interview with Richard Bradford, August 9, 1969, JBP.
15. Interview with Mrs. Roark Bradford, spring 1963, CCP.
16. Interview with Mrs. Vernon Omlie, November 24, 1963, CCP.
17. See the reminiscence of George W. Healy Jr., editor of the *Times-Picayune,* in Webb and Green, eds., *William Faulkner of Oxford,* 59–60: "Although Bill never was, strictly speaking, a member of the *Times-Picayune* staff, he made many a visit to our newsroom to talk with [Roark] Bradford, Lyle Saxon, and others on the staff who, like himself, were turning out books."
18. Parini; Karl, 529.
19. Bassett, ed., 178.
20. Qtd. in Brooks, *William Faulkner: Yoknapatawpha and Beyond,* 402.
21. *EDBS.*
22. *EDBS.*
23. Dardis, *Some Time in the Sun.*
24. For Hawks's difficulties with *Barbary Coast* and the backing he received from Goldwyn, see Rollyson, *A Real American Character,* 43–50.
25. *WFCR,* 132.
26. For my assessment of the film adaptation, see Rollyson, "Faulkner's Shadow."
27. Lurie, *Vision's Immanence,* 16.
28. Qtd. in Lurie, *Vision's Immanence,* 181.
29. Kawin, *Faulkner and Film,* 47.
30. Torchiana, 307.

31. January 23, 1935, in Trotter, 105.

32. February 2, 1935, in Trotter, 106; and February 15, 1935, in Trotter, 108.

33. *SL,* 90.

34. Marshall Maslin, "All of Us," *Xenia (OH) Evening Gazette,* February 23, 1935, https://newspaperarchive.com/xenia-evening-gazette-feb-23-1935-p-4/.

35. *SL,* 88.

36. Bassett, ed., 15.

37. *Charleston (WV) Daily Mail,* March 27, 1935, https://newspaperarchive.com /charleston-daily-mail-mar-27-1935-p-6/, reprinted from *New York Herald Tribune,* March 25, 1935.

38. https://www.newspapers.com/image/202638711/?terms=Pylon%2BFaulkner; interview with Louise Meadow, March 20, 1963, CCP.

39. "DSF," 140–49.

40. "DSF," 161–62.

41. *EDBS.*

42. Interview with Louise Meadow, July 8, 1975, CCP.

43. Trotter, 111.

44. *SL,* 92–93.

45. *SL,* 93.

46. Interview with Louise Meadow, August 3, 1971, CCP.

47. Faulkner is quoted in several newspaper clippings, CCP.

48. Interview with Victoria Fielden, March 13, 1968, CCP.

49. Interview with E. O. Champion, April 12, 1950, CCP.

50. Interview with Louise Meadow, August 3, 1971, CCP.

51. Bleikasten, *William Faulkner: A Life through the Novels,* 254.

52. See Murphet, 30–32, on the romance of flying in Faulkner's work.

53. The details of Dean's death and Faulkner's reaction derive from *EDBS.*

54. Interview with Louise Meadow, August 3, 1971, CCP.

55. *SL,* 93–94.

2. Transcendental Homelessness

1. Wilde, "An Unpublished Chapter from *A Loving Gentleman.*"

2. Cassettes 11 and 12, n.d., MCR. Meta Carpenter's dramatic, retrospective memoir romanticizes her first meeting with Faulkner. I have listened to the recordings of her memories and conversations with her coauthor. A more prosaic account emerges on cassette 18, May 12, 1973, one that does not overturn her book but that includes the mundane aspects of their first meeting. Going over the day Faulkner first walked into the office where Meta was working, she said: "He didn't impress me at all. Nice soft voice. I really wasn't excited. I was meeting big movie stars. Writers were not nearly as glamorous. . . . I probably spoke about it at the Studio Club, saying 'I met William Faulkner. He's a nice little man.'" See also Wilde, "An Unpublished Chapter from *A Loving Gentleman.*" For Carpenter's explanation of how her book was put together, see Broughton, 779. Meta Carpenter Wilde was her married name at the time her book was published. Her maiden name was Doherty. She was also married to Wolfgang Rebner, but throughout my

narrative I refer to her as Meta Carpenter since that was her name when Faulkner met her, and he often used "Carpenter" when addressing her. Unless otherwise noted, quotations of dialogue between Carpenter and Faulkner are from Wilde and Borsten, *A Loving Gentleman.*

3. Interview with Meta Carpenter, December 28, 1963, CCP.
4. Wilde and Borsten, *A Loving Gentleman.*
5. Breen to Colonel Jason S. Joy, January 31, 1936, Academy of Motion Pictures Arts and Sciences.
6. Cassette 14, June 30, 73, MCR.
7. Sayre diary and oral history, NYPL.
8. Interview with Joel Sayre, March 20, 1968, CCP.
9. Interview with Dorothy Parker, April 17, 1965, JBP.
10. Interview with Joel Sayre, March 20, 1963, CCP.
11. Interview with Joel Sayre, March 20, 1968, CCP.
12. Interview with David Hempstead, June 6, 1966, JBP.
13. David Hempstead, television interview transcript, CCP.
14. Interview with Buzz Bezzerides, February 17, 1963, CCP.
15. Stempel, 20.
16. Interview with Lillian Hellman, August 18, 1952; letter from Hellman, February 2, 1952, CCP.
17. Bradford's account is taken from his papers at Tulane University, as transcribed by Carvel Collins.
18. Garrett, afterword to *The Road to Glory,* 163–67.
19. Interview with Ben Wasson, March 28, 1965, JBP.
20. Wilde, "An Unpublished Chapter from *A Loving Gentleman,*" 452–53.
21. Culled from Faulkner's handwritten screenplay at UM.
22. The last names of Paul and Michel change in various versions of the script, and in one version Michel is called Pierre. I have used the names in the released film.
23. Hillier and Wollen, eds., 51.
24. Interview with Meta Carpenter, October 28, 1963, CCP.
25. Although ever-grateful to Howard Hawks, in her recordings Meta could also be critical of the way he exploited her and used other women.
26. Interview with Meta Carpenter, "Hollywood 1963," CCP.
27. Interview with Meta Carpenter, "Hollywood 1963," CCP.
28. I'm indebted to Ramsey's account of Hopkins's career and its relevance to Faulkner's Hollywood reputation. According to Ben Wasson, Hopkins wanted to meet Faulkner. She sent him an invitation to attend a dinner party, but he never replied (interview with Ben Wasson, August 3, 1963, CCP).
29. Wilde, "An Unpublished Chapter from *A Loving Gentleman,*" 453–55.
30. Wilde, "An Unpublished Chapter from *A Loving Gentleman,*" 457–58.
31. Cassette 14, June 30, 1973, MCR.
32. Steve Allen, *Hooked on Books* show, 1977, recording, UM.
33. In *A Loving Gentleman,* Meta has them entering the Larry Edmunds Bookshop. But that shop was not in business until 1940, whereas Stanley Rose, which Faulkner was known to frequent, was located next to Musso & Frank's in 1935.

34. Cassette 13, n.d., MCR. I met Meta in Hollywood in 1987 to interview her and her husband Arthur for my biography of Lillian Hellman. But of course I told her about my dissertation on Faulkner, and we spoke about him as well. My wife, Lisa Paddock, also the author of a book about Faulkner, made this meeting an especially warm one.
35. Interview with Meta Carpenter, "Hollywood 1963," CCP.
36. Interview with Meta Carpenter, December 22, 1963, CCP.
37. Wilde, "An Unpublished Chapter of *A Loving Gentleman*," 455.
38. http://www.bottle-spot.com/posts/10179/manhattan-new-york-other-2-for-sale -chateau-pontet-canet-pauillac-2006.
39. Interview with Meta Carpenter, n.d., CCP.
40. Notes, n.d., CCP; Broughton, 800.
41. Minter, 161.
42. Many have questioned Faulkner's motivations, including Joseph Blotner, writing to Malcolm Cowley (January 13, 1977): "She seems not to have realized how much she was just his doxy, and so she seems self-deluded. But much of the time he was obviously stringing her along, wanting a bed mate, though perhaps somewhat self-deluded that he loved her too" (JBP). I well remember when her memoir first appeared and how much certain Faulkner scholars at a Modern Language Association meeting scorned her testimony. Carvel Collins, on the other hand, regarded her seriously and interviewed her several times. She felt loyal to Collins and distrusted Blotner, the authorized biographer. She published her memoir only when she concluded that Collins would never publish his book, as she told me when I met with her in December 1987. In that same letter to Cowley, Blotner added, "Estelle never gave me problems about her [Meta], or anyone else really." Perhaps not. But judging by Blotner's letters asking for interviews, it was clear that he was prepared to excise passages his interviewees found objectionable, and it is also equally clear that he never put to Estelle many of the basic questions a biographer would like to have answered.
43. Cassette 14, June 30, 1973, MCR.
44. Wilde and Borsten, "A Loving Gentleman," typescript.
45. Carvel Collins seems to be the only scholar who saw the drawings of Meta before she deposited them at the New York Public Library.
46. Telephone interview with Meta Carpenter, April 26, 1989, CCP.
47. Meta Carpenter to Carvel Collins, November 19, 1985, CCP.
48. Interview with Meta Carpenter, December 1963, CCP.
49. Meta Carpenter to Carvel Collins, November 19, 1985, CCP. She objected strongly to David Minter's characterization of her relationship with Faulkner. She hoped Collins would be able to correct many of the misconceptions.
50. Interview with Carvel Collins, December 28, 1963, CCP.
51. Meta Carpenter to Carvel Collins, November 19, 1985, CCP.
52. Broughton, 797.
53. Wilde, "An Unpublished Chapter from *A Loving Gentleman*."
54. Crown later taught generations of performers at the University of Southern California.

55. Interview with John Crown, n.d., CCP.
56. Carpenter misremembers the film, calling Crawford a shop girl.
57. *WFTF*, 190.
58. Grimwood, 279.
59. *WFTF*, 196.
60. UVA. This part of the letter was omitted from *SL*.
61. *WFTF*, 195. Joel Williamson writes: "He conveyed in letters to Oxford the warmth he failed to show in person." Do we know that? Faulkner certainly conveyed that impression in his complaints about Estelle, but that is not the same thing as knowing what the marriage was like when he was not complaining about her.
62. Interview with Howard Hawks, n.d., CCP.
63. UVA.
64. UVA.
65. Trotter, 112, 114, 115. On August 13, 1936, in a note written on Twentieth Century-Fox stationery, Faulkner sent Bryant five hundred dollars, expressing regret that he had not been able to send the money sooner. By December 10, he had sent another five hundred, mentioned in his typed note on Fox letterhead.
66. What part did Malcolm Franklin play in Faulkner's life? His memoir is a loving tribute to his stepfather. On Faulkner's side, the record is mixed. Malcolm's two wives said Faulkner was ambivalent about Malcolm, who was not remembered in Faulkner's will. Dean Faulkner Wells reported Faulkner saying that Malcolm was "weak." One Faulkner friend said Faulkner beat "the hell out of" Malcolm with a switch. Chabrier interprets Faulkner's behavior as a repetition of his own father's rejection of him. Yet Malcolm and Faulkner shared much in their love of nature, and Malcolm, as his mother said and Malcolm's own diaries and letters show, clearly adored his stepfather. Jimmy Faulkner believed his uncle had made an "honest effort" to instill the right values in Malcolm (see Chabrier, 45–46).
67. Judith gives Bon a photograph of herself to carry with him but finds a photograph on Bon's body that is not of her but of the octoroon mistress and his son. Quentin imagines the Sutpens as they would appear in a faded family photograph. Miss Rosa speaks of Charles Bon, "I saw a photograph; I helped to make a grave." She returns obsessively to her impression of Bon as a photograph, a shadow, a projection of her imagination (see Urgo, 62).
68. Interview with Buzz Bezzerides, n.d., CCP.
69. *SL*, 95–96.
70. Interview with Louise Meadow, March 20, 1963, CCP.
71. Estelle Faulkner, n.d., recipient is unclear, JBP.
72. Notes from interview with Mrs. Roark Bradford, spring 1963, CCP: Bradford and his second wife met the Faulkners at the Peabody Hotel in Memphis in 1939. Both of them "threw up their hands and said something to the effect that 'Don't say we must drink again.' However the apartment or set of rooms in the hotel was 2 rooms put together so there were two bathrooms, and Faulkner began to go to one of the bathrooms and his wife, Estelle, began to go to the other one. They began to make continual trips to their two bathrooms. And it turned out Estelle's bathroom had a bottle of gin in it and Faulkner's bathroom had a bottle

of bourbon in it, and they were both drinking privately in this way while seeming not to take part in drinking the Bradfords' liquids in the Bradfords' room."

73. *SL*, 96.
74. Wilde and Borsten, "A Loving Gentleman," typescript.
75. Cassette 15, February 1974, MCR.
76. Broughton, 790.
77. Black.
78. Broughton, 790.
79. Interview with John Crown, December 23, 1963, CCP. Meta corroborated Crown's testimony.
80. The documents I rely on are in the Berg Collection, NYPL.
81. Bleikasten, *William Faulkner: A Life through the Novels*, 237.
82. Walton, 6–7.
83. Elisabeth Muhlenfeld, introduction to *William Faulkner's "Absalom, Absalom!":* *A Critical Casebook* (Garland, 1984), xii–xiii. For the old-school view of Hollywood as only a distraction and worse, see Williamson: "In many ways, Hollywood as Hollywood was simply another disaster in Faulkner's life. It affected his writing, but there is no sign that it added anything really substantial to his talent, and it certainly sponged up his diminishing energies." Unfortunately, even after the splendid scholarship of Gleeson-White, Solomon, Robbins, and others, a recent biography by Kirk Curnutt calls Faulkner's work in Hollywood "lackadaisical."
84. *SL*, 83–84.
85. Rudy Behlmer discusses Faulkner's various drafts in his commentary on the DVD release of *Gunga Din*, warnervideo.com, 2004. See also Rudy Behlmer Papers, Academy of Motion Pictures Arts and Sciences.
86. "Das" is the name of Major Blynt's "colored" double in Faulkner's MGM screenplay "Manservant," also set in India. Das in both of Faulkner's treatments has a fraught identification with the white people he serves, sacrificing himself by taking poison. In each case, the character seems to represent a repressed love that gives *Absalom, Absalom!* so much of its powerful charge.
87. The *Gunga Din* comment, repeated by biographers without any sense of context of how working on a Rudyard Kipling epic not only suited but enriched Faulkner's sensibility, is another part of the disconnect that a biographical narrative ought to remedy. Here is a typical example from Jay Parini: "The money, not the project [*Gunga Din*], excited him, as well as the prospect of spending more time with Meta." Others, like Fred Karl, 573, get distracted by observing that Faulkner went boar hunting with Nathanael West on Catalina Island. André Bleikasten, *William Faulkner: A Life through the Novels*, 225, does not even know that "Gunga Din" is a poem, not a novel, although he does realize that Faulkner "knew Kipling's work well and believed that he understood the film's hero—'a colored man'—better than most." But what Faulkner understood is missing in Bleikasten. See Solomon, 77–79, for a discussion of Faulkner's work on *Gunga Din*.
88. See Polk's introduction to *"Absalom, Absalom!": Typesetting Copy and Miscellaneous Material*, William Faulkner Manuscripts 13.

89. Urgo and Polk, eds. Muhlenfeld still provides the best short account of the book's genesis (introduction to *William Faulkner's "Absalom, Absalom!": A Critical Casebook*).

90. Millgate, 152. This remains the most succinct account of the novel's composition.

91. In *Children of the Dark House*, Polk notes: "The fact that certain pages of the manuscript of *Absalom, Absalom!* are written in the same green ink that he used to write the entire *Pylon* manuscript suggests that even though he put his problems with *Absalom* aside long enough to write *Pylon,* he didn't completely abandon the former."

92. See Muhlenfeld, introduction to *William Faulkner's "Absalom, Absalom!": A Critical Casebook,* xvii.

93. The gangster is Popeye. "A Dull Tale," in Faulkner, *Uncollected Stories of William Faulkner,* provides a slightly different version of Dal Martin's rejection at the big house door.

94. "Evangeline" is included in Faulkner, *Uncollected Stories of William Faulkner.*

95. *SL,* 79.

96. "Evangeline" is confusing and not fully worked-out fiction. In a detailed analysis of the story, Schoenberg, 41, observes that Faulkner "must have intended the child's Negro blood to have come from his mother, at least at this point in the development of the story; Charles Bon's lack of parents, however, makes the matter ambiguous. Bon's appearance is left to the imagination of the reader, but it seems never to have troubled any of the Sutpens."

97. Gwin, *The Feminine and Faulkner,* 84.

98. Irwin, *Doubling and Incest/Repetition and Revenge,* 37, 150.

99. Ford, 150–51.

100. Lurie, *Vision's Immanence,* 2. Lurie's guiding principle is derived from his epigraph citations of Theodor Adorno's "Cultural Criticism and Society": "The cultural critic is not happy with civilization, to which alone he owes his discontent. He speaks as if he represented either unadulterated nature or a higher historical stage. Yet he is necessarily of the same essence as that to which he feels superior." Although Faulkner regretted what he called his "whoring"—writing commercial stories and film scripts—that very word is a palpable admission that he could not extricate himself from the knowledge of that which he abhorred. See also Urgo, 58: "Primarily, *Absalom, Absalom!* is a celebration of collaboration as a fruitful human exercise toward creating new works of art and reaching new levels of comprehension. Faulkner learned this in Hollywood." True enough, although several of his short stories directly related to the novel are also tributes to collaboration, as are Faulkner's experiences with Sherwood Anderson, William Spratling, Howard Hawks, and Joel Sayre.

101. Although Shreve is speaking in 1910 and so could not have seen the movie, readers in 1936 would have recalled the 1925 movie even if they had not read Lew Wallace's 1880 novel.

102. Urgo, 60.

103. Matthews, *William Faulkner: Seeing through the South.*

104. Matthews, *William Faulkner: Seeing through the South.*

105. Weinstein, "Marginalia: Faulkner's Black Lives."

106. T. M. Davis, *Faulkner's Negro: Art and the Southern Context*, 180.

107. Weinstein, *Becoming Faulkner,* provides another eloquent explanation of Bon's significance: "Half French in his sophistication, half American in his vulnerability; half female in his charm, half male in his strength; half white by his father, part black by his mother: Bon blends elegance and power, unillusioned shrewdness and generosity of spirit. These come together to produce a suppleness of being that no pure line of descent could make available. He is the text's utopian image of what miscegenation might really enable, though no one in the story is prepared to consider this possibility once he is 'outed' as black. Identified thus— his history exposed and communicated—Bon cannot be loved, nor admired, nor admitted into the precincts of his white family. Once racially fixed, he must either submit to be 'nigger' or die the death."

108. T. M. Davis, *Faulkner's Negro: Art and the Southern Context,* 235.

109. Interview with Larry Wells.

110. After first identifying her as Miss Rosa, critics tend to call her Rosa. I continue to call her Miss Rosa because I think the title, like Mr. Compson, is important. It defines her status in relation to him, to Quentin, to the other Sutpens, and to her community.

111. Saunders, 69: "a large portion of the narrative itself—that produced by Quentin and Shreve—is conditioned by the Compsons' exchange of a piece of property for a room at Harvard."

112. Coleman, 423: "It is all too easy to let Mr. Compson read Rosa for us."

113. Godden, "*Absalom, Absalom!* and Rosa Coldfield," 43, goes so far as to suggest she "does not seek to bring down the mansion of Patriarchy . . . but to live in a planter's house." She seeks to "maximize her claims to possession."

114. Handley, 139.

115. Polk, *Children of the Dark House.*

116. A good deal of recent Faulkner criticism has been invested in rehabilitating Miss Rosa, demonstrating that hers is the foundation narrative without which the other narrators could not progress, as I argued decades ago in *Uses of the Past in the Novels of William Faulkner.* For a Barthian rehabilitation, see Kaufman, 175–95.

117. Urgo and Polk, eds.: "The 'almost' stops one. Henry is a murderer whether a fratricide or not and a good deal of the novel is based on an assumption (which it does not prove) that Henry and Bon are at least half brothers. Does Rosa mean that she knows they were not brothers but that Henry thought he was killing a brother? If so, and perhaps more important, how does she know this? The novel does not explain" (see Polk's "Faulkner: The Artist as Cuckold," in his *Children of the Dark House).* Godden, "*Absalom, Absalom!* and Rosa Coldfield," 42–43, has quite another gloss on Miss Rosa's reference to fratricide: "Prior to 1865, Rosa knows exactly who Bon is; and . . . in 1865, she has class-based reasons for deploying that knowledge in a minimally articulated form." I deal with Godden's argument when I get to the denouement of the novel.

118. Porter, *Seeing & Being,* 273, observes that Sutpen "virtually treats his failed design as if it were itself a book, over which he pores, 'tedious and intent,' trying to locate the missing fact he had forgotten, the 'mistake' he had made, so as to explain 'a result absolutely and forever incredible.'"

119. The entry for Bon in the genealogy section of the novel supports the findings of Quentin and Shreve, and though certain critics may wish to see Faulkner as fallible—as only one source to consult—I don't see how there can be doubt in his mind, at least, as to how we are to read Bon as a brother with black blood. See also Singal, 201–2: "The overall architecture of the work ... demands that Bon's 'taint' be racial and that he be Sutpen's child; otherwise the pieces will not fit into the structure as Faulkner plainly intended.... [P]assages explicitly establishing Bon's racial ancestry and parentage appeared in draft versions of the novel until very late in the composition process, when Faulkner apparently decided for reasons of narrative technique to make the reader play detective and put the story together him- or herself." I side with Gray, 210: "Working both with and against the grain of the different stories that comprise the novel, Faulkner aims precisely to show that we can 'narrativize' the past: which is to say, come to terms with it as a force both controversial and innate—something open to argument and yet also inward, an understanding or impulse latent within us."

120. I cannot recall in reading the critical literature on the novel an explanation as to why General Compson takes such an interest in Sutpen. I put the question to Hortense Spillers at the 2019 Faulkner and Yoknapatawpha Conference. She suggested that Sutpen, as a failed patriarch, musing over the failure of his design, considers General Compson, another failed patriarch, the only candidate for his confidence. But I'm still not sure why General Compson finds Sutpen so compelling.

121. Latham, 461.

122. Godden, "*Absalom, Absalom!* and Faulkner's Erroneous Dating of the Haitian Revolution," 494–95: "Southerners might recognise that when Sutpen 'enter[s] the ring' with one of his slaves, he does so with 'deadly forethought,' not merely to retain 'supremacy' [and] 'domination' but to enact the pre-emptive counter-revolution, crucial to the authority of his class." Knox, 22, notes that Faulkner was "doubtless drawing on the accounts of the bloody slave rebellion which occurred in August, 1791, when the effects of the French Revolution combined with a history of brutal exploitation to lead to much the same result as in France." Knox cites T. Lothrop Stoddard, *The French Revolution in San Domingo* (Boston, 1914), 138. "The uprising experienced by Sutpen occurred, however, in 1827, at a time when there was no longer slavery in Haiti. It is worth noting that Faulkner avoids the use of 'Slave' to describe the insurgents, but it would certainly be assumed by the unsuspecting (ignorant would be too harsh a term) reader that a slave rebellion was in progress." Knox's work is one of several valuable theses and dissertations on microfilm in UVA.

123. Urgo and Polk, eds.

124. Urgo and Polk are similarly baffled: "Mr. Compson claims 'two exceptions' as sons: does he here mean Bon? If so, how does he know that Bon is Sutpen's son? Is it possible that Sutpen has other children?"

125. There are so many nuances in the narrator's commentary that Urgo and Polk believe the novel has more than one unnamed narrator, although I believe there is only one supple voice who records and ruminates on what the character-narrators have to say.

126. Urgo and Polk go to the trouble of glossing the phrase, pointing out that it originates in logging: A "strong spiked timber by which logs are canted in a saw-mill"

and strewn among other logs was called a "nigger" and could injure an inattentive worker. So the "nigger" in Mr. Compson's terms is "something hidden and dangerous; it's also a secret from the past, like a skeleton in the closet which, if known, would compromise the present."

127. Brister, 49, suggests that the letter is a condensation of Bon himself, that the "stove polish, which is meant to approximate blackness (or blackface), is inscribed over the French watermark on the white page suggesting the taint of darkness which has begun to eclipse the house of Sutpen."

128. The wording recalls Wash Jones's reply to Sutpen: *I'm going to kill you, Kernel.*

129. See Urgo and Polk's introduction to chapter 5. They canvas the different explanations of who is narrating.

130. Lurie, *Vision's Immanence,* 104, 115.

131. D. Robbins, 321.

132. I am closely paraphrasing Fowler, *Faulkner: The Return of the Repressed,* 122.

133. Snead, 13.

134. Snead, 13.

135. Toni Morrison qtd. in Gwin, "Racial Wounding and the Aesthetics of the Middle Voice," 29.

136. Urgo and Polk, eds.

137. James G. Watson, "'If Was Existed': Faulkner's Prophets and the Patterns of History," 62.

138. I examined these drafts, part of the Rowan Oak Papers, UM.

139. Polk, ed., *"Absalom, Absalom!": Typesetting Copy and Miscellaneous Material,* William Faulkner Manuscripts 13.

140. For the full rationale of my argument, see Rollyson, *Uses of the Past in the Novels of William Faulkner.*

141. Sullens.

142. Shreve's question is a statement as much as it is a question, which is perhaps why Faulkner did not use a question mark.

143. Urgo and Polk, eds.: "whites can thus never overcome the fear that that one genetic drop of black blood will someday assert itself in the birth of a child."

144. One of the most remarkable aspects of the novel's ending is that it continues to sustain new and insightful readings, a process of advancing reinterpretation similar to the hermeneutical dialectic that drives *Absalom, Absalom!* My reading of Jim Bond has been powerfully influenced by Aliyyah I. Abdur-Rahman: "By disappearing behind the haunting cry, Jim Bond absents himself from both the conceptual and the visual logics of racial othering. He is not caught, that is, not captive. He is not stationary, that is, not made to occupy the gestures, shapes, and practices of racist subjugation. He is not available for use; that is, he is self-possessed, nearly free. Understanding Jim Bond this way, as both the novel and the nation's redemptive promise, sheds necessary light on the conclusion to *Absalom, Absalom!*: when Shreve prophesies that 'the Jim Bonds are going to conquer the western hemisphere,' it is not a lament; it is a prayer." This interpretation is a fascinating reversal of the earliest generation of Faulkner critics, who saw in Jim Bond Faulkner's own horror of miscegenation. How they could square this interpretation with that other idiot, Benjy Compson, never seems to have occurred to them. By their logic, Benjy would be Faulkner's condemnation of what? See

Campbell; and Kartiganer, 28: "One might say that although Faulkner is aware of the necessity for the South to recognize its 'natural heir,' which is the freed Negro slave, he is unwilling to admit that the products of such miscegenation can approach the magnificence of the pure-blooded if unforeseeing giants who engendered the system." Critics who set aside race see another Jim Bond, who "represents the entire story: he is potential meaning, always just out of reach, but asserting in his idiot howling the negation of meaning. The suggestiveness of his presence is denied by the very quality that establishes it, his incomprehensibility," writes James Guetti, 86. Guetti takes his argument too far when he adds: "Bond represents the constant tension that haunts Quentin, the story that must be meaningful and cannot be." But isn't the story for Quentin all too meaningful?

145. Singal, 221.
146. Abdur-Rahman. For another treatment of *Absalom, Absalom!* as a Reconstruction novel, see Saunders, 66–96.
147. Many historians have remarked upon the medieval ambiance of the antebellum South. See also Rollyson, *Uses of the Past in the Novels of William Faulkner*, 235.
148. Abdur-Rahman.
149. Singal, 211.
150. L. M. Jones, 29: "Significantly, Judith, the one who witnessed, enjoyed and seemed to understand the fights between her father and the 'wild niggers' in the barn (as opposed to Henry's revulsions to those affairs), is able to form a compatible relationship with her mulatto sister, Clytie. Perhaps she comprehends what her father and the system really stand for via these fights, i.e. that these Negroes are in subservience only because of her father's power to defeat them in physical conflict." In Faulkner's treatment of Judith and Clytie in his screenplay "Revolt in the Earth," he makes this bond between Judith and Clytie even stronger. See also Morland.
151. Stecopoulos, 135, observes that "as the Caribbean subplot of *Absalom, Absalom!* suggests, early in his career the writer demonstrated extraordinary sensitivity to the white South's odd status as a society at once colonized (oppressed by the northern metropole and federal state) and colonizing (exploitative of both African Americans and hemispheric Americans)." Like Faulkner, Quentin is a traditionalist under duress, not wanting to hate the South because then he has no basis on which to stand, and yet having to stand on foundations shaped by evils such as slavery. For Quentin, telling the Sutpen story is bearable to begin with because Shreve is Canadian, and so a northerner once removed from the War between the States. But when Shreve turns on Quentin at the very end of the novel, that degree of separation between the roommates no longer obtains, and Quentin's plight is dire as he tries to negate a negation.

3. The Dividing Line

1. *SL,* 98.
2. This paragraph draws directly on Barry Hudek, "'Mississippi on the Potomac': Sutpen's Hundred as Washington, D.C.," in *Faulkner and Hemingway,* ed. Rieger and Leiter.

3. *SL,* 97.

4. By July 24, 1937, Faulkner had instructed his agent, Morton Goldman, to sell "An Odor of Verbena" (*SL,* 100). On August 7 he was assigned to *The Last Slaver,* and he completed his revision of a Sam Hellman and Gladys Lehman screenplay on September 1 (*WFTF,* 221).

5. *WFTF,* 320. Solomon, 79–87, like Karem, sees parallels between *The Last Slaver* and *Absalom, Absalom!,* but Faulkner was just about done with the novel, now in galleys, and his work on *The Unvanquished* seems much more relevant in considering how he developed Lovett's character.

6. Faulkner's work on *Slave Ship* is collected in *WFTF.* The film is available on DVD, Twentieth Century-Fox, Cinema Archives.

7. For a very different interpretation, casting Faulkner as complicit in Hollywood's elimination of "black agency and voice altogether," see Karem, 171.

8. *WFTF,* 376.

9. *WFTF,* 403.

10. *WFTF,* 427.

11. Wilde and Borsten, "A Loving Gentleman," typescript.

12. Postmarked June 28, 37, Twentieth Century-Fox envelope, UVA.

13. For parallels between *Drums along the Mohawk* and *The Unvanquished,* see Solomon, 95.

14. Trotter, 118–23.

15. Interview with Henriette Martin, December 31, 1963, CCP.

16. The film is available on YouTube: https://youtu.be/fowIlhHLcoQ.

17. See Delson, 177–78. Solomon corrects Blotner and subsequent scholars and biographers who assumed "Revolt in the Earth" was written in 1943 because of Robert Buckner's Warner Brothers memo rejecting the script. Solomon provides a learned explanation of the technical innovations of the script that stem in large part from Murphy's earlier films.

18. Interoffice memo, January 6, 1943, Buckner to Faulkner, UVA.

19. Owada, 161.

20. See, for example, Kawin, *Faulkner and Film,* 131–35.

21. Did Orson Welles's 1936 "Voodoo *Macbeth,*" using voodoo rather than Scottish witchcraft to bring down a usurper, have an impact on "Revolt in the Earth"?

22. Owada, 174.

23. The constant laughter in the film is also reminiscent of O'Neill's *Lazarus Laughed,* in which laughter is employed as an elemental force, representing not only the joy that Lazarus takes in existence but also the rebuke his resurrection administers to those who do not participate in the joy of the spirit that he represents. The all-encompassing laughter is the affirmative, all-accepting nature of life that Sutpen denies by rejecting part of his family.

24. *LITG,* 33–34.

25. Trotter, 124.

26. Interview with Wolfgang Rebner, July 1965, CCP.

27. *SL,* 102.

28. *SL,* 101.

29. Interview with Donald Klopfer, February, 8, 1977, CCP.

30. Interview with Phyllis Cerf, December 10, 1965, CCP.

31. Brooks, *William Faulkner: The Yoknapatawpha Country*, 75–99, has one of the most compelling defenses of *The Unvanquished* as a significant example of Faulkner's art. For a contrary view, see Gray, 225–28.

32. See my review of two Sherman biographies: https://www.wsj.com/articles/the-magnitude-of-his-achievement-1466192373.

33. This passage is taken from the Rowan Oak Papers, UM.

34. Rowan Oak Papers, UM.

35. January 7, 1935, UVA.

36. Eric Foner's précis of the early twentieth-century view of Reconstruction is what Faulkner had to work with in *The Unvanquished*: "When the Civil War ended, the white South accepted the reality of military defeat, stood ready to do justice to the emancipated slaves, and desired above all a quick reintegration into the fabric of national life. Before his death, Abraham Lincoln had embarked on a course of sectional reconciliation, and during Presidential Reconstruction (1865–67) his successor, Andrew Johnson, attempted to carry out Lincoln's magnanimous policies. Johnson's efforts were opposed and eventually thwarted by the Radical Republicans in Congress. Motivated by an irrational hatred of Southern 'rebels' and the desire to consolidate their party's national ascendancy, the Radicals in 1867 swept aside the Southern governments Johnson had established and fastened black suffrage on the defeated South. There followed the sordid period of Congressional or Radical Reconstruction (1867–77), an era of corruption presided over by unscrupulous 'carpetbaggers' from the North, unprincipled Southern white 'scalawags,' and ignorant blacks unprepared for freedom and incapable of properly exercising the political rights Northerners had thrust upon them. After much needless suffering, the South's white community banded together to overthrow these governments and restore 'home rule' (a euphemism for white supremacy). All told, Reconstruction was the darkest page in the saga of American history." The novel is not as partisan as this account. Faulkner elides several key events. It is not clear that in his telling the South is "ready to do justice to the emancipated slaves," but his great-grandfather certainly reflected the view that the South should be quickly reintegrated into national life, and Colonel Sartoris is clearly depending on the continuance of Lincoln's reconciliation policies. Very little is said specifically about the Burdens as Radical Republicans or about carpetbaggers and scalawags. "Home rule" entailed violence that Faulkner did not condone. Faulkner generally avoids the period of so-called "ignorant blacks" and worse who harry white people in *Birth of a Nation* and *Gone with the Wind*.

37. Pruitt.

38. "Faulkner Novel Will Be Screened," *Charleston Gazette*, February 22, 1938, https://newspaperarchive.com/charleston-gazette-feb-22-1938-p-5/.

39. Matthews, *William Faulkner: Seeing through the South*, 221.

40. Wittenberg, *The Transfiguration of Biography*, 157, notes that *The Unvanquished* "dramatizes the arrival of its protagonist at a stage of maturity not achieved by any of Faulkner's previous young males and makes a final cathartic gesture toward significant parental and surrogate-parent figures in Faulkner's past."

41. Interview with Estelle Faulkner, September 9, 1965, JBP.
42. Bleikasten, *William Faulkner: A Life through the Novels,* 276.
43. Pruitt. Elnora, Ringo's sister, does not appear in *The Unvanquished;* in "There Was a Queen" she is described as Bayard's half sister, making it just possible that Ringo is also Bayard's half brother.

4. Grief

1. Zender, 538.
2. *SL,* 106.
3. The comment was made at the Faulkner and Yoknapatawpha Conference, July 22, 2019, during a panel discussion of a presentation by Gary Bertholf, "Faulkner's 'Negroes,' The McJunkins's Faulkner, and My Search for Greenfield Farm: Southern Literature from Below."
4. UVA.
5. *B,* 33, 47–50.
6. Interview with Robert Daniel, 1951, CCP. Chabrier, 53, reports the rumor mentioned in an interview with Lewis Dollarhide, who taught at the University of Mississippi from the 1950s through the 1980s.
7. VJR: According to Cho-Cho's daughter, Vicki, Claude Selby later made several visits to Oxford attempting to reclaim Vicki, but Faulkner, in effect, stood guard, picking her up at school and making sure Selby's efforts were thwarted.
8. My account of Cho-Cho is drawn from *LG,* 140–43.
9. Gray, 241, 245.
10. Gray, 246.
11. August 24, 1938, UVA.
12. *SL,* 107.
13. *Harrisburg Sunday Courier,* March 12, 1939.
14. Nelson and Goforth, 80. Charles Nelson saw Faulkner reading the novel and asked him about it. Faulkner said he "enjoyed it" but made no other comment.
15. *WFTF,* 607.
16. In Faulkner's script, the name is Blue Black, but I use the character's name in the released film to avoid confusion.
17. *WFTF,* 705.
18. *WFTF,* 751.
19. *WFTF,* 579: "Here is the paradox of frontier mythology in a nutshell."
20. Miss Reba in *Sanctuary* also wears a veil, and Claude in *Today We Live* announces: "there's not any Eden anymore, and they wear khaki and not veils." Veils are the sign of propriety that Caddy and Charlotte cast off and that Miss Reba appropriates in her parody of propriety.
21. Berg collection, NYPL.
22. Gray, 243.
23. Interview with Wolfgang Rebner, July 1965, CCP.
24. Interview notes, n.d., CCP.
25. McHaney, *William Faulkner's "The Wild Palms,"* 10–12, suggests that Sherwood Anderson's second wife, Tennessee Mitchell, a sculptor who created "grotesque,

satirical figurines" and was attracted to impecunious men, served as a model for Charlotte Rittenmeyer.

26. See McHaney's first chapter of *William Faulkner's "The Wild Palms"* for extensive parallels between *The Wild Palms* and *A Farewell to Arms*.
27. McHaney, *William Faulkner's "The Wild Palms*," 18, likens McCord to Sherwood Anderson.
28. *WFTF*, 224.
29. Gray, 252, supposes Harry is masturbating.
30. Gwin, *The Feminine and Faulkner*, 133–34.
31. Faulkner's erotica drawings are in the Berg Collection, NYPL.
32. Weinstein, *Becoming Faulkner*, 189, speaks of Meta's "well-bred docility." That is nowhere in evidence in the drawings. For a contrary view, see A. G. Jones, "The Kotex Age," 144: "It seems likely that this [the love affair with Meta] was Faulkner's first sustained and intimate encounter with a woman who was both profoundly sexual and increasingly autonomous."

5. Up from Feudalism

1. I was startled when I read this account from Mrs. Agnes McComb Kimbrough to Robert H. Moore, July 14, 1970, RHMP, because it was almost word for word what Kathy Smith, Dana Andrews's daughter, told me about what it was like growing up with an alcoholic father. She would tell her friends to just step over her father, who had passed out in the living room (see Rollyson, *Hollywood Enigma: Dana Andrews*).
2. "TO THE PRESIDENT OF THE LEAGUE OF AMERICAN WRITERS," *ESPL*.
3. Robert Haas to William Faulkner, March 22, 1940, UVA: "This is just to let you know that Mrs. Doherty came in yesterday and that in accordance with your instructions we handed her $150.00 in cash."
4. Interview with Dorothy Commins, January 18, 1964, CCP.
5. Snell, 243.
6. Joel Sayre oral history, NYPL.
7. *SL*, 111.
8. James G. Watson, *William Faulkner: Self-Presentation and Performance*.
9. *LITG*, 17.
10. Weinstein, *Becoming Faulkner*, 299.
11. FWP.
12. Trotter, 136.
13. Pruitt, 193.
14. James G. Watson, *The Snopes Dilemma*, 12.
15. Pruitt, 194.
16. James G. Watson, *William Faulkner: Self-Presentation and Performance*.
17. James G. Watson, *William Faulkner: Self-Presentation and Performance*.
18. I have resisted any deeper probing of Ratliff's motivations, since I think his reactions to the cow episode have a good deal to do with his offended sense of propriety. But if you are in the market for a Freudian take on Ratliff as bugger-man, see Polk, *Children of the Dark House*, 190.

19. Gray, 263.
20. http://faulkner.drupal.shanti.virginia.edu/node/10403?canvas#.
21. Interview with Maud Falkner, April 13, 1950, CCP.
22. Listen to clips from Faulkner talking about *The Hamlet:* http://faulkner.drupal
   .shanti.virginia.edu/node/10403?canvas#.
23. Pruitt, 195.
24. Matthews, *William Faulkner: Seeing through the South,* 125.
25. James G. Watson, *William Faulkner: Self-Presentation and Performance.*
26. http://faulkner.drupal.shanti.virginia.edu/node/10403?canvas#.

6. Was

1. Faulkner to Mary Bell, May 7, 1940, UVA.
2. Faulkner's hunting companion Ike Roberts said that Faulkner, "slightly intoxicated," spoke at the funeral of a black man and spoke so long the "colored preach-
   ers" had no opportunity to speak and the casket was carried out of the church
   while Faulkner was still speaking (interview with Ike Roberts, spring 1950, CCP).
3. *SL,* 117–18.
4. *FL.*
5. Karl, 634.
6. *CGBC,* vol. 2, 27.
7. Faulkner, *Thinking of Home,* ed. Watson, 61.
8. *SL,* 122–23.
9. See, for example, *SL,* 124–25.
10. *SL,* 125.
11. *SL,* 126–29.
12. *FB* (1974), 1050.
13. See *SL,* 130–32, for the business details.
14. *SL,* 136–37.
15. *SL,* 138.
16. For more on *Sergeant York,* see Rollyson, *A Real American Character,* 91–95; and
   Solomon, 119–20.
17. Peek and Hamblin, eds., 283.
18. See Trotter, 137. Faulkner mentions borrowing from Will Bryant John Spencer
   Bassett's *The Southern Plantation Overseer as Revealed in His Letters.* In *The Ledgers of History,* Sally Wolff posits another important source for the commissary
   books, the Francis Terry Leak diaries, which Faulkner may have read while visiting friends in Holly Springs, Mississippi. Several Faulkner scholars have endorsed
   and disputed Wolff's findings. The main problem I have with Wolff's evidence is
   that much of what she attributes to the Leak diaries can also be derived from Bassett's book, which we know for certain Faulkner consulted. As to the testimony of
   Edgar Wiggin Francisco III, who claimed a firsthand connection with Faulkner,
   I could not make a determination. Wolff's critics note that Francisco does not
   appear in the other Faulkner biographies and that much of Wolff's evidence is
   hearsay. That no biographer knew about Francisco's existence is not in itself dispositive. Such occurrences do happen in biography. One of Amy Lowell's lovers,

an important figure in her life, does not make a single appearance in Lowell's massive Houghton Library archive, and yet letters turned up in the Massachusetts Historical Society that made it possible for me to rewrite a significant period in Lowell's biography that none of her several biographers knew about. Perhaps more evidence will yet come to light regarding Faulkner's experiences in Holly Springs, where Francisco's family lived (see Maria Bustillos, "The Faulkner Truthers," *The Awl*, April 22, 2014: https://www.theawl.com/2014/04/the-faulkner-truthers/; and Wolff's rebuttal: "'Everybody Knew': *Ledgers of History:* Questions and Answers," *South Atlantic Review*, December 22, 2016, 66–88).

19. June 23, 1942, CCP. Wiley was then a professor of history at the University of Mississippi and a friend of Faulkner's.
20. Matthews, *William Faulkner: Seeing through the South,* 200, may be right that "Ike solves a mystery that is already known by the community to be part of its unmentionable past," but not until Ike's effort is the enormity of the mystery and its cover-up palpably exposed.
21. Polk, *Children of the Dark House.*
22. *FB* (1984).

7. War

1. Interview with W. J. Van Santen, New Orleans, March 27, 1963, CCP.
2. Interview with Bell Wiley, November 8, 1963, CCP.
3. Jill's report card, UVA.
4. *LITG,* 42–51.
5. January 23, 1940, UVA.
6. Interview with Joan Williams, in Hickman, *William Faulkner and Joan Williams.*
7. Carter, 147–48.
8. Wasson, 159–62.
9. Beck, *Faulkner,* 21. The three Beck articles are collected in this volume.
10. Beck, *Faulkner,* 37.
11. Beck, *Faulkner,* 43.
12. *SL,* 142.
13. *FB* (1974), 364.
14. *FB* (1974), 1103.
15. "Death of William Faulkner Recalls Visit to Author's Home 20 Years Ago," *New York Times,* July 10, 1962.
16. Interview with Richard Charles Rippin, June 2, 1963, about a visit to Rowan Oak on November 30, 1941, CCP.
17. *CGBC,* vol. 2, 23–24.
18. *CGBC,* vol. 2, 25.
19. *EDBS.*
20. *SL,* 149.
21. *SL,* 152.
22. *EDBS.*
23. *EDBS.*
24. *EDBS.*

25. Nelson and Goforth, 57–61.
26. Interviews with Sandra Baker Moore and Larry Wells.
27. Larry Wells, July 2014, interview by the author.
28. *SL*, 153.
29. William Lewis Jr., the current owner of Neilson's, gave me a copy of the letter.
30. *SL*, 154.
31. Cerf to Faulkner, June 3 and 30, 1942, UVA.
32. *SL*, 155.
33. See *SL*, 156–61, for the Herndon fiasco, and 157 for the letter to Geller.

8. Soldiering On

1. Montagu, 34.
2. See also *SL*, 162.
3. Cassette 9, August 11, 1975, MCR.
4. August 20 and September 25, 1942, UVA.
5. N.d., UVA.
6. August 1, 1942, UVA.
7. August 17, 1942, UVA.
8. Cassette 13, n.d., MCR.
9. Interview with Meta Carpenter, n.d., CCP.
10. Interview with Stephen Longstreet, June 12, 1965, JBP.
11. Interview with Meta Carpenter, n.d., CCP.
12. *CWF*, 45.
13. Interviews with Jo Pagano, June 4 and 5, 1966, JBP.
14. Interview with Stephen Longstreet, June 12, 1965, JBP.
15. Interview with Meta Carpenter, n.d., CCP.
16. Interview with Jo Pagano, June 5, 1966, JBP.
17. February 13, 1977, Sound roll 7B, sound 21. Camera roll 13B, CCP.
18. *LG*, 57.
19. Interview with Meta Carpenter, n.d., CCP.
20. Interview with John Fante, June 8, 1966, JBP.
21. Warner, 290.
22. Interview with Robert Buckner, June 9, 1965, JBP.
23. *SL*, 162.
24. Interview with Buzz Bezzerides, June 14, 1965, JBP.
25. Jackson, "If It Still Is France, It Will Endure," 40–41. Blotner reports that at one point Buckner did pair Faulkner with Max Brand, author of *Destry Rides Again* and other pulp stories, to soup up the action, but it is difficult to detect Brand's influence. He apparently accomplished little, except for matching Faulkner drink for drink, and soon he departed for a war-correspondent assignment in Italy, where he was killed (see *FB* [1984]).
26. *SL*, 173.
27. *CGBC*, vol. 3, 6.
28. *CGBC*, vol. 3, 335.
29. *SL*, 164.

30. *CGBC*, vol. 3, 353.

31. *CGBC*, vol. 3, 362.

32. *CGBC*, vol. 3, 395–98.

33. Nigel Hamilton to Carl Rollyson, March 23, 2018. Jackson, "If It Still Is France, It Will Endure," anticipates some of my conclusions, although he links Faulkner's work on the De Gaulle scripts to his Nobel Prize address and to a decline in Faulkner's fiction, whereas I see the Warner Brothers phase as part of his emerging commitment to public service and to a different kind of fiction that should be viewed on its own terms and not be read as simply inferior to his pre–World War II writing.

34. *LG*, 71.

35. *LG*, 71.

36. *LG*, 72.

37. *LG*, 59.

38. *LG*, 59.

39. *SL*, 165–66.

40. Interview with James and Margaret Silver, September 23, 1962, CCP.

41. http://www.earlyblues.com/Yellow%20Dog.htm.

42. The Christmas and New Year's details are drawn from *B*, 69–80.

43. Warner Brothers collection, University of Southern California. The treatment has been published in Faulkner, *Country Lawyer*, ed. Brodsky and Hamblin.

44. Warner Brothers collection, University of Southern California.

9. Yoknapatawpha Comes to Hollywood

1. *SL*, 167.

2. Interview with Dorothy Parker, n.d., CCP.

3. Interview with John Crown, December 22, 1963, CCP.

4. *LG*, 70.

5. Interview with Jo Pagano, winter 1963, CCP.

6. Interview with Meta Carpenter, December 1963, CCP.

7. https://northshorepipes.com/listing/541700111/a-very-unique-historical-straight.

8. Interviews with Meta Carpenter, n.d., CCP.

9. Starr, 347–48.

10. *SL*, 167.

11. http://www.imdb.com/title/tt0036218/?ref_=fn_al_tt_1.

12. *FB* (1974), 1140.

13. *SL*, 167.

14. https://en.m.wikipedia.org/wiki/North_Atlantic_air_ferry_route_in_World_War_II.

15. See Rollyson, *Lillian Hellman: Her Legend and Her Legacy*, 207.

16. March 1, 1943, UVA.

17. *LG*, 104.

18. *SL*, 170–71.

19. *SL*, 173–74.

20. *CGBC*, vol. 4, x–xii.

21. N.d., JBP.
22. *CGBC,* vol. 4, ix.
23. The only film that approaches Faulkner's panoramic visualization of the war is Frank Capra's *Why We Fight,* a seven-part documentary that covers every battle theater of World War II.
24. See Solomon, 119, for Faulkner's work on *God Is My Co-Pilot,* including the creation of a Hawksian hero along the lines of Fonda.
25. Fonda enlisted in the navy and was not available for the film.
26. Faulkner was not able to get those men in Abbeville to listen to a talk about the war, but he put their listening to a Joe Louis heavyweight title match to good use.
27. *CGBC,* vol. 4, xxxv–vi.
28. *CGBC,* vol. 4, xxx.
29. *SL,* 175–76. Was Faulkner referring to the Silver Shirt Legion of America?
30. Larry Wells, interview by the author, July 2017.
31. *SL,* 175.
32. *SL,* 177.
33. JBP. In *FB* (1984), Blotner supposes that Estelle's letter "must have seemed perverse" to Faulkner. Beware of those "must have beens" in biography, which only signal what the biographer does not know.
34. MFP.
35. August 18, 1943, MFP.
36. *CGBC,* vol. 4, xxxix.
37. *SL,* 178.
38. Interview with Henry Hathaway, February 26, 1977, CCP.
39. Interview with Stephen Longstreet, June 8, 1965, JBP.

10. Fables of Fascism

1. December 2, 1943, MFP.
2. November, 4, 1943, MFP.
3. December 21, 1943, MFP.
4. October 8, 1943, JBP.
5. Interview with Vicki and Dean, March 18, 1965, JBP.
6. *SL,* 178–79.
7. *SL,* April 22, 1944, 180–81.
8. *LG,* 60–61.
9. Postmarked April 14, 1944, JBP.
10. Kawin, ed., *To Have and Have Not,* 32.
11. McBride, ed., *Hawks on Hawks,* 78.
12. McCarthy, 372.
13. Kawin, ed., *To Have and Have Not,* interviewed Carpenter about her work on the picture. For a critique of Kawin, see B. Robbins, "The Pragmatic Modernist," 244.
14. McCarthy, 373.
15. Longstreet to Joseph Blotner, n.d., JBP.
16. N.d., JBP.
17. See Rollyson, *A Real American Character,* 109–13.

18. Kawin, introduction to *To Have and Have Not,* ed. Kawin.
19. Williamson.
20. Crowther was not alone. Marcy Townsley (*Austin American*, January 27, 1945) uses the same word.
21. Farber, *Farber on Film,* ed. Polito, 196–97.

11. Hollywoodism

1. *LG,* 63, 75, 77.
2. *SL,* 181.
3. N.d., MFP.
4. February 22, 1944, MFP.
5. May 22, 1944, MFP.
6. Interview with Jo Pagano, winter 1963, CCP.
7. VJR.
8. *CGBC,* vol. 2, 27–29.
9. Blotner, "Faulkner in Hollywood," 291.
10. McClelland, 356.
11. Wald, 130.
12. September 30, 1944, MFP.
13. *LG,* 66–67.
14. *LG,* 58.
15. McCarthy, 379.
16. Dardis, *Some Time in the Sun.*
17. Farber, 287.
18. Agee, 502.
19. Solomon, 183–84.
20. Wood, 170. Furthman worked mainly on the last part of the script, after Faulkner and Brackett had concluded their work. I have concentrated on the parts Faulkner and Brackett worked on together, although Furthman's material fits the Faulkner-Brackett conception of the story quite well (see Kawin, *Faulkner and Film,* 113).
21. Solomon, 181.
22. McBride, ed., *Focus on Howard Hawks,* 51.
23. *SL,* 186–87. Phillips, 49, may be right that this is Faulkner's wry farewell to Hollywood, but it is also an expression of affection for a film he had wanted to work on with Howard Hawks from the moment they had considered doing so.

12. Hollywood and Horror, Home and Horses

1. See the discussion of Faulkner's work on *Mildred Pierce* in LaValley, 34–36; B. Robbins, "The Pragmatic Modernist," 249–55; and Solomon, 172–74.
2. Faulkner's treatment is included in Faulkner, *Country Lawyer,* ed. Brodsky and Hamblin. See Solomon, 160–64, for more discussion of *The Damned Don't Cry* and its impact on Faulkner's fiction, especially *Go Down, Moses.*
3. Zanuck's response is in the Howard Hawks Papers, Brigham Young University.
4. McCarthy, 535.

5. Lee Caplin to Carl Rollyson, email, May 26, 2018.

6. Rose, 96.

7. Moore.

8. Rose, 105, states that Miss Rosa is draining men of their blood, reflecting Faulkner's fear of women, but this is not what the novel reveals about Rosa or about southern women, as Rosa's relations with her sister Ellen and Judith make clear.

9. Vera and the countess may actually be the same person, in which case the Faulknerian idea of perpetuating family behavior by giving different generations the same name becomes a literal truth in the vampire tale.

10. See Kawin, *Faulkner and Film,* 136–43; and McCarthy, 403–4.

11. Wald, 130.

12. *SL,* 189.

13. *SL,* 186.

14. *SL,* 188.

15. *SL,* 189–90, 201.

16. *SL,* 187.

17. *SL,* 191.

18. Faulkner to Geller, Warner Brothers Archives, University of Southern California.

19. Malcolm's letters home, February 2, 23, and March 19, 1945, MFP.

20. *B,* 81–83.

21. *SL,* 192.

22. The script is available at the Academy of Motion Pictures Arts and Sciences.

23. *SL,* 194–95.

24. Blotner, "Faulkner in Hollywood," 294–95.

25. Interview with Malcolm Cowley, April 23, 1965, CCP.

26. Purcell does not appear in Faulkner's unrevised first draft.

27. Faulkner, *Stallion Road,* ed. Brodsky and Hamblin, xv–xvi.

28. Faulkner, *Stallion Road,* ed. Brodsky and Hamblin, xvi.

29. *CGBC,* vol. 2, 31–33.

30. *CGBC,* vol. 2, 33–34.

31. Faulkner, *Stallion Road,* ed. Brodsky and Hamblin, xxvi.

32. Faulkner, *Stallion Road,* ed. Brodsky and Hamblin, xxvi. In another version, *CWF,* 48, Longstreet has Faulkner quoting D. H. Lawrence: "Culture in Southern California is the jade arse of the world."

33. *CGBC,* vol. 2, 34.

34. Brodsky and Hamblin, *Stallion Road,* xvi.

13. "A Golden Book"

1. Wolff and Watkins, *Talking about William Faulkner,* 24.

2. In another version Dean Faulkner Wells remembered, Judith's father forbid her to marry a Yankee, and the brokenhearted girl threw herself off the Rowan Oak balcony, landed on the steps, and broke her neck (see Bezzerides, 71).

3. VJR.

4. *B,* 86–88.

5. Faulkner to A. P. Hudson, August 16, 1945, CCP.

6. *EDBS.*

7. Interview with Jill Faulkner, May 15, 1971, JBP.
8. Bezzerides, 92.
9. Bezzerides, 67.
10. Interview with Jill Faulkner, December 1969, JBP. See also Chabrier, 43.
11. *B*, 89–93.
12. Bezzerides, 94.
13. Bezzerides, 95.
14. N.d., JBP.
15. Bezzerides, 94.
16. *ESPL*.
17. *SL*, 211.
18. *SL*, 223.
19. *SL*, 217–18.
20. *CGBC*, vol. 2, 35.
21. Faulkner to McDermid, January 29, 1946, Warner Brothers Archives, University of Southern California.
22. *CGBC*, vol. 2, 39–40.
23. *SL*, 233.
24. *SL*, 182.
25. *SL*, 184–85.
26. *SL*, 196–98.
27. *FC*, 30.
28. *SL*, 205.
29. *FC*, 47.
30. *SL*, 222–23.
31. *FC*, 57.
32. Interview with Leo Rosten, July 10, 1966, JBP.
33. *SL*, 211–13.
34. *SL*, 217.
35. *SL*, 222.
36. https://www.christies.com/lotfinder/Lot/faulkner-william-the-portable -faulkner-edited-with-5331762-details.aspx.
37. *SL*, 233.
38. This review by Edwin Seaver and Robin McKown was reprinted in the *Arlington (IL) Heights Herald* (July 26); *Chicago Daily Herald* (July 26); *Delphi (IN) Citizen* (August 1); *Odessa (TX) American* (August 4); and *Lubbock (TX) Avalanche Journal* (August 25, 1946); Gordon's review is extensively quoted in the *Kingsport (TN) Times News* (May 26).
39. *SL*, 222.
40. *SL*, 222.

14. Impasse

1. Simons's account: n.d., CCP.
2. On March 17, 1965, Jimmy Faulkner told Blotner that William Faulkner had wanted a son and that Estelle's inability to provide one had disturbed the marriage. The basis for this statement is not clear.

3. These master's theses are conveniently available at UVA.
4. *SL,* 234–35.
5. *FC,* 97.
6. *SL,* 238.
7. Interviews with Ike Roberts, spring 1950 and August 21, 1951, CCP.
8. *SL,* 244.
9. *SL,* 245.
10. See Trotter, 136–48.
11. *SL,* 246.
12. *SL,* 247.
13. *SL,* 248–49.
14. *CWF,* 67.
15. *CWF,* 82.
16. *SL,* 249.
17. *SL,* 251–52.
18. See Hemingway, *Selected Letters,* ed. Baker, 623–25.
19. *SL,* 253.
20. Interview with Phil Stone, April 5, 1950, CCP.
21. VJR.
22. *LG,* 145.
23. *LG,* 147.
24. Sandra Moore and William Lewis Jr., n.d., interviews with the author.
25. William Lewis Jr., n.d., interview with the author.
26. *LG,* 66–69.
27. *LG,* 148.
28. N.d., JBP.
29. N.d., JBP.
30. *B,* 116. See Hamblin, "Lucas Beauchamp, Ned Barnett, and William Faulkner's 1940 Will."
31. *SL,* 257.
32. *FB* (1974), 1242.

15. New Audiences

1. Interview with Eric Devine, Autumn 1965, CCP.
2. *SL,* 262.
3. *SL,* 266.
4. *SL,* 262.
5. *FC,* 100.
6. Broach, LDBP.
7. July 17, 1948, CCP.
8. *EDBS.*
9. *SL,* 276.
10. *SL,* 276.
11. Both interviews are included in *LITG,* 59–62.
12. Cowley's notes and Blotner's interview with Bill Fielden, October 13, 1964, are in JBP.

13. On the first edition of *Go Down, Moses,* Faulkner wrote, "For Muriel Cowley a charming & delightful Lady with gratitude," signing his name and adding "Sherman, Conn 25 Oct. 1948" (see Brodsky and Hamblin, eds., *Selections from the William Faulkner Collection,* 95).

14. *FC,* 108–14.

15. *SL,* 277–79.

16. The heading is quoted from the *Philadelphia Inquirer,* September 26, 1948.

17. Malcolm Cowley in the *New Republic* (October 18, 1948) took a line similar to Wilson's—accusing Faulkner of preachiness. Some critics still find Wilson's critique persuasive (see, for example, Sundquist, 148–52).

18. http://faulkner.drupal.shanti.virginia.edu/node/9852?canvas#.

19. Matthews, *William Faulkner: Seeing through the South,* 227.

20. Jenkins, 278. See also Monaghan, 54: "When he makes use of such stereotyped and insulting terms as 'Sambo,' Stevens shows quite clearly that even a man consciously dedicated to racial equality can, if he adopts a generalising habit of mind, quickly translate generalisation into dehumanisation and deprecation, a mental progression which forms the basis of much racial prejudice." Faulkner, so far as I know, never used the word "Sambo" in his correspondence.

21. Polk, "Man in the Middle: Faulkner and the Southern White Moderate," in *Children of the Dark House.*

22. Towner, *Faulkner on the Color Line,* 55.

23. *SL,* 262.

24. For more on Faulkner's revisions, see Stephen Railton, "Manuscripts &c: *Intruder in the Dust,*" Digital Yoknapatawpha, University of Virginia, http://faulkner.drupal.shanti.virginia.edu/node/10659?canvas (date added to project: 2016).

25. West's classic essay, first published in the *New Yorker,* is reprinted in her collection *A Train of Powder.* See also Rollyson, *Rebecca West,* 255–56.

26. FWP.

27. For examples of Faulkner's work on the film, see Stephen Railton, "Manuscripts &c: *Intruder in the Dust,*" Digital Yoknapatawpha, University of Virginia, http://faulkner.drupal.shanti.virginia.edu/node/10659?canvas (date added to project: 2016).

28. Degenfelder, 138; Fadiman, 27.

29. Philip K. Schemer, "Brown Champions Work on Location," *Los Angeles Times,* October 30, 1949, https://www.newspapers.com/image/381266839/.

30. Interview with Emily Stone, April 11, 1950, CCP.

31. Interview with Phil Stone, April 11, 1950, CCP.

32. *Kingsport (TN) News,* April 9, 1948, quoting an item in the *Jackson (MS) Daily News,* https:xwww.newspapers.com/image/68635042/.

33. Fadiman, 29.

34. Interview with Ben Maddow, February 25, 1977, CCP.

35. Bob Thomas, "Picture with Negro Theme Is Finished," *Pampa (TX) Daily News,* May 8, 1949, https://newspaperarchive.com/pampa-daily-news-may-08–1949-p-4/.

36. Interview with Phil Stone, April 11, 1950, CCP.

37. Fadiman, 37.

38. Fadiman, 32.

39. *LG,* 158.

40. Parini, 307.

41. Snell, 265.

42. *SL,* 286.

43. G. Allen Johnson, "Star Presents a New Look at a 1949 Film about a Lynching," https://www.sfchronicle.com/movies/article/Star-presents-a-new-look-at-1949 -film-about-a-11183938.php#photo-12992542.

44. Broach.

45. *LG,* 158.

46. Fadiman, 36.

47. *LG,* 159.

48. Interview with Dean Faulkner Wells, January 1964, CCP.

49. Elizabeth Spencer, "Film Premiere of 'Intruder' Described by Novelist Spencer," *Delta Democrat-Times,* October 16, 1949, https://www.newspapers.com/image /21421513/.

50. Snell, 269.

51. Bess Condon to Aaron Condon, n.d., CCP.

52. Interview with Dean Faulkner Wells, January 1964, CCP.

53. *LG,* 159.

54. Faulkner wrote as much in a presentation copy of *A Green Bough,* inscribed to his cousin Vance Carter Broach (see Brodsky and Hamblin, eds., *Selections from the William Faulkner Collection,* 74).

55. *LG,* 161.

56. Fadiman, 31.

57. *EDBS.*

58. Gene Roper Sr., "Oxford Blazes with Glory for Premier of 'Intruder,'" *Jackson Clarion-Ledger,* October 12, 1949, https://www.newspapers.com/image /179715276/.

59. "Memphis Censors Approve 'Intruder' with Reservations," *Tennessean,* September 9, 1949, https://www.newspapers.com/image/112041978/; Fadiman, 38.

60. "Film Industry Is Showing Maturity, *Akron Beacon Journal,* November 11, 1949.

61. Jenkins, 267.

62. Helen Bower, "Star Gazing," *Detroit Free Press,* December 4, 1949, https://www .newspapers.com/image/97717741/.

63. Fadiman, 36.

64. Fadiman, 38–39.

65. *SL,* 293.

66. Schwartz, *Creating Faulkner's Reputation,* 57.

67. For these examples and others, see Inge, "William Faulkner, James Avati, and the Art of the Paperback Novel."

68. Schwartz, *Creating Faulkner's Reputation,* 59.

69. Earle, 241, suggests that Lucas is not immediately recognizable as a black man, especially since his head and backside are viewed from a distance. Perhaps, although the four-color cover shows the flesh tones of the white people as opposed to the black head. A cursory glance at the cover, however, might not take in the black-white opposition.

70. Inge, "William Faulkner," 52; see also Earle, 235–38.

16. Coded Autobiography

1. *SL*, 280.
2. Snell, 267–68.
3. *CGBC*, vol. 2, 46.
4. For Stone's correspondence with Carey and Collins, see *CGBC*, vol. 2, 48–56.
5. Brodsky and Hamblin, eds., *Selections from the William Faulkner Collection*, 109.
6. The section heading is taken from the cover of the Signet edition of *Knight's Gambit*.
7. See Jay Watson.
8. Gray, 306.
9. *SL*, 292, 296.

17. Acclaim and Fame and Love

1. *SL*, 278–79.
2. *SL*, 274.
3. *SL*, 304.
4. Skei, *William Faulkner: The Short Story Career*, 106.
5. Critics have engaged in a wide range of arguments about the internal consistencies, inconsistencies, and themes within the six sections and between them. See, for example, Ferguson, 155–60; Carothers, 59–60; and Millgate, 270–75.
6. See Kinney, "Faulkner's Narrative Poetics and *Collected Stories*," for one of the most detailed accounts of the book's unity.
7. Paddock, *Contrapuntal in Integration*, 121.
8. *SL*, 299.
9. Interview with Meta Carpenter, n.d., CCP.
10. Interview with Judge S. B. Thomas of Greenville, MS, September 22, 1962, CCP.
11. Webb and Green, eds., *William Faulkner of Oxford*, 186.
12. *Jacksonville (IL) Daily Journal*, December 3, 1950, https://www.newspapers.com/image/48438126/?terms=Faulkner%2BNobel%2BPrize.
13. FWP.
14. "In Mississippi Everyone Has a Faulkner Story," *Southern Register*, Summer 2007.
15. "I Know William Faulkner," *Oxford Eagle*, November 16, 1950.
16. Snell, 275–76.
17. Interview, August 10, 1951, CCP.
18. *CGBC*, vol. 2, 64.
19. *Hattiesburg American*, December 6, 1950, https://www.newspapers.com/image/277075302/?terms=Faulkner%2BNobel%2BPrize.
20. Interview with Phyllis Cerf, December 10, 1965, CCP.
21. https://newspaperarchive.com/carbondale-southern-illinoisan-dec-13-1950-p-4/.
22. *St. Louis Post-Dispatch*, December 9, 1950, https://www.newspapers.com/image/140018035/?terms=Faulkner%2BNobel%2BPrize.
23. *CGBC*, vol. 2, 59.
24. Interview with Judge S. B. Thomas of Greenville, MS, September 22, 1962, CCP.
25. Cassette 16, July 14, 1973, MCR.
26. *SL*, 311.

27. *CGBC*, vol. 2, 59. Like her nephew, Bama did not use apostrophes in her contractions.

28. *SL*, 311.

29. *Portland Press Herald*, January 20, 1951, https://newspaperarchive.com/portland -press-herald-jan-20–1951-p-9/.

30. Minter, 219: "Many artists carefully avoid articulating their simpler convictions. Some do so out of fear of evoking ridicule—of being termed an aging scout master or a doddering fool. But Faulkner has always been better at taking chances than at exercising caution."

31. Marguerite McMillin, "Nobel Prizewinner Faulkner Prefers His Own Little World," *Corpus Christi Caller Times*, December 4, 1950, https://newspaperarchive .com/corpus-christi-caller-times-dec-10–1950-p-21/.

32. https://newspaperarchive.com/troy-record-nov-15–1950-p-6/; see also *Jackson Daily News*, November 11, 1950, assigning Faulkner to the "privy school of literature."

33. *St. Louis Post-Dispatch*, November 12, 1950, https://www.newspapers.com/image /138184330/?terms=Faulkner%2BNobel%2BPrize.

34. *Miami News*, November 14, 1950, https://www.newspapers.com/image/298551571/ ?terms=Faulkner%2BNobel%2BPrize.

35. *SL*, 312.

36. Interview with Else Jonsson, March 27, 1974, JBP.

37. Aunt Bama enjoyed a comment by Mrs. Collins, Carvel's wife: "Mr. Faulkner made the King of Sweden look like a peasant" (Aunt Bama to Carvel Collins, n.d., CCP).

38. Interview with Else Jonsson, September 12, 1967, JBP.

39. Gresset, "A Public Man's Private Voice," 70, suggests as much.

40. Interview with Else Jonsson, March 28, 1964, JBP.

41. Interview with Else Jonsson, March 28, 1964, JBP.

42. Interview with Else Jonsson, March 27, 1964, JBP.

43. *SL*, 314.

44. *SL*, 315. Faulkner as farmer has often been treated as a joke, a ruse on his part to fend off intruders into his literary life, which he safeguarded as a trade secret. Rose C. Fleming, a public information specialist for the Mississippi Soil Conservation Service, remarked that Faulkner "took seriously the admonition to 'use each acre according to its capabilities and treat it according to its needs.'" Henry Butler, a soil conservation technician, remembered that Faulkner "carried his lunch and stayed with us all one day when we installed the dragline ditch." The technicians were creating "diversion terraces and ditches round the bottom-land fields so they could be worked. . . . He was interested in knowing about all aspects of conservation—why we located the ditch the way we did—how we used the instruments. He was always interesting to talk to, but in the out-of-doors he seemed to open up." Fleming's report is in RHMP.

45. *SL*, 321.

46. *SL*, 318.

47. *SL*, 339.

48. *SL*, 342.

49. *SL*, 381.
50. https://www.antikvariat.net/en/pat32653-jealousy-and-episode-two-stories
-faulkner-william-patrik-andersson-antikvaria; http://patrikandersson.net/bilder
/catalogue-patrik-andersson-no4.pdf.

18. What Mad Pursuit

1. See James G. Watson, *William Faulkner: Letters & Fictions,* for an astute interpretation of the role letters play in Faulkner's life and work.
2. Williams to Karl, n.d., Fred Karl Papers, Special Collections, Thomas Cooper Library, University of South Carolina.
3. N.d., UVA. Unless otherwise noted, all the quotations in this chapter are from *SL* and Hickman.
4. October 2, 1952, UVA.
5. Hickman, ed., *Remembering.*
6. Hickman, *William Faulkner and Joan Williams.*
7. Hickman, *William Faulkner and Joan Williams.*
8. Hickman, *William Faulkner and Joan Williams.*
9. Gray, 322–23.
10. Hickman, *William Faulkner and Joan Williams.*
11. JBP.
12. Hickman, *William Faulkner and Joan Williams.*
13. *CGBC,* vol. 2, 95.
14. Interview with Estelle Faulkner, March 2, 1965, JBP.
15. *CGBC,* vol. 2, 94.
16. *CGBC,* vol. 2, 96.
17. Sandra Moore, Kate Baker's daughter, n.d., interview by the author.
18. *CGBC,* vol. 2, 116; Mullener, 14.
19. Postmarked July 31, 1952.
20. VJR.
21. *CGBC,* vol. 2, 135.
22. *CGBC,* vol. 2, 135.
23. *CGBC,* vol. 2, 135.
24. *CGBC,* vol. 2, 136; Silver, 38–39.
25. *CGBC,* vol. 2, 136.
26. *CGBC,* vol. 2, 138.
27. Minter, 231.
28. Hickman, ed., *Remembering.*
29. *ESPL.* Faulkner had told Jill's high school principal and history teacher, Charles Nelson Sr., that "he had done more for Jill than any other person" (see Nelson and Goforth, 44).
30. Interview with Phil Mullen, November 18, 1966, JBP.
31. Interview with Charles Nelson Sr., August 10, 1951, CCP.
32. *ESPL.* UVA holds Faulkner's letters to his daughter. I have put the dates of letters in the text in parentheses. I am indebted to Marcella Sohm for sharing with me

her essay "'She Was My Heart's Darling': Faulkner as Father, through Letters to his Daughter Jill at College," based on her reading of the UVA letters.

33. *ESPL.*
34. *ESPL.*
35. *CGBC,* vol. 2, 93.
36. *CGBC,* vol. 2, 94.
37. *CGBC,* vol. 2, 116.
38. *CGBC,* vol. 2, 134.
39. *CGBC,* vol. 2, 135.
40. *CGBC,* vol. 2, 136.
41. *CGBC,* vol. 2, 138.
42. Hickman, *William Faulkner and Joan Williams.*
43. Hickman, *William Faulkner and Joan Williams.*
44. Hickman, *William Faulkner and Joan Williams.*
45. Bezzerides, *William Faulkner: A Life on Paper,* 104.
46. Williams's memoir is included in the Open Road ebook edition of her novel.
47. *SL,* 328. Part of the letter was used as a blurb for Greene's novel.

19. Two Lives / Two Faulkners

1. See https://3times.org/a-door-ajar-purser-and-mayfield/.
2. For Purser's reminiscence, see *CWF,* 90–93.
3. *SL,* 75, 78, 84.
4. *SL,* 298.
5. Interview transcript, n.d., CCP.
6. *SL,* 302–7, 311; *Louisville (KY) Courier Journal,* November 19, 1950, https://www.newspapers.com/image/108364063/.
7. McCarthy, 485.
8. Interview with Aunt Bama, October 5 or 6, 1951, CCP.
9. *CGBC,* vol. 2, 61–62.
10. http://www.sothebys.com/en/auctions/ecatalogue/2013/books-manuscripts-n09066/lot.259.html.
11. Faulkner's letter: CCP.
12. McCarthy, 486.
13. "Hommage à Dean Faulkner Wells," by Francois Busnel, Le Grande Librairie, France 5 Television, interview, July 10, 2011, made available by Larry Wells on vimeo: https://vimeo.com/312333051.
14. *CGBC,* vol. 2, 62.
15. Cassette 3, October 27, 1973, UM.
16. George Sidney's dissertation remains a useful study of the tensions inherent in Faulkner's effort to conform to studio standards. See, for example, 184: "Thus twice during his screen writing career Faulkner repudiated Hollywood's 'manual of style,' his obligations to his employers, his assumed role—and wrote for himself." Sidney is referring to *Banjo on My Knee* and "Country Lawyer," underestimating how many times Faulkner went against Hollywood orthodoxy in *Sutter's*

Gold, Drums along the Mohawk, and *The Left Hand of God,* although I am not certain Sidney saw Faulkner's adaptation of Barrett's novel.

17. Karl, 819, mistakenly assumes that Faulkner was "reunited" with Bogart, but the released film is based on another writer's script, with a different director, long after Faulkner had departed from Hollywood.

18. Faulkner and Brennan shared the same anti–New Deal, anticollectivist views. They only cared about individuals and enjoyed the company of all types, who taught Faulkner and Brennan so much of what they needed to know in order to write and to perform.

19. *WFTF,* 923; Solomon, 13–14, 197–98.

20. Maud Falkner to Sallie Burns, January 16, 1951, CCP.

21. Solomon, 211, compares Hank's narration, especially at the beginning of the film, to Faulkner's "anxious habit of qualification" and his long, conjunction-filled sentences that wind through *Requiem for a Nun.*

22. Lowrey to Stone, February 28, 1951, *CGBC,* vol. 2, 63.

23. The film was not released until July 1952, but I think one reason Faulkner liked it is because it accorded with his redemptive vision in *The Left Hand of God.*

24. Solomon, 204.

25. See Robbins, 356, for more parallels between *Mildred Pierce* and *Requiem for a Nun.*

26. Roberts, 218.

27. Rampton, 162.

28. Wittenberg, *The Transfiguration of Biography,* 218.

29. Gray, 314.

30. Snell, 281.

31. Gray, 314–15.

32. Polk, *Faulkner's "Requiem for a Nun,"* 19–20.

33. Weinstein, *Becoming Faulkner,* 216.

34. Gavin Stevens also elicited an ambivalence in Howe that would fuel critical debate for decades to come: "I still don't know whether he is wisdom incarnate or a monster of cruelty." See, for example, Polk's critical study of *Requiem for a Nun* and Jay Watson's book on Stevens's career in Faulkner's fiction.

20. In and Out of Phase

1. William Faulkner to Meta Carpenter, August 8, 1951, CCP.

2. *SL,* 318. For a discussion of the differences between the produced play and the novel, see Polk, ed., *"Requiem for a Nun": Preliminary Holograph and Typescript Materials,* William Faulkner Manuscripts 19, ix.

3. William Faulkner to Meta Carpenter, August 8, 1951, CCP.

4. https://www.bonhams.com/auctions/23477/lot/568/.

5. Interview with Edmund Kohn, n.d., JBP.

6. Interview with Aunt Bama, August 5 or 6, 1951, CCP; Collins to Aunt Bama, January 21, 1952, CCP.

7. Ober to Ray Stark at Famous Artists, April 6, 1951, UVA.

8. *SL,* 319–21.

9. Chabrier, 43–44.

10. Ober to William Faulkner, December 18, 1952, UVA.

11. During one Princeton class when questioned about some difficulties with a literary text, Faulkner observed that he did not think "literature was written for Princeton sophomores" (interview with Richard Ludwig, January 1964, CCP).

12. Kaledin's meetings with Faulkner occurred on October 10 and 12, 1951. He wrote about them for Carvel Collins. Kaledin became an American studies scholar at MIT, which is perhaps where he met Collins, who also taught there. For Kaledin, see http://news.mit.edu/2016/professor-emeritus-arthur-kaledin-dies-1206.

13. *LITG*, 65–67.

14. Interview with Ike Roberts, August 21, 1951, CCP.

15. Interviews with Vicki and Dean, March 18, 1965, CCP; and with Christine Drake, August 19, 1964, JBP.

16. *CGBC*, vol. 2, 71.

17. *SL*, 331–32.

18. *SL*, 340.

19. *SL*, 330–32.

20. *WFCR*, 94–95.

21. James Silver, footnote 7 in his paper "William Alexander Percy: The Aristocrat and the Anthropologist," 10, CCP.

22. *SL*, 339.

23. The doctors' notes and Commins's diary entries from September 18 to late October (Estelle's note is undated) are in LDBP.

24. *SL*, 342.

25. Stone to Collins, November 13, 1952, JBP.

26. *CGBC*, vol. 2, 99.

27. *CGBC*, vol. 2, 104.

28. *SL*, 344.

21. Steal Away

1. *SL*, 344.

2. *CGBC*, vol. 2, 105; *SL*, 345.

3. Malcolm's diary for this period is at UVA.

4. Coughlan, 24–25.

5. The story is included in *Uncollected Stories of William Faulkner*.

6. Interview with Joan Williams, August 22, 1965, JBP.

7. This is Michel Gresset's view as well (see Gresset, "Weekend, Lost and Revisted," 175).

8. *WFCR*, 96–97.

9. Commins, 199–200.

10. *SL*, 346–47.

11. Malcolm Franklin's diary, UVA.

12. *SL*, 348.

13. William Faulkner to Meta Carpenter, May 15, 1953, CCP.

14. *SL*, 349.

15. *CGBC*, vol. 2, 112–13.

16. See Hickman, *William Faulkner and Joan Williams*.
17. *CGBC*, vol. 2, 113.
18. *SL*, 352.
19. *SL*, 354. The letter is undated but appears to have been written in mid-October 1953.
20. JBP.
21. *CGBC*, vol. 2, 120.
22. *CGBC*, vol. 2, 121.
23. Nelson and Goforth, 90.
24. *SL*, 354.
25. Chabrier, xiii.
26. Nelson and Goforth, 17.
27. The striking aspect of the Nelson and Goforth book is its evocation of Faulkner as performance artist.
28. Commins, 208.
29. Interview with Estelle Faulkner, March 12, 1965, JBP.
30. *CGBC*, vol. 2, 124.
31. *CGBC*, vol. 2, 125.
32. *CGBC*, vol. 2, 126.
33. *CGBC*, vol. 2, 141.
34. *CGBC*, vol. 2, 129.
35. *SL*, 356.
36. *SL*, 358.
37. *CGBC*, vol. 2, 129.

22. Civilization and Its Discontents

1. Stein, 295.
2. *CGBC*, vol. 2, 138.
3. WF to Saxe Commins, January 15, 1954, JBP.
4. Jean Stein Van den Heuvel, Dec 6, 1976, CCP.
5. John Waters, August 1, 2018, interview with the author.
6. Chabrier, 56.
7. Kennedy Fraser, "American Parnassus: Jean Stein and Her Friends," http://www.sothebys.com/en/news-video/blogs/all-blogs/sotheby-s-at-large/2017/11/american-parnassus-jean-stein-friends.html.
8. Philip Weiss, "Remembering Jean Stein," http://mondoweiss.net/2017/05/remembering-jean-stein/.
9. https://catalogue.swanngalleries.com/asp/fullCatalogue.asp?salelot=2462+++++121+&refno=++736415&saletype=.
10. *CGBC*, vol. 2, 136.
11. *CGBC*, vol. 2, 130.
12. *CGBC*, vol. 2, 133.
13. Stein, 295.
14. *WFCR*, 118.
15. March 19, 1954, UVA.

16. Commins, 206.
17. *SL*, 362; McCarthy, 517–24.
18. See Solomon, 245.
19. April 13 and April 15, 1954, *CGBC*, vol. 2, 140–42.
20. *CGBC*, vol. 2, 144.
21. *LITG*, 162.
22. *CGBC*, vol. 2, 144; *SL*, 364.
23. UVA.
24. *SL*, 363.
25. *SL*, 365.
26. Jane Eads, "Wm Faulkner Attends Party on Maryland Estate," *Greenwod (SC) Index Journal*, July 2, 1954, https://www.newspapers.com/image/69463435/?terms=Paul %2BSummers%2BJill%2BFaulkner.
27. *LITG*, 77–79.
28. Cerf to William Faulkner, June 28, 1954, UVA.
29. Interview with V. P. Ferguson, June 29, 1965, CCP. Faulkner made this comment in the summer of 1954. I have not been able to identify Dr. Busby.
30. See Bleikasten, *William Faulkner*, 432; Wittenberg, *The Transfiguration of Biography*, 221–22; Minter 229; Parini, 361; Rampton, 165; Karl 754, 880. See Kodat, 82, for a summary of critical response to *A Fable*.
31. See, for example, *SL*, 233.
32. Gray, 333.
33. *SL*, 262.
34. Karl, 879, suggests that "Faulkner was being influenced by the heuristic quality of movies he was working on." Rampton, 164–65, inadvertently describes Faulkner's approach to *A Fable* in terms that would make for a good, wacky Hollywood movie: "a scrambled story, set in a foreign country that he had visited only a few times, about a war that he had tried to serve in but could not, centered around a quasi-supernatural manifestation of Christ during the trench warfare at Easter in 1918, complete with a cast of thousands, including a clutch of abstractions to serve as characters, and an account of the vicissitudes of racing a three-legged horse in America thrown in." Stefan Solomon's book has begun the long overdue process of integrating Faulkner's film work with his fiction.
35. Bleikasten, *William Faulkner*, 432, complains about "page upon page about uniforms," but Cecil B. DeMille would have been delighted.
36. Kodat, 84–85.
37. *SL*, 238.
38. In *The Wintering*, Almoner tells Amy, "I don't ever want you to be embarrassed by sentiment. That's one thing wrong with the world today."
39. *SL*, 178; see also Solomon, 148.
40. Solomon, 149.

23. Ambassador Faulkner

1. *SL*, 367.
2. *CGBC*, vol. 2, 152.

3. *WFCR,* 103.
4. *CGBC,* vol. 2, 151.
5. JBP.
6. *LITG,* 81.
7. *CWF,* 103.
8. *CGBC,* vol. 2, 157.
9. *CGBC,* vol. 2, 158–60.
10. *EDBS.*
11. Interview with Shelby Foote, November 20, 1965, JBP.
12. Interview with Bern Keating, March 25, 1963, CCP.
13. Collins to Sallie Burns Faulkner, June 28, 1963, CCP.
14. Sanderson, 15, 17.
15. Interview with James Silver, March 1963, CCP.
16. *LG,* 169.
17. Interview with Ella Somerville, September 24, 1962, CCP.
18. Interview with Ella Somerville, September 24, 1962, CCP.
19. *LG,* 170.
20. *CGBC,* vol. 2, 161.
21. *CGBC,* vol. 2, 169.
22. *CGBC,* vol. 2, 169.
23. October 31, 1954, *CGBC,* vol. 2, 170–71.
24. *CGBC,* vol. 2, 173–74.
25. Written December 13, postmarked December 16, *CGBC,* vol. 2, 174–75.
26. *SL,* 372.
27. *LITG,* 80–82.

24. Past and Present

1. *LITG,* 83.
2. See Ragan for a detailed discussion of Faulkner's significant alterations of the stories in order to shape *Big Woods* into an integrated work of art.
3. *SL,* 376–77.
4. Johnson, 250.
5. Interview with Robert Farley, n.d., CCP.
6. Faulkner's letters are included in *ESPL.*
7. McEwen did become a leader, serving as president of Alcorn's Student Council, but perhaps not the kind of leader Love envisioned. When a black faculty member attacked the NAACP, claiming the organization was alienating white people and limiting opportunities for black people, McEwen led a student protest and boycott of classes. He was expelled (see *Time,* March 18, 1957, http://content.time.com/time/magazine/article/0,9171,809204,00.html).
8. Eagles, 54.
9. My account of Earnest McEwen Jr. is drawn from conversations with his daughter, Gloria Burgess, and from her book *Pass It On!* (Two Sylvias Press, 2018). See also https://www.eomega.org/article/legacy-living.
10. The speech/essay is included in *ESPL.*

11. Interview with Dean William C. Jones of the University of Oregon, one of Faulkner's hosts, August 9, 1963, CCP.
12. Linscott to Fiedler, March 4 and 21, 1955, UVA.
13. Both articles are in *ESPL*.
14. *SL*, 378.
15. *SL*, 382.
16. Stone to Starr, October 12, 1955, NYPL.

25. East and West

1. See his question-and-answer sessions at Mary Washington University: http://faulkner.lib.virginia.edu/display/wfaudio08_2.
2. The film is available on YouTube: https://youtu.be/oNJP3cRq4lk. The voice-over narration is taken from a somewhat longer Faulkner text included in *ESPL*.
3. *LITG*, 86.
4. *LITG*, 89–90.
5. *LITG*, 98.
6. *LITG*, 100–101.
7. *LITG*, 101.
8. *LITG*, 144.
9. *LITG*, 131.
10. *LITG*, 122.
11. *LITG*, 175.
12. *LITG*, 149.
13. *LITG*, 165.
14. http://faulkner.lib.virginia.edu/display/wfaudio08_2.
15. *WFCR*, 121.
16. *SL*, 386.
17. *LITG*, 205.
18. *LITG*, 213.
19. https://www.vanityfair.com/style/2017/05/remembering-jean-stein.
20. https://www.nytimes.com/2017/05/20/style/remembering-jean-stein.html.
21. Henry Butler, who worked for the Soil Conservation Service that did work on Faulkner's farm, is quoted in a March 1970 press release from Rose C. Fleming, public information specialist with the Soil Conservation Service, RHMP.
22. RHMP, 354.
23. Grenier's interview is included in *LITG*, 215–27.
24. Chapsal's interview is included in *LITG*, 228–31.
25. Qtd. in *FB* (1984).
26. *FB* (1984).
27. Qtd. in RHMP. J. R. Cofield, Faulkner's Oxford photographer, also supplied this gloss in RHMP, 441, August 12, 1970: "I will say, however, that 'friend William' felt very strong about the mistreatment of (WORTHY) darkies (but like the balance of we Southerners), he had no use what-so-ever for a 'trifling Negro' (with his hand poked out) and not willing to work for his 'daily-bread,' as all humans are supposed to do. . . . I too have very dear friends among the Colored-race."

28. McCarthy, 523: Harold Jack Bloom reported Faulkner said "things about blacks that were, to say the least, not very nice, although publicly he cultivated a paternalistic stance toward them."
29. RHMP, 238.
30. Donald Nuechterlein to Patricia Garcia, email, forwarded to Carl Rollyson, April 17, 2017.
31. Nuechterlein, 75.
32. *SL,* 388.
33. I have found no letters from Howland after Faulkner returned home to Mississippi in the fall of 1955.
34. *SL,* 387.

26. North and South

1. *ESPL.* Till had been afflicted with polio and a stutter.
2. Fargnoli and Golay, 234.
3. Interview with James Silver, April 1963, CCP.
4. Interview with Mrs. James Silver, March 23, 1963, CCP. Other details are derived from Silver, *Running Scared,* 36–43.
5. Interview with Ashford Little, n.d., CCP.
6. March 29, 1966, JBP.
7. *CGBC,* vol. 2, 185.
8. Silver, 43–44.
9. *SL,* 388.
10. Stecopoulos, 127–28.
11. For John Faulkner's letters and Faulkner's three replies, see Meriwether, ed., *A Faulkner Miscellany,* 135–38.
12. *ESPL.*
13. C. Adler to William Faulkner, March 17, 1956, JBP.
14. Akia to William Faulkner, March 27, 1956, JBP.
15. The interview appeared in two different versions: on March 4 in the Sunday *Times* and in the *Reporter* on March 22. The *Reporter* version is included in *LITG,* 258–64.
16. To Joan Williams, *SL,* 408, Faulkner admitted, "I don't know why I thought then that drinking could help, but that's what I was doing, a lot of it."
17. *FC,* 111.
18. Weinstein, *Becoming Faulkner,* 116.
19. For Faulkner's letter and Howe's reply, see *LITG,* 265–66.
20. *SL,* 391.
21. "The Life and Times of Fr. David Kirk," *Road to Emmaus* 9, no. 2 (Spring 2008): 11–12, http://www.roadtoemmaus.net/back_issue_articles/RTE_33/THE_ROAD_TO_EMMAUS_RUNS_THR_HARLEM.pdf.
22. *SL,* 398.
23. Williamson.
24. Silver, 60–61.
25. Williamson.

26. *SL,* 393.
27. *SL,* 396.
28. Towner, 127.
29. *SL,* 390.
30. *EDBS.*

27. Going On

1. *SL,* 390.
2. *SL,* 391.
3. Aimee Bell to the author, email, June 30, 2018.
4. *SL,* 393.
5. George Christy Talks about Rupert Murdoch, Jean Stein, West of Eden, Old Hollywood and More!, *Beverly Hills Courier,* http://bhcourier.com/george-christy-talks-about-rupert-murdoch-jean-stein-west-of-eden-old-Hollywood-and-more/.
6. The interview is included in *LITG,* 237–55.
7. *SL,* 398.
8. Maud Falkner to Sallie Burns, June 19, 1956, CCP.
9. *CGBC,* vol. 2, 195.
10. *SL,* 402.
11. Faulkner's letter is included in *SL,* 404, and the responses to his letters and questionnaire are at UVA.
12. Hall.
13. *CGBC,* vol. 2, 199.
14. *LG,* 169.
15. *LG,* 171.
16. WF to Saxe Commins, January 25, 1957, JBP.
17. Interview with Truman Capote, December 29, 1967, JBP.
18. http://faulkner.lib.virginia.edu/display/wfaudio10#wfaudio10.30.
19. For the details from Commins's diary, see LDBP.
20. Saxe Commins to Benjamin Gilbert, February 21 and March 11, 1957, LDBP.
21. Postmarked February 18, 1956, LDBP.
22. Interview with James Silver, September 21, 1962, CCP.

28. Writer-in-Residence

1. Maud Falkner to Sallie Burns, CCP. The details of Faulkner's Virginia life are taken from my conversations with those who came in contact with him in Charlottesville, and also from the university's excellent website: http://faulkner.lib.virginia.edu. I have drawn on several reminiscences posted on the website: http://faulkner.lib.virginia.edu/page?id=essays&section=intro.
2. For Faulkner's letter and Churchill's reply, see http://faulkner.lib.virginia.edu/page?id=essays&section=intro.
3. For Faulkner's 1931 and 1956 letters, see http://faulkner.lib.virginia.edu/page?id=essays&section=intro.

4. http://faulkner.lib.virginia.edu/page?id=essays&section=intro.

4. http://faulkner.lib.virginia.edu/page?id=essays&section=intro.

5. Blotner, *An Unexpected Life,* 159.

6. Blotner, *An Unexpected Life,* 161.

7. Blotner, *An Unexpected Life,* 162.

8. Said to me on one of my visits to Richmond.

9. *WFCR,* 135–46.

10. Interview with Maud Falkner, April 2, 1950, CCP.

11. http://faulkner.lib.virginia.edu/display/wfaudio08_2.

12. March 12, 1957, CCP.

13. Bess Lyon Eager to Lucy Somerville Howarth, July 16, 1965, CCP.

14. http://faulkner.lib.virginia.edu/display/wfaudio09_2#wfaudio09_2.9.

15. Izard and Hieronymus, 246, 243.

16. http://faulkner.lib.virginia.edu/display/wfaudio12_2#wfaudio12_2.14.

17. Beck, *Man in Motion,* 15–16.

18. Jay Watson, 213.

19. Karl, 962.

20. Blotner, *An Unexpected Life,* 175.

21. Wittenberg, *The Transfiguration of Biography,* 229.

22. *CGBC,* vol. 2, 213.

23. *SL,* 407.

24. We don't even learn McCarron's first name until *The Mansion.*

25. See Rampton, 142–43, for a subtle exegesis of this passage and of the late Faulkner who had not "written himself out."

26. Merve Emre, "On William Faulkner's Short Turn as a Cold War PR Man," https://thebaffler.com/latest/reading-like-a-bureaucrat-emre.

27. Estelle Faulkner to Joseph Blotner, April 6, 1967, JBP.

28. Faulkner usually signed Malcolm's books "To Malcolm Franklin" or to "Buddy," but on March 20, 1946, the inscription reads "For My Son" (see *Selections from the William Faulkner Collection of Louis Daniel Brodsky,* 92).

29. VJR.

30. *CGBC,* vol. 2, 214–15.

31. The two-hundred-word speech is in *ESPL.* For an account of the ceremony, see *FC,* 146–47.

32. George Thomas, April 20, 2017, interview by the author.

33. *EDBS.*

34. *LITG,* 267–69, 77–79.

35. White to Robert H. Moore, April 3, 1973, RHMP.

36. Maud Falkner to Sallie Burns, n.d., CCP.

37. *EDBS.*

38. Faulkner's letter is included in *ESPL* and *CGBC,* vol. 2, 219–20.

39. http://uvamagazine.org/articles/a_segregated_charlottesville.

40. For the question-and-answer session, see http://faulkner.lib.virginia.edu/display /wfaudio20_2#wfaudio20_2.10.

41. *SL,* 411.

42. Leslie Aldridge Westoff, "A Faulkner Flirtation," *New York Times Magazine,* May 10, 1987. I interviewed John Aldridge for my biography of Norman Mailer

and would never have supposed that this almost regal figure would have been quite so in awe of Faulkner, but then Aldridge's testimony reflects the impact of the Faulkner mystique (see Aldridge, 145–46).

43. April 17, 1958, UVA.
44. Ace Barber to Carvel Collins, December 2, 1966, CCP.
45. *CGBC*, vol. 2, 240.
46. The novel was published in 1955, but I have no evidence that Faulkner read it.
47. June 11, 1958, CCP.
48. *SL*, 413.
49. Commins, 225–26.
50. *SL*, 415.
51. https://www.nj.com/mercer/2010/11/lahieres_a_landmark_princeton.html.
52. Interview with Harry Celatano, n.d., CCP.
53. Interviews with Harry Celetano and Earl Miller, February 10, 1964, CCP.
54. *SL*, 418.
55. *SL*, 419.
56. *SL*, 425.
57. Interview with Mrs. Mary Winslow Chapman, November 21, 1973, CCP.
58. *ESPL*.
59. Interview with Carvel Collins, n.d., CCP.
60. *SL*, 432–33. Some of the off-the-cuff remarks were deleted in the book.

29. Full Circle

1. January 30, 1959, UVA.
2. Interview with Zachary Scott, December 30, 1964; interview with Estelle Faulkner, August 1963, JBP.
3. For accounts of the productions, see R. Davis; and Izard and Hieronymus; see also Arnold Weissberger to Harold Ober, February 12, 1959, UVA.
4. Izard and Hieronymus, 173–74.
5. Izard and Hieronymus, 172.
6. *SL*, 439.
7. Interview with William Clontz, March 28, 1968, CCP.
8. *CGBC*, vol. 2, 267.
9. *CGBC*, vol. 2, 267.
10. In 1958, Freeland came into a firm that had been a going concern since the 1890s, so well known, Stone thought, that he did not need a sign, saying people knew where to find him. But Freeland convinced him to put up a metal sign. A month later Faulkner came by, and when he learned Stone was not there, he sat on the front steps with Freeland and said, "Hal, it's great how some things never change." Freeland agreed, "Yes, sir." After a long pause, Faulkner said: "That sign, for instance. It's been there for as long as I can remember." Freeland wondered what to say and finally said, "Yes, sir." He never did know what that was about (Tommy Freeland, Hal Freeland's son, July 2014, interview with the author).
11. *CGBC*, vol. 2, 264.
12. Snell, 314.

13. Fanny Butcher, "Faulkner's 'Final' Snopes Novel by Far the Best in the Trilogy," *Chicago Tribune,* November 15, 1959, https://www.newspapers.com/image /370853483/?terms=Faulkner%2BThe%2BMansion.

14. Chabrier, 45.

15. For the rehabilitation of Linda Snopes Kohl as one of Faulkner's most strongly conceived characters, see, for example, Kang; Fulton; and Hagood, 82–86.

16. Oates, 310.

17. Broncano, 110, argues that Linda sides with the "dispossessed versus the capitalist, honor versus shameless ambition. Linda sides with Mink, as she sided with the Republican cause, and hers is a fight for justice, even if it requires allowing the murder of her own putative father, victimizing him and what he represents." But Faulkner was hardly this schematic. Mink is a misogynist and, in effect, a fascist, a wife beater, and a racist. History in Faulkner is more complex and ironic than Broncano allows.

18. *FAWP,* 60, 78, 89.

19. The references to Hollywood in the novel show how much it had become ingrained in Faulkner's imagination. Montgomery Ward Snopes, for example, "was now in Los Angeles, engaged in some quite lucrative adjunct or correlant to the motion picture industry or anyway colony."

20. See Matthews, "Many Mansions," 14–15, for a comparison of *The Mansion* and *Lolita.*

21. Fulton, 431.

22. See Towner, *Faulkner on the Color Line,* 112–13.

23. Roberts, 169.

24. https://en.m.wikipedia.org/wiki/Jaguar_Cars.

25. Roberts, 175.

26. Beck, *Man in Motion,* 183.

27. James G. Watson, *The Snopes Dilemma,* 178.

28. Roberts, 167.

29. James G. Watson, *The Snopes Dilemma,* 223.

30. See Hagood, 85.

30. Renascence

1. VJR.

2. Chabrier, 47.

3. VJR.

4. Emily Balch had provided the funding for Faulkner's writer-in-residence appointment. For the letter of offer, see http://faulkner.lib.virginia.edu/page?id=essays& section=intro.

5. *SL,* 450.

6. *SL,* 450.

7. Interview with Jimmy Falkner, n.d., JBP.

8. *EDBS.*

9. *SL,* 452.

10. VJR. For a summary of the way the State Department touted Faulkner's trip, see https://smallnotes.library.virginia.edu/2017/05/10/more-popular-than-an-astronaut/.

11. *WFCR,* 176–81.

12. VJR.

13. Barclay Rives to the author, email, April 20, 2017, enclosing an undated letter from Faulkner to his father.

14. June 29, 1962, UVA.

15. Article in *Memphis Commercial Appeal,* July 12 [no year], by Richard A Gentry; interview with Wortham, JBP. Jack Falkner also identified Carruthers in an interview, March 31, 1965, JBP.

16. Phil Mullen, "Faulkner's Gotta Let Oxford Be Proud of a Nobel Prize Winner, *Oxford Eagle,* November 16, 1950.

17. *B,* 97.

18. Yoshida, 198.

19. October 23, 1961, Bennett Cerf Papers, Butler Library, Rare Books and Manuscripts, Columbia University.

20. Interview with Taylor McElroy, March 23, 1965, JBP.

21. Wittenberg, *The Transfiguration of Biography,* 241.

22. For Faulkner's many uses of the word, see Carothers, "The Road to *The Reivers,"* 111–12.

23. https://en.m.wikipedia.org/wiki/Winton_Motor_Carriage_Company.

24. Peek and Hamblin, eds., 317.

25. Yoshida, 197.

26. See, for example, Karl; Gray; and Taylor, who deplore Ned as a racial stereotype.

27. Yoshida, 197–98.

28. Inge, *William Faulkner,* 91.

29. William Lewis Jr., July 2014, interview by the author.

30. JBP.

31. Peek and Hamblin, eds., 183–84.

32. *SL,* 458.

33. *LITG,* 270–81.

34. *FAWP,* 3–5.

35. *FAWP,* 71.

36. *FAWP,* 59.

37. *FAWP,* 68.

38. *FAWP,* 79.

39. *FAWP,* 82.

40. *FAWP,* 83.

41. *FAWP,* 99.

42. *FAWP,* 112.

43. Estelle Faulkner to Jim Silver, April 23, 1962, JBP.

44. *SL,* 461.

45. *SL,* 461–62.

46. Weinstein, *Becoming Faulkner.*

47. Parini, 415.

48. Parini, 415; Karl, 1030. Bleikasten, *William Faulkner: A Life through the Novels,* 469, notes: "Kennedy was unpopular in the South, and many white Mississippians saw him as an enemy of the United States or even a communist sympathizer." True, but would this have bothered Faulkner that much? He had deplored McCarthyism and had been willing to offend certain southerners with his stand on integration. Kennedy carried most of the old slaveholding South: Alabama, Arkansas, Georgia, Louisiana, Missouri, North Carolina, South Carolina, and Texas. Virginia voted for Richard Nixon, and Mississippi had a slate of unpledged electors, but Kennedy won the popular vote in the state by a 2-to-1 margin (see https://en.m.wikipedia.org/wiki/United_States_presidential_election,_1960 #Results_by_state).

49. *FC,* 148–49.

50. *ESPL.*

31. End of Days

1. *FAWP,* 62.
2. Interview with Emily Stone, January 27, 1963, CCP.
3. *CGBC,* vol. 2, 306.
4. *CGBC,* vol. 2, 307.
5. *MBB,* 203.
6. Interview with Meta Carpenter, n.d., CCP.
7. "Mr. Mack Remembers," *Oxford Eagle,* July 12, 1962.
8. Blotner, *An Unexpected Life,* 179.
9. My account of Faulkner's last day derives from Wolff and Watkins, *Talking about William Faulkner,* 176–78; Carvel Collins's interview with Ella Somerville, September 24, 1962; and Elliott and Bondurant, "Death on a Summer Night: Faulkner at Byhalia," which corrects errors in previous accounts, including material in Blotner's biographies.
10. Pulmonary edema is another strong possibility that Elliott and Bondurant discuss in their detailed examination of Faulkner's death. Their article provides extensive records of both Estelle and William Faulkner's treatments.
11. *MBB,* 3.
12. Falkner, *The Falkners of Mississippi,* 199–200.
13. My references to Dean in this section are from *EDBS.*
14. *MBB,* 5.
15. Snell, 321.
16. Interview with Jim Silver, n.d., CCP.
17. Klopfer's oral history, Butler Library, Columbia University.
18. From a draft of a letter responding to the August 4, 1963, article about Faulkner in *Vogue* by Nancy Hale, UVA.
19. Interview with Earl Wortham, March 23, 1963, CCP.

Bibliography

Abdur-Rahman, Aliyyah I. "What Moves at the Margin: William Faulkner and Race." In *The New Cambridge Companion to William Faulkner,* edited by John T. Matthews. Cambridge University Press, 2015. Kindle.

Adams, Franklin Pierce. *The Diary of Our Own Samuel Pepys.* Vol. 2. Simon and Schuster, 1935.

Adams, Richard. "Myth and Motion." In *"Light in August" and the Critical Spectrum,* edited by John B. Vickery and Olga W. Vickery. Wadsworth, 1971.

Agee, James. *Film Writing and Selected Journalism.* Library of America, 1996.

Aldridge, John. *The Devil in the Fire: Retrospective Essays on American Literature and Culture, 1951–1971.* Harper and Row, 1972.

Alexander, Marshall. "Faulkner's Metaphysics of Absence." In *Faulkner and Religion,* edited by Doreen Fowler and Ann J. Abadie. University Press of Mississippi, 1991.

Anderson, Elizabeth, and Gerald R. Kelly. *Miss Elizabeth: A Memoir.* Little, Brown, 1969.

Anderson, Sherwood. *Sherwood Anderson: Selected Letters.* Edited by Charles E. Modlin. University of Tennessee Press, 1984.

———. *Sherwood Anderson's Memoirs: A Critical Edition.* Edited by Ray Lewis White. University of North Carolina Press, 1969.

Arnheim, Rudolf. *Film as Art.* University of California Press, 2006.

Arnold, Edwin T. *Annotations to "Mosquitoes."* Garland, 1989.

Atkinson, Ted. *Faulkner and the Great Depression: Aesthetics, Ideology, and Cultural Politics.* University of Georgia Press, 2006.

Bacigalupo, Massimo. "New Information on William Faulkner's First Trip to Italy." *Journal of Modern Literature* 24 (Winter 2000–2001): 321–25.

Bailey, Kevin. "*Flags in the Dust* and the Material Culture of Class." In *Faulkner and Material Culture,* edited by Joseph R. Urgo and Ann J. Abadie. University Press of Mississippi, 2004.

Barker, Deborah. "Demystifying the Modern Mammy in *Requiem for a Nun.*" In *Faulkner and Film,* edited by Peter Lurie and Ann J. Abadie. University Press of Mississippi, 2014.

Bassett, John, ed. *William Faulkner: The Critical Heritage.* Routledge and Kegan Paul, 1975.

Beck, Warren. *Faulkner: Essays.* University of Wisconsin Press, 1976.

———. *Man in Motion: Faulkner's Trilogy.* University of Wisconsin Press, 1961.

Bezzerides, A. I. *William Faulkner: A Life on Paper.* University Press of Mississippi, 1980.

Black, Victoria Fielden. "Faulkner and Women." In *The South and Faulkner's Yoknapa-tawpha,* edited by Evans Harrington and Ann J. Abadie. University Press of Missis-sippi, 1977.

Bledsoe, Erik. "Margaret Mitchell's Review of *Soldiers' Pay." Mississippi Quarterly* 49.3 (Summer 1996): 591–93.

Bleikasten, André. *The Ink of Melancholy: Faulkner's Novels from "The Sound and the Fury" to "Light in August."* Indiana University Press, 2016. Nook.

——. *Most Splendid Failure: Faulkner's "The Sound and the Fury."* Indiana University Press, 1976.

——. *William Faulkner: A Life through the Novels.* Indiana University Press, 2017.

Bloom, Harold, ed. *Bloom's Major Short Story Writers: William Faulkner.* Chelsea House, 1999.

Blotner, Joseph. *Faulkner: A Biography.* Random House, 1974.

——. *Faulkner: A Biography.* University Press of Mississippi, 2005. Kindle.

——. "Faulkner in Hollywood." In *Man and the Movies,* edited by W. R. Robinson. Penguin, 1969.

——. *An Unexpected Life.* Louisiana State University Press, 2005.

——. *William Faulkner's Library: A Catalogue.* University Press of Virginia, 1964.

Bradford, Melvin J. "An Aesthetic Parable: Faulkner's 'Artist at Home.'" *Georgia Review* 27 (Summer 1973): 175–81.

Brinkmeyer, Robert H., Jr. *The Fourth Ghost: White Southern Writers and European Fascism (1930–1950).* Louisiana State University Press, 2009.

Brister, J. G. "*Absalom, Absalom!* and the Semiotic Other." *Faulkner Journal* (Fall 2006/Spring 2007): 39–55.

Broach, Vance. *Grande Dame: A Tribute to Bama Falkner McLean.* Privately printed, n.d.

Brodsky, Louis Daniel. "A Textual History of William Faulkner's *The Wishing-Tree* and *The Wishing Tree." Studies in Bibliography* 38 (1985): 330–74.

——. *William Faulkner, Life Glimpses.* University of Texas Press, 1990.

Brodsky, Louis Daniel, and Robert W. Hamblin, eds. *Faulkner: A Comprehensive Guide to the Brodsky Collection.* Vol. 1: *The Bibliography.* University Press of Mis-sissippi, 1982.

——, eds. *Faulkner: A Comprehensive Guide to the Brodsky Collection.* Vol. 2: *The Letters.* University Press of Mississippi, 1984.

——, eds. *Faulkner: A Comprehensive Guide to the Brodsky Collection.* Vol. 3: *The De Gaulle Story.* University Press of Mississippi, 1984.

——, eds. *Faulkner: A Comprehensive Guide to the Brodsky Collection.* Vol. 4: *Battle Cry.* University Press of Mississippi, 1985.

——, eds. *Faulkner: A Comprehensive Guide to the Brodsky Collection.* Vol. 5: *Manu-scripts and Documents.* University Press of Mississippi, 1988.

——, eds. *Selections from the William Faulkner Collection of Louis Daniel Brodsky.* University Press of Mississippi, 1979.

Broncano, Manuel. "Reading Faulkner in Spain, Reading Spain in Faulkner." In *Global Faulkner,* edited by Annette Trefzer and Ann J. Abadie. University Press of Missis-sippi, 2009.

Brooks, Cleanth. *William Faulkner: The Yoknapatawpha Country.* Yale University Press, 1966.

———. *William Faulkner: Toward Yoknapatawpha and Beyond*. Yale University Press, 1978.

Broughton, Panthea Reid. "An Interview with Meta Carpenter Wilde." *Southern Review* 18.4 (October 1976): 776–801.

Brown, Calvin S. "Faulkner's Manhunts." *Georgia Review* 20.4 (Winter 1966): 388–95.

Brown, May Cameron. "Voice in 'That Evening Sun': A Study of Quentin Compson." In *Critical Essays on William Faulkner: The Compson Family,* edited by Arthur F. Kinney. G. K. Hall, 1982.

Campbell, William K. "A Consideration of the Contrasting Opinions of William Faulkner's Attitude toward the Negro." Master's thesis, State University of Iowa, June 1951. UVA.

Capula, Michelangelo. *Jean Negulesco: His Life and Films*. McFarland, 2017.

Carothers, James. B. "Faulkner's Short Story Writing and the Oldest Profession." In *Faulkner and the Short Story,* edited by Evans Harrington and Ann J. Abadie. University Press of Mississippi, 1992.

———. "The Road to *The Reivers*." In *A Cosmos of My Own: Faulkner and Yoknapatawpha 1980,* edited by Doreen Fowler and Ann J. Abadie. University Press of Mississippi, 1981.

———. *William Faulkner's Short Stories*. UMI Research Press, 1985.

Carter, William C., ed. *Conversations with Shelby Foote*. University Press of Mississippi, 1989.

Chabrier, Gwendolyn. *Faulkner's Families: A Southern Saga*. Gordian, 1993.

Cohen, Martin. "The Novel in Woodcuts: A Handbook." *Journal of Modern Literature* 6.2 (1977): 171–95.

Coleman, Rosemary. "Family Ties: Generating Narratives in *Absalom, Absalom!*" *Mississippi Quarterly* 41.3 (Summer 1998): 421–31.

Collins, Carvel. "Biographical Sources of Faulkner's War Fiction." In *Faulkner and the Short Story,* edited by Evans Harrington and Ann J. Abadie. University Press of Mississippi, 1992.

Commins, Dorothy. *What Is an Editor? Saxe Commins at Work*. University of Chicago Press, 1978.

Cooperman, Stanley. *World War I and the American Novel*. Johns Hopkins University Press, 1967.

Coughlan, Robert. *The Private World of William Faulkner*. Harper and Brothers, 1954.

Cowley, Malcolm. *The Faulkner-Cowley File: Letters and Memories, 1944–1962*. Viking, 1966.

Cullen, John B. *Old Times in the Faulkner Country*. University of North Carolina Press, 1961.

Curnutt, Kirk. *William Faulkner*. Reaktion, 2018. Kindle.

Dabney, Lewis M. *The Indians of Yoknapatawpha: A Study in Literature and History*. Louisiana State University Press, 1974.

Dahl, James. "A Faulkner Reminiscence: Conversations with Mrs. Maud Falkner." *Journal of Modern Literature* 3 (April 1974): 1026–30.

Dardis, Tom. *Firebrand: The Life of Horace Liveright*. Random House, 1995.

———. "Harrison Smith: The Man Who Took a Chance on *The Sound and the Fury*." In *Faulkner and Popular Culture*, edited by Doreen Fowler and Ann J. Abadie. University Press of Mississippi, 1990.

———. *Some Time in the Sun: The Hollywood Years of F. Scott Fitzgerald, William Faulkner, Nathanael West, Aldous Huxley, and James Agee*. Limelight Editions, 2004. Kindle.

———. *The Thirsty Muse: Alcohol and the American Writer*. Ticknor and Fields, 1989.

Davis, Ronald L. *Zachary Scott: Hollywood Sophisticated Cad*. University Press of Mississippi, 2006.

Davis, Thadious M. *Faulkner's Negro: Art and the Southern Context*. Louisiana State University Press, 1983.

———. "From Jazz Syncopation to Blues Elegy: Faulkner's Development of Black Characterization." In *Faulkner and Race,* edited by Doreen Fowler and Ann J. Abadie. University Press of Mississippi, 1988.

Degenfelder, E. Pauline. "The Film Adaptation of Faulkner's *Intruder in the Dust*." *Literature/Film Quarterly* 1 (Spring 1973): 138–49.

Delson, Susan. *Dudley Murphy: Hollywood Wild Card*. University of Minnesota Press, 2006.

Dickerson, Mary Jane. "'The Magician's Wand': Faulkner's *Compson Appendix*." *Mississippi Quarterly* 28 (1975): 317–37.

Ditsky, John. "William Faulkner's *The Wishing Tree*." *Lion and the Unicorn* 2.1 (1978): 56–64.

Doyle, Don H. *Faulkner's County: The Historical Roots of Yoknapatawpha*. University of North Carolina Press, 2001.

Duclos, Donald Philip. *Son of Sorrow: The Life Works and Influence of Colonel William C. Falkner, 1825–1889*. International Scholars Publications, 1999.

Eagles, Charles W. *The Price of Defiance: James Meredith and the Integration of Ole Miss*. University of North Carolina Press, 2014.

Earle, David M. "Faulkner and the Paperback Trade." In *William Faulkner in Context,* edited by John T. Matthews. Cambridge University Press, 2015.

Elliott, Jack D., Jr., and Sidney W. Bondurant. "Death on a Summer Night: Faulkner at Byhalia." *Journal of Mississippi History* 79 (Fall/Winter 2017): 101–36.

Erikson, Erik. *Childhood and Society*. Norton, 2013. Kindle.

Fadiman, Regina K. *Faulkner's "Intruder in the Dust": Novel into Film*. University of Tennessee Press, 1978.

Falkner, Murry C. *The Falkners of Mississippi: A Reminiscence*. Louisiana State University Press, 1968.

Fant, Joseph L., and Robert Ashley. *Faulkner at West Point*. University Press of Mississippi, 2002.

Farber, Manny. *Farber on Film: The Complete Film Writings of Manny Farber*. Edited by Robert Polito. Library of America, 2009.

Fargnoli, A. Nicholas, ed. *William Faulkner: A Literary Companion*. Pegasus, 2008.

Fargnoli, A. Nicholas, and Michael Golay. *William Faulkner A to Z*. Checkmark, 2002.

Faulkner, John. *My Brother Bill*. University of South Carolina Press, 2010.

Faulkner, William. *The Collected Stories of William Faulkner*. Random House, 1950. Kindle.

———. *"Country Lawyer" and Other Stories for the Screen.* Edited by Louis Daniel Brodsky and Robert W. Hamblin. University Press of Mississippi, 1987.

———. *Early Prose and Poetry.* Random House, 1963. Kindle.

———. *Elmer.* Edited by Dianne L. Cox. Seajay, 1983.

———. *Essays, Speeches, and Public Letters.* Random House, 2011. Kindle.

———. *Father Abraham.* Edited by James B. Meriwether. Random House, 1983.

———. *Faulkner's MGM Screenplays.* Edited by Bruce Kawin. University of Tennessee Press, 1982.

———. *The Marionettes.* Edited by Noel Polk. University Press of Virginia, 1977.

———. *Mayday.* Introduction by Carvel Collins. University of Notre Dame Press, 1976.

———. *New Orleans Sketches.* Edited by Carvel Collins. University Press of Mississippi, 2002. Kindle.

———. *"Stallion Road": A Screenplay by William Faulkner.* Edited by Louis Daniel Brodsky and Robert W. Hamblin. University Press of Mississippi, 1989.

———. *Thinking of Home: William Faulkner's Letters to His Mother and Father, 1918–1925.* Edited by James G. Watson. Norton, 1992.

———. *"To Helen: A Courtship" and "Mississippi Poems."* Introductory essays by Carvel Collins and Joseph Blotner. Tulane University and Yoknapatawpha Press, 1981.

———. *The Uncollected Stories of William Faulkner.* Edited by Joseph Blotner. Vintage, 2011. Kindle.

———. *Vision in Spring.* Edited by Judith Sensibar. University of Texas Press, 1984.

———. *William Faulkner at Twentieth Century-Fox: The Annotated Screenplays.* Edited by Sarah Gleeson-White. Oxford University Press, 2017.

Ferguson, James. *Faulkner's Short Fiction.* University of Tennessee Press, 1991.

Fletcher, Matthew L. M. "Red Leaves and the Dirty Ground: The Cannibalism of Law and Economics." *American Indian Law Review* 33 (2008–9): 33–52.

Folks, Jeffrey J. "William Faulkner and the Silent Film. In *The South and Film,* edited by Warren French. University Press of Mississippi, 1981.

Ford, Corey. *The Time of Laughter.* Little, Brown, 1967.

Fowler, Doreen. *Faulkner: The Return of the Repressed.* University Press of Virginia, 1997.

———. "Joe Christmas and 'Womanshenegro.'" In *Faulkner and Women,* edited by Fowler and Ann J. Abadie. University Press of Mississippi, 1986.

Fowler, Doreen, and Ann J. Abadie, eds. *Fifty Years of Yoknapatawpha.* University Press of Mississippi, 1980.

Franklin, Malcolm. *Bitterweeds: Life with William Faulkner at Rowan Oak.* Society for the Study of Traditional Culture, 1977.

Fulton, Keith Louise. "Linda Snopes Kohl: Faulkner's Radical Woman." *Modern Fiction Studies* 34 (1988): 425–36.

Garrett, George. Afterword to *The Road to Glory,* by Joel Sayre and William Faulkner. Southern Illinois University Press, 1981.

———. An Examination of the Poetry of William Faulkner." In *William Faulkner: Four Decades of Criticism.* Michigan State University Press, 1973.

Gleeson-White, Sarah. "Auditory Exposures: Faulkner, Eisenstein, and Film Sound." *PMLA* 128.1 (2013): 187–200.

———. "William Faulkner, Screenwriter: 'Sutter's Gold' and 'Drums along the Mohawk.'" *Mississippi Quarterly* 62.3–4 (Summer 2009): 427–42.

Glick, Evelyn Harper. *The Making of William Faulkner's Books, 1929–1937: An Interview with Evelyn Harper Glick.* Southern Studies Program, University of South Carolina, 1979.

Godden, Richard. "*Absalom, Absalom!* and Faulkner's Erroneous Dating of the Haitian Revolution." *Mississippi Quarterly* 47.3 (Summer 1994): 489–95.

———. "*Absalom, Absalom!* and Rosa Coldfield: Or, What Is in the Dark House?" *Faulkner Journal* 8.2 (Spring 1993): 31–66.

Godwin, Hannah. "Modernism, Childhood, Historical Consciousness in *The Wishing Tree.*" In *Faulkner and History,* edited by Jay Watson and James G. Thomas Jr. University Press of Mississippi, 2017.

Gray, Richard. *The Life of William Faulkner: A Critical Biography.* Blackwell, 1994.

Grider, John MacGavock. *War Birds: Diary of an Unknown Aviator.* Texas A&M Press, 2000. Kindle.

Gresset, Michel. *Fascination: Faulkner's Fiction, 1919–1936.* Duke University Press, 1989.

———. *A Faulkner Chronology.* University Press of Mississippi, 1985.

———. "Faulkner's 'The Hill.'" *Southern Literary Journal* (Spring 1974): 3–18.

———. "A Public Man's Private Voice." In *Faulkner: After the Nobel Prize,* edited by Gresset and Kenzaburo Ohashi. Yamaguchi, 1987.

———. "Weekend, Lost and Revisited." *Mississippi Quarterly* 31 (1968): 173–78.

Grimwood, Michael. "Faulkner's 'Golden Land' as Autobiography." *Studies in Short Fiction* 23.3 (Summer 1986): 275–80.

Guetti, James. "*Absalom, Absalom!:* The Extended Simile." In *William Faulkner's "Absalom, Absalom!": A Critical Casebook,* edited by Elisabeth Muhlenfeld. Garland, 1984.

Guttman, Sondra. "Who's Afraid of the Corncob Man: Masculinity, Race, and Labor in the Preface to *Sanctuary.*" *Faulkner Journal* 15.1/2 (Fall 1999/Spring 2000): 15–34.

Gwin, Minrose C. *The Feminine and Faulkner: Reading (Beyond) Sexual Difference.* University of Tennessee Press, 1990.

———. "*Mosquitoes'* Missing Bite: The Four Deletions." *Faulkner Journal* 9 (Fall 1993/Spring 1994): 31–41.

———. "Racial Wounding and the Aesthetics of the Middle Voice." *Faulkner Journal* 20.1–2 (Fall 2004): 21–35.

Gwynn, Frederick L., and Joseph Blotner, eds. *Faulkner in the University: Class Conferences at the University of Virginia, 1957–1958.* University Press of Virginia, 1959.

Hagood, Taylor. *Faulkner, Writer of Disability.* Louisiana State University Press, 2014.

Hall, Donald. *A Carnival of Losses: Notes Nearing Ninety.* Houghton Mifflin Harcourt, 2018. Kindle.

Hamblin, Robert W. "Biographical Fact or Fiction? William Faulkner, Estelle Oldham Franklin, and Abortion." *Mississippi Quarterly* 60.3 (Summer 1997): 579–87.

———. "Faulkner and Hollywood: A Call for Reassessment." In *Faulkner and Film,* edited by Peter Lurie and Ann J. Abadie. University Press of Mississippi, 2014.

———. "Lucas Beauchamp, Ned Barnett, and William Faulkner's 1940 Will." *Studies in Bibliography* 32 (1979): 281–83.

———. *Myself and the World: A Biography of William Faulkner.* University Press of Mississippi, 2016.

Hamilton, Ian. *Writers in Hollywood: 1915–1951.* Harper and Row, 1990.

Handley, George B. *Postslavery Literature in the Americas: Family Portraits in Black and White.* University Press of Virginia, 2000.

Hannon, Charles. "The Filming of *Intruder in the Dust.*" In *Essays on William Faulkner's "Intruder in the Dust": A Gathering of Evidence,* edited by Michel Gresset and Patrick Samway. St. Joseph's University Press, 2004.

Harrington, Gary. *Faulkner's Fables of Creativity: The Non-Yoknapatawpha Novels.* University of Georgia Press, 1990.

Hemingway, Ernest. *Ernest Hemingway: Selected Letters 1917–1961.* Edited by Carlos Baker. Scribner's, 1981.

Hickman, Lisa C., ed. *Remembering: Joan Williams' Uncollected Pieces.* Open Road, 2016.

———. *William Faulkner and Joan Williams: The Romance of Two Writers.* McFarland, 2006.

Hillier, Jim, and Peter Wollen, eds. *Howard Hawks: American Artist.* British Film Institute, 1996.

Hirsch, Arthur. "Ghosts of the South." *Baltimore Sun,* September 21, 1997.

Hlavsa, Virginia H. "Crucifixion in *Light in August.*" In *Faulkner and Religion,* edited by Doreen Fowler and Ann J. Abadie. University Press of Mississippi, 1991.

Holditch, W. Kenneth. "William Faulkner and Other Famous Creoles." In *Faulkner and His Contemporaries,* edited by Joseph R. Urgo and Ann J. Abadie. University Press of Mississippi, 2010.

Hönnighausen, Lothar. *Faulkner: Masks and Metaphors.* University Press of Mississippi, 1997.

———. *William Faulkner: The Art of Stylization in His Early Graphic and Literary Work.* Cambridge University Press, 1987.

Hyams, Joe. "An 'Interview' With 'Pappy' Faulkner." *Journal of the Screen Producers Guild* 6.3 (September 1959): 17–20.

Inge, M. Thomas, ed. *Conversations with William Faulkner.* University Press of Mississippi, 1999.

———. *The Dixie Limited: Writers on William Faulkner and His Influence.* University Press of Mississippi, 2016.

———. *William Faulkner.* Overlook, 2006.

———, ed. *William Faulkner: The Contemporary Reviews.* Cambridge: Cambridge University Press, 1995.

———. "William Faulkner, James Avati, and the Art of the Paperback Novel." *Illustration* 56 (2017): 46–58.

Irwin, John T. *Doubling and Incest/Repetition and Revenge: A Speculative Reading of Faulkner.* Expanded ed. Johns Hopkins University Press, 1996.

———. "Not the Having but the Waiting: Faulkner's Lost Loves." In *Faulkner at 100: Retrospect and Prospect,* edited by Donald M. Kartiganer and Ann J. Abadie. University Press of Mississippi, 2000.

Izard, Barbara, and Clara Hieronymus. *"Requiem for a Nun": On Stage and Off.* Aurora, 1970.

Jackson, Robert. "'If It Still Is France, It Will Endure': Faulknerian Projections from Hollywood to Stockholm." For the "Faulkner and World Cinema" program arranged by the William Faulkner Society, Modern Language Association of America Convention, December 28, 2007. http://faulknersociety.com/mla07jackson.doc.

———. "Images of Collaboration: William Faulkner's Motion Picture Communities." In *Faulkner and Film,* edited by Peter Lurie and Ann J. Abadie. University Press of Mississippi, 2014.

Jenkins, Lee. *Faulkner and Black-White Relations: A Psychoanalytic Approach.* Columbia University Press, 1981.

Johnson, Glen M. "*Big Woods:* Faulkner's Elegy for Wilderness." *Southern Humanities Review* 14 (1980): 249–58.

Jones, Anne Goodwyn. "Faulkner and the Ideology of Penetration." In *Faulkner and Ideology,* edited by Donald M. Kartiganer and Ann J. Abadie. University Press of Mississippi, 1995.

———. "Faulkner's War Stories and the Construction of Gender." In *Faulkner and Psychology,* edited by Donald M. Kartiganer and Ann J. Abadie. University Press of Mississippi, 1994.

———. "'The Kotex Age': Women, Popular Culture, and *The Wild Palms.*" In *Faulkner and Popular Culture,* edited by Doreen Fowler and Ann J. Abadie. University Press of Mississippi, 1990.

Jones, Diane Brown. *A Reader's Guide to the Short Stories of William Faulkner.* G. K. Hall, 1994.

Jones, Dorothy B. "Novel into Film." *Quarterly of Film, Television, and Radio* 8.1 (Autumn 1953): 51–70.

Jones, Lennis Miears. "Racial Relations in the Fiction of William Faulkner: A Study of Meaning." Master's thesis, University of Iowa, August 1957. UVA.

Kang, Hee. "A New Configuration of Faulkner's Feminine." *Faulkner Journal* 8 (1992): 21–41.

Karem, Jeff. "Fear of a Black Atlantic? African Passages in *Absalom, Absalom!* and *The Last Slaver.*" In *Global Faulkner,* edited by Annette Trefzer and Ann J. Abadie. University Press of Mississippi, 2009.

Karl, Frederick. *William Faulkner, American Writer: A Biography.* Ballantine, 1990.

Kartiganer, Donald M. "The Role of Myth in *Absalom, Absalom!*" In *Faulkner and His Critics,* edited by John N. Duvall. Johns Hopkins University Press, 2010.

Kaufman, Linda. "A Lover's Discourse in *Absalom, Absalom!*" In *Faulkner and His Critics,* edited by John N. Duvall. Johns Hopkins University Press, 2010.

Kawin, Bruce. *Faulkner and Film.* Ungar, 1977.

———, ed. *To Have and Have Not.* University of Wisconsin Press, 1980.

Keiser, Merle Wallace. "*Flags in the Dust* and *Sartoris.*" In *Fifty Years of Yoknapatawpha,* edited by Doreen Fowler and Ann J. Abadie. University Press of Mississippi, 1980.

Kinney, Arthur F., ed. *Critical Essays on William Faulkner: The Compson Family.* G. K. Hall, 1982.

———. "Faulkner and Racism." *Connotations* 3.3 (1993/94).

———. "Faulkner's Narrative Poetics and *Collected Stories.*" *Faulkner Studies* 1 (1980): 58–79.

———. "Unscrambling Surprises." *Connotations* 15.1–3 (2005/2006): 17–29.

Knox, Robert Hilton. "William Faulkner's *Absalom, Absalom!*" Ph.D. diss., Harvard University, April 1959.

Kodat, Catherine Gunther. "Writing *A Fable* for America." In *Faulkner in America,* edited by Joseph E. Urgo and Ann J. Abadie. University Press of Mississippi, 2001.

Kreiswirth, Martin. *William Faulkner: The Making of a Novelist.* University of Georgia Press, 1983.

Ladd, Barbara. *Nationalism and the Color Line in George W. Cable, Mark Twain, and William Faulkner.* Louisiana State University Press, 1996.

La Farge, Oliver. *Raw Material.* Houghton, Mifflin, 1945.

Lang, Beatrice. "'Dr. Martino': The Conflict of Life and Death." *Delta* 3 (1976): 23–32.

Langford, Gerald. *Faulkner's Revision of "Sanctuary": A Collation of the Unrevised Galleys and the Published Book.* University of Texas Press, 1972.

Latham, Sean. "Jim Bond's America: Denaturalizing the Logic of Slavery in *Absalom, Absalom!*" *Mississippi Quarterly* 51.3 (Summer 1998): 453–63.

LaValley, Albert J., ed. *Mildred Pierce.* University of Wisconsin Press, 1980.

Lawrence, John, and Dan Hise. *Faulkner's Rowan Oak.* University Press of Mississippi, 1993.

Limon, John. *Writing after War: American War Fiction from Realism to Postmodernism.* Oxford University Press, 1994.

Lind, Ilse Dusoir. "The Calvinistic Burden." In *"Light in August" and the Critical Spectrum,* edited by John B. Vickery and Olga Vickery. Wadsworth, 1971.

———. "Faulkner's Uses of Poetic Drama." In *Faulkner, Modernism, and Film,* edited by Evans Harrington and Ann J. Abadie. University Press of Mississippi, 1978.

Lowe, John. "Fraternal Fury: Faulkner, World War I, and Myths of Masculinity." In *Faulkner and War,* edited by Noel Polk and Ann J. Abadie. University Press of Mississippi, 2004.

Luce, Diane Cox. *William Faulkner: Annotations to the Novels: "As I Lay Dying."* Garland, 1990.

———, ed. *William Faulkner's "As I Lay Dying": A Critical Casebook.* Garland, 1985.

Luddington, Townsend. *John Dos Passos: A Twentieth-Century Odyssey.* Dutton, 1980.

Lurie, Peter. "Inside and Outside Southern Whiteness: Film Viewing, the Frame and the Racing of Space in Yoknapatawpha." In *Faulkner and Whiteness,* edited by Jay Watson. University Press of Mississippi, 2011.

———. *Vision's Immanence: Faulkner, Film, and the Popular Imagination.* Johns Hopkins University Press, 2004.

Matthews, John T. "Faulkner and the Culture Industry." In *The Cambridge Companion to William Faulkner,* edited by Philip Weinstein. Cambridge University Press, 1995.

———. "Faulkner's Narrative Frames." In *Faulkner and the Craft of Fiction,* edited by Doreen Fowler and Ann J. Abadie. University Press of Mississippi, 1989.

———. "Many Mansions: Faulkner's Cold War Conflicts. In *Global Faulkner,* edited by Annette Trefzer and Ann J. Abadie. University Press of Mississippi, 2009.

———, ed. *The New Cambridge Companion to William Faulkner.* Cambridge University Press, 2015.

———. *William Faulkner: Seeing through the South.* Wiley-Blackwell, 2012. Kindle.

McAlexander, Hubert, Jr. "William Faulkner—The Young Poet in Stark Young's *The Torches Flare*." *American Literature* 43 (January 1972): 647–49.

McBride, Joseph, ed. *Focus on Howard Hawks*. Prentice Hall, 1972.

———. *Hawks on Hawks*. University of California Press, 1982.

McCarthy, Todd. *Howard Hawks: The Grey Fox of Hollywood*. Grove, 1997.

McClelland, Doug. *Forties Film Talk: Oral Histories of Hollywood with 120 Lobby Posters*. McFarland, 1992.

McDaniel, Linda Elkins. *Annotations to William Faulkner's "Flags in the Dust."* Garland, 1991.

McHaney, Thomas L. "The Elmer Papers." In *A Faulkner Miscellany,* edited by James B. Meriwether. University Press of Mississippi, 1974.

———. *William Faulkner's "The Wild Palms": A Study*. University Press of Mississippi, 1975.

McMillen, Neil R. *Dark Journey: Black Mississippians in the Age of Jim Crow*. University of Illinois Press, 1989.

Meade, Marion. *Dorothy Parker: What Fresh Hell Is This?* Villard, 1988.

Meriwether, James B. "Early Notices of Faulkner by Phil Stone and Louis Cochran." *Mississippi Quarterly* 17 (Summer 1964): 136–48.

———, ed. *A Faulkner Miscellany*. University Press of Mississippi, 1974.

———, ed. "Faulkner's Correspondence with *Scribner's Magazine*." *Proof* 3: 256–60.

———, ed. "Faulkner's Correspondence with the *Saturday Evening Post*. *Mississippi Quarterly* 30 (Summer 1977): 464–66.

———. *The Literary Career of William Faulkner*. University of North Carolina Press, 1971.

Meriwether, James B., and Michael Millgate, eds. *Lion in the Garden: Interviews with William Faulkner*. Random House, 1968.

Michel, Fran. "Faulkner as Lesbian Author." *Faulkner Journal* 4.1/2 (Fall 1988/Spring 1989): 5–18.

Millgate, Michael. *The Achievement of William Faulkner*. University of Georgia Press, 1989.

Minter, David. *William Faulkner: His Life and Work*. Johns Hopkins University Press, 1980.

Momberger, Philip. "Faulkner's 'The Village' and 'That Evening Sun': The Tale in Context." In *Bloom's Major Short Story Writers: William Faulkner,* edited by Harold Bloom. Chelsea House, 1999.

———. "A Reading of Faulkner's 'The Hill.'" *Southern Literary Journal* (Spring 1977): 16–29.

Monaghan, David M. "Faulkner's Relationship to Gavin Stevens in *Intruder in the Dust*." *Dalhousie Review* 52 (1972): 449–57.

Montagu, Ivor. *With Eisenstein in Hollywood*. International, 1969.

Moore, Michelle. "Vampires, Detectives, and Hawks: A History and Analysis of William Faulkner's Unpublished Screenplay *Dreadful Hollow*." *Literature/Film Quarterly*. http://www.salisbury.edu/lfq/_issues/45_3/vampires_detectives_and_hawks.html.

Morell, Giliane. "The Last Scene of *Sanctuary*." *Mississippi Quarterly* 25.3 (Summer 1972): 351–55.

Morland, Agnes Louise. "The Negro in the Fiction of William Faulkner." Master's thesis, University of Washington, 1953. UVA.

Moser, Thomas C. "Faulkner's Muse: Speculations on the Genesis of *The Sound and the Fury.*" In *Critical Reconstructions: The Relationship of Fiction and Life,* edited by Robert M. Polhemus and Roger B. Henkel. Stanford University Press, 1994.

Mullener, Elizabeth. "Joan Williams and William Faulkner: A Romance Remembered." *New Orleans Times-Picayune,* September 19, 1982, 8–18.

Murphet, Julian. *Faulkner's Media Romance.* Oxford University Press, 2017.

Nauman, Hilda. "How Faulkner Went His Way and I Went Mine." *Esquire,* December 1967.

Nelson, Charles, and David Goforth. *Our Neighbor, William Faulkner.* Adams, 1977.

Nuechterlein, Donald E. *A Cold War Odyssey.* University Press of Kentucky, 1997.

Oates, Stephen B. *William Faulkner: The Man and the Artist: A Biography.* Harper, 1987.

Owada, Eiko. *Faulkner, Haiti, and Questions of Imperialism.* Sairyusha, 2002.

Paddock, Lisa. *Contrapuntal in Integration: A Study of Three Faulkner Short Story Volumes.* International Scholars, 2000.

———. "'Trifles with a Tragic Profundity': The Importance of 'Mistral.'" *Mississippi Quarterly* (Summer 1979): 413–22.

Parini, Jay. *One Matchless Time: A Life of William Faulkner.* HarperCollins, 2009. Kindle.

Parker, Robert Dale. "Red Slippers and Cottonmouth Moccasins: White Anxieties in Faulkner's Indian Stories." *Faulkner Journal* 18 (Fall 2002/Spring 2003): 81–100.

Peek, Charles A., and Robert W. Hamblin, eds. *A Companion to Faulkner Studies.* Greenwood, 2004.

Peters, Erskine. *William Faulkner: The Yoknapatawpha World and Black Being.* Norwood, 1983.

Peterson, Richard F. "An Early Judgement of Anderson and Joyce in Faulkner's 'Artist at Home.'" *Kyushu American Literature* 18 (1977): 19–23.

Phillips, Gene D. *Fiction, Film, and Faulkner: The Art of Adaptation.* University of Tennessee Press, 1988.

Pilkington, John. *Stark Young.* Twayne, 1985.

Polchin, James. "Selling a Novel: Faulkner's *Sanctuary* as a Psychosexual Text." In *Faulkner and Gender,* edited by Donald M. Kartiganer and Ann J. Abadie. University Press of Mississippi, 1996.

Polk, Noel, ed. *"Absalom, Absalom!": Typesetting Copy and Miscellaneous Material.* William Faulkner Manuscripts 13. Garland, 1987.

———. *Children of the Dark House.* University Press of Mississippi, 1998. Kindle.

———. "Faulkner: The Artist as Cuckold." In *Faulkner and Gender,* edited by Donald M. Kartiganer and Ann J. Abadie. University Press of Mississippi, 1996. Reprinted in *Children of the Dark House,* by Polk.

———. *Faulkner's "Requiem for a Nun": A Critical Study.* Indiana University Press, 1981.

———, ed. *"Requiem for a Nun": Preliminary Holograph and Typescript Materials.* William Faulkner Manuscripts 19. Garland, 1987.

———, ed. *William Faulkner: "Sanctuary": The Original Text*. Random House, 1981.

Polk, Noel, and Neil R. McMillen. "Faulkner on Lynching." *Faulkner Journal* 8 (1992): 3–14.

Porter, Carolyn. *Seeing & Being: The Plight of the Participant Observer in Emerson, James, Adams, and Faulkner*. Wesleyan University Press, 1981.

———. *William Faulkner*. Oxford University Press, 2007.

Pruitt, Claude. *The Well-Wrought Urn: Faulkner and Jefferson on the Practice of Freedom*. CreateSpace Direct, 2015. Kindle.

Putzel, Max. *Genius of Place: William Faulkner's Triumphant Beginnings*. Louisiana State University Press, 1985.

Rado, Lisa. "'A Perversion That Builds Chartres and Invents Lear Is a Pretty Good Thing': *Mosquitoes* and Faulkner's Androgynous Imagination." *Faulkner Journal* 9.1 (Fall 1993): 13–30.

Ragan, David Paul. "'Belonging to the Business of Mankind': The Achievement of Faulkner's *Big Woods*." *Mississippi Quarterly* 36 (Summer 1983): 301–17.

Rampton, David. *William Faulkner: A Literary Life*. Palgrave Macmillan, 2008.

Ramsey, Matthew. "'All That Glitters': Reappraising 'Golden Land.'" *Faulkner Journal* 21.1/2 (Fall 2005/Spring 2006): 51–68.

———. "Stars, Fashion, and Authorship in *Today We Live*." In *Faulkner and Material Culture*, edited by Joseph R. Urgo and Ann J. Abadie. University Press of Mississippi, 2007.

———. "'Turnabout' Is Fair(y) Play: Faulkner's Queer War Story." *Faulkner Journal* 15.1 (Fall 1999/Spring 2000): 61–81.

Ravitz, Abe C. *Leane Zugsmith: Thunder on the Left*. International, 1992.

Reed, John Shelton. *Dixie Bohemia: A French Quarter Circle in the 1920s*. Louisiana State University Press, 2012.

Rhodes, Pamela E. "Who Killed Simon Strother and Why? Race and Counterplot in *Flags in the Dust*." In *Faulkner and Race*, edited by Doreen Fowler and Ann J. Abadie. University Press of Mississippi, 2007.

Richards, Gary. "Male Homosexuality and Faulkner's Early Prose. In *Faulkner's Sexualities*, edited by Annette Trefzer and Ann J. Abadie. University Press of Mississippi, 2010.

Richardson, H. Edward. *William Faulkner: The Journey to Self-Discovery*. University of Missouri Press, 1969.

Rieger, Christopher, and Andrew B. Leiter, eds. *Faulkner and Hemingway*. Southeast Missouri State University Press, 2018.

Robbins, Ben. "The Pragmatic Modernist: William Faulkner's Craft and Hollywood's Networks of Production." *Journal of Screenwriting* 5.2 (2014): 239–57.

———. "William Faulkner's *Requiem for a Nun* and Hollywood Cold War Melodrama." *Genre* 50.3 (2017): 343–70.

Robbins, Deborah. "The Desperate Eloquence of *Absalom, Absalom!*" *Mississippi Quarterly* 34.3 (Summer 1981): 315–25.

Roberts, Diane. "Eula, Linda, and the Death of Nature." In *Faulkner and the Natural World*, edited by Donald M. Kartiganer and Ann J. Abadie. University Press of Mississippi, 1999.

Robinson, W. R. *Man and the Movies*. Penguin, 1969.

Rollyson, Carl. "Faulkner's First Biographers: Early Notices." In *Faulkner and Print Culture,* edited by Jay Watson, Jaime Harper, and James G. Thomas Jr. University Press of Mississippi, 2017.

———. "Faulkner's Shadow: Hollywood, Hemingway, and *Pylon.*" In *Faulkner and Hemingway,* edited by Christopher Rieger and Andrew B. Leiter. Southeast Missouri State University Press, 2018.

———. *Lillian Hellman: Her Legend and Her Legacy.* St. Martin's, 1988.

———. *A Real American Character: The Life of Walter Brennan.* University Press of Mississippi, 2015.

———. *Rebecca West: A Modern Sibyl.* iUniverse, 2009.

———. *Uses of the Past in the Novels of William Faulkner.* Open Road, 2016.

Rose, Julie. "Faulkner's Horror and the American Gothic Cultural Imagination (1930–1945)." Ph.D. diss., New York University, 1999.

Rouselle, Melinda McLeod. *William Faulkner: Annotations to the Novels: Sanctuary.* Garland, 1989.

Ryan, Tim. "Fabbulous Monsters: Faulkner, Alexander Woollcott, and American Literary Culture." In *Faulkner and Print Culture,* edited by Jay Watson, Jaime Harker, and James G. Thomas Jr. University Press of Mississippi, 2017.

Sanderson, Jane. "A Kind of Greatness." *Delta Review* 1 (July/August 1965): 15, 17.

Saunders, Rebecca. "Faulkner's *Absalom, Absalom!* and the New South." In *Faulkner and His Critics,* edited by John N. Duvall. Johns Hopkins University Press, 2010.

Schoenberg, Estella. *Old Tales and Talking: Quentin Compson in William Faulkner's "Absalom, Absalom!" and Related Works.* University Press of Mississippi, 1977.

Schwartz, Lawrence H. *Creating Faulkner's Reputation: The Politics of Modern Literary Criticism.* University of Tennessee Press, 1988.

Scott, Susan. "*As I Lay Dying* and the Modern Aesthetics of Ecological Crisis." In *The New Cambridge Companion to William Faulkner,* edited by John T. Matthews. Cambridge University Press, 2015.

Sensibar, Judith. *Faulkner and Love: The Women Who Shaped His Art, A Biography.* Yale University Press, 2009. Kindle.

———. *The Origins of Faulkner's Art.* University of Texas Press, 1984.

———. "Writing for Faulkner, Writing for Herself: Estelle Oldham's Postcolonial Fiction." *Prospects* 22 (October 1997): 357–78.

Shawhan, Dorothy S., and Martha H. Swain. *Lucy Somerville Howorth: New Deal Lawyer, Politician, and Feminist from the South.* Louisiana State University Press, 2006.

Sidney, George. "Faulkner in Hollywood: A Study of His Career as a Scenarist." Ph.D. diss., University of New Mexico, 1959.

Silver, James. *Running Scared: Silver in Mississippi.* University Press of Mississippi, 1984.

Simross, Lynn. "Memories of a Bohemian in Paris, 1924." *Los Angeles Times,* April 14, 1977.

Singal, Daniel J. *William Faulkner: The Making of a Modernist.* University of North Carolina Press, 1997.

Skei, Hans. *William Faulkner: The Novelist as Short Story Writer.* Universitetsforlaget, 1985.

———. *William Faulkner: The Short Story Career.* Universitetsforlaget, 1981.

Snead, James A. "The 'Joint' of Racism: Withholding the Black in *Absalom, Absalom!*" In *William Faulkner's "Absalom, Absalom!,"* edited by Harold Bloom. Chelsea House, 1987.

Snell, Susan. *Phil Stone of Oxford: A Vicarious Life.* University of Georgia Press, 1991.

Solomon, Stefan. *William Faulkner in Hollywood: Screenwriting for the Studios.* University of Georgia Press, 2017.

Spiegelman, Art, ed. *Lynd Ward: "Gods' Man," "Madman's Drum," "Wild Pilgrimage."* Library of America, 2010.

Spoth, Daniel. "Totalitarian Faulkner: The Nazi Interpretation of *Light in August* and *Absalom, Absalom!*" *English Literary History* 78 (Spring 2011): 239–78.

Spoto, Donald. *Possessed: The Life of Joan Crawford.* HarperCollins, 2010. Kindle.

Spratling, William. *File on Spratling: An Autobiography.* Little, Brown, 1967.

Starr, Kenneth. *Material Dreams: Southern California through the 1920s.* Oxford University Press, 1990.

Stecopoulos, Harilaos. *Reconstructing the World: Southern Fictions and U.S. Imperialisms, 1898–1976.* Cornell University Press, 2008.

Stein, Jean. *West of Eden: An American Place.* Jonathan Cape, 2016.

Stempel, Tom. *Screenwriter: The Life and Times of Nunnally Johnson.* A. S. Barnes, 1980.

Storey, Robert. *Pierrots on the Stage of Desire: Nineteenth-Century French Literary Artists and the Comic Pantomime.* Princeton University Press, 1985.

Sullens, Idelle. "A Study of the Incest Theme in Two Works of William Faulkner: *The Sound and the Fury* and *Absalom, Absalom!*" Master's thesis, University of Washington, 1954. UVA.

Sundquist, Eric. *Faulkner: The House Divided.* Johns Hopkins University Press, 1983.

Taylor, Herman E. *William Faulkner's Oxford: Recollections and Reflections.* Rutledge Hill, 1990.

Taylor, Walter. "Faulkner's *Reivers:* How to Change the Joke without Slipping the Yoke." In *Faulkner and Race,* edited by Doreen Fowler and Ann J. Abadie. University Press of Mississippi, 1986.

Theroux, Paul. *Deep South: Four Seasons on Back Roads.* Houghton Mifflin Harcourt, 2015.

Torchiana, Donald T. "Faulkner's *Pylon* and the Structure of Modernity." In *Faulkner and His Critics,* edited by John N. Duvall. Johns Hopkins University Press, 2010.

Towner, Theresa M. *Faulkner on the Color Line: The Later Novels.* University Press of Mississippi, 2000.

Towner, Theresa M., and James B. Carothers. *Reading Faulkner: Collected Stories.* University Press of Mississippi, 2006.

Trotter, Sally Stone. *Rowan Oak: A History of the William Faulkner Home.* Nautilus, 2017.

Urgo, Joseph R. "*Absalom, Absalom!:* The Movie." *American Literature* 62.1 (1990): 56–73.

Urgo, Joseph R., and Ann J. Abadie, eds. *Faulkner and Material Culture.* University Press of Mississippi, 2007.

——, eds. *Faulkner's Inheritance.* University Press of Mississippi, 2007.

Urgo, Joseph R., and Noel Polk, eds. *Reading Faulkner: "Absalom, Absalom!"* University Press of Mississippi, 2010.

Vickery, John B., and Olga W. Vickery, eds. *"Light in August" and the Critical Spectrum.* Wadsworth, 1971.

Vickery, Olga. *The Novels of William Faulkner: A Critical Interpretation.* Louisiana State University Press, 1964.

Volpe, Edmond L. *A Reader's Guide to William Faulkner.* Octagon, 1964.

———. *A Reader's Guide to William Faulkner: The Short Stories.* Syracuse University Press, 2004. Kindle.

Waggoner, Hyatt H. *William Faulkner: From Jefferson to the World.* University of Kentucky Press, 1959.

Waid, Candace. *The Signifying Eye: Seeing Faulkner's Art.* University of Georgia Press, 2013.

Wald, Jerry. "Faulkner and Hollywood." *Films in Review* (March 1959): 129–33.

Walton, Anthony. *Mississippi: An American Journey.* Knopf, 1996.

Warner, Jack L. *My First Hundred Years in Hollywood.* Random House, 1965.

Wasson, Ben. *Count No 'Count: Flashbacks to Faulkner.* University Press of Mississippi, 1983.

Watson, James G. "'If Was Existed': Faulkner's Prophets and the Patterns of History." In *Faulkner and His Critics,* edited by John N. Duvall. Johns Hopkins University Press, 2010.

———. *The Snopes Dilemma: Faulkner's Trilogy.* University of Miami Press, 1968.

———. *William Faulkner: Letters & Fictions.* University of Texas Press, 1987.

———. *William Faulkner: Self-Presentation and Performance.* University of Texas Press, 2000. Kindle.

Watson, Jay. *Forensic Fictions: The Lawyer Figure in Faulkner.* University of Georgia Press, 1993.

Webb, James, and A. Wigfall Green, eds. *William Faulkner of Oxford.* Louisiana State University Press, 1965.

Weinstein, Philip. *Becoming Faulkner.* Oxford University Press, 2009. Kindle.

———. "Marginalia: Faulkner's Black Lives." In *Faulkner and Race,* edited by Doreen Fowler and Ann J. Abadie. University Press of Mississippi, 1987. Kindle.

———. *Simply Faulkner.* Simply Charly, 2016. Kindle.

Welling, Bart H. "Faulkner's Library Revisited." *Mississippi Quarterly* 52 (1999): 365–420.

Wells, Dean Faulkner. "Dean Swift Faulkner: A Biographical Study." Master's thesis, University of Mississippi, 1975.

———. *Every Day by the Sun: A Memoir of the Faulkners of Mississippi.* Crown, 2010. Kindle.

———. "Faulkner Helped Young Brother Dean with Vocabulary Lesson." *Faulkner Newsletter & Yoknapatawpha Review* 2 (January–March 1982).

Wilde, Meta Carpenter. "An Unpublished Chapter from *A Loving Gentleman.*" *Mississippi Quarterly* 30 (1977): 449–60.

Wilde, Meta Carpenter, and Orin Borsten. "A Loving Gentleman." Typescript. Berg Collection, New York Public Library.

———. *A Loving Gentleman: The Love Story of William Faulkner and Meta Carpenter.* Simon and Schuster, 1976.

Williamson, Joel. *William Faulkner and Southern History.* Oxford University Press, 1993. Kindle.

Wittenberg, Judith. *Faulkner: The Transfiguration of Biography.* University of Nebraska Press, 1979.

———. "*The Reivers:* A Conservative Fable?" In *Faulkner: After the Nobel Prize,* edited by Michel Gresset and Kensaburo Ohashi. Yamaguchi, 1987.

Wolff, Sally. *Ledgers of History: William Faulkner, an Almost Forgotten Friendship, and an Antebellum Plantation Diary.* Louisiana State University Press, 2010.

Wolff, Sally, and Floyd Watkins. *Talking about William Faulkner: Interviews with Jimmy Faulkner and Others.* Louisiana State University Press, 1996.

Wood, Robin. *Howard Hawks.* Doubleday, 1968.

Yonce, Margaret. "'Shot Down Last Spring': The Wounded Aviators of Faulkner's Wasteland." In *Critical Essays on William Faulkner: The Sartoris Family,* edited by Arthur F. Kinney. G. K. Hall, 1985.

———. *William Faulkner: Annotations to the Novels: "Soldiers' Pay."* Garland, 1990.

Yoshida, Michiko. "Faulkner's Comedy of Motion: *The Reivers.*" In *Faulkner: After the Nobel Prize,* edited by Michel Gresset and Kensaburo Ohashi. Yamaguchi, 1987.

Young, Stark. *The Pavilion: Of People and Times Remembered, of Stories and Places.* Scribner's, 1951.

———. *Heaven Trees.* Scribner's, 1926.

———. *So Red the Rose.* J. S. Sanders, 1993. Kindle.

———. *Stark Young: A Life in the Arts: Letters, 1900–1962.* 2 vols. Edited by John Pilkington. Louisiana State University Press, 1975.

———. *The Torches Flare.* Scribner's, 1928.

Zender, Karl. "Two Unpublished Letters from William Faulkner to Helen Baird." *American Literature* 63.3 (September 1991): 535–38.

Illustration Credits

Index

Americans, 63, 72, 101, 112, 115, 130, 189,
    215, 220, 227, 231, 232, 234, 235, 291,
    329, 337, 362, 380–81, 396, 407, 411,
    420, 421, 425–26, 431, 433, 440, 452,
    458, 462, 472, 473, 550n151, 552n36
American soldiers, 106, 112, 113, 116, 197,
    217, 220, 230, 231, 233, 235, 238, 257,
    276, 286, 294, 363, 369, 406, 503, 504
American writers, 96, 189, 204, 458, 459
Anderson, Sherwood, 27, 145, 302,
    334, 389, 436, 457, 546n100, 553n25,
    554n27; *Dark Laughter,* 109
anti-Communism, 459, 529
Armstrong, Louis, 462
Arnold, Edward, 134
Arthur, Jean, 48
As I Lay Dying, 18, 207, 285, 356, 414,
    470. *See also* Bundren family

Bacall, Lauren, 245, 246, 247, 373
Bacher, William, 232, 236, 239, 240, 269,
    408
Bailey, Ellen, 295
Bailey, Sallie, 18, 155
Bailey's Woods, 13, 52, 110, 217, 294, 451
Baird, Helen, 46
Balzac, Honoré, 151, 283, 317, 332, 385, 436
Bankhead, Tallulah, 168, 239
Barber, Ace, 488
Barnett, Ned, 192, 296, 298, 299, 306,
    307, 422, 523, 524
barnstormers, 1, 3, 17, 20, 37
Barr, Caroline (Callie), 23, 112, 170–72,
    185, 187, 225, 299, 303, 422, 521, 536,
    538
Barrett, William E., 358
Barth, J. Robert, 502
Bassett, John, 15
Bassett, John Spencer, 555n18
Basso, Hamilton, 2, 301
Baxter, Warner, 100, 117
Beale, Betty, 483
Beauchamp family (*Go Down, Moses;
    Intruder in the Dust*): Bobo, 524;
    Butch, 186, 188, 309; Hubert, 176, 182;
    Lucas, 85, 176, 178, 224, 296, 298, 304,

305, 306, 307, 309, 311, 313, 314, 318,
    423, 479, 480, 486, 523; Mollie, 185;
    Sophonsiba, 176, 180; Tennie, 181
Beery, Wallace, 141
Bell, Mary, 171
Ben-Hur (film), 70, 86, 521
Berkeley, Annie Churchill, 465
Bergson, Henri, 384
Berry, Joe, 22
Bessie, Alvah, 205, 222, 223
Best Years of Our Lives, The (film), 227
Bezzerides, Al ("Buzz"), 205–6, 207, 208,
    209, 216, 222, 228, 244, 250–51, 253,
    254–55, 256, 270, 293
Bezzerides, Zoe, 252
Big Woods, 418–19; reviews of, 419–20
Birth of a Nation (film), 211, 213, 450,
    552n36
Black, Victoria Fielden, 56, 122
Black Boy (Wright), 267
Black Buster (bull), 192, 296
Bleikasten, André, 545n87, 573n35,
    582n48
Blockade (film), 230
Bloom, Jack Harold, 397, 576n28
Blotner, Joseph, 302, 339, 346, 393, 433,
    467–68, 473, 475, 485, 490, 515,
    518, 531, 532, 543n42, 551n17, 557n25,
    559n33, 562n2
Bogart, Humphrey, 243, 245–47, 248,
    256, 258, 359, 361, 456, 570n17
Boojack, 219, 278
Borsten, Orin, 36, 54, 55, 204, 337
Bouvard, Loïc, 384–85
Brackett, Leigh, 255, 257, 258, 560n20
Bradford, Melvin, 165
Bradford, Lydia, 5
Bradford, Mary Rose, 544–45n72
Bradford, Roark, 5, 29, 540n17,
    544–45n72
Brazil, 403, 410, 411, 412
Breen, Joseph, 11, 26, 235, 272
Breit, Harvey, 304, 459
Brennan, Dan, 192–93
Brennan, Walter, 47, 570n18
Broach, Vance, 171, 337

Broadus, 219, 242

brothels, 144, 260, 371, 456, 500, 522, 525.
  See also whores

brotherhood, 17, 31, 60, 231, 306, 405,
  408, 520

brothers, 68, 70, 72, 74, 76, 81–82, 85, 92,
  93, 94, 97, 105, 112, 115, 119, 121, 149,
  150, 167, 175, 176, 182, 184, 197, 199,
  200, 209–10, 211, 214, 216, 229, 235,
  252, 283, 287, 302, 305, 306, 324, 325,
  330, 355, 361, 408, 413, 445, 446, 451,
  482, 508, 514, 515–16, 519, 535–36, 537

Brown, Clarence, 312–13, 314, 316, 318,
  323

Brown, Joe C., 267

Brown, Margaret (Maggie), 300

Brown, Ross, 300

Brown v. Board of Education, 421, 444,
  448

Bryant, Carolyn, 440

Bryant, Sallie Bailey, 13, 18, 155–56

Bryant, William, 13, 18, 50, 103, 110,
  155–56, 179, 292, 420, 555n18

Buchenwald, 482

Buck, Pearl, 334

Buckner, Mrs., 205

Buckner, Robert, 103, 202, 204, 208–9,
  212, 213, 214, 215, 216, 221, 551n17,
  557n25

Bunche, Ralph, 443, 485

Bundren family (*As I Lay Dying*), 436,
  437, 457, 517; Addie, 370, 480, 517;
  Anse, 470; Jewel, 527

Bunyan, Paul, 382

Burcham, Milo, 3

Burgess, Gloria, 423, 424

Burgess, Guy, 443

Busby, Dr., 403

Butler, Charlie, 51, 200

Butler, Henry, 567n44

Butterworth, Charlie, 28

Byhalia, Wright's Sanatorium in, 414,
  515, 534–35

Byron, George Gordon, Lord, 478

Byronic hero, 98

Byron Society, 478

Cabell, James Branch, 27

Cabinet of Dr. Caligari, The (film), 12

Cain, James M., 259

Cairo, Egypt, 395

Caldwell, Erskine, 293, 334, 459

Cambridge, Massachusetts, 70, 377

Cambridge spies, 443

Camus, Albert, 384, 385, 438, 473

Canada, 73, 89, 223, 328

Cantwell, Robert, 124–27, 299, 524

Capote, Truman, 459, 462

Carey, Glenn O., 323, 324, 326, 327

Carmichael, Hoagy, 246

Carpenter, Meta, 23–27, 30–51, 52, 53,
  54–56, 58, 59, 60, 61, 62–63, 64, 65,
  72–73, 78, 86, 91, 102–3, 110, 119, 120,
  123, 133, 134–35, 136–37, 143, 146, 147–
  48, 149–50, 161, 203–4, 205, 206, 207,
  222, 223, 228, 229, 244, 245, 246, 247,
  248, 250, 251, 252, 254, 274, 314, 323,
  334, 337, 344–45, 348, 351, 353, 359, 360,
  375, 378, 390, 396, 434, 476, 492, 494,
  495, 534, 541n2, 542n25, 542–43nn33–
  34, 543n42, 543n49, 554n32

Carroll, Joe, 470

Carruthers, Chester, 529

Carter, Hodding, 301, 333

Cartier-Bresson, Henri, 528

Carver, George Washington, 433, 507

Casablanca (film), 216, 248, 256

Catcher in the Rye (Salinger), 379

Catullus, 326

Ceiling Zero (film), 11

Celetano, Harry, 493–94

Cerf, Bennett, 13, 18, 98, 99, 110–11, 123,
  150, 174, 197, 201, 206, 207, 301, 336,
  401, 411, 520, 528, 537

Cerf, Phyllis, 110–11

Champion, E. O., 20

Chandler, Raymond, 255, 257

Chapel Hill, North Carolina, 432

Chaplin, Charlie, 223; *The Great Dictator,*
  229–30

Charlottesville, Virginia, 457–58, 461,
  463, 464, 465, 466, 468, 470, 471,
  472, 473, 483, 485, 489–90, 493, 494,

291, 299, 301, 302, 303–4, 317, 323, 335, 343, 369, 374, 403, 405, 449, 457, 459, 481, 482, 532

Cowley, Muriel, 564n13

Crane, Stephen, 16

Crash Dive (film), 234

Crawford, Joan, 4, 45, 143–44, 259, 260

Crosby, Bing, 239

Crown, John, 42–43, 49, 56, 135, 222

Cullen, John, 155, 291, 311, 335

Culley, John, 218, 383

Culloden, 285, 286

Cunning of History, The (Rubenstein), 24

Cyrano de Bergerac, 138, 345

Daniel, Robert, 196

Darden, Colgate, 466, 485, 487

Dardis, Tom, 11

"Dark House," 66, 67, 68

Dark Laughter (Anderson), 109

Death Valley, 273

de Gaulle, Charles, 202, 208, 235

"De Gaulle Story, The," 209–17, 224

Depression, the, 230, 159, 230

detective story, 80, 258, 110, 322, 362

Détroyat, Michel, 3

Deutsch, Herman, 4–5, 9, 97

Devine, Eric (Jim), 298, 301, 302, 314, 390

Dixiecrats, 301, 450

Docherty, Jack, 470, 471

Doherty, Thomas, 34

doom, 15, 63, 72, 78, 83, 92, 97, 105, 113, 115, 118, 136, 140, 141, 167, 180, 237, 266, 286, 287, 305, 337, 338, 342, 387, 389, 502

Dos Passos, John, 293, 482

Dostoevsky, Fyodor, 294

Double Dealer, 323

Dreiser, Theodore, 27, 334

Dressler, Marie, 141

Dr. Jekyll and Mr. Hyde (Stevenson), 199

Drums along the Mohawk (film), 3, 111, 120, 130–32, 133, 134, 137, 138, 144, 230, 361, 366, 551n13, 569–70n16

"Dry September," 307, 333, 440

Dumas, Alexander, 117

Dunkirk, 217, 230, 235

Durward, Quentin, 94

Eager, Bess Lyon, 471

Eastland, James, 451

Edie: American Girl (J. Stein), 396

Ehrenberg, Ilya, 290

Eisenhower, Dwight, 458, 459

Eisenstein, Sergei, xi, 142

Eliot, T. S., 12, 94; "The Love Song of J. Alfred Prufrock," 6, 9, 16; "Tradition and the Individual Talent," 456; *The Waste Land,* 2, 6

Ellery Queen's Mystery Magazine, 279, 318

Elliott, Jack, 582n10

Ellison, Ralph, 316, 488; *Invisible Man,* 486

Ellmann, Richard, 481

Emerson, O. B., 450

Emperor Jones, The (O'Neill), 15, 105–6

End of the Affair, The (Greene), 353–54

Erskine, Albert, 495

Escape (film), 229

Europe, 24, 103, 105, 108, 149–50, 173, 174, 212, 213, 215, 217, 234, 268, 279, 303, 323, 325, 326, 327, 328–29, 339, 340, 346, 347, 360, 363, 376, 390, 394, 395, 396, 400, 411, 426, 435, 439, 443, 447, 452, 473, 496, 506, 530

Evans, Hugh, 278, 300, 442

Evans, Mary, 300, 442

Fable, A, xi, xii, 215, 240, 242, 243, 266, 290, 334, 340, 347, 359, 378, 379, 384, 385–86, 388, 391, 393, 396, 399, 401–9, 411, 412, 414, 416, 432, 457, 475, 523, 529, 573n3

Fadiman, 237, 239, 286, 316

Falkner, Alabama Leroy (Bama, Mrs. Walter McLean), 171–72, 196, 242, 314, 315, 336, 337, 358, 376, 411, 432, 567n37

Falkner, J. W. T. (John Wesley Thompson, grandfather; the young Colonel), 521

Falkner, Maud Butler (mother), 10, 16, 17–18, 19, 75, 197, 198–99, 200, 218,

Faulkner, William (*continued*)
308, 311, 420, 421, 426, 444–48, 450,
451, 466, 472, 485, 487, 512, 524, 536;
servants of (*see* Boojack; Broadus;
McEwen, Narcissus; Norfleet; Oliver,
Jack); and sex, 8, 11, 39, 40, 41, 55, 82,
121, 128, 131, 135, 137, 140, 153, 160, 262,
295, 318, 344, 346, 363, 367, 429, 455,
474, 475, 478, 487, 492, 509, 522,
554n32; and sexism, 503; and slavery,
34, 59, 67, 71, 72, 77–78, 80, 81, 82, 86,
88, 90, 94, 99, 100, 105, 109, 111–13,
114–16, 118, 119, 154–55, 171, 172, 173,
176, 180, 182, 183–84, 188, 191, 213,
230–32, 238, 301–2, 317, 393, 397, 398,
418, 443–44, 449, 450, 523–24, 525,
548n122, 549–50n144, 550n151; and
silent film, 72, 86; as southern novelist, 158, 281, 283, 284, 288; as stepfather, 121–22, 296, 376, 482, 544n66,
553n7; and time, 26, 43, 60, 76, 80, 83,
85, 138, 141, 180, 187, 188–89, 197, 229,
368–69, 371, 384, 398, 498; and uniforms, 173, 197, 199, 227, 228, 276, 282,
326, 327, 342, 403, 406–7, 529, 573n36;
and World War I, 1, 21, 27, 36, 37, 65,
100, 115, 173, 210, 226, 243, 323, 330,
378, 402, 467; and World War II, 101,
185, 212, 226, 231, 284, 334, 405, 482,
500, 506, 507, 512, 558n33, 559n23
—, characters of: Aleck Sander, 226,
306, 307, 310, 311, 316, 476; America,
231, 234, 235; Mrs. Armstid, 166, 168;
Horace Benbow, 157, 195, 330; Narcissa
Benbow, 330; Mr. Binford, 526;
Major Blynt, 545n86; Bogard, 429;
Charles Bon, 21, 24, 52, 59, 60–63,
65, 66, 68–69, 70, 72, 73, 74, 79–80,
84, 85, 92, 94, 105, 109, 112, 172, 186,
305, 325, 449, 511, 544n67, 546n96;
Jim Bond, 22, 87, 93; Bookright,
167, 549n144; Buck (in *The Wild
Palms*), 141, 142, 143; Byron Bunch,
305; Lucas Burch, 457; Burdens, 116,
552n36; Joe Christmas, 63, 285, 305,
318, 337, 408, 523; Rosa Coldfield, 24,

39, 44, 59, 68, 72, 74, 75, 76–77, 78,
80, 84–86, 87, 89, 90, 92, 99, 195, 262,
372, 544n67, 547n110, 547nn112–13,
547nn116–17, 561n8; Miss Corrie, 522,
525, 526; Das, 545n86; Major (Mayor)
de Spain, 156, 182, 198, 429, 474–75,
476, 477, 478, 509; Dilsey, 285, 305;
Doom (Ikkemotubbe), 285, 286, 287,
300, 419, 479; Temple Drake, 33–34,
260, 314, 357, 366–68, 370, 371–73,
374, 497; Jenny Du Pre, 103, 313, 318,
432, 478; Eddie, 247–48, 249, 510;
Roth Edmonds, 34, 177, 187, 527; Zack
Edmonds, 177, 178; Elnora, 553n43;
Eunice, 183–85, 186; Cecilia Farmer,
370; Sam Fathers, 179, 180, 181, 381,
418, 419, 489; Colonel H. I. Feinman,
2–3, 6, 9; Fibby, 183; French architect,
25, 76, 88, 305, 337, 372, 436; Jackie
Gordon, 345; Crawford Gowrie, 311;
Vincent Gowrie, 306; Louis Grenier,
322, 369; Mrs. Grier, 198; Pete Grier,
197; Percy Grimm, 50, 337; Lonnie
Grinnup, 321, 322; Lena Grove, 305,
404, 457; Captain Gualdres, 325, 327,
328, 329; Doctor Habersham, 368;
Miss Habersham, 305, 306, 310, 311,
313, 314, 316, 404, 479; Max Harriss, 325, 327, 328; Miss Harriss, 325,
328; Mr. Harriss, 325, 326, 327; Mrs.
Melisandre Backus Harris, 326, 328,
329; Drusilla Hawk, 116, 117, 372, 504;
Gail Hightower, 31, 195; Doc Hines,
367; Alec Holston, 369; Jack Houston,
161, 162–63, 487, 499, 502, 527; Jack
(in *Pylon*), 4, 6, 8, 12; Al Jackson, 145;
Jiggs, 4, 6, 9, 12, 247; Milly Jones, 84,
85; Wash Jones, 66, 80, 84, 85, 86,
92, 549n128; Barton Kohl, 500, 507;
Labove, 160; Loosh, 111–13, 114, 119,
449; Butch Lovemaiden, 526; Captain
Lovett, 100; Julian Lowe, 101; Charles
(Chick) Mallison, xii, 226, 299, 305,
306–10, 311, 313–14, 316, 320, 324–25,
327–29, 346, 404, 437, 476, 478,
486, 502, 503, 504, 506, 507, 508–9;

Hale, Nancy, 467–68
Hall, Donald, 459, 460
Halloween, 241, 276, 277
Hamlet, 195
Hamlet, The, 152–69, 170, 174, 175, 195,
    289, 305, 470, 474, 480, 481, 498,
    502, 523; reviews of, 152–54. *See also*
    Snopeses; Snopes trilogy
Hammett, Dashiell, 18, 29, 40, 501
Handy, W. C., 48, 219
Hardy, Thomas, 523
Harlem, 124, 235, 316, 447
Harlow, Jean, 475, 476
Hart, Basil Liddell, 98
Hathaway, Henry, 240, 269, 407, 408,
    475
Harvard University, 24, 59, 73, 75, 81,
    86–87, 98, 101, 150, 287, 299, 311, 377,
    547n111
Hawks, Howard, 3–4, 8, 11, 23, 24, 25,
    26, 27, 29, 31–33, 35, 37, 38, 43, 44, 46,
    48–49, 73, 138, 209, 216, 228, 229, 230,
    236, 239, 240, 243, 244–46, 248, 254,
    255, 260, 261, 264, 266, 270, 279, 318,
    358, 359, 360, 361, 365, 375, 393–94,
    397–98, 407, 408, 540n24, 542n25,
    546n100, 559n24, 560n23
Hayward, DuBose, 494
Hayward, Leland, 194
Heilpern, John, 434
Hellman, Lillian, 29, 40, 227, 501, 532;
    The North Star, 212; *The Searching
    Wind,* 226; *Watch on the Rhine,* 214
Hemingway, Ernest, 8, 58, 139, 189, 246,
    247, 248, 279, 280, 293, 334, 338, 428,
    431, 517, 529; *Across the River and into
    the Trees,* 344
Hempstead, David, 28, 47, 72, 314
Henry IV (Shakespeare), 126
Hernandez, Juano, 311, 314, 315
Herndon, William, 202, 269, 273, 280
He Who Gets Slapped (film), 104
Hicks, Granville, 117–18, 374, 403–4,
    481, 499–500, 533
High Noon (film), 365, 390
His Girl Friday (film), 4

Hiss, Alger, 443
History of Henry Esmond, The, 111, 126
Hitchcock, Alfred, 455
Holly Springs, Mississippi, 122, 125, 193,
    515, 555–56n18
Hollywood, 3, 8, 12, 18, 22, 24, 35, 44, 48,
    53, 65, 110, 133, 168, 173, 194, 208, 266,
    273, 315, 342, 398, 404, 545n83, 560n23
Holmes, Edwin R., 397
Holmes, Sherlock, 329
"Hong Kong Blues" (song), 246
Hopkins, Harry, 506
Hopkins, Miriam, 34, 54, 194, 542n28
House, Mrs., 251
Housman, A. E., 38, 353
Howe, Russell, 445, 447
Howland, Harold E., 411, 427, 439
Huck Finn, 518, 524
Hume, Branham, 196
Hurston, Zora Neale, 61

Iceland, 438–39
I Cover the Waterfront (film), 5–6, 8, 10
Impressions of Japan: William Faulkner
    (film), 428
Indian subcontinent (Indians), 64, 65,
    172, 448
Intruder in the Dust (novel), xi, 157, 173,
    224, 226, 299, 301, 302, 303, 310–11,
    317, 318, 321, 323, 330, 333, 346, 357, 369,
    404, 446; reviews of, 305–10. *See also*
    Beauchamp family; Stevens, Gavin
Intruder in the Dust (film), 260, 271,
    312–16, 336, 360, 442, 490
Invisible Man (Ellison), 486
Irving, Washington, 160
Italy, 73, 394, 432, 435, 440, 501, 502
I Wanted Wings (film), 230

Jackson, Andrew, 285, 286
Jackson, Charles, *The Lost Weekend,* 303,
    387
Jackson, Mississippi, 368
Jackson Park (New Orleans), 144
Jackson, Robert, 232
Jackson, Stonewall, 34

James, Henry, 126, 129, 294, 373
Japan, 427–34, 435, 440–41, 468, 479, 512
Japanese, 197, 199, 200, 232, 233, 236, 253, 269, 428, 429, 430–31, 433, 440–41
Japanese-American relations, 433
Japanese culture, 428, 433
Japanese literature, 432
Japanese women, 429, 432
Jarman, Claude, Jr., 313, 314
Jefferson, Mississippi, 59, 62, 73, 77, 78, 151, 152, 154–55, 168, 176, 188, 196, 197, 224, 283, 286, 312, 366, 368–69, 371, 372, 374, 435, 437, 473, 474, 476, 477, 478, 479, 481, 500, 502, 503, 505, 510, 521
Jefferson Society, 468
Jefferson, Thomas, 381, 485, 486
Jim Crow, 93, 190, 235, 422, 423
Joan of Arc, 350
Johnny Belinda (film), 509
Johnson, Andrew, 552n36
Johnson, Nunnally, 26, 28–29, 32, 47, 271
Johnson, Samuel, x, 46, 96
Johnson, Susie Paul, 12
Joice, John, 84
Jones, Henry, 218
Jonsson, Else, 338–40, 351, 359, 360, 364, 378, 384, 389, 390, 426, 434, 439, 477, 534
Jonsson, Thorsten, 334
Joyce, James, 43; *Ulysses*, 296
June Lake, California, 229

Kaledin, Arthur, 377–78, 571n12
Kaltenborn, H. V., 199
Karl, Fred, 342, 531, 545n87, 570n17, 573n34
Karlova, Irina, 260
Kawin, Bruce, 248
Kawin, Alfred, 481
Keating, Bern, 412
Keats, John, 4, 122, 152, 267, 506, 540n10; "Ode on a Grecian Urn," 46, 104, 284
Keel, Pinckney, 379
Keller, 381

Kempton, Murry, 480
Kennedy, John, 529, 531, 582n48
Kentucky Derby, 242, 426
Kentucky limestone, 493
Kentucky tobacco, 126
Keswick Hunt Club, 495
King, Martin Luther, Jr., 453
Kipling, Rudyard, 64, 65, 100, 545n87
Kirk, David, 450
Klopfer, Donald, 18, 110, 393, 537–38
Knickerbocker Hotel, 38, 222
Knight, Salley, 494–95
Knight's Gambit, 225, 271, 309, 318, 320–29, 348; reviews of, 329–31. *See also* Stevens, Gavin
Korea, 428
Korean War, 399, 404
Ku Klux Klan, 487, 507, 509
Kurnitz, Harry, 398, 513
Kurtz, 107

Lady Eve, The (film), 375
Lahiere, 492
Lanham, Buck, 293
La Rue's, 38, 222
Last Tycoon, The (Fitzgerald), 8
Latin America, 410
Latin Americans, 517
Lay of the Last Minstrel, The (Scott), 45–46
Lecky, William, 470
Lee, Muna, 410, 411, 494, 517
Lee, Robert E., 34, 99, 381, 446, 527
Legion of Honor, 378
Lewis, John L., 506–7
Lewis, Sinclair, 8, 27, 294, 334
Lewis, William, Jr., 527, 557n29
liberty, 175, 217, 229, 237, 307, 380–81, 425, 436, 441, 443–44, 452, 457, 484
Life, 324, 376, 413
Light in August, xi, 18, 116, 156, 305, 309, 367, 404, 412
Lincoln, Abraham, 233–34, 238, 381, 408, 485
Lincoln Brigade, 116, 211, 213, 230, 507, 552n36

Modern Library, 201
Moll, Erik, 254–55
Mondadori, Alberto, 435
Monroe, Marilyn, 396, 428, 434, 475,
   476, 477, 478, 481
Moore, Marianne, 459
Moore, Robert H., 437
Moore, Sandra Baker, 294, 453
Morehouse College, 441
Morrison, Toni, 90
Mortal Storm, The (film), 229
Mosquitoes, 135, 311, 317, 436, 501
Mouse That Roared, The (film), 490
Mullen Phil, 349
Mumford, Lewis, 459
Murphy, Dudley, 104–5, 107, 109, 551n17
Musso & Frank's, 34, 40, 204, 212, 222,
   223, 226, 228, 252, 542n33
Mussolini, Benito, 28, 501
"Mythical Latin-American Kingdom
   Story," 510

NAACP, 7, 316, 423, 444–46, 447–48,
   451–53
Nagano, Japan, 429
National Recovery Act, 506
National Velvet (film), 313
Native Americans (Indians), 50, 65, 68,
   77, 130–31, 131, 138, 155, 176, 179, 223,
   283, 286, 361, 394, 418, 419, 422, 435
NATO, 439
Neal, Patricia, 344, 396
Neilson's Department Store, 201, 267,
   527
Nelson, Charles, Sr., 199, 200, 336,
   568n29
Nelson, Charles, Jr., 199, 553n14, 572n27
New Albany, Mississippi, 61
New Deal, 130, 175, 199, 214, 380, 451,
   570n18
New Haven, Connecticut, 479
New Orleans, 1–2, 4, 5, 6, 14, 24, 37, 47,
   48, 59, 60, 61, 62, 63, 67, 69, 73, 74, 79,
   82, 91, 106, 107, 109, 135, 143, 144, 145,
   150, 183, 184, 248, 303, 323, 326, 328,
   359, 378, 393, 418, 436, 457, 482

New York City, 17, 18, 37, 55, 110–11, 123,
   149, 152, 200, 206, 207, 224, 238, 241,
   248, 252, 282, 292, 301–3, 308, 314, 336,
   343, 344, 346, 347, 350, 353, 357, 359,
   364, 375, 383, 385, 386–89, 390, 391, 393,
   411, 412, 413–14, 426, 427, 447, 451,
   459, 464, 468, 477, 478, 482, 501, 502,
   503, 504–6, 509, 514, 517, 519, 532, 537
Niagara, 475
nonwhite people, 443, 444, 448, 452
Norfleet, 218, 219, 242, 278, 382
North (U.S.), 61, 73, 99, 115, 152, 174, 186,
   187, 190, 192, 198, 212, 298, 299, 307,
   308, 369, 447, 449, 485, 486, 490,
   550n151, 552n36
northerners, 99, 106, 238, 291, 301–2,
   306, 307, 369, 408, 447, 485, 486, 487,
   550n151, 552n36
northern liberals, 306, 307, 312, 447, 452
northern newspapers, 100, 126, 446
Nuremberg trials, 232
Nuechterlein, Donald, 439

Obed, 191
Ober, Harold, 174, 200, 203, 242, 243,
   267, 273, 291, 292, 293, 298, 310, 343,
   376, 377, 451, 492
O'Brien, Pat, 6
"Ode on a Grecian Urn" (Keats), 43, 46,
   284, 456
Odiorne, William, 53
O'Donnell, George Marion, 128–29, 153,
   283
Oldham, Dorothy, 276, 278, 536
Oldham, Lemuel E., 241–42
Oldham family, 51, 172, 241, 269, 277,
   322, 482, 538
Old Taylor Road, 242, 277
Oliver, Jack, 119, 125
Omlie, Phoebe, 2, 5
Omlie, Vernon, 2, 17, 20
O'Neill, Eugene, 27, 102, 109, 357; *The
   Emperor Jones*, 15, 105–6; *Lazarus
   Laughed*, 551n23
"Opera in Greenville" (West), 311
Oppenheimer, Robert, 425, 492

Smith & Haas, 13, 14

Snopeses, 27, 129, 156, 159, 163, 166, 169, 283, 284, 286, 419, 437, 455, 480–81, 496, 498, 499, 502, 515; Ab, 156, 158, 159; Clarence, 500, 503, 509, 525; Eck, 165, 166; Eula Varner, 153, 159–61, 162, 163, 167, 168, 474, 477, 475–76, 501; Flem, 155–56, 157, 159, 160, 161, 165, 166, 167–68, 476, 479, 480, 495, 499, 500, 505, 506–7, 509, 510; Ike, 153, 159, 161; Linda, 150, 500, 502, 503, 504, 580n15; Lump, 162–63, 167; Mink, 159, 162, 163, 487, 499, 503; Montgomery Ward, 500, 580n19; Virgil, 525; Wall, 500

Snopes trilogy, xi, 150–52, 156, 162, 164, 169, 382, 472, 497, 502, 514. See also *Hamlet, The; Mansion, The;* Snopeses; *Town, The*

"Snows of Kilimanjaro" (Hemingway), 138

Sohm, Clem, 3

Soldiers' Pay, 101, 244

Somerville, Ella, 413, 414, 536

Sontag, Susan, 504

So Red the Rose (Young), 68–69

Soul of the Cypress (film), 104

Sound and the Fury, The, 18, 40, 59, 64, 70, 75, 92, 94, 157, 233, 260, 261, 263, 282, 284, 285, 288, 401, 414, 424, 457, 468, 490; "Compson Appendix," 75, 236, 279, 282, 285–88, 308, 368, 404, 469. *See also* Compson, Quentin; Compson family

South (U.S.), 22, 23–24, 34, 42, 59–60, 72, 74, 75, 78, 80, 86, 87, 89, 92–93, 94, 97–98, 99, 116, 119, 127, 131, 152, 154, 168, 174, 188, 189, 194, 210, 212, 224, 235, 247, 281–82, 292, 298, 301, 303, 306, 307–8, 310, 311, 312, 320, 330, 333–34, 352, 369, 422, 423, 432, 445, 446, 447, 448–49, 472, 481, 485, 496

South America, 411, 426, 429

Southern Agrarians, 15

southern belles, 50, 352, 442

southern gentlemen. *See* Faulkner, William: and gentleman's code

Southern Gothic, 24, 68, 48, 199

Southern Historical Association, 439, 441

southern history, 1, 59, 68, 77, 198, 230, 466

southern identity, 24, 99, 103, 113, 129, 204, 224, 263, 307, 440, 449, 486

southern ladies, 14, 26, 218–19, 318, 351, 379, 392, 456, 465

southern liberals, 225, 307, 309, 321, 449, 510

southern literature, 69, 126–27, 283, 367, 431, 490

southern newspapers, 317, 338

Southerner, The (film), 271–72, 274, 496

southerners, xi, 24, 28, 32, 42, 68, 73, 118, 195, 206, 214, 225, 231, 238, 301, 307, 311, 313, 316, 357, 380, 408, 434, 443, 444, 448, 450, 451, 461, 465, 485, 496, 500, 502, 503, 507, 508, 516, 548n122, 549–50n144, 550n147, 550n151, 552n36, 575n27, 582n48

Southern Reposure, 451

southern white mythology (identity), 263, 549n43

Soviet Union, 223, 417, 439, 491, 508

Sowell, Navy, 19

Spanish Civil War, 150, 222, 230, 248, 293, 500, 507

Spratling, William, 546n100

Stalin, Josef, 24, 28

Stalingrad, 232

Stallings, Laurence, 8

Starr, Hubert, 57, 58, 427

State Department, 215, 290, 403, 410, 411, 412, 416, 426, 427, 433, 435, 439, 443, 444, 459, 462, 473, 491, 494, 508, 512, 517

Stein, Gertrude, 256

Stein, Jean, 351, 360, 394, 395–96, 397, 398, 399, 414, 415, 416, 432, 434, 438, 444, 447, 452, 455, 457, 458, 461–62, 477, 484, 501, 504, 505

Stein, Jules, 477

Steinbeck, John, 334, 459, 460; *The Grapes of Wrath,* 230